W9-CLL-752

New York
State Road Atlas

Table of Contents

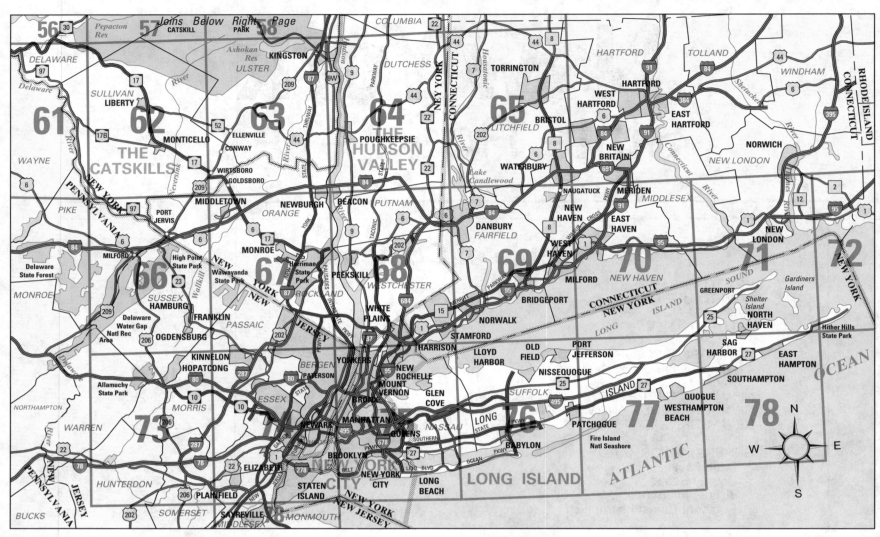

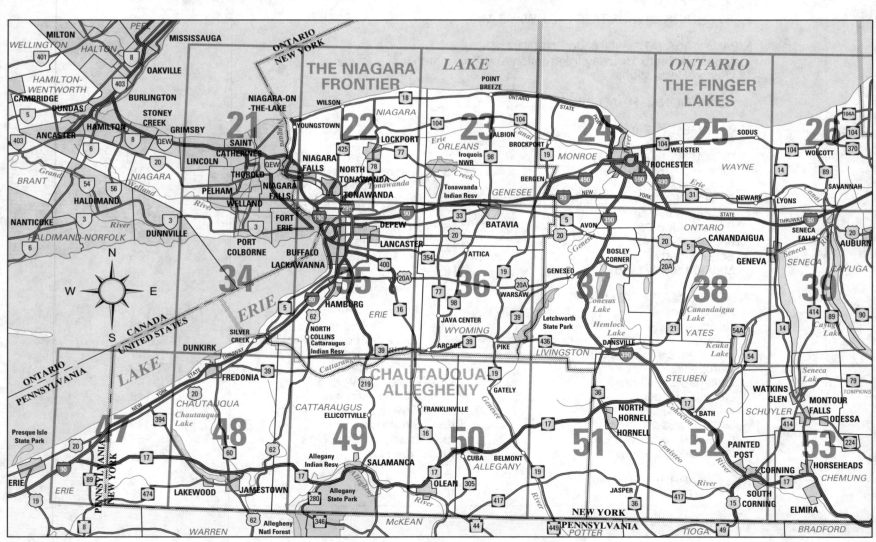

Regional Divisions of New York Referred to in Text

Key To Map Pages

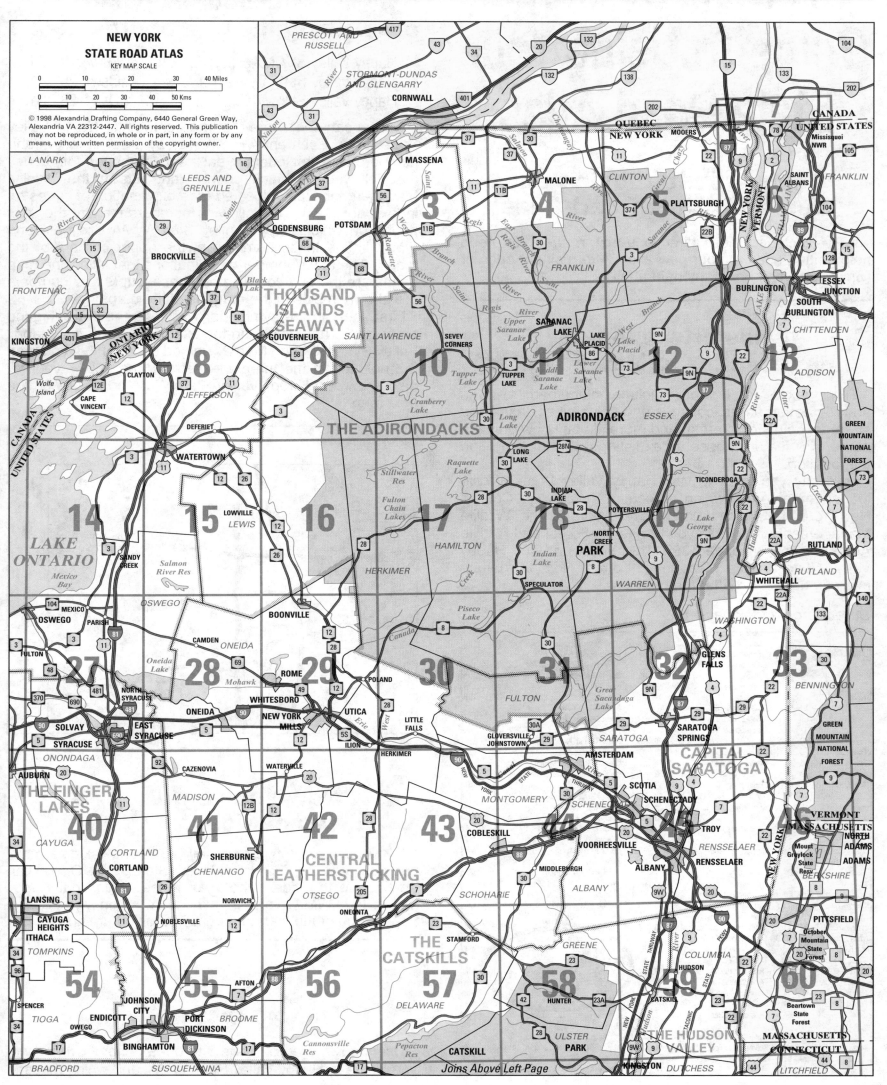

NEW YORK STATE ROAD ATLAS

KEY MAP SCALE

Regional Divisions of New York Referred to in Text

A Step-By-Step Guide To Using Your State Road Atlas

Thank you for buying our New York State Road Atlas

We've included these directions just in case you need help getting used to your new atlas. After using it once or twice, you won't need any help at all.

1. It all starts with the Index to Map Features.

The Index to Map Features includes place names, parks and recreation areas, colleges and universities, lakes and streams, points of interest, and more. If you know only the name of a feature, these index listings will help you find the location.

Let's say you want to visit Happy Valley State Wildlife Management Area, which is located in Oswego County, New York, but don't know the location of the Wildlife Management Area. First, you turn to the Forest and Wildlife Areas section on page 138 of the index and find Happy Valley State Wildlife Management Area. Note the letters and numbers listed after the name.

Section from index page 138

Forest & Wildlife Areas								
...vitt St				Cockaponset St Forest................Mdx	70	F2	Golden Beach Preserve...............Hml	17	E3
...........Pas	67	B4	Cockaponset St Forest................Mdx	71	A1	Goose Egg St Forest Preserve...............Whg	33	C6
...........Hrk	17	B4	Cockaponset St Forest................Mdx	71	A2	Graves Pt Preserve.......Nsu	75	E2
t Forest......Lch	60	F6	Cockaponset St Forest................NHv	70	D2	Great Barrington St Forest...............Brk	60	B4
t Forest......Lch	65	E1	Cockaponset St Forest................NHv	70	D3	Great Is Mgmt Area.......NLn	71	C3
es.............Cat	49	A5	Collins Ldg St WMA....Jfs	8	A3	Great Swamp Mgmt Area...............Wgn	72	E1
Natl Wildlife			Conesus Inlet St WMA...............Lvg	37	D4	Great Swamp Natl Wildlife Ref...............Mrr	73	F4
...........Sfk	78	E1	Connecticut Hill St WMA...............Scy	53	D2	Great Swamp Natl Wildlife Ref...............Mrr	74	A4
egion St			Connecticut Hill St WMA...............Tmk	53	D2	Green Mtn Natl Forest...............Add	13	F6
...........Lch	65	F1	Conscience Pt Natl Wildlife Ref...............Sfk	78	A1	Green Mtn Natl Forest...............Add	20	F1
Forest.......Ben	33	D6	Cornwall Swamp WMA...............Add	20	D1	Green Mtn Natl Forest...............Ben	33	F5
s St			Cortland Natl Fish Hatchery...............Crt	40	C6	Green Mtn Natl Forest...............Ben	46	E1
...........Jfs	7	D4	Cranberry Lake Forest Preserve...............SL	10	C4	Haddam Neck Mgmt Area...............Mdx	71	A1
wamp St			Crumhorn Mtn St WMA...............Ots	43	A6	Hainesville WMA.......Ssx	66	C3
...........NLn	72	B1	David Sarnoff St Pine Barrens Preserve...Sfk	77	E2	Hamburg Mtn WMA.......Ssx	66	F5
rsh St			Dead Cr St WMA........Add	13	B6	Hanging Bog Game Management Area..Agy	50	C3
...........Cln	6	B6	Dead Cr St WMA........Add	13	C4	Happy Valley St WMA................Osw	27	F1
onservation			Dead Cr St WMA........Add	13	C5	Happy Valley St WMA................Osw	28	A1
...........Ont	21	B5	Deer Cr Marsh St WMA...............Osw	14	D5	Happy Valley St WMA................Osw	28	B1
nt Area.......NLn	72	B2	Delaware & Raritan Canal St Forest......Sms	73	E6	Hearthstone Pt Forest Preserve...............Wrr	32	D1
WMA.........Slv	62	F6	Delaware St Forest....Pke	66	A2	High Tor Game Mgmt Area...............Yts	38	C5
Mtn Forest			Delaware St Forest....Pke	66	A3	Highland Co Forest......Ono	41	A3
...........Dlw	56	F5	Delaware St Forest....Pke	66	A5	Honeyville St WMA.....Jfs	15	A2
Mtn Game			Delaware St Forest....Pke	66	C2	Hooker Mtn St WMA.....Ots	43	B5
...........Dlw	56	F5						
t Forest.....Brk	60	C4						
t Forest.....Brk	60	D4						
t Forest.....Brk	60	E4						
rest								
...........Slv	62	B1						
alley								
...........Mrr	73	E1						
MA.........Rut	20	E6						

2. Finding your map and using the grid coordinates.

Happy Valley St WMA ....Osw 27 F1
Happy Valley St WMA ....Osw 28 A1
Happy Valley St WMA ....Osw 28 B1

As you can see, there are three entries for Happy Valley State WMA. Each entry is followed by a set of letters and numbers. The first letters in each set are the territory codes that tell you in which county (and State) the Wildlife Management Area is located (see explanation of codes on index page 124). The following numbers identify the map pages on which Happy Valley State WMA can be found (you will find these numbers at the upper corners of the maps). The letter/number combinations that follow the map pages are the grid coordinates (these letters and numbers are shown in blue in the margins of the maps).

First, look up the symbol for wildlife areas in the legend on page 5. Then, following the example above, find Happy Valley State WMA on Map 27, in grid square F1. If you read the notation in the margin — "Joins Map 28" — you will also know that Happy Valley State WMA continues on the next map.

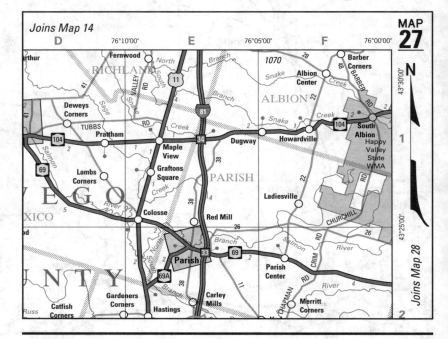

3. Now you've got two choices.

If you wish, you can just turn to Map 28 and, taking a visual cue from Map 27, find Happy Valley State WMA. Or you can go back to the index where you'll see again, that Happy Valley State WMA is also in grid square A1 on Map 28. But how do you get to that area from where you are now?

4. The big picture.

Use the Key Map on page 3 to get a general overview of your route to Happy Valley State WMA, and which maps to use. You know that you're headed for the part of Happy Valley State WMA, which is on Map 28. Assuming you're in Utica, you will see that your current location is in square 29 (square numbers correspond to map numbers) and your destination is in square 28.

5. There is more.

You'll find that the front pages of this atlas contain visitor's information on state regions, points of interest, parks, golf courses, wineries, mileage charts, and general information for the driver. Browse these pages and you'll see that this is the only book you need to travel New York.

You'll find it particularly useful if you study the map legend below. Familiarity with the various symbols will permit you to more quickly find any information on the maps.

Finally, let us hear from you. We appreciate getting ideas and information from our atlas users. This helps us to improve the product's usefulness and value.

Write to: Hagstrom Map Company, 46-35 54th Road, Maspeth, NY 11378. Your suggestions are always welcome.

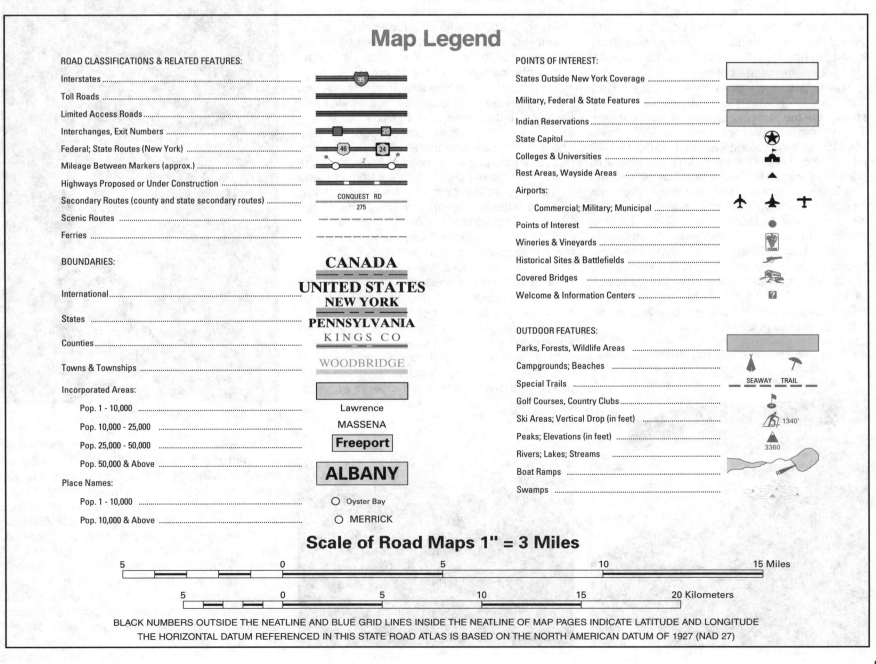

Map Legend

ROAD CLASSIFICATIONS & RELATED FEATURES:

Interstates

Toll Roads

Limited Access Roads

Interchanges, Exit Numbers

Federal; State Routes (New York)

Mileage Between Markers (approx.)

Highways Proposed or Under Construction

Secondary Routes (county and state secondary routes)

CONQUEST RD
275

Scenic Routes

Ferries

BOUNDARIES:

International

States

Counties

Towns & Townships

Incorporated Areas:

  Pop. 1 - 10,000

  Pop. 10,000 - 25,000

  Pop. 25,000 - 50,000

  Pop. 50,000 & Above

Place Names:

  Pop. 1 - 10,000

  Pop. 10,000 & Above

CANADA
UNITED STATES
NEW YORK
PENNSYLVANIA
KINGS CO
WOODBRIDGE

Lawrence
MASSENA
Freeport
ALBANY

○ Oyster Bay
○ MERRICK

POINTS OF INTEREST:

States Outside New York Coverage

Military, Federal & State Features

Indian Reservations

State Capitol

Colleges & Universities

Rest Areas, Wayside Areas

Airports:

  Commercial; Military; Municipal

Points of Interest

Wineries & Vineyards

Historical Sites & Battlefields

Covered Bridges

Welcome & Information Centers

OUTDOOR FEATURES:

Parks, Forests, Wildlife Areas

Campgrounds; Beaches

Special Trails

SEAWAY TRAIL

Golf Courses, Country Clubs

Ski Areas; Vertical Drop (in feet)

1340'

Peaks; Elevations (in feet)

3360

Rivers; Lakes; Streams

Boat Ramps

Swamps

Scale of Road Maps 1" = 3 Miles

5   0   5   10   15 Miles

5   0   5   10   15   20 Kilometers

BLACK NUMBERS OUTSIDE THE NEATLINE AND BLUE GRID LINES INSIDE THE NEATLINE OF MAP PAGES INDICATE LATITUDE AND LONGITUDE

THE HORIZONTAL DATUM REFERENCED IN THIS STATE ROAD ATLAS IS BASED ON THE NORTH AMERICAN DATUM OF 1927 (NAD 27)

Salute to New York

Scenic Hudson River from Bear Mountain Overlook

The astonishing diversity of the Empire State often takes visitors by surprise, but it's also what makes New York one of the most popular and exciting travel destinations in America. Although it ranks 30th in terms of size, New York continues to lead the nation — some would say the world — in the bounty of cultural, scenic, and recreational opportunities to be found within its 11 distinct tourist regions. Consider some of the contrasts:

The largest metropolis in America — New York City — lies in the southern part of the state with the Atlantic Ocean at its doorstep. The rugged Adirondack wilderness, three times the size of Yellowstone National Park, with 42 peaks above 4,000 feet, claims the northern portion of the state. Two Great Lakes, Ontario and Erie, the mighty Saint Lawrence River with its fabled "Thousand Islands," and the thundering majesty of Niagara Falls are found to the northwest and west. These are only highlights in a state blessed with some 8,000 lakes, vast forests, 200 state parks and historic sites, spectacular rivers, exciting cities, picturesque villages, rural farmland, and more than 3500 buildings or sites that have been registered as national historic places.

American, Bridal Veil, and Horseshoe Falls, Niagara Falls

New York changes with the seasons, and each season can be enjoyed for the special pleasures and beauties it brings.

In winter, the alpine slopes of Whiteface Mountain near Lake Placid and resorts in the Catskills and western New York attract skiers of all ages and skill levels. Ice fishing, cross-country skiing, skating, and snowmobiling are popular activities in parks throughout the state, with winter carnivals adding to the snowy fun.

In the spring, New York's rushing streams and rivers provide opportunities for whitewater kayaking and canoeing, while cities like Albany and Rochester celebrate the season with tulip and lilac festivals and the Hudson Valley shimmers in a pink-and-white haze of apple blossom.

Summer fishers cast their reels from one end of the state to the other, for New York's lakes and the Atlantic Ocean provide some of the finest fishing waters in North America — as well as superb beaches, bays, and harbors for swimming, boating, and water sports of all kinds. There are more than 800 miles of hiking trails, superb campsites, thermal ridges for soaring, numerous golf courses, and summer music and theater festivals.

A mellow glow fills the air as New York's autumn foliage turns the countryside into a brilliant tapestry of red and gold. Grapes ripen in the lakeside vineyards, apples are ready to be picked in the orchards, fresh cider is pressed,

Manhattan skyline, New York City

roadside produce stands are loaded with the harvest of summer.

New York's long, fascinating, and often turbulent history has been preserved in a multitude of state and national historic landmarks and museums. Scattered across the state, in towns and villages, you'll find 17th-century stone houses, early 18th-century manors and churches, literally dozens of sites dating from the period of the Revolutionary War, as well as famous resorts like Saratoga Springs, where the Victorian past is not a dusty memory but a living part of today.

The pleasures New York offers range from the simple to the spectacular. Tour award-winning vineyards, reacquaint yourself with legendary American personalities at historic sites, see a new Broadway show, explore pristine wilderness areas, look up at Niagara Falls from the *Maid of the Mist,* or down on the crowded streets of Manhattan from a skyscraper — it's all here. In the process of discovering New York you'll come to expect the unexpected.

New York City

Lady Liberty at New York Harbor

New York City, sometimes called "the greatest metropolis ever built," offers an inexhaustible feast of urban sights and experiences. With more than 7.5 million people living in its five boroughs of Manhattan, Brooklyn, Queens, the Bronx, and Staten Island, New York is the nation's most populous city, followed by Los Angeles, and also one of the most ethnically diverse. It's a national and international epicenter of art, finance, education, fashion, entertainment, publishing, and communications — all of which helps to explain the incredible energy that is a vital characteristic of "the city that never sleeps."

Lincoln Center at night, Manhattan

For most visitors, New York City means Manhattan. From New York Harbor at its southernmost tip — where the Statue of Liberty stands with her torch held aloft — to leafy Fort Tryon Park at its northernmost boundary, this 13.4-mile-long and 2.3-mile-wide island, with its famous skyline of soaring skyscrapers, is home to some of the world's greatest cultural institutions and most well-known landmarks.

Several important historic sites — including Federal Hall, where George Washington was sworn in as the first President of the United States in 1789 — are tucked away amidst the towers of Lower Manhattan. But for all its history, New York is not a city that lives in the past. A stroll through any one of its myriad business, shopping, or residential neighborhoods will always provide an eye-opening glimpse into what's going on today.

There's the Wall Street area, home of the New York Stock Exchange and the 110-story World Trade Center; the art galleries and trendy restaurants of the burgeoning TriBeCa and SoHo areas; the cafes and exotic shops that are the hallmarks of Greenwich Village. The two most notable ethnic neighborhoods in Manhattan are Little Italy around Broadway and Canal Street and Chinatown around Bowery and Canal Street.

Legendary Broadway between Times Square and 50th Street remains a mecca for theatergoers, while midtown on the east side boasts the landmark Empire State Building, the Art Deco Chrysler Building, and the United Nations Headquarters alongside the East River. Upper Fifth Avenue provides a sophisticated backdrop for some of the world's most glamorous shopping, as well as for Rockefeller Center and Saint Patrick's Cathedral. The Lincoln Center for the Performing Arts, another New York cultural institution, is the home of two prestigious opera companies and the New York Philharmonic.

Scattered throughout the city's five boroughs are more than 200 world-famous and one-of-a-kind museums encompassing a vast spectrum of art forms, world cultures, and historical epochs. In Manhattan alone you'll find the Metropolitan Museum of Art; the Museum of Modern Art; the Frick Collection, housed in a Fifth Avenue mansion; the Solomon R. Guggenheim Museum, designed by Frank Lloyd Wright; and the American Museum of Natural History, which awes visitors with its enormous collection of natural science exhibits.

New York City's parks, gardens, and zoos offer leafy respite from the challenging rigors of the urban scene. Most popular and well known, of course, is Central Park — 840 acres in the heart of Manhattan — with a new zoo and miles of landscaped walks and vistas.

And that's only the beginning in New York City.

Long Island

On Long Island, which extends some 118 miles into the Atlantic Ocean east of New York City, you'll find historic seaside communities steeped in the salty atmosphere of the past, fabulous mansions, museums, gardens, glamorous resort towns, wineries, and some of the most beautiful beaches in the world.

The best of Long Island's famed white-sand beaches are found on the Atlantic Ocean along the Island's South Shore, many of them in state parks. Jones Beach, a popular summertime destination for sun- and surf-loving New Yorkers, offers six miles of ocean beach surrounded by 2,400 acres of parkland. Fire Island, with its 17 summer resort communities, is a 32-mile-long and half-mile-wide barrier island with protected National Seashore status.

Montauk Point Lighthouse, Montauk

Old Westbury Gardens, Westbury

Rocky and less dramatic, with water that is calmer and warmer, the North Shore beaches fronting on Long Island Sound are well-suited for families with young children. One of the most popular family-style public beaches here is the 1,230-acre Governor Alfred E. Smith/Sunken Meadow State Park, which boasts three golf courses and miles of hiking trails.

For over 100 years the North Shore of Long Island — dubbed the Gold Coast — has been a summer playground and retreat for the rich. The 24-room Beaux-Arts style Vanderbilt Mansion in Centerport is a perfect example of the lifestyle of one rich and famous Long Island family. Sagamore Hill, a 23-room Victorian mansion on a small peninsula east of Oyster Bay, was the summer White House and eventually the permanent residence of President Theodore Roosevelt.

The towns of Sag Harbor and Cold Spring Harbor were important whaling centers in the 19th century, an era whose architectural heritage is vividly evoked by their saltbox architecture. The Sag Harbor Whaling and Historical Museum, one of Long Island's most important attractions, is entered through the jawbones of a whale.

Sports fishermen enjoy record catches off Montauk, where charter and party fishing boats are readily available. Of special interest, too, is the Okeanos Whale Watch, which allows close-up viewing of whales, dolphins, sea turtles, and seabirds in their natural habitat. The much-photographed Montauk Point Lighthouse, built in 1792 on Long Island's easternmost point by order of George Washington, is one of the nation's oldest.

The south shore seaside towns of East Hampton, Bridgehampton, and Southampton — collectively known as the Hamptons — are filled with elegant mansions, fine restaurants, and enticing shops. Many historic homes and buildings add to the appeal of this contemporary resort community.

Closer to New York City, the Long Island Game Farm and Zoological Park in Manorville features exotic and tame animals, sea lion shows and amusement rides. Old Westbury Gardens, a National Historic Site, has 100 acres of formal gardens, fields, woods, and a Stuart-style mansion. Fans of Thoroughbred horse racing can place their bets at Belmont Park Race Track, watch work-outs while dining, and tour the backstretch and horse clinic.

The Hudson Valley

The Hudson Valley region to the north of New York City follows the course of the majestic Hudson River, named after Henry Hudson, the first European to sail up the river in 1609. The lush countryside on both sides of the Hudson is filled with breathtaking vistas, state parks, apple orchards and wineries, historic 17th-and 18th-century Dutch and English homes and churches, fabled Hudson Valley mansions, charming riverside towns and inns, and several of the nation's most important Revolutionary War sites.

The Hudson Valley and the nearby Catskills were immortalized by Washington Irving, whose personality is vividly evoked at Sunnyside, his home in Tarrytown. The author

Beekman Arms Inn, America's oldest, at Rhinebeck

of *Rip Van Winkle* and *The Legend of Sleepy Hollow* is buried in Tarrytown's Sleepy Hollow Cemetery.

Several state historic sites within the Hudson Valley region bear testament to the area's importance during the American Revolution. George Washington set up head-quarters in the Hasbrouck house, known today as Washington's Headquarters, in Newburgh. Knox Headquarters, a spacious 18th-century stone house in the village of Vails Gate, pro-vided living quarters for several American gen-erals, while the men of the Continental Army spent the last months of the war at nearby New Windsor Cantonment, which contains the only known wooden camp structure built by Revolutionary soldiers.

Art and music lovers flock to the Caramoor Center for Music & the Arts in Katonah, where a summer music and arts festival is held in the house and grounds of a 117-acre estate. On the west side of the Hudson more alfresco art is to be found at the 500-acre Storm King Art Center in Mountainville, a sculpture park with more than 120 permanent works.

On a high bluff overlooking the river is one of the Hudson Valley's most famous institutions, the United States Military Academy at West Point, whose graduates include Robert E. Lee, Ulysses S. Grant, and Douglas MacArthur.

Bear Mountain and Harriman State Parks provide year-round outdoor recreational opportunities. Boating, hiking, picnicking, swimming, fishing, and cross-country skiing are the favorite pastimes here, and the drives along Lake Welch and the Seven Lakes — spectacular at any time of year — are down-right glorious in the fall.

The boyhood home of Franklin Delano Roosevelt, 32nd President of the United States, is located in Hyde Park, a few miles to the north of Poughkeepsie. Nearby Val-Kill cot-tage, where Eleanor Roosevelt lived from 1945 to 1962, is the only historic site in America devoted to a first lady.

The scenic wonders of the Hudson Valley region provided inspiration to a group of 19th-century artists known as the Hudson River School. Foremost amongst them was Frederic E. Church, whose picturesque villa, Olana, in the town of Hudson, is a 37-room Middle Eastern fantasy, with sweeping valley and river views. A drive northeast will take you to Old Chatham, and a very different sensibili-ty. Here, the Shaker Museum is filled with the austere, no-frills objects and artifacts made famous by the late-18th-century English reli-gious sect known as Shakers.

Franklin Delano Roosevelt Home, Hyde Park

The Catskills

Rock climbing in Catskill Park

Resorts and wilderness typify the scenic Catskills region west of the Hudson Valley. Sports lovers and outdoor enthusiasts flock to the Catskills to enjoy some of the best trout fishing in America, as well as hunting, camp-ing, golfing, skiing, hiking, rock climbing, and hang gliding. Countless hotels and inns — from the well-known resorts in the "Borscht Belt" to cozy bed-and-breakfasts and rustic lodges — cater to those seeking a respite from city life. Add museums, historic sites, wineries, and summer festivals and you'll begin to see why the Catskills are one of the most popular and fun-filled destinations in New York State.

The living "centerpiece" of the region is the 688,660-acre Catskill State Park encircling the Catskill Mountains. Slide Mountain, near Shandaken in the central Catskills, is the high-est peak, at 4,190 feet. Hunter Mountain, Belleayre Mountain, and Highmount Ski Center offer the best skiing in the area.

The heart of the Catskills busy resort region is Monticello, where giant resort hotels feature top-name entertainers year-round. For genera-tions this popular area has drawn vacationers who come to fish in its lakes and trout streams, play golf on one of the area's numerous cours-es, and enjoy summer theater and nightclubs. To the southwest is the Delaware River, pro-viding opportunities for whitewater canoeing, kayaking, rafting, and, of course, more fishing.

Fly-fishers cast for the big ones throughout the Catskills, which boasts over 2,200 miles of trout streams. In fact, American fly-fishing was "invented" here in the mid-1800s, at Junction Pool near Roscoe. Called "Trout Town, USA," Roscoe and Junction Pool remain a mecca for anglers.

Airplanes and hang gliders soar through the skies above Ellenville in Ulster County, and fur-ther south at Wurtsboro. After riding the ther-mals above Ellenville you can explore the underground caves of nearby Ice Caves Mountain.

Country shopping in Woodstock

Woodstock, perhaps the most famous town in the Catskills, is filled with arts and crafts gal-leries, antique shops, and restaurants. Summer performances of music and theater add to the town's continuing popularity. The legendary 1969 "Woodstock Nation" music fes-tival was actually held in Bethel, some 50 miles to the southwest.

A special Catskills attraction loved by chil-dren and adults alike is the Delaware & Ulster Rail Ride, which runs between Arksville and Fleischmanns along the Catskill Scenic Trail.

Capital — Saratoga

Capital — Saratoga, situated between the Hudson Valley, the Adirondacks, and the Central — Leatherstocking region to the west, is quintessential New York — a region that's as American as "Uncle Sam," as picturesque as a Grandma Moses painting, as up-to-date as Albany, and as exciting as the race track at Saratoga.

Albany, the capital of the Empire State, is the oldest continuous settlement of America's original 13 colonies and provides visitors with a host of varied attractions, from tours of his-toric homes and buildings to performances at the "Egg," the city's modernistic performing arts center. Albany's governmental office com-plex, the 42-story Empire State Plaza, is also home to the New York State Museum and the New York State Modern Art collection. The adjacent State Capitol building is a century-old structure noted for its intricate carving and "Million Dollar Staircase."

Fort Crailo State Historic Landmark, located in Rensselaer, is another architectural and his-torical gem. Erected in 1704, the house — where "Yankee Doodle" is reputed to have been written — is now a Museum of Hudson Valley Dutch culture.

Empire State Plaza, Albany

Albany, Troy, and Schenectady comprise what is known as the tri-city area of Capital-Saratoga. Troy was the home of meat-packer Sam Wilson, who supplied beef to the U.S. Army during the War of 1812 and became known as "Uncle Sam," the personification of America. While in Troy be sure to visit the unique River Spark Visitor Center, a 28-mile heritage trail with more than 60 significant points of interest.

Schenectady, with its array of 18th-century architecture, is a surprising architectural "find" for many modern-day explorers. Head for the Stockade, a small downtown area that contains over 60 houses and churches built between 1700 and 1850, then stroll through the beautiful grounds of Union College, the first planned campus in America.

The rolling hills of Rensselaer County near the Vermont border provided inspiration for the landscapes of Grandma Moses, one of America's best-loved primitive artists, who lived and painted in the pre-Revolutionary hamlet of White Creek and is buried in Maple Grove Cemetery in Hoosick Falls.

The gambling is gone, but Saratoga still bubbles over with excitement every summer when the Saratoga Performing Arts Center plays host to an acclaimed season of ballet, symphony concerts, theater and jazz. Horse racing fans still converge at beautiful Saratoga Race Course, the nation's oldest Thoroughbred track, every August to watch the best racehorses in the country compete in daily flat-track trials. Any

Saratoga Race Course, Saratoga

season is a good time to visit Saratoga, though, for the town has parks, antique stores, museums, and over 700 structures listed on the National Register of Historic Places.

One of the Capital-Saratoga's most unique natural attractions is the geological trail in the 1,347-acre John Boyd Thacher State Park, which winds among the richest fossil-bearing formations in the world and provides breathtaking vistas of the Hudson and Mohawk valleys and the Green and Adirondack mountains.

The Adirondacks

Ausable Chasm Scenic Gorge, Ausable Chasm

The Adirondacks region in upper New York State is one of the greatest recreational areas in the world, a majestic land with millions of acres of forested wilderness, mountains, lakes, waterfalls, rushing rivers and streams teeming with fish. Lake George and Lake Placid are popular Adirondack resort destinations, but visitors to the region can also savor the quiet solitude of small towns or pitch a tent in remote lakeside campgrounds where the native wildlife provides a morning wake-up call.

Adirondack Park, established by New York State in 1892, encompasses nearly 6 million acres (over 9,375 square miles) of land and is nearly three times the size of Yellowstone National Park. Future development has been prohibited on 2.3 million acres, which are designated "forever wild."

Lake George, at the southern tip of the 32-mile-long lake of the same name, is the region's largest and most popular summer resort town. The attractions here run the gamut — from historic Fort William Henry to Great Escape Fun Park, the largest amusement park in the Adirondacks. You can cruise through the island-studded waters of Lake George on a steamboat and drive or hike the 5.5-mile Prospect Mountain Veterans Memorial Highway for a 100-mile view of 5 states. There's hot-air ballooning, theater and, from mid-July to mid-August, the acclaimed Lake George Opera Festival, which performs opera in English.

The Adirondack region is bounded on the east by Lake Champlain, where historic sites

and natural wonders compete for attention. Fort Ticonderoga, built by the French in 1755, has been restored to its original appearance and contains a noteworthy museum. One of the region's most exciting scenic marvels is Ausable Chasm, massive stone formations formed near Lake Champlain over 500 million years ago.

The excellent sports facilities at Lake Placid, an official Olympic training center and the other resort hub of the Adirondacks, ensures a steady stream of year-round visitors. Whiteface Mountain, site of the Olympic Alpine competitions in 1932 and 1980, is New York's largest ski area. Summer visitors can ice skate in the Olympic arena, play golf and tennis, go horseback riding, and attend theater and concert performances at the Lake Placid Center for the Arts.

Saranac Lake, Tupper Lake, and Raquette Pond are ideal for canoeing, and farther west, in the Saint Regis Canoe Area, power boats are entirely prohibited. In pristine areas like these, where the dip of an oar and the cry of a loon are the only sounds, the wilderness magic of the Adirondacks is at its most profound.

Thousand Islands — Seaway

The northwest corner of upper New York State along the island-studded Saint Lawrence River and northeastern shore of Lake Ontario is known as the Thousand Islands — Seaway. Throughout the region, often called "America's 4th seacoast" international bridges span the mighty Saint Lawrence River, connecting New York State to the Canadian province of Ontario. Boating, fishing, exploring the islands, and camping in one of the area's many fine state campgrounds are popular activities here, but there are also historic port towns and interesting museums to explore.

The Seaway Trail, part of the National Recreational Trail System, is a scenic and historic motor route that winds along the Saint Lawrence River and Lake Ontario as far as Niagara Falls and the Pennsylvania border. It begins (or ends) in Rooseveltown near Massena, the "home" of the Saint Lawrence Seaway, the longest navigable inland waterway in the world, stretching some 2,300 miles from the Atlantic Ocean to the Great Lakes.

Ogdensburg was the first settlement in northern New York (1749), and its Federal Customs House is the oldest active federal building in America. The town is also the home of the Frederic Remington Art Museum, which houses the country's largest single collection of paintings, bronzes, and sketches by this artistic master of the Old West. Excellent state campgrounds can be found at regular intervals along the Seaway Trail south of Ogdensburg.

If you want to explore some of the Thousand Islands (actually, there are closer to 1,800 of them) within the Saint Lawrence, you'll find tour boats at Alexandria Bay, a busy resort hub, offering a variety of exciting excursion possibilities. One of the region's signature landmarks, the 6-story, 120-room Boldt

Boldt Castle, near Alexandria Bay

Castle, is a featured stop-off point on most of these cruises.

Clayton, like Alexandria Bay, acts as a river excursion center and port town for those who have summer homes on the islands. Boat lovers shouldn't miss the Thousand Island Museum, with nautical displays that range from a small launch owned by Ulysses S. Grant to a collection of early outboard motors.

Horne's Ferry, the only international ferry in New York State, leaves from Cape Vincent for round-trip tours to Wolfe Island and Canada. A picturesque harbor, well-preserved historic district, and public beach make Sackets Harbor on Black River Bay a popular stop-over destination. Sackets Harbor Battlefield, scene of heavy fighting between the Americans and the British during the War of 1812, is one of the region's outstanding historical sites.

Central — Leatherstocking

The Central — Leatherstocking region is the heartland of New York State, 7,000 square miles that summarize the state's long history and varied character. With its surprising wealth of museums, stately homes, zoos, historic sites, and recreational spots, Central — Leatherstocking is a region that can be savored in every season.

The unspoiled hamlet of Cooperstown, on the shores of Lake Otsego, boasts three of the region's best museums. Visit the National Baseball Hall of Fame and Museum for an exciting multi-media look at the origins, history, and greatest players of America's national pastime; then stroll down to Doubleday Field where the sport began in 1839 and the annual Hall-of-Fame game is held every summer. The Farmers' Museum features exhibits and demonstrations of 19th-century farm life, while a superb collection of American folk art is on display in the colonnaded, red-brick Fenimore House Museum. There's also a resident theater company and the famed Glimmerglass Opera,

which performs in a new partially open-air theater at the north end of Otsego Lake.

Historic Utica, with its colonial, Revolutionary, and Erie Canal monuments and attractions, appeals to all ages. One of New York's finest art collections is housed at the Munson-Williams-Proctor Institute. Kids love the Utica Zoo and the "hands-on" exhibits at Utica's Children's Museum of History, Natural History, and Science.

In the center of Rome stands Fort Stanwix National Monument, one of the region's most outstanding Revolutionary War sites. With the building of the Erie Canal, Rome surged to life as one of New York's busiest canalside trading towns. This era comes vividly to life at the Erie Canal Village with its tavern, blacksmith shop, schoolhouse, and other period buildings.

The picturesque lakeside town of Cazenovia, founded in 1793, is noted for its maple sugar farms, apple orchards and cider mills, cozy country inns, sailing regattas, antique shops, and historic homes. One "must-see" here is

Baseball Hall of Fame, Cooperstown

"Lorenzo," a handsome Federal-style mansion constructed in 1806.

Hundreds of family farms characterize the rural lifestyle of the Central — Leatherstocking region. Stopping at one of the area's many roadside stands for a selection of fresh fruits and vegetables, tasting fresh-pressed cider at a cider mill, or visiting one of the numerous maple sugar farms will add to your enjoyment of New York's heartland. Outdoor enthusiasts can camp, picnic, and hike at over a dozen state parks, canoe in the rushing waters of Schoharie Creek near Middleburgh, fish in one of the area's well-stocked streams and lakes, and, in the winter, ski, skate, and snowmobile.

The Finger Lakes

Retreating Ice Age glaciers carved out the deep valleys, lakes, and nearly 1,000 waterfalls that characterize the natural beauty and uncrowded landscape of the Finger Lakes region. Bordered on the north by Lake Ontario and on the south by Pennsylvania, this 9,000-square-mile area is home to Rochester and Syracuse, New York's third and fourth largest cities, dozens of vineyards and wineries, and an exciting array of museums, cultural events, and recreational possibilities.

Boating, fishing, waterskiing, swimming, and wind-surfing are understandably popular activities on the 11 Finger Lakes. In addition, the region offers outdoor lovers a spectacular bevy of parks, campgrounds, and other scenic areas to explore. These include the 13,232-acre Finger Lakes National Forest, the only national forest in New York State; the Genesee River Gorge in Letchworth State Park, known as the "Grand Canyon of the East;" Montezuma National Wildlife Refuge near Seneca Falls, with a self-guided auto route; and the thundering 215-foot waterfall in Taughannock Falls State Park, the highest straight-drop falls east of the Rockies. For a truly unique experience visit Watkins Glen State Park near Corning, where you can view 19 waterfalls, and attend a

Corning Glass Center, Corning

fascinating sound, light, and laser show called Timespell that recreates the natural history of the area over some 45 million centuries.

Salt was what brought the Indians and later settlers to Syracuse, which is still known as "Salt City." The reconstructed 1856 salt factory in Syracuse's Salt Museum shows how this once-valuable commodity was produced, while historical reminders of Syracuse's past as an Erie Canal town can be found at the Erie Canal Museum; Clinton and Hanover Squares, where the canal intersected Syracuse in 1820; and the Canal Education Center, located on a 35-mile stretch of the original canal between Syracuse and Rome.

Rochester, on Lake Ontario, is at its best in late May when it hosts its annual Lilac Festival. Known as "The Picture City" because the Kodak Company was founded here, Rochester is home to the International Museum of Photography, the largest and most outstanding collection of photographic art and technology in the world. The museum is located in a new building next to the George Eastman House, the restored 50-room residence of Kodak's founder. Fabulous period architecture and several fine museums add to Rochester's appeal.

What Rochester is to photography, Corning is to glass. The exhibits at the fabulous Corning Glass Center depict the art, history, science, and industry of glass from prehistoric to contemporary times. The Center is also home to the Steuben Glass Factory, where you can watch craftspeople blow molten glass into works of art.

Mark Twain spent over 20 summers in Elmira, southeast of Corning in the Chemung Valley, working on such classic works as *The Adventures of Huckleberry Finn*. Twain memorabilia, including his octagonal study, built like the cabin of a Mississippi riverboat, can be seen in Cowles Hall at Elmira College. Elmira is now a famous sailplane and soaring center and its National Soaring Museum, exhibiting historic gliders and sailplanes and offering simulated cockpit flights, is one of the most exciting in the region.

Seneca Falls, at the northern end of Cayuga Lake, became the birthplace of America's women's rights movement in 1848 when the first women's rights convention was held there. Visitors can tour the Elizabeth Cady Stanton Home in the Women's Rights National Historical Park and the National Women's Hall of Fame, which honors famous American women from Jane Addams and Eleanor Roosevelt to Billie Jean King.

The Niagara Frontier

A visit to Niagara Falls is certainly the high point of any trip to the Niagara Frontier region in the far northwestern corner of New York State, but in this five-county area, bounded on the north by Lake Ontario and on the west by Lake Erie and the Niagara River, you'll also find New York's second-largest city, Buffalo. In addition, there are many scenic villages, scores of amusement centers for the kids, splendid parks and gardens, unusual museums, and the best "antiquing" around.

For sheer size and power, Niagara Falls,

Genesee River, Letchworth State Park

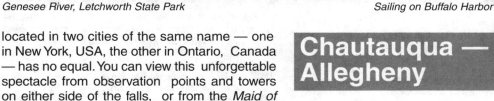
Sailing on Buffalo Harbor

located in two cities of the same name — one in New York, USA, the other in Ontario, Canada — has no equal. You can view this unforgettable spectacle from observation points and towers on either side of the falls, or from the *Maid of the Mist* boat tour, in operation since 1846. Surrounding the falls is Niagara Reservation State Park, the oldest state park in the country, with an excellent visitor orientation center.

The historic village of Lewiston is the home of Artpark, the only state park in the country devoted to the visual and performing arts. Farther north, at the tip of Lake Ontario, is Old Fort Niagara, a pre-Revolutionary fort whose original stone buildings have been remarkably preserved.

The windy, waterfront city of Buffalo is filled with important Victorian and Art Deco architectural treasures. With over a dozen theaters, a zoo, museums, concerts by the Buffalo Philharmonic at Kleinhans Music Hall, sports events in Orchard Park and Marine Midland Arena, nightclubs, and elegant restaurants, New York's second-largest city stays busy around the clock. One of the world's greatest collections of contemporary art fills the galleries of Buffalo's famous Albright-Knox Art Gallery.

Two wildlife areas in the Niagara Frontier region provide sanctuary for a wide variety of animals and a host of recreational opportunities for outdoor enthusiasts. The 11,000-acre Iroquois National Wildlife Refuge and 10,000-acre Oak Orchard and Tonawanda Wildlife Management Areas have miles of hiking trails, streams for fishing and canoeing, and offer some of the best bird watching in the state. Campers can choose from several scenic state parks along the southern shore of Lake Ontario.

Bicycling in Allegany State Park

Chautauqua — Allegheny

Three counties in the southwestern corner of New York State form the region known as Chautauqua — Allegheny. Lake Erie acts as the western boundary of this peaceful, heavily forested, and predominately rural area. Vineyards, sparkling lakes, ski resorts, Amish and Native American communities, beautiful Allegany State Park, and, of course, the distinguished Chautauqua Institution itself are highlights in this region of unhurried charm and abundant recreational opportunities.

The region's focal point is the Chautauqua Institution on the western shore of Chautauqua Lake. The Institution was founded in 1874 as a summer training camp for Methodist Sunday school teachers and quickly grew in prominence as a summer-long cultural enclave where the public gathered for lectures, concerts, plays, and healthy recreation — a tradition that continues today.

Other points of interest can be found along the shores of 22-mile-long Chautauqua Lake. At Mayville, on the lake's northern tip, you can take a scenic lake cruise aboard the steamboat Chautauqua Belle and tour the Sea Lion, a 90-ton, hand-built replica of a 16th-century English merchant ship.

A number of restored 19th-century buildings add to the appeal of Fredonia, a small college town where the first natural gas well in America was discovered in 1821. Three miles north is the Erie lakeshore community of Dunkirk, dominated by the 95-foot Historic Dunkirk Lighthouse in Veteran's Park.

Three interconnecting lakes — Cassadaga, Conewango, and Leon — make this a prime canoeing, swimming, and fishing area. The Conewango Valley has many Amish settlements where Amish arts and crafts are sold in private homes.

Salamanca, the only city to be located on a Native American reservation, lies adjacent to the 65,000-acre Allegany State Park, the largest state park in New York. Here you'll find cabins, tent and trailer sites for camping, lakes and streams for fishing, and miles of scenic trails for hiking, cross-country skiing, horseback riding, and snowmobiling.

11

Points of Interest

New York City

American Museum of Natural History   212-769-5100
Exhibitions on people and nature, including displays of dinosaurs, exhibits on various cultures, minerals, and gems. Special events and "Naturemax Theater." (Manhattan)   Map 86

Bronx Zoo   718-367-1010
One of America's largest zoos, home to over 3,600 animals, which can be viewed in recreated natural habitats up close or via monorails and "Skyfari" cable cars. (Bronx)   75   B5

Brooklyn Museum   718-638-5000
Collections of Egyptian, Primitive American and European art. Outdoor sculpture garden. (Brooklyn)   75   A4

Carnegie Hall   212-247-7800
Since 1891, this great concert hall has presented the world's greatest orchestra and musicans. Tours available. (Manhattan)   Map 86

Ellis Island National Monument   212-363-3200
Self-guided tours of the Ellis Island Immigration Museum. For ferry information call 212-269-5755. (New York Harbor)   Map 86

Empire State Building   212-736-3100
Atop the famous 1454-foot-high skyscraper, this observatory commands a 50-mile view across New York City and portions of four states. (Manhattan)   Map 86

Federal Hall National Memorial   212-264-8711
The site where George Washington was sworn in as the first President of the United States in 1789. Now houses museums of early New York City. (Manhattan)   Map 86

Fraunces Tavern Museum   212-425-1778
A complex of five historic buildings, including the 18th-century tavern where George Washington bade farewell to his officers in 1783. Museum includes 18th- and 19th-century decorative arts. (manhattan)   Map 86

Frick Collection   212-288-0700
Outstanding collection of 14th- to 19th-century European masterworks housed in a Fifth Avenue mansion. (Manhattan)   Map 86

Guggenheim Museum   212-423-3500
One of the nation's finest collections of modern art is housed in this architectural masterpiece by Frank Lloyd Wright. (Manhattan)   Map 86

Hayden Planetarium   212-769-5100
This branch of the American Museum of Natural History features a spectacular star dome. Programs change triannually. (Manhattan)   Map 86

Intrepid Sea-Air-Space Museum   212-245-0072
900-foot-long WWII aircraft carrier converted into a museum of history and technology. ships, airplanes, and space vehicles are also on display. (Manhattan)   Map 86

Lincoln Center for the Performing Arts   212-875-5400
A cluster of great performance halls that feature the New York Philharmonic, the New York City Ballet and Opera companies, the Metropolitan Opera, two dramatic theaters, and the Juilliard School of Music. (Manhattan)   Map 86

Metropolitan Museum of Art   212-535-7710
The largest museum in the Western Hemisphere. "The Met" houses one of the world's leading collections of art, spanning the history of civilization. (Manhattan)   Map 86

**Museum of Jewish Heritage —
   A Living Memorial to the Holocaust**   212-968-1800
The history of the struggles and triumphs of the Jewish people told through artifacts, films and photographs; New York City's newest museum. (Manhattan)   Map 86

Museum of Modern Art   212-708-9480
Exhibits of a wide range of modern art dating from the 1880's to the present. (Manhattan)   Map 86

New York Botanical Garden   718-817-8779
One of the world's largest gardens, featuring magnificent greenhouses and the Enid A. Haupt conservatory. Adjacent to the Bronx Zoo. (Bronx)   75   B2

New York Public Library   212-661-7220
With one of the greatest collections in the world, this landmark Beaux Arts location offers changing exhibits within a superb research facility. (Manhattan)   Map 86

New York Stock Exchange   212-656-5167
A taped narration describes the view of the trading floor, as seen from the two-tiered observation gallery. (Manhattan)   Map 86

Radio City Music Hall   212-247-4777
A masterpiece of Art Deco architecture located in Rockfeller Center, featuring a variety of performances. Home of the Rockettes dance troup. (Manhattan)   Map 86

Saint Patrick's Cathedral   212-753-2261
The seat of the Catholic Archdiocese of New York, this magnificent Gothic cathedral was completed in 1879. (Manhattan)   Map 86

**Smithsonians George Gustav Heye
   Center of the National Museum of
   the American Indian**   212-668-6624
A diverse collection of artifacts dedicated to the preservation of native American cultures and communities. (Lower Manhattan)   Map 86

South Street Seapot   212-748-8600
An eleven-block indoor/outdoor shopping and eating extravaganza. Also features museums, galleries, historic ships, and seasonal performances. (Manhattan)   Map 86

Statue of Liberty National Monument   212-363-3200
This 152-foot copper statue was presented to the U.S. by France in 1886. Its 150-foot-high island pedestal houses a museum devoted to the immigrant experience and the history of "Lady Liberty." For ferry information call 212-363-5755. (New York Harbor)   74   E4

Studio Museum in Harlem   212-864-4500
Museum celebrating African American culture and heritage. (Manhattan)   Map 86

The Cathedral of Saint John the Divine   212-932-7314
The largest Neo-Gothic cathedral in the world. Grounds include a Biblical Garden, Museum, and gift shop. (Manhattan)   Map 86

Trinity Church   212-602-0800
Reconstructed in 1846 on the original 1697 site. Contains a museum, and is the burial ground of Alexander Hamilton and Robert Fulton. (Manhattan)   Map 86

United National Headquarters   212-963-7713
Guided tours available of the grounds, containing artwork and sculpture from member nations. The "Parliament of Man" chamber is open to the public during General Assembly meetings. (Manhattan)   75   A3

Whitney Museum   212-570-3676
Home to the largest collection of 20th-century American art. Regularly changing exhibits feature the finest in contemporary film, video and visual arts. (Manhattan)   Map 86

World Trade Center   212-323-2340
At 110 stories, this is the highest skyscraper in New York City. The observatory and gallery on the 107th floor are both open daily. (Manhattan)   74   F4

Long Island

African American Museum   516-572-0730
Special exhibits highlight a regular collection that examines the history and cultural heritage of Long Island African Americans. (Hempstead)   75   E4

American Merchant Marine Museum   516-773-5515
Training center for officers of the American Merchant Marine and U.S. Naval Reserve. Tours of memorial chapel, the grounds and museum available. (Kings Point)   75   C3

Falaise-Guggenheim Estate   516-571-7902
On Long Island's "Gold Coast," a nature center and trail complement tours of the estate of Daniel and Harry Guggenheim, and the neighboring estates of Falaise, Hempstead House and Castlegould. (Port Washington)   75   D2

"Home Sweet Home" Museum   516-324-0713
John Howard Payne (1791-1852), author of "Home Sweet Home," resided in this Salt-box-style home, dating from 1680. Grounds include unique windmills, gardens, and a gallery. (East Hampton)   78   D1

Long Island Game Farm   516-878-6644
A farm park with rides and a collection of exotic and domestic animals. Also features sea lion shows at its "Oceanarium Sea School Theater." Picnic area and snack bar. (Manorville)   77   C2

Montauk Point Lighthouse   516-668-2428
Built by decree of George Washington in 1792, this beautiful lighthouse at the eastern tip of Long Island guards waters ideal for surf and deep-sea fishing. Charter and party boat trips available. (Montauk)   72   B6

Museums at Stony Brook   516-751-0066
A restored Federal Period village featuring a local history museum, the Carriage Museum — which has 90 priceless horse-drawn vehicles — and art museum, featuring 19th-century American artists, and other attractions. (Stony Brook)   76   E2

Nassau County Museum of Art   516-484-9338
Turn-of-the-century mansion with indoor and outdoor exhibits by world renowned artists. (Roslyn Harbor)   75   E3

Old Westbury Gardens   516-333-0048
Over 100 acres of formal gardens, fields and woods surround the elegant Stuart-style mansion of John S. Phipps. Summer lawn concerts and picnic areas. Tours available. (Old Westbury)   75   E3

Parrish Art Museum   516-283-2118
Home to a collection of turn-of-the-century etchings, and works by William Merritt Chase and Fairfield Porter. (Southampton)   78   B2

**Sag Harbor Whaling and
   Historical Museum**   516-725-0770
The 19th-century whaling heritage of Sag Harbor is depicted through tools, artifacts and etchings. (Sag Harbor)   71   C6

Sagamore Hill National Historic Site   516-922-4447
This Victorian mansion overlooking Oyster Bay acted as the summer "White House" of President Theodore Roosevelt, and was later his place of retirement. Includes a museum of personal items and audio-visual exhibits. (Oyster Bay)   75   F2

Vanderbilt Museum   516-854-5555
This splendid mansion, with its elegant gardens, contains many fine decorative art objects and a natural history collection. The estate is also home to a marine museum and the Planetarium Sky Theater. (Centerport)   76   A2

Village Green   516-734-6977
Dating back almost 350 years, this restoration features an english Tudor house with period furnishings (1649), Wickham Farmhouse (1740), and a schoolhouse museum (1840). (Cutchoque)   71   A6

**Walt Whitman Birthplace
   State Historic Site**   516-427-5240
The boyhood home of the renowned poet. Museum includes manuscripts, pictures and memorabilia of this great American poet. (Huntington)   76   B3

Whaling Museum   516-692-9626
Exhibits include tools of the trade, artifacts, and over 400 pieces of scrimshaw. Hands-on displays of marine mammal bones, films and dioramas are also featured. (Cold Spring Harbor)   76   A2

The Hudson Valley

American Museum of Firefighting   518-828-7695
The oldest collection of firefighting memorabilia in the U.S. Operated by the Fireman's Association of the State of New York. (Hudson)   59   C3

Caramoor Center for Music & the Arts   914-232-5035
A summer music festival is held on the grounds of this beautiful Italian-style mansion, which has an extensive art collection and gardens. Tours available.
(Katonah)   68   E4

Clermont State Historic Site (Seasonal)   518-537-4240
The family home and gardens of Robert R. Livingston, architect of the Louisiana Purchase. Picnicking and nature trails. (Germantown)   59   B5

Eleanor Roosevelt National Historic Site — Val-Kill   914-229-9115
The private retreat and retirement residence of Mrs. Roosevelt from 1945 to 1962. The home is furnished with her unique cottage-industry furniture, made on-site during the Great Depression. (Hyde Park)   64   B3

Harness Racing Museum & Hall of Fame   914-294-6330
A museum devoted to the history and Standardbred champions of harness racing. Near the site of America's oldest harness racing track. Guided tours and gift shop.
(Goshen)   67   C2

Home of Franklin D. Roosevelt — National Historic Site Museum & Library   914-229-9115
Museum home and burial site of our 32nd President and First Lady. (Hyde Park)   64   A3

John Jay Homestead State Historic Site   914-232-5651
Federal-style estate of John Jay, the first Chief Justice of the Supreme Court, former New York governor, and author of the State's first Constitution. (Katonah)   68   E3

Knox Headquarters State Historic Site   914-561-5498
Historic stone house used as a headquarters for General Washington's commanding officers during the American Revolution. Grist mill and native plant sanctuary on site.
(Vails Gate)   67   F1

Lyndhurst   914-631-4481
The Gothic Revival home 19th-century financier Jay Gould. Contains elegant period furnishings and offers seasonal events. (Tarrytown)   68   B6

Martin Van Buren National Historic Site   518-758-9689
Named "Lindenwald," this was the retirement estate of our eighth President. (Kinderhook)   59   D2

Museum Village   914-782-8247
Re-enactors and craftspersons present a living history of Orange County in an authentic 19th-century setting.
(Monroe)   67   D2

New Windsor Cantonment State Historic Site   914-561-1765
The only remaining wooden camp complex from the Revolutionary War, dating from 1782. Offers reenactments of military life through artillery demonstrations, drills, blacksmithing, and campfire cooking.
(New Windsor)   67   F1

Olana State Historic Site   518-828-0135
This 37-room Persian-style estate was designed by the renowned 19th-century Hudson River School artist Frederic E. Church. Includes nature trails and gardens.
(Hudson)   59   C4

Old Rhinebeck Aerodrome   914-758-8610
A collection of vintage aircraft, dating from 1908 to 1937. The museum also offers rides in open-cockpit biplanes and a regular airshow. (Rhinebeck)   64   B1

Philipsburg Manor   914-631-3992
Restored 18th-century complex includes a stone manor house and gristmill. Period-costumed guides conduct tours.
(Sleepy Hollow)   68   B5

Shaker Museum   518-794-9100
Museum exhibits 200 years of Shaker history and culture. Includes a library, lifestyle education center, herb gardens, and nature trails. (Old Chatham)   59   F1

Storm King Art Center   914-534-3115
A 500-acre open-air sculpture park and museum offering family activities, entertainment and tours.
(Mountainville)   67   E1

Sunnyside   914-591-8763
This English Country-style house was home to the famed 19th-century author, Wahsington Irving. His great work, "The Legend of Sleepy Hollow," is evoked in this restoration and museum honoring his life. (Tarrytown)   68   B6

Sugar Loaf Village   914-469-9181
A festive mix of galleries, antiques, crafts and entertainment. (Sugar Loaf)   67   C3

United States Military Academy at West Point   914-938-2638
The United States Army's military academy, founded in 1802. Features cadet parades and military museums with guided tours. (West Point)   67   F2

Vanderbilt Mansion National Historic Site   914-229-9115
Magnificent Beaux-Arts-style mansion completed in 1900. The mansion contains lavish furnishings and decor rivaling palaces of Europe. (Hyde Park)   64   A3

Washington's Headquarters State Historic Site — Hasbrouck House   914-562-1195
General Washington's strategic headquartes during the American Revolution. Adjoined by a museum of military artifacts. (Newburgh)   68   C6

Young-Morse Historic Site   914-454-4500
The American artist and inventor of Morse Code is immortalized in this 1853 Italianate villa. Includes telegraphy exhibits, hiking trails and wildlife sanctuary. (Poughkeepsie)   64   A4

The Catskills

Catskill Game Farm (Seasonal)   518-678-9595
A zoological adventure featuring some 2,000 rare animals. Travel one-half mile by train through a bird sanctuary. Animal shows daily, and a children's play area. (Catskill)   59   A3

Delaware & Hudson Canal Museum   914-687-9311
Depicts the history of the D & H Canal — in operation from 1828 to 1898 — and the many industries and communities that it spawned. (High Falls)   63   E3

Delaware and Ulster Rail Ride   914-586-3877
Explore the Catskill Scenic Trail on this open-air rail trip that runs from Arkville to Fleischmanns. (Arkville)   57   E5

Hunter Mountain   518-263-4223
Home to downhill skiing in winter, Hunter Mountain is host to numerous ethnic and music festivals in summer. The highest chairlift in the Catskills offers astonishing views year-round. (Hunter)   58   D4

Ice Caves Mountain   914-647-7989
Descend to beautiful underground caverns that took millions of years to form. (Ellenville)   63   B4

Senate House State Historic Site   914-338-2786
Site of the first New York State Senate meeting in 1777. Historic collections and contemporary art museum.
(Kingston)   63   F1

Woodstock   914-679-6234
The most famous town in the Catskills region boasts music, art, theater and unique shops. Highlights include the Center for Photography, Kleinert/James Art Center, Maverick Concert Hall, River Arts Repertory at Byrdcliffe Theater, and the Woodstock Artist's Association. For more information, contact the Chamber of Commerce at the number above.
(Woodstock)   58   E6

Wurtsboro Soaring Planes   914-888-2791
Established in 1927, this is the oldest such site in America, and the base of over 60 sailplanes. Rides, instruction and passive viewing are offered. (Wurtsboro)   63   A5

Capital — Saratoga

Albany Institute of History and Art   518-463-4478
New York State's oldest museum, founded in 1791, featuring changing exhibits, lectures, and research library, all devoted to history and culture of the Upper Hudson River Valley. (Albany)   Map 79

Albany Urban Cultural Park   518-434-5132
Year-round tourist information services center, including exhibits on the history of Albany, the Henry Hudson Planetarium, self-guided and guided tours of the city, and seasonal trolley tour of the downtown area.
(Albany)   Map 79

Bennington Battlefield State Historic Site   518-686-7109
This national historic landmark commemorates the victory of American forces over General Burgoyne's British troops, which invaded from Canada in 1777. Maps and interpretive markers depict the battle. (Hoosick Falls)   46   C1

Cherry Hill   518-434-4791
This Georgian-style mansion was the Van Rensselaer family home from 1787 until 1963. The furnishings and cultural items reflect 200 years of cultural change in America.
(Albany)   Map 79

Empire Center at The Egg   518-473-1845
With its striking egg-shaped design, this world-renowned institute is home to a professional stage company, and features touring performances of drama, dance and music. Educational and cultural programs offered year-round.
(Albany)   Map 79

First Church in Albany   518-463-4449
Originally chartered in 1642, this church contains the oldest pulpit and weathervane in America, dating from 1656.
(Albany)   Map 79

Fort Crailo State Historic Landmark   518-463-8738
Museum of the Hudson Valley Dutch Culture, housed in the former estate of the Van Rensselaer family. Tours and cooking demonstrations available.
(Rensselaer)   Map 79

National Museum of Racing & Thoroughbred Hall of Fame   518-584-0400
This multi-media museum highlights "The Sport of Kings," and decades of Thoroughbred champions.
(Saratoga Springs)   32   D5

Saratoga Performing Arts Center   518-587-3330
At the Saratoga Spa State Park, this world-class center features performances by the New York City Ballet and Opera, top stars on tour, and the annual Jazz Festival.
(Saratoga Springs)   32   C6

Schenectady Museum & Planetarium   518-382-7890
Museum features hands-on displays in technology and natural science, a 93-acre nature preserve, a radio transmitting exhibit, and a planetarium show.
(Schenectady)   45   A3

Schuyler Mansion State Historic Site   518-434-0834
Washington, Franklin, Hamilton and other historic figures were entertained in this 1761 Georgian mansion, originally the home of Revolutionary War General Philip Schuyler. The home and gardens showcase fine furniture, porcelain, glassware, and artwork of the Colonial and Federal periods.
(Albany)   Map 79

Shushan Covered Bridge Museum   518-854-3870
This covered bridge, built in 1858, is now a museum of local history, adjacent to an 1852 restored one-room schoolhouse. (Shushan)   33   B5

Skenesborough Museum   518-499-0716
Whitehall, the birthplace of the US Navy (in 1776), features this museum with models of the first navy, including the War of 1812's "Saratoga," and modern battleships. Includes canal and railroad exhibits of Lake Champlain's South Bay.
(Whitehall)   20   B6

State Capitol   518-474-2418
Guided tours include the famed "Million Dollar Staircase," the State Assembly and State Senate Chamber, Governor's Office, Hall of Governors and a military museum.
(Albany)   45   C5

State Museum   518-474-5877
Located within the Empire State Plaza, this is America's oldest and largest museum of state heritage. Major sound and video exhibits of all types highlight the many splendors of New York State. Changing exhibits on art, history, and technology also featured. (Albany)   Map 79

13

Capital — Saratoga, cont.

Ten Broeck Mansion　518-436-9826
Home of Revolutionay War General Abraham Ten Broeck, this Federal-style house was built in 1798, and is preserved with period furnishings, artwork and personal items. (Albany) Map 79

Troy Savings Bank Music Hall　518-273-0038
One of the finest acoustical theaters in America. This unique structure hosts the Albany Symphony Orchestra, and guest artists, and features the Troy Chromatics. Originally built in 1871. (Troy) 45 D4

Uncle Sam's Grave　518-272-7520
Burial place of Sam Wilson, the man upon whom the caricature "Uncle Sam" was based. (Troy) 45 E3

**Walworth Memorial Museum/Casino/
　Historical Society**　518-584-6920
A beautiful Italianate structure, once part of the late 19th-century gambling casino and mineral spring resort that made Saratoga Springs famous. Museum highlights the gambling era, and exhibits furnishings from the home of New York State's last Chancellor, Reuben Hyde Walworth. (Saratoga Springs) 32 B6

The Adirondacks

Adirondack Center Museum　518-873-6466
Museum explores early Adirondack life, and features an audio-visual show of Lake Champlain history. Includes art galleries and wildflower gardens. (Elizabethtown) 12 F4

Adirondack Museum　518-352-7311
A museum complex of 20 exhibit buildings, overlooking beautiful Blue Mountain Lake. Features displays on history, art, life, work and leisure in the Adirondack region. (Blue Mountain Lake) 18 A2

Adirondack Park Visitors　518-282-2000 (Newcomb)
　Interpretive Centers　518-327-3000 (Paul Smiths)
Visitor orientation to the park preserve highlights the natural history and value of the region, and includes interactive displays, interpretive trails, scenic vistas and a marsh trek. (Newcomb) 18 D1 (Paul Smiths) 11 C1

Akwesasne Museum　518-358-2240
This history museum of Mohawk Indian heritage is located within the Saint Regis Mohawk Reservation. (Hogansburg) 3 D1

Ausable Chasm (Seasonal)　518-834-7454
This spectacular gorge is crossed by bridge trails and lined with scenic overlooks. White-water boat rides available. (Ausable Chasm) 6 A6

Crown Point State Historic Site　518-597-3666
Originally built by the French in 1734, and reconstructed by the British in 1759, Fort Crown Point controlled the narrows of Lake Champlain. Visitor center offers orientation show. (Crown Point) 13 A6

Fort Ticonderoga (Seasonal)　518-585-2821
This restored 1755 fort features artillery drills, fife and drum parades, and a fort history museum. Scenic drive to the top of Mount Defiance Lookout. (Ticonderoga) 20 B2

Fort William Henry (Seasonal)　518-668-5471
Restored fort from the French and Indian War, revitalized with musket and cannon firings and military drills. Large gift shop with memorabilia. (Lake George) 32 D2

Great Camp Sagamore　315-354-5303
The former summer retreat of the Vanderbilt family, near Raquette Lake. Built in 1897, it is now a museum consisting of 29 buildings, with two dozen fireplaces, period furnishings, artwork and craft shops. (Raquette Lake) 17 E3

Hyde Collection　518-792-1761
This beautiful 1912 Italianate villa features European and American masters, including Degas, Picasso, Whistler and Van Gogh. (Glens Falls) 32 E3

Lake George Steamboat Company　518-668-5777
Narrated cruises lasting one to five hours on a fleet of three large steamboats. Available itineraries include dinner & jazz, moonlight entertainment, and fall foliage cruises. (Lake George) 32 D1

Lake Placid Center for the Arts　518-523-2512
Repertory theater and concerts are staged year-round at this mountain resort arts center. Includes an art gallery, classes, and special performances. (Lake Placid) 11 F3

Mount Van Hoevenberg Recreation Area　518-523-1655
U.S. Olympic training center for luge and bobsled. Public luge and bobsled rides available in the winter, and trolley rides to the scenic top in the summer. Hiking trails and cafeteria. (Lake Placid) 12 B4

Natural Stone Bridge & Caves (Seasonal)　518-494-2283
A scenic wonder consisting of caves, gorge, waterfalls, and wilderness above Schroon Lake. Self-guided excursion includes nature trails, trout fishing, rock shops and cave swimming exhibitions. (Pottersville) 19 B3

Olympic Center Ice Arenas　518-523-1655
Site of the 1932 and 1980 Olympic skating events, and current training camp of the U.S. Olympic hockey and figure skating teams. Open to the public for exhibition hockey games and skating performances. (Lake Placid) 12 A3

Santa's Workshop　518-946-2111
Santa Claus, live reindeer, crafts, rides and entertainment are all a part of this wonderful mountain village. (North Pole) 12 B2

Six Nations Indian Museum (Seasonal)　518-891-2299
Iroquois Six Nations Confederacy defined by Pre-Colombian through contemporary artifacts, exhibits on lifestyles, historic leaders, major contributions and events. Special lectures onthe Iroquois cultural heritage offered. (Onchitota) 11 E1

Thousand Islands — Seaway

Antique Boat Museum　315-686-4104
　& Uncle Sam Boat Tours　315-686-3511
Thousand Islands — Seaway nautical history is exhibited through antique boats, motors, and related items. A 45-munite antique boat cruise is also offered. (Clayton) 7 E3

Boldt Castle (Seasonal)　315-482-9724
Located on Heart Island, this six-story replica of a Rhineland castle is accessible only by boat. (Alexandria Bay) 8 A2

Fort Ontario State Historic Site　315-343-4711
Fortified since 1755 by the French, Bristish and Americans. Attractions include military drills and lifestyle demonstrations, a research library and a cemetery. (Oswego) 26 F1

Frederic Remington Art Museum　315-393-2425
Works by the foremost artist of America's western frontier are on display in the largest collection of his art. Additional collections include Dresden china, cut glass, and Victorian furnishings. (Ogdensburg) 2 A4

H. Lee White Marine Museum　315-342-0480
Museum featuring the history and heritage of Port Oswego on the great Lake Ontario. (Oswego) 26 F1

Richardson Bates House Museum　315-343-1342
A Victorian mansion, authentically restored and furnished in the style of the 1890's. Additional exhibits on Oswego County history. (Oswego) 26 F1

Sackets Harbor Battlefield　315-646-3634
A registered state historic site commemorating a War o\f 1812 naval military center. Includes a restored hotel with a visitors' center and orientation program. (Sackets Harbor) 14 E1

**Saint Lawrence — FDR Power Project
　Visitors' Center**　315-764-0226
Located on Barnhart Island, featuring multimedia exhibits and working models of power production along the great seaway. Observation deck offers views of Lake Saint Lawrence and the Moses-Saunders Power Dam. (Massena) 3 C1

Central — Leatherstocking

**Children's Museum of History,
　Natural History & Science**　315-724-6129
Interactive exhibits and displays form the basis of this popular museum. Educational programs and creative craft workshops are also offered. (Utica) Map 92

Erie Canal Village (Seasonal)　315-337-3999
This restored 1840's canal village includes a train station, old tavern, hotel, shops, schoolhouse, farm cabin, and other village amenities. (Rome) 28 F4

Farmer's Museum　607-547-1450
This 19th-century frontier village recreates life in New York State during the years of 1790-1860 in a living history museum. Consists of craftspeople in authentic costumes and work settings. (Cooperstown) 43 A4

Fenimore House Museum　607-547-1400
This historic home of novelist James Fenimore Cooper now displays a superb collection of American folk art and the works of several great 19th-century artists. Includes memorabilia, sculpture and furnishings from the Cooper estate. (Cooperstown) 43 A4

Fly Creek Cider Mill and Orchard　607-547-9692
The oldest water-powered cider mill in Otsego County, in operation since 1856. Apples and cider available. (Cooperstown) 43 A4

Fort Stanwix National Monument　315-336-2090
A reconstructed Revolutionary War fort now operated by the National Park Service. Features costumed guides, film exhibits, and a museum of fort history. (Rome) Map 91

F.X. Matt Brewery Tour Center　315-732-0022
A Victorian-era brewery restored and active. Tour includes a trolley ride to the 1888 tavern for samples and a brewery shop. (Utica) Map 92

Glimmerglass Opera　607-547-2255
A new "park" theater seats 920 in a semi-convertible open-air environment, and is home to this famous professional English-language opera company. (Cooperstown) 43 A3

Herkimer Diamond Mines　315-891-7355
This famous prospecting site for "Herkimer Diamonds" (quartz crystals) includes a gem and mineral shop, museum of area mining history and concessions. (Herkimer) 30 A5

Herkimer Home State Historic Site　315-823-0398
restored residence of Brigadier General Nicholas Herkimer, who led Revolutionary War troops at Oriskany — the bloodiest battle of the war. Visitor center has audio-visual displays, and seasonal activities that include maple sugar gathering and sheep shearing. (Little Falls) 30 B6

Howe Caverns　518-296-8900
Travel 200 feet below the surface to view these geological wonders. Elevators, walkways and brilliantly colored lights lead you through formations that were millions of years in the making. Includes a boat ride on an underground lake. (Howes Cave) 44 A4

Iroquois Indian Museum　518-296-8949
Exhibits and displays on Iroquois history, arts, crafts and contemporary culture. Also includes a museum shop. (Howes Cave) 44 B4

Lorenzo State Historic Site　315-655-3200
A classic example of Federal-style architecture. Tours include the formal gardens, arboretum, and a new Visitor's Center. (Cazenovia) 41 B1

Munson-Williams-Proctor Institute　315-797-0000
An internationally recognized collection of American and European art dating from the 18th - 20th centuries. Institute comprised of Museum of Art, School of Art, and a Victorian museum-house called "Fountain Elms." (Utica) Map 92

National Baseball Hall of Fame & Museum　607-547-7200
A museum honoring America's favorite pastime. Exhibits feature photographs, artifacts, memorabilia and personal items. A new 200-seat theater presents an audio-visual account of baseball's history. (Cooperstown) 43 A4

National Soccer Hall of Fame 607-432-3351
The history of soccer in the United States is told through video presentations, memorabilia, awards and a feature on World Cup '94. (Oneonta) 56 F1

Old Stone Fort Museum 518-295-7192
This Revolutionary War fortified church (1772), has been a museum and library since 1889. It contains an early Americana collection including one of the oldest existing fire engines (1731), and other items from the 18th and 19th centuries. (Schoharie) 44 B4

Roberson Museum & Science Center 607-772-0660
Museum of regional history, art and science, housed in a restored 1910 mansion, with a planetarium and observatory. (Binghamton) Map 82

Ross Park Zoo 607-724-5461
One of America's oldest zoos, dating from the late 1800's, on 75 acres. (Binghamton) Map 82

Utica Zoo 315-738-0472
Home to over 150 animals, featuring a children's zoo. (Utica) Map 92

The Finger Lakes

Burnet Park Zoo 315-435-8511
Over 1,000 animals in recreated natural habitats, spread over 36 acres. Special bus from downtown area available. (Syracuse) Map 93

Corning Glass Center 607-974-2000
A museum complex consisting of the Corning Glass Factory, Steuben Glass Factory, and the Hall of Science & Technology, exhibiting the history, art, and science of the glass industry. (Corning) 52 F5

Elizabeth Cady Stanton Home/
Women's Rights National Historical Park 315-568-2991
The restored home of the great women's suffrage advocate and feminist pioneer. This national park honors all those who have championed the cause of equal rights for women. (Seneca Falls) 39 C1

Empire Expo Center (State Fairgrounds) 315-487-7711
Hosts a wide variety of entertainments, including exhibits, shows, competitions, sporting events, and racing of all types. (Syracuse) Map 93

Erie Canal Museum 315-471-0593
National Landmark restoration of an 1850's canal boat weigh station, along the original Erie Canal. Now a museum illustrating the waterway's historic importance to Syracuse. (Syracuse) Map 93

Everson Museum of Art 315-474-6064
The nation's finest collection of American ceramics. Home to the Syracuse China Center for the Study of American Ceramics. (Syracuse) Map 93

George Eastman House & International
Museum of Photography 716-271-3361
Houses one of the world's greatest collections of photographic art and technology in the world. Exhibits are housed in a new building adjacent to the restored mansion of the Eastman Kodak founder. (Rochester) Map 90

Joseph Smith Home & Sacred Grove 315-597-4383
The founder of the Mormon Church resided in this restored farmhouse from 1825-1827. Features authentic furnishings and kitchenware. (Palmyra) 25 D6

Memorial Art Gallery 716-473-7720
A collection of nearly 10,000 objects, spanning 5,000 years of civilization. Housed in a grand pavilion with indoor sculpture gardens. (Rochester) Map 90

National Soaring Museum 607-734-3128
The history of motorless flight, and the world's largest assembly of sailplanes and gliders are exhibited in this unique museum. (Elmira) 53 A5

National Women's Hall of Fame 315-568-8060
Recognizes and pays tribute to America's most outstanding women and their achievements. (Seneca Falls) 39 B1

New York Museum of Transportation 716-533-1113
Features road and rail vehicles characteristic of Western New York during the period from 1867 to 1956. Facilities include a gallery, visitor center, gift shop and track car rides. (Rush) 24 D6

Rochester Museum & Science Center
& Strasenburgh Plantarium 716-271-1880
Museum of regional and local history, natural science and anthropology. (Rochester) Map 90

Salt Museum (open May-Sept) 315-453-6715
This restoration of an 1856 salt factory illustrates the heritage of Syracuse as an important salt-producing center — earning the nickname "Salt City." (Syracuse) Map 93

Seneca Park Zoo 716-342-2744
This Genessee riverside zoological park is home to some 200 species of animals. Additional information: 716-336-7200. (Rochester) 24 E4

Strong Museum 716-263-2700
Life and times of the Industrial Revolution are illustrated in this unique museum through extensive collections of dolls and other toys, miniatures, and various decorative arts. (Rochester) Map 90

Susan B. Anthony Home 716-235-6124
This 1860 Victorian house was the home of the women's suffrage movement. Original furnishings and historical source materials of the movement are featured. (Rochester) Map 90

Timespell 607-535-4960
Located within Watkins Glen State Park, this laser light and sound spectacle recreates natural and human history of the past 4.5 billion years. (Watkins Glen) 53 B2

Valentown Museum 716-924-2645
A complex of historic sites dating from 1618, located in the restored Fishers Historic District. Includes the oldest railroad building in the state (1845), and the Fisher Homestead (1811), where the Transcontinental Railroad was first planned. (Fishers) 25 A6

Victorian Doll Museum 716-247-0130
Home to an impressive collection of over 1,000 rare dolls, vintage doll houses and puppets. (North Chili) 24 B5

Niagara Frontier

Albright-Knox Art Gallery 716-882-8700
This museum contains over 12,000 works of art spanning 5,000 years of history. Home to a world-famous collection of contemporary art. (Buffalo) Map 83

Aquarium of Niagara 716-285-3575
Marine Research and exhibition park featuring over 2,000 marine animals, regular dolphin and sea lion shows, as well as a three-acre sculpture park and rose garden. (Niagara Falls) Map 87

Artpark 800-659-PARK
This 200-acre state park is dedicated to the arts, and features major music and dance productions, arts and crafts workshops, and an International Indian Village featuring Native American artistry. Bike and nature trails and picnicking are also available. (Lewiston) 21 F5

Buffalo City Hall 716-851-4200
Sweeping panoramic views of the City and Harbor of Buffalo can be seen from this 28th-floor observation area. (Buffalo) Map 83

Buffalo Museum of Science 716-896-5200
Exhibits on natural history, evolution and civilization. Includes an observatory and an interactive discovery room for children. (Buffalo) Map 83

Buffalo Zoological Gardens 716-837-3900
A fine collection of animals, representing 230 species, in a 23-acre park setting. The zoo also includes a children's section and a popular gorilla exhibit. (Buffalo) Map 83

Herschell Carrousel Factory Museum 716-693-1885
The first merry-go-round was created here in 1883 by Allan Herschell. The museum displays vintage carrousels and other artifacts, tracing the history of amusement rides. (Tonawanda) 22 B6

Kleinhans Music Hall 716-885-4632
The home of the Buffalo Philharmonic. (Buffalo) Map 83

Millard Fillmore Museum (Seasonal) 716-652-8875
A National Landmark restoration of the home of our 13th President, Millard Fillmore, and the First Lady, Abigail Fillmore (1850-1853). (East Aurora) 35 E3

Niagara Falls Observation Tower 716-278-1770
This steel tower features a glass elevator that rises above the falls for a spectacular view, then descends to water level for access to various boat tours. (Niagara Falls) Map 87

Niagara Power Project Visitor's Center 716-285-3211
A breathtaking view of the Niagara Gorge combines with multimedia exhibits to tell the story of this awesome hydroelectric power project. (Niagara Falls) Map 87

Old Fort Niagara 716-745-7611
Built in 1679, this is one of America's oldest forts. Events include military drills and demonstrations recreating fort life. (Youngstown) 21 F3

Schoelkopf Geological Museum 716-278-1780
Traces the geologic history and development of Niagara Falls over the last 440 million years. (Niagara Falls) Map 87

Theodore Roosevelt Inaugural
National Historic Site 716-884-0095
Historic site at Wilcox Mansion where our 26th President (1901-1909) took the Oath of Office. (Buffalo) Map 83

The Original American Kazoo Co.
Museum and Factory 716-992-3960
The only metal kazoo factory in the world, in operation since 1916, it now includes a museum dedicated to the amazing kazoo. (Eden) 35 B5

Chautauqua — Allegheny

Chautauqua Institution 716-357-6200
Founded in 1874 as a summer training camp for Methodist Sunday School teachers, this renowned institution now offers retreats, outdoor recreation, sports, and a variety of performing arts productions and programs. (Chautauqua) 48 A4

Dunkirk Historical Lighthouse &
Veterans Park Museum 716-366-5050
This lighthouse, built in 1875, honors each branch of the service with a historic room. The 95-foot-high structure stands guard over Dunkirk Harbor, and dominates the Veterans Park surrounding its base. (Dunkirk) 48 B1

Michael C. Rockefeller Arts Center 716-673-3217
Located at the State University of New York, Fredonia, this complex also contains three theaters and features over 120 exhibits and shows annually. (Fredonia) 48 B1

New York & Lake Erie Railroad 716-532-5716
Rail excursions traveling 20 or more scenic miles across the countryside. Features special dinner theater performance trips. (Gowanda) 49 A1

Salamanca Rail Museum 716-945-3133
Housed in a restored 1912 passenger rail depot, this museum traces the history of Western New York's railroads. Offers scenic rail excursions in the summer and fall. (Salamanca) 49 D5

Seneca-Iroquois National Museum 716-945-1738
The history and culture of the Seneca people — part of the great iroquois Nation — are depicted in this museum on the Allegany Indian Reservation. (Salamanca) 49 C5

Webb's Candy Factory Tour 716-753-2161
Taste confectionary delights made by hand in copper kettles as part of this candy factory tour. (Mayville) 48 A4

Recreation

Downhill Ski Areas

Belleayre Mountain 914-254-5600
1404' vertical drop (Highmount) 57 F5

Big Tupper 518-359-7902
1152' vertical drop (Tupper Lake) 11 A4

Bobcat 914-676-3143
1050' vertical drop (Andes) 57 D4

Brantling 315-331-2365
240' vertical drop (Sodus) 25 F4

Bristol Mountain 716-374-6000
1200' vertical drop (Canandaigua) 38 A4

Catamount 518-325-3200
1000' vertical drop (Hillsdale) 60 A5

Cockaigne 716-287-3223
430' vertical drop (Cherry Creek) 48 D3

Concord 800-431-3850
200' vertical drop (Kiamesha Lake) 62 E5

Cortina Valley 518-589-6500
725' vertical drop (Haines Falls) 58 E4

Dry Hill 315-782-8584
300' vertical drop (Watertown) 15 B1

Four Seasons 315-637-9023
100' vertical drop (Fayetteville) 28 A6

Frost Ridge 716-768-4883
140' vertical drop (Le Roy) 24 A6

Gore Mountain 518-251-2411
2100' vertical drop (North Creek) 18 F4

Greek Peak 607-835-6111
900' vertical drop (Cortland) 40 E6

Hickory 518-623-2825
1230' vertical drop (Schenectady) 32 C1

Holiday Mountain 914-796-3161
400' vertical drop (Monticello) 62 E5

Holiday Valley 716-699-2345
750' vertical drop (Ellicottville) 49 D3

Hunter 518-263-4223
1600' vertical drop (Hunter) 58 D4

Kissing Bridge 716-592-4963
550' vertical drop (Glenwood) 35 E6

Kutsher's Country Club 800-431-1273
150' vertical drop (Monticello) 62 D5

Labrador 607-842-6204
700' vertical drop (Truxton) 40 F4

Maple Ski Ridge 518-381-4700
400' vertical drop (Schenectady) 44 E5

McCauley Mountain 315-369-3225
633' vertical drop (Old Forge) 17 A4

Mount Peter 914-986-4992
450' vertical drop (Warwick) 67 C4

Mount Pisgah 518-891-0970
300' vertical drop (Saranac Lake) 11 E2

Northampton Park 716-352-9995
100' vertical drop (Brockport) 24 B4

Oak Mountain 518-548-7311
650' vertical drop (Speculator) 18 B6

Orange County 914-457-3000
131' vertical drop (Montgomery) 67 C1

Peek 'n Peak 716-355-4141
400' vertical drop (Clymer) 47 D6

Pines Resort 800-367-4637
260' vertical drop (South Fallsburg) 62 E4

Powder Mills 716-586-9209
75' vertical drop (Pittsford) 25 A6

Ridin-Hy 518-494-2742
150' vertical drop (Warrensburg) 19 D5

Rocking Horse 800-647-2624
150' vertical drop (Highland) 64 A4

Royal Mountain 518-835-6445
550' vertical drop (Caroga Lake) 30 F5

Sawkill 914-336-6977
70' vertical drop (Kingston) 63 E2

Scotch Valley 607-652-3132
800' vertical drop (Stamford) 57 E1

Shu-Maker Mountain 315-823-4470
750' vertical drop (Little Falls) 43 B1

Ski Plattekill 607-326-3500
1000' vertical drop (Roxbury) 57 E3

Ski Tamarack 716-941-6821
500' vertical drop (Colden) 35 D4

Ski Windham 518-734-4300
1600' vertical drop (Windham) 58 C3

Snow Ridge 315-348-8456
500' vertical drop (Turin) 16 A5

Song Mountain 315-696-5711
700' vertical drop (Tully) 40 D3

Sterling Forest 914-351-2163
400' vertical drop (Tuxedo) 67 D4

Swain 607-545-6511
650' vertical drop (Swain) 51 B1

Thunder Ridge 914-878-4100
600' vertical drop (Patterson) 64 F6

Titus Mountain 800-848-8766
1200' vertical drop (Malone) 4 D3

Toggenburg 315-683-5842
650' vertical drop (Fabius) 41 A3

Val Bialas 315-738-0328
400' vertical drop (Utica) 29 D5

Villa Roma 800-533-6767
300' vertical drop (Callicoon) 62 A3

West Mountain 518-793-6606
1010' vertical drop (Glens Falls) 32 D3

Whiteface Mountain 518-946-2223
3216' vertical drop (Wilmington) 12 B2

Willard Mountain 518-692-7337
505' vertical drop (Greenwich) 32 F6

Woods Valley 315-827-4721
500' vertical drop (Westernville) 29 B3

Racing Tracks

Accord Speedway 518-756-3633
Stock car racing (Accord) 63 D3

Airborne International Raceway 802-244-6964
Stock car racing (Plattsburgh) 5 F5

Apple Valley Raceway 315-589-3081
Modified stock and street cars (Williamson) 25 D4

Aqueduct Race Track 718-641-4700
Thoroughbred horseracing (Queens) 75 B4

Batavia Downs 716-343-3750
Harness racing (Batavia) 23 D6

Belmont Park Race Track 516-488-6000
Third leg of the Triple Crown of thoroughbred racing.
(Elmont) 75 D4

Black Rock Speedway 607-243-8686
Street, stocks and sprint car racing (Dundee) 39 A6

Bridgehampton Race Circuit 516-537-3770
Auto and motorcycle racing (Bridgehampton) 78 B1

Buffalo Raceway 716-649-1280
Harness racing (Hamburg) 35 C4

Canandaigua Speedway 716-394-0961
Modified stock car racing (Canandaigua) 38 D2

Cayuga County Fair Speedway 315-834-6606
Modified stock car racing (Weedsport) 26 F6

Finger Lakes Race Track 716-924-3232
Thoroughbred racing (Farmington) 38 B1

Fonda Speedway 518-853-3151
Modified stock car racing (Fonda) 44 B1

Goshen Historic Track 914-294-5333
Oldest harness racing track in America. Trotters and Pacers (Goshen) 67 C2

Lancaster National Speedway 716-759-6818
Drag strip racing (Lancaster) 35 E1

Lebanon Valley Speedway and Dragway 518-794-9606
Drag and stock car races (New Lebanon) 60 A1

Monticello Raceway 914-794-4100
Harness racing (Monticello) 62 D5

Orange County Speedway 914-342-2573
Stock car racing (Middletown) 67 B1

Oswego Speedway 315-342-0646
NASCAR super modified race track (Oswego) 27 A1

Ransomville Speedway 716-791-3602
Modified stock car racing (Ransomville) 22 B3

Riverhead Raceway 516-842-7223
Modified stock car racing (Riverhead) 77 D1

Rolling Wheels Raceway Park 315-689-7809
Modified stock car racing (Elbridge) 26 F6

Saratoga Equine Sports Center 518-584-2110
Harness racing (Saratoga Springs) 32 C6

Saratoga Race Course 518-584-6200
The oldest thoroughbred racing track in America
(Saratoga Springs) 32 C6

Vernon Downs 315-829-2201
Harness racing (Vernon) 28 F6

Watkins Glen International Raceway 607-535-2481
World-class auto racing circuit (Watkins Glen) 53 A2

Yonkers Raceway 914-968-4200
Home of two Triple Crowns of Harness racing: the Yonkers Trot and Cane Race. (Yonkers) 75 B2

Public Golf Courses

Adirondack Golf & Country Club 518-643-8403
18 holes (Peru) 5 D5

Afton GC 607-639-2454
18 holes (Afton) 55 F4

Alban Hills CC 518-762-3717
18 holes (Johnstown) 31 C6

Alder Creek GC   315-831-5222
9 holes (Alder Creek) 29 D2

Allegheny Hills GC   716-437-2658
9 holes (Cuba) 50 C2

Amsterdam Municipal GC   518-842-9731
18 holes (Amsterdam) 44 D1

Apalachin GC   607-625-2682
9 holes (Apalachin) 54 D6

Apple Greens GC   914-883-5500
9 holes (Highland) 63 F4

Arrowhead GC   716-352-5500
18 holes (Spencerport) 24 B4

Arrowhead GC   315-656-7563
27 holes (Syracuse) 27 F5

Auburn CC   315-253-3152
18 holes (Auburn) 39 F2

Barberlea GC   716-468-2116
18 holes (Nunda) 37 A5

Barker Brook GC   315-821-6438
18 holes (Oriskany Falls) 42 A1

Batavia CC   716-343-7600
18 holes (Batavia) 36 E1

Bath CC   607-776-5043
18 holes (Bath) 52 B3

Battenkill CC   518 692-9179
9 holes (Greenwich) 33 A5

Battle Island State Park GC   315-593-3408
18 holes (Fulton) 27 A2

Bay Meadows GC   518-792-1650
27 holes (Queensbury) 32 E2

Bay Park GC   516-593-8840
9 holes (East Rockaway) 75 E5

Beaver Island State Park GC   716-773-3271
18 holes (Grand Island) 35 A1

Bedford Creek GC   315-646-3400
9 holes (Sackets Harbor) 14 E2

Beekman CC   914-226-7700
27 holes (Hopewell Junction) 64 C5

Beldon Hill GC   607-693-3257
9 holes (Beldon) 55 D4

Bellport CC   516-286-7045
18 holes (Bellport) 77 A3

Bemus Point GC   716-386-2893
9 holes (Bemus Point) 48 B5

Bend of the River GC   518-696-3415
9 holes (Hadley) 32 B3

Bergen Point GC   516-661-8282
18 holes (West Babylon) 76 B4

Bethpage State Park GC   516-249-0701
5 18-hole courses (Farmingdale) 76 A3

Big Oak GC   315-789-9419
9 holes (Geneva) 39 A2

Birch Run CC   716-373-3113
9 holes (Allegany) 49 F6

Blackhead Mountain Lodge & CC   518-622-3157
9 holes (Roundtop) 58 F2

Blue Stone GC   607-843-8352
9 holes (Oxford) 55 E1

Bluff Point Golf & Country Club   518-563-3420
18 holes (Plattsburgh) 6 A4

Bob O'Link GC   716-662-4311
18 holes (Orchard Park) 35 D3

Bonavista GC   607-869-9909
9 holes (Willard) 39 C4

Brae Burn Recreational GC   716-335-3101
9 holes (Dansville) 37 D6

Braemar CC   716-352-5360
18 holes (Spencerport) 24 C4

Brandy Brook GC   315-363-9879
9 holes (Durhamville) 28 E5

Brentwood CC   516-436-6060
18 holes (Brentwood) 76 D3

Brighton Park GC   716 875 8721
18 holes (Tonawanda) 22 B6

Bristol Harbour GC   716-396-2600
18 holes (Canandaigua) 38 C3

Brockport CC   716-638-6486
18 holes (Brockport) 24 A4

Brookhaven GC   518-893-7458
18 holes (Porter Corners) 32 B5

Brooklawn GC   315-463-1831
18 holes (Syracuse) 27 E5

Brunswick Greens   518-279-3848
9 holes (Troy) 45 E4

Burden Lake CC   518-674-8917
9 holes (Averill Park) 45 F5

Burnet Park GC   315-487-6285
9 holes (Syracuse) 27 D6

Byrncliff Resort & Conference Center   716-535-7300
18 holes (Varysburg) 36 C4

Calverton Links   516-369-5200
9 holes (Calverton) 77 D2

Camillus CC   315-672-3770
18 holes (Camillus) 27 B6

Camroden GC   315-865-5771
9 holes (Rome) 29 B3

Canajoharie GC   518-673-8183
9 holes (Canajoharie) 43 E2

Canasawacta CC   607-336-2685
18 holes (Norwich) 41 F6

Cantiague Park GC   516-571-7061
9 holes (Hicksville) 75 F3

Cardinal Hills CC   716-358-5409
18 holes (Randolph) 49 A4

Casolwood GC   315-697-9164
18 holes (Canastota) 28 C5

Cassadaga CC   716-595-3003
9 holes (Cassadaga) 48 B2

Catatonk GC   607-659-4600
18 holes (Candor) 54 C4

Cato GC   315-626-2291
9 holes (Cato) 26 F5

Catskill GC   518-943-0302
9 holes (Catskill) 59 B4

Cazenovia Park GC   716-825-9811
18 holes (Buffalo) 35 C2

Cedar River GC   518-648-5906
9 holes (Indian Lake) 18 C3

Cedars GC   315-376-6267
9 holes (Lowville) 15 F3

Cedars GC   516-734-6363
9 holes (Cutchogue) 71 A6

Cedar View GC   315-764-9104
18 holes (Roosevelttown) 3 B1

Cee Jay GC   607-263-5291
18 holes (Laurens) 42 E6

Centerpointe CC   716-924-5346
18 holes (Canandaigua) 38 C2

Central Valley GC   914-928-6924
18 holes (Central Valley) 67 E2

Chautauqua GC   716-357-6211
27 holes (Chautauqua) 48 A4

Chautauqua Point GC   716-753-7271
9 holes (Mayville) 48 A4

Chemung GC   607-565-2323
18 holes (Waverly) 53 E6

Chenango Valley State Park GC   607-648-5251
18 holes (Chenango Forks) 55 C4

Chili CC   716-889-9325
18 holes (Scotsville) 24 C6

Christopher Morley Park GC   516-621-9107
9 holes (Roslyn) 75 D3

Churchville GC   716-256-4950
27 holes (Churchville) 24 B5

Clayton CC   315-686-4242
9 holes (Clayton) 7 F3

Clearview Park GC   718-229-2570
18 holes (Queens) 75 C3

Cobble Hill GC   518-873-9974
9 holes (Elizabethtown) 12 E4

Cobleskill GC   518-234-2788
9 holes (Cobleskill) 44 A4

Colgate University Seven Oaks GC   315-824-1432
18 holes (Hamilton) 41 F3

College GC   607-746-4281
9 holes (Delhi) 57 A4

College Hill (Caven) GC   914-486-9112
9 holes (Poughkeepsie) 64 B4

Colonial CC   518-589-9807
9 holes (Tannersville) 58 E4

Colonie Town GC   518-374-4181
27 holes (Schenectady) 45 B3

Concord Hotel GC   914-794-4000
45 holes (Kiamesha Lake) 62 E4

Conewango Forks GC   716-358-5409
18 holes (Randolph) 49 A5

Conklin Player's GC   607-775-3042
18 holes (Conklin) 55 B6

Copake CC   518-325-4338
18 holes (Craryville) 59 E4

Crab Meadow GC   516-757-8909
18 holes (Northport) 76 C1

Craggie Brae GC   716-889-1440
18 holes (Scottsville) 24 C6

Craig Wood GC   518-523-9811
18 holes (Lake Placid) 12 A4

Cranebrook GC   315-252-7887
18 holes (Auburn) 39 E1

Crestwood GC   315-736-0478
18 holes (Marcy) 29 C4

17

Public Golf Courses, cont.

Cronins Golf Resort — 518-623-9336
18 holes (Warrensburg) 19 B5

D.J.'s GC — 607-565-2618
9 holes (Waverly) 53 F6

Dande Farms GC — 716-542-2027
18 holes (Akron) 23 A6

Deerfield CC — 716-329-8080
27 holes (Brockport) 24 B4

Deerwood GC — 716-695-8525
18 holes (North Tonawanda) 22 C6

Delaware Park GC — 518-835-2533
18 holes (Buffalo) 35 B1

Delphi Falls GC — 315-662-3611
18 holes (Delphi Falls) 41 A2

Delta Knolls GC — 315-339-1280
18 holes (Rome) 29 A3

Dinsmore GC — 914-889-4082
18 holes (Staatsburg) 64 A2

Dix Hills GC — 516-499-8055
9 holes (Dix Hills) 76 B3

Dogwood Knolls GC — 914-226-7317
9 holes (Hopewell Junction) 64 B5

Domenicos GC — 315-736-9812
18 holes (Whitesboro) 29 B5

Dotys GC — 315-894-2860
9 holes (Ilion) 29 F6

Douglaston GC — 718-224-6566
18 holes (Brooklyn) 75 D4

Drumlins GC — 315-446-5580
18 holes (Syracuse) 27 E6

Dryden Lake GC — 607-844-9173
9 holes (Dryden) 54 C1

Dunwoodie GC — 914-476-5151
18 holes (Yonkers) 75 B1

Durand-Eastman GC — 716-266-8364
18 holes (Rochester) 24 E4

Dutchers GC — 914-855-9845
18 holes (Pawling) 64 E6

Dyker Beach GC — 718-836-9722
18 holes (Brooklyn) 74 F5

Eagle Crest GC — 518-877-8789
18 holes (Ballston Lake) 45 B2

Eagle Vale GC — 716-377-5200
18 holes (Fairport) 25 A5

Eddy Farm Resort Hotel GC — 914-858-4333
9 holes (Sparrow Bush) 66 D1

Eden Valley GC — 716-337-2190
9 holes (Eden) 35 C6

Edgewood GC — 607-432-2713
9 holes (Laurens) 42 E6

Eisenhower Park CC — 516-452-4528
54 holes (East Meadow) 75 F4

Elkdale CC — 716-945-5553
18 holes (Salamanca) 49 C4

Elma Meadows GC — 716-652-5475
18 holes (Elma) 35 E3

Elms GC — 315-387-5297
18 holes (Sandy Creek) 14 D4

Elm Tree GC — 607-753-1341
18 holes (Cortland) 40 E5

Ely Park GC — 607-772-7231
18 holes (Binghamton) 55 B5

Emerald Crest GC — 315-593-1016
18 holes (Fulton) 27 C2

Endwell Greens GC — 607-785-4653
18 holes (Endwell) 54 F5

En-Joie GC — 607-785-1661
18 holes (Endicott) 54 E5

Evergreen CC — 518-477-6224
27 holes (Castleton) 45 D6

Evergreen GC — 716-688-6204
18 holes (Amherst) 22 C6

Evergreen GC — 716-928-1270
18 holes (Bolivar) 50 E6

Fairview Golf & Country Inn — 716-226-8210
18 holes (Avon) 37 C2

Fallsview GC — 914-647-5100
9 holes (Ellenville) 63 B4

Fillmore GC — 315-497-3145
18 holes (Locke) 40 A4

Fishkill GC — 914-896-5220
9 holes (Fishkill) 64 B6

Ford Hill GC — 607-692-8938
36 holes (Whitney Point) 55 A3

Forest Heights GC — 716-487-0533
9 holes (Jamestown) 48 C5

Forest Park GC — 718-296-0999
18 holes (Woodhaven) 75 B4

Four X Four GC — 315-287-3711
9 holes (Gouverneur) 9 A3

Fox Fire GC — 315-638-2930
18 holes (Baldwinsville) 27 C5

Fox Run GC — 607-535-4413
9 holes (Rock Stream) 53 A1

Frear Park & GC — 518-270-4557
18 holes (Troy) 45 E3

French's Hollow Fairways — 518-861-8837
9 holes (Guilderland Center) 45 A4

Galway GC — 518-882-6395
9 holes (Glenville) 32 A6

Garrison GC & CC — 914-424-3604
18 holes (Garrison) 68 B2

Genegantslet GC — 607-656-8191
18 holes (Green) 55 C3

Genesee Valley County Park GC — 716-274-7775
18 holes (Rochester) 24 E5

Glen Cove GC — 516-671-0033
18 holes (Glen Cove) 75 F3

Glen Oak GC — 716-688-5454
18 holes (East Amherst) 22 D6

Golden Oak GC — 607-655-9961
18 holes (Windsor) 55 E6

Golf Club at Wind Watch — 516-232-9800
18 holes (Hauppauge) 76 D3

Golf Club of Newport — 315-845-8333
18 holes (Newport) 29 F4

Golf Knolls GC — 315-337-0920
9 holes (Rome) 28 F3

Gouverneur GC — 315-287-2130
18 holes (Gouverneur) 9 A3

**Governor Alfred E. Smith/
Sunken Meadow State Park GC** — 516-269-4333
27 holes (Kings Park) 76 C1

Grandview Farms Bed GC — 607-657-2619
9 holes (Berkshire) 54 D3

Grandview GC — 716-549-4930
9 holes (Angola) 34 F5

Green Acres GC — 914-331-2283
9 holes (Kingston) 63 F1

Green Lakes State Park GC — 315-637-6672
18 holes (Fayetteville) 28 A6

Green Mansions GC — 518-494-7222
9 holes (Chestertown) 19 B6

Green Ridge GC — 914-355-1317
9 holes (Johnson) 66 F2

Greenview CC — 315-668-2244
18 holes (West Monroe) 27 F3

Greenwood GC — 716-741-3395
9 holes (Clarence Center) 22 E6

Griffins Greens GC — 315-343-2996
18 holes (Oswego) 27 A5

Grossinger Golf Resort — 914-292-9000
27 holes (Liberty) 62 D3

Grygiel's Pine Hills GC — 315-733-5030
18 holes (Frankfort) 29 E6

Hanah CC — 914-586-4841
18 holes (Margaretville) 57 E4

Harbour Pointe CC — 716-682-3922
18 holes (Waterport) 23 D3

Hauppauge CC — 516-724-7500
18 holes (Hauppauge) 76 D2

Heartland Golf Park — 516-667-7400
9 holes (North Bay Shore) 76 C3

Heatherwood GC — 516-473-9000
18 holes (Centereach) 76 F2

Hiawatha Trails GC — 518-456-9512
18 holes (Guilderland) 45 B4

Hickory Hill GC — 914-986-7100
18 holes (Warwick) 67 C3

Hickory Ridge Golf & Country Club — 716-638-4653
18 holes (Holley) 23 E4

Hidden Valley GC — 315-736-9953
18 holes (Whitesboro) 29 C5

Highland Park GC — 315-252-9605
18 holes (Auburn) 39 F1

Highlands CC — 914-424-3727
9 holes (Garrison) 68 A2

Hiland GC — 518-761-4653
18 holes (Queensbury) 32 E2

Hillcrest GC — 518-355-9817
9 holes (Gifford) 44 F3

Hillendale GC — 607-273-2363
18 holes (Ithaca) 53 E1

Hillview GC — 716-679-4574
18 holes (Fredonia) 48 B1

Holbrook CC — 516-467-3417
18 holes (Holbrook) 76 F3

Holiday Valley GC *18 holes* (Ellicottville) 49 D3	716-699-2346	**Lakeview GC** *9 holes* (Mannsville) 14 E4	315-465-6515	**Mohonk Mountain House GC** *9 holes* (New Paltz) 63 E3	914-255-1000

Holiday Valley GC
18 holes (Ellicottville) 49 D3 — 716-699-2346

Holland Hills GC
18 holes (Glenwood) 35 F5 — 716-537-2345

Holland Meadows GC
18 holes (Broadalbin) 31 D6 — 518-883-3318

Hollow Hills GC
9 holes (Dix Hills) 76 B3 — 516-242-0010

Homowack Hotel GC
9 holes (Spring Glen) 63 A4 — 914-647-6800

Hoosick Falls CC
9 holes (Hoosick Falls) 46 B2 — 518-686-1967

Hornell CC
18 holes (Hornell) 51 E2 — 607-324-4225

Hyde Park GC
36 holes (Niagara Falls) 21 F5 — 716-297-2067

Indian Head GC
9 holes (Cayuga) 39 D1 — 315-253-6812

Indian Hills GC
18 holes (Painted Post) 52 E5 — 607-523-7315

Indian Island GC
18 holes (Riverhead) 77 E1 — 516-727-7776

Ironwood GC
9 holes (Baldwinsville) 27 B5 — 315-635-9826

Ischua Valley CC
9 holes (Franklinville) 50 A2 — 716-676-3630

Island Glenn CC
9 holes (Bethel) 62 B3 — 914-583-9898

Islands End GC
18 holes (Greenport) 71 B5 — 516-477-9457

Island Valley GC
9 holes (Fairport) 25 A5 — 716-586-1300

James Baird State Park GC
18 holes (Pleasant Valley) 64 C4 — 914-452-1489

Jones Beach State Park GC
18 holes (Wantagh) 75 F5 — 516-679-7221

Katsbaan GC
9 holes (Saugerties) 59 A5 — 914-246-8182

Keshequa GC
9 holes (Mount Morris) 37 C4 — 716-658-4545

Kingsboro Golf Club
9 holes (Gloversville) 31 B6 — 516-773-4600

Kissena Park GC
18 holes (Queens) 75 C4 — 908-219-1775

Kiss n Greens GC
9 holes (Alden) 36 A1 — 716-937-6708

Knickerbocker GC
9 holes (Cincinnatus) 41 A6 — 607-863-3800

Kutsher's CC
18 holes (Monticello) 62 D4 — 800-431-1273

Lake Isle CC
18 holes (Eastchester) 75 C1 — 914-337-9645

Lake Pleasant GC
9 holes (Lake Pleasant) 31 A1 — 518-548-7071

Lake Shore CC
18 holes (Rochester) 24 E3 — 716-663-5578

Lakeside CC
18 holes (Penn Yan) 38 F5 — 315-536-7252

Lakeside GC
9 holes (Ripley) 47 D4 — 716-736-7637

Lakeview GC
9 holes (Mannsville) 14 E4 — 315-465-6515

La Tourette GC
18 holes (Staten Island) 74 E5 — 718-351-1889

Leatherstocking GC
18 holes (Cooperstown) 43 B4 — 607-547-5275

LeRoy CC
18 holes (LeRoy) 37 A1 — 716-768-7330

Lido GC
18 holes (Lido Beach) 75 E5 — 516-431-8778

Lima GC
18 holes (Lima) 37 E2 — 716-624-1490

Links at Erie Village
18 holes (East Syracuse) 27 F6 — 315-656-4653

Links at Hiawatha Landing
18 holes (Apalachin) 54 E5 — 607-687-6952

Liverpool GC
18 holes (Liverpool) 27 D5 — 315-457-7170

Livingston CC
18 holes (Geneseo) 37 C3 — 716-243-4430

Lochmor GC
18 holes (Loch Sheldrake) 62 E3 — 914-434-9079

Loon Lake GC
18 holes (Loon Lake) 4 E6 — 518-891-3249

Lyndon GC
18 holes (Fayetteville) 27 F6 — 315-446-1885

Malone GC
36 holes (Malone) 4 C3 — 518-483-2926

Maple Crest GC
9 holes (Frankfort) 29 E6 — 315-894-3970

Maple Hill GC
18 holes (Marathon) 54 F1 — 607-849-3285

Maplehurst CC
18 holes (Lakewood) 48 C6 — 716-763-1225

Maple Moor GC
18 holes (White Plains) 68 D6 — 914-946-1830

Marine Park GC
18 holes (Brooklyn) 75 A5 — 718-338-7113

Mark Twain GC
18 holes (Elmira) 53 B5 — 607-737-5770

Massena CC
18 holes (Massena) 3 A1 — 315-769-2293

McCann Memorial GC
18 holes (Poughkeepsie) 64 B4 — 914-454-1968

McConnellsville GC
18 holes (McConnellsville) 28 D3 — 315-245-1157

Meadowbrook GC
9 holes (Weedsport) 26 F6 — 315-834-9358

Meadowbrook GC
9 holes (Winthrop) 3 C4 — 315-389-4562

Mechanicville GC
9 holes (Mechanicville) 45 E2 — 518-664-3866

Merrick Road GC
9 holes (Merrick) 75 F5 — 516-868-4650

Middle Island CC
27 holes (Middle Island) 77 A2 — 516-924-5100

Mill Road Acres GC
9 holes (Latham) 45 C3 — 516-785-4653

Mohawk Valley CC
9 holes (Herkimer) 30 B6 — 315-866-0204

Mohonk Mountain House GC
9 holes (New Paltz) 63 E3 — 914-255-1000

Monroe CC
9 holes (Monroe) 67 D3 — 914-783-9045

Montauk Downs State Park GC
18 holes (Montauk) 72 A6 — 516-668-5000

Mosholu GC
9 holes (The Bronx) 75 B2 — 718-655-9164

Mountain Top GC
9 holes (Sherburne) 42 A4 — 607-674-4005

Nevele GC
18 holes (Ellenville) 63 B4 — 914-647-7315

Newark Valley GC
18 holes (Newark Valley) 54 D3 — 607-642-3376

New Course at Albany
18 holes (Albany) 45 B5 — 518-489-3526

Newman GC
9 holes (Ithaca) 53 F1 — 607-273-6262

New Paltz GC
9 holes (New Paltz) 63 F3 — 914-255-8282

Niagara County GC
18 holes (Lockport) 22 E4 — 716-439-6051

Niagara Orleans CC
18 holes (Middleport) 23 A4 — 716-735-9000

Nick Stoner GC
18 holes (Caroga Lake) 31 A5 — 518-835-4211

Nine Hole Executive Course
9 holes (Saratoga Springs) 32 C6 — 516-584-2007

North Country GC
18 holes (Rouses Point) 6 B1 — 518-297-5814

Northern Pines GC
9 holes (Syracuse) 27 F4 — 315-699-2939

North Shore GC
18 holes (Cleveland) 28 B3 — 315-675-8101

North Woodmere GC
9 holes (North Woodmere) 75 D5 — 516-791-7705

Oak Ridge GC
19 holes (Wellesley Island) 8 A2 — 315-482-5145

Oak Run GC
18 holes (Lockport) 22 E4 — 716-434-8851

Oakwood GC
9 holes (Buffalo) 22 D6 — 716-689-1421

Old Hickory GC
18 holes (Livonia) 37 E3 — 716-346-2450

Oneida CC
9 holes (Oneida) 28 E6 — 315-363-8879

Orchard Valley GC
9 holes (Lafayette) 40 D2 — 315-677-5180

Oriskany Hills GC
9 holes (Oriskany) 29 B4 — 315-736-4540

Otsego GC
9 holes (Springfield Center) 43 B3 — 607-547-9290

Otterkill CC
18 holes (Campbell Hall) 67 D1 — 914-427-2301

Ouleout Creek GC
9 holes (Franklin) 56 E3 — 607-829-2100

Oyster Bay GC
18 holes (Woodbury) 76 A3 — 516-364-3977

Parkview Fairways
18 holes (Victor) 38 B1 — 716-657-7867

Public Golf Courses, cont.

Peek 'n Peak GC 716-355-4141
36 holes (Clymer) 47 D6

Pelham/Split Rock GC 718-885-1258
36 holes (The Bronx) 75 C2

Peninsula GC 516-798-9776
9 holes (Massapequa) 76 A4

Perinton Golf & Country Club 716-223-7651
9 holes (Fairport) 25 B5

Phillip J Rotella GC 914-354-1616
18 holes (Thiells) 67 F4

Pine Grove Golf & Country Club 315-672-9272
18 holes (Camillus) 27 C6

Pine Hills CC 516-878-4343
18 holes (Manorville) 77 C2

Pine Hills GC 315-733-5030
18 holes (Frankfort) 29 E6

Pinehurst GC 716-326-4424
9 holes (Westfield) 47 F3

Pine Meadows Golf & Country Club 716-741-3970
9 holes (Clarence) 35 E1

Pinewood CC 716-352-5314
9 holes (Spencerport) 24 B4

Pinnacle State Park GC 607-359-2767
9 holes (Addison) 52 D5

Pleasant Knolls GC 315-829-4653
9 holes (Oneida) 28 E5

Pleasantview GC 518-634-2523
9 holes (Freehold) 58 F2

Point East GC 315-445-0963
9 holes (Syracuse) 27 E6

Popes Grove GC 315-487-9075
9 holes (Syracuse) 27 C5

Port Bay GC 315-594-8295
9 holes (Wolcott) 26 C3

Potsdam Town & CC 315-265-2141
9 holes (Potsdam) 3 A5

Pound Ridge GC 914-764-5771
9 holes (Pound Ridge) 68 F4

Poxabogue GC 516-537-0025
9 executive holes (Bridgehampton) 78 C1

Putnam GC 914-628-4200
18 holes (Mahopac) 68 D4

Queensbury GC 518-793-3711
18 holes (Lake George) 32 E2

Radisson Greens GC 315-638-0092
18 holes (Baldwinsville) 27 B5

Rainbow CC 518-966-5343
18 holes (Greenville) 58 F1

Raymondville Golf & Country Club 315-769-2759
9 holes (Massena) 3 B2

Ricci Meadows GC 716-682-3221
18 holes (Albion) 23 E2

Rip Van Winkle GC 518-678-9779
9 holes (Palenville) 58 F4

Riverbend GC 607-847-8481
9 holes (New Berlin) 42 C5

River Oaks GC 716-733-3336
18 holes (Grand Island) 22 A6

Riverside CC 315-676-7714
18 holes (Central Square) 27 D3

Riverton GC 716-334-6196
9 holes (West Henrietta) 24 D6

River View CC 516-399-1920
18 holes (Rexford) 45 B2

Robert Moses GC 516-669-0449
18 holes (Fire Island) 76 C5

Robert T Jones GC at Cornell University 607-257-3661
18 holes (Ithaca) 54 A2

Robert Van Patten GC 516-877-5400
27 holes (Jonesville) 45 C2

Rock Hill CC 516-878-2250
18 holes (Manorville) 77 C2

Rockland Lake North GC 914-268-6250
36 regulation holes;18 par 3 holes (Congers) 68 B5

Rockland Lake South GC 914-268-7930
18 holes (Congers) 68 B5

Rogue's Roost GC 315-633-9406
18 holes (Bridgeport) 28 A5

Rolling Acres GC 716-567-8557
18 holes (Pike) 36 D6

Rome CC 315-336-6464
18 holes (Rome) 28 F3

Rondout GC 914-626-2513
18 holes (Accord) 63 D3

Rosebrook GC 716-934-2825
9 holes (Silver Creek) 34 E6

Rothland GC 716-542-4325
27 holes (Akron) 22 F6

Roxbury GC 607-326-7121
9 holes (Roxbury) 57 F3

Rustic GC & CC 315-639-6800
9 holes (Dexter) 14 E1

Sacandaga GC 518-863-4887
9 holes (Northville) 31 D4

Sagamore Resort & GC 518-644-9400
18 holes (Bolton Landing) 19 E5

Sag Harbor GC 516-725-2503
9 holes (Sag Harbor) 78 D1

Saint Bonaventure GC 716-372-7692
9 holes (Saint Bonaventure) 50 A5

Saint Lawrence State Park GC 315-393-2286
18 holes (Ogdensburg) 1 F5

Saint Lawrence University GC 315-386-4600
18 holes (Canton) 2 E5

Salmon Creek CC 716-352-4300
18 holes (Spencerport) 24 B4

Sanctuary GC 914-962-8050
18 holes (Yorktown Heights) 68 C3

Sandy Pond GC 516-727-0909
9 holes (Riverhead) 77 D1

Saranac Inn Golf & Country Club 518-891-1402
18 holes (Saranac Inn) 11 B2

Saranac Lake GC 518-891-2675
18 holes (Saranac Lake) 11 F3

Saratoga Spa State Park GC 518-584-2007
18 holes (Saratoga Springs) 32 C6

Sauquoit Knolls GC 315-737-8959
9 holes (Sauquoit) 42 D1

Saxon Woods GC 914-723-0949
18 holes (Scarsdale) 75 C1

Scenic Farms GC 914-258-4455
9 holes (Pine Island) 67 C2

Schenectady Municipal GC 518-382-5155
18 holes (Schenectady) 45 A3

Scotts Corner GC 914-457-9141
9 holes (Montgomery) 63 C6

Scott's Oquaga GC 607-467-3094
18 holes (Deposit) 56 A6

Segalla CC 914-373-9200
18 holes (Amenia) 64 F2

Seneca GC 315-635-7571
9 holes (Baldwinsville) 27 C5

Seneca Lake CC 315-789-4681
18 holes (Geneva) 39 A3

Shadow Lake GC 716-385-2010
27 holes (Penfield) 25 A5

Shadow Pines GC 716-385-8550
18 holes (Penfield) 25 A5

Shamrock GC 315-336-9858
18 holes (Oriskany) 29 B5

Shawangunk CC 914-647-6090
9 holes (Ellenville) 63 A4

Shawnee CC 716-731-5177
9 holes (Sanborn) 22 C5

Shelter Island CC 516-749-0416
9 holes (Shelter Island Heights) 71 B6

Sheridan Park GC 716-875-1811
18 holes (Kenmore) 35 B1

Shore Acres GC 716-621-1030
9 holes (Rochester) 24 E3

Silver Creek GC 315-539-8076
18 holes (Waterloo) 39 B2

Silver Lake Park GC 718-447-5640
18 holes (Staten Island) 74 E5

Six-S CC 716-365-2201
27 holes (Belfast) 50 F3

Skene Valley CC 518-499-1685
18 holes (Whitehall) 20 B6

Skyline Golf & Country Club 315-699-5338
18 holes (Brewerton) 27 E4

Skyridge Chalet & GC 315-687-6900
9 holes (Chittenango) 28 B6

Sleepy Hollow GC 315-336-4110
18 holes (Rome) 29 A3

Smithtown Landing CC 516-360-7618
27 holes (Smithtown) 76 D2

Soaring Eagles GC 607-739-0034
18 holes (Horseheads) 53 B4

Sodus Bay Heights GC 315-483-6777
18 holes (Sodus Point) 25 F4

South Hills CC 716-487-1471
18 holes (Jamestown) 48 C6

South Park GC 716-825-9504
9 holes (Buffalo) 35 B2

South Shore GC 718-984-0101
18 holes (Staten Island) 74 D6

South Shore GC 716-649-6674
18 holes (Hamburg) 35 B3

Spook Rock CC 914-357-6466
18 holes (Suffern) 67 E5

Sprain Lake GC 914-779-9827
18 holes (Yonkers) 75 B1

Springbrook Greens GC 315-947-6115 *9 holes* (Fair Haven) 26 D3	**Thousand Islands GC** 315-482-9454 *18 holes* (Wellesley Island) 8 A3	**Watkins Glen GC** 607-535-2340 *9 holes* (Watkins Glen) 53 A2
Spring Lake GC 516-924-5115 *3 9-hole courses* (Middle Island) 77 A2	**Ticonderoga CC** 518-585-2801 *18 holes* (Ticonderoga) 20 A2	**Wayne Hills CC** 315-946-6944 *18 holes* (Lyons) 26 A6
Stadium GC 518-374-9104 *18 holes* (Schenectady) 45 A3	**Timber Point CC** 516-581-2401 *27 holes* (Great River) 76 E4	**Webster GC** 716-265-1920 *36 holes* (Webster) 25 B4
Stamford GC 607-652-7398 *18 holes* (Stamford) 57 E1	**Tioga CC** 607-699-3881 *18 holes* (Nichols) 54 B6	**Wellesley Island State Park GC** 315-482-9622 *18 holes* (Alexandria Bay) 7 F2
Stonebridge Golf & Country Club 315-733-5663 *18 holes* (New Hartford) 29 C6	**Tomacy's GC** 315-232-4842 *9 holes* (Adams) 14 F3	**Wells College GC** 315-364-8024 *9 holes* (Aurora) 39 E4
Stone Dock GC 914-687-9944 *9 holes* (High Falls) 63 E3	**Tomassos GC** 607-656-2323 *18 holes* (Waverly) 53 F6	**Wellsville CC** 716-593-6337 *18 holes* (Wellsville) 51 B4
Stonehedges GC 607-898-3754 *18 holes* (Groton) 40 C6	**Top 'O The World GC** 518-668-2062 *9 holes* (Lake George) 32 E1	**Western Turnpike GC** 518-456-0786 *27 holes* (Guilderland) 45 A4
Stony Ford GC 914-457-3000 *18 holes* (Montgomery) 67 C1	**Town Isle CC** 315-656-3522 *18 holes* (Kirkville) 28 A6	**West Hill Golf & Country Club** 315-672-8677 *18 holes* (Camillus) 27 B6
Suffolk County GC 516-567-1704 *18 holes* (West Sayville) 76 E4	**Town of Hamburg GC** 716-648-4410 *9 holes* (Hamburg) 35 C4	**Westmoreland GC** 315-853-8914 *9 holes* (Westmoreland) 29 A5
Sugar Hill GC 716-326-4653 *9 holes* (Westfield) 47 F2	**Town of Schroon GC** 518-532-9359 *9 holes* (Schroon Lake) 19 D3	**Westport CC** 518-962-4470 *18 holes* (Westport) 13 A4
Sullivan County GC 914-292-9584 *9 holes* (Liberty) 62 C3	**Town of Wallkill GC** 914-361-1022 *18 holes* (Middletown) 63 B6	**West Sayville GC** 516-567-1704 *18 holes* (West Sayville) 76 F4
Sundown Golf & Country Club 607-895-6888 *9 holes* (Bainbridge) 56 A1	**Tri-County CC** 716-965-2053 *18 holes* (Forestville) 48 E1	**Westvale GC** 315-487-0130 *18 holes* (Camillus) 27 C6
Sunnyhill Resort GC 518-634-7698 *18 holes* (Greenville) 58 F1	**Triple Creek GC** 716-468-2116 *18 holes* (Nunda) 37 D5	**Whispering Hills GC** 716-346-2100 *18 holes* (Conesus) 37 D4
Sunset Valley GC 716-664-7508 *18 holes* (Lakewood) 48 C5	**Trumansburg GC** 607-387-8844 *18 holes* (Trumansburg) 39 D6	**Whiteface Inn GC** 518-523-2551 *18 holes* (Lake Placid) 12 A3
Swan Lake GC 516-369-1818 *18 holes* (Manorville) 77 C2	**Tupper Lake GC** 518-359-3701 *18 holes* (Tupper Lake) 11 A4	**Wildwood CC** 716-334-5860 *18 holes* (Rush) 37 E1
Swan Lake Golf & Country Club 914-292-0478 *18 holes* (Swan Lake) 62 C4	**Turin Highlands GC** 315-348-9912 *18 holes* (Turin) 16 B5	**Wildwood GC** 315-699-5255 *18 holes* (Cicero) 27 E5
Sycamore Greens GC 518-355-6145 *18 holes* (Duanesburg) 44 F3	**Twin Brooks GC** 315-388-4480 *18 holes* (Waddington) 2 E2	**Willowbrook GC** 315-782-8192 *27 holes* (Watertown) 8 B6
Tall Tree GC 516-744-3200 *18 holes* (Rocky Point) 77 A1	**Twin Hickory CC** 607-324-1441 *18 holes* (Hornell) 51 E3	**Willowbrook GC** 716-434-0111 *18 holes* (Lockport) 22 D4
Tanner Valley GC 315-492-9856 *18 holes* (Syracuse) 40 C1	**Twin Hills GC** 716-352-4800 *18 holes* (Spencerport) 24 B4	**Willowbrook GC** 607-756-7382 *18 holes* (Cortland) 40 D6
Taranwould Golf Club 315-331-9128 *18 holes* (Newark) 25 E5	**Twin Ponds GC & CC** 315-736-0550 *18 holes* (New York Mills) 29 C5	**Willow Brook Golf & Country Club** 716-434-0111 *18 holes* (Lockport) 22 E4
Tarry Brae GC 914-434-2622 *18 holes* (South Fallsburg) 62 E4	**Vails Grove GC** 914-669-5721 *9 holes* (Brewster) 68 E2	**Willow Creek GC** 607-562-8898 *18 holes* (Big Flats) 53 A5
Tee-Bird GC 518-792-7727 *18 holes* (Fort Edward) 32 E3	**Valley View GC** 315-732-8755 *18 holes* (Utica) 29 D6	**Willow Run GC** 716-789-3162 *9 holes* (Mayville) 48 A4
Tennanah Lake GC 607-498-5502 *18 holes* (Roscoe) 62 A2	**Van Cortlandt Park GC** 718-543-4585 *18 holes* (The Bronx) 75 A2	**Willsboro GC** 518-963-8989 *9 holes* (Willsboro) 13 A2
Terry Hills GC 716-343-0860 *18 holes* (Batavia) 23 E6	**Vassar GC** 914-473-1550 *9 holes* (Poughkeepsie) 64 B4	**Windham CC** 518-734-9910 *18 holes* (Windham) 58 D3
The Heritage CC 607-797-2381 *18 holes* (Johnson City) 55 B5	**Vesper Hills GC** 315-696-8328 *18 holes* (Tully) 40 E3	**Winding Brook CC** 518-758-9117 *18 holes* (Kinderhook) 59 D2
Thendara GC 315-369-3136 *18 holes* (Thendara) 17 A4	**Victor Hills CC** 716-924-3480 *36 holes* (Victor) 38 B1	**Winged Pheasant GC** 716-289-8846 *18 holes* (Shortsville) 38 C1
The Pines GC 315-298-9970 *18 holes* (Pulaski) 14 D6	**Villa Roma GC** 914-887-5097 *18 holes* (Callicoon) 62 A3	**Woodcliff GC** 716-248-4845 *9 holes* (Rochester) 25 A6
The Pines Resort GC 914-434-6000 *9 holes* (South Fallsburg) 62 E4	**Wakely Lodge & GC** 518-648-5011 *9 holes* (Indian Lake) 17 D3	**Woodcrest GC** 716-789-4653 *9 holes* (Mayville) 48 A4
The Ponds at Lake Grove GC 516-737-4649 *18 holes* (Lake Grove) 76 E2	**Walden Oaks GC** 607-753-9452 *18 holes* (Cortland) 40 D6	**Woodgate Pines GC** 315-942-5442 *18 holes* (Boonville) 29 B1
Thomas Carvel CC 518-398-7101 *18 holes* (Pine Plains) 64 E1	**Wa-Noa GC** 315-656-8213 *18 holes* (East Syracuse) 27 F6	**Woodhaven GC** 607-433-2301 *9 holes* (West Oneonta) 56 E1
Thousand Acres GC 518-696-5246 *9 holes* (Stony Creek) 32 B1	**Watertown GC** 315-782-4040 *18 holes* (Watertown) 15 B1	

State Recreation Area Facilities

	Bicycle Trails	Boating — Launch (L), Rentals (R)	Bridle Trails	Camping	Concessions	Cross Country Skiing	Environmental Education and Interpretation	Fishing	Golf (G), Tennis (T)	Handicapped Facilities	Hunting	Ice Skating	Lake (L), River (R)	Picnic Areas	Playgrounds	Restrooms (R), Showers (S)	Snowmobile Trails	Swimming — Beach (B), Pool (P)	Trails — Hiking (H), Nature (N)	Map Number	Grid Location
NEW YORK CITY																					
Clay Pit Ponds Preserve 718-967-1976			●				●			●			L,R	●					H,N	74	D6
Empire-Fulton Ferry State Park 718-858-4708										●			R	●						Map 86	
Riverbank State Park 212-694-3600					●		●		T	●		●		●	●			P	H	75	A3
Roberto Clemente State Park 718-299-8750	●				●		●			●			L,R	●	●			P	H	75	A2
LONG ISLAND																					
Bayard Cutting Arboretum State Park 516-581-1002					●		●			●									N	76	D3
Belmont Lake State Park 516-667-5055	●	R	●		●	●	●	●		●			L	●	●				H,N	76	B4
Bethpage State Park 516-249-0700	●		●		●	●	●		G,T	●				●	●	R,S			H,N	76	A3
Caleb Smith Preserve State Park 516-265-1054			●			●	●	●		●									H,N	76	D2
Captree State Park 516-669-0449		L			●			●		●				●	●					76	D5
Caumsett State Park 516-423-1770	●		●			●		●		●									H,N	76	A1
Connetquot River Preserve State Park 516-581-1005			●			●	●	●		●									H,N	76	E3
Governor Alfred E. Smith/Sunken Meadow State Park 516-269-4333	●		●		●	●	●	●	G	●				●	●	R,S		B	H,N	76	C1
Heckscher State Park 516-581-2100	●	L	●	●	●	●	●	●		●				●	●	R,S		B,P	H	76	E4
Hempstead Lake State Park 516-766-1029	●		●		●	●	●	●	T	●			L	●	●				H	75	D4
Hither Hills State Park 516-668-3781	●		●	●	●	●	●	●		●	●			●	●	R,S		B	H,N	71	F6
Jones Beach State Park 516-785-1600	●				●		●	●	G	●				●	●	R,S		B,P		75	F5
Montauk Downs State Park 516-668-5000					●		●		G,T	●			L			R,S		P		72	A6
Montauk Point State Park 516-668-3781			●		●	●		●		●	●			●					H,N	72	B6
Orient Beach State Park 516-323-2440	●				●		●	●		●				●	●	R,S		B	N	71	D5
Planting Fields Arboretum State Historic Park 516-922-9200							●			●									H,N	75	F2
Robert Moses State Park 516-669-0449					●		●	●	G	●				●	●	R,S		B		76	C5
Valley Stream State Park 516-825-4128	●				●	●				●				●	●				N	75	D4
Wildwood State Park 516-929-4314	●			●	●		●			●				●	●	R,S		B	H,N	77	C1
THE HUDSON VALLEY																					
Bear Mountain State Park 914-786-2701	●	R			●	●	●	●		●		●	L,R	●	●			P	H,N	67	F3
Blauvelt State Park 914-786-2701													R						H	68	A6
Clarence Fahnestock State Park 914-225-7207	●	L,R	●	●	●	●	●	●		●	●		L	●	●	R,S	●	B	H,N	68	B1
Franklin D. Roosevelt State Park 914-245-4434	●	L,R			●	●	●	●		●			L	●			●	P	H,N	68	B3
Goosepond Mountain State Park 914-786-2701			●																H	67	C3
Harriman State Park 914-786-2701			●			●		●		●			L	●					H	67	F3
Harriman St Pk/Anthony Wayne 914-942-2560						●													H	67	F3
Harriman St Pk/Beaver Pond Campgrounds 914-947-2792		L		●				●					L	●		R,S		B	H	67	E4
Harriman St Pk/Lake Sebago Beach 914-351-2583		L,R			●			●					L	●				B	H	67	E4
Harriman St Pk/Lake Tiorati Beach 914-351-2568		L,R			●			●				●	L	●				B	H	67	F3
Harriman St Pk/Lake Welch Beach 914-947-2444		L,R			●			●					L	●				B	H	67	F4
Harriman St Pk/Sebago Cabin Camp 914-351-2360						●		●					L	●	●	R,S		B	H	67	E4
Harriman St Pk/Silver Mine 914-351-2568								●					L						H	67	F3
Highland Lakes State Park 914-786-2701			●										L							63	B6
High Tor State Park 914-634-8074					●									●				P	H	68	A4
Hudson Highlands State Park 914-225-7207							●				●		R						H	68	A1
James Baird State Park 914-452-1489	●				●	●	●		G,T	●				●	●				H,N	64	C4
Lake Taghkanic State Park 518-851-3631	●	L,R		●	●	●	●	●		●	●	●	L	●	●	R,S	●	B	H,N	59	D5

22

Region	Name	Phone	Bicycle Trails	Boating — Launch (L), Rentals (R)	Bridle Trails	Camping	Concessions	Cross Country Skiing	Environmental Education and Interpretation	Fishing	Golf (G), Tennis (T)	Handicapped Facilities	Hunting	Ice Skating	Lake (L), River (R)	Picnic Areas	Playgrounds	Restrooms (R), Showers (S)	Snowmobile Trails	Swimming — Beach (B), Pool (P)	Trails Hiking (H), Nature (N)	Map Number	Grid Location
THE HUDSON VALLEY	Margaret Lewis Norrie State Park	914-889-4646	●	L	●	●	●	●	●	●		●			R	●	●	R,S	●		H	64	A2
	Nyack Beach State Park	914-268-3020	●				●			●		●			R	●					H	68	B5
	Ogden & Ruth Mills State Park	914-889-4646	●			●	●	●	●	●	G	●			R						H	64	B2
	Old Croton Trailway State Park	914-693-5259	●			●															H	68	B6
	Rockefeller State Park	914-631-1470			●		●	●	●	●					L,R						H	68	C5
	Rockland Lake State Park	914-268-3020	●	L,R			●	●	●	●	G,T	●		●	L	●				P	H,N	68	A5
	Storm King State Park	914-786-2701											●		L						H	67	F1
	Taconic/Copake Falls State Park	518-329-3993	●			●	●	●		●		●	●		R	●	●	R,S	●	B	H,N	59	F5
	Taconic/Rudd Pond State Park	518-789-3059	●	L,R		●	●	●		●		●	●		L	●	●	R,S		B	H,N	64	F1
	Tallman Mountain State Park	914-359-0544	●				●			●		●			R	●	●			P	H	68	B6
THE CATSKILLS	Bear Spring Mountain Forest Preserve	607-865-6989		L		●		●		●		●			L	●				B	H	56	F5
	Beaverkill Forest Preserve	914-439-4281				●		●		●		●			R	●		R,S		B	H	62	B1
	Devils Tombstone Forest Preserve	914-688-7160				●				●		●			L						H	58	D5
	Kenneth L. Wilson Forest Preserve	914-679-7020		L,R		●				●		●			L,R	●		R,S		B	H	58	D6
	Lake Superior State Park	914-786-2701		L,R			●			●		●		●	L					B		62	A5
	Little Pond Forest Preserve	914-439-5480		L		●				●		●			L	●		R,S		B	H	57	C6
	Minnewaska State Park	914-255-0752	●	L	●		●	●		●			●		L,R	●						63	C4
	Mongaup Pond Forest Preserve	914-439-4233		L,R		●				●		●			L,R	●		R,S		B	H	62	D1
	North/South Lake Forest Preserve	518-589-5058		L,R		●	●			●		●			L	●		R,S		B	H	58	E4
	Woodland Valley Forest Preserve	914-688-7647				●				●		●			R	●					H	58	B6
CAPITAL — SARATOGA	Cherry Plain State Park	518-733-5400	●	L	●		●	●		●		●			L	●	●		●	B	H,N	46	B5
	Grafton Lakes State Park	518-279-1155	●	L,R	●		●	●		●		●	●	●	L	●	●		●	B	H,N	46	A3
	Hudson River Islands State Park	518-474-0456								●		●	●		R						H	59	C2
	John Boyd Thacher State Park	518-827-1237	●				●	●	●			●				●			●	P	H,N	44	F4
	Max V. Shaul State Park	518-827-1237				●				●		●				●	●	R,S			H,N	44	A6
	Mine Kill State Park	518-827-6111		L			●	●	●	●		●	●		L	●			●	P	H,N	58	A1
	Moreau Lake State Park	518-793-0511		L,R		●	●	●		●		●			L	●		R,S		B	H,N	32	D4
	Peebles Island State Park	518-237-8643						●		●						●					H	45	D3
	Saratoga Spa State Park	518-584-2950					●	●	●		G,T	●		●	R	●	●			P	H,N	32	C6
	Thompson's Lake State Park	518-872-1674		L,R		●	●	●		●		●			L		●	R,S		B	H,N	44	E5
THE ADIRONDACKS	Alger Island Preserve	315-369-3224				●				●					L	●						17	B4
	Ausable Point Forest Preserve	518-561-7080		L,R		●				●		●			L,R	●		R,S		B		6	A6
	Brown Tract Pond Forest Preserve	315-354-4412		L,R		●				●					L	●				B	H	17	D3
	Buck Pond Forest Preserve	518-891-3449		L,R		●				●		●			L,R	●		R,S		B		4	E6
	Caroga Lake Forest Preserve	518-835-4241		L		●	●			●		●			L	●		R,S		B	H	31	A5
	Cranberry Lake Forest Preserve	315-848-2315				●				●		●			L			R,S		B	H	10	C4
	Crown Point Reservation	518-597-3603		L		●				●		●			L			R,S				13	A6
	Cumberland Bay State Park	518-563-5240				●	●	●				●			L	●	●	R,S		B		6	B4
	Eagle Point Forest Preserve	518-494-2220		L		●				●		●			L	●		R,S		B		19	C3
	Eighth Lake Forest Preserve	315-354-4120		L,R		●		●		●		●			L			R,S		B	H	17	D3
	Fish Creek Pond Forest Preserve	518-891-4560		L,R		●				●		●			L,R	●		R,S		B	H	11	B3

THE ADIRONDACKS

Name	Phone	Bicycle Trails	Boating — Launch (L), Rentals (R)	Bridle Trails	Camping	Concessions	Cross Country Skiing	Environmental Education and Interpretation	Fishing	Golf (G), Tennis (T)	Handicapped Facilities	Hunting	Ice Skating	Lake (L), River (R)	Picnic Areas	Playgrounds	Restrooms (R), Showers (S)	Snowmobile Trails	Swimming — Beach (B), Pool (P)	Trails — Hiking (H), Nature (N)	Map Number	Grid Location
Forked Lake Forest Preserve	518-624-6646		L,R		●				●					L	●					H	17	F1
Fourth Lake Picnic Area	315-369-3224		L						●					L	●						17	B4
Golden Beach Preserve	315-354-4230		L,R		●				●		●			L	●		R,S		B	H	17	E3
Hearthstone Point Forest Preserve	518-668-5193				●				●		●			L			R,S		B		32	D1
Hinckley Reservoir Picnic Area	315-826-3800								●		●			L	●				B		29	F3
Indian Lake Islands Preserve	518-648-5300		L,R		●				●					L	●					H	18	A5
Lake Durant Forest Preserve	518-352-7797		L,R		●				●					L	●				B	H	18	A2
Lake Eaton Forest Preserve	518-624-2641		L,R		●				●		●			L	●				B	H	18	A1
Lake George Battlefield Picnic Area	518-623-3671								●						●						32	D2
Lake George Battleground Preserve	518-668-3348				●						●						R,S				32	D2
Lake George Beach Preserve	518-668-3352								●		●			L	●		R,S		B		32	D2
Lake George/Glen Island Preserve	518-644-9696				●				●					L	●					H	19	E6
Lake George/Long Island Preserve	518-656-9426				●				●					L	●					H	32	E1
Lake George/Narrow Island Preserve	518-499-1288				●				●					L	●					H	19	F5
Lake Harris Forest Preserve	518-582-2503		L,R		●				●					L	●		R,S		B	H	18	E1
Lewey Lake Forest Preserve	518-648-5266		L,R		●				●		●			L	●		R,S		B	H	18	B5
Limekiln Lake Forest Preserve	315-357-4401		L,R		●				●		●			L	●		R,S		B	H	17	C4
Lincoln Pond Forest Preserve	518-942-5292		R		●				●		●			L	●		R,S		B		12	F5
Little Sand Point Forest Preserve	518-548-7585		L,R		●				●		●			L					B	H	30	E1
Luzerne Forest Preserve	518-696-2031		L,R		●				●		●			L	●		R,S		B	H	32	C2
Macomb Reservation State Park	518-643-9952				●		●	●	●		●			R	●	●	R,S	●	B	H,N	5	E5
Meacham Lake Forest Preserve	518-483-5116		L,R		●				●		●			L	●		R,S		B	H	4	C5
Meadowbrook Forest Preserve	518-891-4351				●				●						●		R,S				11	F3
Moffitt Beach Preserve	518-548-7102		L,R		●				●		●			L	●		R,S		B	H	31	A1
Nick's Lake Forest Preserve	315-369-3314		L,R		●				●		●			L	●		R,S		B	H	17	A4
Northampton Beach Preserve	518-863-6000		L,R		●				●					L	●		R,S		B	H	31	D4
Paradox Lake Forest Preserve	518-532-7451		L,R		●				●					L	●		R,S		B		19	D2
Point Au Roche State Park	518-563-0369	●	L			●	●	●	●					L	●	●	R,S		B	H,N	6	B3
Point Comfort Forest Preserve	518-598-7586		L,R		●				●		●			L	●				B	H	30	E2
Poke-O-Moonshine Forest Preserve	518-834-9045				●										●		R,S			H	12	F1
Poplar Point Forest Preserve	518-548-8031		L,R		●				●		●			L	●				B		30	F1
Prospect Mountain State Highway	518-668-5198														●					H	32	C1
Putnam Pond Forest Preserve	518-585-7280		L		●				●		●			L	●		R,S		B	H	19	E2
Rogers Rock Forest Preserve	518-585-6746		L		●				●		●			L	●		R,S		B		20	A3
Rollins Pond Forest Preserve	518-891-3239		L,R		●				●		●			L,R			R,S			H	11	B3
Sacandaga Forest Preserve	518-924-4121				●				●		●			R	●		R,S		B	H	31	C2
Saranac Lake Islands Preserve	518-891-3170		L		●				●					L	●						11	D3
Sharp Bridge Forest Preserve	518-532-7538				●				●					R	●					H	12	E6
Taylor Pond Forest Preserve	518-647-5250		L,R		●				●					L	●					H	12	B1
Tioga Point Forest Preserve	315-354-4230		R		●				●					L	●					H	17	E2
Wilmington Notch Forest Preserve	518-946-7172				●				●		●			R	●		R,S				12	B2

Park	Phone	Bicycle Trails	Boating — Launch (L), Rentals (R)	Bridle Trails	Camping	Concessions	Cross Country Skiing	Environmental Education and Interpretation	Fishing	Golf (G), Tennis (T)	Handicapped Facilities	Hunting	Ice Skating	Lake (L), River (R)	Picnic Areas	Playgrounds	Restrooms (R), Showers (S)	Snowmobile Trails	Swimming — Beach (B), Pool (P)	Trails — Hiking (H), Nature (N)	Map Number	Grid Location
THOUSAND ISLANDS — SEAWAY																						
Battle Island State Park	315-593-3408					•	•			G				R	•						27	A2
Burnham Point State Park	315-654-2324		L		•				•		•	•		R	•	•	R,S				7	C3
Canoe-Picnic Point State Park	315-654-2522				•				•		•	•		R	•						7	F2
Cedar Island State Park	315-654-2522				•				•			•		R	•						8	C1
Cedar Point State Park	315-654-2522		L,R		•			•	•		•	•		R	•	•	R,S		B		7	D3
Coles Creek State Park	315-388-5636		L,R		•	•			•		•	•		R	•		R,S		B		2	E2
Dewolf Point State Park	315-482-2012		L		•				•			•		R	•		R,S				8	A3
Eel Weir State Park	315-393-1138		L		•				•			•		R	•		R,S				2	A5
Grass Point State Park	315-686-4472		L		•			•	•		•	•		R	•		R,S		B		7	F2
Higley Flow State Park	315-262-2880		L		•				•		•	•		R	•		R,S	•	B	H,N	3	A6
Jacques Cartier State Park	315-375-6371		L		•	•			•		•	•		R	•		R,S		B		1	D6
Keewaydin Point State Park	315-482-3331		L,R		•			•	•		•			R	•		R,S		P		8	A3
Kring Point State Park	315-482-2444		L		•			•	•		•	•		R	•		R,S		B		8	B2
Long Point State Park	315-649-5258		L		•				•		•			L	•		R,S				7	D5
Mary Island State Park	315-654-2522				•				•					R	•						8	A2
Robert Moses State Park	315-769-8663		L,R		•		•	•	•	T	•			R	•	•	R,S	•	B	H,N	3	B1
Saint Lawrence State Park	315-393-1977					•	•			G	•			R			R,S			H	1	F5
Selkirk Shores State Park	315-298-5737	•	L		•	•	•	•	•		•			L	•		R,S	•	B	H,N	14	D6
Southwick Beach State Park	315-846-5338				•	•	•	•	•		•			L	•		R,S		B	H,N	14	D3
Waterson Point State Park	315-482-2722								•					R							7	F1
Wellesley Island State Park	315-482-2722		L,R		•	•	•	•	•	G	•			R	•	•	R,S		B	H,N	7	F2
Westcott Beach State Park	315-646-2239		L		•	•	•		•		•	•		L	•		R,S		B	H	14	E2
Whetstone Gulf State Park	315-376-6630		L		•	•	•		•		•			L,R	•		R,S		B	H	16	A4
CENTRAL — LEATHERSTOCKING																						
Bowman Lake State Park	607-334-2718	•	L,R		•	•	•	•	•		•	•		L	•	•	R,S		B	H,N	41	E6
Chenango Valley State Park	607-648-5251	•	R		•	•	•	•	•	G	•		•	L,R	•	•	R,S		B	H,N	55	C4
Chittenango Falls State Park	315-655-9620				•		•		•		•			R	•		R,S			H,N	41	B1
Clark Reservation State Park	315-492-1590								•		•			L	•					H,N	27	F6
Delta Lake State Park	315-337-4670	•	L		•	•	•		•		•			L	•		R,S	•	B	H,N	29	B3
Gilbert Lake State Park	607-432-2114	•	L,R		•	•	•	•	•		•	•		L	•	•	R,S		B	H,N	42	E5
Glimmerglass State Park	607-547-8662	•	L		•	•	•		•		•		•	L	•	•	R,S		B	H,N	43	B3
Green Lakes State Park	315-637-6111	•	R		•	•	•	•	•	G	•			L	•	•	R,S		B	H,N	28	A6
Hunts Pond State Park	607-859-2249		L		•				•		•	•		L						H	42	B5
Old Erie Canal State Park	315-687-7821	•	L	•					•		•			R	•	•				H,N	28	E5
Oquaga Creek State Park	607-467-4160	•	L,R		•	•	•		•		•	•		L	•		R,S		B	H,N	56	B4
Pixley Falls State Park	315-942-4713				•	•	•		•		•	•		R	•					N	29	C2
Verona Beach State Park	315-762-4463	•			•	•	•		•		•	•		L	•	•	R,S	•	B	H,N	28	D4
FINGER LAKES																						
Allen H. Treman State Marine Park	607-272-1460		L						•		•			L,R			R,S				Map 84	
Buttermilk Falls State Park	607-273-5761				•	•		•	•		•			L,R	•		R,S		B	H,N	53	F2
Canandaigua Lake State Marine Park	315-789-2331		L						•												38	C2
Cayuga Lake State Park	315-568-5163		L			•		•	•		•			L	•	•	R,S		B	N	39	C2
Conesus Lake State Park	716-493-3600		L								•			L	•						37	D3

State Recreation Area Facilities

Region	Park	Phone	Bicycle Trails	Boating — Launch (L), Rentals (R)	Bridle Trails	Camping	Concessions	Cross Country Skiing	Environmental Education and Interpretation	Fishing	Golf (G), Tennis (T)	Handicapped Facilities	Hunting	Ice Skating	Lake (L), River (R)	Picnic Areas	Playgrounds	Restrooms (R), Showers (S)	Snowmobile Trails	Swimming — Beach (B), Pool (P)	Trails — Hiking (H), Nature (N)	Map Number	Grid Location
FINGER LAKES	Fair Haven Beach State Park	315-947-5205		L,R		•	•	•	•	•		•	•	•	L	•		R,S		B	H,N	26	D2
	Fillmore Glen State Park	315-497-0130				•		•	•	•		•	•		L	•	•	R,S		B	H	40	B4
	Hamlin Beach State Park	716-964-2462	•	L		•	•	•	•	•		•	•		L	•	•	R,S		B	H,N	24	A2
	Harriet Hollister Spencer Rec Area	716-335-8111						•					•			•					H	37	F4
	Irondequoit Bay State Marine Park	716-964-2462		L						•					L							24	F4
	Keuka Lake State Park	315-536-3666		L		•		•		•		•	•		L	•	•	R,S		B	H	38	E6
	Lakeside Beach State Park	716-682-2462	•			•	•	•	•	•		•			L	•	•	R,S	•		H	23	C2
	Letchworth State Park	716-682-4888	•			•	•	•	•	•		•		•	L,R	•	•	R,S	•	P	H,N	36	F5
	Lodi Point State Park	607-582-6392		L						•		•			L	•						39	B5
	Long Point State Park	315-364-8884		L						•				•	L	•				B		39	D4
	Newtown Battlefield State Park	607-732-1096				•						•				•						53	D6
	Oak Orchard Marine Park	716-682-4888		L						•					L,R							23	D2
	Pinnacle State Park	607-359-2767					•	•			G	•	•			•					H	52	D5
	Robert H. Treman State Park	606-273-3440				•	•	•	•	•	G	•	•		R	•	•	R,S		B	H	53	E2
	Sampson State Park	315-585-6392	•	L		•	•	•	•	•	T	•	•		L	•	•	R,S		B		39	B4
	Seneca Lake State Park	315-789-2331	•	L						•		•			L	•	•			B		39	A2
	Stony Brook State Park	716-335-8111				•	•	•			T	•	•		R	•		R,S		B	H,N	37	D6
	Taughannock Falls State Park	607-387-6739		L		•	•	•	•	•		•	•	•	L	•	•	R,S		B	H	39	E6
	Watkins Glen State Park	607-535-4511				•	•	•			G	•	•		L,R	•	•	R,S		P	H	53	A2
THE NIAGARA FRONTIER	Beaver Island State Park	716-773-3271	•			•	•	•	•	•	G	•	•			•	•			B	N	35	A1
	Big Six State Marina	716-773-3271		L						•												21	F6
	Buckhorn Island State Park	716-773-3271						•	•	•		•									H,N	22	A6
	Darien Lake State Park	716-547-9242	•		•	•	•	•	•	•		•	•		L	•	•	R,S	•	B	H	36	A2
	Devil's Hole State Park	716-285-3893	•				•	•	•							•					H,N	Map 87	
	Earl W. Brydges Artpark	716-754-9000					•	•	•			•									H,N	Map 87	
	Evangola State Park	716-549-1802				•	•	•	•	•		•	•			•	•		•	B	H	34	E5
	Fort Niagara State Park	716-745-7273		L			•	•	•	•	T	•			L	•	•			P	H,N	21	F3
	Four Mile State Campsite	716-745-3802				•		•		•		•							•		H,N	22	A3
	Golden Hill State Park	716-795-3885	•			•		•	•	•		•	•			•	•				H,N	23	A2
	Joseph Davis State Park	716-754-4596					•	•	•			•	•			•			•		H	21	F4
	Niagara Reservation State Park	716-278-1770	•				•	•	•			•				•					H,N	Map 87	
	Reservoir State Park	716-285-3893	•					•	•		T	•				•	•				H,N	Map 87	
	Silver Lake State Park	716-493-3600		L						•			•		L	•						36	F4
	Whirlpool State Park	716-285-3893						•	•			•				•	•				H,N	Map 87	
	Wilson-Tuscarora State Park	716-751-6361		L				•	•	•		•				•			•		H,N	22	D2
CHAUTAUQUA — ALLEGHENY	Allegany State Park/Quaker	716-354-2182	•	L,R	•	•	•	•	•	•	T	•	•		L,R	•	•	R,S	•	B	H,N	49	B6
	Allegany State Park/Red House	716-354-9121	•	L		•	•	•	•	•	T	•	•		L,R	•	•	R,S	•	B	H,N	49	C5
	Lake Erie State Park	716-792-9214	•			•	•	•	•	•		•			L	•	•	R,S		B	H,N	48	A1
	Long Point on Lake Chautauqua	716-386-2722	•	L			•	•	•	•		•			L	•	•		•	B	H,N	48	B4

Great Western Winery, Hammondsport

As the second-largest wine-producing state in the nation, New York offers wine lovers unrivaled opportunities to explore new and historic vineyards, and to sample the vintages produced in its four major wine regions. Found in the scenic countryside of Long Island, the Hudson Valley, the Finger Lakes, and along the shores of Lake Erie in Chautauqua — Allegheny, New York's award-winning wineries provide a perfect excuse for a romantic summer or fall getaway. Even if you don't enjoy wine, you'll enjoy New York's wine country.

The history of New York's wine-making industry dates back to the mid-17th century, when early settlers planted grapes on Long Island and today's Manhattan. The Hudson Valley — where the first vineyards were planted near New Paltz by French Huguenots in 1677 — is, in fact, the oldest continuous wine-producing region in the nation. Brotherhood Winery, the oldest commercial winery in America, was founded in the Hudson Valley in 1839. In the Lake Erie region, vineyards were planted in Chautauqua County, near the town of Brocton, in 1818. The dominant grapes used then were native American varieties, especially Concord, Catawba, and Delaware. The Welch brothers set up their famous grape juice business at Westfield in 1897. It was the Welch brothers, aided by wine companies such as Mogen David and Manischewitz, who used Concord grapes from the Lake Erie region for their sweet kosher wines, who first established the sweet Concord flavor as the quintessentially American grape flavor. Keuka Lake in the Finger Lakes region became the center of the state's growing wine industry at the time of the Civil War.

Until fairly recently, New York State wines were primarily the sweet, grapey varieties made from Concord grapes — "jelly glass" wines, as they are often called. It wasn't until 1952 that the first experimental *vinifera* vineyard was planted. (*Vinifera* refers to the common European grape — *Vitis vinifera* — that is the chief source of Old World wine and table grapes.) Once it became apparent that the *vinifera* — especially Chardonnay and Riesling — could not only survive in New York, but thrive, the New York wine industry was off and pruning. New hybrids and European hybrids, which have been used commercially since the 1960s, have added even more variety and flavor to New York State wines.

The most successful New York wines have thus far been the crisp and slightly tart white varieties that do well in the state's relatively cool — and sometimes bitterly cold — climate. If you are scouting out white wines, connoisseurs recommend Riesling, Gewürztraminer, Chardonnay, Seyval Blanc, Cayuga White, Vignoles, and Vidal Blanc as the best. A good New York Riesling, with its lively, fruity flavor, compares favorably with German and Californian Rieslings.

New York State red wines are not as plentiful or successful as the whites, but many vintners are now working on improving them. Merlot, Pinot Noir from Long Island, Cabernet Sauvignon, Chelois, Chancellor, and Baco Noir are considered the most successful reds. Sparkling wines utilizing the *methode champenoise* are enjoying new popularity in New York, and production of wine coolers is growing.

Thanks to its sunny, temperate climate and sandy soil, Long Island has in recent years become one of New York State's fastest-growing wine regions. Promising new vineyards — many of them planted on former potato farms — can be found on both the North and South Forks, about a three-hour drive east of Manhattan. The area around Cutchoque and Peconic, east of Riverhead, has some 12 wineries and 30 commercial vineyards, some of which offer tours and tastings. Look for Chardonnays, Merlots, Pinot Noirs, Sauvignon Blancs, and Cabernet Sauvignons.

Wine cellars, Brotherhood Winery, Washingtonville

America's oldest continuous wine-producing region is the Hudson Valley, where vineyards are planted on the slopes of the Hudson River and stretch as far as the Connecticut border. The soil here is slatey and more complex than Long Island's, and the red wines of the region are generally considered to be a cut above those produced in the Finger Lakes. An aged Baco Noir from the Benmarl Winery & Vineyard in Marlboro is one highly rated red. Few of the wineries in the Hudson Valley have thus far been planted with *vinifera* hybrids, but there are some excellent dry whites to be found — including Rieslings, Pinot Noirs, Seyval Blancs, and Chardonnays. Some of these wines approach the subtlety and complexity of older European wines. If you're driving up the west side of the Hudson River, you'll find wineries — many with magnificent river views — stretching from Marlboro to West Park. Brotherhood Winery, founded by a French shoe maker in 1839, is the oldest continually operating winery in the country and produces a thick, sweet Port. It is located in Washingtonville, about 50 miles north of Manhattan.

The sloping hillsides, glacial soil drainage, and protected microclimates of the Finger Lakes provide ideal conditions for growing grapes, so it's no surprise that the Finger Lakes region has long been one of the top wine producers in the state. In fact, the federal government has officially designated it the "Finger Lakes Wine District." Crisp Rieslings, Chardonnays, and Gewürztraminers are locally available from Finger Lakes' vintners, as are sweeter sparkling whites and reds produced from *vinifera* hybrids. Wine lovers can choose from a variety of routes that allow them to stop, tour, and taste the vintages produced by wineries both small and large. One of the most popular routes is the Cayuga Wine Trail, which begins in Ithaca and passes nine wineries. The southern half of 35-mile-long Seneca Lake is home to several wineries and makes for another good wine tour. Hammondsport, at the southern end of Lake Keuka, is where the Finger Lakes region's wine industry was born in 1829 — the Great Western Winery there is the oldest in the Finger Lakes and is well known for its sparkling wine. Canandaigua Wine Company, the nation's third-largest winery, offers tours at Widmer Wine Cellars in Naples and has a tasting center at Sonnenberg Gardens in Canandaigua.

Wine lovers can also stop for tours and tastings at several wineries located along a scenic 50-mile drive known as the Chautauqua Wine Trail, which hugs the shore of Lake Erie between Ripley and Silver Creek. More Concord grapes of the *lambrusca* variety are grown in the vineyards in this vicinity than anywhere else in the world, and most of them are used to produce jelly, juice, and the sweet kosher wines for which Mogen David, near Westfield, is famous. Most of the newer wineries in the Lake Erie grape-growing region use hybrid varieties for their products, and good Rieslings, Chardonnays, Seyvals, and Gewürztraminers are to be found.

Concord Grapes

The listings below represent a selection of prominent vineyards and wineries in the major wine tour regions of New York State. All of these establishments offer wine tastings. Please call for information, tour hours, and fees.

New York City

Delmonico's Winery 718-768-7020
(Brooklyn) 75 A4

Joseph Zakon Winery 718-604-1430
(Brooklyn) 75 A4

Loukas Wines 718-992-1024
(The Bronx) 75 B2

Schapiro Wine Cellars, Inc. 212-674-4404
(Manhattan) Map 86

Long Island

Banfi Vintners — Old Brookville Vineyards 516-626-9200
(Old Brookville) 75 E2

Bedell Cellars 516-734-7537
(Cutchogue) 71 A6

Bidwell Vineyards 516-734-5200
(Cutchogue) 70 F6

Cory Creek Vineyards 516-323-1224
(Southold) 71 C5

Duck Walk Vineyards 516-726-7555
(Water Mill) 78 B2

Gristina Vineyards 516-734-7089
(Cutchogue) 77 F1

Hargrave Vineyard 516-734-5111
(Cutchogue) 70 F6

Jamesport Vineyards 516-722-5256
(Jamesport) 77 E1

Lenz Winery 516-734-6010
(Peconic) 71 A6

Loughlin Vineyards, Inc. 516-589-0027
(Sayville) 76 F4

Macari Vineyards & Winery 516-298-0100
(Mattituck) 77 F1

Osprey's Dominion Vineyards 516-765-6188
(Peconic) 71 A6

Palmer Vineyards 516-722-9463
(Aquebogue) 77 E1

Paumanok Vineyards, Ltd. 516-722-8800
(Aquebogue) 77 E1

Peconic Bay Vineyards 516-734-7361
(Cutchogue) 71 A6

Pellegrini Vineyards 516-734-4111
(Cutchogue) 71 A6

Pindar Vineyards 516-734-6200
(Peconic) 71 A6

Pugliese Vineyards 516-734-4057
(Cutchogue) 71 A6

Sag Pond Vineyards 516-537-5106
(Bridgehampton) 78 C1

Hudson Valley

Applewood Winery 914-988-9292
(Warwick) 67 B3

Baldwin Vineyards 914-744-2226
(Pine Bush) 63 C5

Benmarl Winery & Vineyard 914-236-4265
(Marlboro) 64 A5

Brimstone Hill Vineyard 914-744-2231
(Pine Bush) 63 B5

Brotherhood — "America's Oldest Winery," Ltd. 914-496-3661
(Washingtonville) 67 E1

Cascade Mountain Winery & Restaurant 914-373-9021
(Amenia) 64 F2

Clinton Vineyards 914-266-5372
(Clinton Corners) 64 C2

El Paso Winery 914-331-8642
(Ulster Park) 64 A2

Hudson Valley Draft Cider 914-266-5967
(Staatsburg) 64 B2

Millbrook Vineyards & Winery 800-662-9463
(Millbrook) 64 D2 · 914-677-8383

North Salem Vineyard 914-669-5518
(North Salem) 68 E2

Regent Champagne Cellars, Inc. 914-691-7296
(Highland) 64 A4

Royal Kedem Wine Company 914-795-2240
(Milton) 64 A5

Warwick Valley Winery 914-258-4858
(Warwick) 67 A3

West Park Wine Cellars 914-384-6709
(West Park) 64 A3

Windsor Vineyards 914-236-4440
(Marlboro) 64 A5

The Catskills

Adair Vineyards 914-255-1377
(New Paltz) 63 E4

Magnanini Winery, Inc. 914-895-2767
(Wallkill) 63 E5

Rivendell Winery 914-255-2494
(New Paltz) 63 D4

Walker Valley Vineyards 914-744-3449
(Walker Valley) 63 B5

Capital — Saratoga

Johnston's Winery 516-882-6310
(Ballston Spa) 32 A6

Larry's Vineyard & Farm Winery 518-355-7365
(Altamont) 44 F4

The Meadery at Greenwich 518-692-9669
(Greenwich) 33 A5

Thousand Islands — Seaway

Pleasant Valley Winery 315-379-0221
(Canton) 2 F6

Central — Leatherstocking

Saint Benedict Winery 607-655-2366
(Windsor) 55 E6

Finger Lakes

Amberg Wine Cellars 716-526-6742
(Clifton Spring) 38 E2

Americana Vineyards Winery 607-387-6801
(Interlaken) 39 D6

Anthony Road Wine Company 800-559-2182
(Penn Yan) 39 A4 · 315-536-2182

Arbor Hill Grapery 716-374-2406
(Naples) 38 B4

Arcadian Estate Vineyards 800-298-1346
(Rock Stream) 53 B1 · 607-535-2068

Barrington Cellars — Buzzard Crest Vineyards 315-536-9686
(Penn Yan) 38 E5

Bully Hill Vineyards 607-868-3610
(Hammondsport) 52 D1

Canandaigua Wine Company 716-394-7900
(Canandaigua) 38 B2

Casa Larga Vineyards 716-223-4210
(Fairport) 25 A6

Cascata Winery at the Professors' Place 607-535-8000
(Watkins Glen) 53 B2

Castel Grisch Estate Winery 607-535-9614
(Watkins Glen) 53 A2

Cayuga Ridge Estate Winery 607-869-5158
(Ovid) 39 D4

Chateau LaFayette Reneau 607-546-2062
(Hector) 53 B1

Dr. Konstantin Frank's Vinifera Wine   800-320-0735
   Cellars   607-868-4884
(Hammondsport) 52 D1

Eagle Crest Vineyards, Inc.   716-346-2321
(Conesus) 37 E4

Earle Estates Meadery   607-243-9011
(Himrod) 40 A5

Four Chimneys Farm Winery   607-243-7502
(Himrod) 39 A5

Fox Run Vineyards   800-636-9786
(Penn Yan) 39 A4   315-536-4616

Frontenac Point Vineyard   607-387-9619
(Trumansburg) 39 D6

Fulkerson's Winery & Juice Plant   607-243-7883
(Dundee) 53 B1

Glenora Wine Cellars   800-243-5511
(Dundee) 53 A1   607-243-5511

Goose Watch Winery   315-549-8326
(Romulus) 39 C3

Great Western Winery Visitor Ctr &
   Pleasant Valley Wine Company   607-569-6292
(Hammondsport) 52 D2

Hazlitt 1852 Vineyards   607-546-9463
(Hector) 39 B6

Hermann J. Wiemer Vineyard, Inc.   800-371-7971
(Dundee) 39 A5   607-243-7971

Heron Hill Vineyards   800-441-4241
(Hammondsport) 52 D1   607-868-4241

Hosmer Wine Cellar   607-869-3393
(Ovid) 39 C4

Hunt Country Vineyard   315-595-2812
(Branchport) 38 E5

Keuka Overlook Wine Cellars   607-292-6877
(Dundee) 38 E6

King Ferry Winery   800-439-5271
(King Ferry) 39 E5   315-364-5100

Knapp Vineyards Winery & Restaurant   607-869-9271
(Romulus) 39 C3

Lakeshore Winery   315-549-7075
(Romulus) 39 C3

Lakewood Vineyards   607-535-9252
(Watkins Glen) 53 B1

Lamoreaux Landing Wine Cellars   607-582-6011
(Lodi) 39 B5

Leidenfrost Vineyards   607-546-2800
(Hector) 39 B6

Lucas Vineyards   800-682-9463
(Interlaken) 39 D5   607-532-4825

McGregor Vineyard & Winery   800-272-0192
(Dundee) 52 F1   607-292-3999

New Land Vineyard   315-585-9844
(Geneva) 39 A2

Olde Germania Wine Cellars   607-569-2218
(Hammondsport) 52 D1

Onondaga Winery, Inc.   315-698-0855
(Cicero) 27 E4

Poplar Ridge Vineyards   607-582-6421
(Valois) 39 B6

Prejean Winery   315-536-7524
(Penn Yan) 39 A5

Rasta Ranch Vineyards   607-546-2974
(Valois) 39 B6

Shalestone Vineyards   607-582-6783
(Lodi) 39 B6

Signore Winery   607-539-7935
(Brooktondale) 54 B2

Silver Thread Vineyard   607-582-6116
(Caywood) 39 B5

Six Mile Creek Vineyard   607-272-9463
(Ithaca) 54 A2

Standing Stone Vineyards   800-803-7135
(Valois) 39 B6

Swedish Hill Vineyard   888-549-9463
(Romulus) 39 C3   315-549-8326

The Barrel People Winery (Squaw Point)   607-243-8602
(Dundee) 39 A6

The Wine Center at Widmer Wine Cellars   800-836-5253
(Naples) 38 A5   716-374-6311

Thorpe Vineyard   315-594-2502
(Wolcott) 26 B3

Wagner Winery & Ginny Lee Cafe   607-582-6450
(Lodi) 39 B5

Niagara Frontier

Batavia Wine Cellars   716-344-1111
(Batavia) 36 E1

Chautauqua — Allegheny

Frederick S. Johnson Vineyards   716-326-2191
(Westfield) 47 E3

Merritt Estate Winery   716-965-4800
(Forestville) 48 D1

Mogen David Wine Corporation   716-326-3151
(Westfield) 47 F2

Roberian Vineyards, Ltd.   716-679-1620
(Forestville) 48 D1

Schloss Doepken Winery   716-326-3636
(Ripley) 47 D3

Vetter Vineyards   716-326-3100
(Westfield) 47 F2

Woodbury Vineyards   888-697-9463
(Dunkirk) 48 C1   716-679-9463

State Facts

State Name:	State of New York (after Duke of York, later James II)
Statehood:	Admitted to the Union July 26, 1788
State Nickname:	Empire State
State Capital:	Albany
State Motto:	*Excelsior* (Ever upward)
State Animal:	Beaver
State Beverage:	Milk
State Bird:	Bluebird
State Fish:	Trout
State Flower:	Rose
State Fruit:	Apple
State Fossil:	Sea Scorpion
State Gem:	Garnet
State Tree:	Sugar Maple

County Seats

County	County Seat	Map	Grid
Albany	Albany	45	C5
Allegany	Belmont	50	F4
Bronx	Bronx	75	C2
Broome	Binghamton	55	B5
Cattaraugus	Little Valley	49	C4
Cayuga	Auburn	39	F1
Chautauqua	Mayville	2	F3
Chemung	Elmira	53	B5
Chenango	Norwich	41	F6
Clinton	Plattsburgh	6	A4
Columbia	Hudson	59	C3
Cortland	Cortland	40	E5
Delaware	Delhi	57	B3
Dutchess	Poughkeepsie	64	A4
Erie	Buffalo	35	B1
Essex	Elizabethtown	12	E4
Franklin	Malone	4	C2
Fulton	Johnstown	31	B6
Genesee	Batavia	36	D1
Greene	Catskill	59	B4
Hamilton	Lake Pleasant	31	B1
Herkimer	Herkimer	29	F6
Jefferson	Watertown	15	B1
Kings	Brooklyn	7	F5
Lewis	Lowville	16	A3
Livingston	Geneseo	37	C3
Madison	Wampsville	28	D6
Monroe	Rochester	24	E4
Montgomery	Fonda	44	B1
Nassau	Mineola	75	E4
New York	Manhattan	75	A4
Niagara	Lockport	22	D4
Oneida	Utica	29	D5
Onondaga	Syracuse	40	D1
Ontario	Canandaigua	38	C2
Orange	Goshen	67	C2
Orleans	Albion	23	D4
Oswego	Oswego	26	F1
Otsego	Cooperstown	43	A4
Putnam	Carmel	68	D1
Queens	Queens	75	C4
Rensselaer	Troy	45	D4
Richmond	Staten Island	74	E5
Rockland	New City	68	A5
Saint Lawrence	Canton	2	D5
Saratoga	Ballston Spa	32	B6
Schenectady	Schenectady	45	A2
Schoharie	Schoharie	44	C5
Schuyler	Watkins Glen	53	B2
Seneca	Waterloo	39	B2
Steuben	Bath	52	C2
Suffolk	Riverhead	77	E1
Sullivan	Monticello	62	D5
Tioga	Owego	54	C5
Tompkins	Ithaca	53	F1
Ulster	Kingston	64	A1
Warren	Lake George	32	D1
Washington	Hudson Falls-Salem	32	F3
Wayne	Lyons	26	A6
Westchester	White Plains	75	C1
Wyoming	Warsaw	36	E3
Yates	Penn Yan	38	F4

New York State Tourist Information	800-225-5697
Bed and Breakfast Association of New York State P.O. Box 387, Syracuse, NY 13208	315-474-4889
Department of Economic Development "I LOVE NY" Publications Albany, NY 12235	518-474-7910
Great New York State Fair and County Fairs 1 Winter Circle Albany, NY 12235	800-554-4501 518-457-3880
New York State Camping Reservations For state operated campgrounds only.	800-456-CAMP
New York State Department of Agriculture and Markets 1 Winners Circle Capitol Plaza Albany, NY 12235	518-457-5981
New York State Department of Environmental Conservation (DEC) DEC Publications 50 Wolf Road Albany, NY 12233	518-457-5400
New York State Department of Tourism Twin Towers 99 Washington Avenue Albany, NY 12245	518-474-4116
New York State Outdoor Guides Association P.O. Box 4704 NYS, Queensbury, NY 12804	518-798-1253
New York State Parks & Historic Sites Office of Parks, Recreation and Historic Preservation Albany, NY 12238	518-474-0456
New York State Tour Boat Association Circle Line Pier 83, W. 42nd Street New York, NY 10036	800-852-0095
New York Wine and Grape Foundation 350 Elm Street Penn Yan, NY 14527	315-536-9996
Seaway Trail National Scenic Byway System (Sackets Harbor)	315-646-1000

New York City

NYC Convention and Visitors Bureau 2 Columbus Circle, New York, NY 10019	800-692-8474 212-397-8222

Free Publications:
New York Visitors Guide
New York Tour Package Directory
New York Visitors Map to NYC
The New York Hotel Guide
The New York Restaurant Guide
The New York Shopping Guide
20 Free Things To Do
Only-In-New York Sights
Quarterly Events Listing

Public Transportation (24 hours a day)	718-330-1234
New York City State Parks	212-694-3608

Long Island

Long Island Convention & Visitors Bureau Nassau Veterans Memorial Coliseum (Uniondale)	800-441-4601
Long Island State Park Region	516-669-1000
Long Island Tours	718-990-7498
Montauk Chamber of Commerce (Montauk)	516-668-2428
Railroad Schedules	718-217-5477
Shelter Island Chamber of Commerce (Manhanset Chapel)	516-749-0399

Hudson Valley

Columbia County Tourism (Hudson)	800-724-1846
Dutchess County Tourism (Poughkeepsie, Hyde Park, Wappingers Falls)	800-445-3131
Greater South Dutchess Chamber of Commerce (Wappingers Falls)	914-897-2067
Orange County Tourism (Goshen, Middletown, Newburgh, West Point)	800-762-8687
Palisades Interstate Park Commission	914-786-2701
Taconic State Park Region	914-889-4100
Westchester County Convention & Visitors Bureau (White Plains)	800-833-9282

The Catskills

Catskills Regional Information	800-697-2287
Delaware County Chamber of Commerce (Delhi, Stamford, Walton)	800-642-4443
East Durham Information Center	518-622-3939
Greene County Tourism (Catskill, Hunter, Windham)	800-950-3656
Hunter Chamber of Commerce (Hunter)	518-263-4900
New Paltz Chamber of Commerce (New Paltz)	914-255-0243
Sullivan County Office of Public Information (Monticello, Liberty)	800-882-CATS
Ulster County Public Information Office (Kingston, New Paltz, Woodstock)	800-DIAL-UCO
Woodstock Chamber of Commerce (Woodstock)	914-679-6234

Capital — Saratoga

Albany County Convention & Visitor Bureau (Albany)	800-732-8259
Capital — Saratoga Region	800-732-8259

Capital — Saratoga
State Park & Recreation   518-584-2000
(Saratoga Springs)

Fulton County Chamber of Commerce   800-676-3858
(Gloversville)

Greater Saratoga
Chamber of Commerce   518-584-3255
(Saratoga Springs)

Rensselaer County Tourism   518-274-7020
(Troy)

Saratoga County Chamber of Commerce   800-526-8970
(Saratoga Springs)

Schenectady County
Chamber of Commerce   800-962-8007
(Schenectady)

Southern Saratoga
Chamber of Commerce   518-371-7748
(Clifton Park)

Washington County Tourism   518-747-2290
(Fort Edward)

The Adirondacks

Adirondack Regional Information   800-648-5239

Adirondack Visitors Information Center   518-597-4646

Essex County Tourist Department   518-942-7794
(Elizabethtown)

Franklin County Tourism   518-483-6767
(Malone)

Hamilton County Tourism Department   518-648-5239
(Indian Lake)

Lake Placid Essex County Visitor Bureau   800-447-5224
(Lake Placid)

Lake Placid Olympic Facilities   800-462-6236
(Lake Placid)

Lewis County Tourism   800-724-0242
(Lowville)

Long Lake Department of Parks,
Recreation and Tourism   518-624-3077
(Long Lake)

Malone Chamber of Commerce   518-483-3760
(Malone)

North Creek Chamber of Commerce   518-251-2612
(North Creek)

Olympic Regional Development
Authority   518-523-1655
(Lake Placid)

Plattsburgh/North Country
Chamber of Commerce   518-563-1000
(Plattsburgh)

Saranac Lake Chamber of Commerce   518-891-1990
(Saranac Lake)

Warren County Tourism   800-365-1050
(Lake George)

Thousand Islands — Seaway

Alexandria Bay Chamber of Commerce   800-541-2110
(Alexandria Bay)

Massena Chamber of Commerce   315-769-3525
(Massena)

Ogdensburg Chamber of Commerce   315-393-3620
(Ogdensburg)

Oswego County Department of
Promotion and Tourism   315-349-8322
(Oswego)

Saint Lawrence County
Chamber of Commerce   315-386-4000
(Canton)

Thousand Islands—Seaway
Regional Information   800-8-ISLAND
(Alexandria Bay)

Thousand Islands State Parks   315-482-2593

Watertown Chamber of Commerce   315-788-4400
(Watertown)

Central — Leatherstocking

Leatherstocking Country, NY   800-233-8778
(Binghamton, Oneonta, Utica, Rome, Little Falls, Norwich, Cazenovia, Herkimer)

Broome County
Chamber of Commerce   800-836-6740
(Binghamton)

Central New York State Park Region   315-473-8400
(Jamesville)

Chenango County
Chamber of Commerce   607-334-1400
(Norwich)

Herkimer County
Chamber of Commerce   315-866-7820
(Mohawk)

Madison County Tourism   800-684-7320
(Madison)

Montgomery County
Chamber of Commerce   800-743-7337
(Amsterdam)

New York State Canal System   800-422-6254
(Albany)

Oneida County
Convention & Visitors Bureau   800-426-3132
(Boonville, Rome, Utica)

Otsego County Chamber of Commerce   800-843-3394
(Oneonta)

Schoharie County
Chamber of Commerce   800-418-4748
(Cobbleskill, Schoharie)

Finger Lakes

Auburn & Cayuga County
Chamber of Commerce   315-252-7291
(Auburn)

Auburn Tourist Information   315-255-1188
(Finger Lakes Mall)

Chemung County Tourism   800-627-5892
(Elmira, Horseheads, Southport)

Finger Lakes Regional Information   800-KIT-4FUN

Finger Lakes State Park Region   607-387-7041
(Trumansburg)

Greater Rochester Visitors Association   800-677-7282
(Rochester)

Ithaca and Tompkins County
Convention & Visitors Bureau   800-284-8422
(Ithaca)

Ontario Chamber of Commerce   315-524-5886
(Ontario)

Ontario County Tourism Bureau   800-654-9798
(Canandaigua, Naples, Geneva)

Schuyler County
Chamber of Commerce   607-535-4300
(Watkins Glen)

Syracuse Convention & Visitors Bureau   315-470-1800
(Syracuse)

Wayne County Tourism   800-527-6510
(Palmyra, Newark, Sodus Point, Lyons)

Niagara Frontier

Genesee County
Chamber of Commerce   800-622-2686
(Batavia)

Genesee State Park Region   716-493-2611
(Castile)

Grand Island Information Center   716-773-6382

Greater Buffalo
Convention & Visitors Bureau   716-852-0511
(Buffalo)

Niagara County
Tourism & Fishing Office   800-338-7890
(Lockport)

Niagara Falls
Convention & Visitors Bureau   716-285-2400
(Niagara Falls)

Niagara Frontier State Park
& Recreation Region   716-278-1770
(Niagara Falls)

Orleans County Tourism   716-589-7004
(Albion)

Wyoming County
Tourist Promotion Agency   716-493-3190
(Warsaw)

Chautauqua — Allegheny

Allegany County Historian   716-268-9293
(Wellsville)

Allegany County Tourism   800-836-1869
(Belmont)

Allegany State Park Region   716-354-9101

Cattaraugus County Tourism Bureau   800-331-0543
(Little Valley)

Chautauqua County
Vacationland Association   800-242-4569
(Mayville)

Chautauqua County (North)
Chamber of Commerce   716-366-6200
(Dunkirk)

Ellicottville Chamber of Commerce   716-699-5046
(Ellicottville)

Jamestown Area
Chamber of Commerce   716-484-1101
(Jamestown)

Olean Chamber of Commerce   716-372-4433
(Olean)

Salamanca Chamber of Commerce   716-945-2034
(Salamanca)

New York Cities

MILEAGE CHART

	Albany	Auburn	Batavia	Binghamton	Buffalo	Canandaigua	Cortland	Deer Park	Dunkirk	Elmira	Glens Falls	Hempstead	Hornell	Ithaca	Jamestown	Kingston	Massena	Montauk	Monticello	New York City	Newburgh	Niagara Falls	Ogdensburg	Oswego	Plattsburgh	Poughkeepsie	Riverhead	Rochester	Rome	Saranac Lake	Saratoga Springs	Schenectady	Syracuse	Utica	Watertown	White Plains
Albany		167	250	133	295	214	151	183	321	188	51	171	246	174	336	51	301	258	99	144	86	295	229	173	161	72	221	219	103	144	31	7	137	89	171	137
Auburn	167		89	78	130	41	34	304	168	65	209	271	92	34	219	199	191	377	161	265	202	143	157	38	264	216	340	65	65	212	164	154	27	75	99	258
Binghamton	133	78	161		202	111	45	225	217	55	157	210	116	45	215	123	233	282	86	186	128	216	199	113	270	127	241	171	99	223	140	120	72	89	141	179
Buffalo	295	130	34	202		82	178	416	38	137	301	404	103	154	68	325	301	489	288	377	332	24	270	144	397	325	452	72	191	349	284	277	147	198	215	377
Deer Park	183	304	368	225	416	334	252		443	262	234	21	323	252	416	128	440	79	121	39	97	440	406	320	344	114	39	378	286	327	214	190	299	272	360	53
Elmira	188	65	106	55	137	72	51	262	181		212	247	55	32	154	178	250	337	141	223	183	161	216	127	325	182	296	113	127	264	195	175	86	134	158	216
Ithaca	174	34	113	45	154	65	22	252	188	32	216	237	82		178	168	215	325	131	213	173	178	182	93	322	172	288	92	96	253	199	165	55	102	127	206
Jamestown	336	219	103	215	68	154	195	416	26	154	387	407	99	178		274	408	495	301	383	343	92	378	260	497	343	458	140	287	455	355	330	246	304	318	376
New York City	144	265	347	186	377	295	235	39	409	223	195	24	302	213	383	89	421	112	82		58	401	390	281	305	75	75	339	247	288	175	151	260	233	332	17
Niagara Falls	295	143	58	216	24	106	202	440	62	161	325	428	127	178	92	349	325	513	312	401	356		294	168	418	383	476	76	215	365	308	294	171	222	239	394
Plattsburgh	161	264	365	270	397	315	278	344	435	325	106	329	364	322	497	212	86	419	260	305	247	418	120	227		233	382	331	213	48	120	154	226	199	174	307
Poughkeepsie	72	216	309	127	325	264	172	114	344	182	123	99	243	172	343	17	319	187	64	75	17	383	329	240	233		150	291	175	216	103	79	199	161	271	62
Rochester	219	65	34	171	72	27	113	378	110	113	260	363	58	92	140	270	219	477	257	339	305	76	185	72	331	291	432		120	253	284	205	82	133	127	359
Rome	103	65	151	99	191	103	72	286	226	127	137	274	181	96	287	154	161	359	161	247	189	215	130	79	213	175	322	120		153	108	93	41	14	72	240
Schenectady	7	154	233	120	277	185	165	190	315	175	55	178	236	165	330	58	294	263	106	151	103	294	219	161	154	79	226	205	93	147	25		123	79	161	144
Syracuse	137	27	110	72	147	62	31	299	185	86	178	284	141	55	246	164	195	372	158	260	200	171	127	38	226	199	335	82	41	178	157	123		51	72	233
Utica	89	75	165	89	198	129	86	272	240	134	123	260	196	102	304	140	175	345	147	233	175	222	144	93	199	161	308	133	14	151	102	79	51		82	226
Watertown	171	99	161	141	215	134	103	360	253	158	222	356	213	127	318	222	89	444	227	332	257	239	58	51	174	271	407	127	72	110	186	161	72	82		302

Interstate Highways

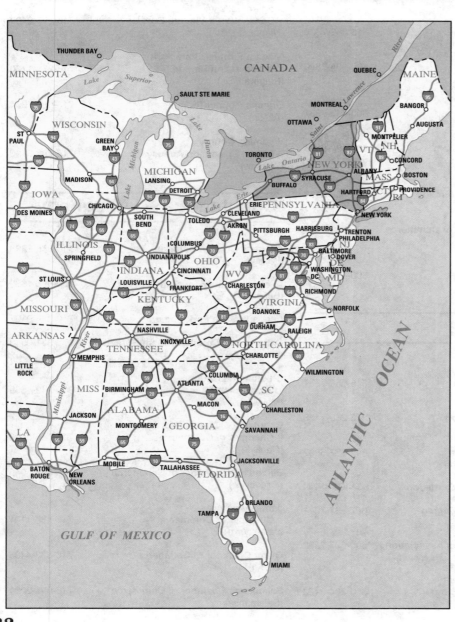

Eastern Cities

MILEAGE CHART

	Atlanta, GA	Boston, MA	Chicago, IL	Detroit, MI	Miami, FL	Montreal, QUE	Nashville, TN	New Orleans, LA	Ottawa, ONT	Pittsburgh, PA	St Louis, MO	Toronto, ONT	Washington, D.C.
Albany	994	170	820	539	1457	220	993	1393	279	471	1028	395	396
Auburn	969	337	655	385	1468	269	825	1333	207	375	906	230	358
Batavia	889	420	584	289	1551	352	729	1259	277	258	810	134	375
Binghamton	836	297	681	457	1390	314	844	1260	258	333	894	302	283
Buffalo	855	465	525	255	1424	389	695	1225	321	219	776	100	370
Canandaigua	987	384	607	337	1440	304	777	1348	242	291	892	182	358
Cortland	881	321	703	433	1435	273	824	1294	211	291	938	278	330
Deer Park	894	249	871	659	1339	403	924	1361	487	420	980	516	289
Dunkirk	856	491	487	293	1386	427	661	1187	352	181	738	138	367
Elmira	915	358	662	392	1396	328	807	1309	274	242	897	237	306
Glens Falls	1045	221	826	587	1508	164	1080	1417	264	538	1101	401	447
Hempstead	874	228	856	644	1324	388	909	1346	472	405	965	504	276
Hornell	970	416	628	358	1413	383	728	1316	321	217	837	203	325
Ithaca	942	344	679	409	1435	297	807	1308	235	269	921	254	333
Jamestown	830	506	491	323	1330	485	629	1217	390	158	743	168	341
Kingston	943	189	850	580	1402	271	903	1411	330	456	1017	425	341
Massena	1172	358	878	556	1623	85	996	1493	90	486	1087	292	517
Monticello	926	235	813	543	1363	319	930	1283	386	419	1023	388	283
New York City	855	203	790	620	1313	364	885	1322	448	381	941	477	252
Niagara Falls	879	465	549	279	1448	411	719	1249	342	243	800	76	394
Oswego	946	324	666	399	1503	218	839	1359	159	347	920	244	393
Plattsburgh	1299	273	928	652	1613	58	1092	1627	179	548	1246	390	557
Poughkeepsie	976	177	850	580	1338	292	972	1397	388	356	1016	425	327
Rochester	927	389	597	327	1440	294	767	1316	235	275	848	172	387
Rome	949	273	716	446	1489	239	886	1376	180	404	943	291	396
Saranac Lake	1138	321	880	604	1601	106	1044	1509	158	500	1229	342	540
Schenectady	1001	177	802	532	1464	212	959	1380	269	453	1021	377	403
Syracuse	908	307	672	402	1462	242	842	1343	180	322	923	247	355
Utica	959	259	723	453	1479	249	893	1330	190	373	983	298	372
Watertown	980	349	740	470	1531	167	910	1410	108	394	995	232	427
White Plains	867	186	807	637	1330	357	902	1339	411	398	958	477	269

New York State Highway Information

New York State Thruway Toll Schedule — Class 1 Vehicles

NEW YORK STATE THRUWAY	Buffalo I-290 50	Depew 49	Pembroke 48A	Batavia 48	Leroy I-490 47	Rochester I-390 46	Rochester E. I-490 45	Canandaigua 44	Manchester 43	Geneva 42	Waterloo 41	Weedsport 40	Syracuse W. I-690 39	Syracuse — Liverpool 38	Electronics Pkwy 37	Syracuse I-81 36	Syracuse E. 35	Syracuse I-481 34A
15 Woodbury	12.10	12.00	11.55	11.15	10.80	10.30	9.95	9.85	9.65.	9.20	9.00	8.50	8.05	7.95	7.90	7.85	7.75	7.65
16 Harriman (Entry)	11.15	11.05.	10.60	10.20	9.85	9.35	9.00	8.90	8.65	8.25	8.05	7.55	7.10	7.00	6.90	6.90	6.75	6.70
16 Harriman (Exit)	11.65	11.55	11.10	10.70	10.35	9.85	9.50	9.40	9.15	8.75	8.55	8.05	7.60	7.50	7.40	7.40	7.25	7.20
17 Newburgh I-84	11.20	11.10	10.60	10.25	9.90	9.40	9.05	8.90	8.70	8.30	8.10	7.60	7.15	7.05	6.95	6.95	6.80	6.75
18 New Paltz	10.70	10.60	10.10	9.75	9.40	8.90	8.55	8.45	8.20	7.80	7.60	7.10	6.65	6.55	6.45	6.45	6.30	6.25
19 Kingston	10.20	10.15	9.65	9.30	8.95	8.45	8.05	7.95	7.75	7.35	7.10	6.60	6.15	6.05	6.00	5.95	5.85	5.75
20 Saugerties	9.90	9.80	9.35	9.00	8.60	8.10	7.75	7.65	7.45	7.05	6.80	6.30	5.85	5.75	5.70	5.65	5.55	5.45
21 Catskill	9.50	9.45	8.95	8.60	8.25	7.75	7.35	7.25	7.05	6.65	6.45	5.90	5.45	5.35	5.30	5.25	5.15	5.05
21B Coxsackie	9.20	9.10	8.60	8.25	7.90	7.40	7.05	6.90	6.70	6.30	6.10	5.60	5.15	5.05	4.95	4.95	4.80	4.75
B1 Hudson-Rensselaer I-90	9.50	9.40	8.95	8.60	8.20	7.70	7.35	7.25	7.05	6.65	6.40	5.90	5.45	5.35	5.30	5.25	5.15	5.05
B2 Taconic Parkway	9.80	9.70	9.20	8.85	8.50	8.00	7.65	7.50	7.30	6.90	6.70	6.20	5.75	5.60	5.55	5.50	5.40	5.30
B3 Canaan (Mass. Line)	10.05	9.95	9.50	9.15	8.75	8.25	7.90	7.80	7.60	7.20	6.95	6.45	6.00	5.90	5.85	5.80	5.70	5.60
22 Selkirk	8.85	8.80	8.30	7.95	7.60	7.10	6.70	6.60	6.40	6.00	5.75	5.25	4.80	4.70	4.65	4.60	4.50	4.40
23 Albany (Downtown)	8.65	8.55	8.10	7.70	7.35	6.85	6.50	6.40	6.15	5.75	5.55	5.05	4.60	4.50	4.40	4.40	4.25	4.20
24 Albany (Northway)	8.45	8.40	7.90	7.55	7.20	6.70	6.30	6.20	6.00	5.60	5.35	4.85	4.40	4.30	4.25	4.20	4.10	4.00
25 Schenectady E. I-890	8.30	8.20	7.70	7.35	7.00	6.50	6.15	6.00	5.80	5.40	5.20	4.70	4.25	4.10	4.05	4.05	3.90	3.85
25A Schenectady I-88	8.05	7.95	7.45	7.10	6.75	6.25	5.90	5.75	5.55	5.15	4.95	4.45	3.95	3.85	3.80	3.75	3.65	3.55
26 Schenectady W. I-890	8.05	7.95	7.45	7.10	6.75	6.25	5.90	5.75	5.55	5.15	4.95	4.45	3.95	3.85	3.80	3.75	3.65	3.55
27 Amsterdam	7.65	7.60	7.10	6.75	6.40	5.90	5.50	5.40	5.20	4.80	4.60	4.05	3.60	3.50	3.45	3.40	3.30	3.20
28 Fultonville	7.40	7.30	6.85	6.45	6.10	5.60	5.25	5.15	4.90	4.50	4.30	3.80	3.35	3.25	3.15	3.15	3.00	2.95
29 Canajoharie	7.05	6.95	6.45	6.10	5.75	5.25	4.90	4.75	4.55	4.15	3.95	3.45	3.00	2.85	2.80	2.80	2.65	2.60
29A Little Falls	6.55	6.45	5.95	5.60	5.25	4.75	4.40	4.25	4.05	3.65	3.45	2.90	2.45	2.35	2.30	2.25	2.15	2.05
30 Herkimer	6.25	6.15	5.65	5.30	4.95	4.45	4.10	3.95	3.75	3.35	3.15	2.65	2.20	2.10	2.00	2.00	1.85	1.80
31 Utica	5.85	5.75	5.25	4.90	4.55	4.05	3.70	3.55	3.35	2.95	2.75	2.25	1.80	1.65	1.60	1.60	1.45	1.40
32 Westmoreland — Rome	5.50	5.40	4.95	4.55	4.20	3.70	3.35	3.25	3.00	2.60	2.40	1.90	1.45	1.35	1.30	1.25	1.15	1.05
33 Verona — Rome	5.20	5.15	4.65	4.30	3.95	3.45	3.05	2.95	2.75	2.35	2.10	1.60	1.15	1.05	1.00	0.95	0.85	0.75
34 Canastota	4.95	4.85	4.35	4.00	3.65	3.15	2.80	2.70	2.45	2.05	1.85	1.35	0.90	0.80	0.70	0.70	0.55	0.50
34A Syracuse I-481	4.50	4.40	3.90	3.55	3.20	2.70	2.35	2.20	2.00	1.60	1.40	0.90	0.45	0.30	0.25	0.20	0.15	
35 Syracuse E.	4.40	4.30	3.85	3.45	3.10	2.60	2.25	2.15	1.90	1.50	1.30	0.80	0.35	0.25	0.15	0.15		
36 Syracuse I-81	4.30	4.20	3.70	3.35	3.00	2.50	2.15	2.00	1.80	1.40	1.20	0.70	0.25	0.15	0.15			
37 Electronics Pkwy	4.25	4.15	3.70	3.30	2.95	2.45	2.10	2.00	1.75	1.35	1.15	0.65	0.20	0.15				
38 Syracuse — Liverpool	4.20	4.10	3.60	3.25	2.90	2.40	2.05	1.90	1.70	1.30	1.10	0.60	0.15					
39 Syracuse W. I-690	4.10	4.00	3.50	3.15	2.80	2.30	1.95	1.80	1.60	1.20	1.00	0.50						
40 Weedsport	3.60	3.55	3.05	2.70	2.35	1.85	1.45	1.35	1.15	0.75	0.55							
41 Waterloo	3.10	3.05	2.55	2.20	1.85	1.35	0.95	0.85	0.65	0.25								
42 Geneva	2.90	2.80	2.35	2.00	1.60	1.10	0.75	0.65	0.45									
43 Manchester	2.50	2.40	1.95	1.55	1.20	0.70	0.35	0.25										
44 Canandaigua	2.30	2.20	1.70	1.35	1.00	0.50	0.15											
45 Rochester E. I-490	2.15	2.10	1.60	1.25	0.90	0.40												
46 Rochester I-390	1.80	1.70	1.25	0.90	0.50													
47 Leroy I-490	1.30	1.20	0.75	0.40														
48 Batavia	0.95	0.85	0.40															
48A Pembroke	0.60	0.50																
49 Depew	0.15																	

NEW YORK STATE THRUWAY	Canastota 34	Verona — Rome 33	32 Westmoreland — Rome	Utica 31	Herkimer 30	Little Falls 29A	Canajoharie 29	Fultonville 28	Amsterdam 27	Schenectady W. 26	Schenectady I-88 25A	Schenectady E. 25	Albany 24	Albany (Downtown) 23	Selkirk 22	Canaan B3	Taconic Pkwy B2	B1 Hudson-Rensselaer I-90	Coxsackie 21B	Catskill 21	Saugerties 20	Kingston 19	New Paltz 18	Newburgh I-84 17
15 Woodbury	7.20	6.90	6.60	6.30	5.90	5.60	5.10	4.75	4.45	4.10	3.65	3.85	3.65	3.50	3.25	4.35	4.10	3.85	2.95	2.60	2.20	1.90	1.45	0.95
16 Harriman (Entry)	6.25	5.95	5.65	5.35	4.95	4.65	4.15	3.75	3.50	3.15	2.70	2.90	2.70	2.50	2.30	3.40	3.15	2.85	2.00	1.65	1.25	0.95	0.50	—
16 Harriman (Exit)	6.75	6.45	6.15	5.85	5.45	5.15	4.65	4.25	4.00	3.65	3.20	3.40	3.20	3.00	2.80	3.90	3.65	3.35	2.50	2.15	1.75	1.45	1.00	0.50
17 Newburgh I-84	6.25	6.00	5.70	5.40	4.95	4.70	4.20	3.80	3.55	3.20	2.75	2.95	2.75	2.55	2.35	3.45	3.15	2.90	2.00	1.70	1.30	1.00	0.50	
18 New Paltz	5.75	5.50	5.20	4.90	4.50	4.20	3.70	3.30	3.05	2.70	2.25	2.45	2.25	2.05	1.85	2.95	2.70	2.40	1.55	1.20	0.80	0.50		
19 Kingston	5.30	5.05	4.75	4.40	4.00	3.70	3.20	2.85	2.55	2.20	1.80	1.95	1.80	1.60	1.35	2.50	2.20	1.95	1.05	0.70	0.35			
20 Saugerties	5.00	4.70	4.45	4.10	3.70	3.40	2.90	2.55	2.25	1.90	1.45	1.65	1.45	1.30	1.05	2.20	1.90	1.65	0.75	0.40				
21 Catskill	4.60	4.35	4.05	3.70	3.30	3.00	2.50	2.15	1.85	1.50	1.10	1.25	1.10	0.90	0.70	1.80	1.50	1.25	0.35					
21B Coxsackie	4.25	4.00	3.70	3.40	2.95	2.70	2.20	1.80	1.55	1.20	0.75	0.95	0.75	0.55	0.35	1.45	1.15	0.90						
B1 Hudson-Rensselaer I-90	4.60	4.30	4.05	3.70	3.30	3.00	2.50	2.15	1.85	1.50	1.05	1.25	1.05	0.90	0.65	0.55	0.30							
B2 Taconic Parkway	4.85	4.60	4.30	3.95	3.55	3.30	2.75	2.40	2.15	1.80	1.35	1.50	1.35	1.15	0.95	0.30								
B3 Canaan (Mass. Line)	5.15	4.85	4.60	4.25	3.85	3.55	3.05	2.70	2.40	2.05	1.60	1.80	1.60	1.45	1.20									
22 Selkirk	3.95	3.70	3.40	3.05	2.65	2.35	1.85	1.50	1.20	0.85	0.45	0.60	0.45	0.25										
23 Albany (Downtown)	3.75	3.45	3.15	2.85	2.45	2.15	1.65	1.25	1.00	0.65	0.20	0.40	0.20											
24 Albany (Northway)	3.55	3.25	3.00	2.65	2.25	1.95	1.45	1.10	0.80	0.45	—	0.20												
25 Schenectady E. I-890	3.35	3.10	2.80	2.45	2.05	1.80	1.25	0.90	0.65	0.30	—													
25A Schenectady I-88	3.10	2.85	2.55	2.20	1.80	1.50	1.00	0.65	0.40	—														
26 Schenectady W. I-890	3.10	2.85	2.55	2.20	1.80	1.50	1.00	0.65	0.40															
27 Amsterdam	2.75	2.50	2.20	1.85	1.45	1.15	0.65	0.30																
28 Fultonville	2.50	2.20	1.90	1.60	1.20	0.90	0.40																	
29 Canajoharie	2.10	1.85	1.55	1.25	0.80	0.55																		
29A Little Falls	1.60	1.35	1.05	0.70	0.30																			
30 Herkimer	1.30	1.05	0.75	0.45																				
31 Utica	0.90	0.65	0.35																					
32 Westmoreland — Rome	0.60	0.30																						
33 Verona — Rome	0.30																							

Erie Section Interchanges

NEW YORK STATE THRUWAY	Ripley 61	Westfield 60	Dunkirk — Fredonia 59	Silver Creek 58	Eden — Angola 57A	Hamburg 57	Blasdell 56
55 Lackawanna	2.10	1.75	1.20	0.85	0.50	0.25	0.15
56 Blasdell	2.00	1.65	1.10	0.75	0.40	0.15	
57 Hamburg	1.90	1.55	1.00	0.60	0.30		
57A Eden — Angola	1.60	1.25	0.75	0.35			
58 Silver Creek	1.30	0.95	0.40				
59 Dunkirk — Fredonia	0.90	0.55					
60 Westfield	0.35						

Class 1 Definition

Class 1 consists of: Passenger cars, motorcycles, taxis, ambulances, and hearses; trucks, motorhomes or recreational vehicles with 2 axles and 4 tires; tractors with 2 axles; vans with 2 axles and 4 tires registered as passenger cars.

Driving Regulations

Seat Belts

Seat belts must be worn by all front seat occupants and all passengers between 4 and 10 years of age. Children under 4 years of age must be secured in federally-approved safety seats.

Speed Limits

State speed limit is 55 mph, unless otherwise posted.

Inclement Weather

State law requires that headlights be on when windshield wipers are in use.

Insurance Regulations

All motorists, including out-of-state drivers, must be able to show proof of liability insurance coverage by a company licensed to cover New York State.

State Police

New York State Governor's Traffic Safety Committee 518-474-5111
Swan Street Building, Room 414
Albany, NY 12228

New York State Department of Motor Vehicles 518-474-0877

Swan Street Building
Albany, NY 12228

New York State Thruway Authority 518-436-2700
P.O. Box 189
Albany, NY 12201-0189

State Police Division Headquarters 518-457-6811
Building 22
New York State Office Campus
Albany, NY 12226

State Police Troop T (Thruway) 518-436-2825
P.O. Box 189
Albany, NY 12201-0189

Thruway Information

For Thruway emergencies 800-842-2233 (*911 Cellular)

For Thruway weather and road conditions 800-847-8929

Out-of-state and Canada 800-847-8929

Service Areas

Northbound:

Location	*Milepost*
Ardsley	6
Sloatsburg	33
Plattekill	65
Malden	103
New Baltimore	127

Southbound:

Location	*Milepost*
New Baltimore	127
Ulster	96
Modena	66
Ramapo	33

Westbound:

Location	*Milepost*
Pattersonville	168
Iroquois	210
Schuyler	227
Chittenango	266
Warners	292
Junius Ponds	324
Seneca	350
Ontario	376
Clarence	412
Angola	447

Eastbound:

Location	*Milepost*
Angola	447
Pembroke	397
Scottsville	366
Clifton Springs	337
Port Byron	310
DeWitt	280
Oneida	244
Indian Castle	210
Mohawk	172
Guilderland	153

Information Centers

Location	*Milepost*	*Location*	*Milepost*
Sloatsburg	33 N	Chittenango	266 W
Malden	103 N	Scottsville	366 E
New Baltimore	127 N/S	Pembroke	397 E
Pattersonville	168 W	Clarence	412 W

Regulatory Signs

STOP

YIELD

DO NOT
ENTER

NO LEFT
TURN

NO RIGHT
TURN

NO U
TURN

LEFT TURN
ONLY

LEFT OR
THROUGH

RIGHT TURN
ONLY

RIGHT OR
THROUGH

KEEP
RIGHT

KEEP
LEFT

NO TRUCKS

2-WAY LEFT
TURN LANE

NO
BICYCLES

NO
PARKING

NO
PEDESTRIANS

NO
HITCHHIKING

RESTRICTED
LANE

ONE WAY
TRAFFIC

TOW AWAY
ZONE

TRUCK
WEIGHT
LIMIT

RESERVED
PARKING FOR
HANDICAPPED

DIVIDED
HIGHWAY

RAILROAD
CROSSING

Service Signs

HOSPITAL

GAS

FOOD

ACCESS FOR
HANDICAPPED

CAMPING
(TRAILER)

INFORMATION

REST
AREA

LODGING

PHONE

DIESEL

CAMPING
(TENT)

TRAILER
SANITARY
STATION

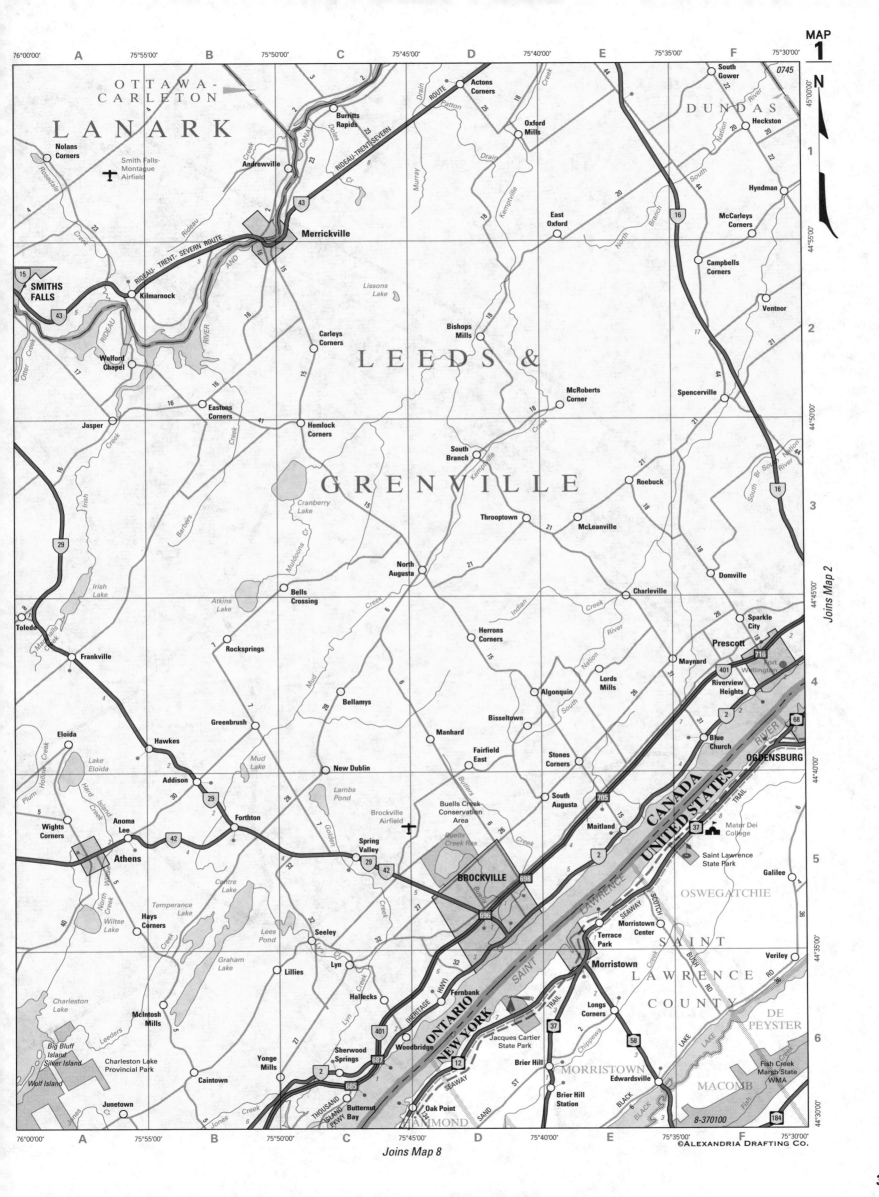

MAP
1
0745
N

OTTAWA-CARLETON

L A N A R K

Nolans Corners

Smith Falls-Montague Airfield

Andrewville

Burritts Rapids

Merrickville

RIDEAU- TRENT- SEVERN ROUTE

RIDEAU-TRENT-SEVERN

Actons Corners

Oxford Mills

D U N D A S

Heckston

Hyndman

South Gower

McCarleys Corners

East Oxford

Campbells Corners

Ventnor

SMITHS FALLS

Kilmarnock

Wolford Chapel

RIDEAU RIVER AND

Lissons Lake

Carleys Corners

Bishops Mills

McRoberts Corner

Spencerville

L E E D S &

Jasper

Eastons Corners

Hemlock Corners

South Branch

Roebuck

G R E N V I L L E

Cranberry Lake

Throoptown

McLeanville

Domville

Toledo

Irish Lake

Bells Crossing

North Augusta

Herrons Corners

Charleville

Sparkle City

Frankville

Rocksprings

Prescott

Maynard

Algonquin

Lords Mills

Riverview Heights

Eloida

Greenbrush

Bellamys

Manhard

Fairfield East

Bisseltown

Stones Corners

Blue Church

OGDENSBURG

Hawkes

Addison

Anoma Lee

Forthton

New Dublin

Lambs Pond

Brockville Airfield

Buells Creek Conservation Area

Buells Creek Res.

South Augusta

Maitland

C A N A D A
U N I T E D   S T A T E S

Mater Dei College

Athens

Wights Corners

Hays Corners

Spring Valley

BROCKVILLE

Saint Lawrence State Park

Galilee

O S W E G A T C H I E

Seeley

Morristown Center

Terrace Park

S A I N T

Lillies

Lyn

Hallecks

Morristown

Veriley

L A W R E N C E

C O U N T Y

McIntosh Mills

Fernbank

Longs Corners

Charleston Lake

Yonge Mills

Sherwood Springs

Woodbridge

Jacques Cartier State Park

Brier Hill

MORRISTOWN

DE PEYSTER

Big Bluff Island

Silver Island

Charleston Lake Provincial Park

Caintown

O N T A R I O
N E W   Y O R K

Brier Hill Station

Edwardsville

Fish Creek Marsh State WMA

M A C O M B

Wolf Island

Junetown

Butternut Bay

Oak Point

HAMMOND

SEAWAY

8-370100

Joins Map 2

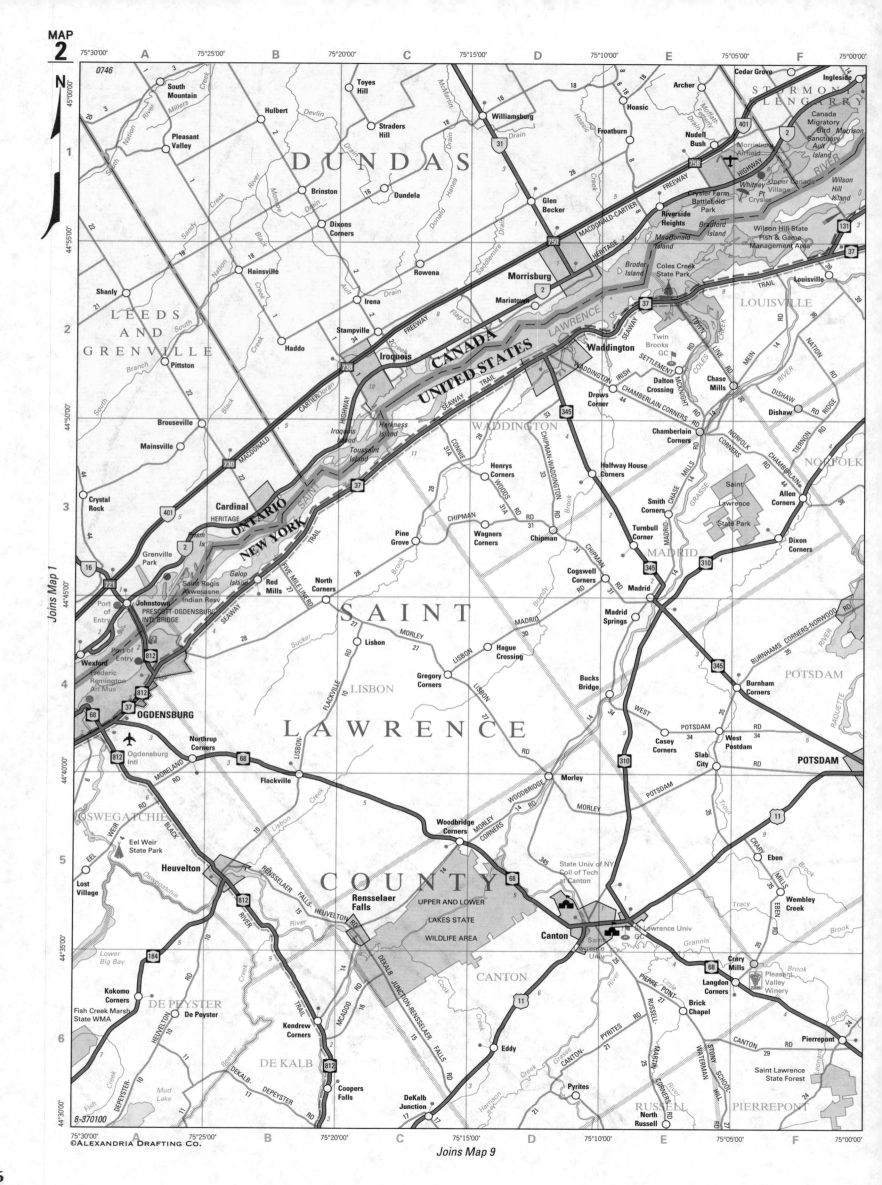

MAP 2

N

DUNDAS

LEEDS AND GRENVILLE

CANADA
UNITED STATES

ONTARIO
NEW YORK

SAINT

LAWRENCE

COUNTY

WADDINGTON

LISBON

MADRID

NORFOLK

POTSDAM

PIERREPONT

RUSSELL

DE KALB

DE PEYSTER

OSWEGATCHIE

Joins Map 1

©Alexandria Drafting Co.

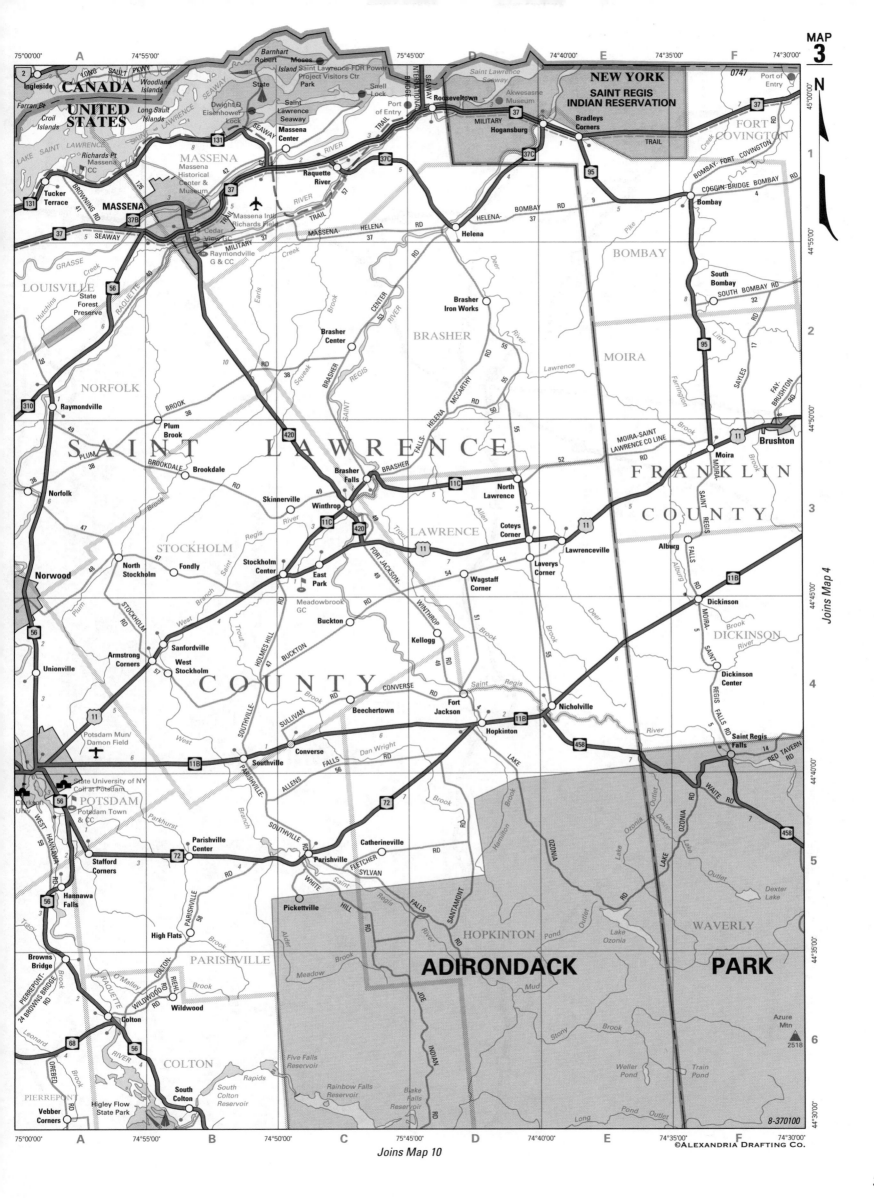

MAP 3

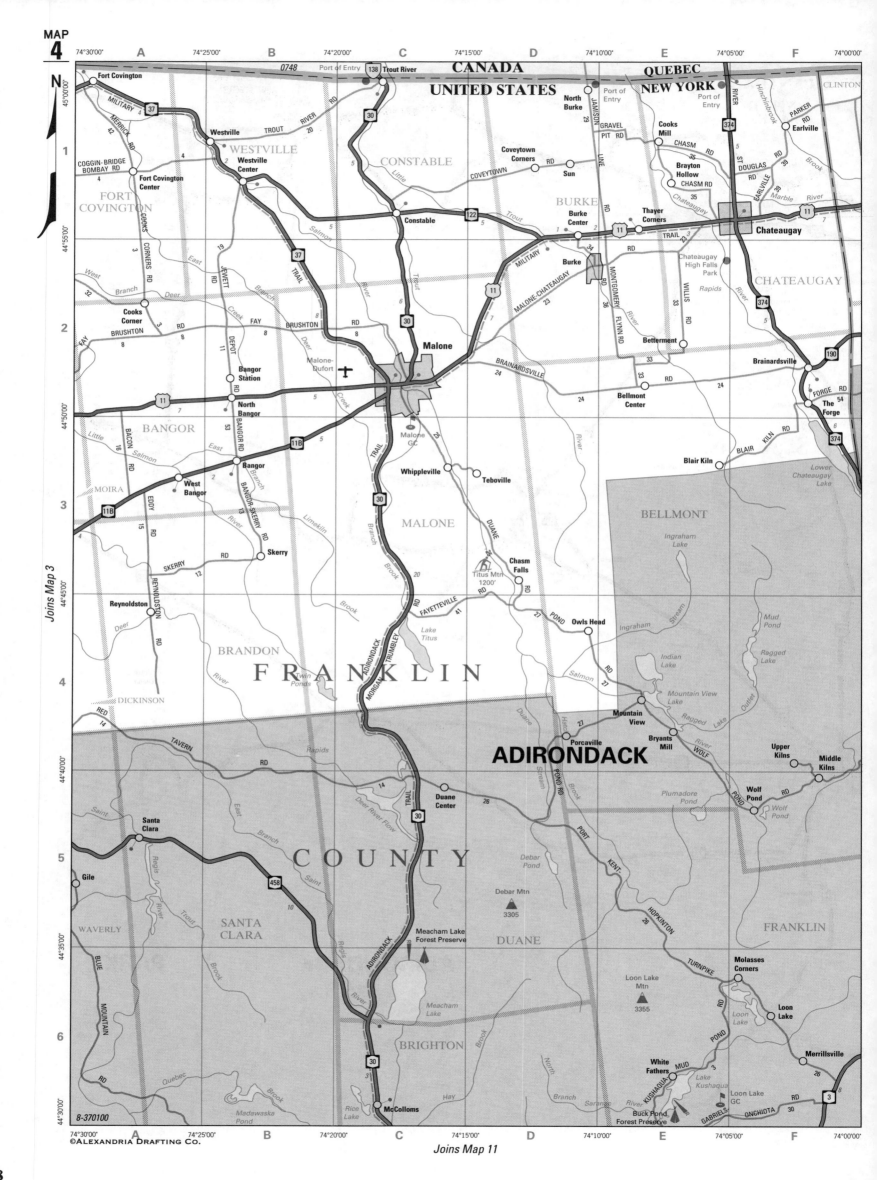

MAP
4
N

CANADA
UNITED STATES
QUEBEC
NEW YORK

Fort Covington
Trout River
North Burke
Port of Entry
Cooks Mill
Earlville
CLINTON

WESTVILLE
Westville
Westville Center
Fort Covington Center
CONSTABLE
Coveytown Corners
Sun
BURKE
Brayton Hollow
Thayer Corners
Chateaugay
CHATEAUGAY

FORT COVINGTON
Cooks Corner
BRUSHTON
Constable
Burke Center
Burke
Chateaugay High Falls Park

Bangor Station
Malone
Betterment
Brainardsville

BANGOR
North Bangor
Bangor
Malone GC
Bellmont Center
The Forge

MOIRA
West Bangor
Whippleville
Teboville
Blair Kiln
BELLMONT

Skerry
MALONE
Chasm Falls
Ingraham Lake
Mud Pond
Ragged Lake

Reynoldston
Titus Mtn 1200'
Owls Head
Indian Lake
Mountain View Lake
Upper Kilns
Middle Kilns

BRANDON
FRANKLIN
Mountain View
Bryants Mill

DICKINSON
Porcaville
ADIRONDACK
Wolf Pond

Santa Clara
Duane Center
Debar Pond
Plumadore Pond
Wolf Pond

COUNTY
Debar Mtn 3305
FRANKLIN

Gile
SANTA CLARA
WAVERLY
Molasses Corners

DUANE
Loon Lake Mtn 3355
Loon Lake

Meacham Lake Forest Preserve
Merrillsville
White Fathers
BRIGHTON
Meacham Lake

McColloms
Buck Pond Forest Preserve
Loon Lake GC

©Alexandria Drafting Co.
8-370100

Joins Map 11
Joins Map 3

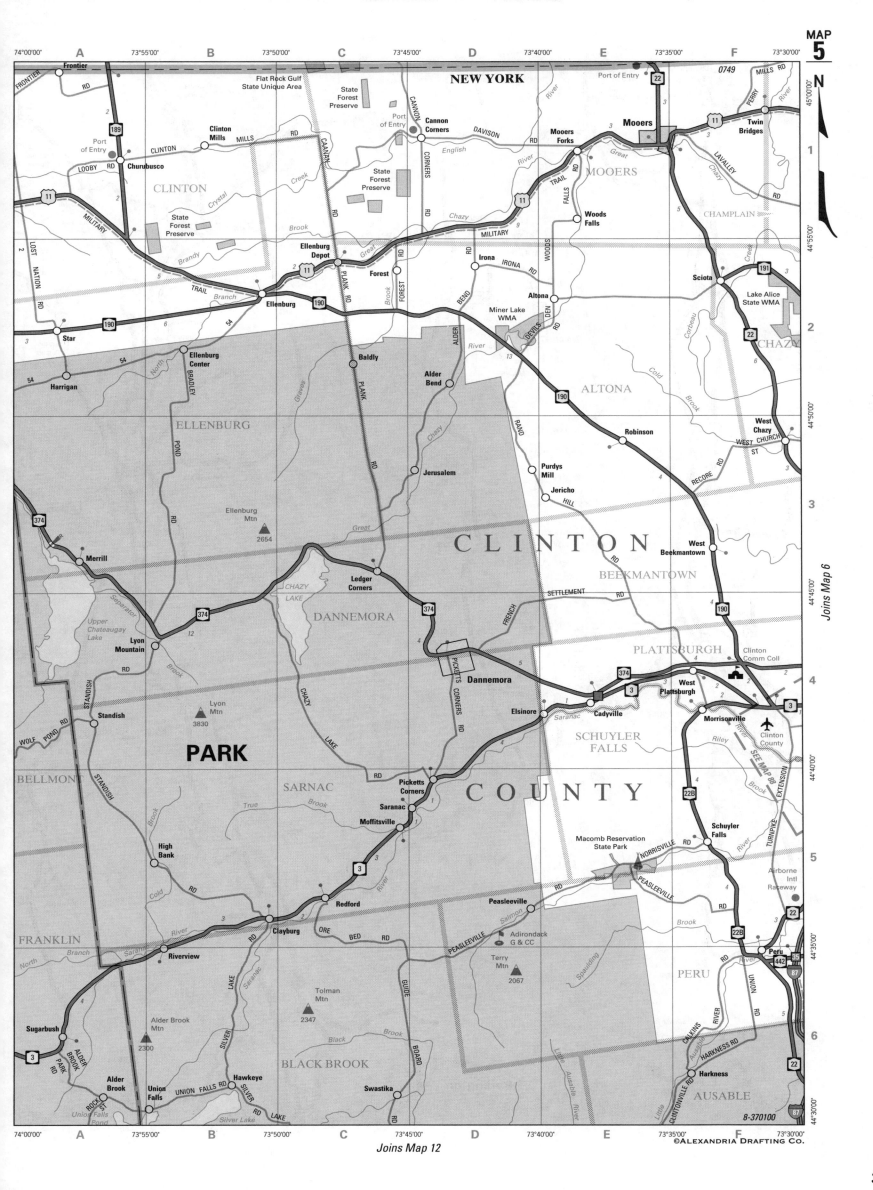

MAP
5

NEW YORK

CLINTON

PARK

CLINTON

COUNTY

ELLENBURG

DANNEMORA

BELLMONT

FRANKLIN

SARNAC

BLACK BROOK

BEEKMANTOWN

ALTONA

MOOERS

CHAZY

SCHUYLER
FALLS

PERU

AUSABLE

Joins Map 6

MAP 6

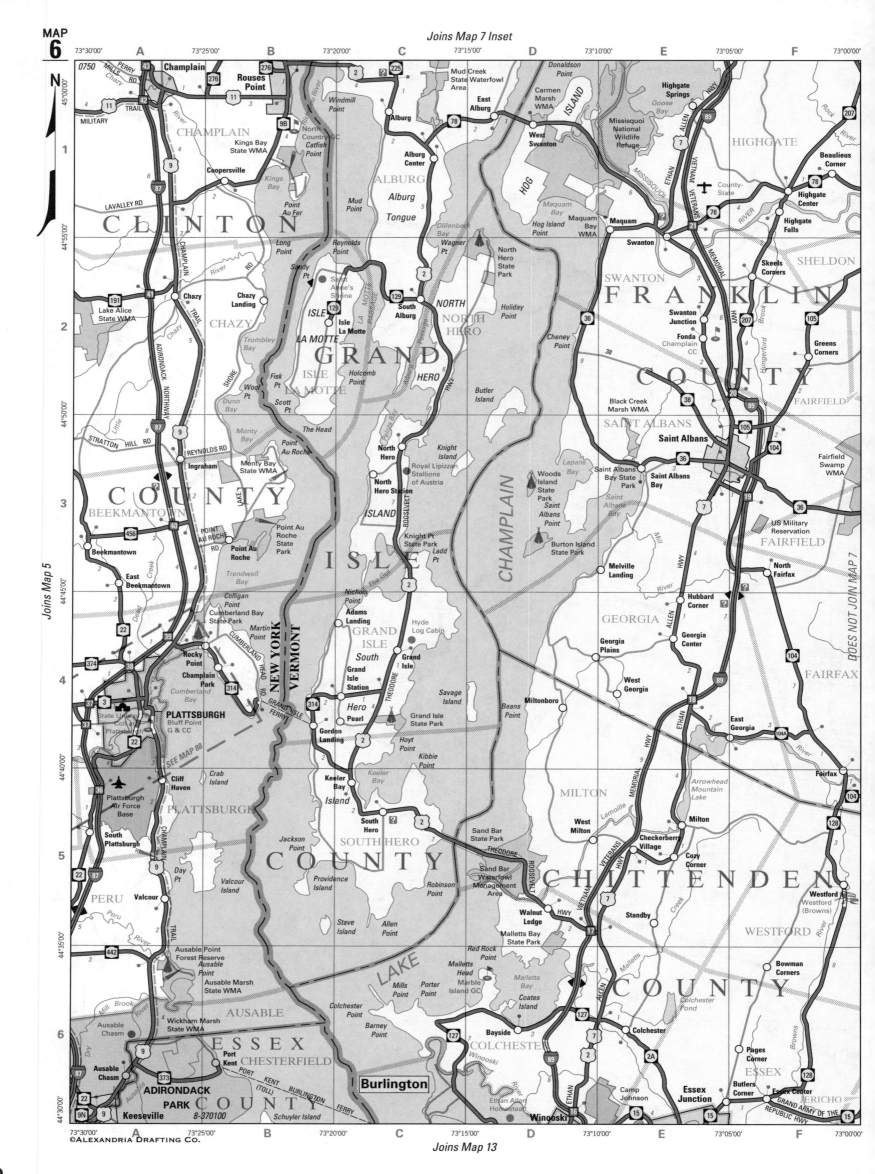

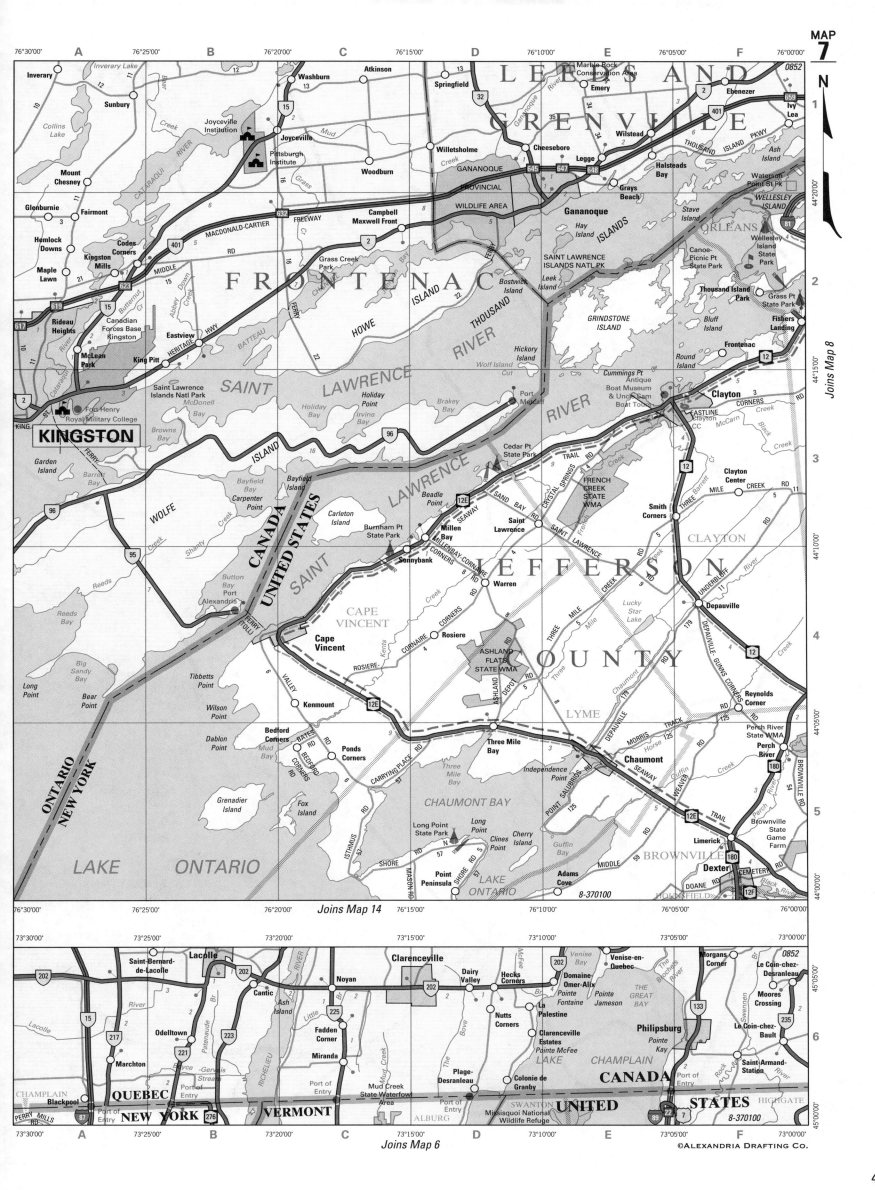

MAP 7

Joins Map 14

Joins Map 6

©Alexandria Drafting Co.

MAP 8

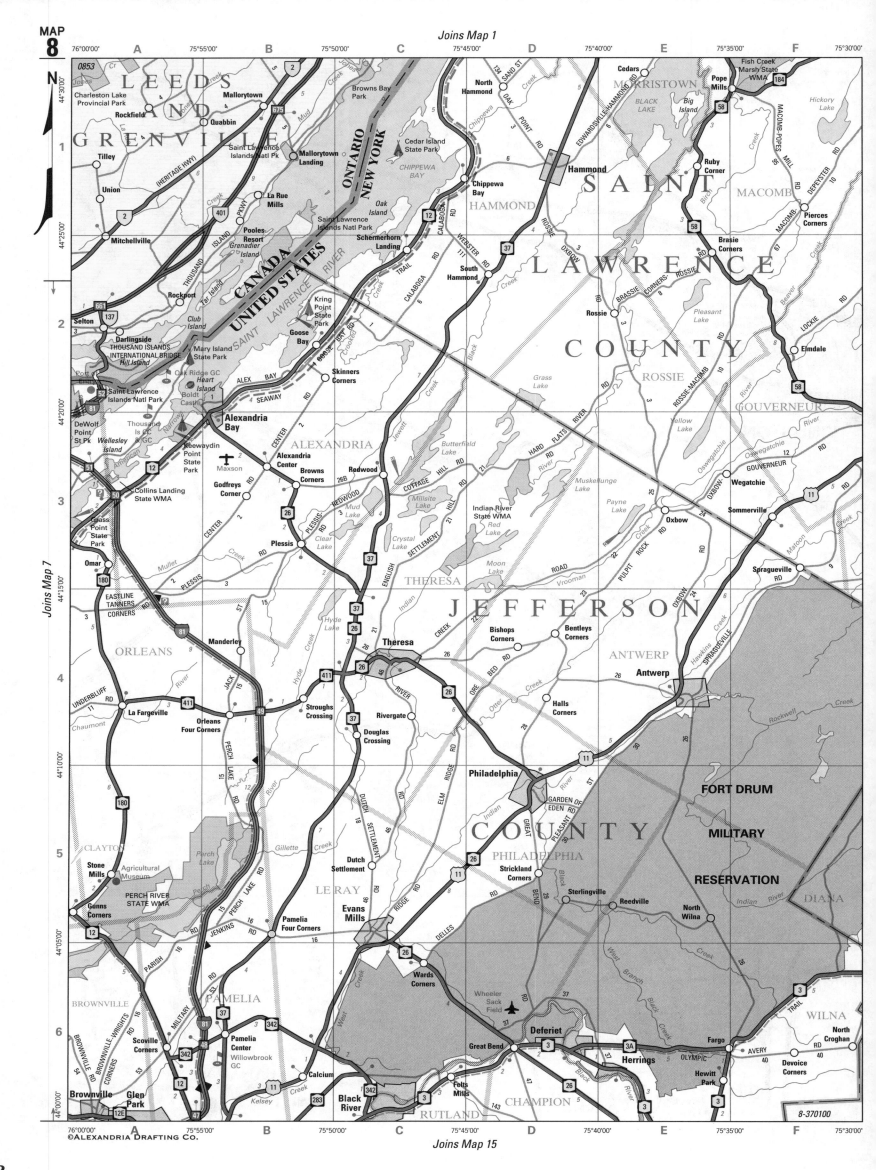

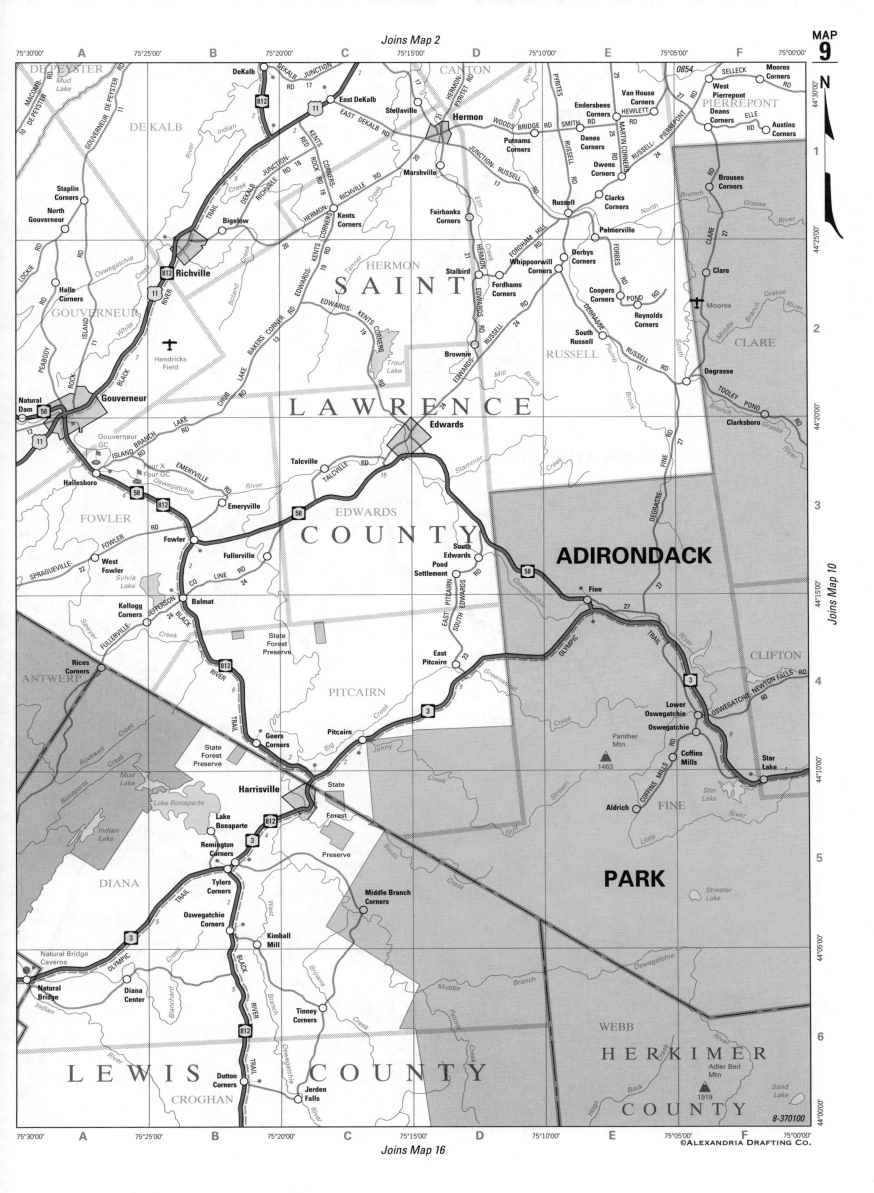

©Alexandria Drafting Co.

8-370100

MAP
10

Joins Map 3

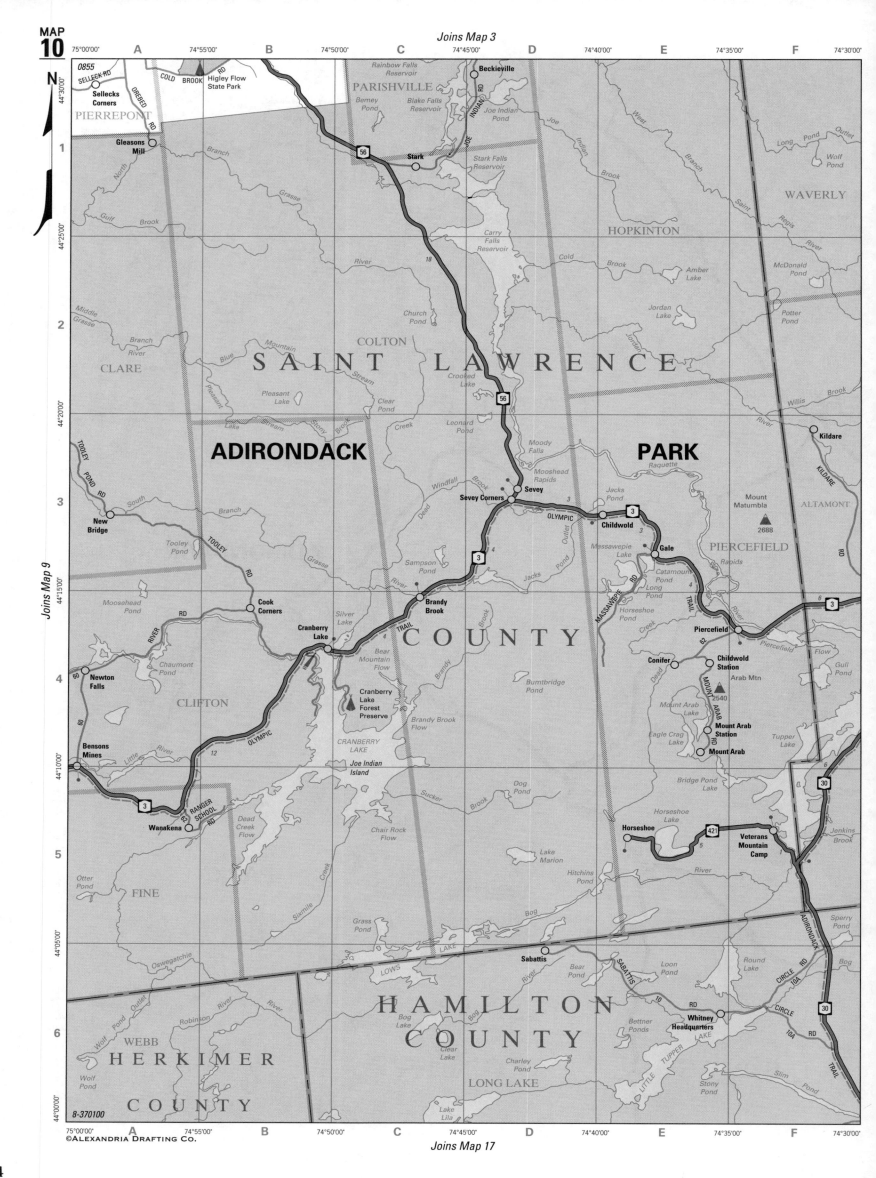

©Alexandria Drafting Co.

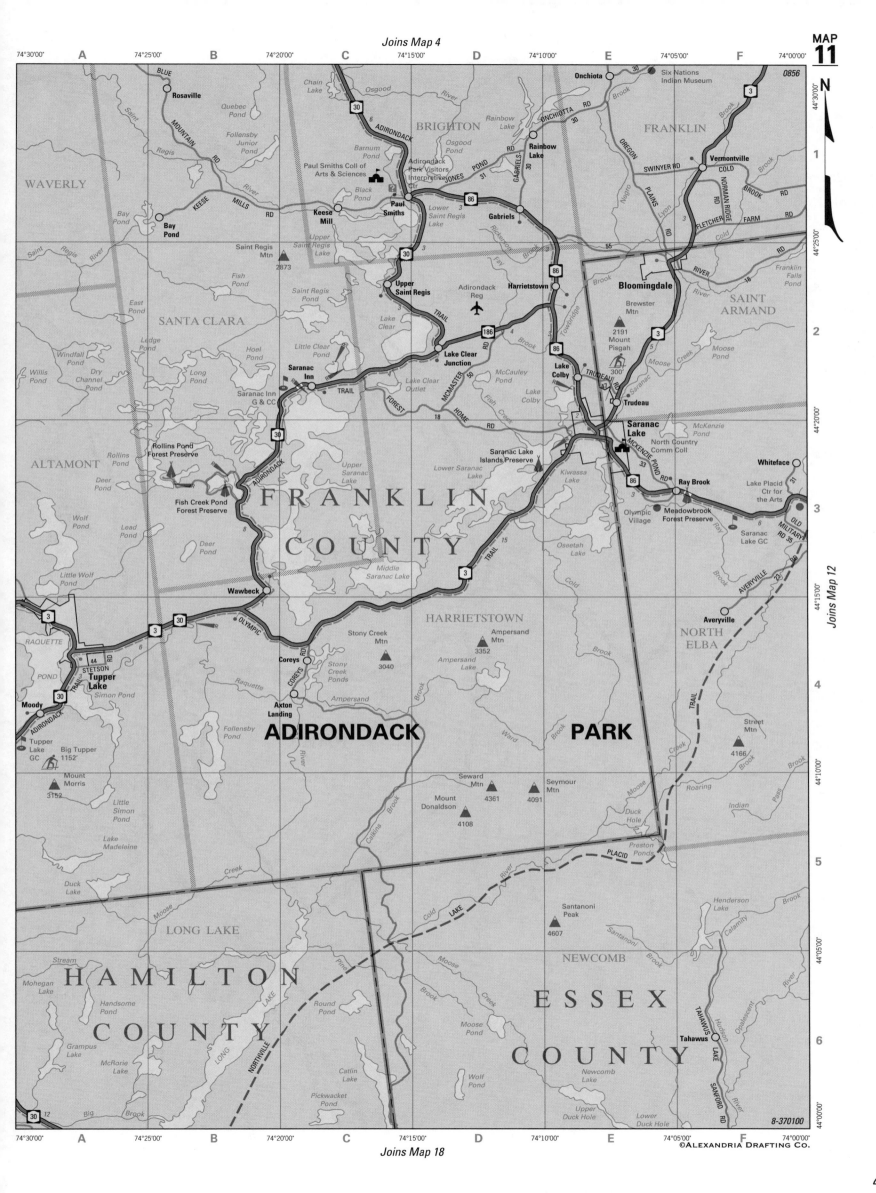

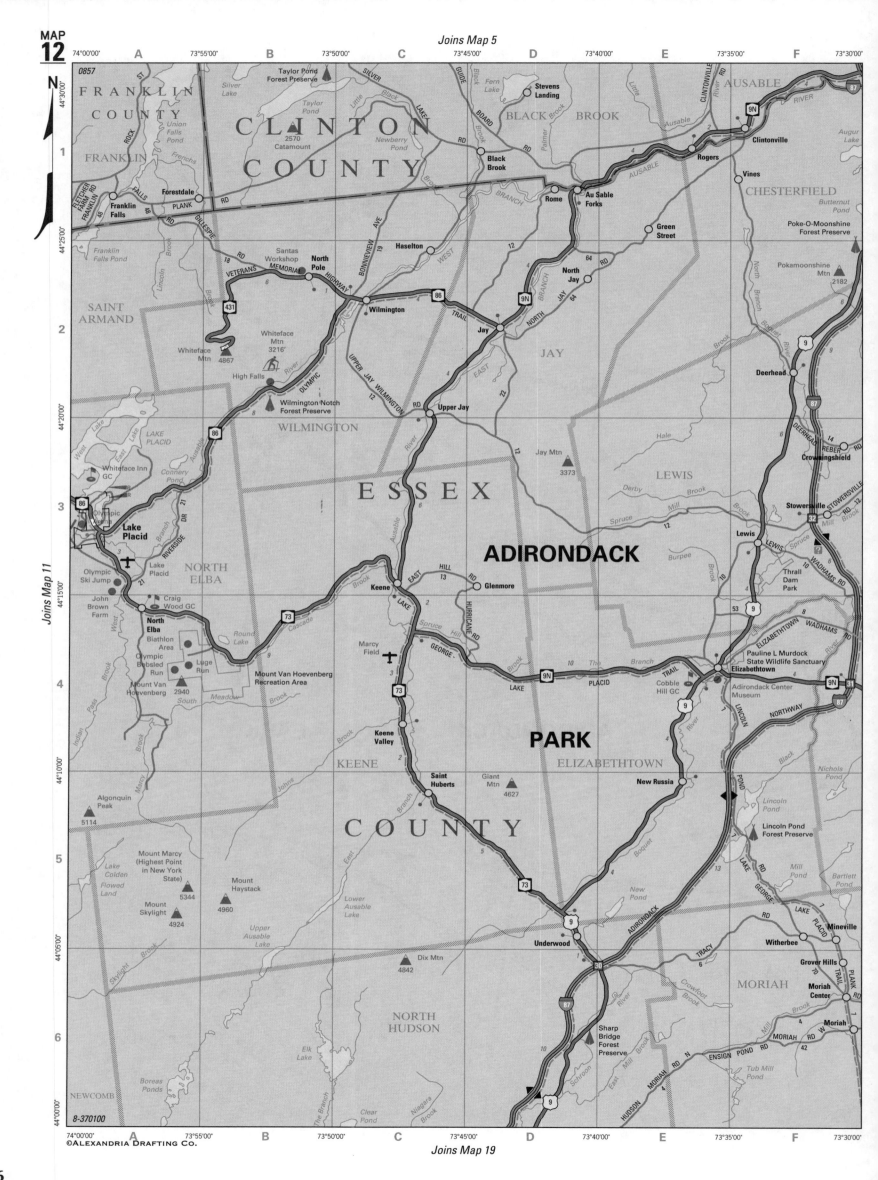

74°00'00" 73°55'00" 73°50'00" 73°45'00" 73°40'00" 73°35'00" 73°30'00"
A   B   C   D   E   F

FRANKLIN
COUNTY

CLINTON

COUNTY

Taylor Pond
Forest Preserve

Silver
Lake

Taylor
Pond

2570
Catamount

Little Black Brook

Newberry
Pond

SILVER

LAKE RD

GUIDE BOARD RD

Black Brook

Fern
Lake

Stevens
Landing

BLACK BROOK

AUSABLE

Ausable

Little Ausable River

CLINTONVILLE

AUSABLE

87

9N

RIVER

Clintonville

Vines

Augur
Lake

FRANKLIN

Union
Falls
Pond

ROCK ST

FLETCHER FARM RD
FRANKLIN

Forestdale

Franklin
Falls

48

48

PLANK   RD

GILLESPIE RD

Black Brook

Rome

Au Sable
Forks

Rogers

2

CHESTERFIELD

Poke-O-Moonshine
Forest Preserve

Butternut
Pond

SAINT
ARMAND

Franklin
Falls Pond

Frenchs

Lincoln Brook

VETERANS RD

431

Santas
Workshop
MEMORIAL

North
Pole

6

1

Haselton

BONNIEVIEW AVE

19

WEST

AUSABLE BRANCH

86

Green
Street

12

North
Jay

64 RD

NORTH BRANCH

North Branch Boquet River

Pokamoonshine
Mtn
2182

9

Whiteface
Mtn
3216'

Whiteface Mtn
4867

High Falls

OLYMPIC

Ausable River

Wilmington

Jay

JAY

9N

64

9

Deerhead

87

Wilmington Notch
Forest Preserve

8

WILMINGTON

UPPER JAY WILMINGTON

12

Upper Jay

RD

EAST

12

4

Jay Mtn
3373

Hale
Pond

LEWIS

DEERHEAD

6

14 RD

REBER

Crowningshield

86

LAKE PLACID

Connery
Pond

West Lake

ESSEX

Ausable River

6

Derby Brook

Mill Brook

Spruce

12

Burpee Brook

Mill Brook

STOWERSVILLE

Stowersville RD

32

STOWERSVILLE RD 12

Mill Brook

86

Olympic
Whiteface Inn
GC

RIVERSIDE DR 21

R

Lake
Placid

ADIRONDACK

Lewis

10

4

Thrall
Dam
Park

8

WADHAMS RD

10

3

John Brown
Farm

Olympic
Ski Jump

Craig
Wood GC

NORTH
ELBA

Lake
Placid

EAST HILL RD

Keene

LAKE

13

Glenmore

Spruce Hill

HURRICANE RD

53

9

ELIZABETHTOWN

WADHAMS RD

Pauline L Murdock
State Wildlife Sanctuary

9N

87

North
Elba
Biathlon
Area

Olympic
Bobsled Run

Luge
Run

73

Round
Lake

9

Cascade

Mount Van Hoevenberg
Recreation Area

Marcy
Field

GEORGE

3

9N

The Branch

LAKE PLACID

TRAIL

Cobble
Hill GC

Elizabethtown

Adirondack Center
Museum

9

LINCOLN

NORTHWAY

9N 31

4

Mount Van
Hoevenberg
2940

South Meadow Brook

73

Keene
Valley

2

KEENE

Johns Brook

Boquet River

PARK

ELIZABETHTOWN

New Russia

Black Brook

Nichols
Pond

Indian Pass Brook

Marcy Brook

Saint
Huberts

Giant
Mtn
4627

POND

LINCOLN

Lincoln Pond
Forest Preserve

Algonquin
Peak
5114

COUNTY

East Branch Ausable River

5

Lincoln Pond

Bartlett
Pond

Mount Marcy
(Highest Point
in New York
State)

Mount
Haystack
4960

73

New
Pond

4

LAKE GEORGE RD

PLACID

13

Mill
Pond

Mineville

Lake
Colden
Flowed
Land

5344

Mount
Skylight
4924

Lower
Ausable
Lake

Upper
Ausable
Lake

5

Boquet River

ADIRONDACK

TRACY RD

Witherbee

7

Grover Hills

MORIAH

PLANK RD

70

Skylight Brook

Dix Mtn
4842

Underwood

1

9

TRAIL

6

Crowfoot Brook

Moriah
Center

MORIAH RD W

Moriah

87

NORTH HUDSON

Elk
Lake

Sharp
Bridge
Forest
Preserve

10

Schroon River

HUDSON

MORIAH RD

ENSIGN POND RD

4

Mill Brook

42

Tub Mill
Pond

6

NEWCOMB

Boreas
Ponds

Clear
Pond

Niagara Brook

9

44°30'00"
44°25'00"
44°20'00"
44°15'00"
44°10'00"
44°05'00"

1
2
3
4
5
6

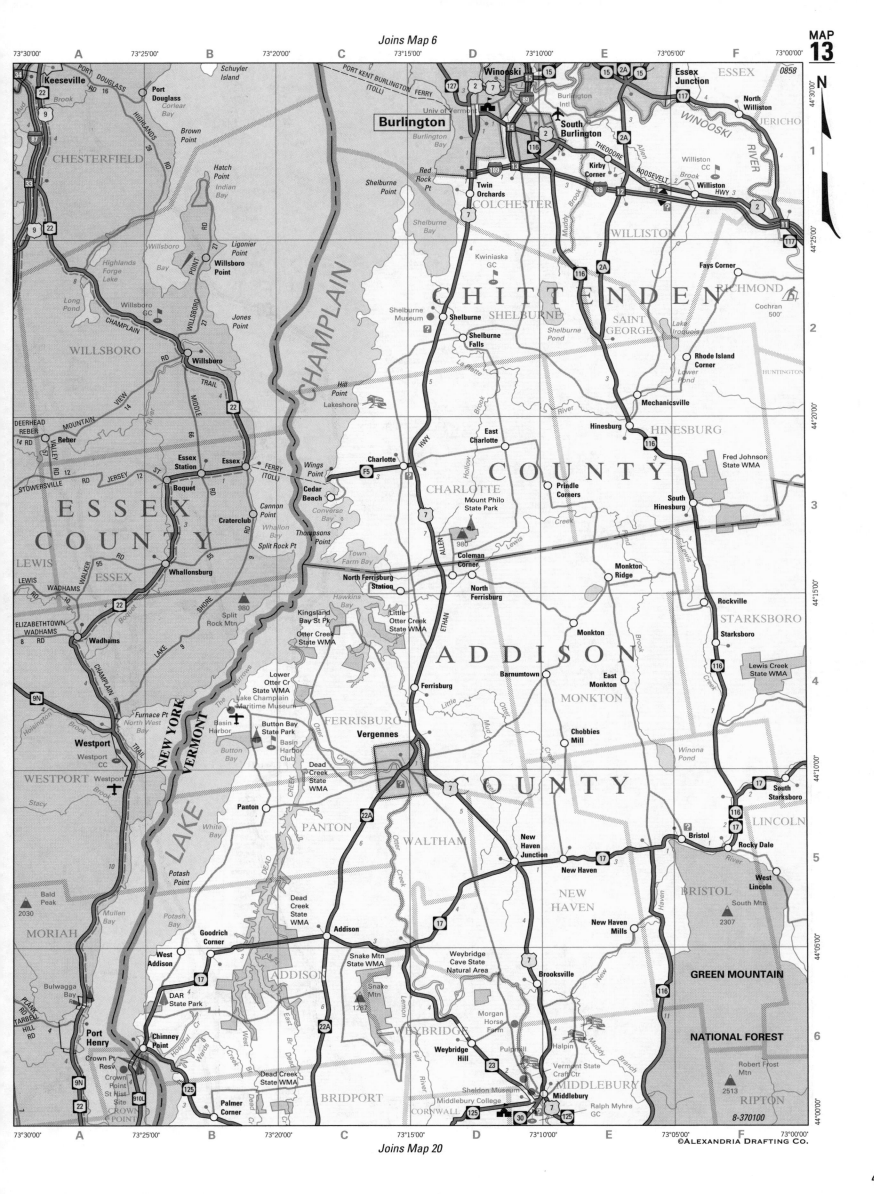

MAP
14
N
Joins Map 7

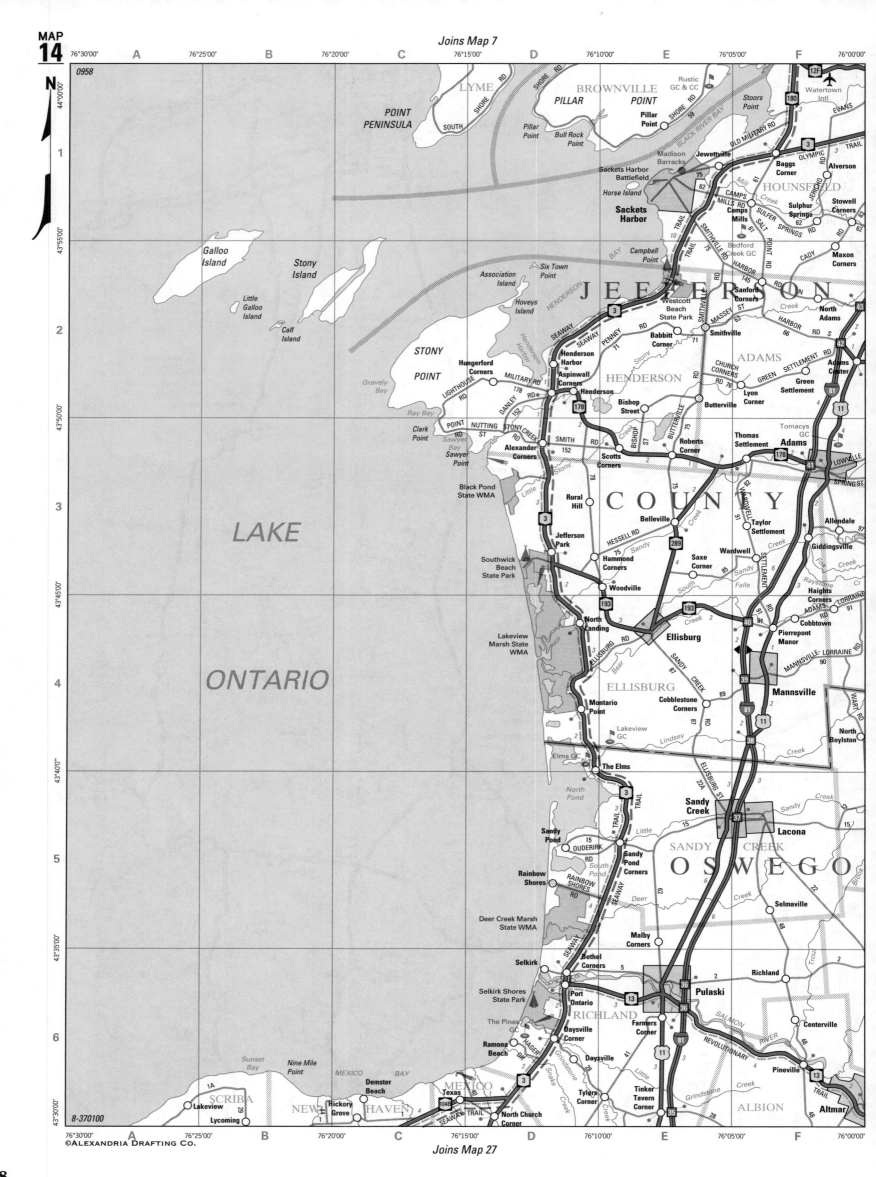

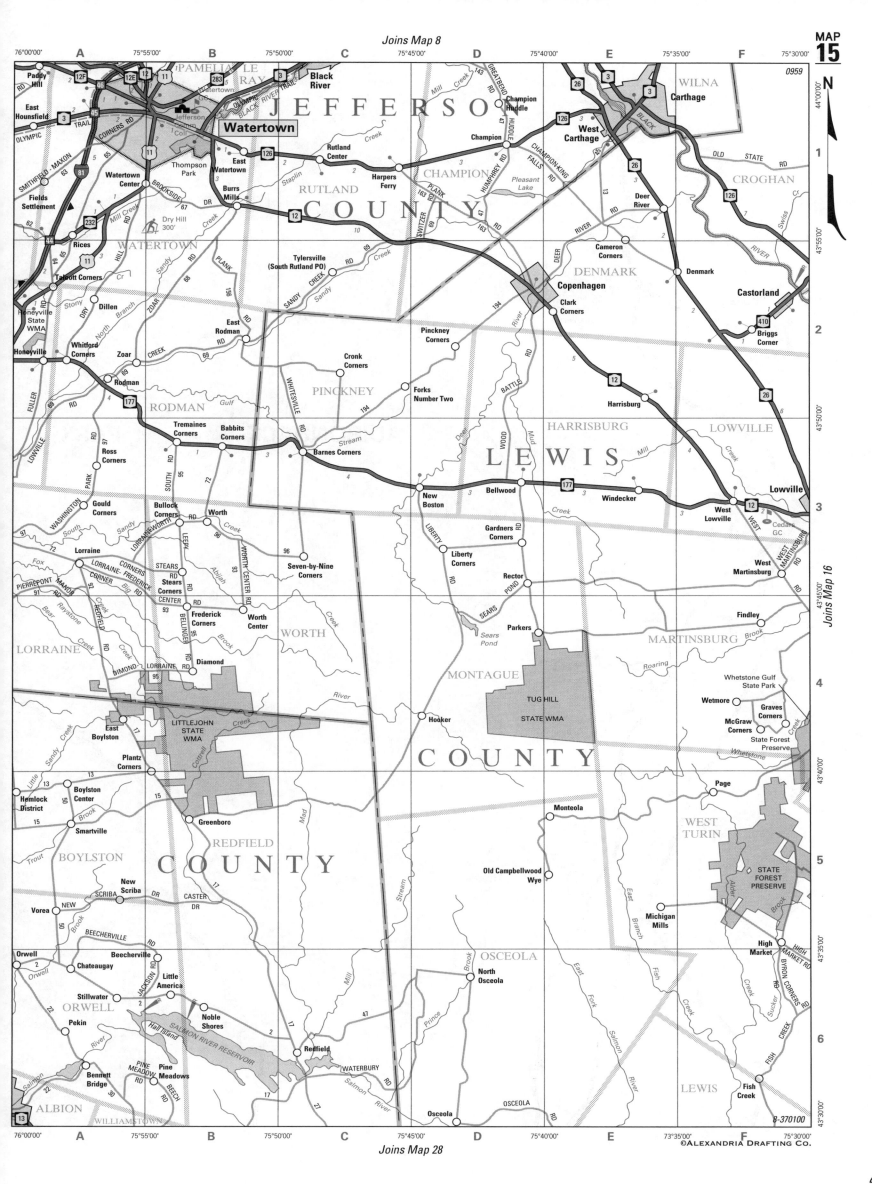

MAP
16

Joins Map 9

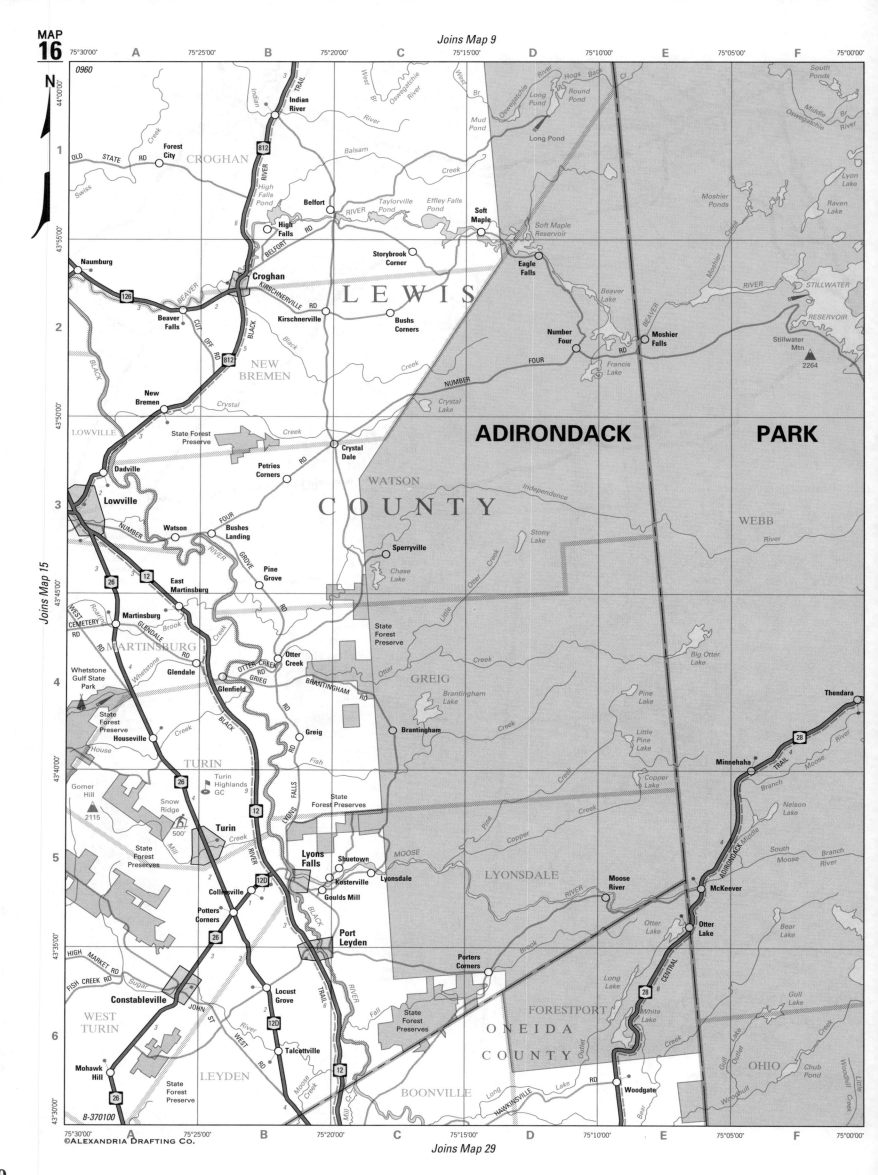

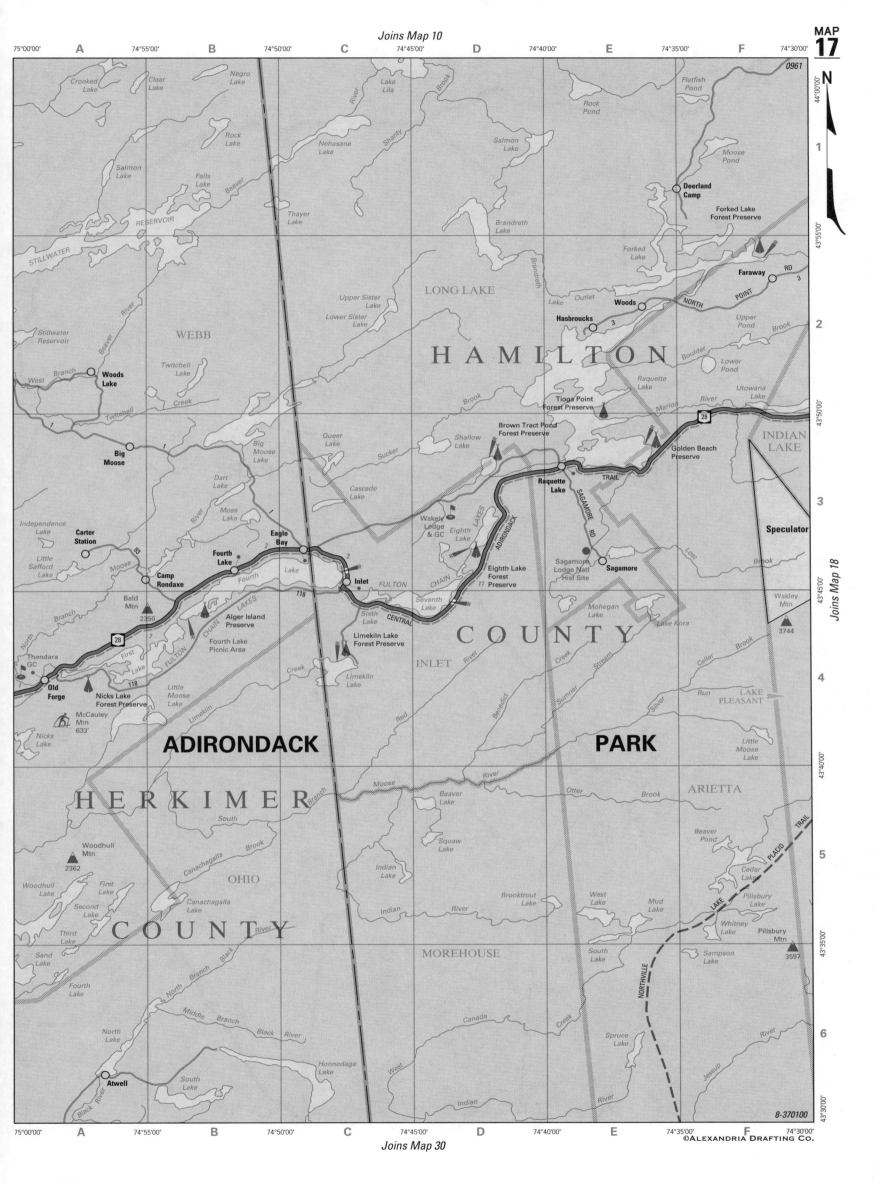

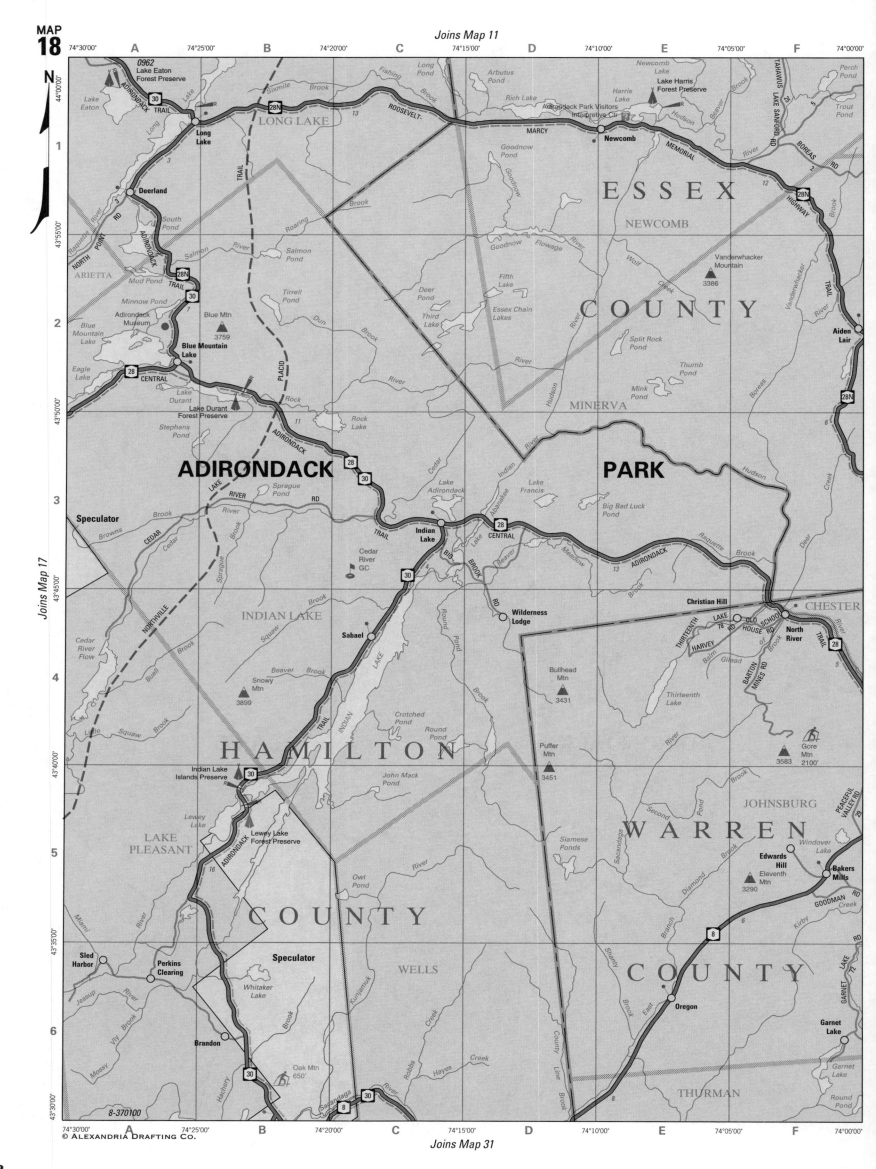

MAP
18

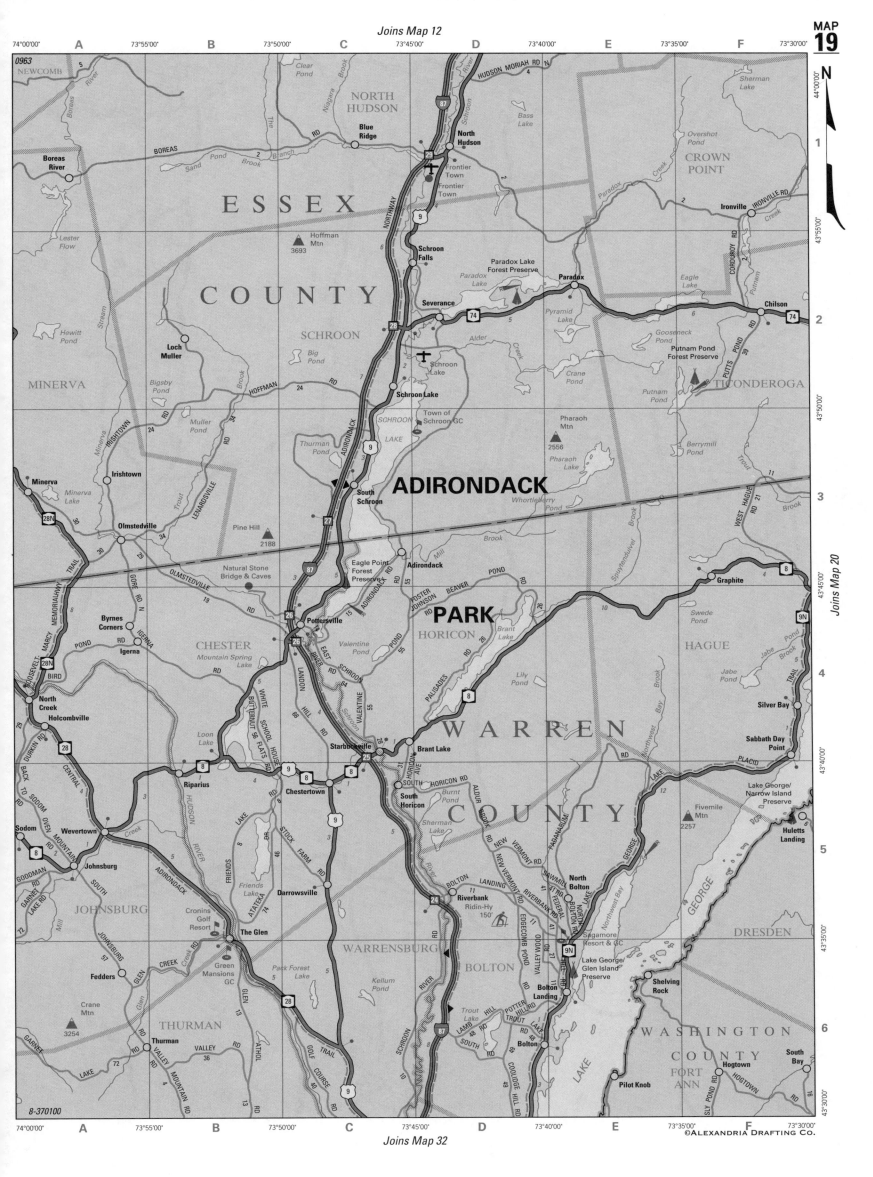

MAP
20

N

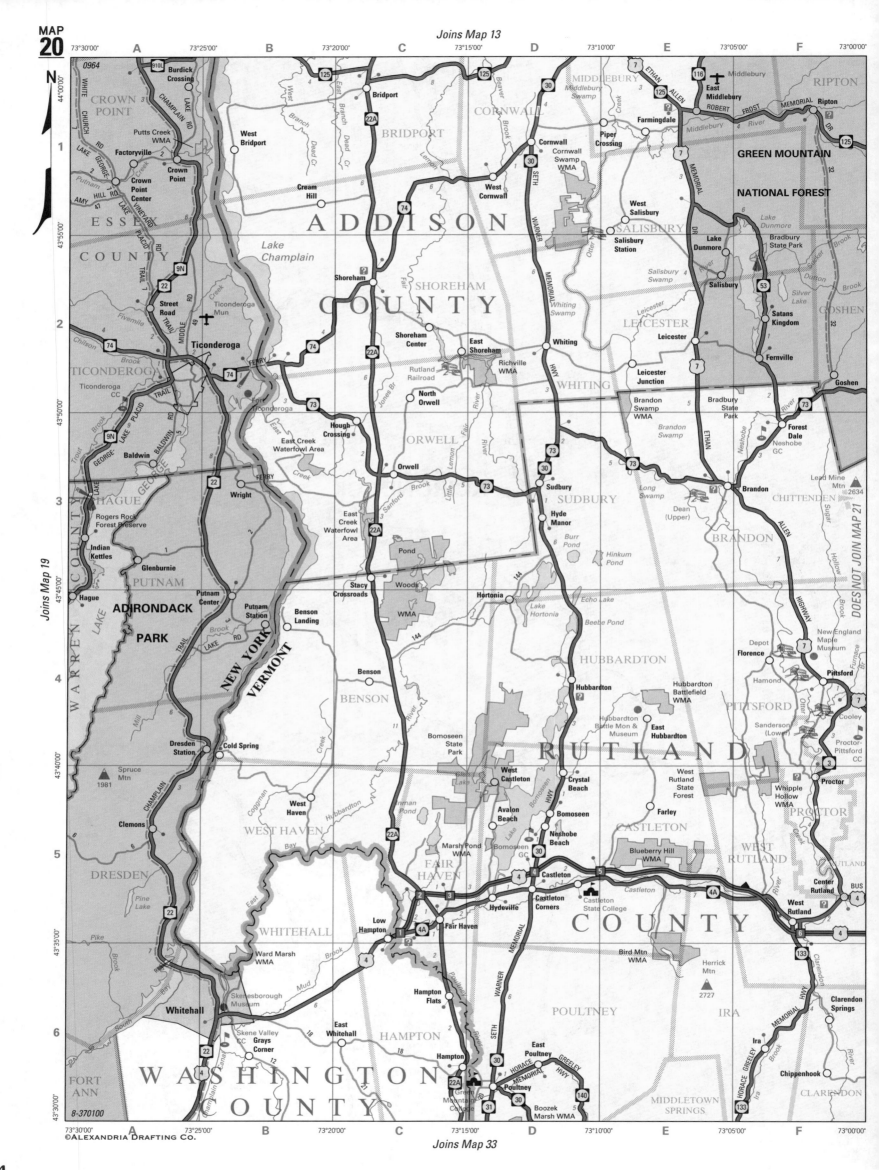

MAP
21

1064

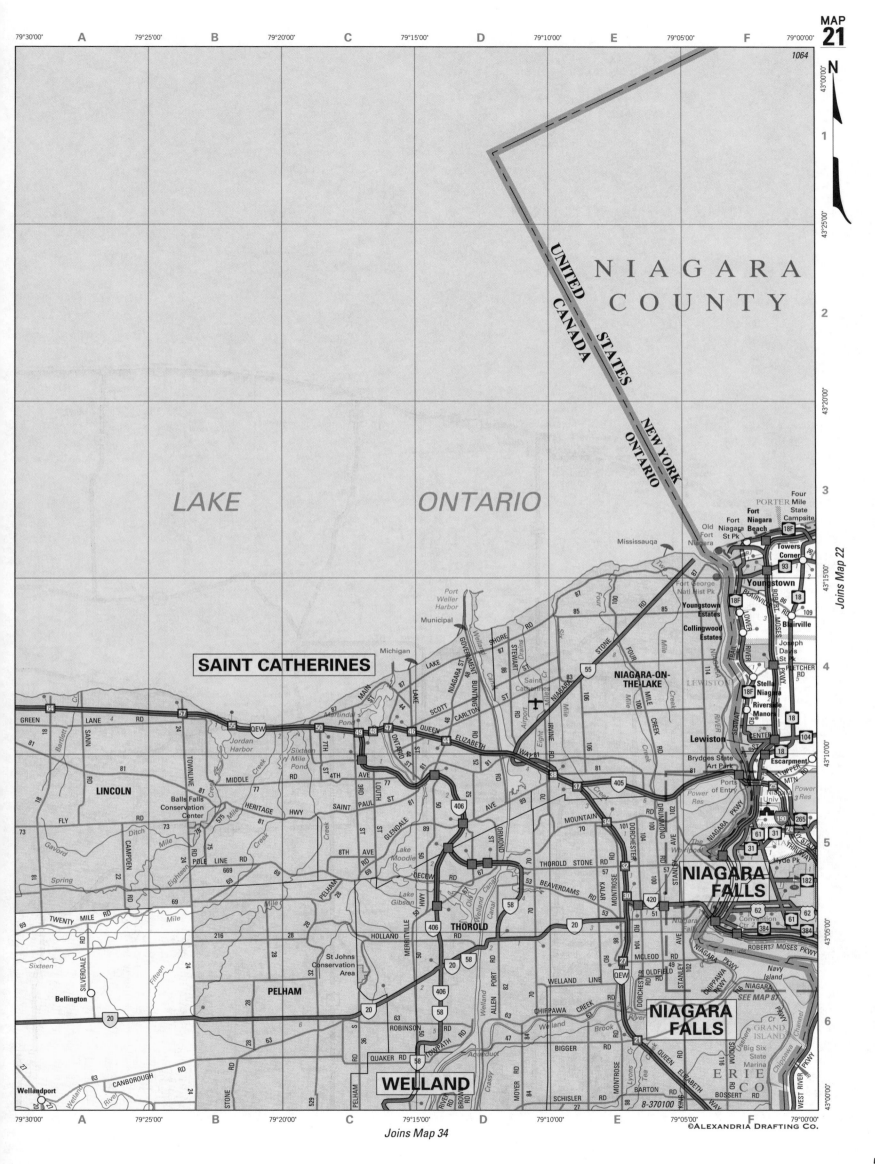

NIAGARA
COUNTY

LAKE ONTARIO

SAINT CATHERINES

NIAGARA-ON-THE-LAKE

LINCOLN

PELHAM

THOROLD

NIAGARA FALLS

NIAGARA FALLS

WELLAND

ERIE CO.

Joins Map 22

Joins Map 34

MAP
22
N

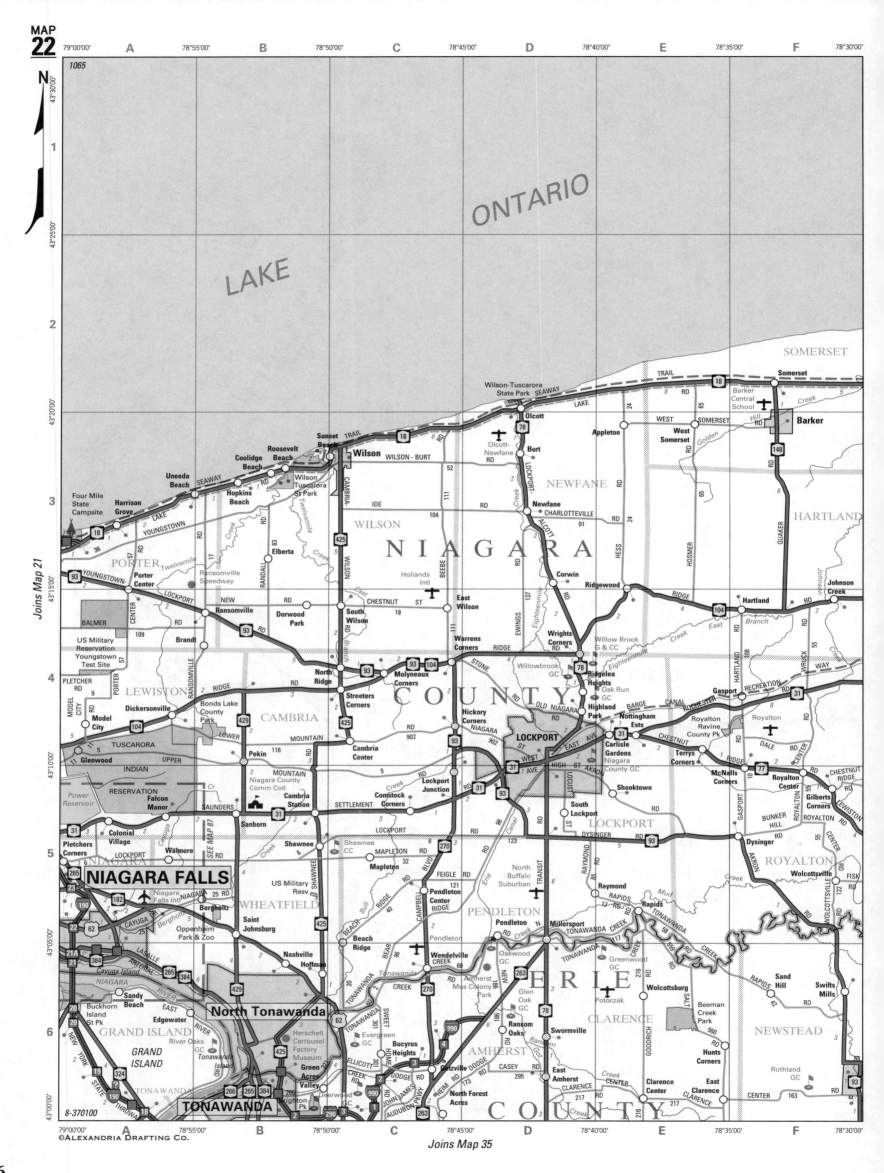

A 78°55'00" B 78°50'00" C 78°45'00" D 78°40'00" E 78°35'00" F 78°30'00"
79°00'00"
43°30'00"
43°25'00"
43°20'00"
43°15'00"
43°10'00"
43°05'00"
43°00'00"

LAKE ONTARIO

Joins Map 21

SEE MAP 87

Joins Map 35

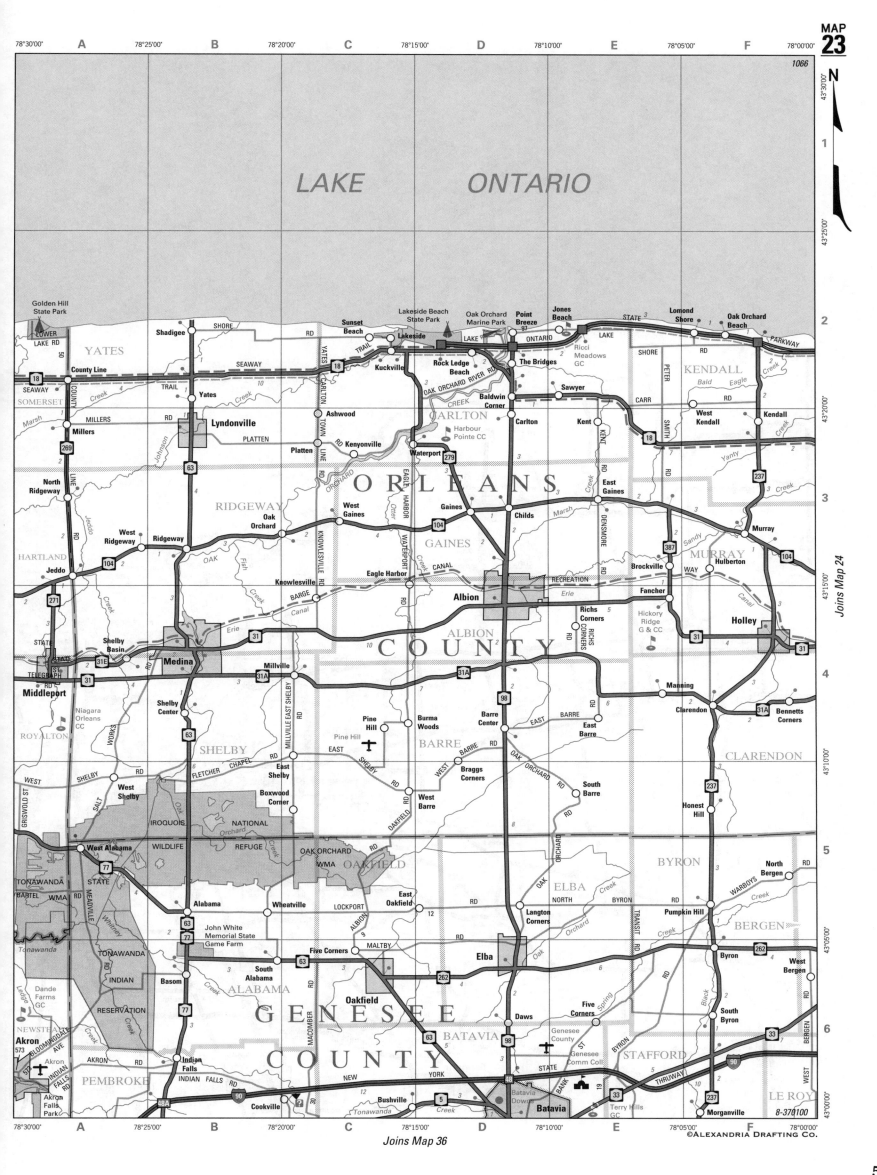

MAP **23**

LAKE ONTARIO

©Alexandria Drafting Co.

MAP
24

1067

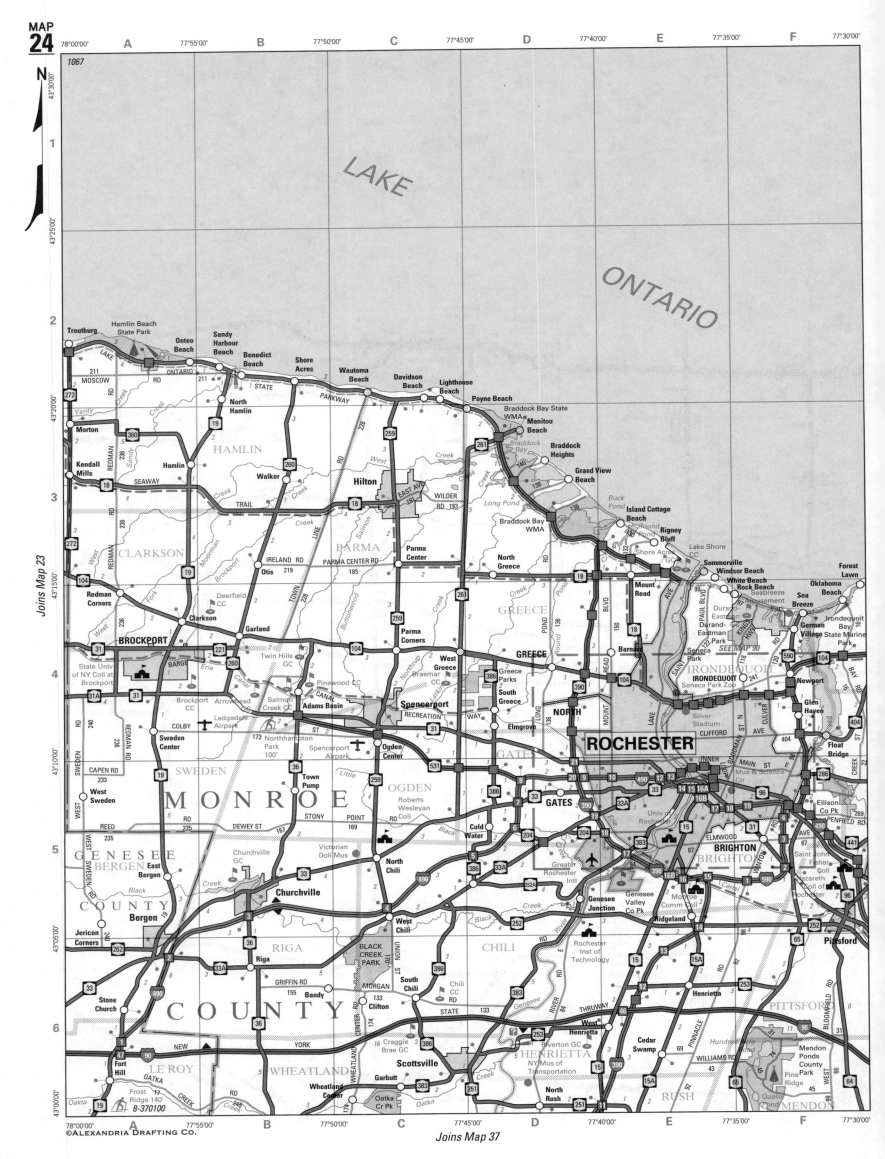

Joins Map 37

MAP
25

1068

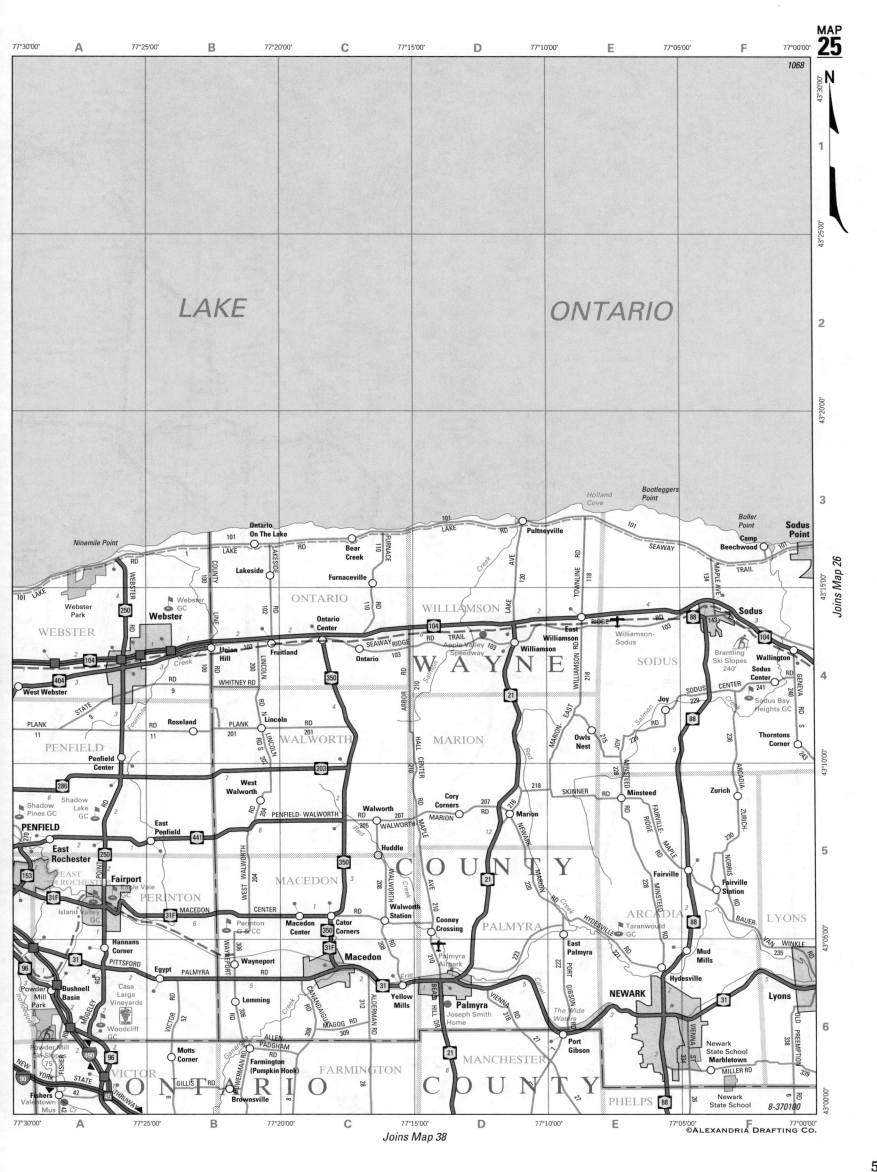

MAP
26

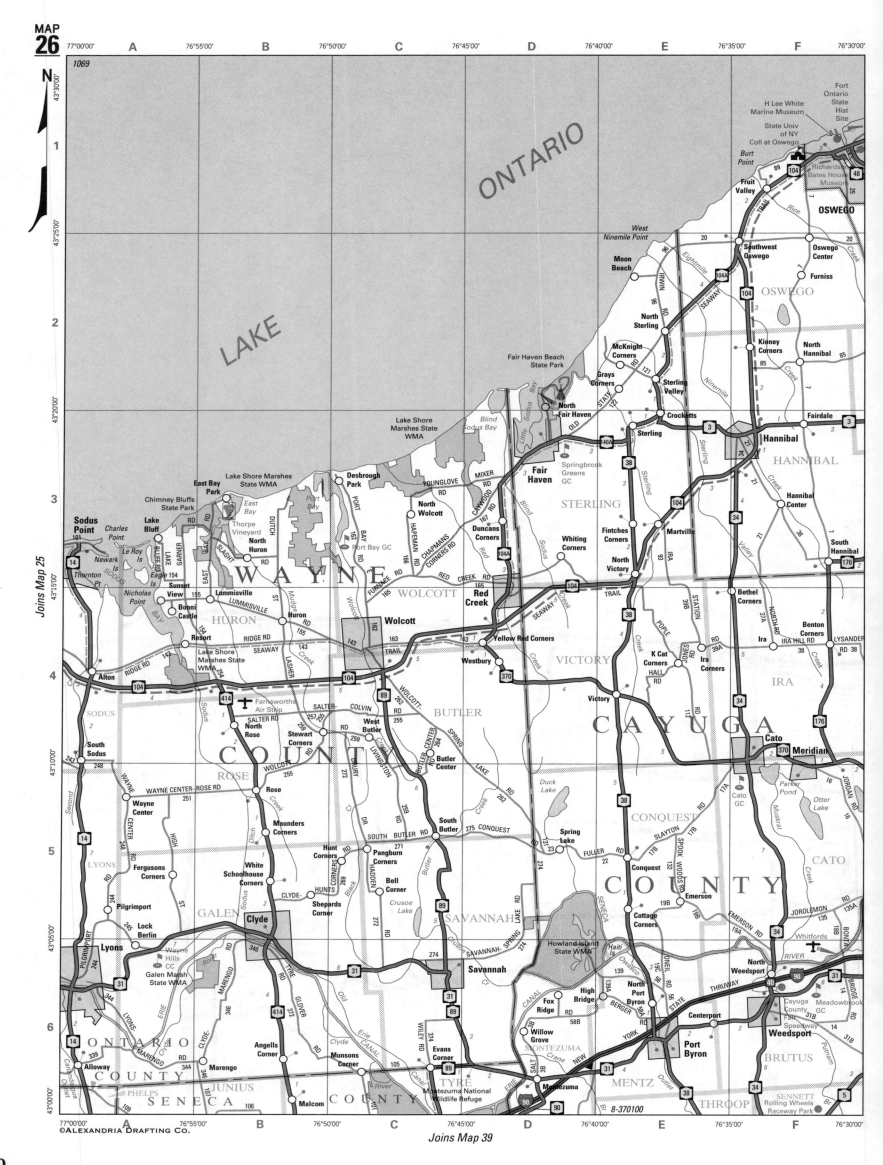

©ALEXANDRIA DRAFTING CO.

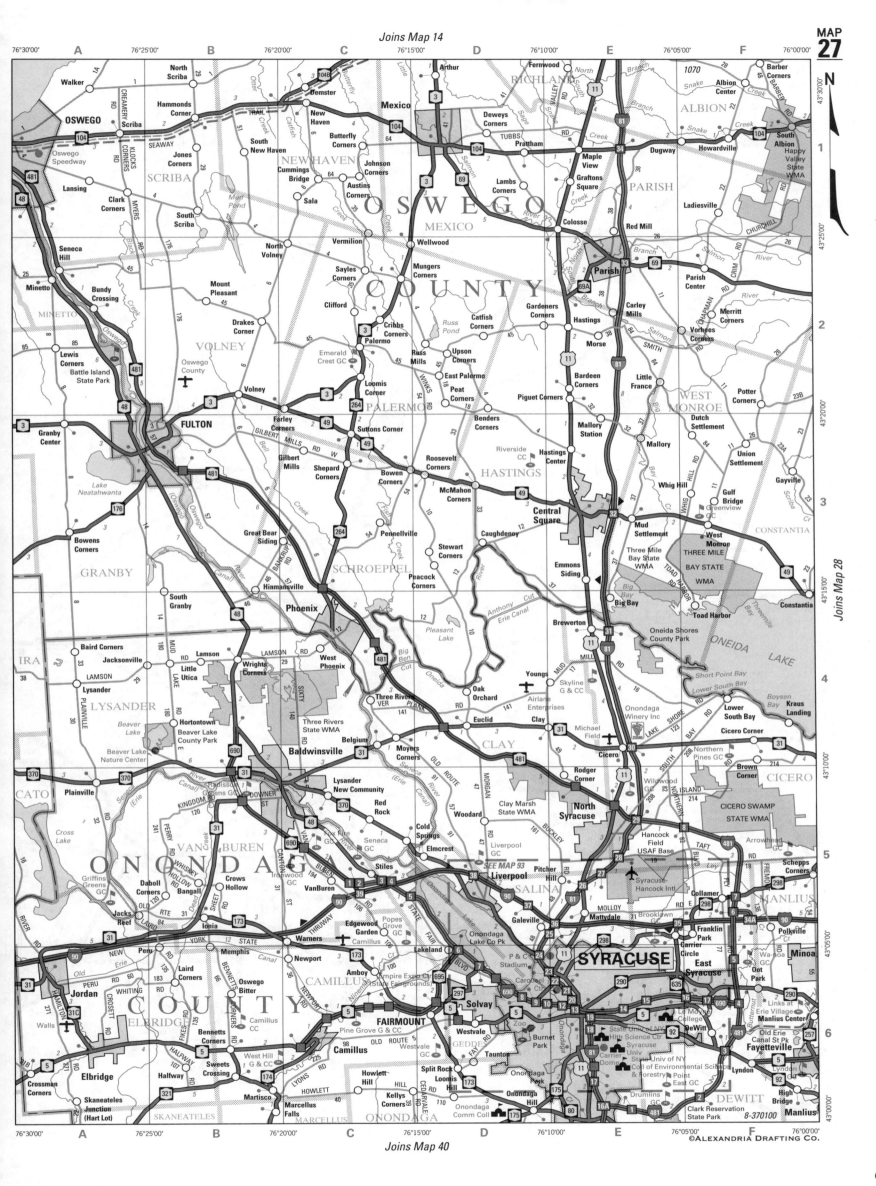

MAP
28

Joins Map 15

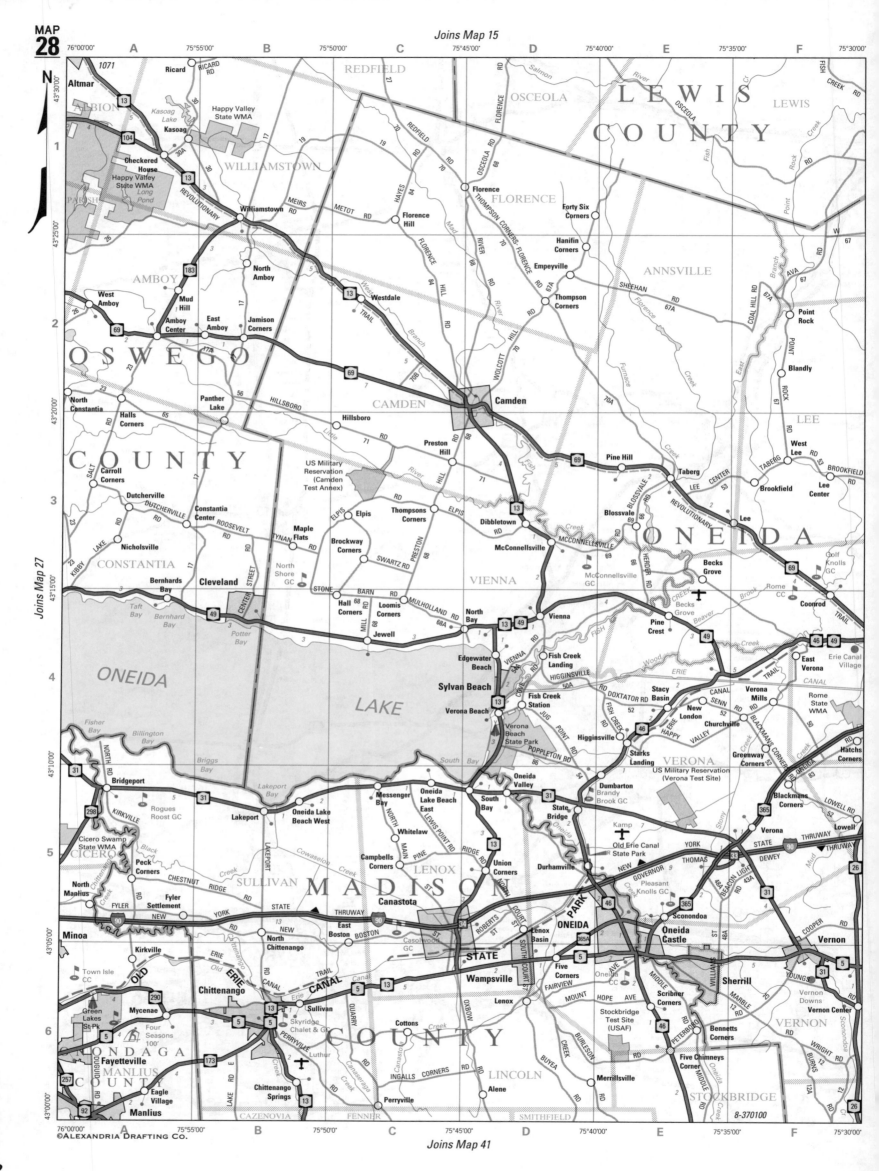

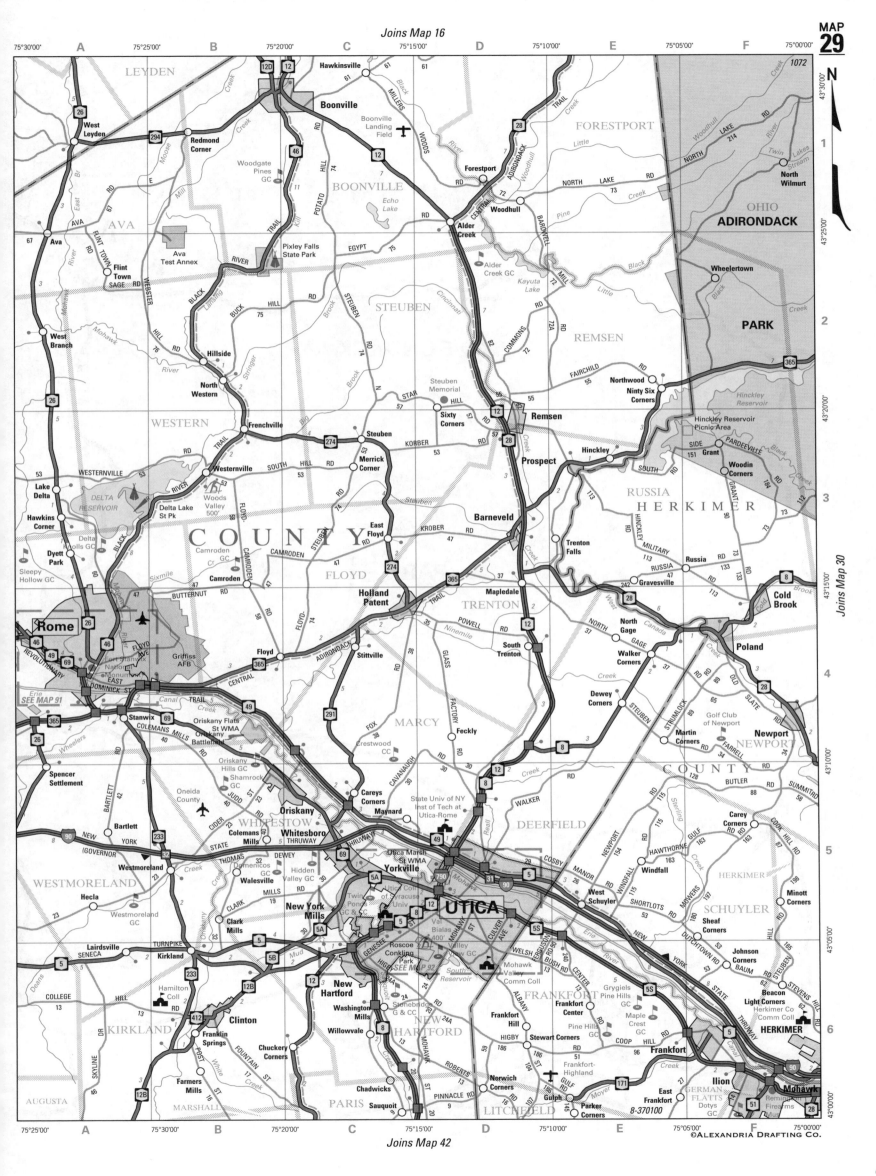

MAP
30

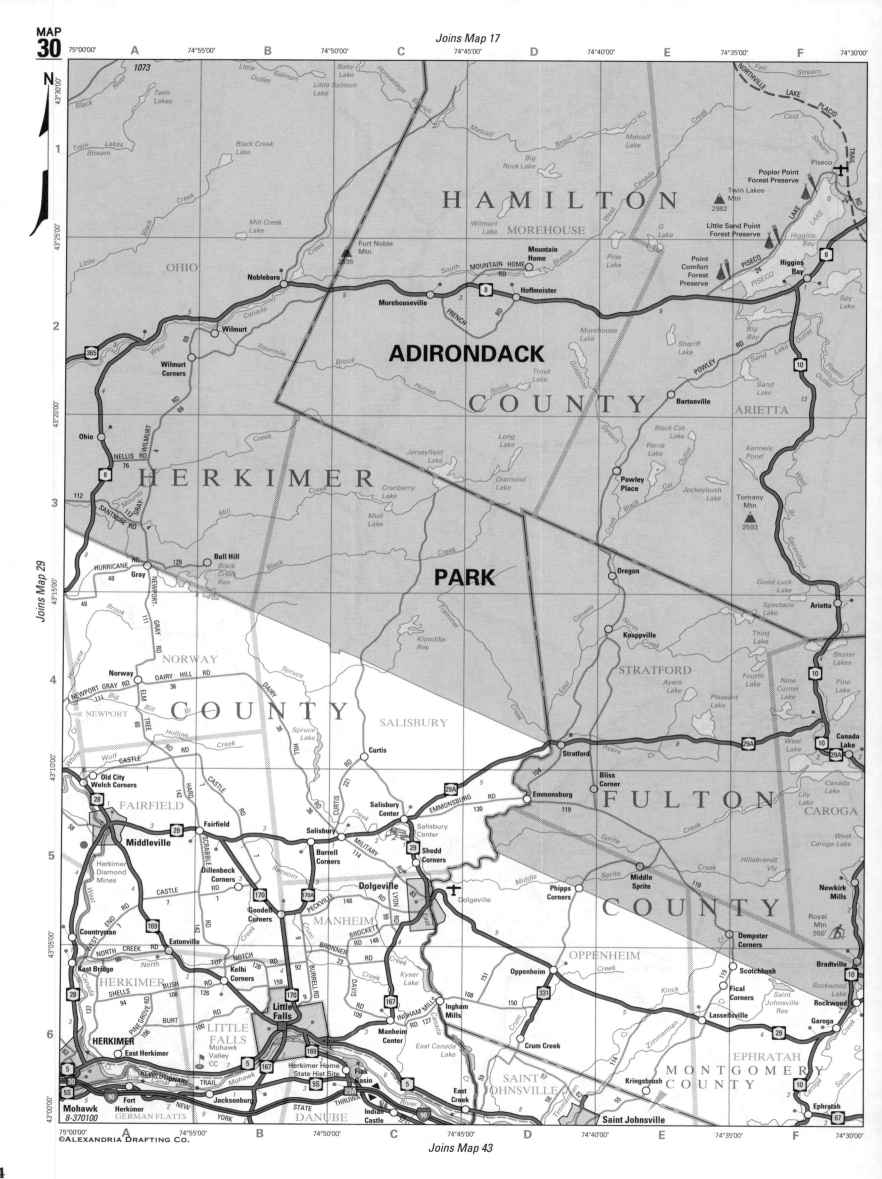

©Alexandria Drafting Co.

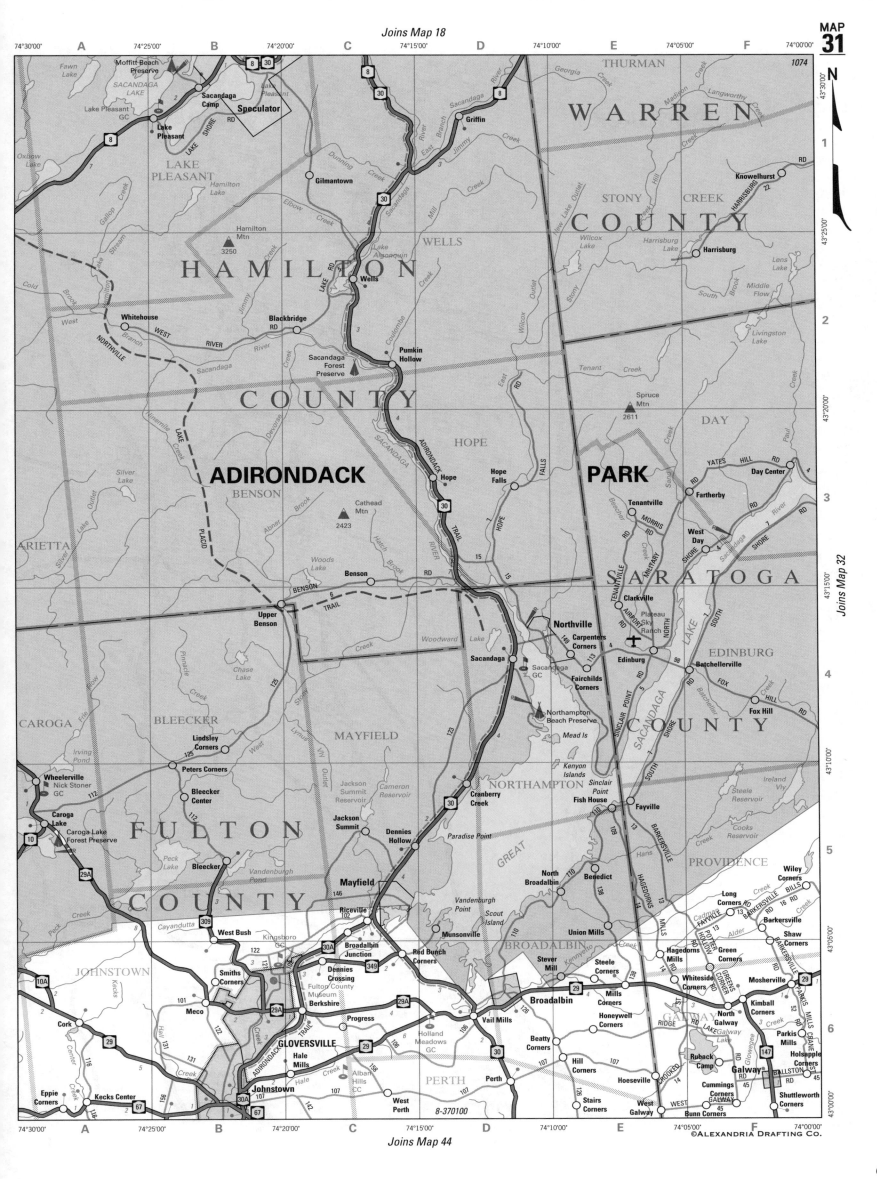

MAP
32

Joins Map 19

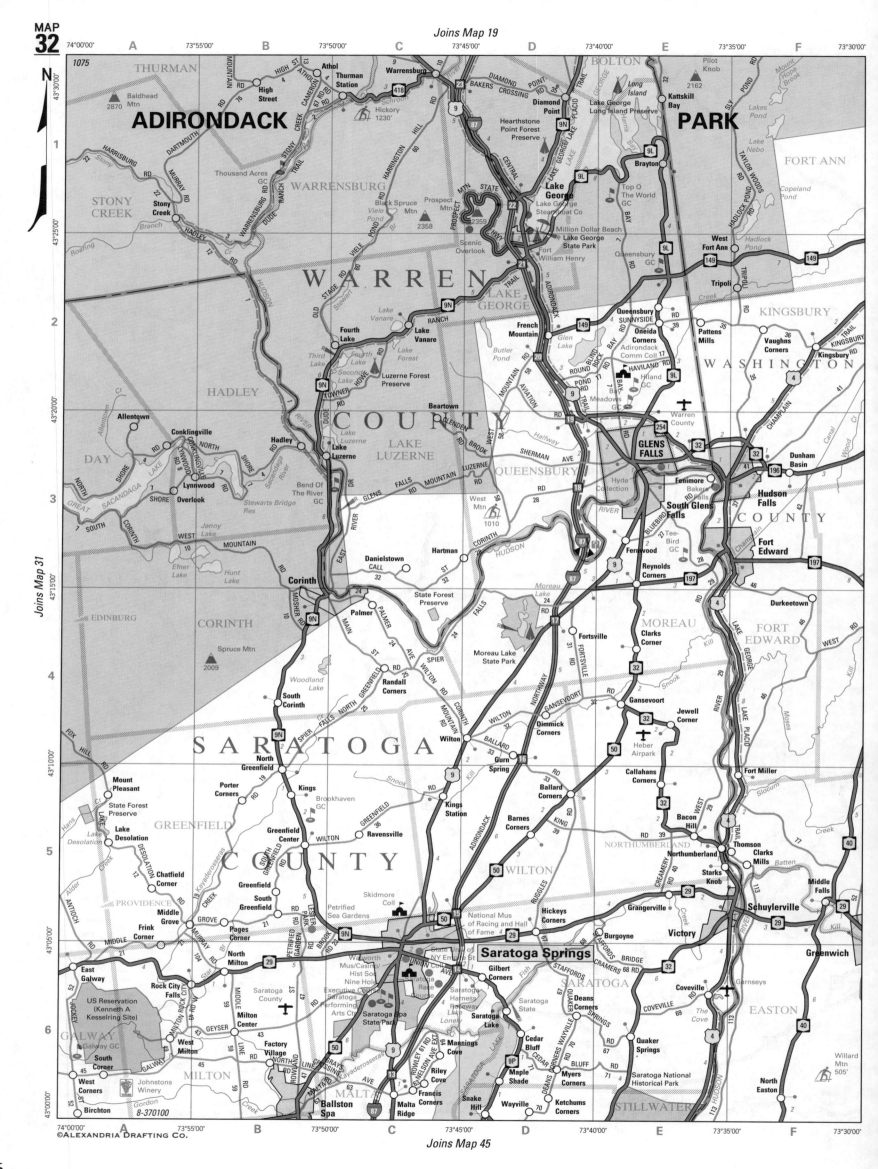

ADIRONDACK **PARK**

Joins Map 31

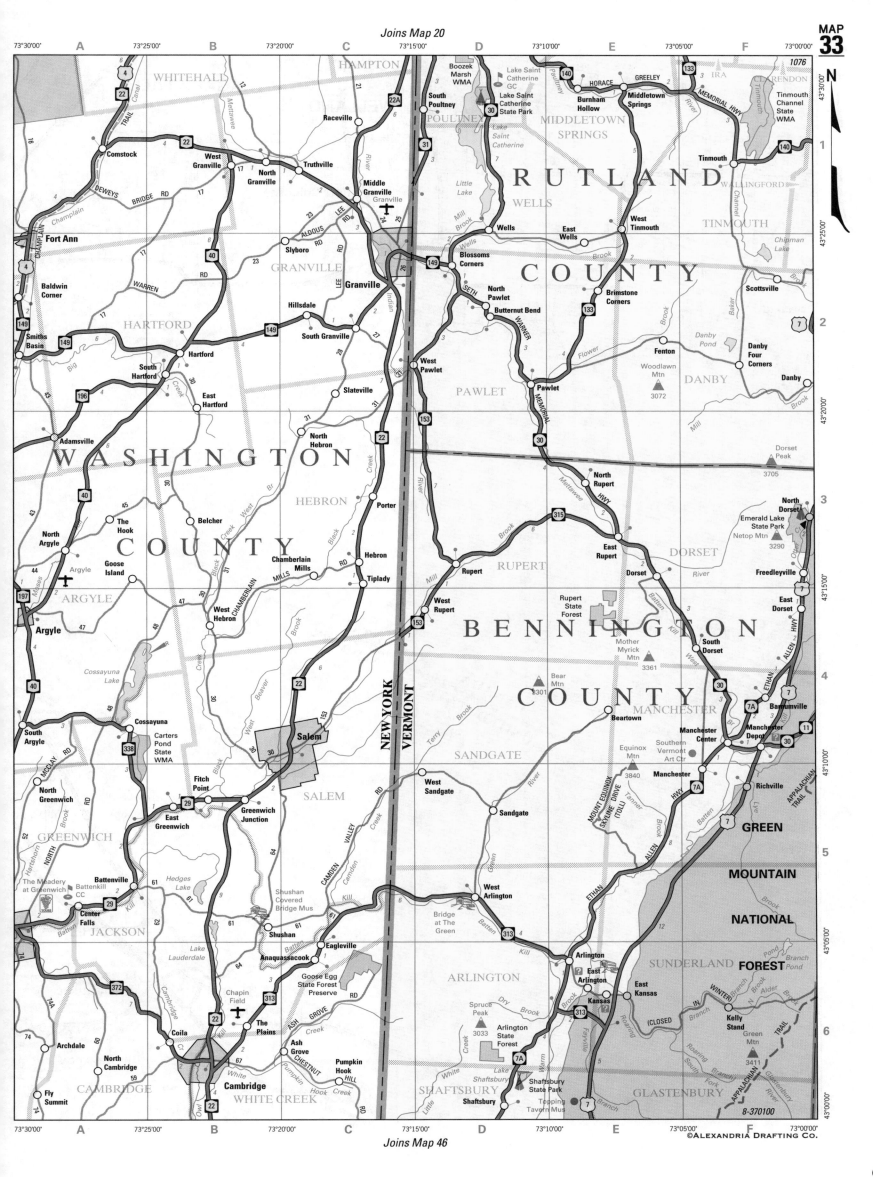

MAP
33

©Alexandria Drafting Co.

MAP
34
N

Joins Map 21

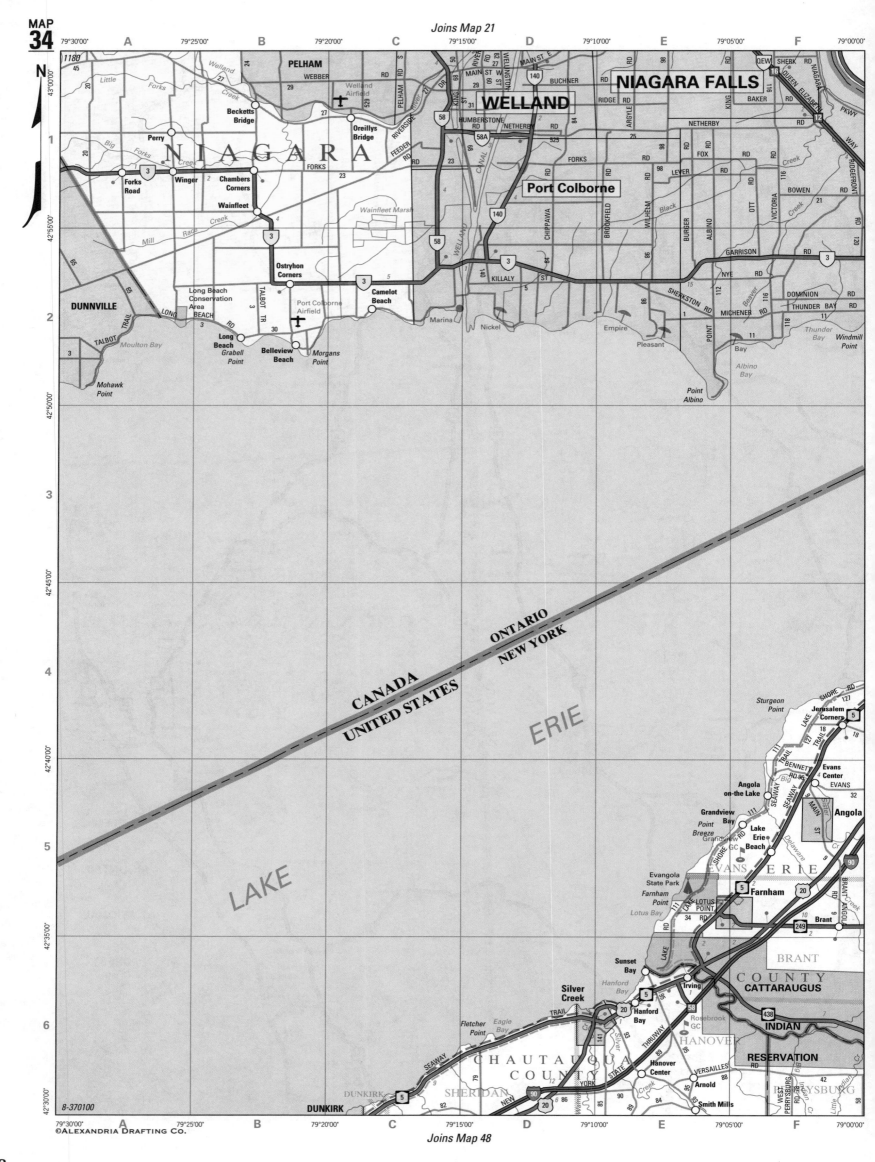

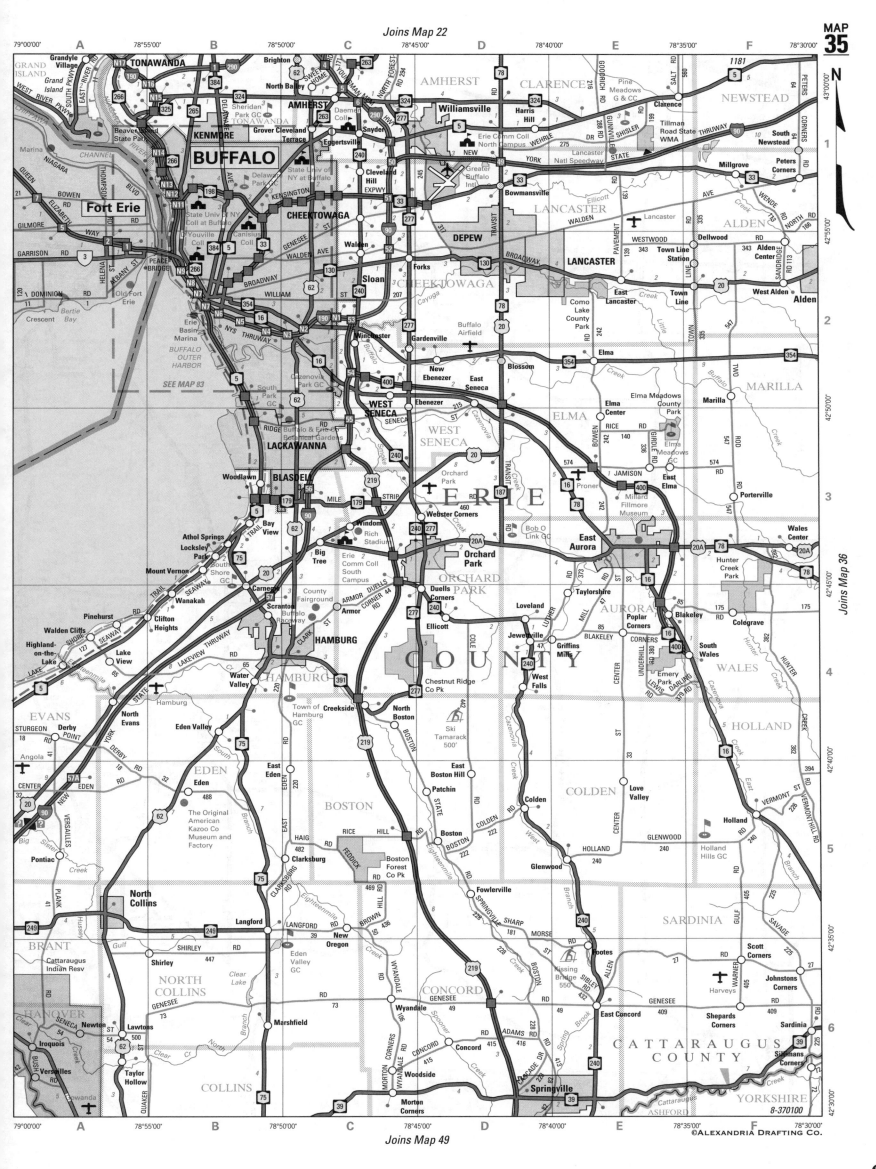

MAP
36

Joins Map 23

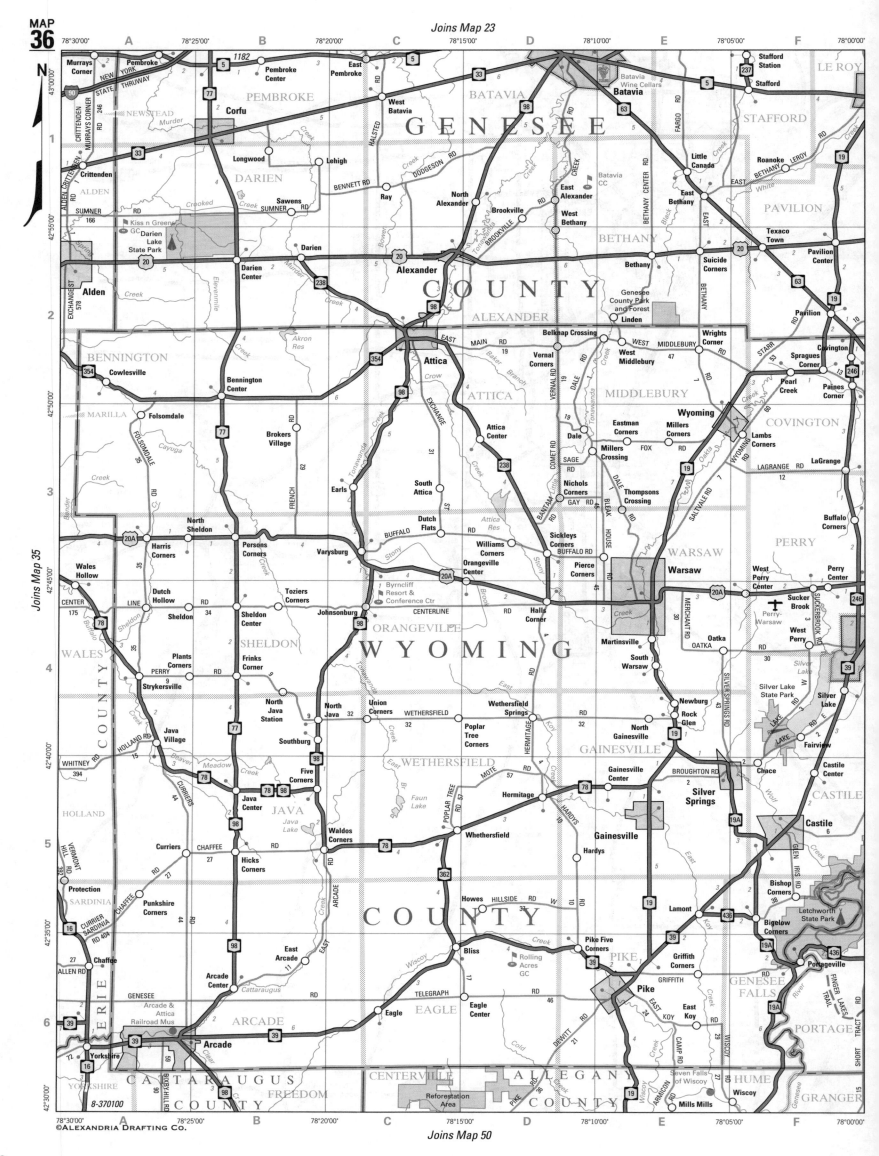

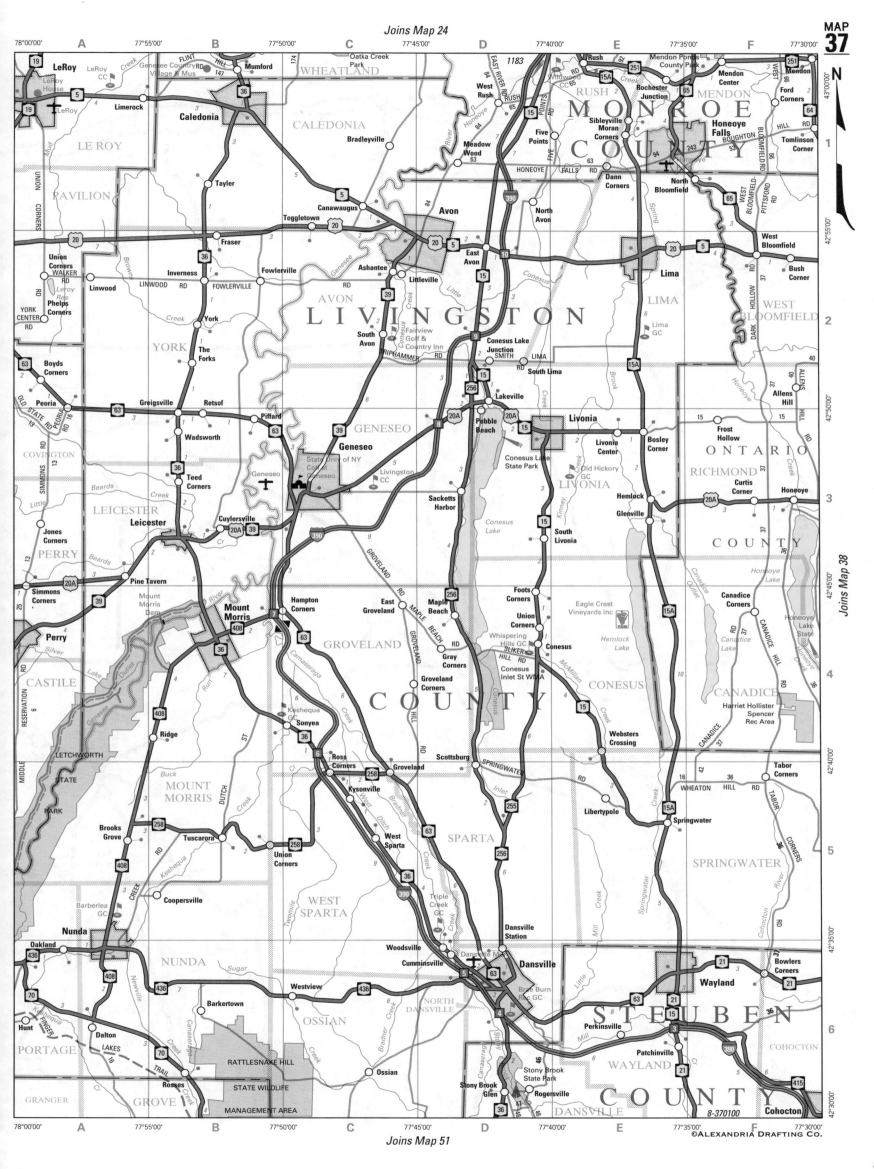

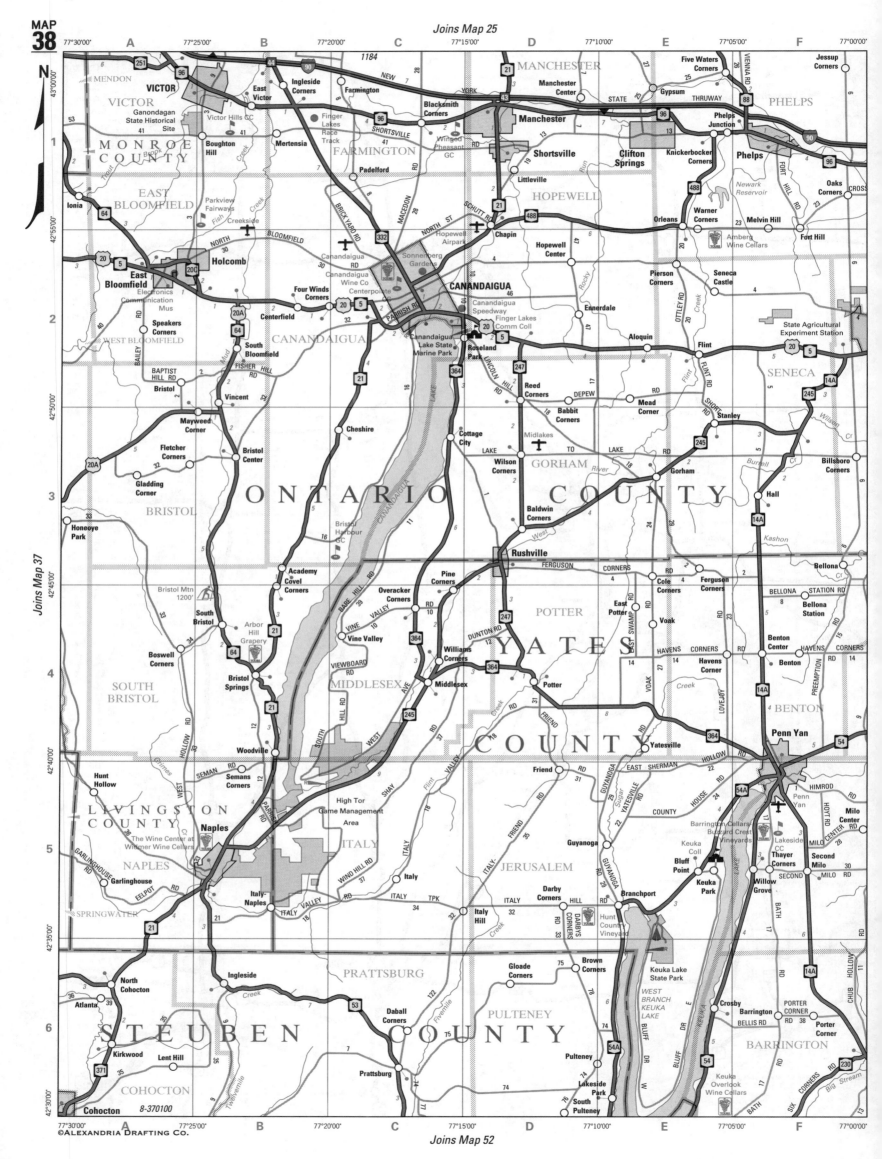

MAP
38

Joins Map 37

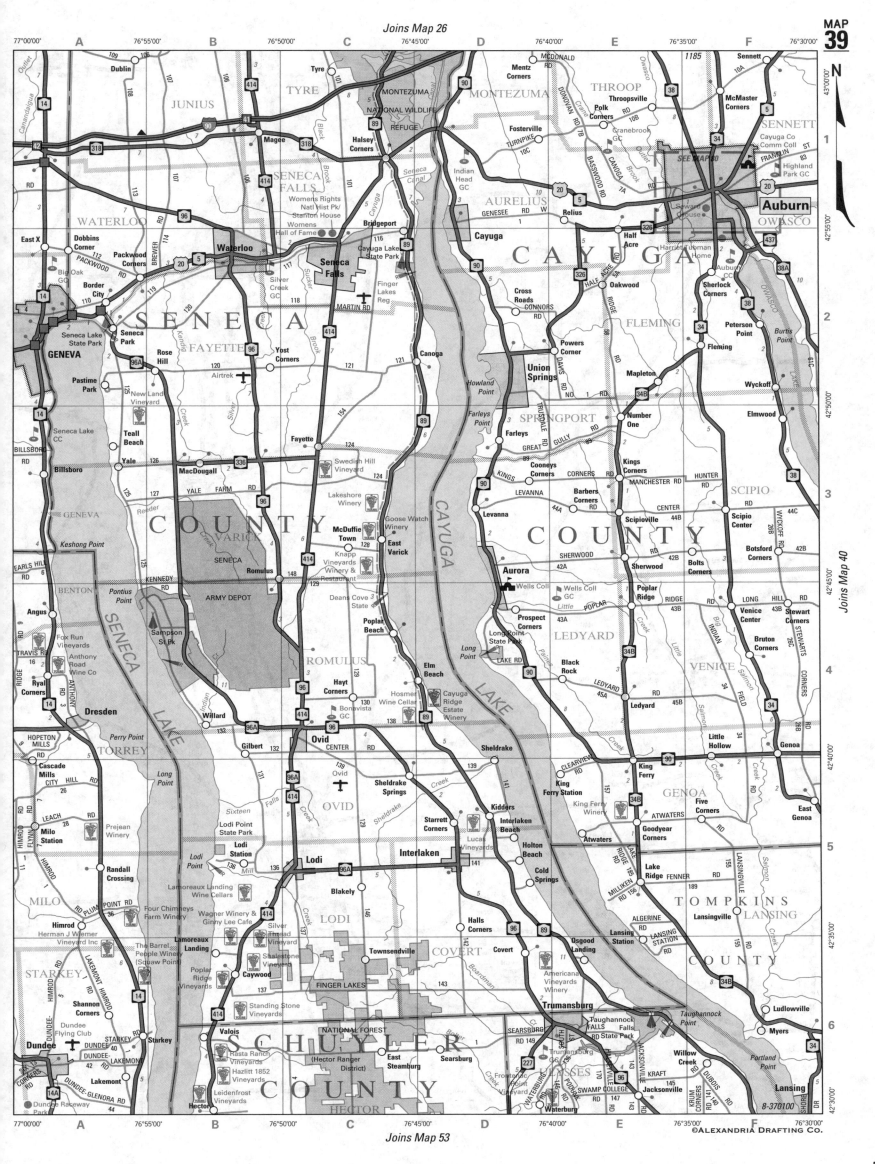

MAP 40

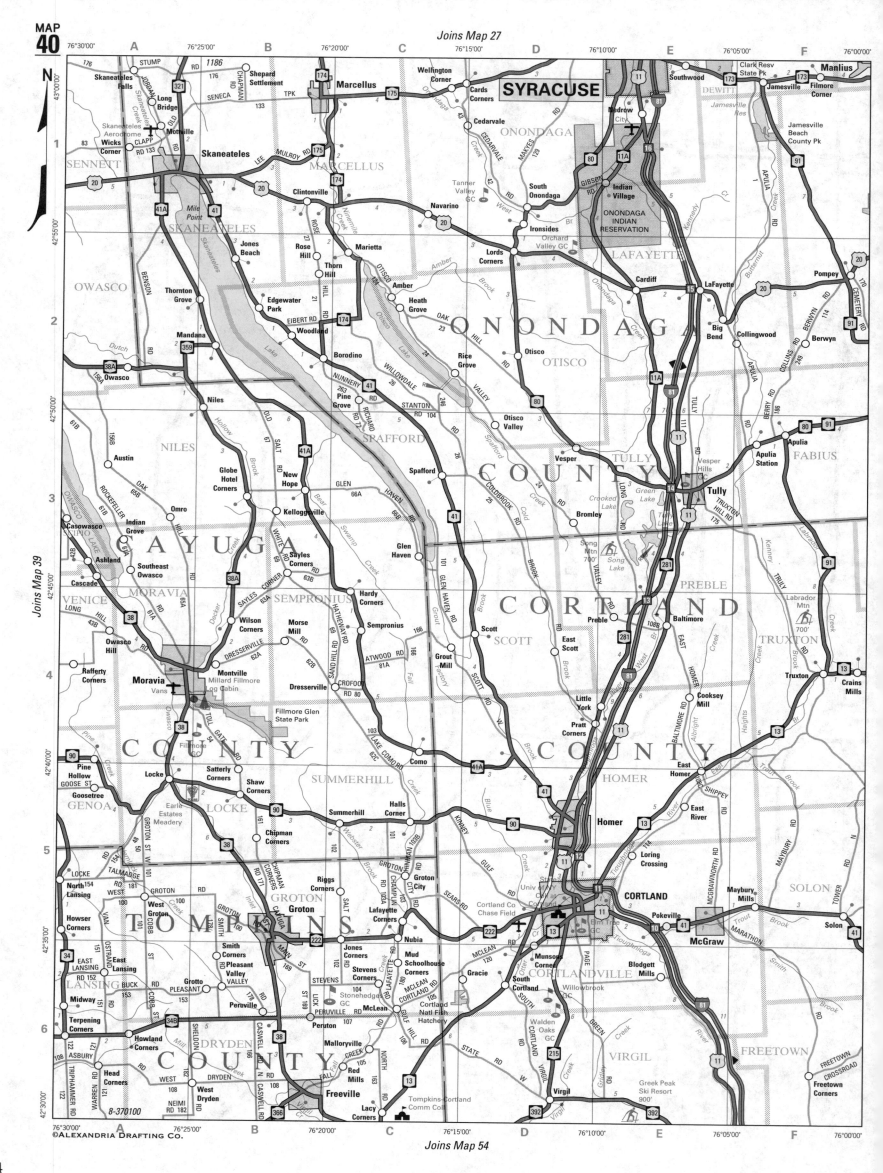

©Alexandria Drafting Co.

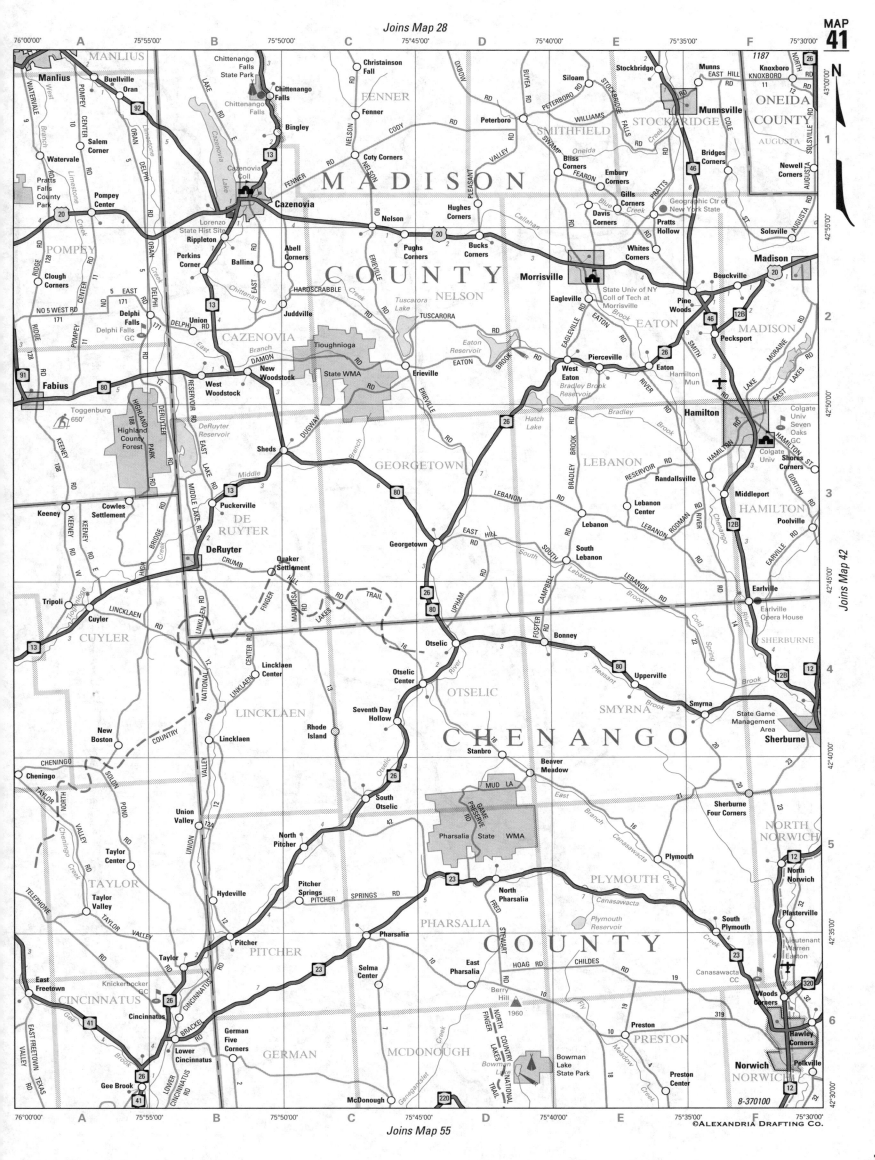

MAP
41
N

©Alexandria Drafting Co.

MAP 42

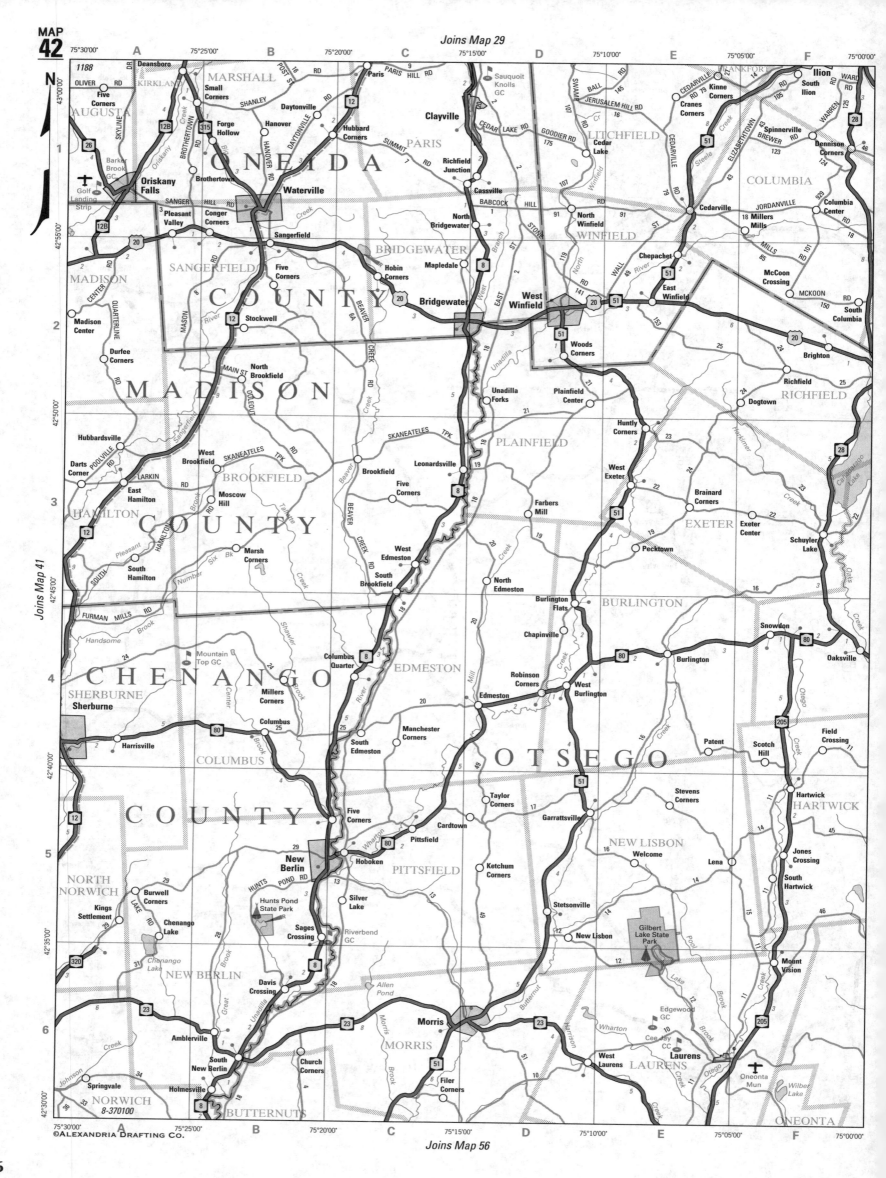

©Alexandria Drafting Co.

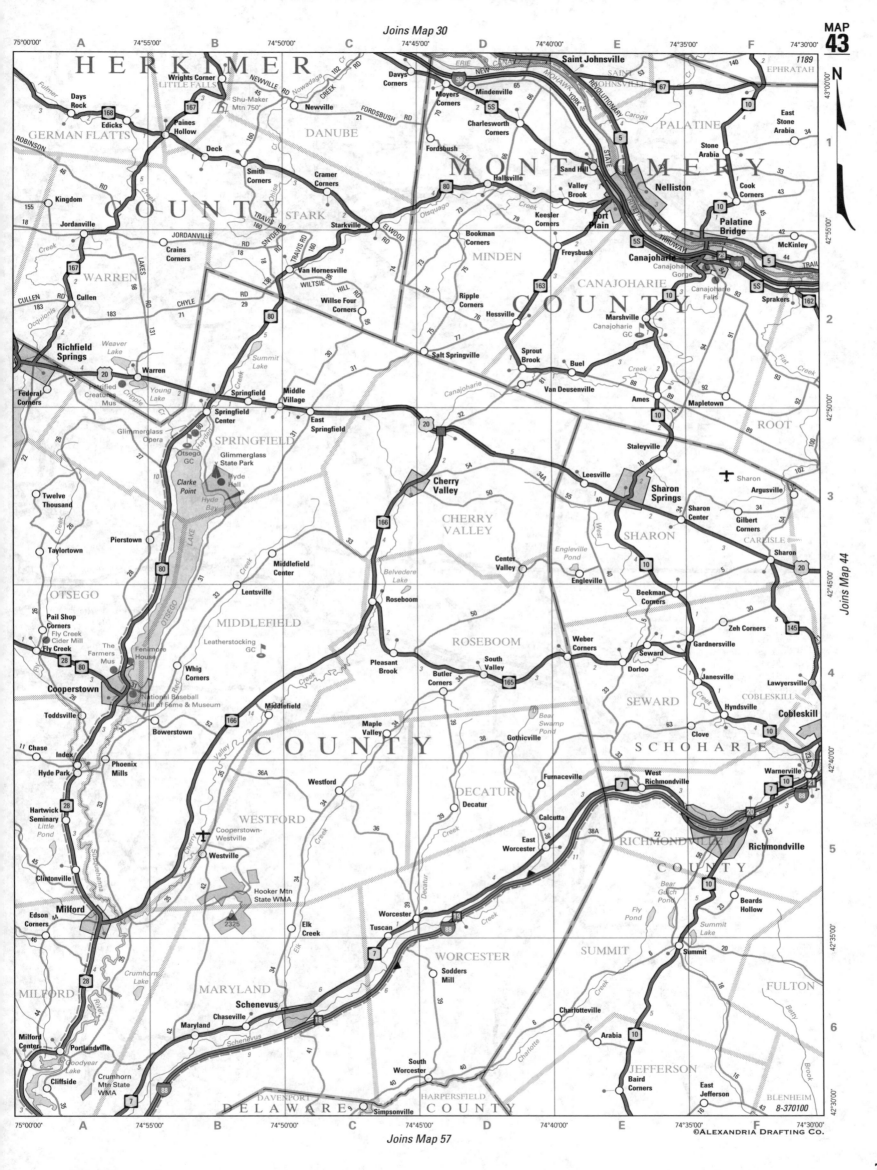

MAP
43
1189
N

©Alexandria Drafting Co.

8-370100

MAP 44

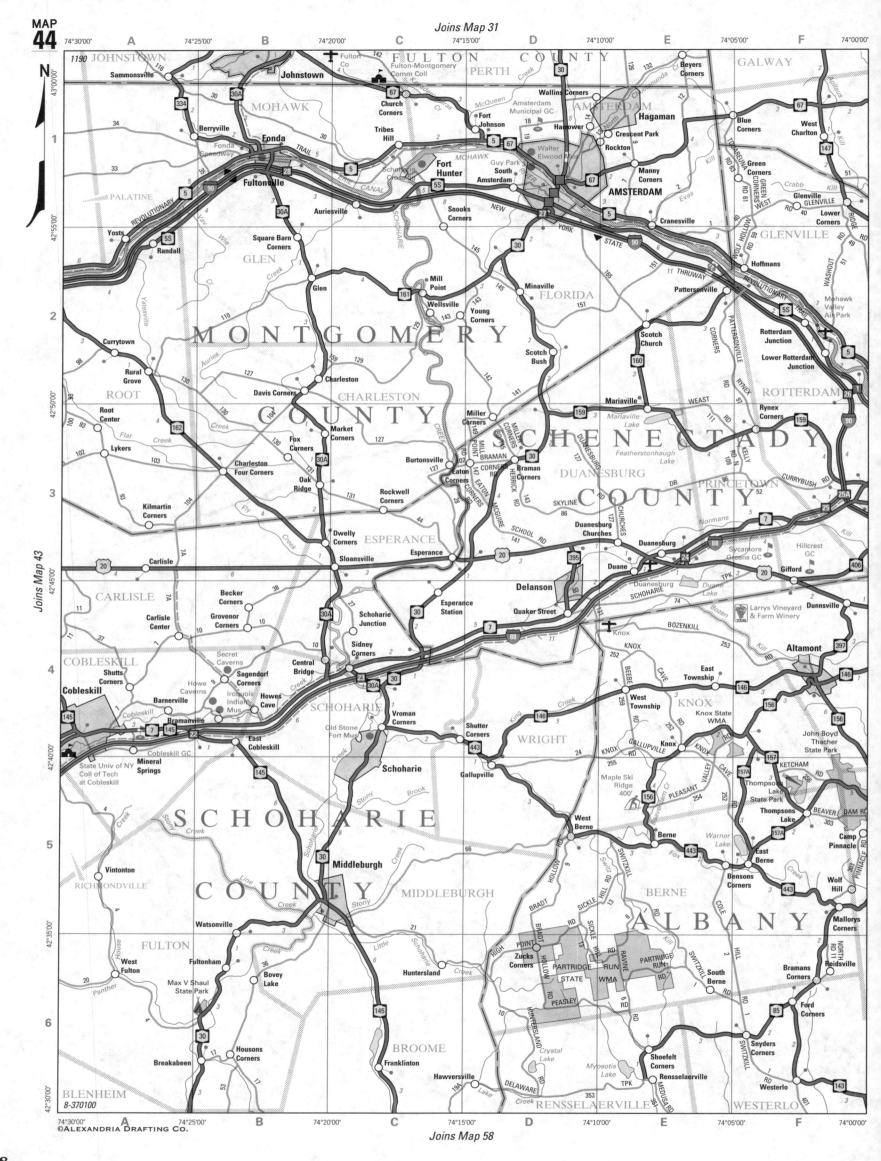

©Alexandria Drafting Co.

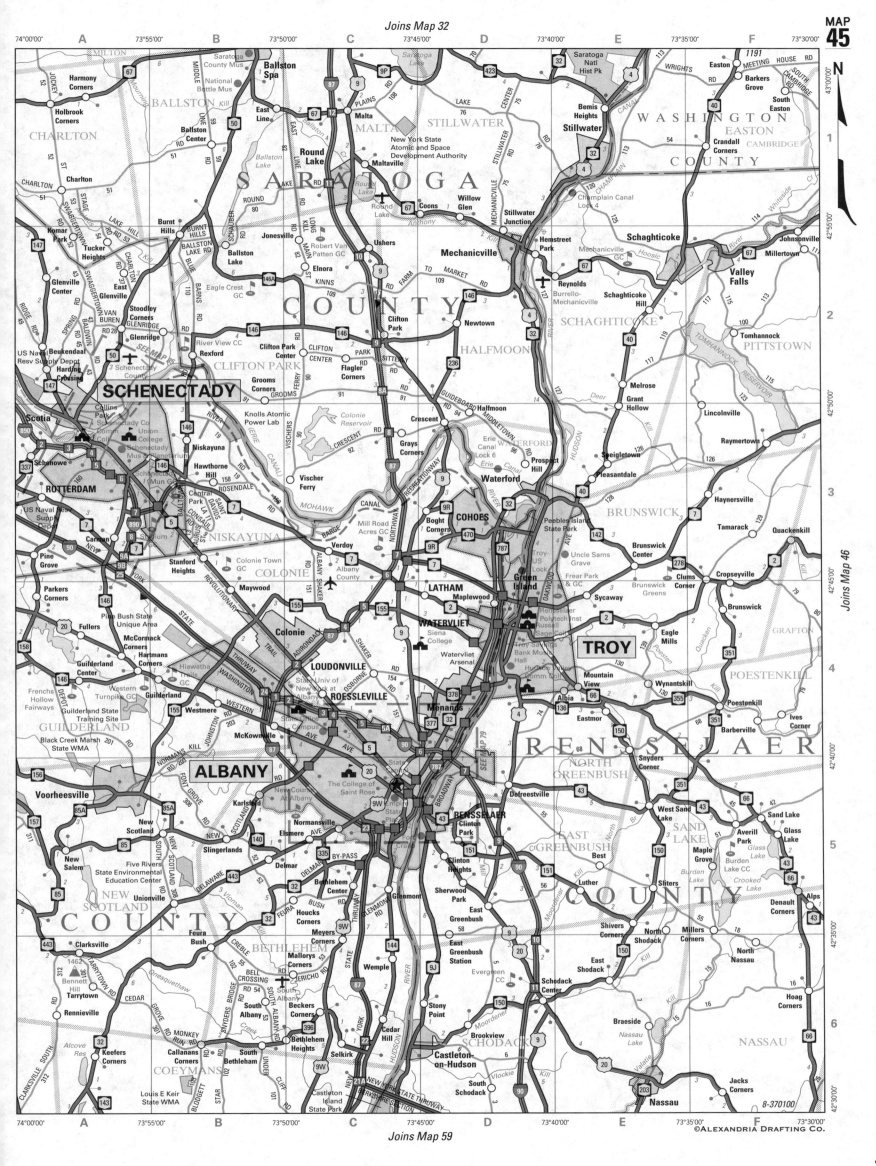

©Alexandria Drafting Co.

MAP
46
Joins Map 33

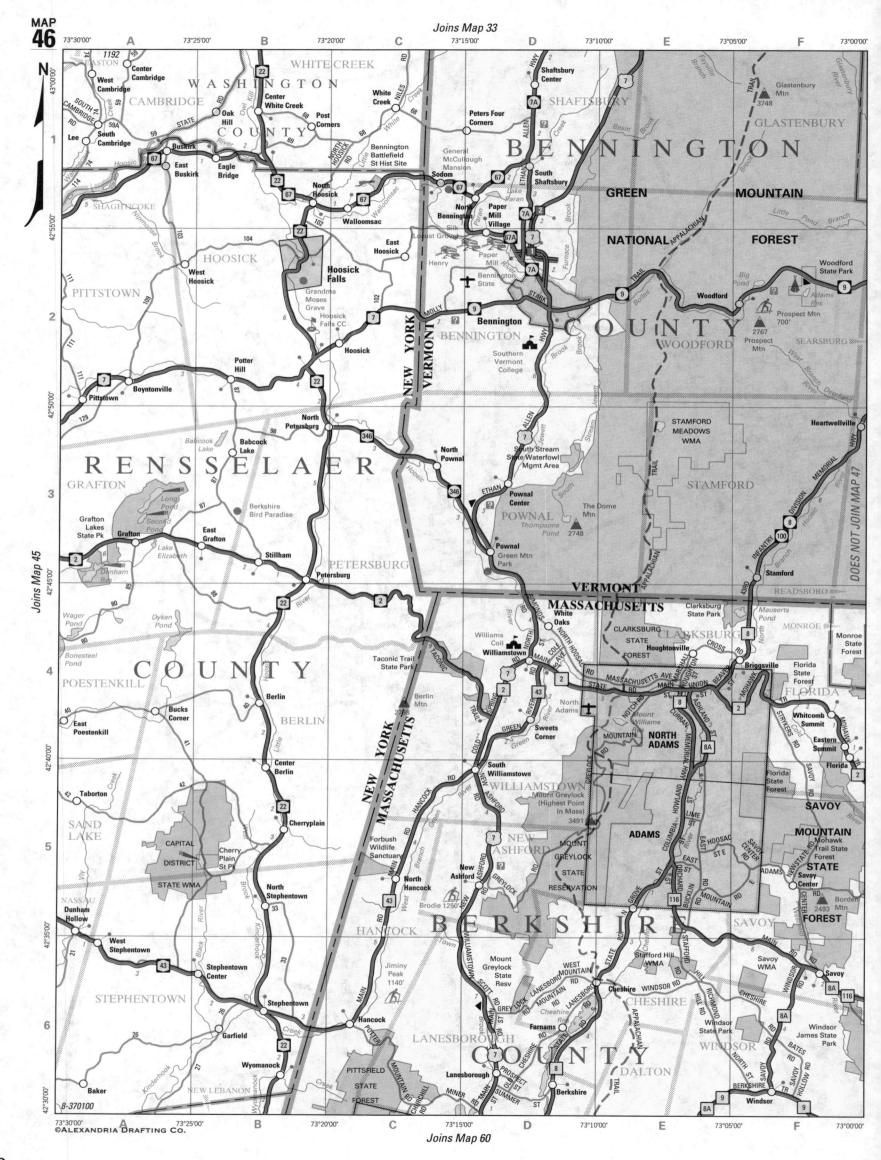

MAP
47

1287

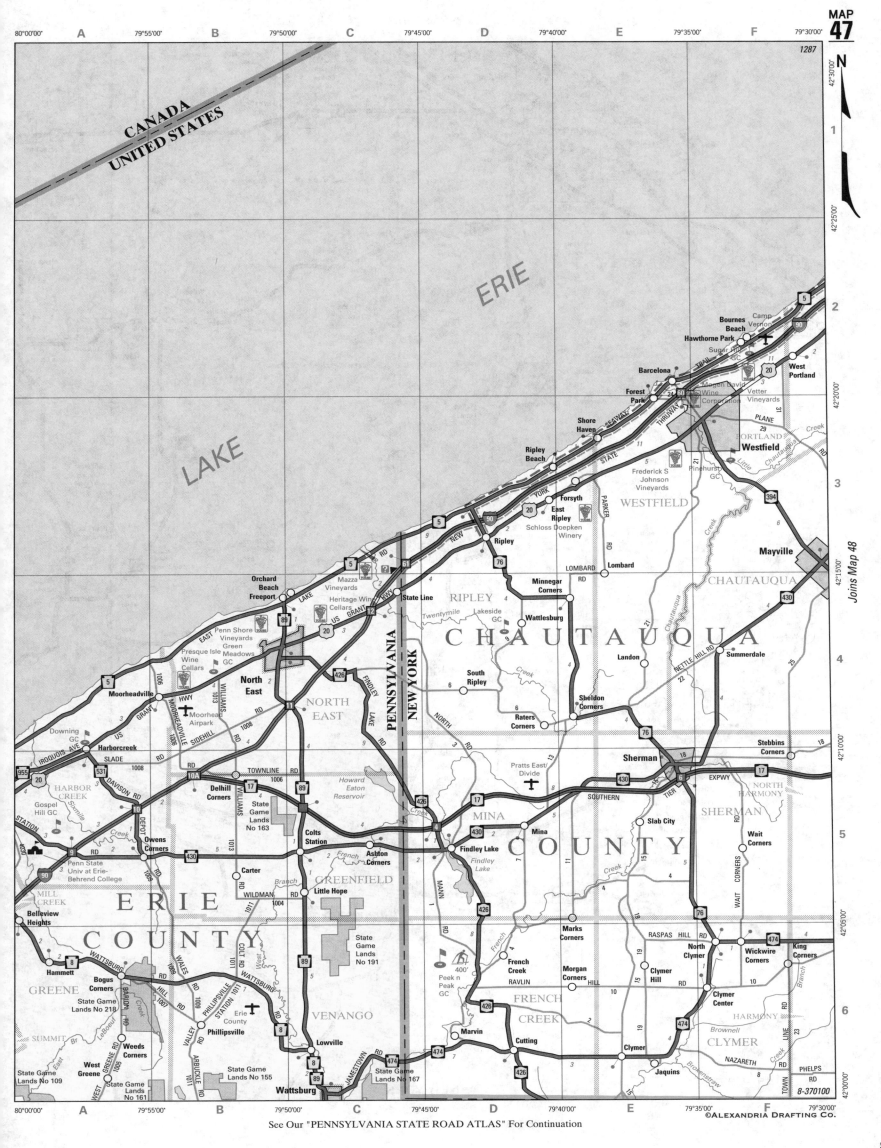

See Our "PENNSYLVANIA STATE ROAD ATLAS" For Continuation

©Alexandria Drafting Co.

MAP 48
Joins Map 34

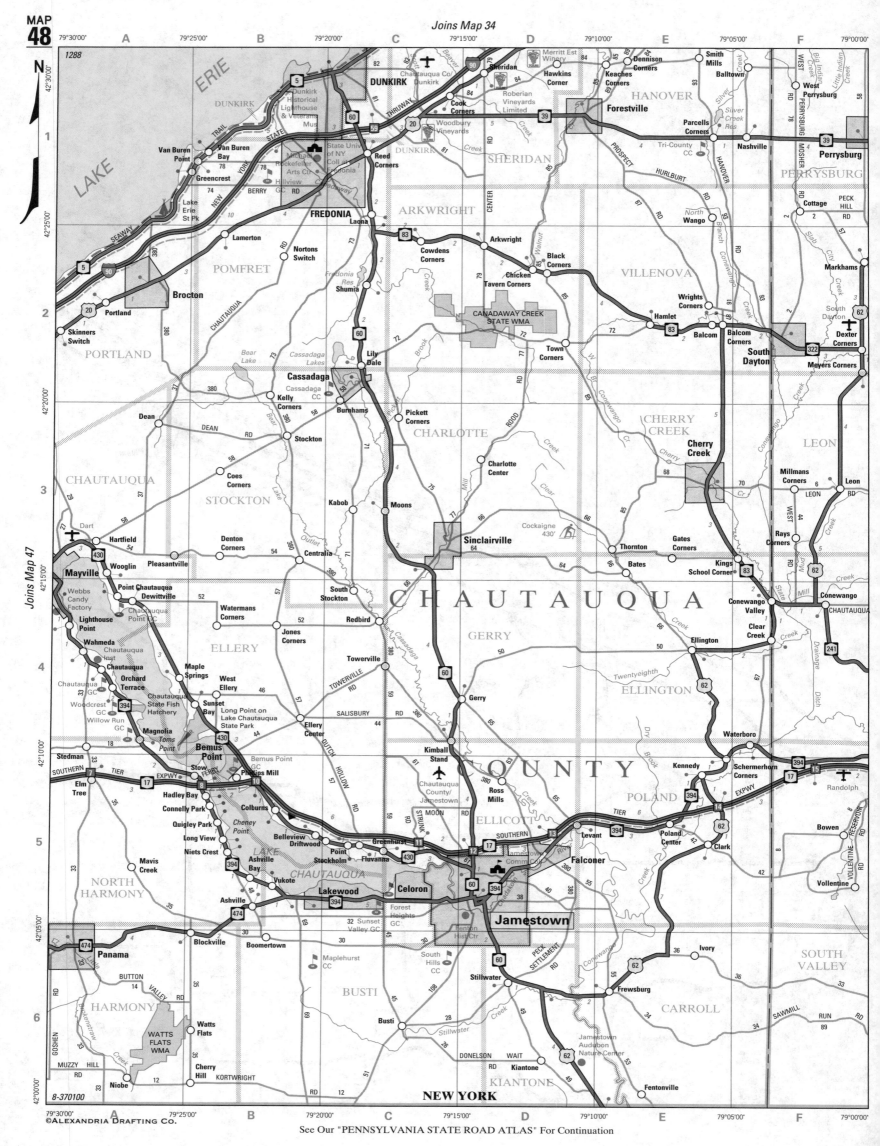

MAP 49

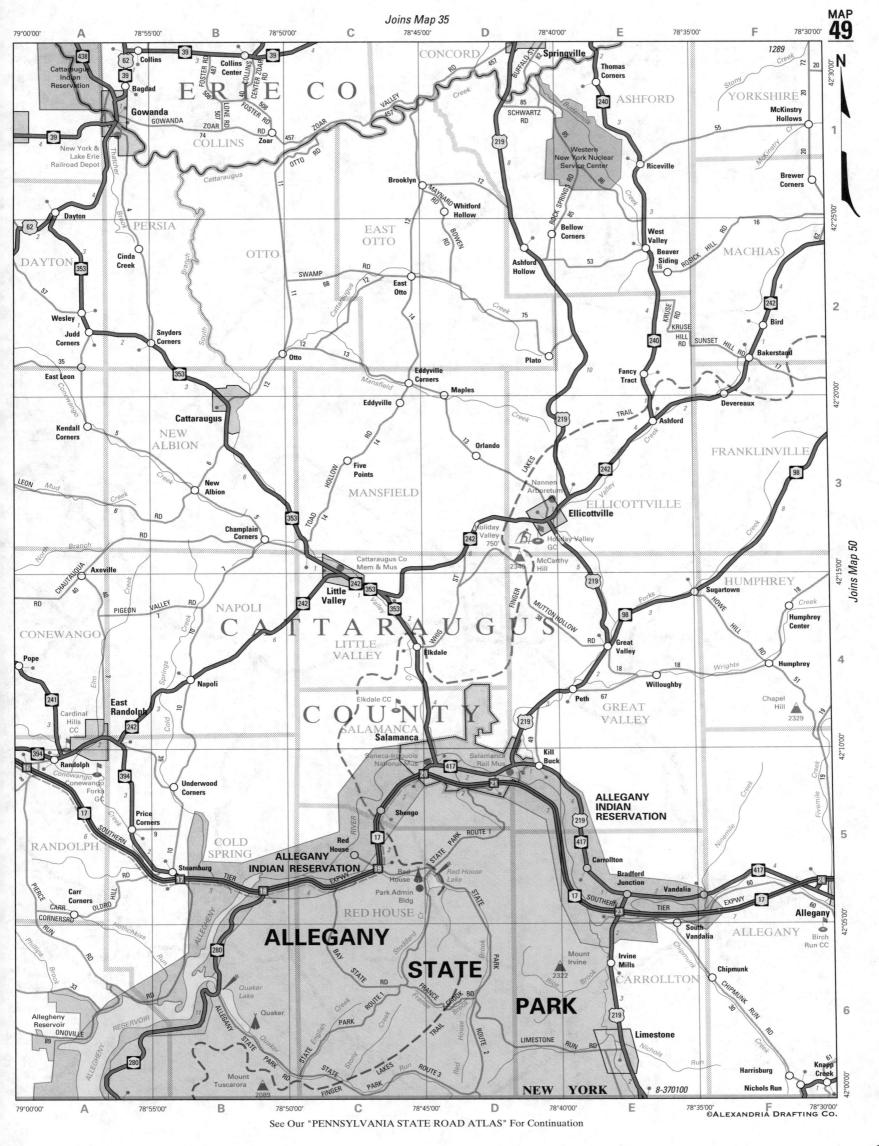

©Alexandria Drafting Co.

MAP
50
Joins Map 36

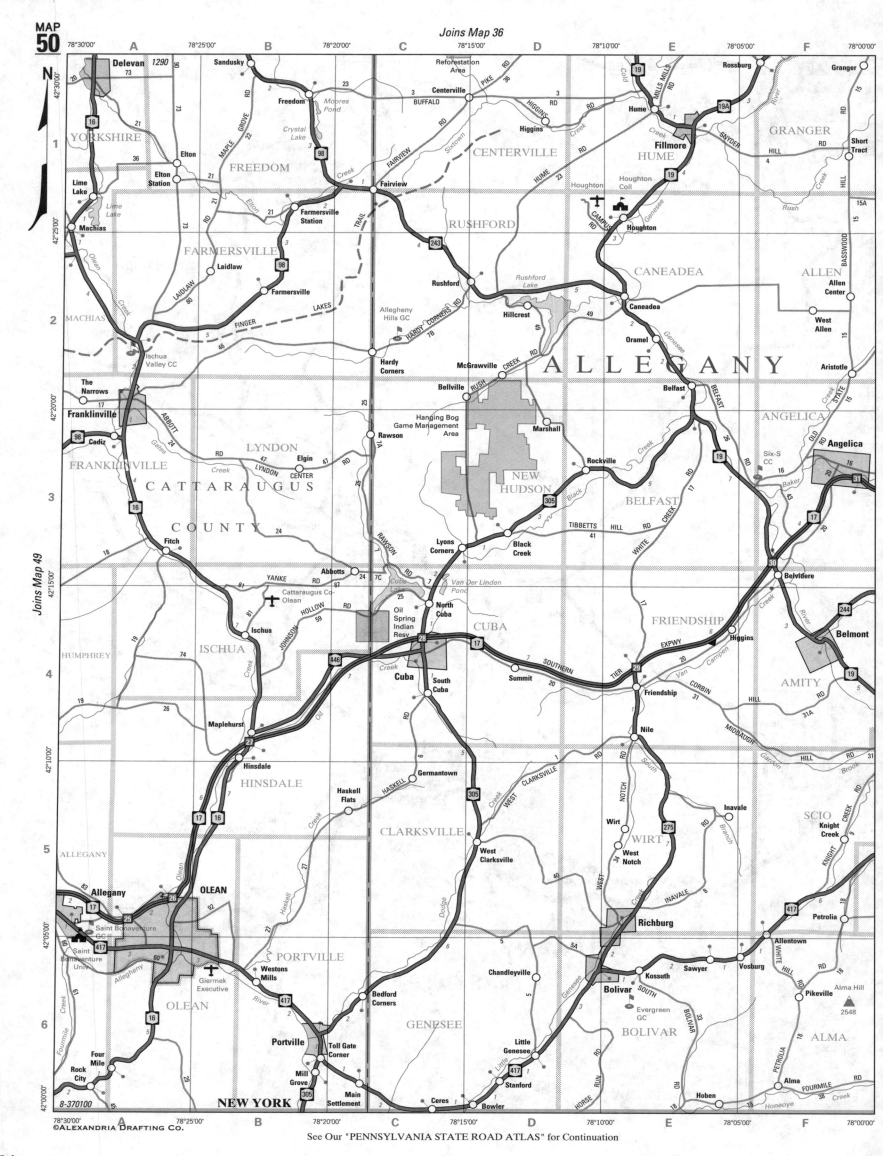

See Our "PENNSYLVANIA STATE ROAD ATLAS" for Continuation

MAP
51

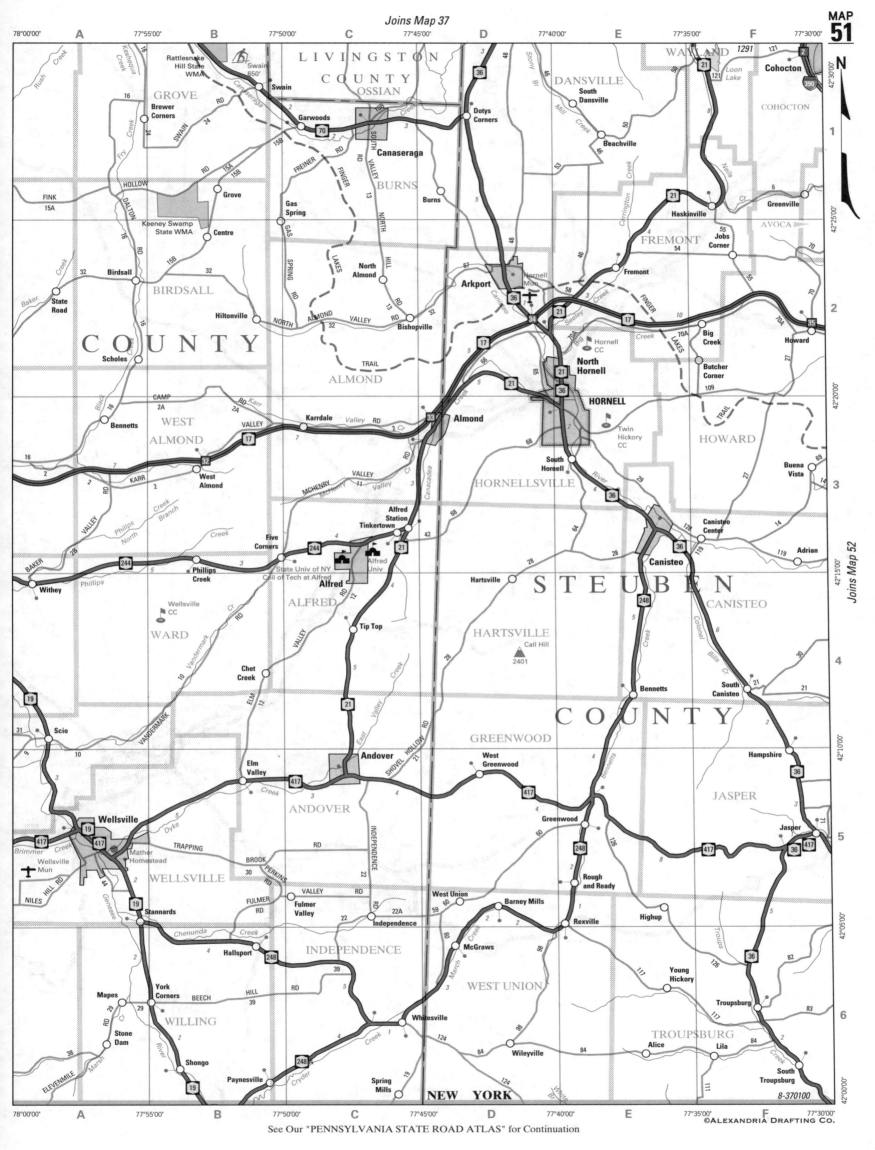

MAP
52

Joins Map 38

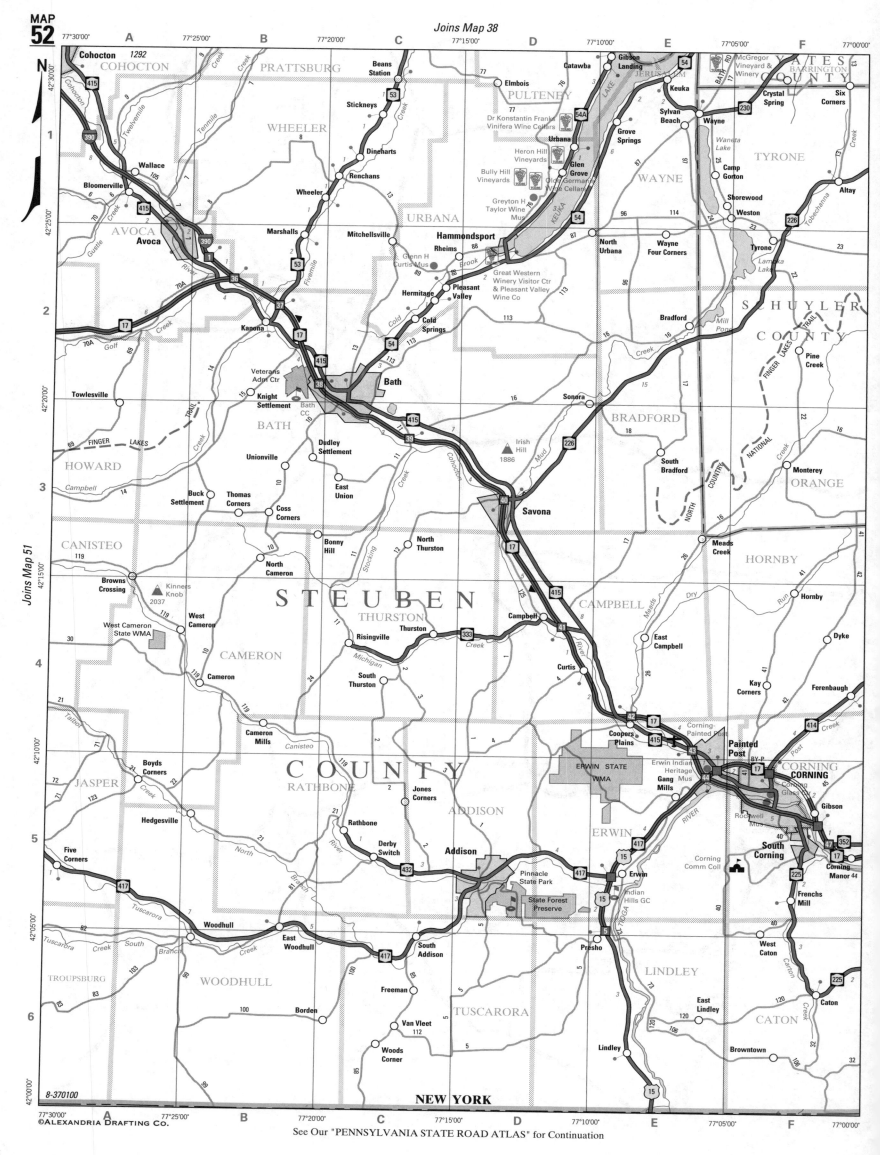

©ALEXANDRIA DRAFTING CO.

NEW YORK

See Our "PENNSYLVANIA STATE ROAD ATLAS" for Continuation

MAP
53

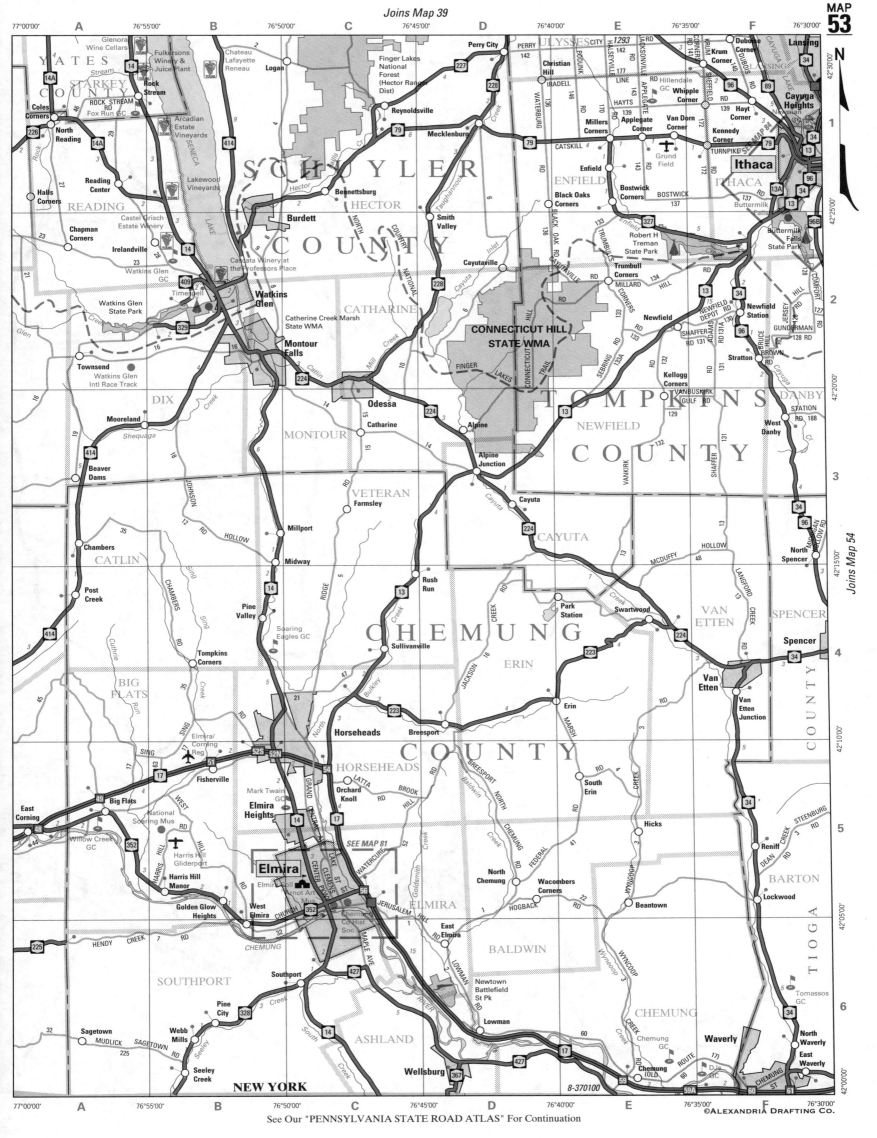

MAP
54
Joins Map 40

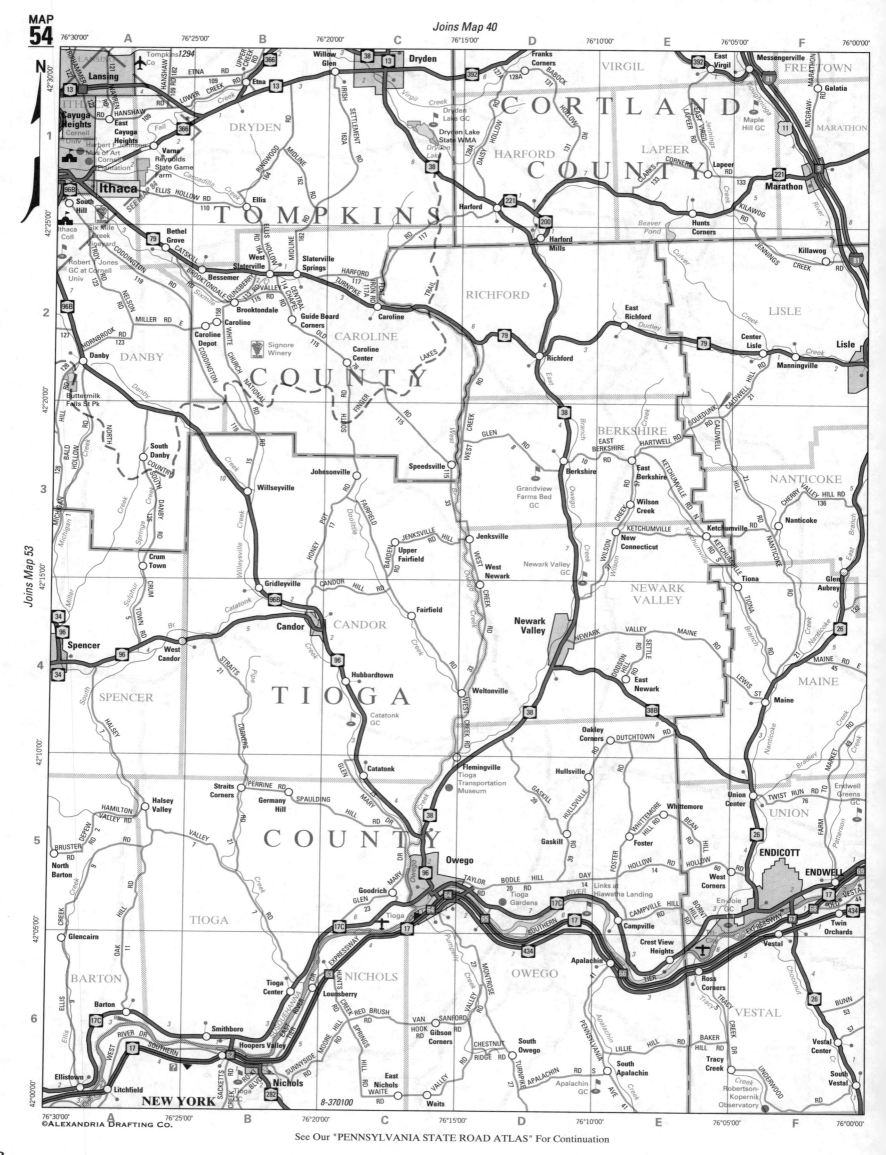

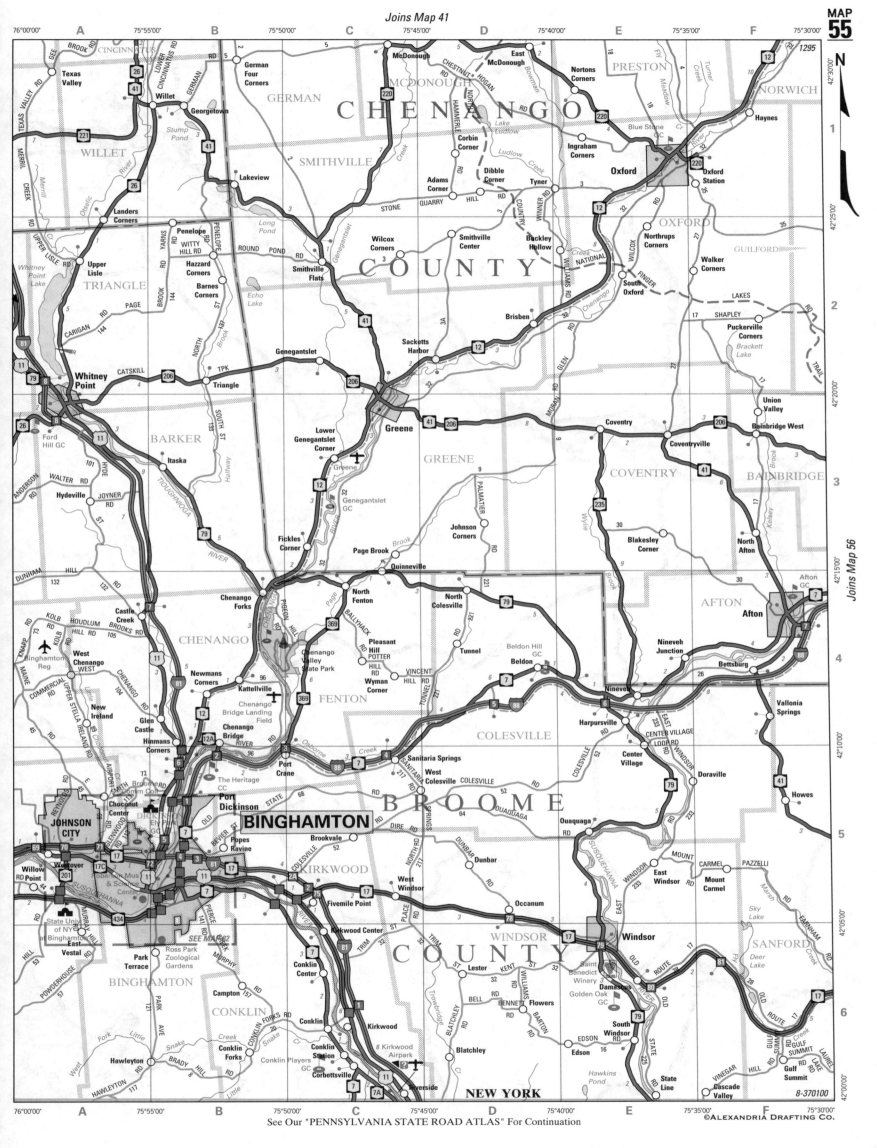

MAP 56

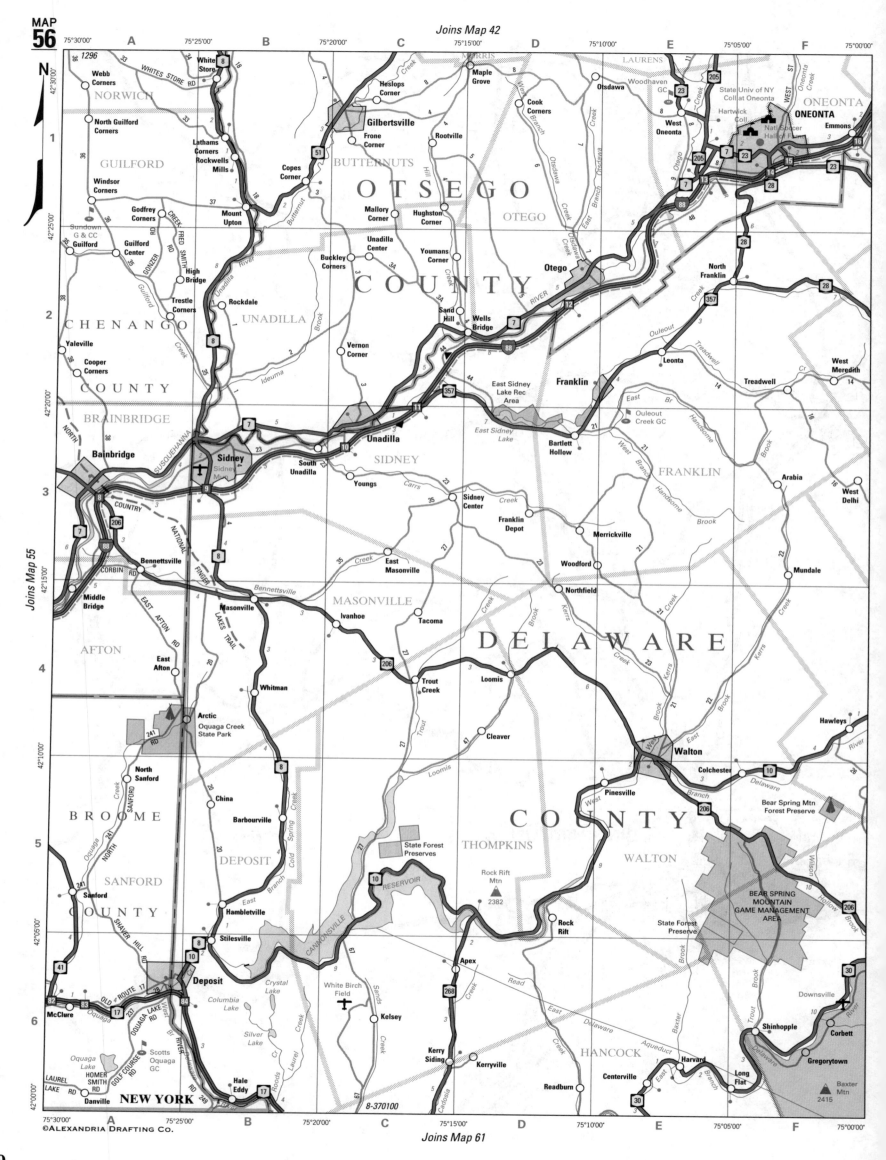

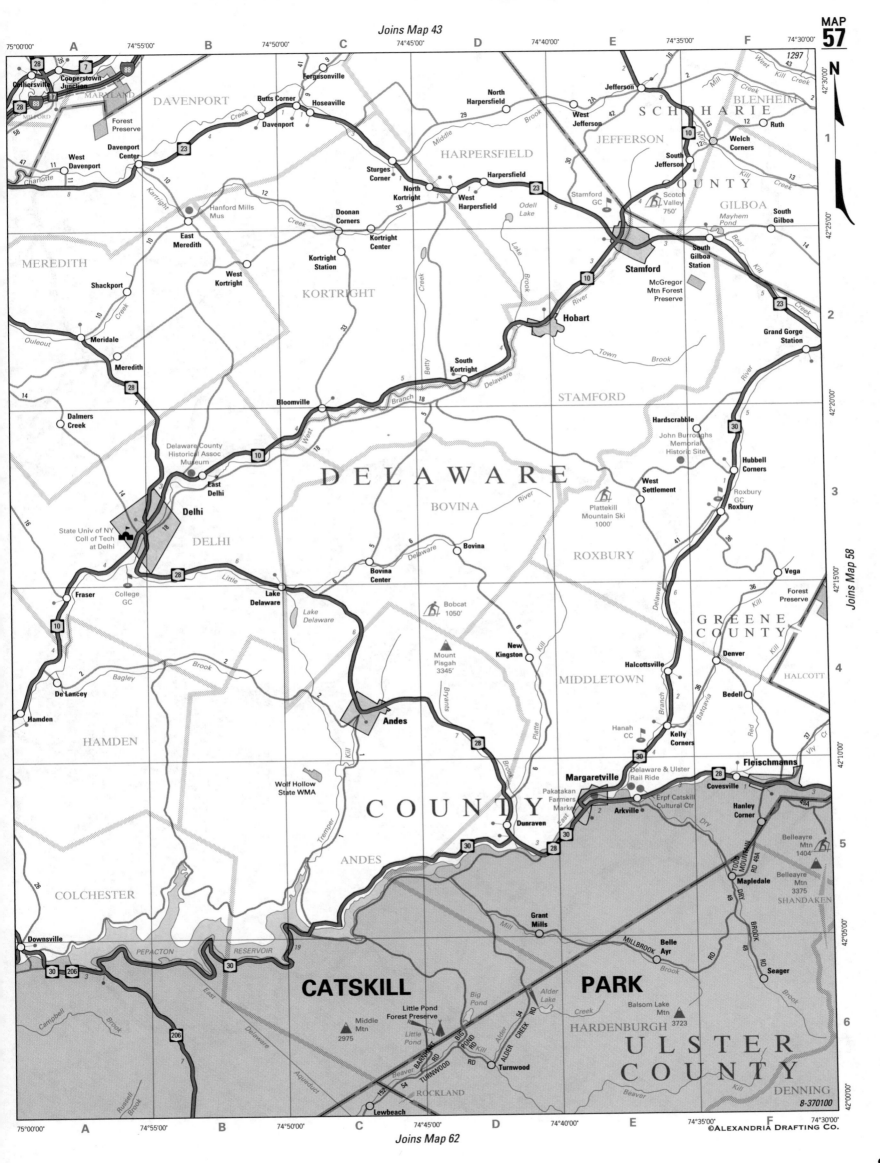

MAP
58
Joins Map 44

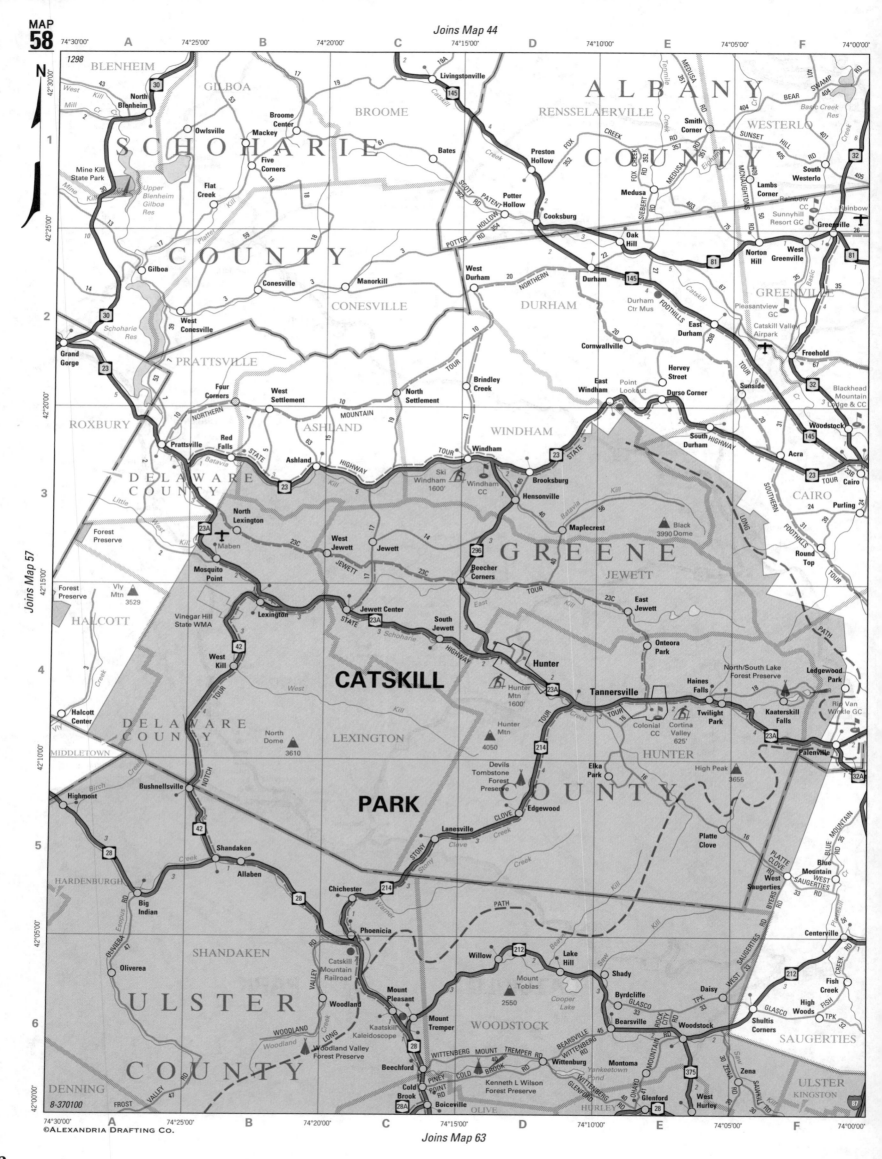

MAP
59

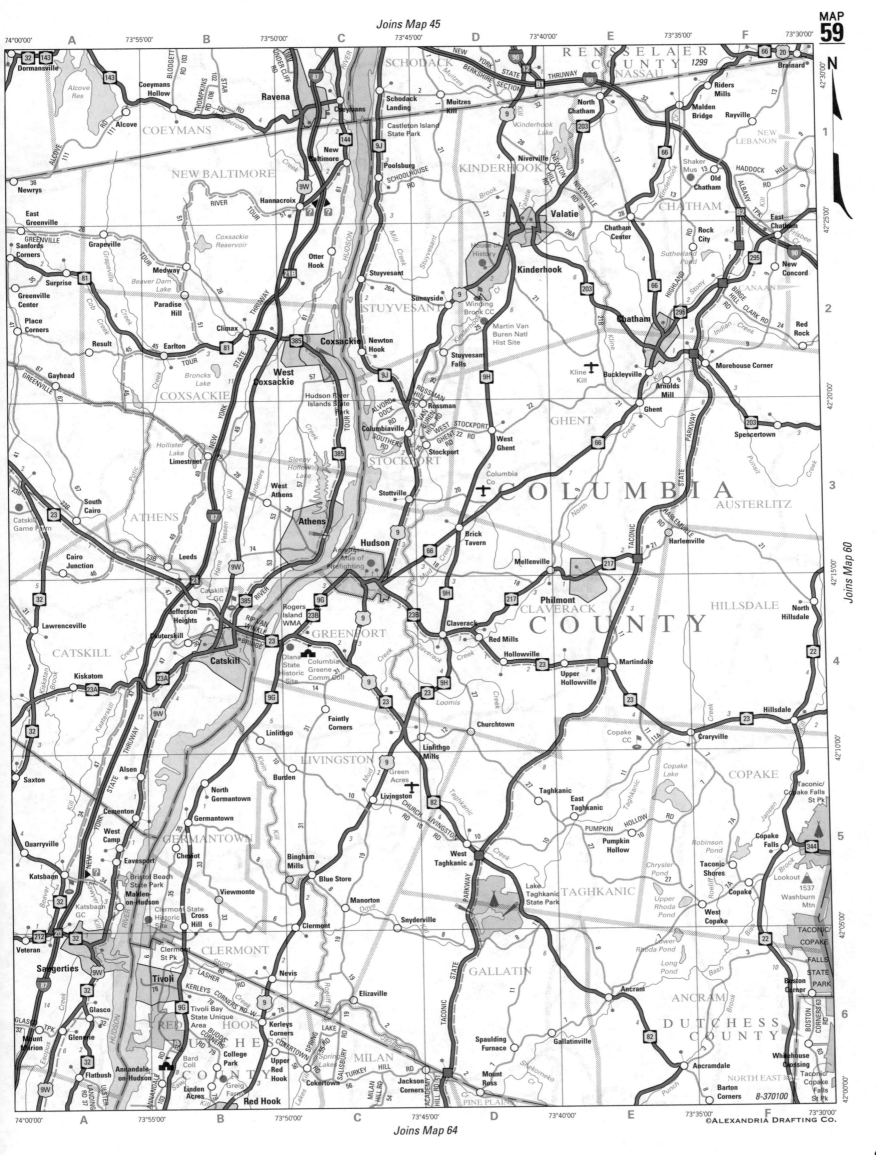

©ALEXANDRIA DRAFTING CO.

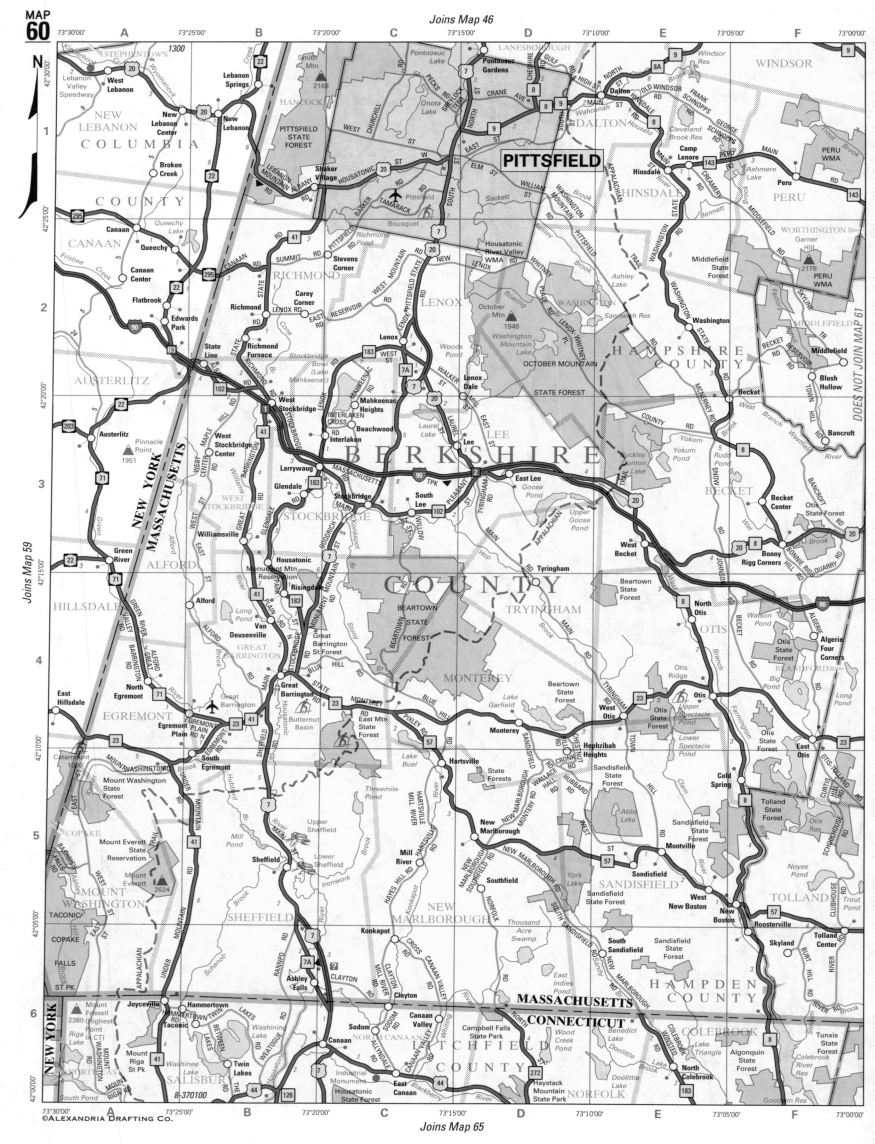

MAP
60
N

©Alexandria Drafting Co.

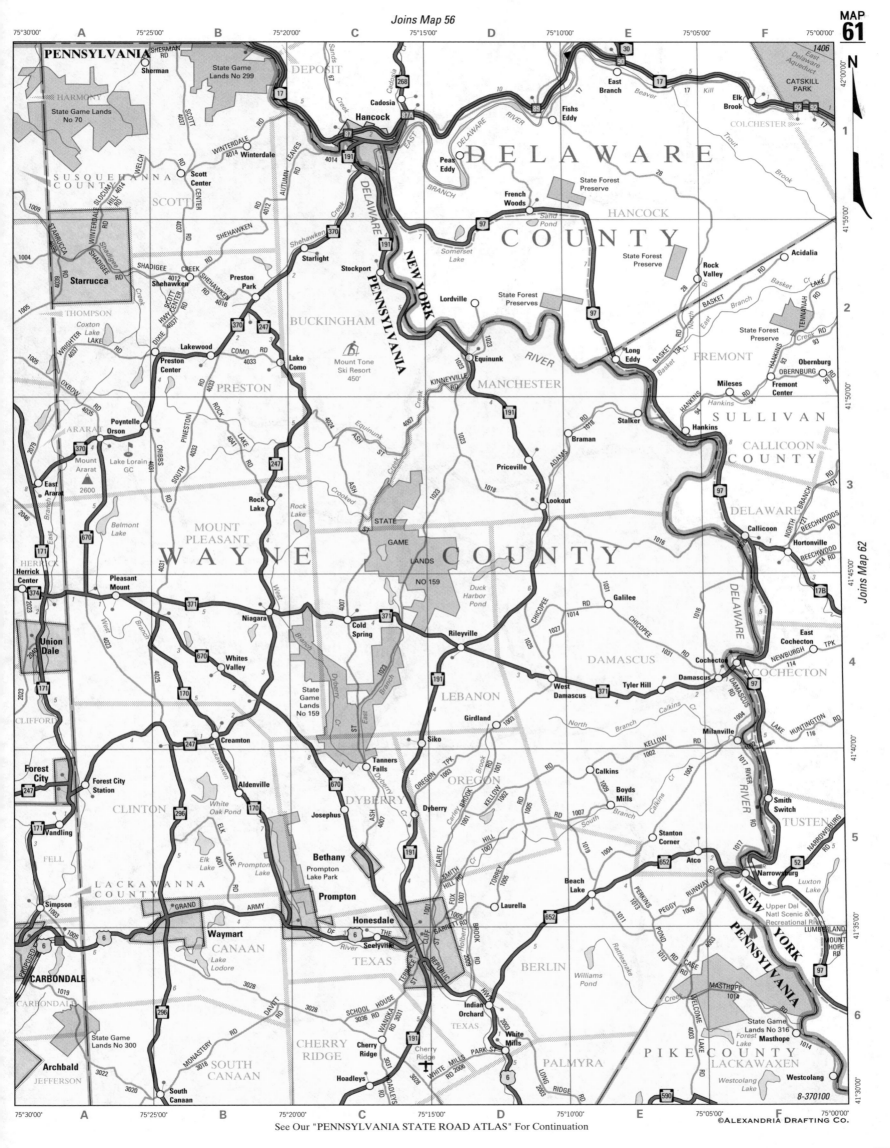

MAP
62
Joins Map 57

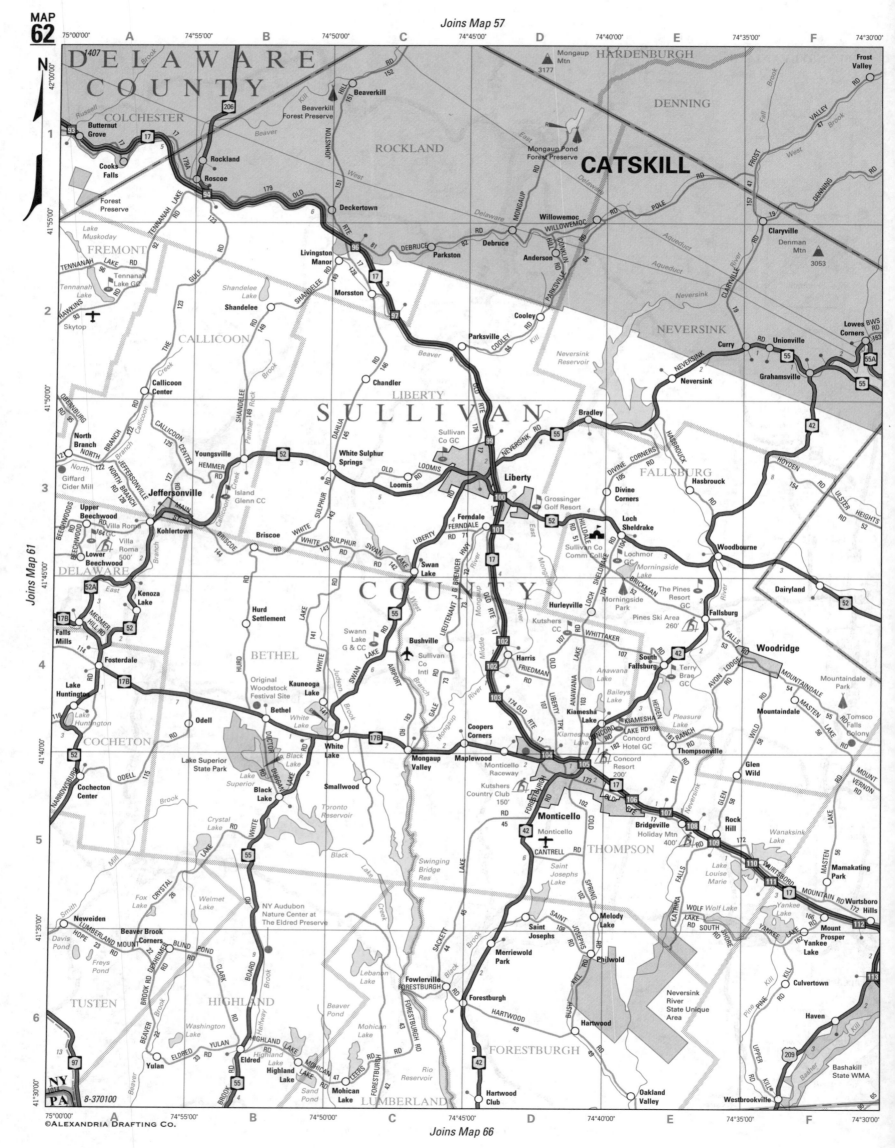

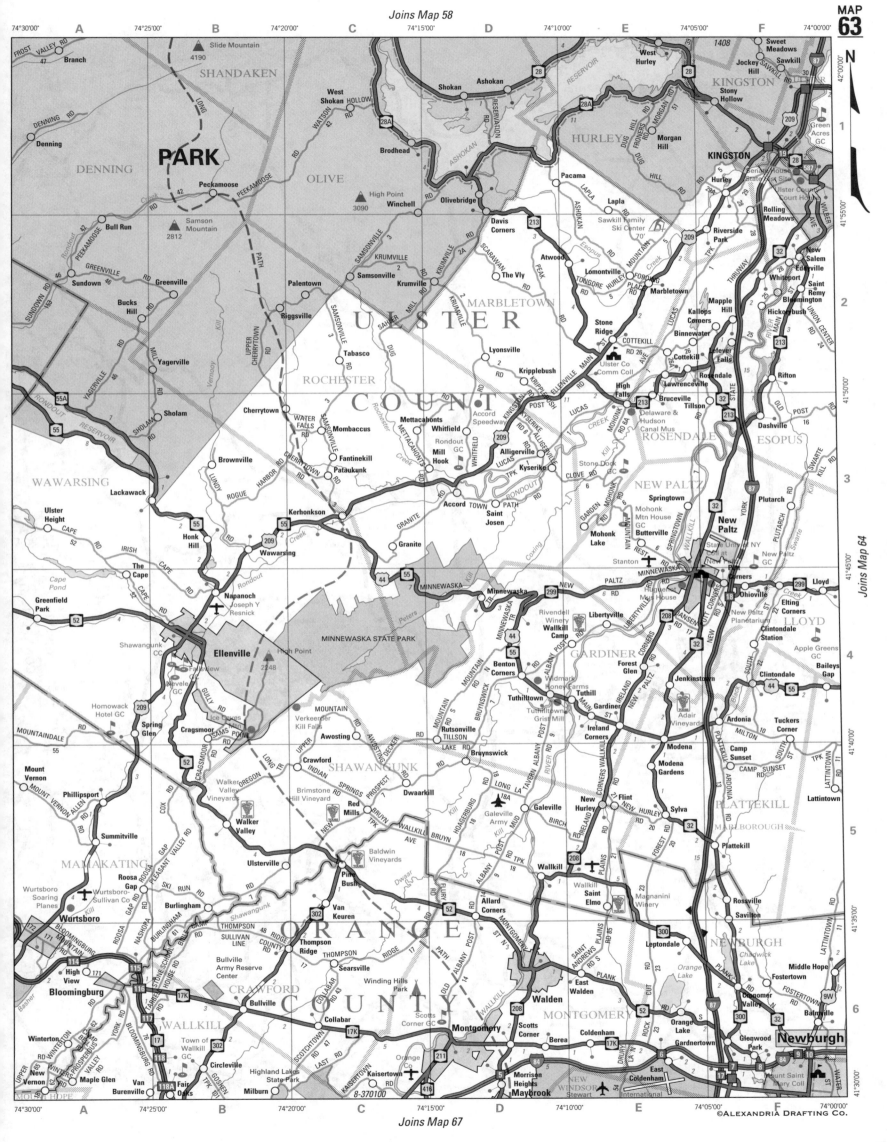

MAP
64
N
Joins Map 59

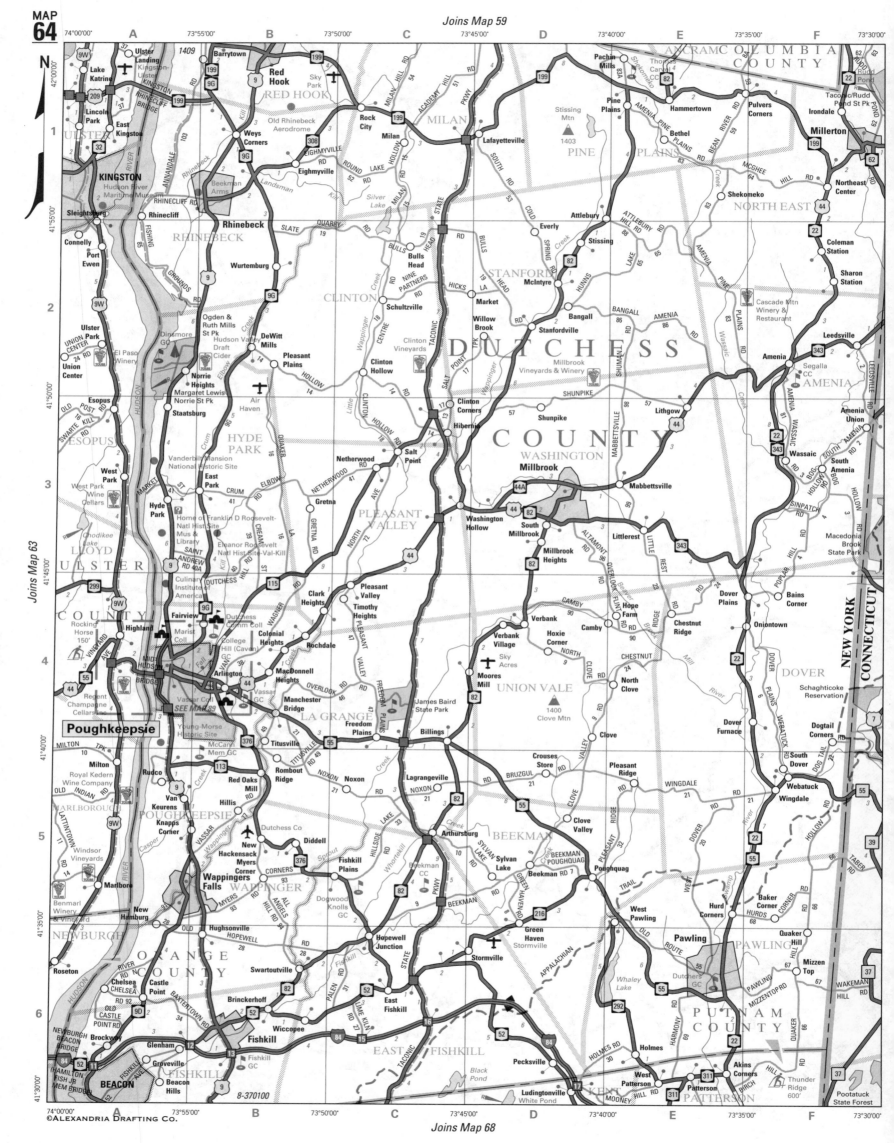

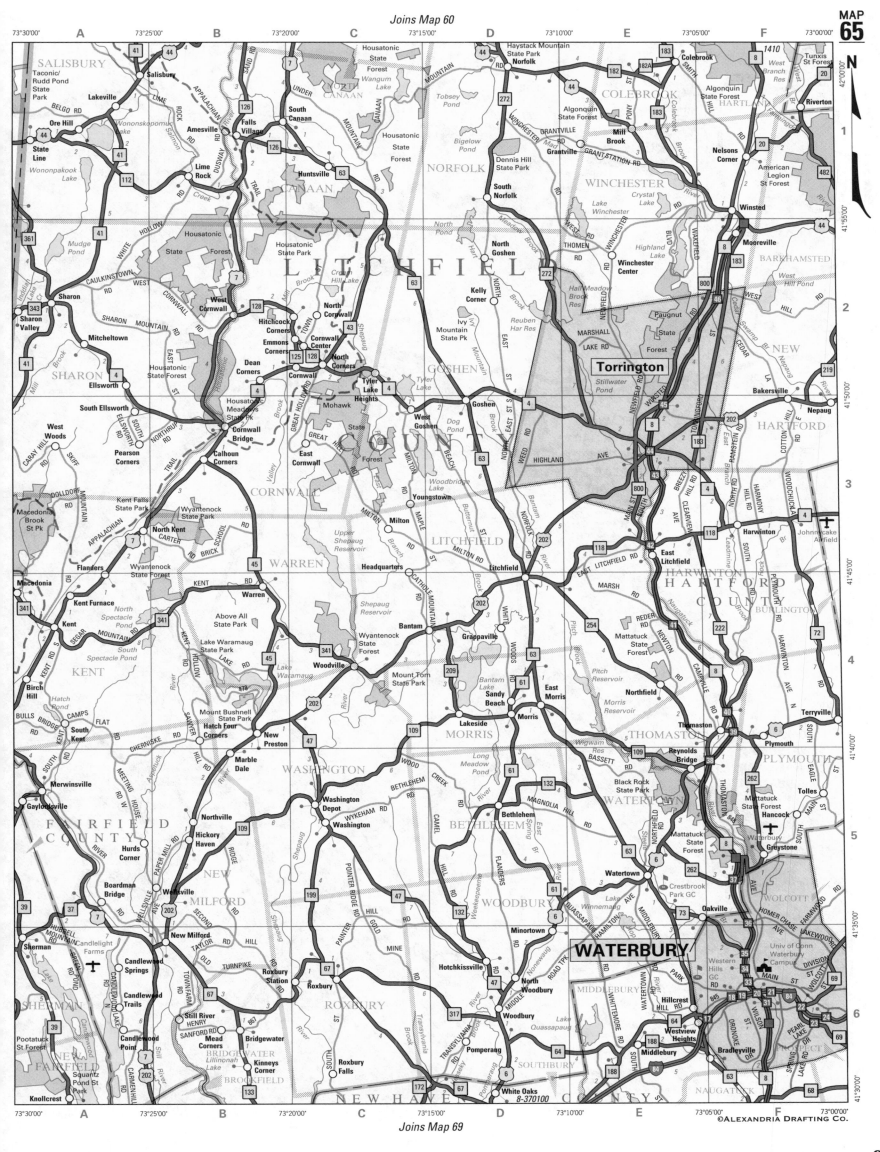

MAP
66
N
Joins Map 62

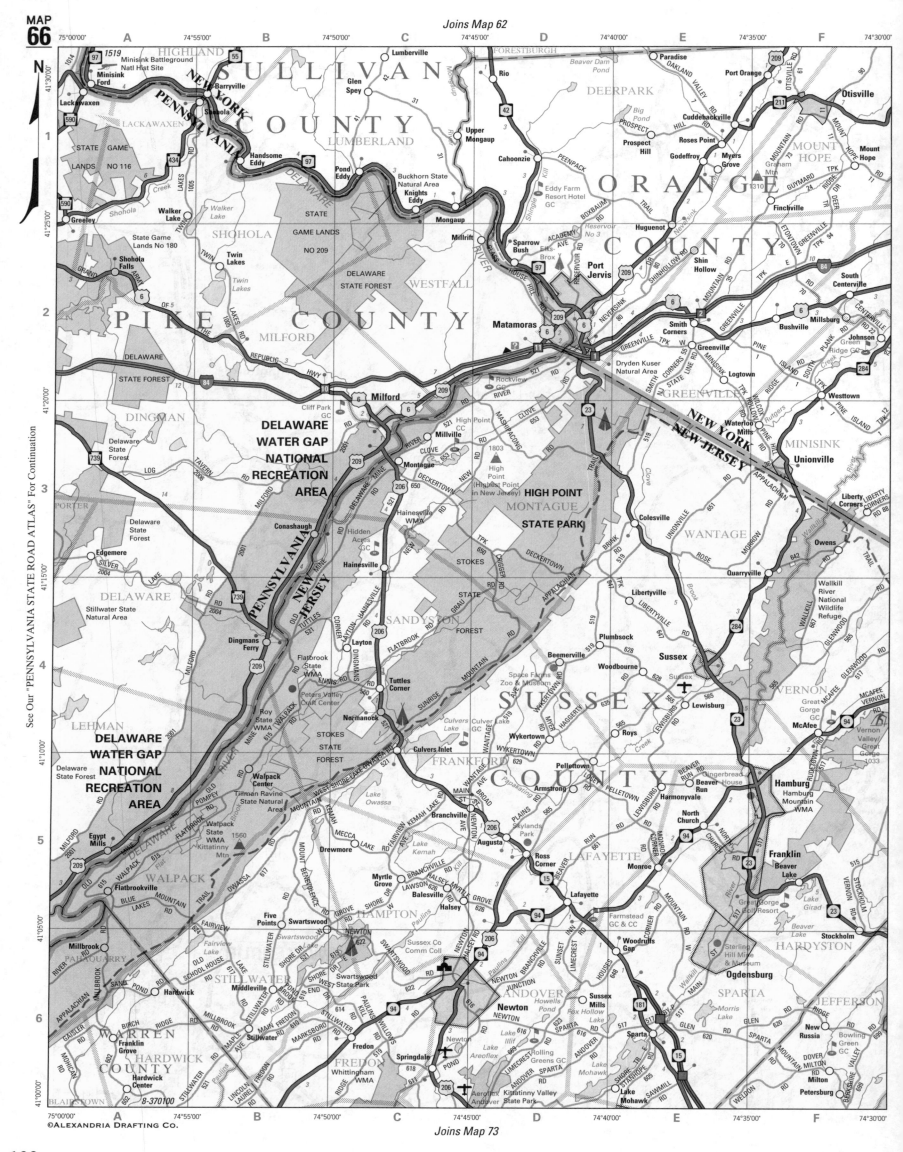

See Our "PENNSYLVANIA STATE ROAD ATLAS" For Continuation

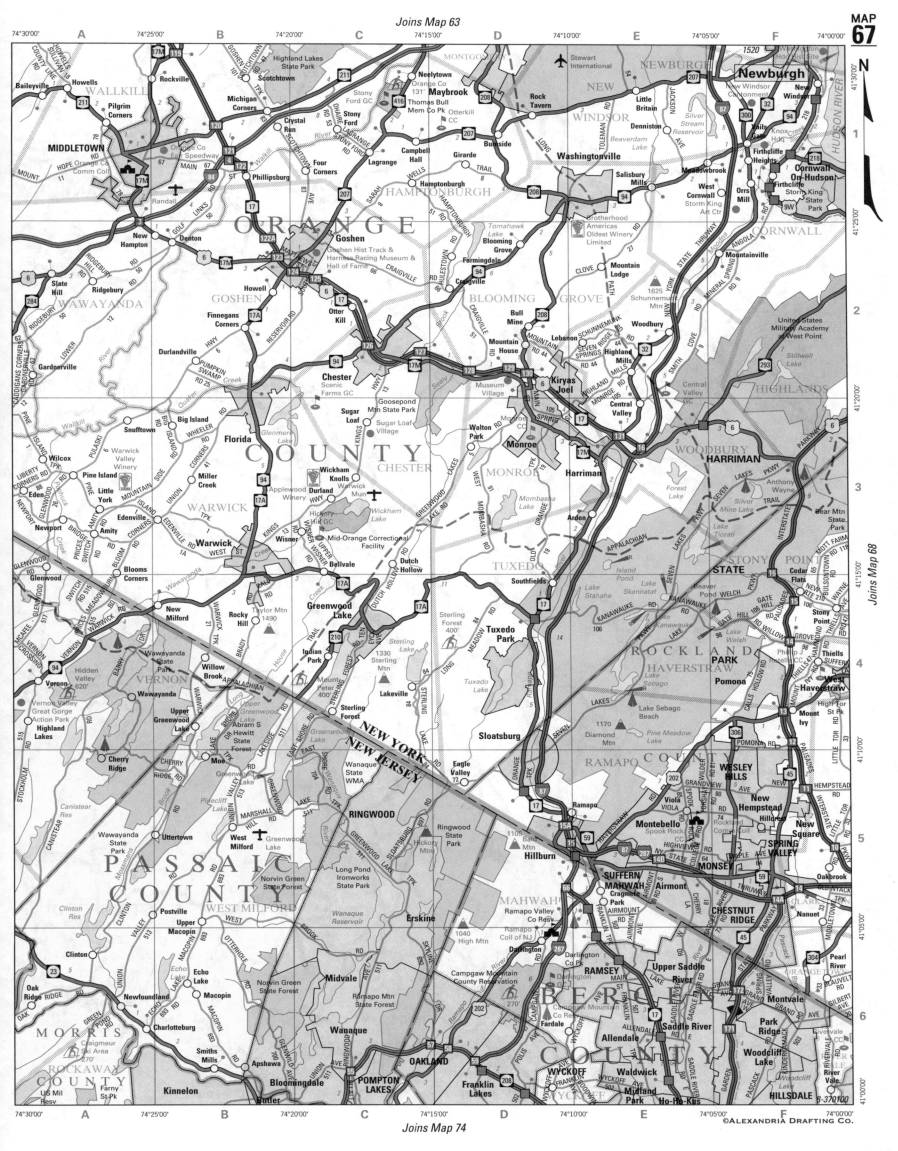

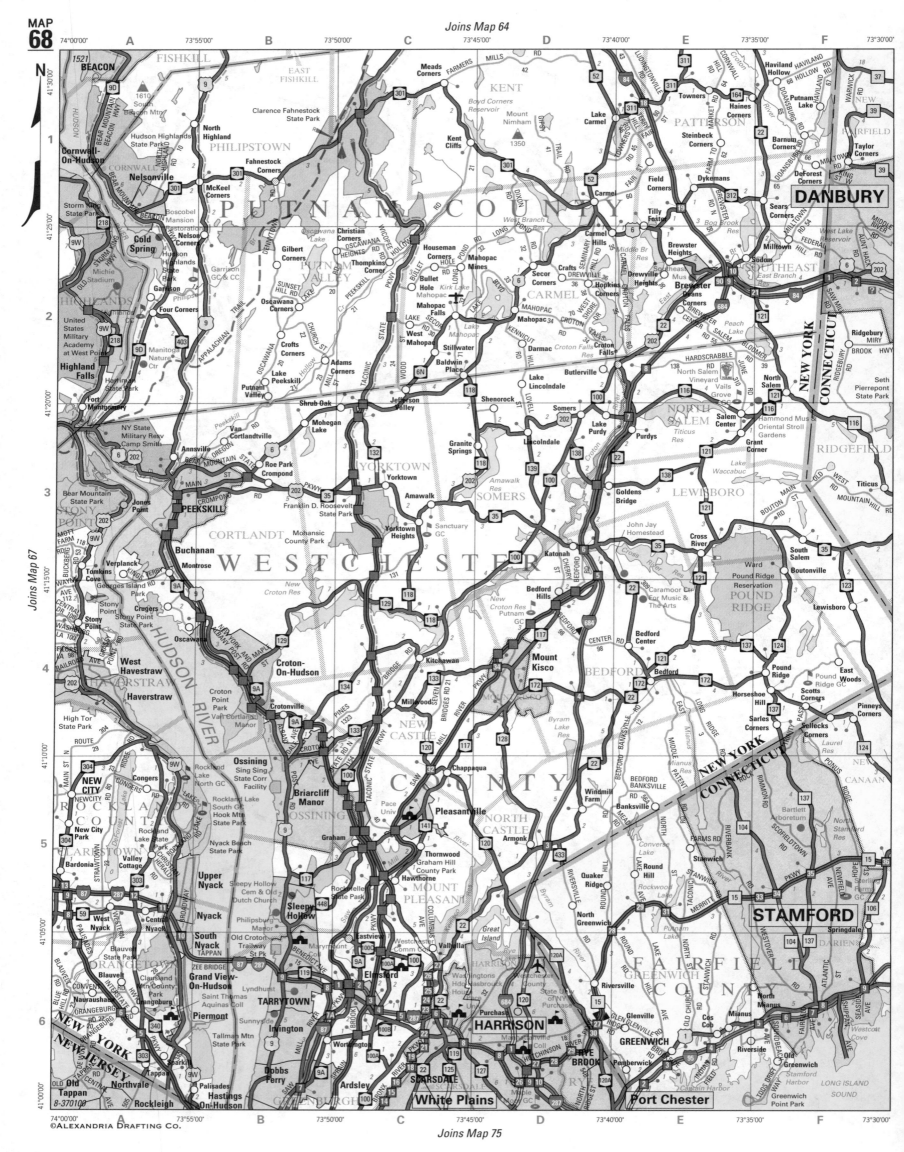

MAP
68

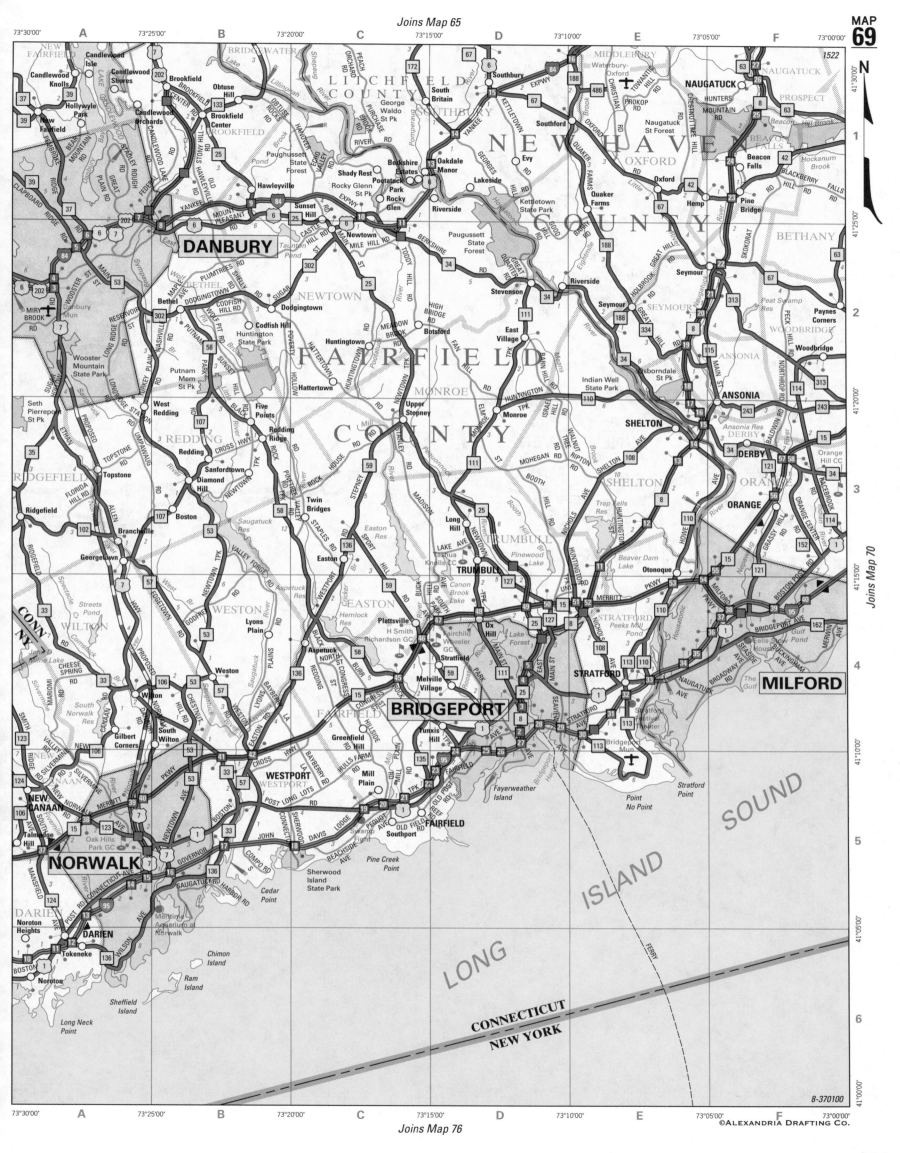

MAP
70

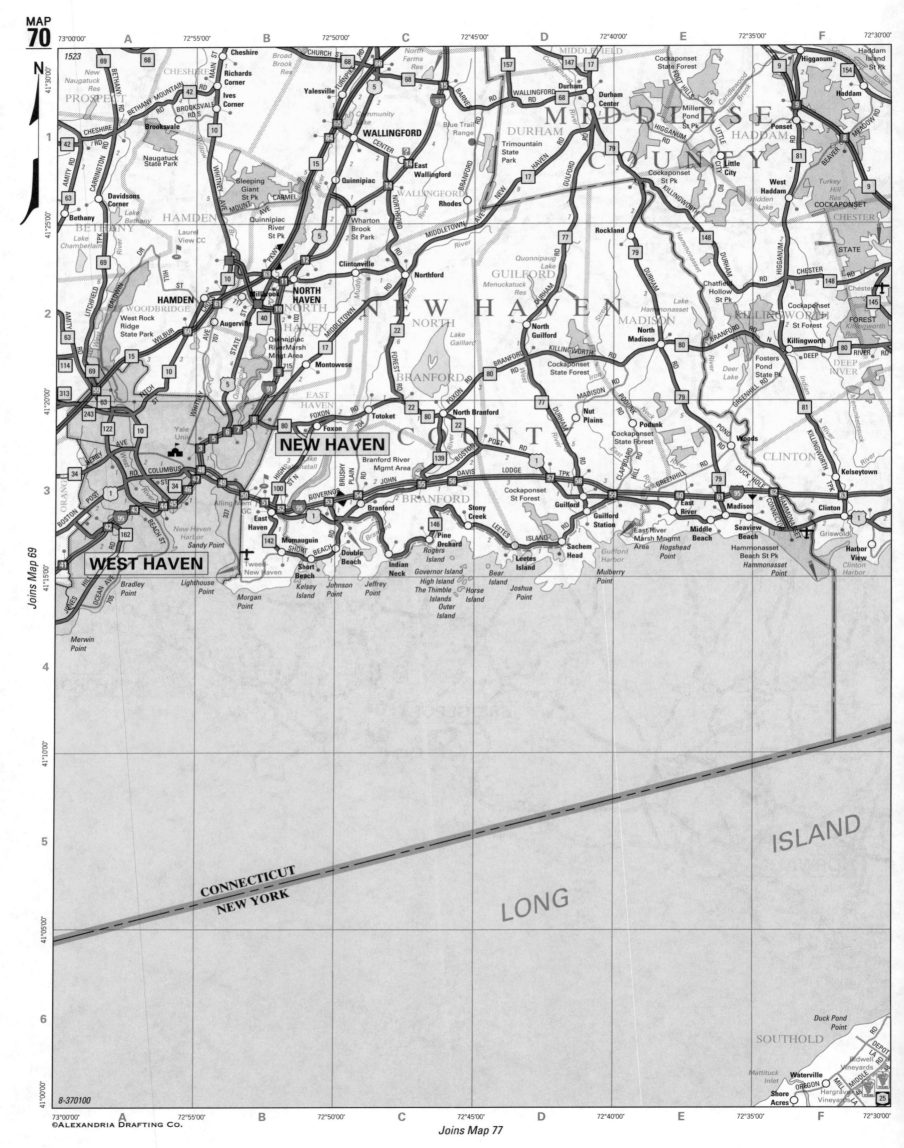

MAP
71

N

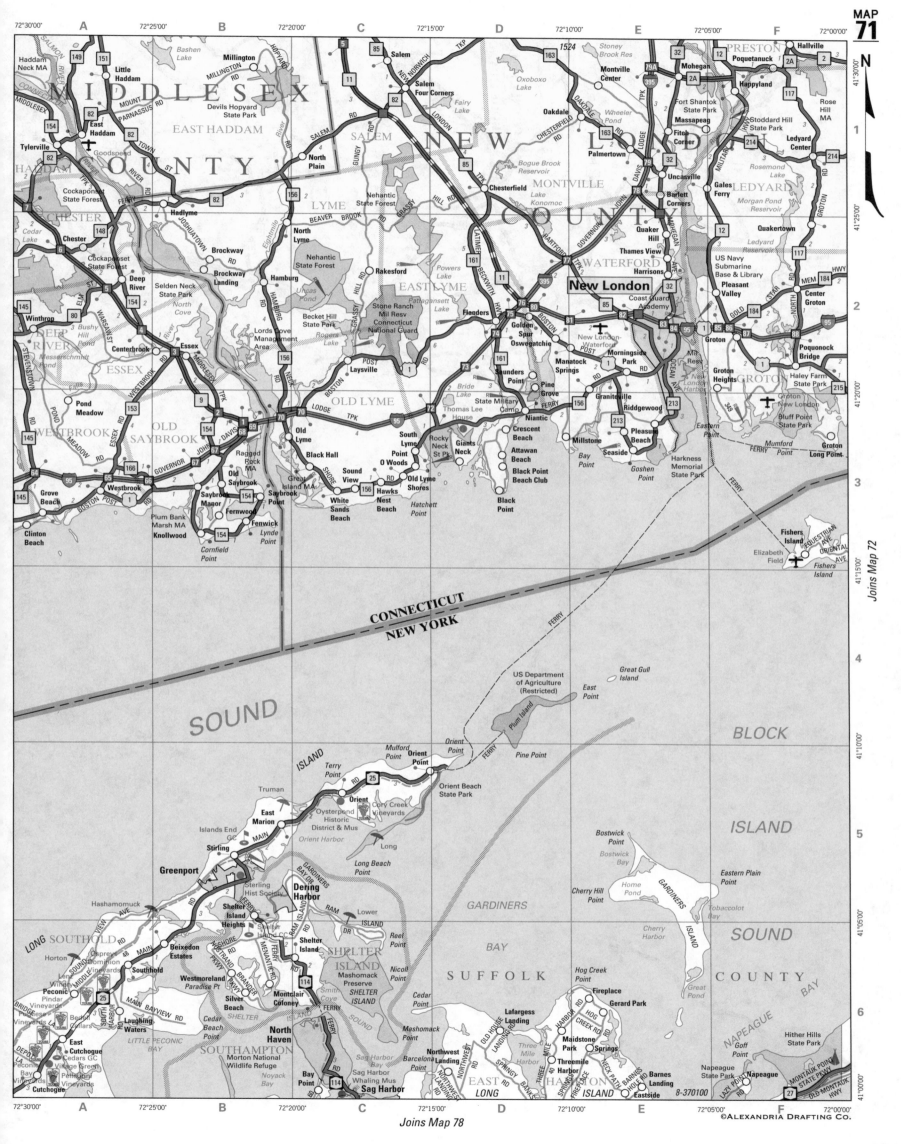

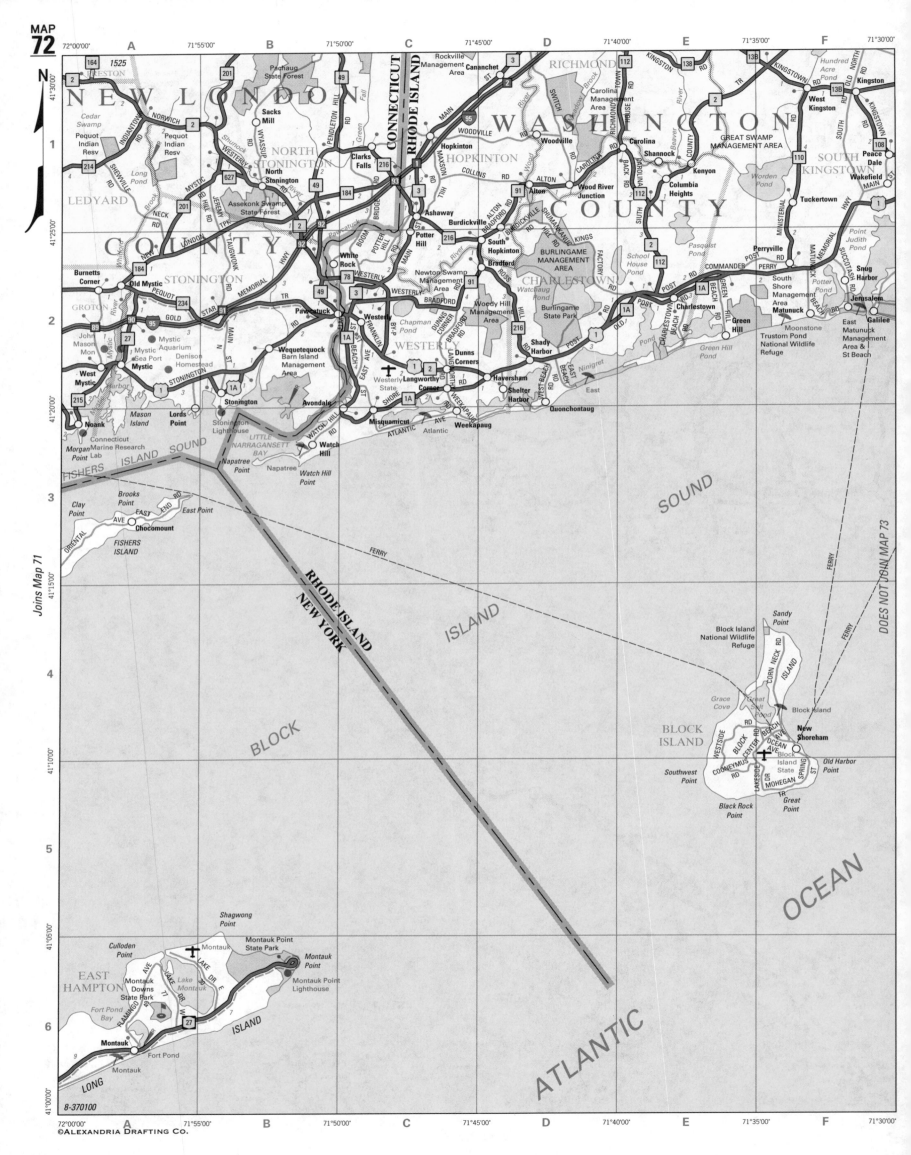

MAP
72

©Alexandria Drafting Co.

8-370100

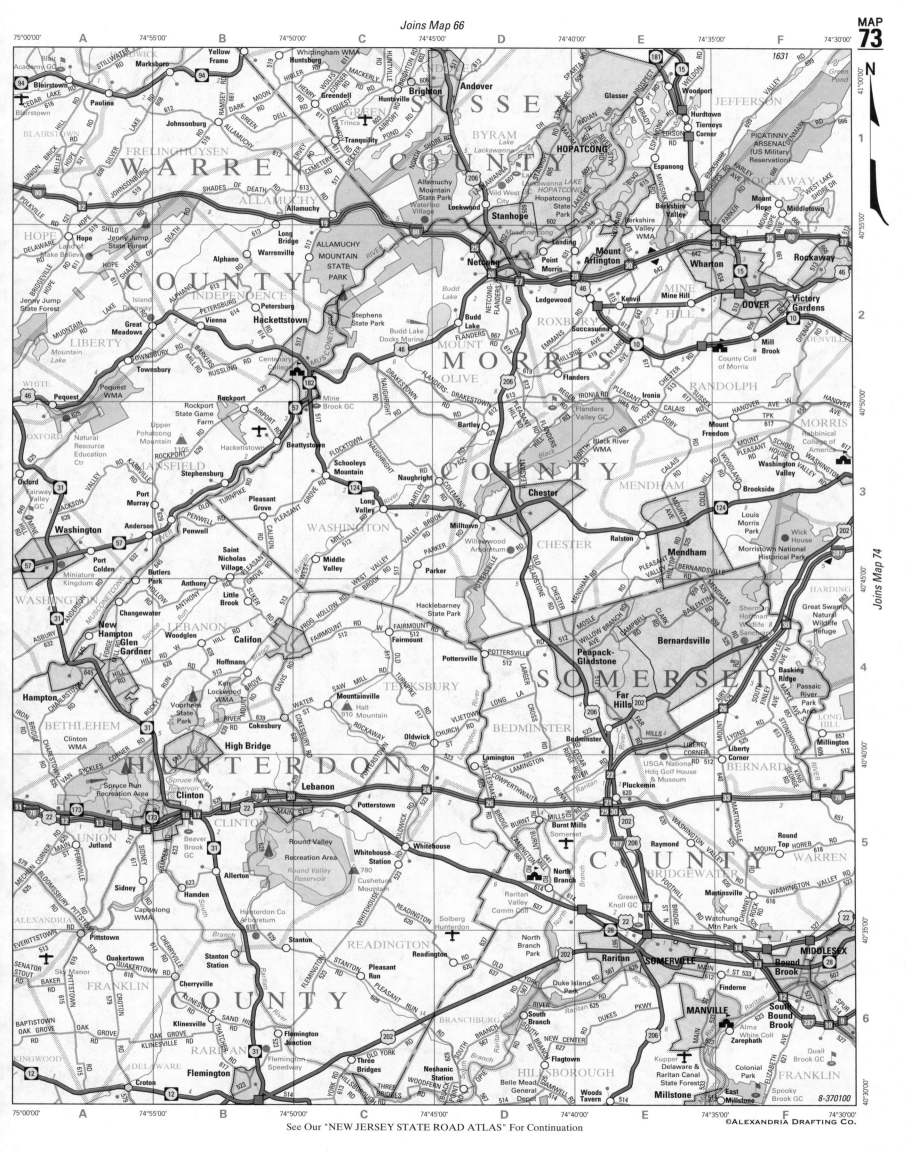

MAP 74

Joins Map 67

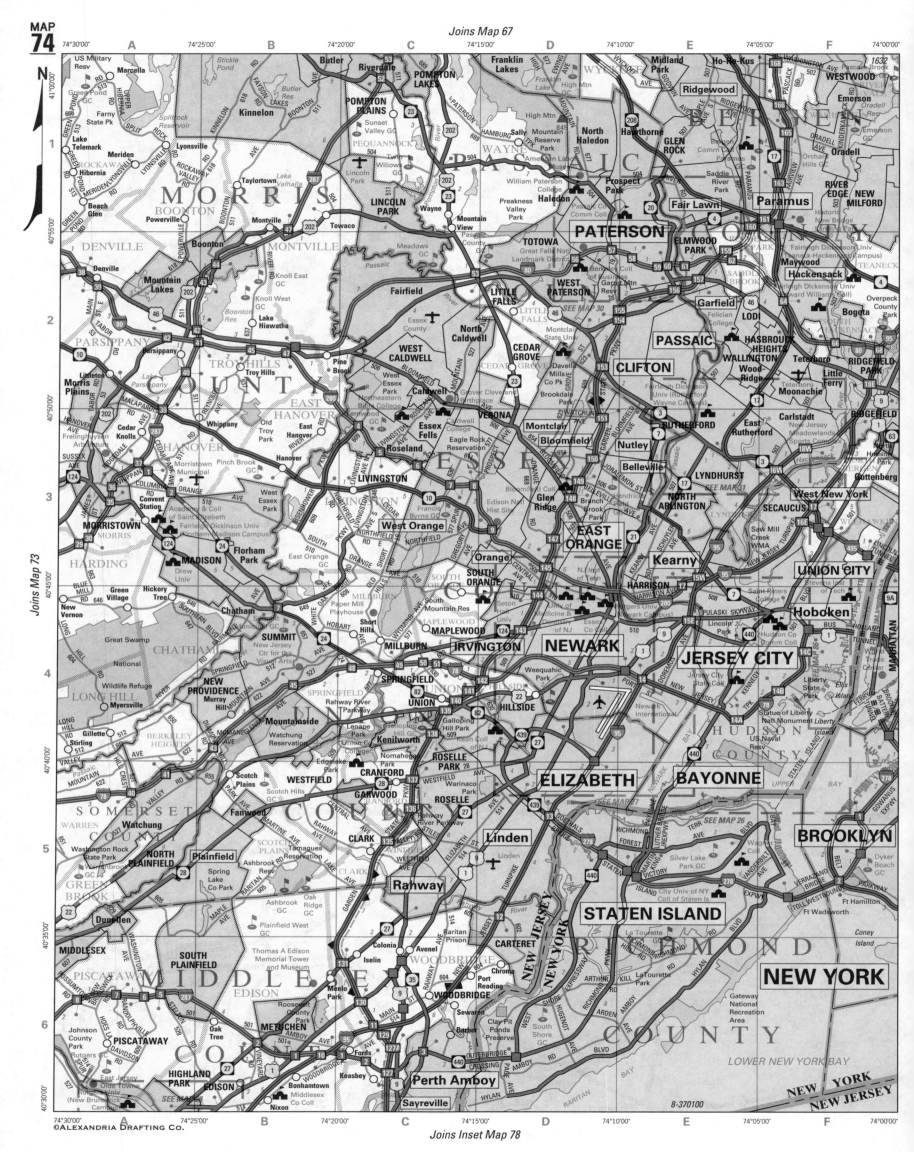

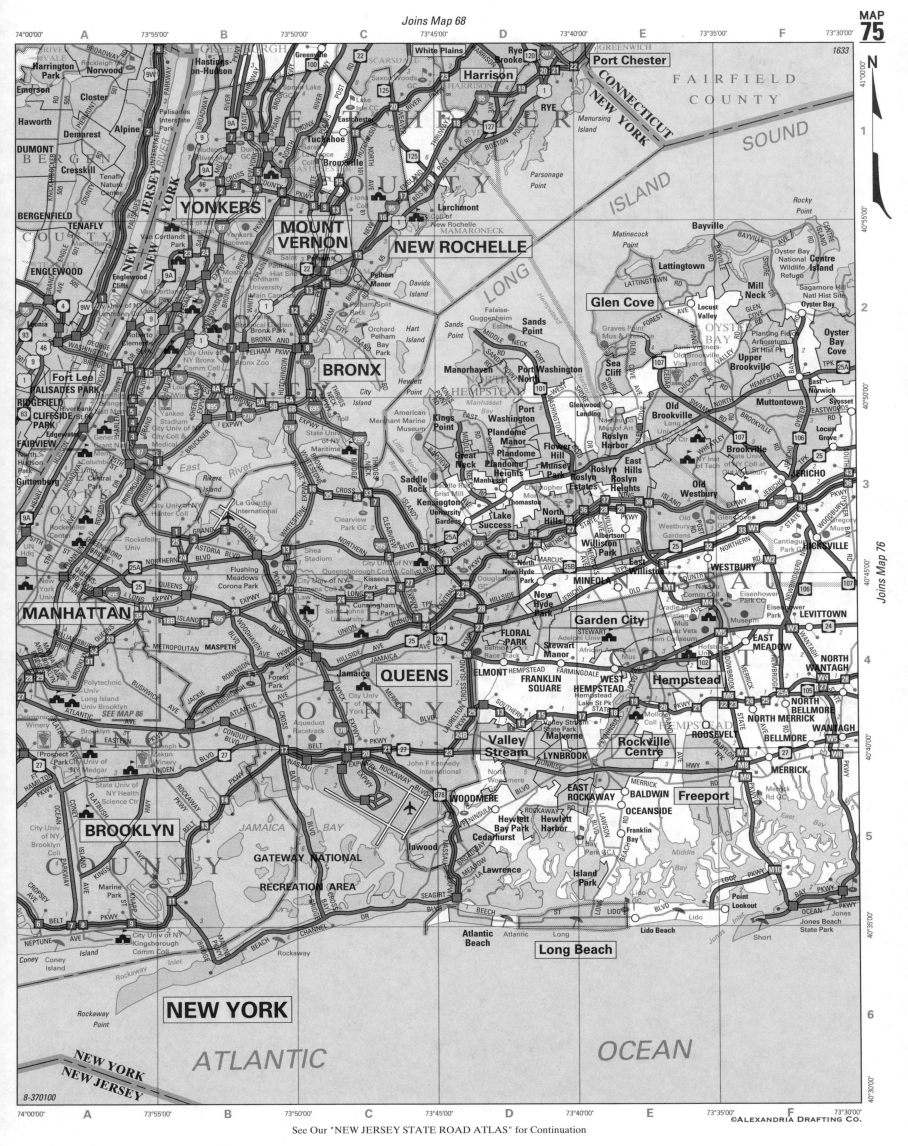

©Alexandria Drafting Co.

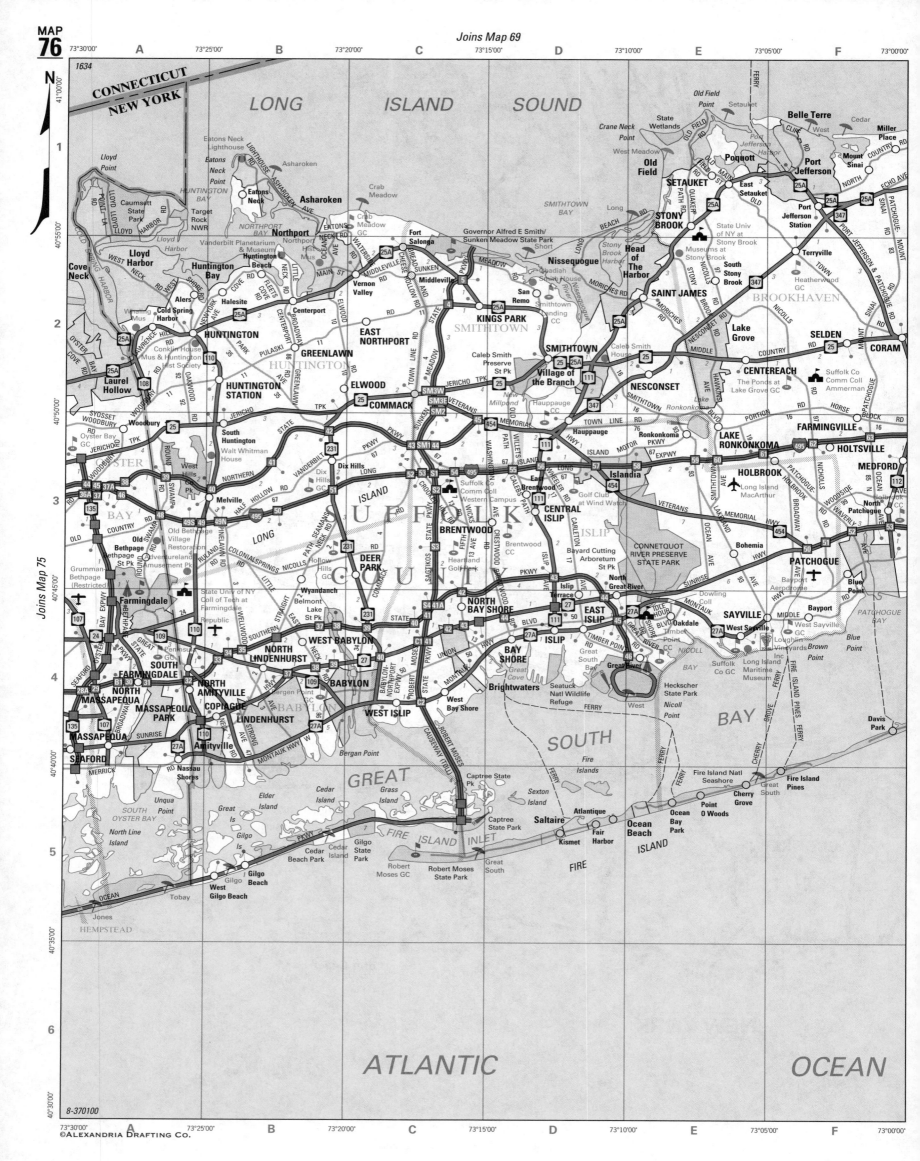

MAP
76
N
Joins Map 69

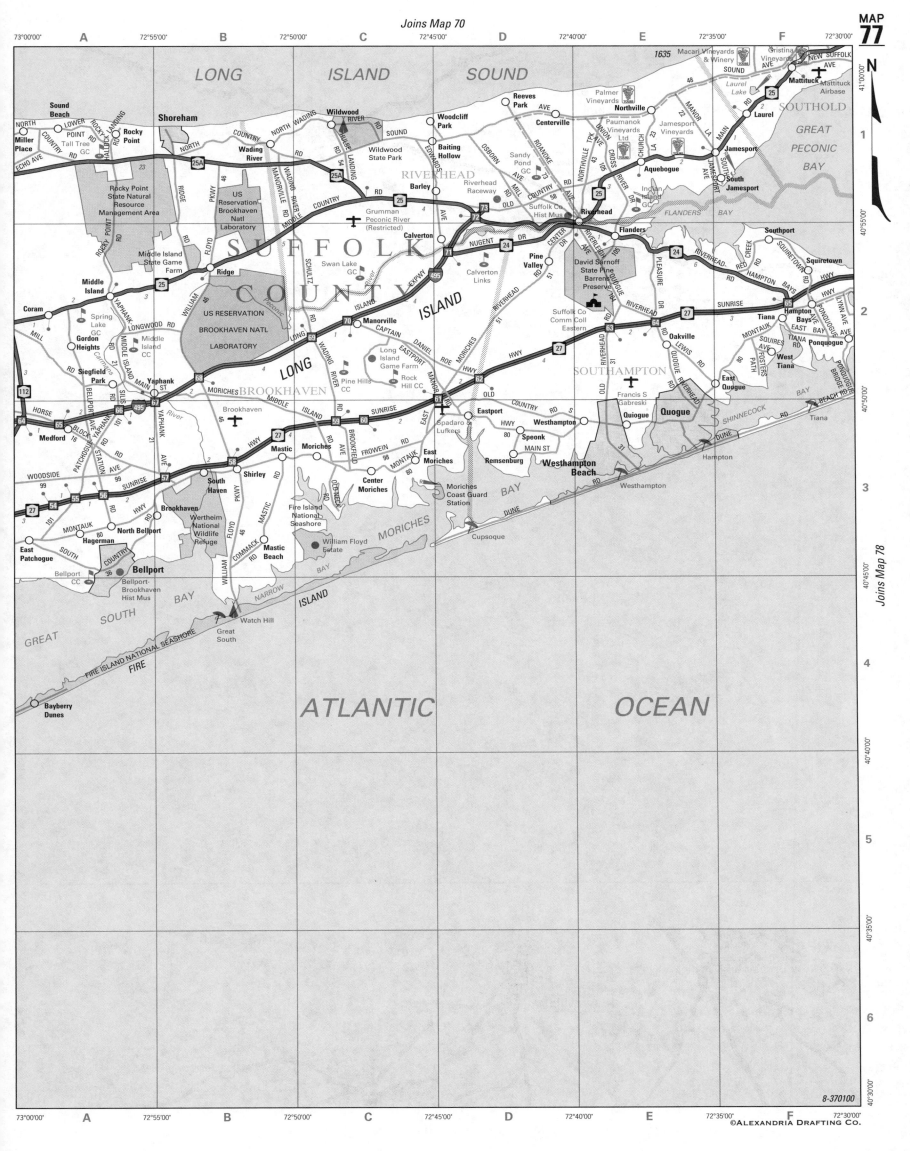

©Alexandria Drafting Co.

MAP
78

Joins Map 71

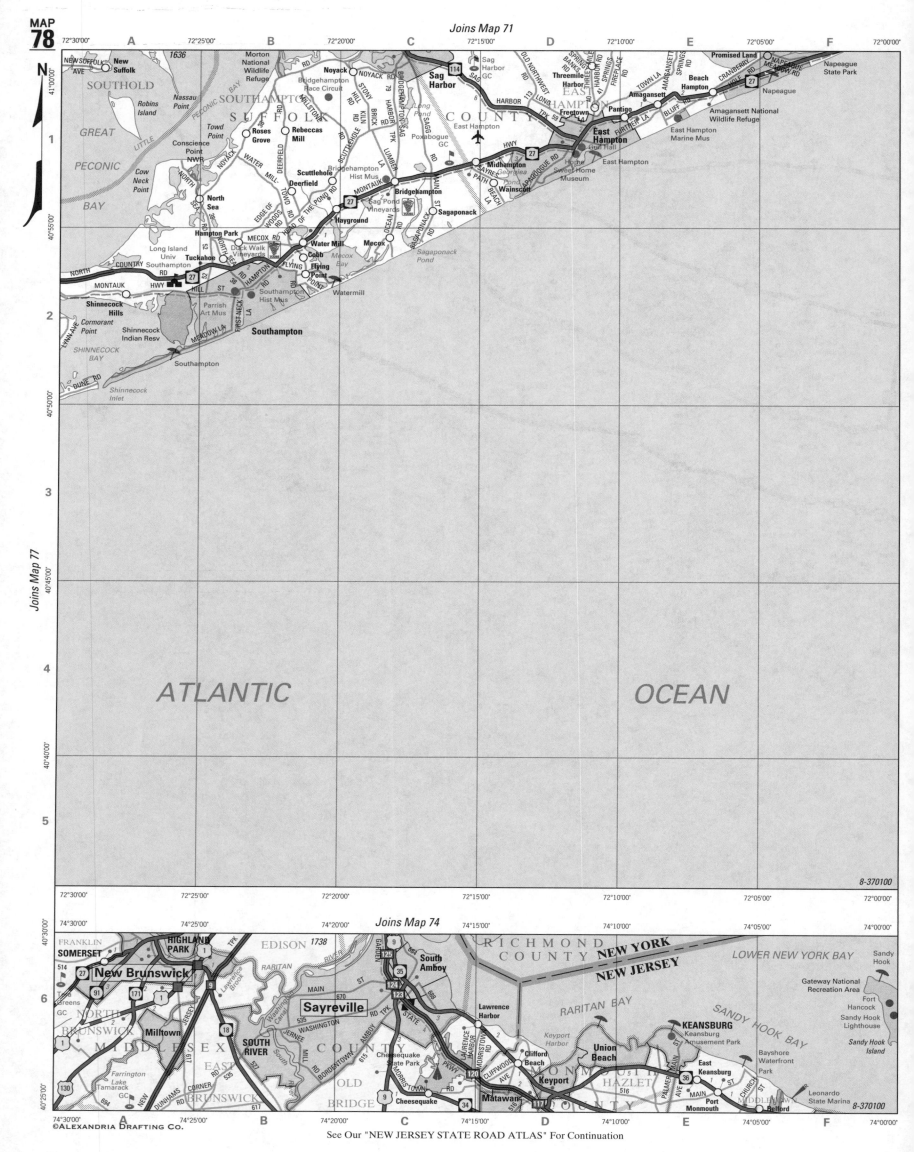

Joins Map 74

Joins Map 77

©ALEXANDRIA DRAFTING CO.

See Our "NEW JERSEY STATE ROAD ATLAS" For Continuation

MAP
79

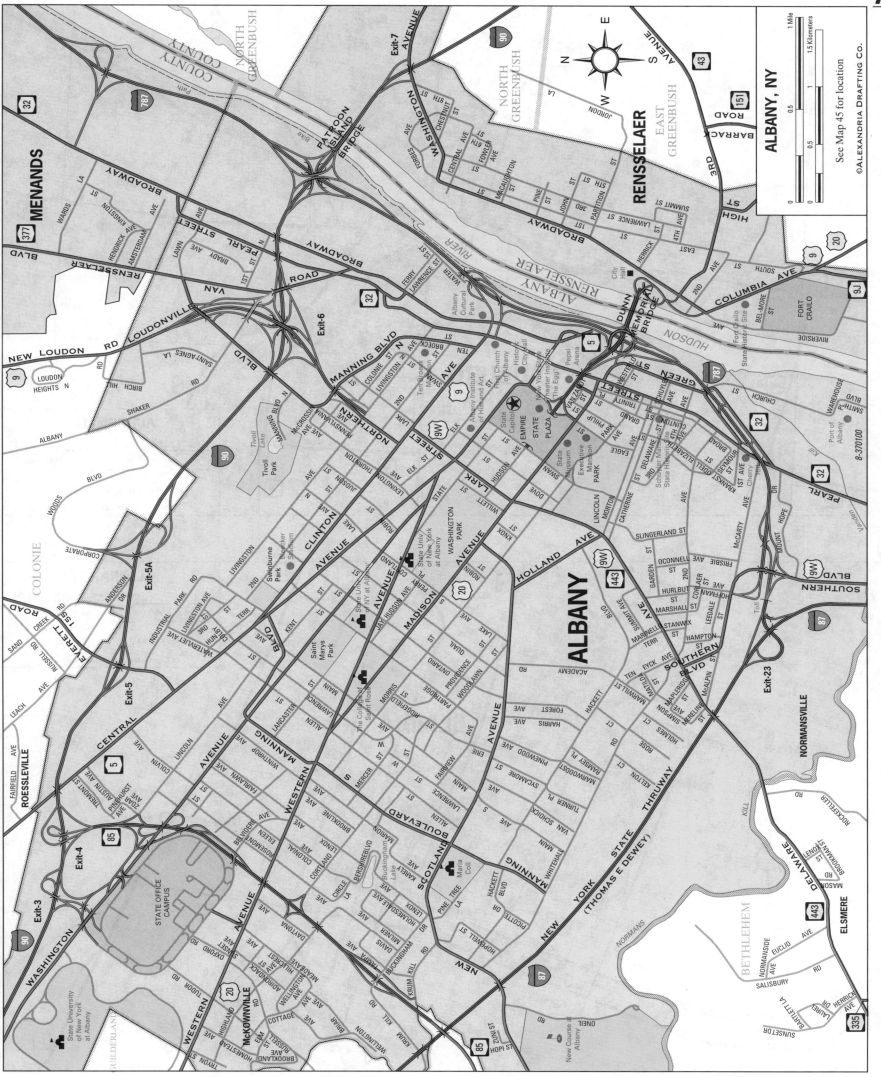

ALBANY, NY

See Map 45 for location

©ALEXANDRIA DRAFTING CO.

MAP 80

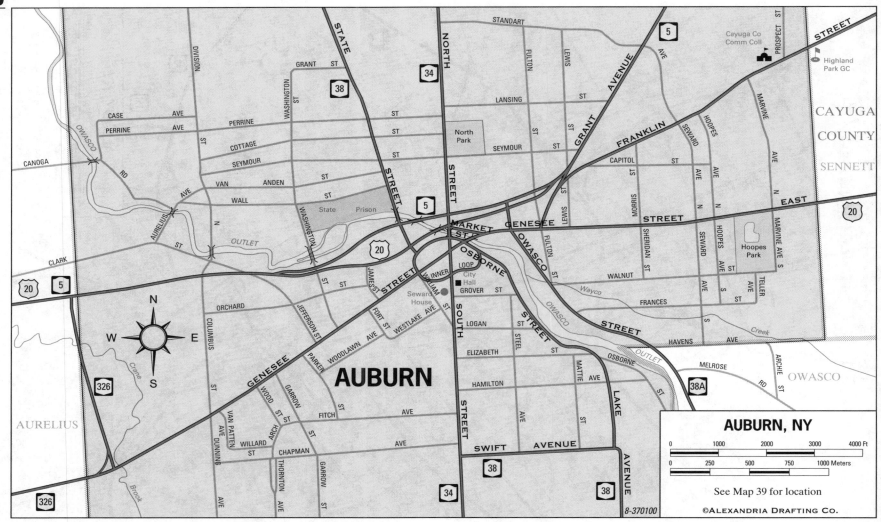

AUBURN, NY

| 0 | 1000 | 2000 | 3000 | 4000 Ft |

| 0 | 250 | 500 | 750 | 1000 Meters |

See Map 39 for location

©Alexandria Drafting Co.

8-370100

MAP 81

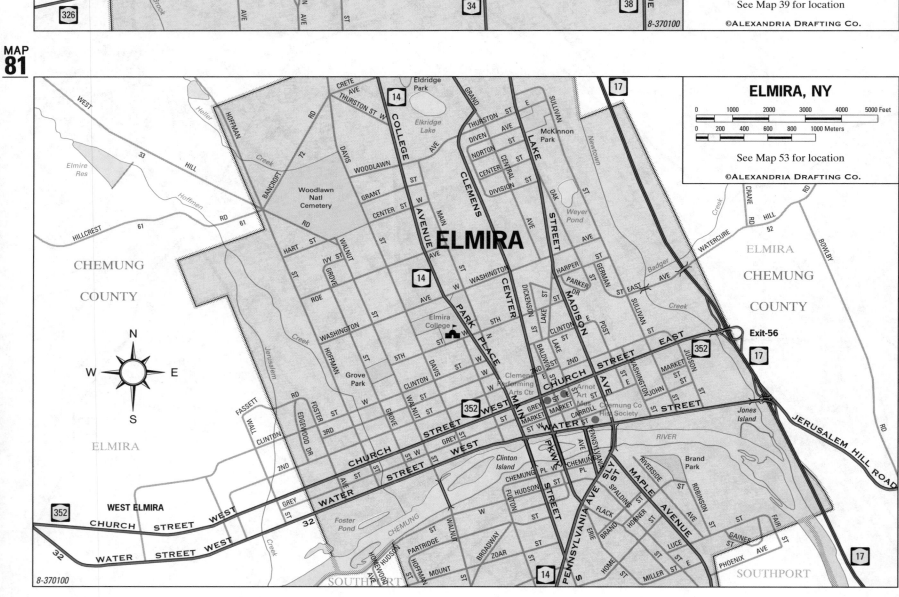

ELMIRA, NY

| 0 | 1000 | 2000 | 3000 | 4000 | 5000 Feet |

| 0 | 200 | 400 | 600 | 800 | 1000 Meters |

See Map 53 for location

©Alexandria Drafting Co.

8-370100

MAP
82

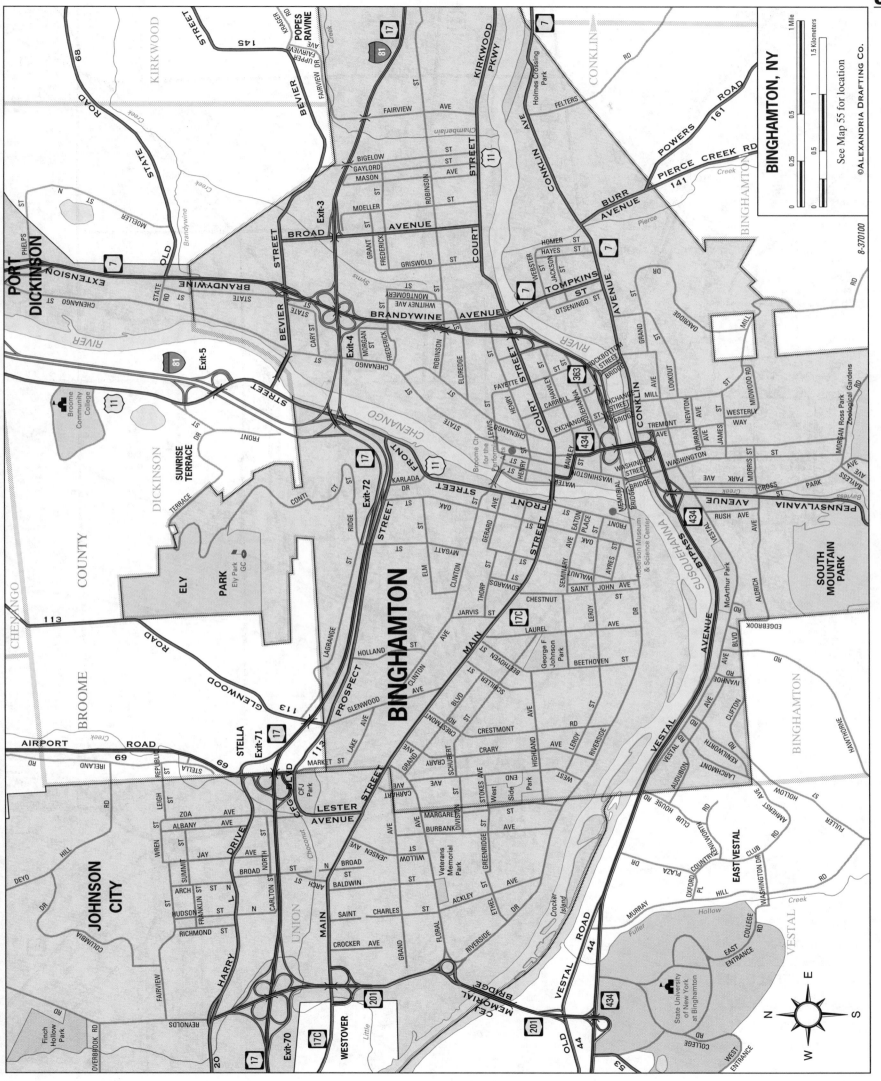

BINGHAMTON, NY

See Map 55 for location

©ALEXANDRIA DRAFTING CO.

8-370100

PORT DICKINSON

POPES RAVINE

KIRKWOOD

CONKLIN

BROOME COUNTY

DICKINSON

SUNRISE TERRACE

BINGHAMTON

Broome Community College

ELY PARK

CHENANGO COUNTY

BROOME

JOHNSON CITY

WESTOVER

Roberson Museum & Science Center

SOUTH MOUNTAIN PARK

Morgan Ross Park Zoological Gardens

EAST VESTAL

State University of New York at Binghamton

BINGHAMTON

VESTAL

MAP
83

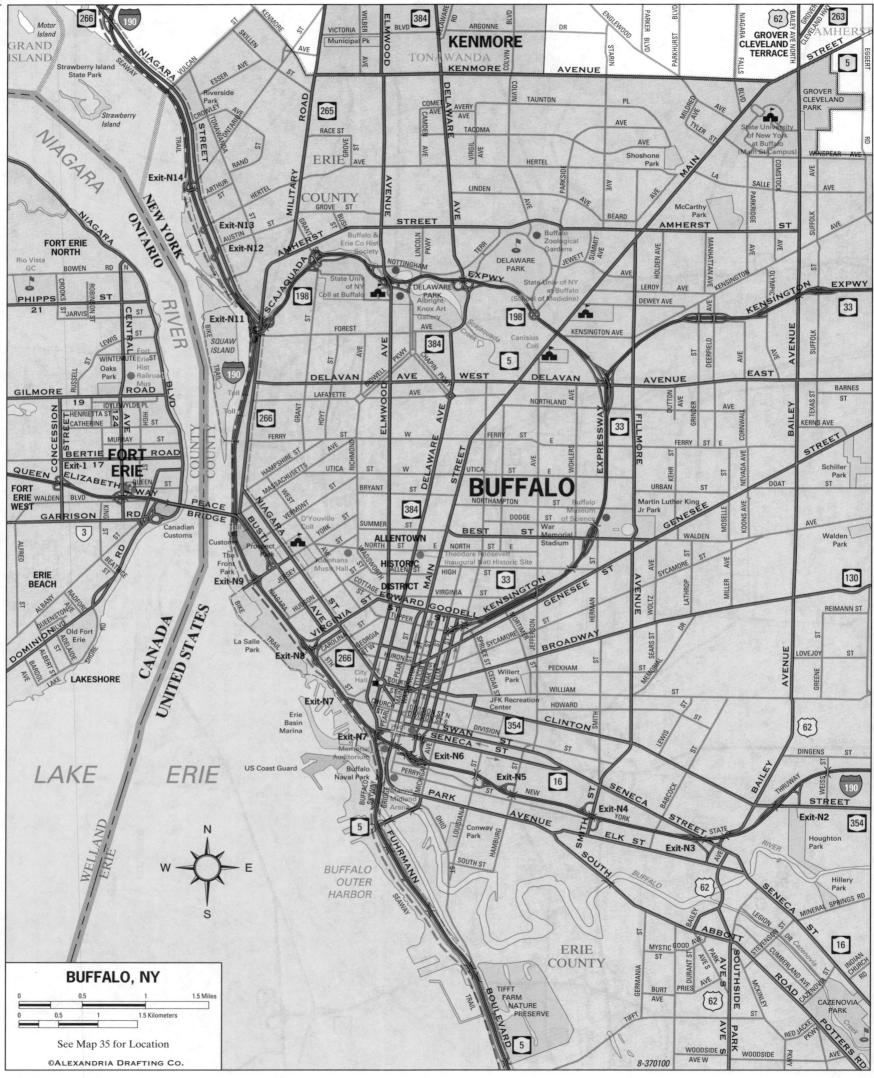

BUFFALO, NY

0   0.5   1   1.5 Miles

0   0.5   1   1.5 Kilometers

See Map 35 for Location

©Alexandria Drafting Co.

8-370100

MAP
84

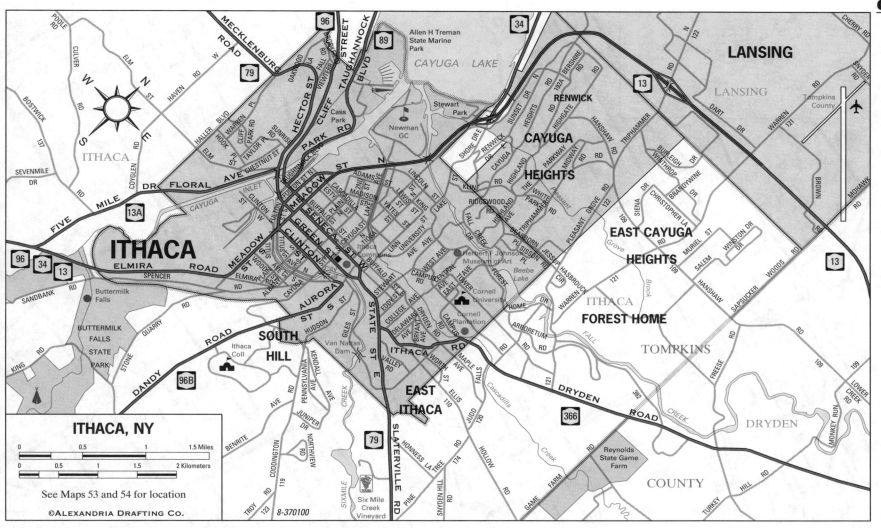

ITHACA, NY

0   0.5   1   1.5 Miles
0   0.5   1   1.5   2 Kilometers

See Maps 53 and 54 for location

©Alexandria Drafting Co.

MAP
85

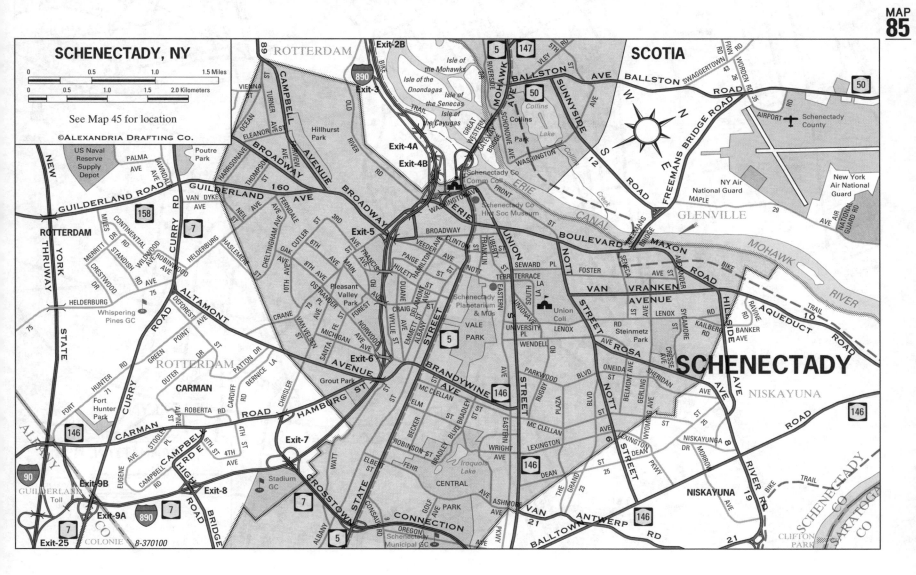

SCHENECTADY, NY

0   0.5   1.0   1.5 Miles
0   0.5   1.0   1.5   2.0 Kilometers

See Map 45 for location

©Alexandria Drafting Co.

MAP
86

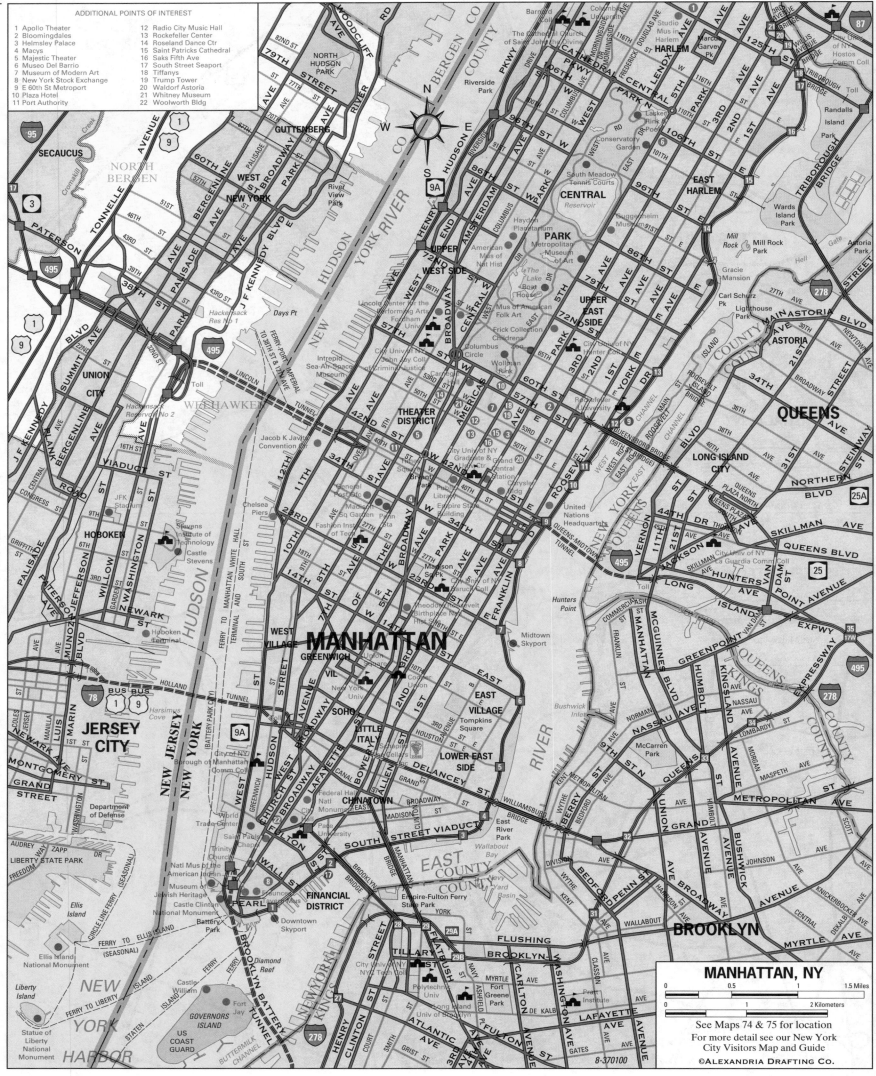

ADDITIONAL POINTS OF INTEREST

1 Apollo Theater
2 Bloomingdales
3 Helmsley Palace
4 Macys
5 Majestic Theater
6 Museo Del Barrio
7 Museum of Modern Art
8 New York Stock Exchange
9 E 60th St Metroport
10 Plaza Hotel
11 Port Authority
12 Radio City Music Hall
13 Rockefeller Center
14 Roseland Dance Ctr
15 Saint Patricks Cathedral
16 Saks Fifth Ave
17 South Street Seaport
18 Tiffanys
19 Trump Tower
20 Waldorf Astoria
21 Whitney Museum
22 Woolworth Bldg

MANHATTAN, NY

| 0 | 0.5 | 1 | 1.5 Miles |

| 0 | 1 | 2 Kilometers |

See Maps 74 & 75 for location
For more detail see our New York
City Visitors Map and Guide
©Alexandria Drafting Co.

8-370100

MAP
87

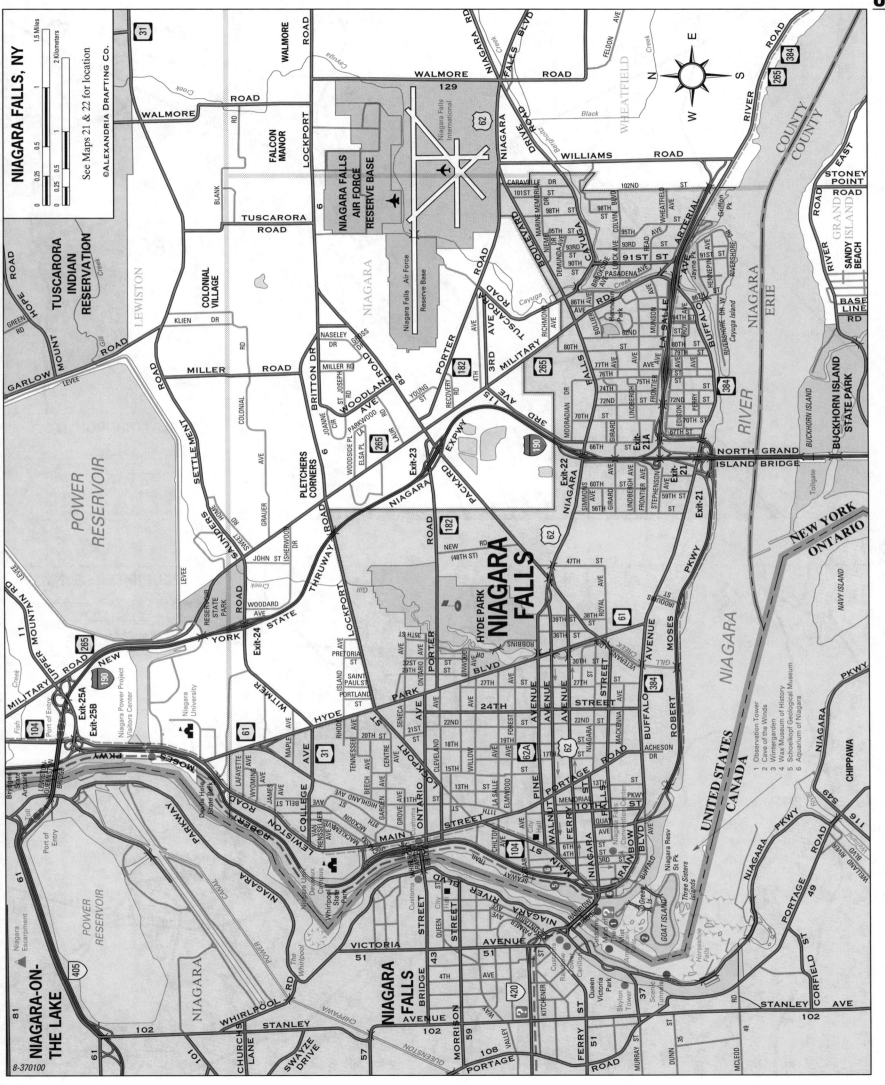

NIAGARA FALLS, NY

See Maps 21 & 22 for location

©Alexandria Drafting Co.

MAP
88

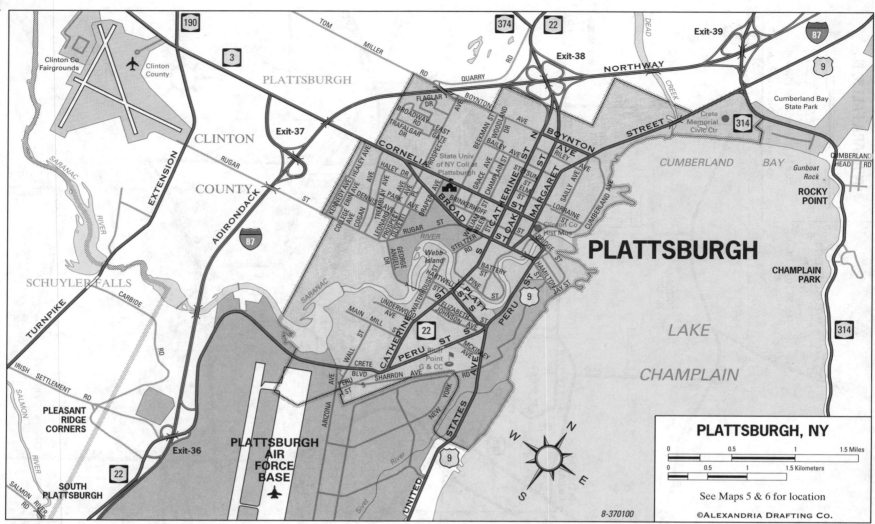

PLATTSBURGH

CLINTON COUNTY

SCHUYLER FALLS

LAKE CHAMPLAIN

ROCKY POINT

CHAMPLAIN PARK

CUMBERLAND BAY

State Univ of NY Coll at Plattsburgh

PLATTSBURGH AIR FORCE BASE

PLEASANT RIDGE CORNERS

SOUTH PLATTSBURGH

Exit-36

Exit-37

Exit-38

Exit-39

PLATTSBURGH, NY

| 0 | | 0.5 | | 1 | | 1.5 Miles |

| 0 | 0.5 | 1 | 1.5 Kilometers |

See Maps 5 & 6 for location

©Alexandria Drafting Co.

8-370100

MAP
89

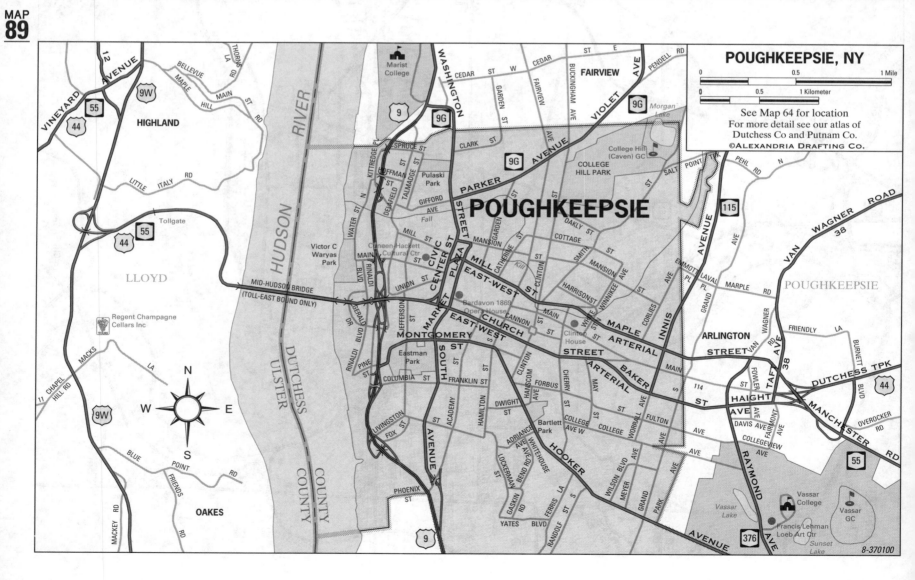

POUGHKEEPSIE

HIGHLAND

HUDSON RIVER

LLOYD

OAKES

ULSTER COUNTY

DUTCHESS COUNTY

Marist College

College Hill (Caven) GC

COLLEGE HILL PARK

FAIRVIEW

ARLINGTON

POUGHKEEPSIE

Regent Champagne Cellars Inc

Victor C Waryas Park

Cuneen-Hackett Cultural Ctr

Bardavon 1869 Opera House

Clinton House

Eastman Park

Bartlett Park

Vassar College

Vassar GC

Vassar Lake

Francis Lehman Loeb Art Ctr

Sunset Lake

MID-HUDSON BRIDGE (TOLL-EAST BOUND ONLY)

POUGHKEEPSIE, NY

| 0 | | 0.5 | | 1 Mile |

| 0 | 0.5 | 1 Kilometer |

See Map 64 for location
For more detail see our atlas of Dutchess Co and Putnam Co.
©Alexandria Drafting Co.

8-370100

MAP
90

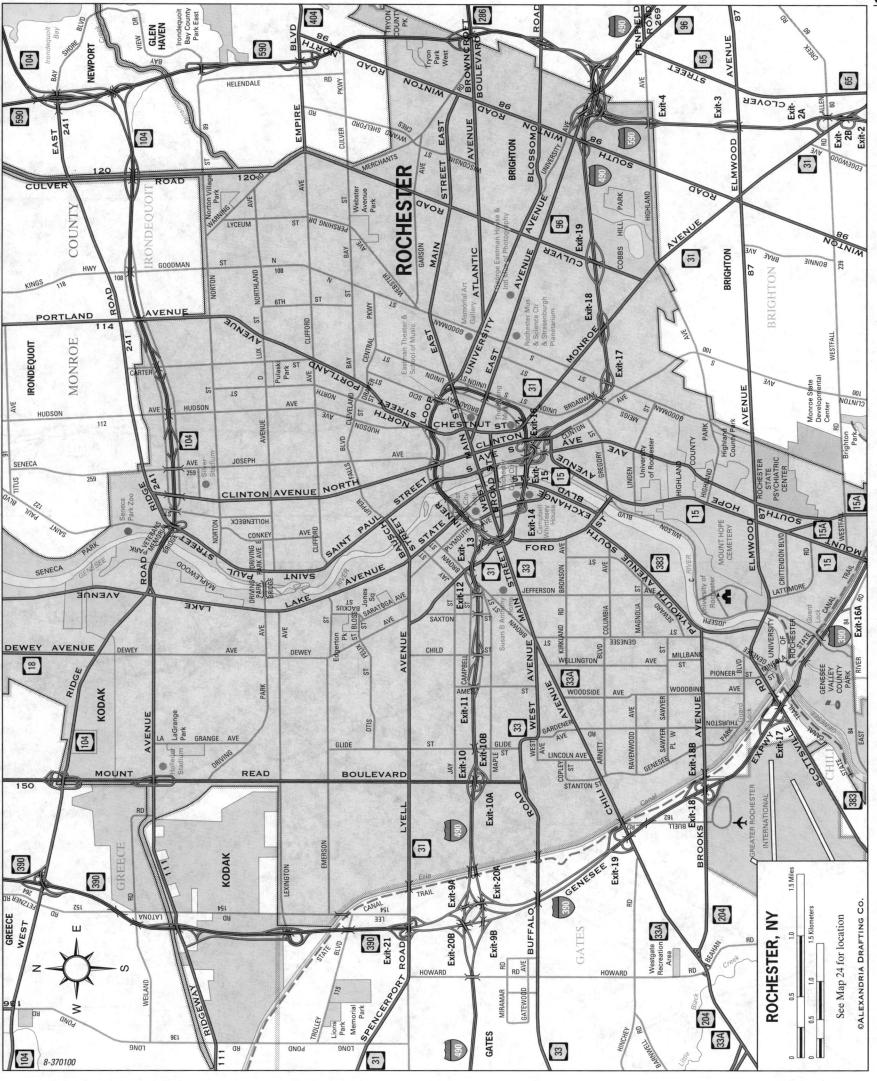

ROCHESTER, NY

See Map 24 for location

©ALEXANDRIA DRAFTING CO.

MAP
91

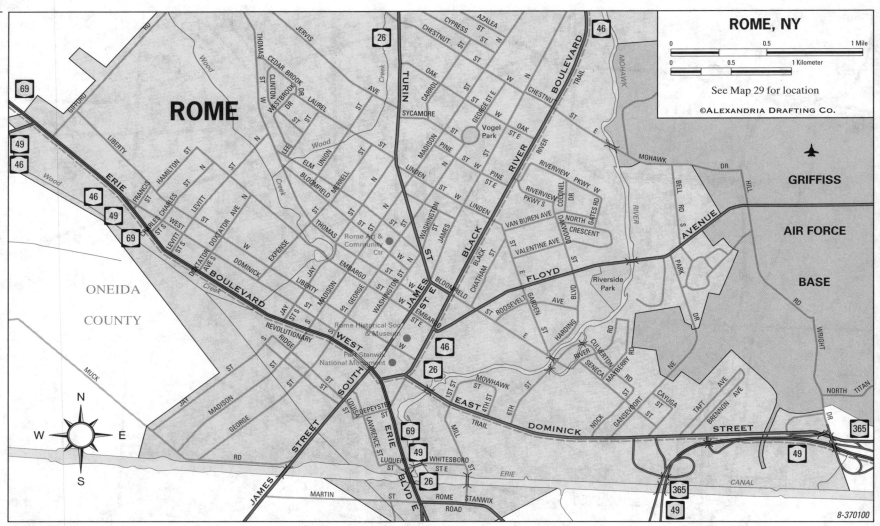

MAP
92

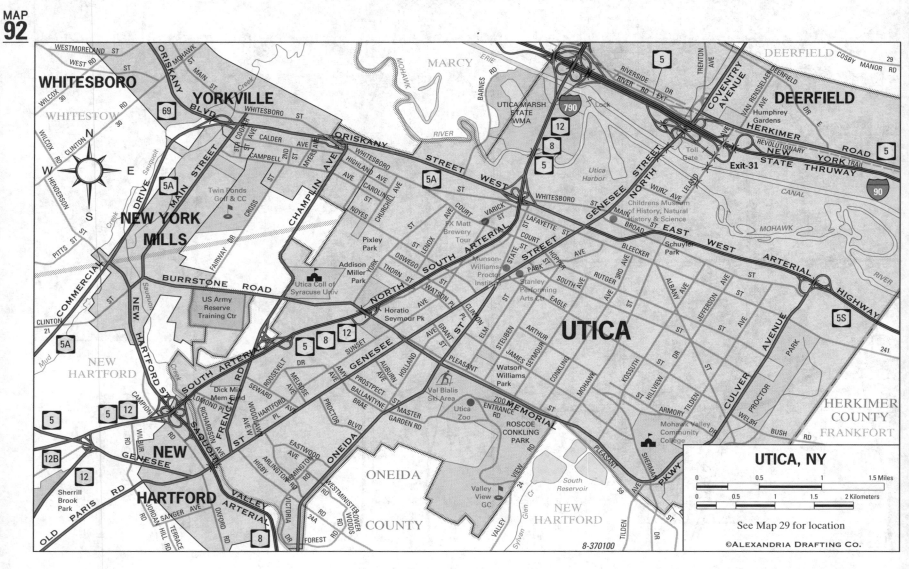

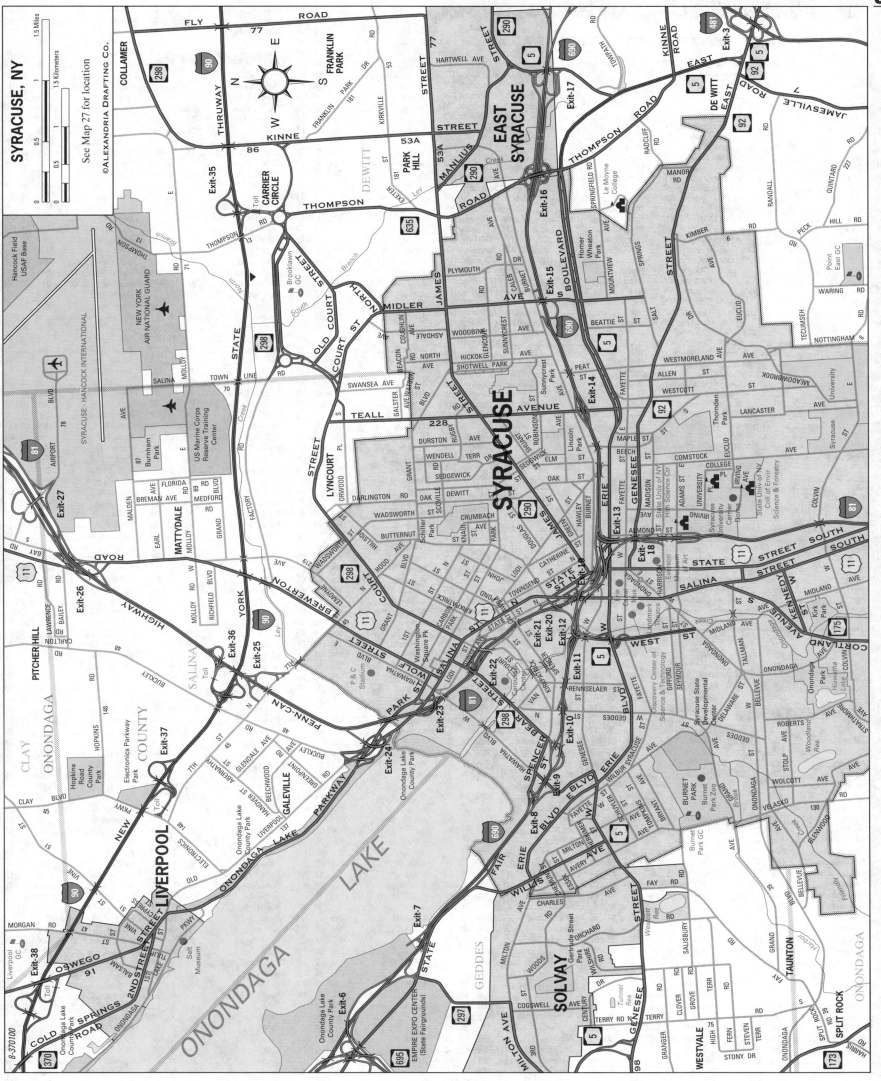

MAP
93

SYRACUSE, NY

See Map 27 for location

©Alexandria Drafting Co.

Index

TERRITORY CODES FOR NEW YORK STATE ATLAS

Place Names

NAME	TERR	MAP	GRID
Bennetts Corners	Mds	28	E6
Bennetts Corners	Ono	27	B6
Bennetts Corners	Orl	23	F4
Bennettsburg	Scy	53	C1
Bennettsville	Cng	56	A3
Bennington	Ben	46	D2
Bennington Center	Wyo	36	B2
Benson	Hml	31	C3
Benson	Rut	20	C4
Benson Landing	Rut	20	B4
Bensons Corners	Alb	44	E5
Bensons Mines	SL	10	A4
Bentleys Corners	Jfs	8	D4
Benton	Yts	38	F4
Benton Center	Yts	38	F4
Benton Corners	Cyg	26	F4
Benton Corners	Uls	63	D4
Berea	Orn	63	D6
Bergen	Gns	24	A5
Bergenfield	Brg	75	A1
Bergholtz	Nia	22	B5
Berkshire	Brk	46	D6
Berkshire	Flt	31	C6
Berkshire	Tio	54	D3
Berkshire Estates	Ffd	69	C1
Berkshire Valley	Ssx	73	E1
Berlin	Rns	46	B4
Bernardsville	Sms	73	E4
Berne	Alb	44	E5
Bernhards Bay	Osw	28	A3
Berryville	Mgy	44	B1
Berwyn	Ono	40	F2
Bessemer	Tmk	54	B2
Best	Rns	45	E5
Bethany	Gns	36	E2
Bethany	NHv	70	A1
Bethany	Wyn	61	C5
Bethel	Dut	64	E1
Bethel	Ffd	69	B2
Bethel	Slv	62	B4
Bethel Corners	Cyg	26	F4
Bethel Corners	Osw	14	D6
Bethel Grove	Tmk	54	A2
Bethlehem	Lch	65	D5
Bethlehem Center	Alb	45	C5
Bethlehem Heights	Alb	45	B6
Betterment	Frl	4	E2
Bettsburg	Cng	55	F4
Beukendaal	Sch	45	A2
Beyers Corners	Flt	44	E1
Big Bay	Osw	27	E4
Big Bend	Ono	40	E2
Big Creek	Stu	51	F2
Big Flats	Chm	53	A5
Big Indian	Uls	58	A5
Big Island	Orn	67	B3
Big Moose	Hrk	17	A3
Big Tree	Ere	35	C3
Bigelow	SL	9	B1
Bigelow Corners	Wyo	36	F5
Billings	Dut	64	C4
Billsboro	Otr	39	A3
Billsboro Corners	Otr	38	F3
Bingham Mills	Clm	59	C5
Binghamton	Brm	55	B5
Bingley	Mds	41	C1
Binnewater	Uls	63	E2
Birch Hill	Lch	65	A4
Birchton	Srg	32	A6
Bird	Cat	49	F2
Birdsall	Agy	51	A2
Bishop Corners	Wyo	36	F5
Bishop Street	Jfs	14	E2
Bishops Corners	Jfs	8	D4
Bishops Mills	Ont	1	D2
Bishopville	Agy	51	C2
Bisseltown	Ont	1	D4
Black Brook	Cln	12	D1
Black Corners	Chu	48	D2
Black Creek	Agy	50	D3
Black Hall	NLn	71	C3
Black Lake	Slv	62	B5
Black Oaks Corners	Tmk	53	E1
Black Point	NLn	71	D3
Black Point Beach Club	NLn	71	D3
Black River	Jfs	8	B6
Black River	Jfs	15	C1
Black Rock	Cyg	39	E4
Blackbridge	Hml	31	B2
Blackmans Corners	Ond	28	F5
Blackpool	Qub	7	A6
Blacksmith Corners	Otr	38	C1
Blair Kiln	Frl	4	E3
Blairstown	War	73	A1
Blairville	Nia	21	F4
Blakeley	Ere	35	E4
Blakely	Sen	39	C5
Blakesley Corner	Cng	55	E3
Blandy	Ond	28	F2
Blasdell	Ere	35	B3
Blatchley	Brm	55	D6
Blauvelt	Rck	68	A6
Bleecker	Flt	31	B5
Bleecker Center	Flt	31	B5
Bliss	Wyo	36	D6
Bliss Corner	Flt	30	E5
Bliss Corners	Mds	41	E1
Blockville	Chu	48	B6
Blodgett Mills	Crt	40	E6
Bloomerville	Stu	52	A1
Bloomfield	Esx	74	D3
Blooming Grove	Orn	67	D2
Bloomingburg	Slv	63	A6
Bloomingdale	Ese	11	E2
Bloomingdale	Pas	67	B6
Bloomington	Uls	63	F2
Blooms Corners	Orn	67	A3
Bloomville	Dlw	57	B2
Blossom	Ere	35	D2
Blossoms Corners	Rut	33	D2
Blossvale	Ond	28	C5
Blue Church	Ont	1	F4
Blue Corners	Srg	44	F1
Blue Mountain	Uls	58	F5
Blue Mountain Lake	Hml	18	A2
Blue Point	Sfk	76	F3
Blue Ridge	Ese	19	C1
Blue Store	Clm	59	C5
Bluff Point	Yts	38	E5
Blush Hollow	Hms	60	F2
Boardman Bridge	Lch	65	A5
Boght Corners	Alb	45	B3
Bogota	Brg	74	F2
Bogus Corners	Eri	47	A6
Bohemia	Sfk	76	E3
Boiceville	Uls	58	C6
Bolivar	Agy	50	D6
Bolton	Wrr	19	D6
Bolton Landing	Wrr	19	D6
Bolts Corners	Cyg	39	F3
Bombay	Frl	3	F1
Bomoseen	Rut	20	D5
Bonhamtown	Mid	74	B6
Bonney	Cng	41	E4
Bonni Castle	Wan	26	A6
Bonny Hill	Stu	52	C3
Bonny Rigg Corners	Brk	60	F3
Bookman Corners	Mgy	43	D2
Boomertown	Chu	48	B6
Boonton	Mrr	74	A2
Boonville	Ond	29	C1
Boquet	Ese	13	B3
Borden	Stu	52	B6
Border City	Sen	39	A2
Boreas River	Ese	19	A1
Borodino	Ono	40	C2
Bosley Corner	Lvg	37	E3
Boston	Ere	35	D5
Boston	Ffd	69	B3
Boston Corner	Clm	59	F6
Bostwick Corners	Tmk	53	E1
Boswell Corners	Otr	38	A4
Botsford	Ffd	69	D2
Botsford Corners	Cyg	39	F3
Bouckville	Mds	41	F2
Boughton Hill	Otr	38	B1
Bound Brook	Sms	73	F6
Bournes Beach	Chu	47	F2
Boutonville	Wch	68	F3
Bovey Lake	Shh	44	B6
Bovina	Dlw	57	D3
Bovina Center	Dlw	57	C3
Bowen	Cat	48	F5
Bowen Corners	Osw	27	C3
Bowens Corners	Osw	27	A3
Bowerstown	Ots	43	B4
Bowler	Agy	50	D6
Bowlers Corners	Stu	37	F6
Bowman Corners	Chi	6	F6
Bowmansville	Ere	35	D1
Boxwood Corner	Orl	23	B5
Boyd Mills	Wyn	61	E5
Boyds Corners	Stu	52	A5
Boyds Corners	Wyo	37	A2
Boylston Center	Osw	15	A5
Boyntonville	Rns	46	A2
Braddock Heights	Mro	24	D3
Bradford	Stu	52	E2
Bradford	Wgn	72	D2
Bradford Junction	Cat	49	F5
Bradley	Slv	62	D3
Bradleys Corners	Frl	3	E1
Bradleyville	Lvg	37	E6
Bradleyville	NHv	65	F6
Bradtville	Flt	30	F6
Braeside	Rns	45	E6
Braggs Corners	Orl	23	D5
Brainard	Rns	59	F1
Brainard Corners	Ots	42	E3
Brainardsville	Frl	4	F2
Braman	Wyn	61	E3
Braman Corners	Sch	44	D3
Bramans Corners	Alb	44	F6
Bramanville	Shh	44	A4
Branch	Uls	63	A1
Branchport	Yts	38	E5
Branchville	Ffd	69	A3
Branchville	Ssx	66	C5
Brandon	Hml	18	B6
Brandon	Rut	20	F3
Brandt	Nia	22	A4
Brandy Brook	SL	10	C4
Brandy Mill	Mid	78	B6
Branford	NHv	70	C3
Brant	Ere	34	F5
Brant Lake	Wrr	19	D4
Brantingham	Lew	16	C4
Brasher Center	SL	3	C2
Brasher Falls	SL	3	C3
Brasher Iron Works	SL	3	D2
Brasie Corners	SL	8	E2
Brayton	Wrr	32	E1
Brayton Hollow	Frl	4	E1
Breakabeen	Shh	44	A6
Breesport	Chm	53	D3
Brentwood	Sfk	76	C3
Brewer Corners	Agy	51	B1
Brewer Corners	Cat	49	F1
Brewerton	Ono	27	D4
Brewster	Put	68	E2
Brewster Heights	Put	68	E2
Briarcliff Manor	Wch	68	B5
Brick Chapel	SL	2	E6
Brick Tavern	Clm	59	D3
Bridgehampton	Sfk	78	C1
Bridgeport	Ffd	69	C4
Bridgeport	Mds	28	A5
Bridgeport	Sen	39	C1
Bridges Corners	Mds	41	F1
Bridgeville	Slv	62	E5
Bridgewater	Lch	65	B6
Bridgewater	Ond	42	C2
Bridport	Add	20	C1
Brier Hill	SL	1	D6
Brier Hill Station	SL	1	E6
Briggs Corner	Lew	15	F2
Briggsville	Brk	46	F4
Brighton	Ere	35	B1
Brighton	Mro	24	E5
Brighton	Ots	42	F2
Brighton	Ssx	73	C1
Brightwaters	Sfk	76	D4
Brimstone Corners	Rut	33	E2
Brinckerhoff	Dut	64	B6
Brindley Creek	Grn	58	D2
Brinston	Ont	2	B1
Brisben	Cng	55	D2
Briscoe	Slv	62	B3
Bristol	Add	13	F5
Bristol	Otr	38	A2
Bristol Center	Otr	38	B3
Bristol Springs	Otr	38	B4
Broadalbin	Flt	31	D6
Broadalbin Junction	Flt	31	C6
Brockport	Mro	24	A4
Brockville	Ont	1	D5
Brockville	Orl	23	E3
Brockway	Dut	64	A6
Brockway	NLn	71	B2
Brockway Corners	Ond	28	C3
Brockway Landing	NLn	71	B2
Brocton	Chu	48	A2
Brodhead	Uls	63	C1
Broken Creek	Clm	60	A1
Brokers Village	Wyo	36	B3
Bromley	Ono	40	D3
Bronx	Brx	75	C2
Bronxville	Wch	75	C1
Brookdale	SL	3	B3
Brookfield	Ffd	69	B1
Brookfield	Mds	42	C3
Brookfield	Ond	28	F3
Brookfield Center	Ffd	69	B1
Brookhaven	Sfk	77	B3
Brooklyn	Cat	49	C1
Brooklyn	Kng	74	F5
Brooklyn	Kng	75	A5
Brooks Grove	Lvg	37	A5
Brooksburg	Grn	58	D3
Brookside	Mrr	73	F3
Brooksvale	NHv	70	A1
Brooksville	Add	13	D6
Brooktondale	Tmk	54	B2
Brookvale	Brm	55	C5
Brookview	Rns	45	D6
Brookville	Gns	36	D1
Brookville	Nsu	75	F3
Broome Center	Shh	58	B1
Brothertown	Ond	42	A1
Brouses Corners	SL	9	F1
Brouseville	Ont	2	A3
Brown Corner	Ono	27	F5
Brown Corners	Stu	38	D6
Brownie	SL	9	D2
Browns Bridge	SL	3	A6
Browns Corners	Jfs	8	B3
Browns Crossing	Stu	52	A4
Brownsville	Otr	25	B6
Browntown	Stu	52	F6
Brownville	Jfs	8	A6
Brownville	Uls	63	B3
Bruceville	Uls	63	E3
Brunswick	Rns	45	F4
Brunswick Center	Rns	45	E3
Brushton	Frl	3	F3
Bruton Corners	Cyg	39	F4
Bruynswick	Uls	63	D5
Bryants Mill	Frl	4	E4
Buchanan	Wch	68	A3
Buck Settlement	Stu	52	B3
Buckley Corners	Ots	56	B2
Buckley Hollow	Cng	55	D2
Buckleyville	Clm	59	E2
Bucks Bridge	SL	2	D4
Bucks Corner	Rns	46	A4
Bucks Corners	Mds	41	D2
Bucks Hill	Uls	63	D2
Buckton	SL	3	C4
Bucyrus Heights	Ere	22	C6
Budd Lake	Mrr	73	D2
Buel	Mgy	43	E2
Buellville	Ono	41	A1
Buena Vista	Stu	51	F3
Buffalo	Ere	35	B1
Buffalo Corners	Wyo	36	F3
Bull Hill	Hrk	30	B3
Bull Mine	Orn	67	D2
Bull Run	Uls	63	A2
Bullet Hole	Put	68	C2
Bullock Corners	Jfs	15	B3
Bulls Head	Dut	64	C2
Bullville	Orn	63	B6
Bundy Crossing	Osw	27	A2
Bunn Corners	Srg	31	E6
Burden	Clm	59	B5
Burdett	Scy	53	C2
Burdick Crossing	Ese	20	A1
Burdickville	Wgn	72	C1
Burgoyne	Srg	32	E5
Burke	Frl	4	D2
Burke Center	Frl	4	D1
Burlingham	Slv	63	B5
Burlington	Chi	6	C6
Burlington	Chi	13	C1
Burlington	Ots	42	E4
Burlington Flats	Ots	42	D4
Burma Woods	Orl	23	D4
Burnetts Corner	NLn	72	A2
Burnham Corners	SL	2	F4
Burnham Hollow	Rut	33	E1
Burnhams	Chu	48	C3
Burns	Agy	51	D1
Burnside	Orn	67	D1
Burnt Hills	Srg	45	B1
Burnt Mills	Hnt	73	D5
Burrell Corners	Hrk	30	B5
Burritts Rapids	Ont	1	C1
Burrs Mills	Jfs	15	B1
Burt	Nia	22	D3
Burtonsville	Mgy	44	C3
Burwell Corners	Cng	42	A5
Bush Corner	Otr	37	F2
Bushes Landing	Lew	16	B3
Bushnell Basin	Mro	25	A6
Bushnellsville	Uls	58	B5
Bushs Corners	Lew	16	C2
Bushville	Gns	23	C6
Bushville	Orn	66	F2
Bushville	Slv	62	C4
Buskirk	Rns	46	A1
Busti	Chu	48	C6
Butcher Corner	Stu	51	F2
Butler	Mrr	67	B6
Butler	Mrr	74	B1
Butler Center	Wan	26	D4
Butler Corners	Ots	43	D4
Butlers Corner	Chi	6	F6
Butlers Park	Hnt	73	A3
Butlerville	Wch	68	D2
Butterfly Corners	Osw	27	C1
Butternut Bay	Ont	1	C6
Butternut Bend	Rut	33	D3
Butternut Grove	Dlw	62	A1
Butterville	Jfs	14	E2
Butterville	Uls	63	E3
Butts Corner	Dlw	57	B1
Byrdcliffe	Uls	58	E6
Byrnes Corners	Wrr	19	A4
Byron	Gns	23	F6
C			
Cadiz	Cat	50	A3
Cadosia	Dlw	61	C1
Cadyville	Cln	5	E4
Cahoonzie	Orn	66	D1
Caintown	Ont	1	B6
Cairo	Grn	58	F3
Cairo Junction	Grn	59	A3
Calcium	Jfs	8	B6
Calcutta	Ots	43	D5
Caldwell	Esx	74	C2
Caledonia	Lvg	37	B1
Calhoun Corners	Lch	65	B3
Califon	Hnt	73	B4
Calkins	Wyn	61	E5
Callahans Corners	Srg	32	E5
Callanans Corners	Alb	45	B6
Callicoon	Slv	61	F3
Callicoon Center	Slv	62	A2
Calverton	Sfk	77	C2
Cambria Center	Nia	22	C4
Cambria Station	Nia	22	B5
Cambridge	Whg	33	B6
Camby	Dut	64	D4
Camden	Ond	28	D2
Camelot Beach	Ont	34	C2
Cameron	Stu	52	B4
Cameron Corners	Lew	15	E2
Cameron Mills	Stu	52	B4
Camillus	Ono	27	C6
Camp Beechwood	Wan	25	F3
Camp Gorton	Scy	52	E1
Camp Lenore	Brk	60	E1
Camp Pinnacle	Alb	44	F5
Camp Rondaxe	Hrk	17	B3
Camp Sunset	Uls	63	F5
Campbell	Stu	52	D4
Campbell Hall	Orn	67	C1
Campbell Maxwell Front	Ont	7	C1
Campbells Corners	Mds	28	C5
Campbells Corners	Ont	1	F2
Camps Mills	Jfs	14	E1
Campton	Brm	55	B6
Campville	Tio	54	E5
Camroden	Ond	29	B3
Canaan	Clm	60	A2
Canaan	Lch	60	C6
Canaan Center	Clm	60	A2
Canaan Valley	Lch	60	C6
Canada Lake	Flt	30	F4
Canadice Corners	Otr	37	F4
Canajoharie	Mgy	43	E2
Cananchet	Wsh	72	C1
Canandaigua	Otr	38	C2
Canaseraga	Agy	51	C1
Canastota	Mds	28	C5
Canawaugus	Lvg	37	C1
Candlewood Isle	Ffd	69	A1
Candlewood Knolls	Ffd	69	A1
Candlewood Orchards	Ffd	69	A1
Candlewood Point	Lch	65	A6
Candlewood Shores	Ffd	69	A1
Candlewood Springs	Lch	65	A6
Candlewood Trails	Lch	65	A6
Candor	Tio	54	B4
Caneadea	Agy	50	E2
Canisteo	Stu	51	E3
Canisteo Center	Stu	51	F3
Cannon Corners	Cln	5	D1
Canoga	Sen	39	D2
Cantic	Qub	7	B6
Canton	SL	2	D5
Cape Vincent	Jfs	7	C4
Carbondale	Lak	61	A6
Cardiff	Ono	40	E2
Cardinal	Ont	2	B3
Cards Corners	Ono	40	D1
Cardtown	Ots	42	C5
Carey Corner	Brk	60	B2
Carey Corners	Hrk	29	F5
Careys Corners	Ond	29	C5
Carley Mills	Osw	27	E2
Carleys Corners	Ont	1	C2
Carlisle	Shh	44	A3
Carlisle Center	Shh	44	A4
Carlisle Gardens	Nia	22	E4
Carlstadt	Brg	74	F3
Carlton	Orl	23	D3
Carman	Sch	45	A3
Carmel	Put	68	D1
Carmel Hills	Put	68	D2
Carnegie	Ere	35	B4
Caroga Lake	Flt	31	A5
Carolina	Wgn	72	E1
Caroline	Tmk	54	B2
Caroline	Tmk	54	C2
Caroline Center	Tmk	54	C2
Caroline Depot	Tmk	54	B2
Carpenters Corners	Flt	31	E4
Carr Corners	Cat	49	A5
Carrier Circle	Ono	27	E6
Carroll Corners	Osw	28	A3
Carrollton	Cat	49	E5
Carter	Eri	47	B5
Carter Station	Hrk	17	A3
Carteret	Mid	74	D6
Carthage	Jfs	15	E1
Cascade	Cyg	40	A3
Cascade Mills	Yts	39	A5
Cascade Valley	Brm	55	F6
Casey Corners	SL	2	E4
Casowasco	Cyg	40	A3
Cassadage	Chu	48	B2
Cassville	Ond	42	D1
Castile	Wyo	36	F5
Castile Center	Wyo	36	F5
Castle Creek	Brm	55	A4
Castle Point	Dut	64	A6
Castleton	Rut	20	D5
Castleton Corners	Rut	20	D5
Castleton-on-Hudson	Rns	45	D6
Castorland	Lew	15	F2
Catatonk	Tio	54	C5
Catawba	Stu	52	D1
Catfish Corners	Osw	27	D2
Catharine	Scy	53	C3
Catherineville	SL	3	C5
Cato	Cyg	26	F4
Caton	Stu	52	F6
Cator Corners	Wan	25	C5
Catskill	Grn	59	B4
Cattaraugus	Cat	49	B3
Caughdenoy	Osw	27	D3
Cauterskill	Grn	59	B4
Cayuga	Cyg	39	D2
Cayuga Heights	Tmk	53	F1
Cayuga Heights	Tmk	54	A1
Cayuta	Scy	53	D3
Cayutaville	Scy	53	D2
Caywood	Sen	39	B6
Cazenovia	Mds	41	B1
Cedar Beach	Chi	13	C3
Cedar Bluff	Srg	32	D6
Cedar Flats	Rck	67	F3
Cedar Grove	Esx	74	D2
Cedar Grove	Ont	2	E1
Cedar Hill	Alb	45	C6
Cedar Knolls	Mrr	74	A3
Cedar Lake	Hrk	42	D1
Cedar Swamp	Mro	24	E6
Cedarhurst	Nsu	75	D5
Cedars	SL	8	E1
Cedarvale	Ono	40	D1
Cedarville	Hrk	42	E1
Celoron	Chu	48	C5
Cementon	Grn	59	A5
Center Berlin	Rns	46	B5
Center Cambridge	Whg	46	A1
Center Falls	Whg	33	A5
Center Groton	NLn	71	F2
Center Lisle	Brm	54	F2
Center Moriches	Sfk	77	C3
Center Rutland	Rut	20	F5
Center Valley	Ots	43	D3
Center Village	Brm	55	E5
Center White Creek	Whg	46	B1
Centerbrook	Mdx	71	A2
Centereach	Sfk	76	F2
Centerfield	Otr	38	B2
Centerport	Cyg	26	E6
Centerport	Sfk	76	B2
Centerville	Agy	50	C1
Centerville	Dlw	56	E6
Centerville	Osw	14	F6
Centerville	Sfk	77	D1
Centerville	Uls	58	F5
Central Bridge	Shh	44	B4
Central Islip	Sfk	76	D3
Central Nyack	Rck	68	A5
Central Square	Osw	27	D3
Central Valley	Orn	67	E3
Centralia	Chu	48	B3
Centre	Agy	51	B2
Centre Island	Nsu	75	F2
Ceres	Agy	50	C6
Chace	Wyo	36	F5
Chadwicks	Ond	29	C6
Chaffee	Ere	36	A6
Chamberlain Corners	SL	2	E3
Chamberlain Mills	Whg	33	B3
Chambers	Chm	53	A3
Chambers Corners	Ont	34	B1
Champion	Jfs	15	D1
Champion Huddle	Jfs	15	D1
Champlain	Cln	6	A1

NAME	TERR	MAP	GRID
Champlain Corners	Cat	49	B3
Champlain Park	Cln	6	A4
Chandler	Slv	62	C2
Chandleyville	Agy	50	D6
Changewater	Hnt	73	A4
Chapin	Otr	38	D2
Chapinville	Ots	42	D4
Chapman Corners	Scy	53	A2
Chappaqua	Wch	68	C5
Charleston	Mgy	44	B2
Charleston Four Corners	Mgy	44	B3
Charlestown	Wgn	72	E2
Charlesworth Corners	Mgy	43	D1
Charleville	Ont	1	E3
Charlotte	Chi	13	C3
Charlotte Center	Chu	48	D3
Charlotteburg	Pas	67	B6
Charlotteville	Shh	43	E6
Charlton	Srg	45	A1
Chase	Ots	43	A4
Chase Mills	SL	2	E2
Chaseville	Ots	43	B6
Chasm Falls	Frl	4	D3
Chateaugay	Frl	4	F1
Chateaugay	Osw	15	A6
Chatfield Corner	Srg	32	A5
Chatham	Clm	59	E2
Chatham	Mrr	74	B4
Chatham Center	Clm	59	E2
Chaumont	Jfs	7	E5
Chautauqua	Chu	48	A4
Chazy	Cln	6	A2
Chazy Landing	Cln	6	B2
Checkerberry Village	Chi	6	E5
Checkered House	Osw	28	A1
Cheektowaga	Ere	35	C1
Cheeseboro	Ont	7	D1
Cheesequake	Mid	78	C6
Chelsea	Dut	64	A6
Chemung	Chm	53	E6
Chenango Bridge	Brm	55	B4
Chenango Forks	Brm	55	B4
Chenango Lake	Cng	42	A5
Cheningo	Crt	41	A5
Chepachet	Hrk	42	E2
Cherry Creek	Chu	48	E3
Cherry Grove	Sfk	76	E5
Cherry Hill	Chu	48	B6
Cherry Ridge	Ssx	67	A5
Cherry Ridge	Wyn	61	C6
Cherry Valley	Ots	43	D3
Cherryplain	Rns	46	B5
Cherrytown	Uls	63	B3
Cherryville	Hnt	73	B6
Cheshire	Brk	46	E6
Cheshire	NHv	70	B1
Cheshire	Otr	38	C3
Chester	Mdx	71	A2
Chester	Mrr	73	D3
Chester	Orn	67	C2
Chesterfield	NLn	71	D1
Chestertown	Wrr	19	B5
Chestnut Ridge	Dut	64	E4
Chestnut Ridge	Rck	67	F5
Chet Creek	Agy	51	B4
Cheviot	Clm	59	B5
Chichester	Uls	58	C5
Chicken Tavern Corners	Chu	48	D2
Childs	Orl	23	D3
Childwold	SL	10	E3
Childwold Station	SL	10	E4
Chili Center	Mro	24	D5
Chilson	Ese	19	F2
Chimney Point	Add	13	B6
China	Dlw	56	B5
Chipman	SL	2	D3
Chipman Corners	Cyg	40	B5
Chipmunk	Cat	49	F6
Chippenhook	Rut	20	F6
Chippewa Bay	SL	8	C1
Chittenango	Mds	28	B6
Chittenango Falls	Mds	41	B1
Chittenango Springs	Mds	28	B6
Chobbies Mill	Add	13	E4
Chocomount	Sfk	72	A3
Choconut Center	Brm	55	A5
Christainson Fall	Mds	41	C1
Christian Corners	Put	68	C2
Christian Hill	Tmk	53	D1
Christian Hill	Wrr	18	E4
Chrome	Mid	74	D6
Chuckery Corners	Ond	29	B6
Church Corners	Mgy	44	C1
Church Corners	Ots	42	B6
Churchtown	Clm	59	D4
Churchville	Mro	24	B5
Churchville	Ond	28	E4

NAME	TERR	MAP	GRID
Churubusco	Cln	5	A1
Cicero	Ono	27	E4
Cicero Corner	Ono	27	F4
Cincinnatus	Crt	41	A6
Cinda Creek	Cat	49	A2
Circleville	Orn	63	B6
Clare	SL	9	F2
Clarence	Ere	35	E1
Clarence Center	Ere	22	E6
Clarenceville	Qub	7	C6
Clarenceville Estates	Qub	7	D6
Clarendon	Orl	23	E4
Clarendon Springs	Rut	20	F6
Clark	Chu	48	E5
Clark	Uni	74	C5
Clark Corners	Lew	15	E2
Clark Corners	Osw	27	A1
Clark Heights	Dut	64	B4
Clark Mills	Ond	29	B6
Clarks Corner	Srg	32	E4
Clarks Corners	SL	9	E1
Clarks Falls	NLn	72	C1
Clarks Mills	Whg	32	F5
Clarksboro	SL	9	F3
Clarksburg	Ere	35	C5
Clarkson	Mro	24	A4
Clarksville	Alb	45	A6
Clarkville	Srg	31	E4
Claryville	Slv	62	F2
Claverack	Clm	59	D4
Clay	Ono	27	D4
Clayburg	Cln	5	B5
Clayton	Jfs	7	F3
Clayton	Lch	60	C6
Clayton Center	Jfs	7	F3
Clayville	Ond	42	C1
Clear Creek	Cat	48	F4
Clear Creek	Chu	48	F4
Cleaver	Dlw	56	D4
Clemons	Whg	20	A5
Clermont	Clm	59	C5
Cleveland	Osw	28	B3
Cleveland Hill	Ere	35	C1
Cliff Haven	Cln	6	A5
Clifford	Osw	27	C2
Cliffside	Ots	43	A6
Cliffside Park	Brg	75	A3
Cliffwood Beach	Mom	78	D6
Clifton	Mro	24	C6
Clifton	Pas	74	E2
Clifton Heights	Ere	35	B4
Clifton Park	Srg	45	C2
Clifton Park Center	Srg	45	B2
Clifton Springs	Otr	38	E1
Climax	Grn	59	B2
Clinton	Hnt	73	B5
Clinton	Mdx	70	F3
Clinton	Ond	29	B6
Clinton	Pas	67	A6
Clinton Beach	Mdx	71	A3
Clinton Corners	Dut	64	C3
Clinton Heights	Rns	45	D5
Clinton Hollow	Dut	64	C2
Clinton Mills	Cln	5	B1
Clinton Park	Rns	45	D5
Clintondale	Uls	63	F4
Clintondale Station	Uls	63	F4
Clintonville	Cln	12	F1
Clintonville	NHv	70	C2
Clintonville	Ono	40	B1
Clintonville	Ots	43	A5
Closter	Brg	75	A1
Clough Corners	Ono	41	A2
Clove	Dut	64	D4
Clove	Shh	43	F4
Clove Valley	Dut	64	D5
Clums Corner	Rns	45	F4
Clyde	Wan	26	B5
Clymer	Chu	47	E6
Clymer Center	Chu	47	F6
Clymer Hill	Chu	47	F6
Cobb	Sfk	78	B2
Cobblestone Corners	Jfs	14	E4
Cobbtown	Jfs	14	F4
Cobleskill	Shh	43	F4
Cobleskill	Shh	44	A4
Cochecton	Slv	61	E4
Cochecton Center	Slv	62	A5
Codes Corners	Ont	7	A2
Codfish Hill	Ffd	69	B2
Coes Corners	Chu	48	C4
Coeymans	Alb	59	C1
Coeymans Hollow	Alb	59	B1
Coffins Mills	SL	9	F4
Cogswell Corners	SL	2	D3
Cohocton	Stu	37	F6
Cohocton	Stu	38	A6
Cohocton	Stu	51	F1
Cohocton	Stu	52	A1
Cohoes	Alb	45	D3

NAME	TERR	MAP	GRID
Coila	Whg	33	B6
Cokertown	Dut	59	C6
Cokesbury	Hnt	73	B4
Colburns	Chu	48	B5
Colchester	Chi	6	E6
Colchester	Dlw	56	E5
Cold Brook	Hrk	29	F4
Cold Brook	Uls	58	C6
Cold Spring	Brk	60	E5
Cold Spring	Put	68	A2
Cold Spring	Rut	20	B4
Cold Spring	Wyn	61	C4
Cold Spring Harbor	Sfk	76	A2
Cold Springs	Ono	27	D5
Cold Springs	Sen	39	D5
Cold Springs	Stu	52	C2
Cold Water	Mro	24	D5
Colden	Ere	35	D5
Coldenham	Orn	63	E6
Cole Corners	Yts	38	E3
Colebrook	Lch	65	F1
Colegrave	Ere	35	F4
Coleman Corner	Add	13	D3
Coleman Station	Dut	64	F2
Colemans Mills	Ond	29	B5
Coles Corners	Scy	53	A1
Colesville	Ssx	66	E3
Collabar	Orn	63	C6
Collamer	Ono	27	F5
College Park	Dut	59	B6
Colliersville	Ots	57	A1
Collingwood	Ono	40	F2
Collingwood Estates	Nia	21	F4
Collins	Ere	49	A1
Collins Center	Ere	49	B1
Collinsville	Lew	16	B5
Colonia	Mid	74	C6
Colonial Heights	Dut	64	B4
Colonial Village	Nia	22	A5
Colonie	Alb	45	B4
Colonie Delaware Granby	Qub	7	D6
Colosse	Osw	27	E1
Colton	SL	3	A6
Colts Station	Eri	47	C5
Columbia Center	Hrk	42	F1
Columbia Heights	Wgn	72	E1
Columbiaville	Clm	59	C3
Columbus	Cng	42	B4
Columbus Quarter	Cng	42	B4
Commack	Sfk	76	C2
Como	Cyg	40	C4
Comstock	Whg	33	A1
Comstock Corners	Nia	22	C5
Conashaugh	Pke	66	B3
Concord	Ere	35	D6
Conesus	Lvg	37	D4
Conesus Lake Junction	Lvg	37	D2
Conesville	Shh	58	B2
Conewango	Cat	48	F4
Conewango Valley	Cat	48	E4
Conewango Valley	Chu	48	E4
Conger Corners	Ond	42	B1
Congers	Rck	68	A5
Conifer	SL	10	E4
Conklin	Brm	55	C6
Conklin Center	Brm	55	C6
Conklin Forks	Brm	55	B6
Conklin Station	Brm	55	C6
Conklingville	Srg	32	A3
Connelly	Uls	64	A2
Connelly Park	Chu	48	A5
Conquest	Cyg	26	E5
Constable	Frl	4	C1
Constableville	Lew	16	A6
Constantia	Osw	27	F4
Constantia Center	Osw	28	B3
Convent Station	Mrr	74	A3
Converse	SL	3	C4
Cook Corners	Chu	48	C1
Cook Corners	Mgy	43	F1
Cook Corners	Ots	56	D1
Cook Corners	SL	10	B4
Cooks Corner	Frl	4	A2
Cooks Falls	Dlw	62	A1
Cooks Mill	Frl	4	E1
Cooksburg	Alb	58	D1
Cooksey Mill	Crt	40	E4
Cookville	Gns	23	B6
Cooley	Slv	62	D2
Coolidge Beach	Nia	22	B3
Cooney Crossing	Wan	25	D5
Cooneys Corners	Cyg	39	D3
Coonrod	Ond	28	F4
Coons	Srg	45	D1
Cooper Corners	Cng	56	A2
Coopers Corners	SL	9	E2
Coopers Corners	Slv	62	D4
Coopers Falls	SL	2	C6

NAME	TERR	MAP	GRID
Coopers Plains	Stu	52	E4
Cooperstown	Ots	43	A4
Cooperstown Junction	Ots	57	A1
Coopersville	Cln	6	B1
Coopersville	Lvg	37	B5
Copake	Clm	59	F5
Copake Falls	Clm	59	F5
Copenhagen	Lew	15	E2
Copes Corner	Ots	56	B1
Copiague	Sfk	76	B4
Coram	Sfk	76	F2
Coram	Sfk	77	A2
Corbett	Dlw	56	F6
Corbettsville	Brm	55	C6
Corbin Corner	Cng	55	D1
Coreys	Frl	11	C4
Corfu	Gns	36	B1
Corinth	Srg	32	B3
Cork	Flt	31	A6
Corning	Stu	52	F5
Corning Manor	Stu	52	F5
Cornwall	Add	20	D1
Cornwall	Lch	65	C2
Cornwall Bridge	Lch	65	B3
Cornwall Center	Lch	65	C2
Cornwall-On-Hudson	Orn	67	F1
Cornwall-On-Hudson	Orn	68	A1
Cornwallville	Grn	58	D2
Cortland	Crt	40	F4
Corwin	Nia	22	D3
Cory Corners	Wan	25	D5
Cos Cob	Ffd	68	E6
Coss Corners	Stu	52	B3
Cossayuna	Whg	33	A4
Coteys Corner	SL	3	D3
Cottage	Cat	48	F1
Cottage City	Otr	38	C3
Cottage Corners	Cyg	26	E5
Cottekill	Uls	63	E2
Cottons	Mds	28	C6
Coty Corners	Mds	41	C1
Countryman	Hrk	30	A5
County Line	Nia	23	A2
County Line	Orl	23	A2
Cove Neck	Nsu	76	A2
Covel Corners	Otr	38	B3
Coventry	Cng	55	E2
Coventryville	Cng	55	E3
Covert	Sen	39	D6
Covesville	Dlw	57	F5
Coveville	Wrr	32	E6
Coveytown Corners	Frl	4	D1
Covington	Wyo	36	F2
Cowdens Corners	Chu	48	C2
Cowles Settlement	Crt	41	A3
Cowlesville	Wyo	36	A2
Coxsackie	Grn	59	C2
Cozy Corner	Chi	6	E5
Crafts	Put	68	D2
Cragmere Park	Brg	67	E6
Cragsmoor	Uls	63	B4
Craigville	Orn	67	C2
Crains Corners	Hrk	43	B2
Crains Mills	Crt	40	F4
Cramer Corners	Hrk	43	C1
Cranberry Creek	Flt	31	D5
Cranberry Lake	SL	10	B4
Crandall Corners	Whg	45	F1
Cranes Corners	Hrk	42	E1
Cranesville	Mgy	44	E1
Cranford	Uni	74	C5
Crary Mills	SL	2	E6
Craryville	Clm	59	F4
Craterclub	Ese	13	B3
Crawford	Uls	63	C5
Cream Hill	Add	20	B1
Creamton	Wyn	61	B4
Creekside	Ere	35	C4
Crescent	Srg	45	C3
Crescent Beach	NLn	71	D3
Crescent Park	Mgy	44	E1
Cresskill	Brg	75	A1
Crest View Heights	Tio	54	E6
Cribbs Corners	Osw	27	C2
Crittenden	Ere	36	A1
Crocketts	Cyg	26	E3
Crofts Corners	Put	68	B2
Croghan	Lew	16	B2
Crompond	Wch	68	B3
Cronk Corners	Lew	15	C2
Cronomer Valley	Orn	63	F6
Cropseyville	Rns	45	F3
Crosby	Yts	38	E6
Cross Hill	Clm	59	B5
Cross River	Wch	68	E3
Cross Roads	Cyg	39	D2
Crossman Corners	Ono	27	A6
Croton	Hnt	73	A6
Croton Falls	Wch	68	D2
Croton-On-Hudson	Wch	68	B4

NAME	TERR	MAP	GRID
Crotonville	Wch	68	B4
Crouses Store	Dut	64	D5
Crown Point	Ese	20	A1
Crown Point Center	Ese	20	A1
Crowningshield	Ese	12	F3
Crows Hollow	Ono	27	B5
Crugers	Wch	68	A4
Crum Creek	Flt	30	D6
Crum Town	Tio	54	A3
Crystal Beach	Rut	20	D5
Crystal Dale	Lew	16	C3
Crystal Rock	Ont	2	A3
Crystal Run	Orn	67	B1
Crystal Spring	Yts	52	F1
Cuba	Agy	50	C4
Cuddebackville	Orn	66	E1
Cullen	Hrk	43	A2
Culvers Inlet	Ssx	66	C4
Culvertown	Slv	62	F6
Cummings Bridge	Osw	27	C1
Cummings Corners	Srg	31	F6
Cumminsville	Lvg	37	C6
Curriers	Wyo	36	A5
Curry	Slv	62	E2
Currytown	Mgy	44	A2
Curtis	Hrk	30	C4
Curtis	Stu	52	D4
Curtis Corner	Otr	37	F3
Cutchogue	Sfk	71	A6
Cutting	Chu	47	D6
Cuyler	Crt	41	A4
Cuylersville	Lvg	37	B3

D

NAME	TERR	MAP	GRID
Daball Corners	Stu	38	C6
Daboll Corners	Ono	27	A5
Dadville	Lew	16	A3
Dairy Valley	Qub	7	D6
Dairyland	Uls	62	F4
Daisy	Uls	58	E6
Dale	Wyo	36	D3
Dalmers Creek	Dlw	57	A3
Dalton	Brk	60	E1
Dalton	Lvg	37	A6
Dalton Crossing	SL	2	E2
Damascus	Brm	55	E6
Damascus	Wyn	61	E4
Danbury	Ffd	68	F1
Danbury	Ffd	69	B2
Danby	Rut	33	F2
Danby	Tmk	54	A2
Danby Four Corners	Rut	33	F2
Danes Corners	SL	9	E1
Danielstown	Srg	32	C3
Dann Corners	Lvg	37	E1
Dannemora	Cln	5	D4
Dansville	Lvg	37	D6
Dansville Station	Lvg	37	D5
Danville	Brm	56	A6
Darby Corners	Yts	38	D5
Darien	Ffd	69	A6
Darien	Gns	36	B2
Darien Center	Gns	36	B2
Darlingside	Ont	8	A2
Darlington	Brg	67	D6
Darmac	Put	68	D2
Darrowsville	Wrr	19	B5
Darts Corner	Mds	42	A3
Dashville	Uls	63	F3
Davenport	Dlw	57	B1
Davenport Center	Dlw	57	A1
Davidson Beach	Mro	24	C2
Davidsons Corner	NHv	70	A1
Davis Corners	Mds	41	E1
Davis Corners	Mgy	44	B2
Davis Corners	Uls	63	D2
Davis Crossing	Cng	42	B6
Davis Park	Sfk	76	F4
Davis Park	Sfk	77	A4
Davys Corners	Hrk	43	C1
Daws	Gns	23	D6
Day Center	Srg	31	F3
Days Rock	Hrk	43	A1
Daysville	Osw	14	D6
Daysville Corner	Osw	14	D6
Dayton	Cat	49	A2
Daytonville	Ond	42	B1
Dean	Chu	48	A3
Dean Corners	Lch	65	B2
Deans Corners	Put	68	E2
Deans Corners	SL	9	F1
Deans Corners	Srg	32	D6
Deansboro	Ond	42	A1
Debruce	Slv	62	D2
Decatur	Ots	43	D5
Deck	Hrk	43	B1
Deckertown	Slv	62	C1
Deep River	Mdx	71	A2

NAME	TERR	MAP	GRID
Deer Park	Sfk	76	C3
Deer River	Lew	15	E1
Deerfield	Sfk	78	B1
Deerhead	Ese	12	F2
Deerland	Hml	18	A1
Deerland Camp	Hml	17	F1
Deferiet	Jfs	8	D6
Deforest Corners	Put	68	F1
Defreestville	Rns	45	D5
Degrasse	SL	9	F2
Dekalb	SL	9	B1
DeKalb Junction	SL	2	C6
Delanson	Sch	44	D4
Delaware Lancey	Dlw	57	A4
Delaware Peyster	SL	2	A6
Delevan	Cat	50	A1
Delhi	Dlw	57	B3
Delhill Corners	Eri	47	B5
Dellwood	Ere	35	F2
Delmar	Alb	45	B5
Delphi Falls	Ono	41	A2
Demarest	Brg	75	A1
Dempster Corners	Flt	30	F5
Demster	Osw	27	C1
Demster Beach	Osw	14	C6
Denault Corners	Rns	45	F5
Denmark	Lew	15	F2
Dennies Crossing	Flt	31	C6
Dennies Hollow	Flt	31	C5
Denning	Uls	63	A1
Dennison Corners	Chu	48	E1
Dennison Corners	Hrk	42	F1
Denniston	Orn	67	E1
Denton	Orn	67	B2
Denton Corners	Chu	48	B3
Denver	Dlw	57	F4
Denville	Mrr	74	A2
Depauville	Jfs	7	F4
Depew	Ere	35	D2
Deposit	Brm	56	B6
Deposit	Dlw	56	B6
Derby	Ere	35	A4
Derby	NHv	69	F3
Derby Switch	Stu	52	C5
Derbys Corners	SL	9	E2
Dering Harbor	Sfk	71	C5
DeRuyter	Mds	41	B3
Desbrough Park	Wan	26	C3
Devereaux	Cat	49	F3
Devoice Corners	Jfs	8	F6
Dewey Corners	Ond	29	E4
Deweys Corners	Osw	27	D1
DeWitt	Ono	27	E6
Dewitt Mills	Dut	64	B2
Dewittville	Chu	48	A4
Dexter	Jfs	7	F5
Dexter Corners	Cat	48	F2
Diamond	Jfs	15	B4
Diamond Hill	Ffd	69	B3
Diamond Point	Wrr	32	D1
Diana Center	Lew	9	A6
Dibble Corner	Cng	55	D1
Dibbletown	Ond	28	D3
Dickersonville	Nia	22	A4
Dickinson	Frl	3	F4
Dickinson Center	Frl	3	F4
Diddell	Dut	64	B5
Dillen	Jfs	15	A2
Dillenbeck Corners	Hrk	30	B5
Dimmick Corners	Srg	32	D4
Dineharts	Stu	52	C1
Dingmans Ferry	Pke	66	B4
Dishaw	SL	2	F2
Divine Corners	Slv	62	E3
Dix Hills	Sfk	76	B3
Dixon Corners	SL	2	F3
Dixons Corners	Ont	2	B1
Dobbins Corner	Otr	39	A2
Dobbins Corner	Sen	39	A2
Dobbs Ferry	Wch	68	B6
Dodgingtown	Ffd	69	B2
Dodtail Corners	Dut	64	F4
Dogtown	Ots	42	F2
Dolgeville	Hrk	30	C5
Domaine-Omer-Alix	Qub	7	E6
Domville	Ont	1	F3
Doonan Corners	Dlw	57	C1
Doraville	Brm	55	F5
Dorloo	Shh	43	E4
Dormansville	Alb	59	A1
Dorset	Ben	33	E3
Dorwood Park	Nia	22	B4
Dotys Corners	Stu	51	D1
Double Beach	NHv	70	C3
Douglas Crossing	Jfs	8	C4
Dover	Mrr	73	F2
Dover Furnace	Dut	64	E4
Dover Plains	Dut	64	E4
Downsville	Dlw	57	A5
Drakes Corner	Osw	27	B2

NAME	TERR	MAP	GRID
Fort Edward	Whg	32	F3
Fort Erie	Ont	35	A1
Fort Herkimer	Hrk	30	A6
Fort Hill	Gns	24	A6
Fort Hill	Otr	38	F2
Fort Hunter	Mgy	44	C1
Fort Jackson	SL	3	D4
Fort Johnson	Mgy	44	D1
Fort Lee	Brg	75	A2
Fort Miller	Whg	32	F5
Fort Montgomery	Orn	68	A2
Fort Niagara Beach	Nia	21	F3
Fort Plain	Mgy	43	E1
Fort Salonga	Sfk	76	C1
Forthton	Ont	1	B5
Fortsville	Srg	32	D4
Forty Six Corners	Ond	28	D1
Foster	Tio	54	E5
Fosterdale	Slv	62	A4
Fostertown	Orn	63	F6
Fosterville	Cyg	39	D1
Four Corners	Grn	58	B2
Four Corners	Orn	67	C1
Four Corners	Put	68	A2
Four Mile	Cat	50	A6
Four Winds Corners	Otr	38	B2
Fourth Lake	Wrr	32	C2
Fowler	SL	9	B3
Fowlerville	Ere	35	D5
Fowlerville	Lvg	37	B2
Fowlerville	Slv	62	C6
Fox Corners	Mgy	44	B3
Fox Hill	Srg	31	F4
Fox Ridge	Cyg	26	D6
Foxon	NHv	70	B3
Francis Corners	Srg	32	C6
Frankfort	Hrk	29	E6
Frankfort Center	Hrk	29	E6
Frankfort Hill	Hrk	29	D6
Franklin	Dlw	56	D2
Franklin	Ssx	66	F5
Franklin Bay	Nsu	75	E5
Franklin Depot	Dlw	56	D3
Franklin Falls	Frl	12	A1
Franklin Grove	War	66	A6
Franklin Lakes	Brg	67	D6
Franklin Lakes	Brg	74	D1
Franklin Park	Ono	27	F5
Franklin Springs	Ond	29	B6
Franklin Square	Nsu	75	D4
Franklinton	Shh	44	C6
Franklinville	Cat	50	A2
Franks Corners	Crt	54	D1
Frankville	Ont	1	A4
Fraser	Dlw	57	A4
Fraser	Lvg	37	B2
Frederick Corners	Jfs	15	B4
Fredon	Ssx	66	C6
Fredonia	Chu	48	B1
Freedleyville	Ben	33	F3
Freedom	Cat	50	B1
Freedom Plains	Dut	64	C4
Freehold	Grn	58	F2
Freeman	Stu	52	C6
Freeport	Eri	47	B4
Freeport	Nsu	75	E5
Freetown	Sfk	78	D1
Freetown Corners	Crt	40	F6
Freeville	Tmk	40	C6
Fremont	Stu	51	E2
Fremont Center	Slv	61	F2
French Creek	Chu	47	D6
French Mountain	Wrr	32	D2
French Woods	Dlw	61	D1
Frenchs Mill	Stu	52	F5
Frenchville	Ond	29	B3
Frewsburg	Chu	48	E6
Freysbush	Mgy	43	E2
Friend	Yts	38	D5
Friendship	Agy	50	E4
Frink Corner	Srg	32	A5
Frinks Corner	Wyo	36	B4
Froatburn	Ont	2	D1
Frone Corner	Ots	56	C1
Frontenac	Jfs	7	F2
Frontier	Qub	5	A1
Frost Hollow	Otr	37	F3
Frost Valley	Uls	62	F1
Fruit Valley	Osw	26	F1
Fruitland	Wan	25	B4
Fullers	Alb	45	A4
Fullerville	SL	9	B3
Fulmer Valley	Agy	51	C5
Fulton	Osw	27	B3
Fultonham	Shh	44	A6
Fultonville	Mgy	44	B1
Furnaceville	Ots	43	D5
Furnaceville	Wan	25	C3
Furniss	Osw	26	F2
Fyler Settlement	Mds	28	A5

G

NAME	TERR	MAP	GRID
Gabriels	Frl	11	D1
Gaines	Orl	23	D3
Gainesville	Wyo	36	E5
Gainesville Center	Wyo	36	E5
Galatia	Crt	54	F1
Gale	SL	10	E3
Gales Ferry	NLn	71	F1
Galeville	Ono	27	D5
Galeville	Uls	63	D5
Galilee	SL	1	F5
Galilee	Wgn	72	F2
Galilee	Wyn	61	E4
Gallatinville	Clm	59	D6
Gallupville	Shh	44	C5
Galway	Srg	31	F6
Gananoque	Ont	7	E2
Gang Mills	Stu	52	E5
Gansevoort	Srg	32	E4
Garbutt	Mro	24	C6
Garden City	Nsu	75	D4
Gardeners Corners	Osw	27	D2
Gardenville	Ere	35	D2
Gardiner	Uls	63	E4
Gardners Corners	Lew	15	D3
Gardnersville	Shh	43	F4
Gardnertown	Orn	63	F6
Gardnerville	Orn	67	A2
Garfield	Brg	74	E2
Garfield	Rns	46	B6
Garland	Mro	24	B4
Garlinghouse	Lvg	38	A5
Garnet Lake	Wrr	18	F6
Garoga	Flt	30	F6
Garrattsville	Ots	42	D5
Garrison	Put	68	A2
Garwood	Uni	74	C5
Garwoods	Agy	51	C1
Gas Spring	Agy	51	C1
Gaskill	Tio	54	D5
Gasport	Nia	22	E4
Gates	Mro	24	D5
Gates Corners	Chu	48	E3
Gayhead	Grn	59	A2
Gaylordsville	Lch	65	A5
Gayville	Osw	27	F3
Gee Brook	Crt	41	A6
Geers Corners	SL	9	B4
Genegantslet	Cng	55	B2
Genesee Junction	Mro	24	D5
Geneseo	Lvg	37	C3
Geneva	Otr	39	A2
Genoa	Cyg	39	F4
Georgetown	Crt	55	B1
Georgetown	Ffd	69	A3
Georgetown	Mds	41	C3
Georgia Center	Fkl	6	E4
Georgia Plains	Fkl	6	E4
Gerard Park	Sfk	71	E6
German Five Corners	Cng	41	B6
German Four Corners	Cng	55	B1
German Village	Mro	24	F4
Germantown	Agy	50	C5
Germantown	Clm	59	B5
Germany Hill	Tio	54	B5
Gerry	Chu	48	D4
Getzville	Ere	22	C6
Ghent	Clm	59	E3
Giants Neck	NLn	71	D3
Gibson	Stu	52	F5
Gibson Corners	Tio	54	C6
Gibson Landing	Stu	52	E1
Giddingsville	Jfs	14	F3
Gifford	Sch	44	F3
Gilbert	Sen	39	B4
Gilbert Corners	Ffd	69	A4
Gilbert Corners	Put	68	B2
Gilbert Corners	Shh	43	F6
Gilbert Corners	Srg	32	D6
Gilbert Mills	Osw	27	C3
Gilberts Corners	Nia	22	F5
Gilbertsville	Ots	56	C1
Gilboa	Shh	58	A2
Gile	Frl	4	A5
Gilgo Beach	Sfk	76	B5
Gillette	Mrr	74	A4
Gills Corners	Mds	41	E1
Gilmantown	Hml	31	C1
Girarde	Orn	67	D1
Girdland	Wyn	61	D4
Gladding Corner	Otr	38	A3
Glasco	Uls	59	A6
Glass Lake	Rns	45	F5
Glasser	Ssx	73	E1
Gleasons Mill	SL	10	A1
Glen	Mgy	44	B2
Glen Aubrey	Brm	54	F3
Glen Becker	Ont	2	D1
Glen Castle	Brm	55	A4
Glen Cove	Nsu	75	E2
Glen Gardner	Hnt	73	A4
Glen Grove	Stu	52	D1
Glen Haven	Cyg	40	C3
Glen Haven	Mro	24	F4
Glen Park	Jfs	8	A6
Glen Ridge	Esx	74	D3
Glen Rock	Brg	74	E1
Glen Spey	Slv	66	C1
Glen Wild	Slv	62	F5
Glenburnie	Ont	7	A2
Glenburnie	Whg	20	A3
Glencairn	Tio	54	A6
Glendale	Brk	60	B3
Glendale	Lew	16	A4
Glenerie	Uls	59	A6
Glenfield	Lew	16	B4
Glenford	Uls	58	E6
Glenham	Dut	64	A6
Glenmont	Alb	45	C5
Glenmore	Ese	12	D3
Glenridge	Sch	45	A2
Glens Falls	Wrr	32	E3
Glenville	Ffd	68	E6
Glenville	Lvg	37	E3
Glenville	Sch	44	F1
Glenville Center	Sch	45	A2
Glenwood	Ere	35	D5
Glenwood	Nia	22	A4
Glenwood	Ssx	67	A4
Glenwood Landing	Nsu	75	D3
Glenwood Park	Orn	63	F6
Gloade Corners	Stu	38	D6
Globe Hotel Corners	Cyg	40	B3
Gloversville	Flt	31	B6
Godeffroy	Orn	66	E1
Godfrey Corners	Cng	56	A1
Godfreys Corner	Jfs	8	B3
Golden Glow Heights	Chm	53	B5
Golden Spur	NLn	71	D2
Goldens Bridge	Wch	68	E3
Goodell Corners	Hrk	30	B5
Goodrich	Tio	54	C5
Goodrich Corner	Add	13	B5
Goodyear Corners	Cyg	39	E5
Goose Bay	Jfs	8	B2
Goose Island	Whg	33	A3
Goosetree	Cyg	40	A5
Gordon Heights	Sfk	77	A2
Gordon Landing	GIC	6	B4
Gorham	Otr	38	E3
Goshen	Add	20	F2
Goshen	Lch	65	D3
Goshen	Orn	67	C2
Gothicville	Ots	43	D4
Gould Corners	Jfs	15	A3
Goulds Mill	Lew	16	B5
Gouverneur	SL	9	A2
Gowanda	Cat	49	A1
Gowanda	Ere	49	A1
Gracie	Crt	40	D6
Grafton	Rns	46	A3
Graftons Square	Osw	27	E1
Graham	Wch	68	B5
Grahamsville	Slv	62	F2
Granby Center	Osw	27	A3
Grand Gorge	Dlw	58	A2
Grand Gorge Station	Dlw	57	F2
Grand Isle	GIC	6	C4
Grand Isle Station	GIC	6	C4
Grand View Beach	Mro	24	D3
Grand View-On-Hudson	Rck	68	B6
Grandview Bay	Ere	34	E5
Grandyle Village	Ere	35	A1
Granger	Agy	50	F1
Grangerville	Srg	32	E5
Granite	Uls	63	C3
Granite Springs	Wch	68	C3
Graniteville	NLn	71	E3
Grant	Hrk	29	F3
Grant Corner	Wch	68	E3
Grant Hollow	Rns	45	E2
Grant Mills	Dlw	57	D5
Grantville	Lch	65	D1
Granville	Whg	33	C2
Grapeville	Grn	59	A2
Graphite	Wrr	19	F3
Grappaville	Lch	65	D4
Graves Corners	Lew	15	F4
Gravesville	Hrk	29	E3
Gray	Hrk	30	A3
Gray Corners	Lvg	37	D4
Grays Beach	Ont	7	E1
Grays Corner	Whg	20	B6
Grays Corners	Cyg	26	E2
Grays Corners	Srg	45	C3
Great Barrington	Brk	60	B4
Great Bear Siding	Osw	27	B3
Great Bend	Jfs	8	D6
Great Meadows	War	73	A2
Great Neck	Nsu	75	D3
Great River	Sfk	76	D4
Great Valley	Cat	49	E4
Greece	Mro	24	D4
Greeley	Pke	66	A1
Green Acres Valley	Ere	22	B6
Green Corners	Sch	44	F1
Green Corners	Srg	31	F6
Green Haven	Dut	64	D6
Green Hill	Wgn	72	E2
Green Island	Alb	45	D3
Green River	Clm	60	A3
Green Settlement	Jfs	14	F2
Green Street	Ese	12	E1
Green Village	Mrr	74	A4
Greenboro	Osw	15	B5
Greenbrush	Ont	1	B4
Greencrest	Chu	48	B1
Greendell	Ssx	73	C1
Greene	Cng	55	C3
Greenfield	Srg	32	B5
Greenfield Center	Srg	32	B5
Greenfield Hill	Ffd	69	C4
Greenfield Park	Uls	63	A4
Greenhurst	Chu	48	C5
Greenlawn	Sfk	76	B2
Greenport	Sfk	71	B5
Greens Corners	Fkl	6	F2
Greenville	Grn	58	F1
Greenville	Orn	66	E2
Greenville	Stu	51	F1
Greenville	Uls	63	B2
Greenville	Wch	75	C1
Greenville Center	Grn	59	A2
Greenway Corners	Ond	28	F4
Greenwich	Ffd	68	E6
Greenwich	Whg	32	F6
Greenwich Junction	Whg	33	B5
Greenwood	Stu	51	D5
Greenwood Lake	Orn	67	C4
Gregory Corners	SL	2	C4
Gregorytown	Dlw	56	F6
Greig	Lew	16	B4
Greigsville	Lvg	37	A2
Gretna	Dut	64	B3
Greystone	Lch	65	F5
Gridleyville	Tio	54	B4
Griffin	Hml	31	D1
Griffins Mills	Ere	35	E4
Griffith Corners	Wyo	36	E6
Grooms Corners	Srg	45	B2
Groton	NLn	71	F2
Groton	Tmk	40	B5
Groton City	Tmk	40	C5
Groton Heights	NLn	71	F2
Groton Long Point	NLn	71	F3
Grotto	Tmk	40	A6
Grout Mill	Crt	40	C4
Grove	Agy	51	B1
Grove Beach	Mdx	71	A3
Grove Springs	Stu	52	E1
Groveland	Lvg	37	C5
Groveland Corners	Lvg	37	D4
Grovenor Corners	Shh	44	B4
Grover Cleveland Terrace	Ere	35	B1
Grover Hills	Ese	12	F6
Groveville	Dut	64	A6
Guide Board Corners	Tmk	54	B2
Guilderland	Alb	45	A4
Guilderland Center	Alb	45	A4
Guilford	Cng	56	A2
Guilford	NHv	70	D3
Guilford Center	Cng	56	A2
Guilford Station	NHv	70	D3
Gulf Bridge	Osw	27	F3
Gulf Summit	Brm	55	F6
Gulph	Hrk	29	D6
Gunns Corners	Jfs	8	A5
Gurn Spring	Srg	32	D4
Guttenberg	Hud	74	F3
Guttenberg	Hud	75	A3
Guyanoga	Yts	38	D5
Gypsum	Otr	38	E1

H

NAME	TERR	MAP	GRID
Hackensack	Brg	74	F2
Hackettstown	War	73	B2
Haddam	Mdx	70	F1
Haddo	Ont	2	B2
Hadley	Srg	32	B3
Hadley Bay	Chu	48	A5
Hadlyme	NLn	71	B1
Hagaman	Mgy	44	E1
Hagedorns Mills	Srg	31	E6
Hagerman	Sfk	77	A3
Hague	Wrr	20	A4
Hague Crossing	SL	2	D4
Haights Corners	Jfs	14	F3
Hailesboro	SL	9	A3
Haines Corners	Put	68	E1
Haines Falls	Grn	58	E4
Hainesville	Ssx	66	C3
Hainsville	Ont	2	B2
Halcott Center	Grn	58	A4
Halcottsville	Dlw	57	E4
Hale Eddy	Dlw	56	B6
Hale Mills	Flt	31	C6
Haledon	Pas	74	D1
Halesite	Sfk	76	B2
Half Acre	Cyg	39	E2
Halfmoon	Srg	45	D3
Halfway	Ono	27	B6
Halfway House Corners	SL	2	E3
Hall	Otr	38	F3
Hall Corners	Ond	28	B4
Hallecks	Ont	1	C6
Halls Corner	Cyg	40	C5
Halls Corner	Wyo	36	D4
Halls Corners	Jfs	8	D4
Halls Corners	Osw	28	A3
Halls Corners	SL	9	A2
Halls Corners	Scy	53	A1
Halls Corners	Sen	39	D5
Hallsport	Agy	51	B6
Hallsville	Mgy	43	D1
Hallville	NLn	71	F1
Halsey	Ssx	66	C5
Halsey Corners	Sen	39	C1
Halsey Valley	Tio	54	A5
Halsteads Bay	Ont	7	C1
Hambletville	Dlw	56	B5
Hamburg	Ere	35	C4
Hamburg	NLn	71	B2
Hamburg	Ssx	66	F5
Hamden	Dlw	57	A4
Hamden	Hnt	73	B5
Hamden	NHv	70	A2
Hamilton	Mds	41	F3
Hamlet	Chu	48	E2
Hamlin	Mro	24	A3
Hammertown	Dut	64	E1
Hammertown	Lch	60	B6
Hammett	Eri	47	A6
Hammond	SL	8	D1
Hammond Corners	Jfs	14	E3
Hammonds Corner	Osw	27	B1
Hammondsport	Stu	52	C2
Hampshire	Stu	51	F4
Hampton	Hnt	73	A4
Hampton	Whg	20	C6
Hampton Bays	Sfk	77	F2
Hampton Corners	Lvg	37	C4
Hampton Flats	Whg	20	C6
Hampton Park	Sfk	78	A2
Hamptonburgh	Orn	67	C1
Hancock	Brk	46	C6
Hancock	Dlw	61	C1
Hancock	Lch	65	F5
Handsome Eddy	Slv	66	B1
Hanford Bay	Chu	34	E6
Hanifin Corners	Ond	28	D2
Hankins	Slv	61	E3
Hanley Corner	Dlw	57	F5
Hannacroix	Grn	59	B1
Hannans Corner	Mro	25	A6
Hannawa Falls	SL	3	A5
Hannibal	Osw	26	F3
Hannibal Center	Osw	26	F3
Hanover	Mrr	74	B3
Hanover	Ond	42	B1
Hanover Center	Chu	34	E6
Happyland	NLn	71	F1
Harbor View	Mdx	70	F3
Harborcreek	Eri	47	A4
Harding Crossing	Sch	45	A5
Hardscrabble	Dlw	57	E3
Hardwick	War	66	A6
Hardwick Center	War	66	A6
Hardy Corners	Agy	50	C2
Hardy Corners	Cyg	40	C4
Hardys	Wyo	36	D5
Harford	Crt	54	D1
Harford Mills	Crt	54	D2
Harkness	Cln	5	F6
Harlemville	Clm	59	E3
Harmony Corners	Srg	45	A1
Harmonyvale	Ssx	66	E5
Harpers Ferry	Jfs	15	E1
Harpersfield	Dlw	57	D1
Harpursville	Brm	55	E4
Harrietstown	Frl	11	D2
Harrigan	Cln	5	A2
Harriman	Orn	67	D3
Harrington Park	Brg	75	A1
Harris	Slv	62	D4
Harris Corners	Wyo	36	A3
Harris Hill	Ere	35	D1
Harris Hill Manor	Chm	53	B5
Harrisburg	Cat	49	F6
Harrisburg	Lew	15	E2
Harrisburg	Wrr	31	F2
Harrison	Hud	74	E4
Harrison	Wch	68	D6
Harrison	Wch	75	D1
Harrison Grove	Nia	22	A3
Harrisons	NLn	71	E2
Harrisville	Cng	42	A4
Harrisville	Lew	9	B5
Harrower	Mgy	44	D1
Hart Lot	Ono	27	E6
Hartfield	Chu	48	A3
Hartford	Whg	33	B2
Hartland	Nia	22	F4
Hartman	Wrr	32	C3
Hartmans Corners	Alb	45	A4
Hartsville	Brk	60	C5
Hartsville	Stu	51	D4
Hartwick	Ots	42	F5
Hartwick Seminary	Ots	43	A5
Hartwood	Slv	62	D6
Hartwood Club	Slv	62	D6
Harvard	Dlw	56	E6
Harwinton	Lch	65	F3
Hasbrouck	Slv	62	E3
Hasbrouck Heights	Brg	74	E2
Hasbroucks	Hml	17	E2
Haselton	Ese	12	C2
Haskell Flats	Cat	50	C5
Haskinville	Stu	51	E1
Hastings	Osw	27	E2
Hastings Center	Osw	27	D3
Hastings-on-Hudson	Wch	68	B6
Hastings-on-Hudson	Wch	75	B1
Hatch Four Corners	Lch	65	B4
Hatchs Corners	Ond	28	F4
Hattertown	Ffd	69	C2
Hauppauge	Sfk	76	D3
Haven	Slv	62	F6
Havens Corner	Yts	38	E4
Haversham	Wsh	72	D2
Haverstraw	Rck	68	A4
Haviland Hollow	Put	68	F1
Hawkes	Ont	1	B4
Hawkeye	Cln	5	B6
Hawkins Corner	Chu	48	D1
Hawkins Corner	Ond	29	A3
Hawkinsville	Ond	29	C1
Hawks Nest Beach	NLn	71	C3
Hawley Corners	Cng	41	F6
Hawleys	Dlw	56	F4
Hawleyton	Brm	55	A6
Hawleyville	Ffd	69	B1
Haworth	Brg	75	A1
Hawthorne	Pas	74	E1
Hawthorne	Wch	68	C5
Hawthorne Hill	Sch	45	B3
Hawthorne Park	Chu	47	E2
Hawversville	Shh	44	C6
Hayground	Sfk	78	C1
Haynersville	Rns	45	F3
Haynes	Cng	55	F1
Hays Corners	Ont	1	A5
Hayt Corner	Tmk	53	F1
Hayt Corners	Sen	39	C4
Hazzard Corners	Brm	55	B2
Head Corners	Tmk	40	A6
Head Of The Harbor	Sfk	76	E2
Headquarters	Lch	65	C3
Heartwellville	Ben	46	F3
Heath Grove	Ono	40	C2
Hebron	Whg	33	C3
Hecks Corners	Qub	7	D6
Heckston	Ont	1	F1
Hecla	Ond	29	A5
Hector	Scy	39	B6
Hedgesville	Stu	52	A5
Helena	SL	3	D1
Hemlock	Lvg	37	E3
Hemlock Corners	Ont	1	C3
Hemlock District	Osw	15	A5
Hemlock Downs	Ont	7	A2
Hemp	NHv	69	E1
Hempstead	Nsu	75	E4
Hemstreet Park	Rns	45	D2
Henderson	Jfs	14	D2
Henderson Harbor	Jfs	14	D2
Henrietta	Mro	24	E6
Henrys Corners	SL	2	D3
Hensonville	Grn	58	D3
Hephzibah Heights	Brk	60	D4

NAME	TERR	MAP	GRID
Herkimer	Hrk	29	F6
Herkimer	Hrk	30	A6
Hermitage	Stu	52	C2
Hermitage	Wyo	36	D5
Hermon	SL	9	D1
Herrick Center	Sqh	61	A3
Herrings	Jfs	8	E6
Herrons Corners	Ont	1	D4
Hervey Street	Grn	58	E2
Heslops Corner	Ots	56	C1
Hessville	Mgy	43	D2
Heuvelton	SL	2	A5
Hewitt Park	Jfs	8	E6
Hewlett Bay Park	Nsu	75	D5
Hewlett Harbor	Nsu	75	D5
Hibernia	Dut	64	C3
Hibernia	Mrr	74	A1
Hickeys Corners	Srg	32	D5
Hickory Corners	Nia	22	D4
Hickory Grove	Osw	14	B6
Hickory Haven	Lch	65	B5
Hickory Tree	Mrr	74	A4
Hickorybush	Uls	63	F2
Hicks	Chm	53	E5
Hicks Corners	Wyo	36	B5
Hicksville	Nsu	75	F3
Higganum	Mdx	70	F1
Higgins	Agy	50	D1
Higgins	Agy	50	F4
Higgins Bay	Hml	30	F2
Higginsville	Ond	28	D4
High Bank	Cln	5	B5
High Bridge	Cng	56	A2
High Bridge	Cyg	26	D6
High Bridge	Hnt	73	B4
High Bridge	Ono	27	F6
High Falls	Lew	16	B1
High Falls	Uls	63	E2
High Flats	SL	3	A5
High Market	Lew	15	F5
High Ridge	Ffd	68	F5
High Street	Wrr	32	B1
High View	Slv	63	A6
High Woods	Uls	58	F6
Highgate Center	Fkl	6	F1
Highgate Falls	Fkl	6	F1
Highgate Springs	Fkl	6	E1
Highland	Uls	64	A4
Highland Falls	Orn	68	A2
Highland Lake	Slv	62	B6
Highland Lakes	Ssx	67	A4
Highland Mills	Orn	67	E2
Highland Park	Mid	74	A6
Highland Park	Mid	78	A6
Highland Park	Nia	22	D4
Highland-on-the-Lake	Ere	35	A4
Highmont	Uls	58	A5
Highup	Stu	51	E5
Hill Corners	Flt	31	E6
Hillburn	Brg	67	D5
Hillcrest	Agy	50	D2
Hillcrest	NHv	65	F6
Hillcrest	Rck	67	F5
Hillis	Dut	64	B5
Hillsboro	Ond	28	C3
Hillsdale	Brg	67	F6
Hillsdale	Clm	59	F4
Hillsdale	Whg	33	C2
Hillside	Ond	29	B2
Hillside	Uni	74	D4
Hilton	Mro	24	C3
Hiltonville	Agy	51	B2
Himrod	Yts	39	A5
Hinckley	Ond	29	E3
Hinesburg	Chi	13	E3
Hinmans Corners	Brm	55	A4
Hinmansville	Osw	27	B3
Hinsdale	Brk	60	E1
Hinsdale	Cat	50	B5
Hitchcock Corners	Lch	65	B2
Ho-Ho-Kus	Brg	67	E6
Ho-Ho-Kus	Brg	74	E1
Hoadleys	Wyn	61	C6
Hoag Corners	Rns	45	F6
Hoasic	Ont	2	E1
Hobart	Dlw	57	E2
Hoben	Agy	50	E6
Hobin Corners	Ond	42	C2
Hoboken	Hud	74	F4
Hoboken	Ots	42	C5
Hoeseville	Flt	31	E6
Hoffman	Nia	22	B6
Hoffmans	Hnt	73	B4
Hoffmans	Sch	44	F2
Hoffmeister	Hml	30	D2
Hogansburg	Frl	3	D1
Hogtown	Whg	19	F6
Holbrook	Sfk	76	E3
Holbrook Corners	Srg	45	A1
Holcomb	Otr	38	B2
Holcombville	Wrr	19	A4
Holland	Ere	35	F5
Holland Patent	Ond	29	C4
Holley	Orl	23	F4
Hollowville	Clm	59	D4
Hollywyle Park	Ffd	69	A1
Holmes	Dut	64	E6
Holmesville	Cng	42	A6
Holsapple Corners	Srg	31	F6
Holton Beach	Sen	39	D5
Holtsville	Sfk	76	F3
Homer	Crt	40	E5
Honeoye	Otr	37	F3
Honeoye Falls	Mro	37	F1
Honeoye Park	Otr	38	A3
Honesdale	Wyn	61	C5
Honest Hill	Orl	23	E5
Honeyville	Jfs	15	A2
Honeywell Corners	Flt	31	E6
Honk Hill	Uls	63	B3
Hooker	Lew	15	D4
Hoopers Valley	Tio	54	B6
Hoosick	Rns	46	C2
Hoosick Falls	Rns	46	B2
Hopatcong	Ssx	73	D1
Hope	Hml	31	D3
Hope	War	73	A2
Hope Falls	Hml	31	D3
Hope Farm	Dut	64	E4
Hopewell Center	Otr	38	D2
Hopewell Junction	Dut	64	C6
Hopkins Beach	Nia	22	B3
Hopkins Corners	Put	68	D2
Hopkinton	SL	3	D4
Hopkinton	Wgn	72	C1
Hornby	Stu	52	F4
Hornell	Stu	51	E3
Horseheads	Chm	53	C4
Horseshoe	SL	10	B1
Horseshoe Hill	Wch	68	E4
Hortonia	Rut	20	D4
Hortontown	Ono	27	B4
Hortonville	Slv	61	F3
Hoseaville	Dlw	57	C1
Hotchkissville	Lch	65	D6
Houcks Corners	Alb	45	C5
Hough Crossing	Add	20	B3
Houghton	Agy	50	E1
Houghtonville	Brk	46	E4
Housatonic	Brk	60	B3
Houseman Corners	Put	68	C2
Houseville	Lew	16	A4
Housons Corners	Shh	44	B5
Howard	Stu	51	F2
Howardville	Osw	27	F1
Howell	Orn	67	B2
Howells	Orn	67	A1
Howes	Brm	55	F5
Howes	Wyo	36	C5
Howes Cave	Shh	44	B4
Howland Corners	Tmk	40	A6
Howlett Hill	Ono	27	C6
Howser Corners	Tmk	40	A5
Hoxie Corner	Dut	64	D4
Hubbard Corner	Fkl	6	E4
Hubbard Corners	Ond	42	C1
Hubbardsville	Mds	42	A3
Hubbardton	Rut	20	D4
Hubbardtown	Tio	54	C4
Hubbell Corners	Dlw	57	F3
Huddle	Wan	25	C5
Hudson	Clm	59	C3
Hudson Falls	Whg	32	F3
Hughes Corners	Mds	41	D1
Hughsonville	Dut	64	B6
Hughston Corner	Ots	56	C1
Huguenot	Orn	67	B6
Hulbert	Ont	2	B1
Hulberton	Orl	23	F3
Huletts Landing	Whg	19	E5
Hullsville	Tio	54	D5
Hume	Agy	50	E1
Humphrey	Cat	49	F4
Humphrey Center	Cat	49	F4
Hungerford Corners	Jfs	14	C2
Hunt	Lvg	37	A6
Hunt Corners	Wan	26	B5
Hunt Hollow	Lvg	38	A5
Hunter	Grn	58	D4
Huntersland	Shh	44	C6
Huntington	Sfk	76	B2
Huntington Bay	Sfk	76	A2
Huntington Beach	Sfk	76	B2
Huntington Station	Sfk	76	B2
Huntingtown	Ffd	69	C2
Huntly Corners	Ots	42	E3
Hunts Corners	Crt	54	E1
Hunts Corners	Ere	22	E6
Huntsburg	Ssx	73	B1
Huntsville	Lch	65	C1
Huntsville	Ssx	73	C1
Hurd Corners	Dut	64	E5
Hurd Settlement	Slv	62	B4
Hurds Corner	Lch	65	A5
Hurdtown	Ssx	73	E1
Hurley	Uls	63	F1
Hurleyville	Slv	62	D4
Huron	Wan	26	B4
Hyde Manor	Rut	20	D3
Hyde Park	Dut	64	A3
Hyde Park	Ots	43	A5
Hydesville	Wan	25	E6
Hydeville	Brm	55	A3
Hydeville	Cng	41	B5
Hydeville	Rut	20	D5
Hyndman	Ont	1	F1
Hyndsville	Shh	43	F4

I

NAME	TERR	MAP	GRID
Igerna	Wrr	19	A4
Ilion	Hrk	29	F6
Ilion	Hrk	42	F1
Inavale	Agy	50	E5
Independence	Agy	51	C5
Index	Ots	43	A4
Indian Castle	Hrk	30	C6
Indian Falls	Gns	23	B6
Indian Grove	Cyg	40	A3
Indian Kettles	Wrr	20	A3
Indian Lake	Hml	18	C3
Indian Neck	NHv	70	C3
Indian Orchard	Wyn	61	D6
Indian Park	Orn	67	C4
Indian River	Lew	16	B1
Indian Village	Ono	40	E1
Ingham Mills	Flt	30	C6
Ingham Mills	Hrk	30	C6
Ingleside	Ont	2	F1
Ingleside	Ont	3	A1
Ingleside	Stu	38	B6
Ingleside Corners	Otr	38	B1
Ingraham	Cln	6	A3
Ingraham Corners	Cng	55	E1
Inlet	Hml	17	C3
Interlaken	Brk	60	C3
Interlaken	Sen	39	C5
Interlaken Beach	Sen	39	D5
Inverary	Ont	7	A1
Inverness	Lvg	37	B2
Inwood	Nsu	75	C5
Ionia	Ono	27	B5
Ionia	Otr	38	A1
Ira	Cyg	26	F4
Ira	Rut	20	F6
Ira Corners	Cyg	26	E4
Ireland Corners	Uls	63	E4
Irelandville	Scy	53	A2
Irena	Ont	2	C2
Irishtown	Ese	19	A3
Irona	Cln	5	D2
Irondale	Dut	64	F1
Irondequoit	Mro	24	E4
Ironia	Mrr	73	E2
Ironsides	Ono	40	D1
Ironville	Ese	19	F1
Iroquois	Ere	35	A6
Iroquois	Ont	2	C2
Irvine Mills	Cat	49	E6
Irving	Chu	34	E6
Irvington	Esx	74	C4
Irvington	Wch	68	B6
Ischua	Cat	50	B4
Iselin	Mid	74	C6
Island Cottage Beach	Mro	24	B2
Island Park	Nsu	75	D5
Islandia	Sfk	76	D3
Isle La Motte	GIC	6	C2
Islip	Sfk	76	D4
Islip Terrace	Sfk	76	D3
Italy	Yts	38	C5
Italy Hill	Yts	38	D5
Italy-Naples	Lvg	38	B5
Itaska	Brm	55	B3
Ithaca	Tmk	53	F1
Ithaca	Tmk	54	A1
Ivanhoe	Dlw	56	C4
Ives Corner	NHv	70	B1
Ives Corner	Rns	45	F4
Ivory	Chu	48	E6
Ivy Lea	Ont	7	F1

J

NAME	TERR	MAP	GRID
Jacks Corners	Rns	45	F6
Jacks Reef	Ono	27	A5
Jackson Corners	Dut	59	C6
Jackson Summit	Flt	31	C5
Jacksonburg	Hrk	30	B6
Jacksonville	Ono	27	A4
Jacksonville	Tmk	39	E6
Jamaica	Que	75	C4
Jamesport	Sfk	77	F1
Jamestown	Chu	48	D5
Jamesville	Ono	40	F1
Jamison Corners	Osw	28	B2
Jamison Road	Ere	35	E3
Janesville	Shh	43	F4
Jaquins	Chu	47	E6
Jasper	Ont	1	A3
Jasper	Stu	51	F5
Java Center	Wyo	36	B5
Java Village	Wyo	36	B5
Jay	Ese	12	D2
Jeddo	Nia	23	A3
Jeddo	Orl	23	A3
Jefferson	Shh	57	E1
Jefferson Heights	Grn	59	B4
Jefferson Park	Jfs	14	D3
Jefferson Valley	Wch	68	C2
Jeffersonville	Slv	62	A3
Jenkinstown	Uls	63	E4
Jenksville	Tio	54	D3
Jerden Falls	Lew	9	C6
Jericho	Cln	5	E3
Jericho	Nsu	75	F3
Jericon Corners	Gns	24	A5
Jersey City	Hud	74	E4
Jerusalem	Cln	5	D3
Jerusalem	Wgn	72	F2
Jerusalem Corners	Ere	34	F4
Jessup Corners	Otr	38	F1
Jewell	Ond	28	C4
Jewell Corner	Srg	32	E4
Jewett	Grn	58	C3
Jewett Center	Grn	58	C4
Jewettville	Ere	35	D4
Jewettville	Jfs	14	E1
Jobs Corner	Stu	51	F2
Jockey Hill	Uls	63	E2
Johnsburg	Wrr	19	A5
Johnson	Orn	66	F2
Johnson City	Brm	55	A5
Johnson Corners	Cng	55	D3
Johnson Corners	Hrk	29	F6
Johnson Corners	Osw	27	C1
Johnson Creek	Nia	22	F3
Johnsonburg	War	73	B1
Johnsonburg	Wyo	36	B4
Johnsonville	Rns	45	F2
Johnsonville	Tio	54	B5
Johnstons Corners	Ere	35	F6
Johnstown	Flt	31	B6
Johnstown	Flt	44	B1
Johnstown	Ont	2	A4
Jones Beach	Ono	40	B2
Jones Beach	Orl	23	E2
Jones Corners	Chu	48	B4
Jones Corners	Osw	27	B1
Jones Corners	Stu	52	C5
Jones Corners	Tmk	40	C6
Jones Corners	Wyo	37	A3
Jones Crossing	Ots	42	F5
Jones Point	Orn	68	A3
Jonesville	Srg	45	B2
Jordan	Ono	27	A6
Jordanville	Hrk	43	A1
Josephus	Wyn	61	C5
Joy	Wan	25	E4
Joyceville	Lch	60	A6
Joyceville	Ont	7	C1
Judd Corners	Cat	49	A2
Juddville	Mds	41	C2
Junetown	Ont	1	A6
Jutland	Hnt	73	A5

K

NAME	TERR	MAP	GRID
K Cat Corners	Cyg	26	E4
Kaaterskill Falls	Grn	58	F4
Kabob	Chu	48	C3
Kaisertown	Orn	63	C6
Kallops Corners	Uls	63	E2
Kanona	Stu	52	B2
Kansas	Ben	33	E6
Karlsfeld	Alb	45	B5
Karrdale	Agy	51	C3
Kasoag	Osw	28	A1
Kast Bridge	Hrk	30	A6
Katonah	Wch	68	D3
Katsbaan	Uls	59	A5
Kattellville	Brm	55	B4
Kattskill Bay	Whg	32	E1
Kattskill Bay	Wrr	32	E1
Kauneoga Lake	Slv	62	B4
Kay Corners	Stu	52	F4
Keaches Corners	Chu	48	E1
Keansburg	Mom	78	E6
Kearny	Hud	74	E3
Keasbey	Mid	74	B6
Kecks Center	Flt	31	A6
Keefers Corners	Alb	45	A6
Keeler Bay	GIC	6	B5
Keene	Ese	12	C3
Keene Valley	Ese	12	C4
Keeney	Crt	41	A3
Keese Mill	Frl	11	C1
Keeseville	Cln	6	A6
Keeseville	Ese	6	A6
Keeseville	Ese	13	A1
Keesler Corners	Mgy	43	D1
Kelhi Corners	Hrk	30	B6
Kellogg	SL	3	C4
Kellogg Corners	SL	9	A4
Kellogg Corners	Tmk	53	E2
Kelloggsville	Cyg	40	B3
Kelly Corner	Lch	65	D2
Kelly Corners	Chu	48	B2
Kelly Corners	Dlw	57	E4
Kelly Stand	Ben	33	F6
Kellys Corners	Ono	27	C6
Kelsey	Dlw	56	C6
Kelseytown	Mdx	70	F3
Kendall	Orl	23	F3
Kendall Corners	Cat	49	A3
Kendall Mills	Mro	24	A3
Kendrew Corners	SL	2	B6
Kenilworth	Uni	74	C4
Kenmore	Ere	35	B1
Kenmount	Jfs	7	C4
Kennedy	Chu	48	E5
Kennedy Corner	Tmk	53	F1
Kenoza Lake	Slv	62	A4
Kensington	Nsu	75	C3
Kent	Lch	65	A4
Kent	Orl	23	E3
Kent Cliffs	Put	68	C1
Kent Furnace	Lch	65	A4
Kents Corners	SL	9	C1
Kenvil	Mrr	73	E2
Kenyon	Wgn	72	E1
Kenyonville	Orl	23	C3
Kerhonkson	Uls	63	C3
Kerleys Corners	Dut	59	B6
Kerry Siding	Dlw	56	C6
Kerryville	Dlw	56	D6
Ketchum Corners	Ots	42	D5
Ketchums Corners	Srg	32	D6
Ketchumville	Tio	54	E3
Keuka	Stu	52	E1
Keuka Park	Yts	38	E5
Keyport	Mom	78	D6
Kiamesha Lake	Slv	62	D4
Kiantone	Chu	48	D6
Kidders	Sen	39	D5
Kildare	Frl	10	F3
Kill Buck	Cat	49	D5
Killawog	Brm	54	F2
Killingworth	Mdx	70	F2
Kilmarnock	Ont	1	A2
Kilmartin Corners	Mgy	44	A3
Kimball Corners	Srg	31	F6
Kimball Mill	Lew	9	B5
Kimball Stand	Chu	48	C4
Kinderhook	Clm	59	D2
King Corners	Chu	47	F6
King Ferry	Cyg	39	E5
King Ferry Station	Cyg	39	E5
King Pitt	Ont	7	A2
Kingdom	Hrk	43	A1
Kings	Srg	32	B5
Kings Corners	Cyg	39	E3
Kings Park	Sfk	76	C2
Kings Point	Nsu	75	C3
Kings School Corner	Chu	48	E3
Kings Settlement	Cng	42	A5
Kings Station	Srg	32	C5
Kingsbury	Whg	32	F2
Kingston	Ont	7	A3
Kingston	Uls	63	F1
Kingston	Uls	64	A1
Kingston	Wgn	72	F1
Kingston Mills	Ont	7	A2
Kinne Corners	Hrk	42	E1
Kinnelon	Mrr	67	B6
Kinnelon	Mrr	74	B1
Kinney Corners	Osw	26	F2
Kinneys Corner	Lch	65	B6
Kirby Corner	Chi	13	E1
Kirkland	Ond	29	B6
Kirkville	Ono	28	A6
Kirkwood	Brm	55	C6
Kirkwood	Stu	38	A6
Kirkwood Center	Brm	55	C6
Kirschnerville	Lew	16	B2
Kiryas Joel	Orn	67	E2
Kiskatom	Grn	59	A4
Kismet	Sfk	76	D5
Kitchawan	Wch	68	C4
Klinesville	Hnt	73	B6
Knapp Creek	Cat	49	F6
Knapps Corner	Dut	64	A5
Knappville	Flt	30	E4
Knickerbocker Corners	Otr	38	E1
Knight Creek	Agy	50	F5
Knight Settlement	Stu	52	B2
Knights Eddy	Slv	66	C1
Knollcrest	Ffd	65	A6
Knollwood	Mdx	71	B3
Knowelhurst	Wrr	31	F1
Knowlesville	Orl	23	B3
Knox	Alb	44	E4
Knoxboro	Ond	41	F1
Kohlertown	Slv	62	A3
Kokomo Corners	SL	2	A6
Komar Park	Srg	45	A2
Konkapot	Brk	60	C6
Kortright Center	Dlw	57	C2
Kortright Station	Dlw	57	C2
Kossuth	Agy	50	E6
Kosterville	Lew	16	C5
Kraus Landing	Ono	27	F4
Kringsbrush	Flt	30	D6
Kripplebush	Uls	63	D2
Krum Corner	Tmk	53	F1
Krumville	Uls	63	D2
Kuckville	Orl	23	C2
Kyserike	Uls	63	E3
Kysonville	Lvg	37	C5

L

NAME	TERR	MAP	GRID
La Fargeville	Jfs	8	A4
La Grange	Orn	67	C1
La Palestine	Qub	7	D6
La Rue Mills	Ont	8	B1
Lackawack	Uls	63	A3
Lackawanna	Ere	35	B3
Lackawaxen	Pke	66	A1
Lacolle	Qub	7	B6
Lacona	Osw	14	F5
Lacy Corners	Tmk	40	C6
Ladiesville	Osw	27	E1
Lafargeys Landing	Sfk	71	D6
Lafayette	Ono	40	E2
Lafayette	Ssx	66	D5
Lafayette Corners	Tmk	40	C5
Lafayetteville	Dut	64	D1
LaGrange	Wyo	36	F3
Lagrangeville	Dut	64	C5
Laidlaw	Cat	50	B2
Laird Corners	Ono	27	B6
Lairdsville	Ond	29	A6
Lake Bluff	Wan	26	A3
Lake Bonaparte	Lew	9	B5
Lake Carmel	Put	68	D1
Lake Clear Junction	Frl	11	D2
Lake Colby	Frl	11	E2
Lake Como	Wyn	61	C2
Lake Delaware	Dlw	57	C3
Lake Delta	Ond	29	A3
Lake Desolation	Srg	32	A5
Lake Dunmore	Add	20	E2
Lake Erie Beach	Ere	34	E5
Lake Grove	Sfk	76	E2
Lake Hiawatha	Mrr	74	B2
Lake Hill	Uls	58	D6
Lake Huntington	Slv	62	A4
Lake Katrine	Uls	64	A1
Lake Lincolndale	Wch	68	D2
Lake Luzerne	Wrr	32	C3
Lake Mohawk	Ssx	66	E6
Lake Peekskill	Put	68	B2
Lake Placid	Ese	12	A3
Lake Pleasant	Hml	31	B1
Lake Purdy	Wch	68	D3
Lake Ridge	Tmk	39	E5
Lake Ronkonkoma	Sfk	76	E3
Lake Success	Nsu	75	D3
Lake Telemark	Mrr	74	A1
Lake Vanare	Wrr	32	C2
Lake View	Ere	35	A4
Lakeland	Ono	27	C6
Lakemont	Yts	39	A6
Lakeport	Mds	28	B5
Lakeside	Lch	65	D4
Lakeside	NHv	69	D1
Lakeside	Orl	23	C2
Lakeside	Wan	25	B3
Lakeside Park	Stu	38	D6
Lakeview	Cng	55	B1
Lakeview	Osw	14	A6
Lakeville	Lch	65	A1
Lakeville	Lvg	37	D2
Lakeville	Orn	67	C4

NAME	TERR	MAP	GRID
Millington	Mdx	71	B1
Millington	Mrr	73	F4
Millmans Corners	Cat	48	F3
Millport	Chm	53	C3
Millrift	Pke	66	C2
Mills Corners	Flt	31	E6
Mills Mills	Agy	36	E6
Millsburg	Orn	66	F2
Millstone	NLn	71	E3
Millstone	Sms	73	E6
Milltown	Mid	78	A6
Milltown	Mrr	73	D3
Milltown	Put	68	F2
Millville	Orl	23	B4
Millville	Ssx	66	C3
Millwood	Wch	68	C4
Milo Center	Yts	38	F5
Milo Station	Yts	39	A5
Milton	Chi	6	E5
Milton	Lch	65	C3
Milton	Mrr	66	F6
Milton	Uls	64	A5
Milton Center	Srg	32	B6
Miltonboro	Chi	6	D4
Mina	Chu	47	D5
Minaville	Mgy	44	D2
Mindenville	Mgy	43	D1
Mine Hill	Mrr	73	E2
Mineola	Nsu	75	D4
Mineral Springs	Shh	44	A5
Minerva	Ese	19	A3
Minetto	Osw	27	A2
Mineville	Ese	12	F5
Minisink Ford	Slv	66	A1
Minnegar Corners	Chu	47	D4
Minnehaha	Hrk	16	E4
Minnewaska	Uls	63	D4
Minoa	Ono	27	F6
Minoa	Ono	28	A5
Minortown	Lch	65	D6
Minott Corners	Hrk	29	F5
Minsteed	Wan	25	E5
Miranda	Qub	7	C6
Misquamicut	Wgn	72	C3
Mitchellsville	Stu	52	C2
Mitchellville	Ont	8	A2
Mitcheltown	Lch	65	A2
Mizzen Top	Dut	64	F6
Model City	Nia	22	A4
Modena	Uls	63	E5
Modena Gardens	Uls	63	E5
Moe	Pas	67	B5
Moffitsville	Cln	5	C5
Mohawk	Hrk	29	F6
Mohawk	Hrk	30	A6
Mohawk Hill	Lew	16	A6
Mohegan	NLn	71	E1
Mohegan Lake	Wch	68	B3
Mohican Lake	Slv	62	B6
Mohonk Lake	Uls	63	E3
Moira	Frl	3	F3
Molasses Corners	Frl	4	F6
Molyneaux Corners	Nia	22	C4
Momauguin	NHv	70	B3
Mombaccus	Uls	63	C3
Mongaup	Slv	66	C1
Mongaup Valley	Slv	62	C5
Monkton	Add	13	E4
Monkton Ridge	Add	13	E3
Monroe	Ffd	69	D3
Monroe	Orn	67	D3
Monroe	Ssx	66	E5
Monsey	Rck	67	E5
Montague	Ssx	66	C3
Montario Point	Jfs	14	D4
Montauk	Sfk	72	A6
Montclair	Esx	74	D3
Montclair Coloney	Sfk	71	B6
Montebello	Rck	67	E5
Monteola	Lew	15	E5
Monterey	Brk	60	D4
Monterey	Scy	52	F3
Montezuma	Cyg	26	D6
Montgomery	Orn	63	D6
Monticello	Slv	62	D5
Montoma	Uls	58	E6
Montour Falls	Scy	53	C2
Montowese	NHv	70	B2
Montrose	Wch	68	A3
Montvale	Brg	67	F6
Montville	Brk	60	E5
Montville	Cyg	40	B4
Montville	Mrr	74	B1
Montville Center	NLn	71	E1
Moody	Frl	11	A4
Mooers	Cln	5	E1
Mooers Forks	Cln	5	E1
Moon Beach	Cyg	26	E2
Moonachie	Brg	74	F2
Moons	Chu	48	C3
Mooreland	Scy	53	A3
Moores Corners	SL	9	F1
Moores Crossing	Qub	7	F6
Moores Mill	Dut	64	D4
Mooreville	Lch	65	F2
Moorheadville	Eri	47	A4
Moose River	Lew	16	E5
Moran Corners	Mro	37	E1
Moravia	Cyg	40	A4
Morehouse Corner	Clm	59	F2
Morehouseville	Hml	30	C2
Morgan Corners	Chu	47	E6
Morgan Hill	Uls	63	E1
Morgans Corner	Qub	7	F6
Morganville	Gns	23	F6
Moriah	Ese	12	F6
Moriah Center	Ese	12	F6
Moriches	Sfk	77	C3
Morley	SL	2	D5
Morningside Park	NLn	71	E2
Morris	Lch	65	D4
Morris	Ots	42	C6
Morris Plains	Mrr	74	A3
Morrisburg	Ont	2	D2
Morrison Heights	Orn	63	D6
Morrisonville	Cln	5	F4
Morristown	Mrr	74	A3
Morristown	SL	1	E6
Morristown Center	SL	1	E5
Morrisville	Mds	41	D2
Morse	Osw	27	E2
Morse Mill	Cyg	40	B4
Morsston	Slv	62	C2
Morton	Mro	24	A3
Morton	Orl	24	A3
Morton Corners	Ere	35	C6
Moscow Hill	Mds	42	B3
Mosherville	Srg	31	F6
Moshier Falls	Hrk	16	E2
Mosquito Point	Grn	58	B3
Motts Corner	Otr	25	B6
Mottville	Ono	40	A1
Mount Arab	SL	10	E4
Mount Arab Station	SL	10	E4
Mount Arlington	Mrr	73	E2
Mount Carmel	Brm	55	F5
Mount Chesney	Ont	7	A1
Mount Freedom	Mrr	73	E3
Mount Hope	Mrr	73	F1
Mount Hope	Orn	66	F1
Mount Ivy	Rck	67	F4
Mount Kisco	Wch	68	D4
Mount Marion	Uls	59	A6
Mount Morris	Lvg	37	B4
Mount Morris Dam	Lvg	37	A4
Mount Pleasant	Osw	27	B2
Mount Pleasant	Srg	32	A5
Mount Pleasant	Uls	58	C6
Mount Prosper	Slv	62	F5
Mount Read	Mro	24	E4
Mount Ross	Dut	59	D6
Mount Sinai	Sfk	76	F1
Mount Tremper	Uls	58	C6
Mount Upton	Cng	56	B1
Mount Vernon	Ere	35	B3
Mount Vernon	Slv	63	A5
Mount Vernon	Wch	75	B2
Mount Vision	Ots	42	F6
Mountain Home	Hml	30	D2
Mountain House	Orn	67	D2
Mountain Lakes	Mrr	74	A2
Mountain Lodge	Orn	67	E2
Mountain View	Frl	4	E4
Mountain View	Pas	74	C1
Mountain View	Rns	45	E4
Mountaindale	Slv	62	F4
Mountainside	Uni	74	B4
Mountainville	Hnt	73	C4
Mountainville	Orn	67	F2
Moyers Corners	Mgy	43	D1
Moyers Corners	Ono	27	C4
Mud Hill	Osw	28	A2
Mud Mills	Wan	25	F6
Mud Schoolhouse Corners	Tmk	40	C6
Mud Settlement	Osw	27	E3
Muitzes Kill	Rns	59	D1
Mumford	Mro	37	B1
Mundale	Dlw	56	F3
Mungers Corners	Osw	27	D2
Munns	Mds	41	F1
Munnsville	Mds	41	F1
Munsey Park	Nsu	75	D3
Munsons Corners	Crt	40	D6
Munsons Corner	Sen	26	C6
Munsons Corner	Wan	26	C6
Munsonville	Flt	31	D6
Murray	Orl	23	F3
Murray Hill	Uni	74	B4
Murrays Corner	Ere	36	A1
Muttontown	Nsu	75	F3
Mycenae	Ono	28	A6
Myers	Tmk	39	F6
Myers Corner	Dut	64	B5
Myers Corners	Srg	32	D6
Myers Grove	Orn	66	E1
Myersville	Mrr	74	A4
Myrtle Grove	Ssx	66	C5
Mystic	NLn	72	A2

N

NAME	TERR	MAP	GRID
Nanticoke	Brm	54	F3
Nanuet	Rck	67	F5
Napanoch	Uls	63	B4
Napeague	Sfk	71	F6
Naples	Lvg	38	B5
Napoli	Cat	49	B4
Narrowsburg	Slv	61	F5
Nashville	Chu	48	F1
Nashville	Nia	22	B6
Nassau	Rns	45	E6
Nassau Shores	Nsu	76	A5
Natural Bridge	Jfs	9	A6
Natural Dam	SL	9	A2
Naugatuck	NHv	65	E6
Naugatuck	NHv	69	E1
Naughright	Mrr	73	C3
Naumburg	Lew	16	A2
Nauraushaun	Rck	68	A6
Navarino	Ono	40	C1
Nedrow	Ono	40	E1
Neelytown	Orn	67	C1
Nelliston	Mgy	43	E1
Nelson	Mds	41	C1
Nelson Corners	Put	68	A2
Nelsons Corner	Lch	65	F1
Nelsonville	Put	68	A1
Nepaug	Lch	65	F3
Nesconset	Sfk	76	E2
Neshanic Station	Sms	73	C6
Neshobe Beach	Rut	20	D5
Netcong	Mrr	73	D2
Netherwood	Dut	64	C3
Neversink	Slv	62	E2
Nevis	Clm	59	B6
New Albion	Cat	49	B3
New Ashford	Brk	46	D5
New Baltimore	Grn	59	C1
New Berlin	Cng	42	B5
New Boston	Brk	60	E5
New Boston	Crt	41	A4
New Boston	Lew	15	D3
New Bremen	Lew	16	A2
New Bridge	SL	10	A3
New Brunswick	Mid	78	A6
New Canaan	Ffd	69	A5
New City	Rck	68	A5
New City Park	Rck	68	A5
New Concord	Clm	59	F2
New Connecticut	Tio	54	E3
New Dublin	Ont	1	C4
New Ebenezer	Ere	35	D2
New Fairfield	Ffd	69	A1
New Hackensack	Dut	64	B5
New Hamburg	Dut	64	A5
New Hampton	Hnt	73	A4
New Hampton	Orn	67	A2
New Hartford	Ond	29	C6
New Haven	Add	13	E5
New Haven	NHv	70	B3
New Haven	Osw	27	C1
New Haven Junction	Add	13	D5
New Haven Mills	Add	13	E5
New Hempstead	Rck	67	F5
New Hope	Cyg	40	B3
New Hurley	Uls	63	E5
New Hyde Park	Nsu	75	D4
New Ireland	Brm	55	A4
New Kingston	Dlw	57	D4
New Lebanon	Clm	60	B1
New Lebanon Center	Clm	60	A1
New Lisbon	Ots	42	D5
New London	NLn	71	E2
New London	Ond	28	E4
New Marlborough	Brk	60	D5
New Milford	Brg	74	F1
New Milford	Lch	65	B6
New Milford	Orn	67	B4
New Oregon	Ere	35	C5
New Paltz	Uls	63	F3
New Preston	Lch	65	B4
New Providence	Uni	74	B4
New Rochelle	Wch	75	C2
New Russia	Ese	12	E5
New Russia	Ssx	66	F6
New Salem	Alb	45	A5
New Salem	Uls	63	F2
New Scotland	Alb	45	A5
New Scriba	Osw	15	A5
New Shoreham	Wgn	72	F4
New Square	Rck	67	F5
New Suffolk	Sfk	78	A1
New Vernon	Mrr	74	A4
New Vernon	Orn	63	A6
New Vernon	Slv	63	A6
New Windsor	Orn	67	F1
New Woodstock	Mds	41	B2
New York	Kng	75	B6
New York	NYC	74	F6
New York	NYC	75	B6
New York Mills	Ond	29	C5
Newark	Esx	74	D4
Newark	Wan	25	E6
Newark Valley	Tio	54	D4
Newburg	Wyo	36	E4
Newburgh	Orn	63	F6
Newburgh	Orn	67	F1
Newcomb	Ese	18	E1
Neweiden	Slv	62	A5
Newell Corners	Ond	41	F1
Newfane	Nia	22	D3
Newfield	Ffd	68	F5
Newfield	Tmk	53	E2
Newfield Station	Tmk	53	F2
Newfoundland	Pas	67	A6
Newkirk Mills	Flt	30	F5
Newmans Corners	Brm	55	B4
Newport	Hrk	29	F4
Newport	Mro	24	F4
Newport	Ono	27	C6
Newport	Orn	67	A3
Newrys	Grn	59	A1
Newton	Ere	35	A6
Newton	Ssx	66	D6
Newton Falls	SL	10	A4
Newton Hook	Clm	59	C2
Newtown	Ffd	69	C2
Newtown	Srg	45	D2
Newville	Hrk	43	C1
Niagara	Wyn	61	B4
Niagara Falls	Nia	21	F5
Niagara Falls	Nia	22	A5
Niagara Falls	Ont	21	E6
Niagara Falls	Ont	34	E1
Niagara-on-the-Lake	Ont	21	E4
Niantic	NLn	71	D3
Nichols	Tio	54	B6
Nichols Corners	Wyo	36	D3
Nichols Run	Cat	49	F6
Nicholsville	Osw	28	A3
Nicholville	SL	3	E4
Niets Crest	Chu	48	B5
Nile	Agy	50	E4
Niles	Cyg	40	B2
Nineveh	Brm	55	E4
Nineveh Junction	Cng	55	E4
Ninty Six Corners	Ond	29	E2
Niobe	Chu	48	A6
Niskayuna	Sch	45	B3
Nissequogue	Sfk	76	D2
Niverville	Clm	59	D1
Nixon	Mid	74	B6
Noank	NLn	72	A3
Noble Shores	Osw	15	B6
Nobleboro	Hrk	30	B2
Nolans Corners	Ont	1	A1
Norfolk	Lch	65	D1
Norfolk	SL	3	A3
Normanock	Ssx	66	C4
Normansville	Alb	45	A6
Noroton	Ffd	69	A6
Noroton Heights	Ffd	69	A5
Norrie Heights	Dut	64	A2
North Adams	Brk	46	E4
North Adams	Jfs	14	F2
North Afton	Cng	55	F3
North Alexander	Gns	36	C1
North Almond	Agy	51	C2
North Amboy	Osw	28	B2
North Amityville	Sfk	76	A4
North Argyle	Whg	33	A3
North Arlington	Brg	74	E3
North Augusta	Ont	1	C3
North Avon	Lvg	37	D1
North Bailey	Ere	35	C1
North Bangor	Frl	4	B2
North Barton	Tio	54	A5
North Bay	Ond	28	D4
North Bay Shore	Sfk	76	C4
North Bellmore	Nsu	75	F4
North Bellport	Sfk	77	A3
North Bennington	Ben	46	C1
North Bergen	Gns	23	F5
North Blenheim	Shh	58	A1
North Bloomfield	Lvg	37	E1
North Bolton	Wrr	19	E5
North Boston	Ere	35	C4
North Boylston	Osw	14	F4
North Branch	Slv	62	A3
North Branch	Sms	73	D5
North Branford	NHv	70	C3
North Bridgewater	Ond	42	C1
North Broadalbin	Flt	31	D5
North Brookfield	Mds	42	B2
North Burke	Frl	4	D1
North Caldwell	Esx	74	C2
North Cambridge	Whg	33	A6
North Cameron	Stu	52	B3
North Chatham	Clm	59	E1
North Chemung	Chm	53	D5
North Chili	Mro	24	C5
North Chittenango	Mds	28	B5
North Church	Ssx	66	E5
North Church Corner	Osw	14	D6
North Clove	Dut	64	E4
North Clymer	Chu	47	E6
North Cohocton	Stu	38	A6
North Colebrook	Lch	60	E6
North Colesville	Brm	55	D4
North Collins	Ere	35	A5
North Constantia	Osw	28	A2
North Corners	Lch	65	C2
North Corners	SL	2	B3
North Cornwall	Lch	65	C2
North Creek	Wrr	19	A4
North Croghan	Jfs	8	F6
North Cuba	Agy	50	C4
North Dorset	Ben	33	F3
North East	Eri	47	B4
North Eastond	Whg	32	F6
North Edmeston	Ots	42	D3
North Egremont	Brk	60	A4
North Elba	Ese	12	A4
North Evans	Ere	35	A4
North Fair Haven	Cyg	26	D2
North Fairfax	Fkl	6	F3
North Fenton	Brm	55	C4
North Ferrisburg	Add	13	D3
North Ferrisburg Station	Add	13	C3
North Forest Acres	Ere	22	C6
North Franklin	Dlw	56	E2
North Gage	Ond	29	E4
North Gainesville	Wyo	36	E4
North Galway	Srg	31	F6
North Germantown	Clm	59	B5
North Goshen	Lch	65	D2
North Gouverneur	SL	9	A1
North Granville	Whg	33	B1
North Great River	Sfk	76	D3
North Greece	Mro	24	D3
North Greenfield	Srg	32	B4
North Greenwich	Ffd	68	D5
North Greenwich	Whg	33	A5
North Guilford	NHv	70	D2
North Guilford Corners	Cng	56	A1
North Haledon	Pas	74	D1
North Hamlin	Mro	24	B2
North Hammond	SL	8	D1
North Hancock	Brk	46	C5
North Hannibal	Osw	26	F2
North Harpersfield	Dlw	57	D1
North Haven	NHv	70	B2
North Haven	Sfk	71	B6
North Hebron	Whg	33	C3
North Hero	GIC	6	C3
North Hero Station	GIC	6	C3
North Highland	Put	68	B1
North Hills	Nsu	75	D3
North Hillsdale	Clm	59	F4
North Hoosick	Rns	46	B1
North Hornell	Stu	51	E2
North Hudson	Ese	19	D1
North Huron	Wan	26	B3
North Java	Wyo	36	B4
North Java Station	Wyo	36	B4
North Jay	Ese	12	D2
North Kent	Lch	65	B3
North Kortright	Dlw	57	C1
North Landing	Jfs	14	D4
North Lansing	Tmk	40	A5
North Lawrence	SL	3	D3
North Lexington	Grn	58	B3
North Lindenhurst	Sfk	76	B4
North Lyme	NLn	71	C2
North Madison	NHv	70	E2
North Manlius	Ono	28	A5
North Massapequa	Nsu	76	A4
North Merrick	Nsu	75	F4
North Mianus	Ffd	68	F6
North Milton	Srg	32	B6
North Nassau	Rns	45	F6
North New Hyde Park	Nsu	75	D3
North Norwich	Cng	41	F5
North Orwell	Add	20	C2
North Osceola	Lew	15	D6
North Otis	Brk	60	E4
North Patchogue	Sfk	76	F3
North Pawlet	Rut	33	D2
North Petersburg	Rns	46	B3
North Pharsalia	Cng	41	D5
North Pitcher	Cng	41	B5
North Plain	Mdx	71	C1
North Plainfield	Sms	74	A5
North Pole	Ese	12	B2
North Port Byron	Cyg	26	E6
North Pownal	Ben	46	C3
North Reading	Scy	53	A1
North Ridge	Nia	22	B4
North Ridgeway	Nia	23	A3
North Ridgeway	Orl	23	A3
North River	Wrr	18	F4
North Rose	Wan	26	B4
North Rupert	Ben	33	E3
North Rush	Mro	24	D6
North Russell	SL	2	E6
North Salem	Wch	68	F2
North Sanford	Brm	56	A5
North Scriba	Osw	27	B1
North Sea	Sfk	78	B1
North Settlement	Grn	58	C2
North Sheldon	Wyo	36	A3
North Shodack	Rns	45	E5
North Spencer	Tio	53	F3
North Stamford	Ffd	68	F5
North Stephentown	Rns	46	B5
North Sterling	Cyg	26	E2
North Stockholm	SL	3	A3
North Stonington	NLn	72	B1
North Syracuse	Ono	27	E5
North Thurston	Stu	52	C3
North Tonawanda	Nia	22	B6
North Urbana	Stu	52	E2
North Victory	Cyg	26	E3
North Volney	Osw	27	C2
North Wantagh	Nsu	75	F4
North Waverly	Tio	53	F6
North Weedsport	Cyg	26	F6
North Western	Ond	29	B2
North Williston	Chi	13	F1
North Wilmurt	Hrk	29	F1
North Wilna	Jfs	8	E5
North Winfield	Hrk	42	D1
North Wolcott	Wan	26	C3
North Woodbury	Lch	65	D6
Northeast Center	Dut	64	F1
Northfield	Dlw	56	D4
Northfield	Lch	65	E4
Northford	NHv	70	C2
Northport	Sfk	76	B1
Northrup Corners	SL	2	A4
Northrups Corners	Cng	55	E2
Northumberland	Srg	32	E5
Northvale	Brg	68	A6
Northville	Flt	31	E4
Northville	Lch	65	B5
Northville	Sfk	77	E1
Northwest Landing	Sfk	71	C6
Northwood	Ond	29	E2
Norton Hill	Grn	58	F2
Nortons Corners	Cng	55	E1
Nortons Switch	Chu	48	B2
Norwalk	Ffd	69	A5
Norway	Hrk	30	A4
Norwich	Cng	41	F6
Norwich Corners	Hrk	29	D6
Norwood	Brg	75	A1
Norwood	SL	3	A3
Nottingham Estates	Nia	22	E4
Noxon	Dut	64	C5
Noyack	Sfk	78	B1
Noyan	Qub	7	C6
Nubia	Tmk	40	C5
Nudell Bush	Ont	2	E1
Number Four	Lew	16	D2
Number One	Cyg	39	E3
Nunda	Lvg	37	A5
Nut Plains	NHv	70	D3
Nutley	Esx	74	E3
Nutts Corners	Qub	7	D6
Nyack	Rck	68	B5

O

NAME	TERR	MAP	GRID
Oak Hill	Grn	58	E2
Oak Hill	Whg	46	B1
Oak Orchard	Ono	27	D4
Oak Orchard	Orl	23	B3
Oak Orchard Beach	Orl	23	F2
Oak Point	SL	1	D6
Oak Ridge	Mgy	44	B3
Oak Ridge	Pas	67	A6
Oak Tree	Mid	74	B6
Oakbrook	Rck	67	F5

NAME	TERR	MAP	GRID
Quarryville	Uls	59	A5
Queechy	Clm	60	A2
Queens	Que	75	C4
Queensbury	Wrr	32	E2
Quigley Park	Chu	48	A5
Quinneville	Brm	55	C3
Quinneville	Cng	55	C3
Quinnipiac	NHv	70	C1
Quiogue	Sfk	77	E3
Quogue	Sfk	77	E3
Quonchontaug	Wgn	72	D3

R

NAME	TERR	MAP	GRID
Raceville	Whg	33	C1
Rafferty Corners	Cyg	40	A4
Rahway	Uni	74	C5
Rainbow Lake	Frl	11	D1
Rainbow Shores	Osw	14	D5
Rakesford	NLn	71	C2
Ralston	Mrr	73	E3
Ramapo	Rck	67	E5
Ramona Beach	Osw	14	D6
Ramsey	Brg	67	E6
Randall	Mgy	44	A2
Randall Corners	Srg	32	C4
Randall Crossing	Yts	39	A5
Randallsville	Mds	41	E3
Randolph	Cat	49	A5
Ransom Oaks	Ere	22	D6
Ransomville	Nia	22	B4
Rapids	Nia	22	E5
Raquette Lake	Hml	17	D3
Raquette River	SL	3	C1
Raritan	Sms	73	E6
Raters Corners	Chu	47	D4
Rathbone	Stu	52	C5
Ravena	Alb	59	B1
Ravensville	Srg	32	C5
Rawson	Agy	50	C3
Rawson	Cat	50	C3
Ray	Gns	36	C1
Ray Brook	Ese	11	E3
Raymertown	Rns	45	F3
Raymond	Nia	22	E5
Raymond	Sms	73	E5
Raymondville	SL	3	A2
Rays Corners	Cat	48	F3
Rayville	Clm	59	F1
Readburn	Dlw	56	D6
Reading Center	Scy	53	A1
Readington	Hnt	73	C6
Rebeccas Mill	Sfk	78	B1
Reber	Ese	13	A3
Rector	Lew	15	D3
Red Bunch Corners	Flt	31	C6
Red Creek	Wan	26	D4
Red Falls	Grn	58	B3
Red Hook	Dut	59	B6
Red Hook	Dut	64	B1
Red House	Cat	49	C5
Red Mill	Osw	27	E1
Red Mills	Clm	59	D4
Red Mills	SL	2	B3
Red Mills	Tmk	40	C6
Red Mills	Uls	63	C5
Red Oaks Mill	Dut	64	B5
Red Rock	Clm	59	F2
Red Rock	Ono	27	C5
Redbird	Chu	48	C4
Redding	Ffd	69	B3
Redding Ridge	Ffd	69	B3
Redfield	Osw	15	C6
Redford	Cln	5	C5
Redman Corners	Mro	24	A4
Redmond Corner	Ond	29	B1
Redwood	Jfs	8	C3
Reed Corners	Chu	48	C1
Reed Corners	Otr	38	D2
Reedville	Jfs	8	E5
Reeves Park	Sfk	77	D1
Reidsville	Alb	44	F6
Relius	Cyg	39	E1
Remington Corners	Lew	9	B5
Remsen	Ond	29	D3
Remsenburg	Sfk	77	D3
Renchans	Stu	52	C1
Reniff	Tio	53	F5
Rennieville	Alb	45	A6
Rensselaer	Rns	45	D5
Rensselaer Falls	SL	2	C5
Rensselaerville	Alb	44	E6
Resort	Wan	26	A4
Result	Grn	59	A2
Retsof	Lvg	37	B2
Rexford	Srg	45	B2
Rexville	Stu	51	E5
Reynolds	Rns	45	E2
Reynolds Bridge	Lch	65	E5
Reynolds Corner	Jfs	7	F4
Reynolds Corners	SL	9	E2
Reynolds Corners	Srg	32	E3
Reynoldston	Frl	4	A4
Reynoldsville	Scy	53	C1
Rheims	Stu	52	C2
Rhinebeck	Dut	64	B2
Rhinecliff	Dut	64	A1
Rhode Island	Cng	41	C4
Rhode Island Corner	Chi	13	F2
Rhodes	NHv	70	C1
Ricard	Osw	28	A1
Rice Grove	Ono	40	C2
Rices	Jfs	15	A2
Rices Corners	Jfs	9	A4
Rices Corners	Lew	9	A4
Riceville	Cat	49	E1
Riceville	Flt	31	C5
Richards Corner	NHv	70	B1
Richburg	Agy	50	E5
Richfield	Ots	42	F2
Richfield Junction	Ond	42	C1
Richfield Springs	Ots	43	A2
Richford	Tio	54	D2
Richland	Osw	14	F6
Richmond	Brk	60	B2
Richmond Furnace	Brk	60	B2
Richmondville	Shh	43	F5
Richs Corners	Orl	23	E4
Richville	Ben	33	F5
Richville	SL	9	B2
Riddgewood	NLn	71	E3
Rideau Heights	Ont	7	A2
Riders Mills	Clm	59	F1
Ridge	Lvg	37	B4
Ridge	Sfk	77	B2
Ridgebury	Ffd	68	F2
Ridgebury	Orn	67	A2
Ridgefield	Brg	74	F3
Ridgefield	Brg	75	A3
Ridgefield	Ffd	69	A3
Ridgefield Park	Brg	74	F2
Ridgeland	Mro	24	E5
Ridgelea Heights	Nia	22	D4
Ridgeway	Ffd	68	E6
Ridgeway	Orl	23	B3
Ridgewood	Brg	74	E1
Ridgewood	Nia	22	D3
Rifton	Uls	63	F2
Riga	Mro	24	B6
Riggs Corners	Tmk	40	B5
Riggsville	Uls	63	C6
Rigney Bluff	Mro	24	E3
Riley Cove	Srg	32	C6
Rileyville	Wyn	61	D4
Ringwood	Pas	67	C5
Rio	Orn	66	D1
Riparius	Wrr	19	B5
Ripley	Chu	47	D3
Ripley Beach	Chu	47	D3
Ripple Corners	Mgy	43	D2
Rippleton	Mds	41	B2
Ripton	Add	20	F1
Risingdale	Brk	60	B4
Risingville	Stu	52	C4
River Edge	Brg	74	F1
River Vale	Brg	67	F6
Riverbank	Wrr	19	D5
Riverdale	Mrr	74	C1
Rivergate	Jfs	8	C4
Riverhead	Sfk	77	E1
Riverside	Brm	55	C6
Riverside	Ffd	68	E6
Riverside	Ffd	69	D1
Riverside	NHv	69	E2
Riverside Heights	Ont	2	F2
Riverside Manors	Nia	21	F4
Riverside Park	Uls	63	F2
Riversville	Ffd	68	D6
Riverton	Htf	65	F1
Riverview	Cln	5	B6
Riverview Heights	Ont	1	F4
Roanoke	Gns	36	F1
Roberts Corner	Jfs	14	E3
Robinson	Cln	5	E3
Robinson Corners	Ots	42	D4
Rochdale	Dut	64	B4
Rochester	Mro	24	D4
Rochester Junction	Mro	37	E1
Rock Beach	Mro	24	F4
Rock City	Cat	50	A6
Rock City	Clm	59	F2
Rock City	Dut	64	C1
Rock City Falls	Srg	32	A6
Rock Glen	Wyo	36	E4
Rock Hill	Slv	62	E5
Rock Lake	Wyn	61	B3
Rock Ledge Beach	Orl	23	D2
Rock Rift	Dlw	56	D5
Rock Stream	Yts	53	A1
Rock Tavern	Orn	67	D1
Rock Valley	Dlw	61	F2
Rockaway	Mrr	73	F2
Rockdale	Ots	56	B2
Rockfield	Ont	8	A1
Rockland	NHv	70	D2
Rockland	Slv	62	B1
Rockleigh	Brg	68	A6
Rockport	Ont	8	A2
Rockport	War	73	B2
Rocksprings	Ont	1	B4
Rockton	Mgy	44	E1
Rockville	Add	13	F4
Rockville	Agy	50	D3
Rockville	Orn	67	A1
Rockville Centre	Nsu	75	E4
Rockwell Corners	Mgy	44	C3
Rockwell Corners	Shh	44	C3
Rockwells Mills	Cng	56	B1
Rockwood	Flt	30	F6
Rocky Dale	Add	13	F5
Rocky Glen	Ffd	69	C1
Rocky Hill	Orn	67	B4
Rocky Point	Cln	6	A4
Rocky Point	Sfk	77	A1
Rodger Corner	Ono	27	E5
Rodman	Jfs	15	A2
Roe Park	Wch	68	B3
Roebuck	Ont	1	E3
Roessleville	Alb	45	C4
Rogers	Cln	12	E1
Rogersville	Stu	37	D6
Rolling Meadows	Uls	63	F1
Rombout Ridge	Dut	64	B5
Rome	Ese	12	D1
Rome	Ond	29	A4
Romulus	Sen	39	B3
Ronkonkoma	Sfk	76	E3
Roosa Gap	Slv	63	A5
Roosevelt	Nsu	75	E4
Roosevelt Beach	Nia	22	B3
Roosevelt Corners	Osw	27	D3
Rooseveltown	SL	3	D1
Roosterville	Brk	60	F5
Root Center	Mgy	44	A3
Rootville	Ots	56	C1
Rosaville	Frl	11	B1
Roscoe	Slv	62	B1
Rose	Wan	26	B5
Rose Hill	Ono	40	B2
Rose Hill	Sen	39	B2
Roseboom	Ots	43	C4
Roseland	Esx	74	C3
Roseland	Mro	25	B4
Roseland Park	Otr	38	D2
Roselle	Uni	74	C5
Roselle Park	Uni	74	C4
Rosendale	Uls	63	F2
Roses Grove	Sfk	78	B1
Roses Point	Orn	66	E1
Roseton	Orn	64	A6
Rosiere	Jfs	7	D4
Roslyn	Nsu	75	E3
Roslyn Estates	Nsu	75	D3
Roslyn Harbor	Nsu	75	E3
Roslyn Heights	Nsu	75	E3
Ross Corner	Ssx	66	D5
Ross Corners	Brm	54	E6
Ross Corners	Jfs	15	A3
Ross Corners	Lvg	37	C4
Ross Mills	Chu	48	D5
Rossburg	Agy	50	E1
Rosses	Agy	37	B6
Rossie	SL	8	D2
Rossman	Clm	59	D3
Rossville	Orn	63	F5
Rotterdam	Sch	45	A3
Rotterdam Junction	Sch	44	F2
Rough And Ready	Stu	51	E5
Round Hill	Ffd	68	E5
Round Lake	Srg	45	C1
Round Top	Grn	58	F3
Round Top	Sms	73	F5
Rouses Point	Cln	6	B1
Rowena	Ont	2	C2
Roxbury	Dlw	57	F3
Roxbury	Lch	65	C6
Roxbury Falls	Lch	65	C6
Roxbury Station	Lch	65	B6
Royalton Center	Nia	22	F5
Roys	Ssx	66	E4
Ruback Camp	Srg	31	E6
Ruby Corner	SL	8	E1
Rudco	Dut	64	A5
Rupert	Ben	33	D3
Rural Grove	Mgy	44	A2
Rural Hill	Jfs	14	D3
Rush	Mro	37	E1
Rush Run	Chm	53	D4
Rushford	Agy	50	C2
Rushville	Otr	38	D3
Rushville	Yts	38	D3
Russ Mills	Osw	27	D2
Russell	SL	9	E1
Russia	Hrk	29	F3
Ruth	Shh	57	F1
Rutherford	Brg	74	E3
Rutland Center	Jfs	15	C1
Rutsonville	Uls	63	D4
Ryal Corners	Yts	39	A4
Rye	Wch	75	D1
Rye Brook	Wch	68	D6
Rye Brook	Wch	75	D1
Rynex Corners	Sch	44	F3

S

NAME	TERR	MAP	GRID
Sabael	Hml	18	C4
Sabattis	Hml	10	D6
Sabbath Day Point	Wrr	19	F4
Sacandaga	Flt	31	D4
Sacandaga Camp	Hml	31	B1
Sachem Head	NHv	70	D3
Sackets Harbor	Jfs	14	E1
Sacketts Harbor	Cng	55	C2
Sacketts Harbor	Lvg	37	D3
Sacks Mill	NLn	72	B1
Saddle River	Brg	67	E6
Saddle Rock	Nsu	75	C3
Sag Harbor	Sfk	71	C6
Sag Harbor	Sfk	78	C1
Sagamore	Hml	17	E3
Sagaponack	Sfk	78	C3
Sagendorf Corners	Shh	44	B4
Sages Crossing	Cng	42	B5
Sagetown	Chm	53	A6
Saint Albans	Fkl	6	E3
Saint Albans Bay	Fkl	6	E3
Saint Catherines	Ont	21	B4
Saint Elmo	Uls	63	D3
Saint Huberts	Ese	12	C5
Saint James	Sfk	76	E2
Saint Johnsburg	Nia	22	B5
Saint Johnsville	Mgy	30	E6
Saint Johnsville	Mgy	43	E1
Saint Josen	Uls	63	D3
Saint Josephs	Slv	62	D5
Saint Lawrence	Jfs	7	D3
Saint Nicholas Village	Hnt	73	B3
Saint Regis Falls	Frl	3	F4
Saint Remy	Uls	63	F2
Saint-Armand-Station	Qub	7	F6
Saint-Bernard-de-Lacolle	Qub	7	A6
Sala	Osw	27	C1
Salamanca	Cat	49	C4
Salem	NLn	71	C1
Salem	Whg	33	C4
Salem Center	Wch	68	E3
Salem Corner	Ono	41	A1
Salem Four Corners	NLn	71	C1
Salisbury	Add	20	E2
Salisbury	Hrk	30	B5
Salisbury	Lch	65	B1
Salisbury Center	Hrk	30	C5
Salisbury Mills	Orn	67	E1
Salisbury Station	Add	20	E2
Sally	Pas	74	D1
Salt Point	Dut	64	C3
Salt Springville	Mgy	43	D2
Saltaire	Sfk	76	D5
Sammonsville	Flt	44	A1
Samsonville	Uls	63	C2
San Remo	Sfk	76	D2
Sanborn	Nia	22	B5
Sand Hill	Ere	22	F6
Sand Hill	Mgy	43	E1
Sand Hill	Ots	56	C2
Sand Lake	Rns	45	F5
Sandgate	Ben	33	D5
Sandisfield	Brk	60	E5
Sands Point	Nsu	75	D2
Sandusky	Cat	50	B1
Sandy Beach	Ere	22	A6
Sandy Beach	Lch	65	D4
Sandy Creek	Osw	14	E5
Sandy Harbour Beach	Mro	24	B2
Sandy Pond	Osw	14	D5
Sandy Pond Corners	Osw	14	E5
Sanford	Brm	56	A5
Sanford Corners	Jfs	14	F2
Sanfords Corners	Grn	59	A2
Sanfordtown	Ffd	69	B3
Sanfordville	SL	3	B4
Sangerfield	Ond	42	B1
Sanitaria Springs	Brm	55	C5
Santa Clara	Frl	4	A5
Saranac	Cln	5	C5
Saranac Inn	Frl	11	C2
Saranac Lake	Ese	11	E3
Saranac Lake	Frl	11	E3
Saratoga Lake	Srg	32	D6
Saratoga Springs	Srg	32	D6
Sardinia	Ere	35	F6
Sarles Corners	Wch	68	E4
Satans Kingdom	Add	20	F2
Satterly Corners	Cyg	40	B5
Saugerties	Uls	59	A6
Saunders Point	NLn	71	D2
Sauquoit	Ond	29	C6
Savannah	Wan	26	D6
Savilton	Orn	63	F5
Savona	Stu	52	D3
Savoy	Brk	46	F6
Savoy Center	Brk	46	F5
Sawens	Gns	36	B1
Sawkill	Uls	63	F1
Sawyer	Agy	50	E6
Sawyer	Orl	23	E2
Saxe Corner	Jfs	14	E3
Saxton	Uls	59	A5
Saybrook Manor	Mdx	71	B3
Saybrook Point	Mdx	71	B3
Sayles Corners	Cyg	40	B3
Sayles Corners	Osw	27	C2
Sayreville	Mid	74	C6
Sayreville	Mid	78	B6
Sayville	Sfk	76	E4
Scarsdale	Wch	68	C6
Scarsdale	Wch	75	C1
Schaghticoke	Rns	45	E2
Schaghticoke Hill	Rns	45	E2
Schenectady	Sch	45	A2
Schenevus	Ots	43	B6
Schepps Corners	Ono	27	F5
Schermerhorn Corners	Chu	48	F5
Schermerhorn Landing	SL	8	C2
Schodack Center	Rns	45	D6
Schodack Landing	Rns	59	C1
Schoharie	Shh	44	C5
Schoharie Junction	Shh	44	C4
Scholes	Agy	51	A2
Schonowe	Sch	45	A3
Schooleys Mountain	Mrr	73	C3
Schroon Falls	Ese	19	D2
Schroon Lake	Ese	19	C2
Schultzville	Dut	64	C2
Schuyler Falls	Cln	5	F5
Schuyler Lake	Ots	42	F3
Schuylerville	Srg	32	F5
Scio	Agy	51	A4
Sciota	Cln	5	F2
Scipio Center	Cyg	39	F3
Scipioville	Cyg	39	E3
Sconondoa	Ond	28	E5
Scotch Bush	Mgy	44	D2
Scotch Church	Mgy	44	E2
Scotch Church	Sch	44	E2
Scotch Hill	Ots	42	F4
Scotch Plains	Uni	74	B5
Scotchbush	Flt	30	F6
Scotchtown	Orn	67	B1
Scotia	Sch	45	A3
Scott	Crt	40	D4
Scott Center	Wyn	61	B1
Scott Corners	Ere	35	F6
Scotts Corner	Orn	63	D6
Scotts Corners	Jfs	14	D3
Scotts Corners	Wch	68	F4
Scottsburg	Lvg	37	D4
Scottsville	Mro	24	C6
Scottsville	Rut	33	F2
Scoville Corners	Jfs	8	A6
Scranton	Ere	35	B4
Scriba	Osw	27	A1
Scribner Corners	Mds	28	E6
Scuttlehole	Sfk	78	B1
Sea Breeze	Mro	24	F4
Sea Cliff	Nsu	75	E2
Seaford	Nsu	76	A4
Seager	Uls	57	F6
Sears Corners	Put	68	F1
Searsburg	Scy	39	D6
Searsville	Orn	63	C6
Seaside	NLn	71	E3
Seaview Beach	NHv	70	E3
Secaucus	Hud	74	E3
Second Milo	Yts	38	F5
Secor Corners	Put	68	D2
Seeley	Ont	1	C5
Seeley Creek	Chm	53	B6
Seelyville	Wyn	61	C6
Selden	Sfk	76	F2
Selkirk	Alb	45	C6
Selkirk	Osw	14	D6
Sellecks Corners	Ffd	68	F4
Sellecks Corners	SL	10	A1
Selma Center	Cng	41	C6
Selmaville	Osw	14	F5
Selton	Ont	8	A2
Semans Corners	Lvg	38	B5
Sempronius	Cyg	40	C4
Seneca Castle	Otr	38	E2
Seneca Falls	Sen	39	C2
Seneca Hill	Osw	27	A2
Seneca Park	Sen	39	A2
Sennett	Cyg	39	F1
Setauket	Sfk	76	E1
Seven-by-Nine Corners	Jfs	15	C3
Seventh Day Hollow	Cng	41	C4
Severance	Ese	19	D2
Sevey	SL	10	D3
Sevey Corners	SL	10	C3
Seward	Shh	43	E4
Sewaren	Mid	74	C6
Seymour	NHv	69	E2
Shackport	Dlw	57	A2
Shadigee	Orl	23	B2
Shady	Uls	58	E6
Shady Harbor	Wgn	72	D2
Shady Rest	Ffd	69	C1
Shaftsbury	Ben	33	D6
Shaftsbury Center	Ben	46	D1
Shahola Falls	Pke	66	A2
Shaker Village	Brk	60	B1
Shandaken	Uls	58	B5
Shandelee	Slv	62	B2
Shanly	Ont	2	A2
Shannock	Wgn	72	E1
Shannon Corners	Yts	39	A6
Sharon	Lch	65	A2
Sharon	Shh	43	F3
Sharon Center	Shh	43	F3
Sharon Springs	Shh	43	E3
Sharon Station	Dut	64	F2
Sharon Valley	Lch	65	A2
Shaw Corners	Cyg	40	B5
Shaw Corners	Srg	31	F5
Shawnee	Nia	22	B5
Sheaf Corners	Hrk	29	F5
Shedd Corners	Hrk	30	C5
Sheds	Mds	41	B3
Sheffield	Brk	60	B5
Shehawken	Wyn	61	B2
Shekomeko	Dut	64	E1
Shelburne	Chi	13	D2
Shelburne Falls	Chi	13	D2
Shelby Basin	Orl	23	A4
Shelby Center	Orl	23	B4
Sheldon	Wyo	36	A4
Sheldon Center	Wyo	36	B4
Sheldon Corners	Chu	47	D4
Sheldrake	Sen	39	D4
Sheldrake Springs	Sen	39	C5
Shelter Harbor	Wgn	72	D2
Shelter Island	Sfk	71	C6
Shelter Island Heights	Sfk	71	B5
Shelton	Ffd	69	E3
Shelving Rock	Whg	19	E6
Shenorock	Wch	68	D3
Shepard Corners	Osw	27	C3
Shepard Settlement	Ono	40	B1
Shepards Corner	Wan	26	B5
Shepards Corners	Ere	35	F6
Sherburne	Cng	41	F4
Sherburne	Cng	42	A4
Sherburne Four Corners	Cng	41	F5
Sheridan	Chu	48	D1
Sherlock Corners	Cyg	39	F2
Sherman	Chu	47	E5
Sherman	Ffd	65	A6
Sherman	Wyn	61	A1
Sherrill	Ond	28	E6
Sherwood	Cyg	39	E3
Sherwood Park	Rns	45	D5
Sherwood Springs	Ont	1	C6
Shin Hollow	Orn	66	E2
Shinhopple	Dlw	56	F6
Shinnecock Hills	Sfk	78	A2
Shirley	Ere	35	B6
Shirley	Sfk	77	B3
Shivers Corners	Rns	45	E5
Shoefelt Corners	Alb	44	E6
Shohola	Pke	66	B1
Shohola Falls	Pke	66	A2
Shokan	Uls	63	D1
Sholam	Uls	63	B3
Shongo	Agy	51	B6
Shongo	Cat	49	C5
Shooktown	Nia	22	E5

134

NAME	TERR	MAP	GRID
Thorn Hill	Ono	40	B2
Thornton	Chu	48	E3
Thornton Grove	Ono	40	A2
Thorntons Corner	Wan	25	F4
Thornwood	Wch	68	C5
Thorold	Ont	21	D5
Thousand Island Park	Jfs	7	F2
Three Bridges	Hnt	73	C6
Three Mile Bay	Jfs	7	D5
Three Rivers	Ono	27	C4
Threemile Harbor	Sfk	71	E6
Threemile Harbor	Sfk	78	D1
Throopsville	Cyg	39	E1
Throoptown	Ont	1	D3
Thurman	Wrr	19	B6
Thurman Station	Wrr	32	C1
Thurston	Stu	52	C4
Tiana	Sfk	77	F2
Ticonderoga	Ese	20	A2
Tierneys Corner	Ssx	73	E1
Tilley	Ont	8	A1
Tillson	Uls	63	E3
Tilly Foster	Put	68	E1
Timothy Heights	Dut	64	C4
Tinker Tavern Corner	Osw	14	E6
Tinkertown	Agy	51	C3
Tinmouth	Rut	33	F1
Tinney Corners	Lew	9	C6
Tioga Center	Tio	54	B6
Tiona	Brm	54	E3
Tip Top	Agy	51	C4
Tiplady	Whg	33	C3
Titicus	Ffd	68	F3
Titusville	Dut	64	B4
Tivoli	Dut	59	B6
Toad Harbor	Osw	27	F4
Toddsville	Ots	43	A4
Toggletown	Lvg	37	C2
Tokeneke	Ffd	69	A6
Toledo	Ont	1	A4
Toll Gate Corner	Cat	50	C6
Tolland Center	Hmp	60	F6
Tolles	Lch	65	F5
Tomhannock	Rns	45	F2
Tomkins Cove	Rck	68	A3
Tomlinson Corner	Mro	37	F1
Tompkins Corners	Chm	53	B4
Tonawanda	Ere	22	B6
Tonawanda	Ere	35	B1
Topstone	Ffd	69	A3
Torrington	Lch	65	E2
Totoket	NHv	70	C3
Totowa	Pas	74	D2
Towaco	Mrr	74	B1
Towers Corner	Nia	21	F3
Towerville	Chu	48	C4
Towlesville	Stu	52	A2
Town Corners	Chu	48	D2
Town Line	Ere	35	E2
Town Line Station	Ere	35	E2
Town Pump	Mro	24	B6
Towners	Put	68	E1
Townsbury	War	73	A2
Townsend	Scy	53	A2
Townsendville	Sen	39	C6
Toyes Hill	Ont	2	C1
Toziers Corners	Wyo	36	B4
Tracy Creek	Brm	54	E6
Tranquility	Ssx	73	C1
Treadwell	Dlw	56	F2
Tremaines Corners	Jfs	15	B3
Trenton Falls	Ond	29	E3
Trestle Corners	Cng	56	A2
Triangle	Brm	55	B2
Tribes Hill	Mgy	44	C1
Tripoli	Crt	41	A4
Tripoli	Whg	32	E2
Trout Creek	Dlw	56	C4
Trout River	Frl	4	C1
Troutburg	Mro	24	A2
Troy	Rns	45	D4
Troy Hills	Mrr	74	B2
Trudeau	Ese	11	E2
Trumansburg	Tmk	39	D6
Trumbull	Ffd	69	D3
Trumbull Corners	Tmk	53	E2
Truthville	Whg	33	C1
Truxton	Crt	40	F4
Tuckahoe	Sfk	78	A2
Tuckahoe	Wch	75	C1
Tucker Heights	Srg	45	A2
Tucker Terrace	SL	3	A1
Tuckers Corner	Uls	63	F4
Tuckertown	Wgn	72	F1
Tully	Ono	40	E3
Tunnel	Brm	55	D4
Tunxis Hill	Ffd	69	C4
Tupper Lake	Frl	11	A4
Turin	Lew	16	B5
Turnbull Corner	SL	2	E3
Turnwood	Uls	57	D6
Tuscan	Ots	43	C5
Tuscarora	Lvg	37	B5
Tuthill	Uls	63	E4
Tuthilltown	Uls	63	D4
Tuttles Corner	Ssx	66	C4
Tuxedo Park	Orn	67	D4
Twelve Thousand	Ots	43	A3
Twilight Park	Grn	58	E4
Twin Bridges	Cln	5	F1
Twin Bridges	Ffd	69	C3
Twin Lakes	Lch	60	B6
Twin Lakes	Pke	66	B2
Twin Orchards	Brm	54	F5
Twin Orchards	Chi	13	D1
Tyler Hill	Wyn	61	E4
Tyler Lake Heights	Lch	65	C2
Tylers Corner	Osw	14	D6
Tylers Corners	Lew	9	B5
Tylersville	Jfs	15	C2
Tylerville	Mdx	71	A1
Tyner	Cng	55	D1
Tyre	Sen	39	C1
Tyringham	Brk	60	D3
Tyrone	Scy	52	F2

U

NAME	TERR	MAP	GRID
Ulster Height	Uls	63	A3
Ulster Landing	Uls	64	A1
Ulster Park	Uls	64	A2
Ulsterville	Uls	63	B5
Unadilla	Ots	56	C3
Unadilla Center	Ots	56	C2
Unadilla Forks	Ots	42	D2
Uncasville	NLn	71	E1
Underwood	Ese	12	D5
Underwood Corners	Cat	49	B5
Uneeda Beach	Nia	22	A3
Union	Mds	41	B2
Union	Ont	8	A1
Union	Uni	74	C4
Union Beach	Mom	78	E6
Union Center	Brm	54	F5
Union Center	Uls	64	A2
Union City	Hud	74	F3
Union Corners	Gns	37	A2
Union Corners	Lvg	37	B5
Union Corners	Lvg	37	D4
Union Corners	Mds	28	D5
Union Corners	Wyo	36	C4
Union Dale	Sqh	61	A4
Union Falls	Cln	5	B6
Union Hill	Mro	25	B4
Union Hill	Wan	25	B4
Union Mills	Flt	31	E6
Union Settlement	Osw	27	F3
Union Springs	Cyg	39	D2
Union Valley	Cng	55	F3
Union Valley	Crt	41	B5
Unionville	Alb	45	A5
Unionville	Orn	66	F3
Unionville	SL	3	A4
Unionville	Slv	62	F4
Unionville	Stu	52	B3
University Gardens	Nsu	75	C3
Upper Beechwood	Slv	62	A3
Upper Benson	Hml	31	B4
Upper Brookville	Nsu	75	F2
Upper Fairfield	Tio	54	C3
Upper Greenwood Lake	Pas	67	B4
Upper Hollowville	Clm	59	E4
Upper Jay	Ese	12	C4
Upper Kilns	Frl	4	F4
Upper Lisle	Brm	55	A2
Upper Macopin	Pas	67	B5
Upper Mongaup	Orn	66	C1
Upper Mongaup	Slv	66	C1
Upper Nyack	Rck	68	A5
Upper Red Hook	Dut	59	B6
Upper Saddle River	Brg	67	E6
Upper Saint Regis	Frl	11	C2
Upper Stepney	Ffd	69	C3
Upperville	Cng	41	E4
Upson Corners	Osw	27	D2
Urbana	Stu	52	D1
Ushers	Srg	45	A2
Utica	Ond	29	D5
Uttertown	Pas	67	B5

V

NAME	TERR	MAP	GRID
Vail Mills	Flt	31	D6
Vails Gate	Orn	67	F1
Valatie	Clm	59	E1
Valcour	Cln	6	A5
Valhalla	Wch	68	C6
Valley Brook	Mgy	43	E1
Valley Cottage	Rck	68	A5
Valley Falls	Rns	45	F2
Valley Stream	Nsu	75	D4
Vallonia Springs	Brm	55	F4
Valois	Scy	39	B6
Van Buren Bay	Chu	48	B1
Van Buren Point	Chu	48	A1
Van Burenville	Orn	63	A6
Van Cortlandtville	Wch	68	B3
Van Deusenville	Brk	60	B4
Van Deusenville	Mgy	43	D2
Van Dorn Corner	Tmk	53	E1
Van Etten	Chm	53	F4
Van Etten Junction	Chm	53	F4
Van Hornesville	Hrk	43	C2
Van House Corners	SL	9	E1
Van Keuren	Orn	63	C5
Van Keurens	Dut	64	A5
Van Vleet	Stu	52	C6
VanBuren	Ono	27	C5
Vandalia	Cat	49	E5
Vandling	Lak	61	A5
Varna	Tmk	54	A1
Varysburg	Wyo	36	B3
Vaughns Corners	Whg	32	F2
Vebber Corners	SL	3	A6
Vega	Dlw	57	F3
Venice Center	Cyg	39	F4
Venise-en-Quebec	Qub	7	E6
Ventnor	Ont	1	F2
Verbank	Dut	64	D4
Verbank Village	Dut	64	D4
Verdoy	Alb	45	C3
Vergennes	Add	13	C4
Veriley	SL	1	F6
Vermilion	Osw	27	D1
Vermontville	Frl	11	F1
Vernal Corners	Wyo	36	D2
Vernon	Ond	28	F5
Vernon	Ssx	67	A4
Vernon Center	Ond	28	F6
Vernon Corner	Ots	56	C2
Vernon Valley	Sfk	76	C2
Verona	Esx	74	C3
Verona	Ond	28	F5
Verona Beach	Ond	28	C4
Verona Mills	Ond	28	F4
Verplanck	Wch	68	A3
Versailles	Ere	35	A6
Vesper	Ono	40	D3
Vestal	Brm	54	F6
Vestal Center	Brm	54	F6
Veteran	Uls	59	A6
Veterans Mountain Camp	SL	10	F5
Victor	Otr	38	B1
Victory	Cyg	26	D4
Victory	Srg	32	E5
Victory Gardens	Mrr	73	F2
Vienna	Ond	28	D4
Vienna	War	73	B2
Viewmonte	Clm	59	B5
Village of the Branch	Sfk	76	D2
Vincent	Otr	38	F2
Vine Valley	Yts	38	C4
Vines	Ese	12	F1
Vintonton	Shh	44	A5
Viola	Rck	67	E5
Virgil	Crt	40	D6
Vischer Ferry	Srg	45	C3
Voak	Yts	38	E4
Vollentine	Cat	48	F5
Volney	Osw	27	B2
Voorheesville	Alb	45	A5
Vorea	Osw	15	A5
Vorhees Corners	Osw	27	F2
Vosburg	Agy	50	F6
Vroman Corners	Shh	44	C4
Vukote	Chu	48	B5

W

NAME	TERR	MAP	GRID
Wacombers Corners	Chm	53	D5
Waddington	SL	2	D2
Wadhams	Ese	13	A4
Wading River	Sfk	77	B1
Wadsworth	Lvg	37	B3
Wagners Corners	SL	2	D3
Wagstaff Corner	SL	3	D3
Wahmeda	Chu	48	A4
Wainfleet	Ont	34	B1
Wainscott	Sfk	78	D1
Wait Corners	Chu	47	F5
Waits	Tio	54	C6
Wakefield	Wgn	72	F1
Walden	Ere	35	C2
Walden	Orn	63	D6
Walden Cliffs	Ere	35	A4
Waldos Corners	Wyo	36	C5
Waldwick	Brg	67	E6
Wales Center	Ere	35	F3
Wales Hollow	Ere	36	A3
Walesville	Ond	29	B5
Walker	Mro	24	B3
Walker	Osw	27	A1
Walker Corners	Cng	55	F2
Walker Corners	Ond	29	E4
Walker Lake	Pke	66	A1
Walker Valley	Uls	63	B5
Wallace	Stu	52	A1
Wallingford	NHv	70	C1
Wallington	Brg	74	E2
Wallington	Wan	25	F4
Wallins Corners	Mgy	44	D1
Wallkill	Uls	63	D5
Wallkill Camp	Uls	63	E4
Walloomsac	Rns	46	C1
Walmore	Nia	22	A5
Walnut Ledge	Chi	6	D5
Walpack Center	Ssx	66	B5
Walton	Dlw	56	E4
Walton Park	Orn	67	D3
Walworth	Wan	25	C5
Walworth Station	Wan	25	C5
Wampsville	Mds	28	D6
Wanakah	Ere	35	B4
Wanakena	SL	10	A5
Wanaque	Pas	67	C6
Wango	Chu	48	E1
Wantagh	Nsu	75	F4
Wappingers Falls	Dut	64	B5
Wards Corners	Jfs	8	C6
Wardwell	Jfs	14	E3
Warner Corners	Otr	38	E1
Warners	Ono	27	C5
Warnerville	Shh	43	F5
Warren	Hrk	43	A2
Warren	Jfs	7	D4
Warren	Lch	65	B4
Warrens Corners	Nia	22	C4
Warrensburg	Wrr	32	C1
Warrenville	War	73	B2
Warsaw	Wyo	36	E3
Warwick	Orn	67	B3
Washburn	Ont	7	C1
Washington	Brk	60	E2
Washington	Lch	65	C5
Washington	War	73	A3
Washington Depot	Lch	65	C5
Washington Hollow	Dut	64	C3
Washington Mills	Ond	29	C6
Washington Valley	Mrr	73	F3
Washingtonville	Orn	67	D1
Wassaic	Dut	64	F3
Watch Hill	Wgn	72	B3
Watchung	Sms	74	A5
Water Mill	Sfk	78	B2
Water Valley	Ere	35	B4
Waterboro	Chu	48	E4
Waterburg	Tmk	39	D6
Waterbury	NHv	65	E6
Waterford	Srg	45	D3
Waterloo	Sen	39	B2
Waterloo Mills	Orn	66	E3
Watermans Corners	Chu	48	B4
Waterport	Orl	23	C3
Watertown	Jfs	15	B1
Watertown	Lch	65	E5
Watertown Center	Jfs	15	A1
Watervale	Ono	41	A1
Waterville	Ond	42	B1
Waterville	Sfk	70	F6
Watervliet	Alb	45	D4
Watkins Glen	Scy	53	B2
Watson	Lew	16	A3
Watsonville	Shh	44	B5
Wattlesburg	Chu	47	D4
Watts Flats	Chu	48	B6
Wattsburg	Eri	47	B6
Wautoma Beach	Mro	24	C2
Waverly	Chm	53	F6
Waverly	Tio	53	F6
Wawarsing	Uls	63	B3
Wawayanda	Ssx	67	A4
Wawbeck	Frl	11	B3
Wayland	Stu	37	F6
Waymart	Wyn	61	B6
Wayne	Pas	74	C1
Wayne	Scy	52	E1
Wayne Center	Wan	26	A5
Wayne Four Corners	Stu	52	E2
Wayneport	Wan	25	B6
Wayville	Srg	32	D6
Webatuck	Dut	64	F5
Webb Corners	Cng	56	A1
Webb Mills	Chm	53	B6
Weber Corners	Ots	43	E4
Webster	Mro	25	A6
Webster Corners	Ere	35	D3
Websters Crossing	Lvg	37	E4
Weeds Corners	Eri	47	A6
Weedsport	Cyg	26	F6
Weekapaug	Wgn	72	C3
Wegatchie	SL	8	F3
Welch Corners	Hrk	30	A5
Welch Corners	Shh	57	F1
Welcome	Ots	42	E5
Welland	Ont	21	C6
Welland	Ont	34	D1
Wellandport	Ont	21	A6
Wellington Corner	Ono	40	C1
Wells	Hml	31	C2
Wells	Rut	33	D1
Wells Bridge	Ots	56	D2
Wellsburg	Chm	53	C6
Wellsville	Agy	51	A5
Wellsville	Lch	65	B5
Wellsville	Mgy	44	C2
Wellwood	Osw	27	D2
Weltonville	Tio	54	D4
Wembley Creek	SL	2	F5
Wemple	Alb	45	C6
Wendelville	Nia	22	C6
Wequetequock	NLn	72	B2
Wesley	Cat	49	A2
Wesley Hills	Rck	67	E5
West Addison	Add	13	B6
West Alabama	Gns	23	A5
West Alden	Ere	35	F2
West Allen	Agy	50	F2
West Almond	Agy	51	B3
West Amboy	Osw	28	A2
West Arlington	Ben	33	D5
West Athens	Grn	59	B3
West Babylon	Sfk	76	B4
West Bangor	Frl	4	A3
West Barre	Orl	23	D5
West Batavia	Gns	36	C1
West Bay Shore	Sfk	76	C4
West Becket	Brk	60	E3
West Beekmantown	Cln	5	F3
West Bergen	Gns	23	F6
West Berne	Alb	44	D5
West Bethany	Gns	36	D1
West Bloomfield	Otr	37	F2
West Branch	Ond	29	A2
West Bridport	Add	20	B1
West Brookfield	Mds	42	B3
West Burlington	Ots	42	D4
West Bush	Flt	31	B6
West Butler	Wan	26	C4
West Caldwell	Esx	74	C2
West Cambridge	Whg	46	A1
West Cameron	Stu	52	B4
West Camp	Uls	59	A5
West Candor	Tio	54	A4
West Carthage	Jfs	15	E1
West Castleton	Rut	20	D5
West Caton	Stu	52	F6
West Charlton	Srg	44	F1
West Chazy	Cln	5	F3
West Chenango	Brm	55	A4
West Chili	Mro	24	C5
West Clarksville	Agy	50	D5
West Colesville	Brm	55	D5
West Conesville	Shh	58	A2
West Copake	Clm	59	F5
West Corners	Brm	54	E5
West Corners	Srg	32	A6
West Cornwall	Add	20	D1
West Cornwall	Lch	65	B2
West Cornwall	Orn	67	E1
West Coxsackie	Grn	59	B2
West Damascus	Wyn	61	D4
West Danby	Tmk	53	F3
West Davenport	Dlw	57	A1
West Day	Srg	31	E3
West Delhi	Dlw	56	F3
West Dryden	Tmk	40	B6
West Durham	Grn	58	D2
West Eaton	Mds	41	E2
West Edmeston	Mds	42	C3
West Ellery	Chu	48	B4
West Elmira	Chm	53	B5
West Exeter	Ots	42	E3
West Falls	Ere	35	D4
West Fort Ann	Whg	32	E2
West Fowler	SL	9	A3
West Fulton	Shh	44	A6
West Gaines	Orl	23	C3
West Galway	Flt	31	E6
West Georgia	Fkl	6	E4
West Ghent	Clm	59	D3
West Gilgo Beach	Sfk	76	B5
West Goshen	Lch	65	C3
West Granville	Whg	33	B1
West Greece	Mro	24	C4
West Greene	Eri	47	A6
West Greenville	Grn	58	F2
West Greenwood	Stu	51	D5
West Groton	Tmk	40	A5
West Haddam	Mdx	70	F1
West Harpersfield	Dlw	57	D1
West Haven	NHv	70	A3
West Haven	Rut	20	B5
West Haverstraw	Rck	67	F4
West Haverstraw	Rck	68	A4
West Hebron	Whg	33	B4
West Hempstead	Nsu	75	E4
West Henrietta	Mro	24	D6
West Hoosick	Rns	46	A2
West Hurley	Uls	58	E6
West Hurley	Uls	63	E1
West Islip	Sfk	76	C4
West Jefferson	Shh	57	E1
West Jewett	Grn	58	C3
West Kendall	Orl	23	F3
West Kill	Grn	58	B4
West Kingston	Wgn	72	F1
West Kortright	Dlw	57	B2
West Laurens	Ots	42	E6
West Lebanon	Clm	60	A1
West Lee	Ond	28	F3
West Leyden	Lew	29	A1
West Lincoln	Add	13	F5
West Lowville	Lew	15	F3
West Mahopac	Put	68	C2
West Martinsburg	Lew	15	F3
West Meredith	Dlw	56	F2
West Middlebury	Wyo	36	E2
West Milford	Pas	67	B5
West Milton	Chi	6	D5
West Milton	Srg	32	A6
West Monroe	Osw	27	E2
West Mystic	NLn	72	A2
West New Boston	Brk	60	E5
West New York	Hud	74	F3
West Newark	Tio	54	D3
West Notch	Agy	50	E5
West Nyack	Rck	68	A5
West Oneonta	Ots	56	E1
West Orange	Esx	74	C3
West Otis	Brk	60	E4
West Park	Uls	64	A3
West Paterson	Pas	74	D2
West Patterson	Put	64	E6
West Pawlet	Rut	33	D2
West Pawling	Dut	64	E5
West Perry	Wyo	36	F4
West Perry Center	Wyo	36	F3
West Perrysburg	Cat	48	F1
West Perth	Flt	31	C6
West Phoenix	Ono	27	C4
West Pierrepont	SL	9	F1
West Plattsburgh	Cln	5	F4
West Portland	Chu	47	F2
West Postdam	SL	2	E4
West Redding	Ffd	69	B3
West Richmondville	Shh	43	E5
West Ridgeway	Orl	23	A3
West Rupert	Ben	33	D4
West Rush	Mro	37	D1
West Rutland	Rut	20	F5
West Salisbury	Add	20	E1
West Sand Lake	Rns	45	E5
West Sandgate	Ben	33	D5
West Saugerties	Uls	58	F5
West Sayville	Sfk	76	E4
West Schuyler	Hrk	29	E5
West Seneca	Ere	35	C2
West Settlement	Dlw	57	E3
West Settlement	Grn	58	B2
West Shelby	Orl	23	A5
West Shokan	Uls	63	C1
West Slaterville	Tmk	54	B2
West Somerset	Nia	22	E3
West Sparta	Lvg	37	C5
West Stephentown	Rns	46	A6
West Stockbridge	Brk	60	B3
West Stockbridge Center	Brk	60	B3
West Stockholm	SL	3	B4
West Swanton	Fkl	6	D1
West Sweden	Mro	24	A5
West Taghkanic	Clm	59	D5
West Tiana	Sfk	77	F2
West Tinmouth	Rut	33	E1
West Township	Alb	44	E4
West Union	Stu	51	D5
West Valley	Cat	49	E2
West Walworth	Wan	25	B5
West Webster	Mro	25	A4
West Windsor	Brm	55	C5
West Winfield	Hrk	42	D2

Y

Z

Airports

Beaches

NAME	TERR	MAP	GRID
Setauket	Sfk	76	E1
Short	Nsu	75	F6
Short	Sfk	76	D2
Southampton	Sfk	78	A2
Tiana	Sfk	77	F3
Tobay	Nsu	76	A5
Truman	Sfk	71	B5
Union Beach	Mom	78	D6
Watermill	Sfk	78	C2
West	Sfk	76	E4
West	Sfk	76	F1
West Meadow	Sfk	76	D1
Westhampton	Sfk	77	E5

Boat Ramps

NAME	TERR	MAP	GRID
Alder Lake	Uls	57	D6
Ausable Pt Forest Preserve	Cln	6	A6
Barn Is Mgmt Area	NLn	72	B2
Bay Pt	NLn	71	E3
Big Six St Marina	Ere	21	F6
Bowman Lake St Pk	Cng	41	D6
Branford River	NHv	70	C3
Brown Tract Pond Forest Preserve	Hml	17	D3
Buck Pond Forest Preserve	Frl	4	E6
Budd Lake Docks Marina	Mrr	73	C2
Bulwagga Bay	Ese	13	A6
Burnham Pt St Pk	Jfs	7	C4
Butterfield Lake	Jfs	8	C3
Canandaigua Lake	Otr	38	C2
Canandaigua Lake St Marine Pk	Otr	38	C2
Candlewood Hill Brook	Mdx	70	E1
Capital District St WMA	Rns	46	A5
Captree St Pk	Sfk	76	C5
Caroga Lake Forest Preserve	Flt	31	A5
Castorland	Lew	15	F2
Cayuga Lake St Pk	Sen	39	C2
Cedar Pt	Ffd	69	B5
Cedar Pt St Pk	Jfs	7	D3
Cherry Plain St Pk	Rns	46	B5
Chodikee Lake	Uls	64	A3
Clarence Fahnestock St Pk	Put	68	B1
Cochecton	Slv	61	F4
Coles Cr St Pk	SL	2	E2
Conesus Lake St Pk	Lvg	37	D3
Cossayuna Lake	Whg	33	B4
Coxsackie	Grn	59	C2
Cranberry Lake	SL	10	B4
Crown Pt Resv	Ese	13	A6
Danbury	Ffd	69	A2
Day Pt	Cln	6	A5
Deans Cove St	Sen	39	C4
Delta Lake St Pk	Ond	29	B3
DeWolf Pt St Pk	Jfs	8	A3
Dunham Res	Rns	46	A3
Eastern Pt	NLn	71	F3
Eaton Res	Mds	41	D2
Eighth Lake	Hml	17	D3
Elizabeth City	Uni	74	D5
Erie Basin Marina	Ere	35	B2
Fair Haven Beach St Pk	Cyg	26	D2
Fayerweather Is	Ffd	69	D5
Fish Cr Pond Forest Preserve	Frl	11	B3
Forked Lake Forest Preserve	Hml	17	F1
Fort Erie Marina	Ont	35	A1
Fort Niagara St Pk	Nia	21	F3
Fort Pond	Sfk	72	A6
Fourth Lake	Hml	17	C3
Fourth Lake	Wrr	32	B2
Fourth Lake Picnic Area	Hrk	17	B4
Glimmerglass St Pk	Ots	43	B3
Golden Beach Preserve	Hml	17	E3
Grass Pt St Pk	Jfs	8	A3
Great Is Mgmt Area	NLn	71	C3
Great Peconic Bay	Sfk	77	F1
Great South Bay	Sfk	76	D4
Greenwood Lake	Pas	67	B5
Guilford Hbr	NHv	70	E3
Hamlin Beach St Pk	Mro	24	A2
Hammonasset Beach St Pk	NHv	70	F3
Harris Lake	Ese	18	E1
High Tor Game Mgmt Area	Yts	38	B5
Higley Flow St Pk	SL	3	A6
Honeoye Cr	Mro	37	D1
Honeoye Lake St	Otr	37	F4
Housatonic River	Ffd	69	E3
Housatonic River	NHv	69	E4
Hudson River	Grn	59	C2
Hudson River	Grn	59	C3
Hudson River	Wrr	32	C3
Hunts Pond St Pk	Cng	42	B5
Indian Lake	Hml	18	B5
Irondequoit Bay St Marine Pk	Mro	24	F4
Island Pond	Orn	67	E3
Jacques Cartier St Pk	SL	1	D6
Johnson Co Pk	Mid	74	A6
Keewaydin Pt St Pk	Jfs	8	A3
Kenneth L Wilson Forest Preserve	Uls	58	D6
Keuka Lake St Pk	Yts	38	E6
Kings Bay St WMA	Cln	6	B1
Kring Pt St Pk	Jfs	8	B2
Lake Candlewood	Ffd	69	A1
Lake Champlain	Ese	20	B2
Lake Colby	Frl	11	D2
Lake Durant	Hml	18	A2
Lake Eaton	Hml	18	A1
Lake George	Wrr	20	A3
Lake George St Pk	Wrr	32	D2
Lake Kanawauke	Orn	67	E4
Lake Lillinonah	Ffd	69	B1
Lake Musconetcong	Mrr	73	D2
Lake Placid	Ese	12	A3
Lake Ronkonkoma	Sfk	76	E3
Lake Sebago	Rck	67	E4
Lake Skannatat	Orn	67	E4
Lake Superior St Pk	Slv	62	B5
Lake Taghkanic St Pk	Clm	59	D5
Lake Tiorati	Orn	67	F3
Lakeview Marsh St WMA	Jfs	14	D3
Laurel Lake	Sfk	77	F1
Leonardo State Marina	Mom	78	F6
Lewey Lake	Hml	18	B5
Liberty St Pk	Hud	74	F4
Limekiln Lake	Hml	17	C4
Little Clear Pond	Frl	11	C2
Little Pond Forest Preserve	Dlw	57	C6
Little Sand Pt Forest Preserve	Hml	30	E1
Lodi Pt St Pk	Sen	39	B5
Long Lake	Hml	18	A1
Long Pond	Lew	16	D1
Long Pond	NLn	72	A1
Long Pond	Rns	46	A3
Long Pt on Lake Chautauqua St Pk	Chu	48	B4
Long Pt St Pk	Cyg	39	D4
Long Pt St Pk	Jfs	7	D5
Lower Saranac Lake	Frl	11	E3
Margaret Lewis Norrie St Pk	Dut	64	A2
Meacham Lake Forest Preserve	Frl	4	C6
Mexico Bay	Osw	14	C6
Milanville	Slv	61	F5
Mine Kill St Pk	Shh	58	A1
Moffitt Beach Preserve	Hml	31	A1
Mongaup Pond Forest Preserve	Slv	62	D1
Moreau Lake St Pk	Srg	32	D4
Moriches Coast Guard Station	Sfk	77	C3
Nanticoke Cr	Brm	54	E2
Narrowsburg	Slv	61	F5
Nehantic St Forest	NLn	71	C2
Nelliston	Mgy	43	E1
Newark Bay	Uni	74	D5
Newburgh	Orn	67	F1
Niantic	NLn	71	D3
North Farms Res	NHv	70	C1
North West Bay	Ese	13	A4
North/South Lake Forest Preserve	Grn	58	E4
Northampton Beach Preserve	Flt	31	D4
Northwest Bay Lake George	Wrr	19	E5
Oak Orchard Marine Pk	Orl	23	D2
Old Erie Canal St Pk	Ond	28	E5
Ontario Marina	Ont	34	C2
Orient Hbr	Sfk	71	B5
Otisco Lake	Ono	40	C2
Paradox Lake	Ese	19	D2
Passaic River	Esx	74	C2
Pattagansett Lake	NLn	71	C2
Payne Lake	Jfs	8	E3
Point Au Roche	Cln	6	B3
Point Au Roche St Pk	Cln	6	B3
Point Comfort Forest Preserve	Hml	30	E2
Pond Brook	Ffd	69	C1
Poplar Pt Forest Preserve	Hml	30	F1
Powers Lake	NLn	71	D2
Putnam Pond	Ese	19	E2
Quaker Lake	Cat	49	B6
Quonnipaug Lake	NHv	70	D2
Ragged Rock Mgmt Area	Mdx	71	B3
Raquette River	Frl	11	B4
Raritan River	Mid	74	A6
Red House Lake	Cat	49	D5
Robert Moses St Pk	SL	3	B1
Rocky Neck St Pk	NLn	71	D3
Rogers Lake	NLn	71	C2
Rollins Pond Forest Preserve	Frl	11	B3
Rudd Pond	Dut	64	F1
Salmon River Res	Osw	15	B6
Sampson St Pk	Sen	39	B4
Sandy Cr	Mro	24	B2
Saratoga St	Srg	32	D6
Saunders Pt	NLn	71	D2
Schroon Lake	Wrr	19	C4
Scottsville	Mro	24	D6
Second Pond	Rns	46	A3
Selkirk Shores St Pk	Osw	14	D6
Seneca Lake St Pk	Sen	39	A2
Seneca River	Cyg	26	F6
Seneca River	Ono	27	C4
Seventh Lake	Hml	17	D4
Silver Lake St Pk	Wyo	36	F4
South Bay	Whg	20	A6
South End	NHv	70	B3
Spruce Run St Pk	Hnt	73	A5
Stillwater Res	Hrk	16	F2
Stony Cr	Jfs	14	D3
Susquehanna River	Ots	43	A6
Susquehanna River	Ots	56	E1
Susquehanna River	Tio	54	A6
Taughannock Falls St Pk	Tmk	39	E6
Thames River	NLn	71	F1
Thames River	NLn	71	F2
Thompsons Lake St Pk	Alb	44	E5
Tully Lake	Crt	40	E3
Upper Chateaugay Lake	Cln	5	A3
Upper Saranac Lake	Frl	11	C2
Welch Lake	Rck	67	E4
Wellesley Is St Pk	Jfs	7	F2
West Essex Pk	Esx	74	C2
Westcott Beach St Pk	Jfs	14	E2
Whetstone Gulf St Pk	Lew	16	A4
White Lake	Slv	62	B4
White Pond	Put	64	D6
Whitney Pt Lake	Brm	55	A2
Willsboro Bay	Ese	13	B2
Wilson Hill Is	SL	2	F1
Wilson-Tuscarora St Pk	Nia	22	D2

Campsites

NAME	TERR	MAP	GRID
Alger Is Preserve	Hrk	17	B4
Allegany St Pk Quaker	Cat	49	B6
Allegany St Pk Red House	Cat	49	C5
Anthony Wayne	Orn	67	F3
Ausable Pt Forest Preserve	Cln	6	A6
Bear Spring Mtn Forest Preserve	Dlw	56	F5
Beaver Pond	Rck	67	E4
Beaverkill Forest Preserve	Slv	62	B1
Bethpage St Pk	Nsu	76	A3
Bowman Lake St Pk	Cng	41	D6
Bradbury St Pk	Add	20	F2
Brown Tract Pond Forest Preserve	Hml	17	D3
Buck Pond Forest Preserve	Frl	4	E6
Bulwagga Bay	Ese	13	A6
Burnham Pt St Pk	Jfs	7	C3
Burton Is St Pk	Fkl	6	D3
Buttermilk Falls St Pk	Tmk	53	F2
Button Bay St Pk	Add	13	B4
Campgaw Mtn Co Resv	Brg	67	D6
Caroga Lake Forest Preserve	Flt	31	A5
Cayuga Lake St Pk	Sen	39	C2
Cedar Is St Pk	SL	8	C1
Cedar Pt St Pk	Jfs	7	D3
Cheesequake St Pk	Mid	78	C6
Chenango Valley St Pk	Brm	55	C4
Chittenango Falls St Pk	Mds	41	B1
Clarence Fahnestock St Pk	Put	68	B1
Coles Cr St Pk	SL	2	E2
Cranberry Lake Forest Preserve	SL	10	C4
Crown Pt Resv	Ese	13	A6
Cumberland Bay St Pk	Cln	6	A4
Dar St Pk	Add	13	B6
Darien Lake St Pk	Gns	36	A2
Delta Lake St Pk	Ond	29	B3
Devils Tombstone Forest Preserve	Grn	58	D5
DeWolf Pt St Pk	Jfs	8	A2
Eagle Pt Forest Preserve	Wrr	19	C3
Eel Weir St Pk	SL	2	A5
Eighth Lake Forest Preserve	Hml	17	D3
Elks-Brox	Orn	66	D2
Emerald Lake St Pk	Ben	33	F3
Evangola St Pk	Ere	34	E5
Fair Haven Beach St Pk	Cyg	26	D2
Fillmore Glen St Pk	Cyg	40	B4
Fish Cr Pond Forest Preserve	Frl	11	B3
Forked Lake Forest Preserve	Hml	17	F1
Four Mile St	Nia	21	F3
Four Mile St	Nia	22	A3
Gilbert Lake St Pk	Ots	42	E5
Glimmerglass St Pk	Ots	43	B3
Golden Beach Preserve	Hml	17	E3
Golden Hill St Pk	Nia	23	A2
Grand Isle St Pk	GIC	6	C4
Grass Pt St Pk	Jfs	7	F2
Green Lakes St Pk	Ono	28	A6
Hamlin Beach St Pk	Mro	24	A2
Hearthstone Pt Forest Preserve	Wrr	32	D1
Heckscher St Pk	Sfk	76	E4
High Pt St Pk	Ssx	66	D3
Higley Flow St Pk	SL	3	A6
Higley Flow St Pk	SL	10	B1
Hither Hills St Pk	Sfk	71	F6
Hunts Pond St Pk	Cng	42	B5
Indian Lake Islands Preserve	Hml	18	A5
Jacques Cartier St Pk	SL	1	D6
Jenny Jump St Forest	War	73	A2
Keewaydin Pt St Pk	Jfs	8	A3
Kenneth L Wilson Forest Preserve	Uls	58	D6
Keuka Lake St Pk	Yts	38	E6
Kring Pt St Pk	Jfs	8	B2
Lake Durant Forest Preserve	Hml	18	A2
Lake Eaton Forest Preserve	Hml	18	A1
Lake Erie St Pk	Chu	48	A1
Lake George St Pk	Wrr	32	D2
Lake George/Glen Is Preserve	Wrr	19	E6
Lake George/Long Is Preserve	Wrr	32	E1
Lake George/Narrow Is Preserve	Wrr	19	F5
Lake Harris Forest Preserve	Ese	18	E1
Lake Saint Catherine St Pk	Rut	33	D1
Lake Sebago Beach	Rck	67	E4
Lake Taghkanic St Pk	Clm	59	D5
Lakeside Beach St Pk	Orl	23	C2
Letchworth St Pk	Wyo	36	F5
Lewey Lake Forest Preserve	Hml	18	B5
Limekiln Lake Forest Preserve	Hml	17	C4
Lincoln Pond Forest Preserve	Ese	12	F5
Little Pond Forest Preserve	Dlw	57	C6
Little Sand Pt Forest Preserve	Hml	30	E1
Long Pt St Pk	Jfs	7	D5
Luzerne Forest Preserve	Wrr	32	C2
Macomb Resv St Pk	Cln	5	E5
Mary Is St Pk	Jfs	8	A2
Max V Shaul St Pk	Shh	44	A6
Meacham Lake Forest Preserve	Frl	4	C5
Meadowbrook Forest Preserve	Ese	11	E3
Moffitt Beach Preserve	Hml	31	A1
Mongaup Pond Forest Preserve	Slv	62	D1
Moreau Lake St Pk	Srg	32	D4
Morningside Pk	Slv	62	E4
Mount Philo St Pk	Chi	13	D3
Mountaindale Pk	Slv	62	F4
Nicks Lake Forest Preserve	Hrk	17	A4
North Hero St Pk	GIC	6	D2
North/South Lake Forest Preserve	Grn	58	E4
Northampton Beach Preserve	Flt	31	D4
Ogden & Ruth Mills St Pk	Dut	64	B2
Oquaga Cr St Pk	Brm	56	B4
Paradox Lake Forest Preserve	Ese	19	D2
Pine Ridge	Mro	24	F6
Pixley Falls St Pk	Ond	29	C2
Point Comfort Forest Preserve	Hml	30	E2
Poke-o-Moonshine Forest Preserve	Ese	12	F2
Poplar Pt Forest Preserve	Hml	30	F1
Putnam Pond Forest Preserve	Ese	19	E2
Ramapo Valley Co Resv	Brg	67	D5
Robert H Treman St Pk	Tmk	53	E2
Robert Moses St Pk	SL	3	B1
Rogers Rock Forest Preserve	Wrr	20	A3
Rollins Pond Forest Preserve	Frl	11	B3
Round Valley Rec Area	Hnt	73	B5
Sacandaga Forest Preserve	Hml	31	C2
Sampson St Pk	Sen	39	B4
Saranac Lake Islands Preserve	Frl	11	D3
Selkirk Shores St Pk	Osw	14	D6
Seneca Lake St Pk	Sen	39	A2
Shaftsbury St Pk	Ben	33	D6
Sharp Bridge Forest Preserve	Ese	12	E6
Silver Mine Lake	Orn	67	F3
Southwick Beach St Pk	Jfs	14	D3
Spruce Run Rec Area	Hnt	73	A5
Stephens St Pk	Mrr	73	C2
Stokes St Forest	Ssx	66	C4
Stony Brook St Pk	Stu	37	D6
Swartswood St Pk	Ssx	66	C6
Taconic/Copake Falls St Pk	Clm	59	F5
Taughannock Falls St Pk	Tmk	39	E6
Taylor Pond Forest Preserve	Cln	12	B1
Tioga Pt Forest Preserve	Hml	17	E2
Upper Delaware Natl Scenic & Rec River	Pke	61	F6
Verona Beach St Pk	Ond	28	D4
Voorhees St Pk	Hnt	73	B4
Watch Hill	Sfk	77	B4
Watkins Glen St Pk	Scy	53	A2
Wawayanda St Pk	Pas	67	A4
Wellesley Is St Pk	Jfs	7	F2
Westcott Beach St Pk	Jfs	14	E2
Whetstone Gulf St Pk	Lew	16	A4
Wildwood St Pk	Sfk	77	C1
Wilmington Notch Forest Preserve	Ese	12	B2
Winding Hills Pk	Orn	63	C6
Woodford St Pk	Ben	46	F2
Woodland Valley Forest Preserve	Uls	58	B6
Woods Is St Pk	Fkl	6	D3

Colleges & Universities

NAME	TERR	MAP	GRID
Academy & Coll of Saint Elizabeth	Mrr	74	A3
Adelphi Univ	Nsu	75	D4
Adirondack Comm Coll	Wrr	32	E2
Alfred Univ	Agy	51	C3
Alma White Coll	Sms	73	F6
Bard Coll	Dut	59	B6
Bergen Comm Coll	Brg	74	E1
Berkeley Coll of Bus	Pas	74	D2
Bloomfield Coll	Esx	74	D3
Broome Comm Coll	Brm	55	A5
Caldwell Coll	Esx	74	C3
Canisius Coll	Ere	35	B2
Castleton St Coll	Rut	20	D5
Cayuga Co Comm Coll	Cyg	39	F1
Cazenovia Coll	Mds	41	B1
Centenary Coll	War	73	B2
City Univ of New York Bronx Comm Coll	Brx	75	B2
City Univ of New York Brooklyn Coll	Kng	75	A5
City Univ of New York City Coll & Medical Sch	NYC	75	A3
City Univ of New York Coll of Staten Is	Rmd	74	E5
City Univ of New York Hunter Coll	NYC	75	A3
City Univ of New York Kingsborough Comm Coll	Kng	75	A6
City Univ of New York Lehmann Coll	Brx	75	A2
City Univ of New York Medgar Evers Coll	Kng	75	A5
City Univ of New York Queens Coll & Law Sch	Que	75	C4
City Univ of New York Queensborough Comm Coll	Que	75	C3
City Univ of New York York Coll	Que	75	C4
Clarkson Univ	SL	3	A5
Clinton Comm Coll	Cln	5	F4
Colgate Univ	Mds	41	F3
College Of Mt Saint Vincent	Brx	75	B2
College Of New Rochelle	Wch	75	C1
Columbia Univ	NYC	75	A3
Columbia-Greene Comm Coll	Clm	59	C4
Cornell Univ	Tmk	54	A1
Corning Comm Coll	Stu	52	E5
County Coll of Morris	Mrr	73	F2
D'Youville Coll	Ere	35	B2
Daemen Coll	Ere	35	C1
Dowling Coll	Sfk	76	E4
Drew Univ	Mrr	74	A3
Dutchess Comm Coll	Dut	64	B4
Elmira Coll	Chm	53	B5
Erie Comm Coll North Campus	Ere	35	D1
Erie Comm Coll South Campus	Ere	35	C3
Essex Co Coll	Esx	74	D4
Fairleigh Dickenson Univ Edward Williams Coll	Brg	74	F2
Fairleigh Dickinson Univ Teaneck-Hackensack Campus	Brg	74	F2
Fairleigh Dickinson Univ Florham-Madison Campus	Mrr	74	A3
Fairleigh Dickinson Univ Rutherford-Wayne Campus	Brg	74	E2
Felician Coll	Brg	74	E2

Covered Bridges

Forest & Wildlife Areas

NAME	TERR	MAP	GRID
Monroe St Forest	Fkl	46	F4
Montezuma Natl Wildlife Ref	Sen	26	C6
Montezuma Natl Wildlife Ref	Sen	39	C1
Monty Bay St WMA	Cln	6	B3
Monument Mtn Resv	Brk	60	B3
Morton Natl Wildlife Ref	Sfk	71	B6
Morton Natl Wildlife Ref	Sfk	78	B1
Mount Everett St Resv	Brk	60	A5
Mount Greylock St Resv	Brk	46	D5
Mount Greylock St Resv	Brk	46	D6
Mount Washington St Forest	Brk	60	A5
Mud Cr St Waterfowl Area	GIC	6	C1
Mud Cr St Waterfowl Area	GIC	7	C6
Natural Resource Education Ctr	War	73	A3
Naugatuck St Forest	NHv	69	E1
Nehantic St Forest	NLn	71	C1
Nehantic St Forest	NLn	71	C2
Neversink River St Unique Area	Slv	62	E6
New York Audubon Nature Ctr at The Eldred Preserv	Slv	62	B5
Newton Swamp Mgmt Area	Wgn	72	C2
Nicks Lake Forest Preserve	Hrk	17	A4
North/South Lake Forest Preserve	Grn	58	E4
Northampton Beach Preserve	Flt	31	D4
Norvin Green St Forest	Pas	67	B5
Norvin Green St Forest	Pas	67	B6
Oak Orchard WMA	Gns	23	C5
October Mtn St Forest	Brk	60	D2
Oriskany Flats St WMA	Ond	29	B4
Otis St Forest	Brk	60	E4
Otis St Forest	Brk	60	F3
Otis St Forest	Brk	60	F4
Otter Cr St WMA	Add	13	C4
Oyster Bay Natl Wildlife Ref	Nsu	75	F2
Pachaug St Forest	NLn	72	B1
Paradox Lake Forest Preserve	Ese	19	D2
Partridge Run St WMA	Alb	44	D6
Paughussett St Forest	Ffd	69	B1
Paugnut St Forest	Lch	65	E2
Paugussett St Forest	Ffd	69	D2
Pauline L Murdock St Wildlife Sanctuary	Ese	12	F4
Peoples St Forest	Lch	65	F1
Pequest WMA	War	73	A2
Perch River St WMA	Jfs	7	F5
Perch River St WMA	Jfs	8	A5
Peru WMA	Brk	60	F1
Peru WMA	Brk	60	F2
Pharsalia St WMA	Cng	41	D5
Pine Bush St Unique Area	Alb	45	A4
Pittsfield St Forest	Brk	46	C6
Pittsfield St Forest	Brk	60	B1
Plum Bank Marsh Mgmt Area	Mdx	71	A3
Point Comfort Forest Preserve	Hml	30	E2
Poke-O-Moonshine Forest Preserve	Ese	12	F1
Pond Woods WMA	Add	20	C3
Pootatuck St Forest	Ffd	64	F6
Pootatuck St Forest	Ffd	65	A6
Poplar Point Forest Preserve	Hml	30	F1
Putnam Pond Forest Preserve	Ese	19	E2
Putts Cr WMA	Ese	20	A1
Quinnipiac River Marsh Mgmt Area	NHv	70	B2
Ragged Rock Mgmt Area	Mdx	71	B3
Ramapo Mtn St Forest	Pas	67	C6
Ramapo Valley Co Resv	Brg	67	D5
Rattlesnake Hill St WMA	Agy	37	B6
Rattlesnake Hill St WMA	Agy	51	B1
Rattlesnake Hill St WMA	Lvg	37	B6
Reforestation Area	Agy	36	C6
Reynolds St Game Farm	Tmk	54	A1
Richville WMA	Add	20	D2
Rockport St Game Farm	War	73	B3
Rockville Mgmt Area	Wgn	72	C1
Rocky Pt St Nat Resource Mgmt Area	Sfk	77	A1
Rogers Is WMA	Clm	59	C4
Rogers Rock Forest Preserve	Wrr	20	A3
Rollins Pond Forest Preserve	Frl	11	B3
Rome St WMA	Ond	28	F4
Rose Hill Mgmt Area	NLn	71	F1
Roy St WMA	Ssx	66	B4
Rupert St Forest	Ben	33	E4
Sacandaga Forest Preserve	Hml	31	C2
Saint Johns Conservation Area	Ont	21	C6
Saint Lawrence St Forest	SL	2	F6
Sand Bar Waterfowl Mgmt Area	Chi	6	D5
Sandisfield St Forest	Brk	60	D5
Sandisfield St Forest	Brk	60	E5
Sandisfield St Forest	Brk	60	E6
Saranac Lake Islands Preserve	Frl	11	D3
Savoy Mtn St Forest	Brk	46	F5
Savoy WMA	Brk	46	F6
Saw Mill Cr WMA	Hud	74	E3
Seatuck Natl Wildlife Ref	Sfk	76	D4
Sharp Bridge Forest Preserve	Ese	12	E6
Sherman-Hoffman Wildlife Sanctuary	Sms	73	F4
Snake Mtn St WMA	Add	13	C6
South Shore Mgmt Area	Wgn	72	F2
South Stream St Waterfowl Mgmt Area	Ben	46	D3
Stafford Hill WMA	Brk	46	E6
Stamford Meadows WMA	Ben	46	E3
State Forest Preserve	Brk	60	D5
State Forest Preserve	Cln	5	B1
State Forest Preserve	Cln	5	C1
State Forest Preserve	Dlw	56	E5
State Forest Preserve	Dlw	61	E1
State Forest Preserve	Dlw	61	E2
State Forest Preserve	Lew	9	B4
State Forest Preserve	Lew	15	F4
State Forest Preserve	Lew	15	F5
State Forest Preserve	Lew	16	A3
State Forest Preserve	Lew	16	A4
State Forest Preserve	Lew	16	A6
State Forest Preserve	Lew	16	C4
State Forest Preserve	SL	3	A2
State Forest Preserve	SL	9	B4
State Forest Preserve	SL	9	C5
State Forest Preserve	Slv	61	F2
State Forest Preserve	Srg	32	A5
State Forest Preserve	Wrr	32	C4
State Forest Preserves	Dlw	56	C5
State Forest Preserves	Dlw	61	D2
State Forest Preserves	Lew	16	A5
State Forest Preserves	Lew	16	B5
State Forest Preserves	Lew	16	C6
State Game Lands No 70	Wyn	61	A1
State Game Lands No 109	Eri	47	A6
State Game Lands No 116	Pke	66	A1
State Game Lands No 155	Eri	47	B6
State Game Lands No 159	Wyn	61	C3
State Game Lands No 159	Wyn	61	C4
State Game Lands No 161	Eri	47	A6
State Game Lands No 163	Eri	47	B5
State Game Lands No 167	Eri	47	C6
State Game Lands No 180	Pke	66	A2
State Game Lands No 191	Eri	47	C6
State Game Lands No 209	Pke	66	B1
State Game Lands No 218	Eri	47	A6
State Game Lands No 299	Wyn	61	B1
State Game Lands No 300	Lak	61	A6
State Game Lands No 300	Wyn	61	A6
State Game Lands No 316	Pke	61	F6
State Game Mgmt Area	Cng	41	F4
State Wetlands	Sfk	76	E1
Stillwater St Nat Area	Pke	66	A4
Stokes St Forest	Ssx	66	B4
Stokes St Forest	Ssx	66	C3
Stokes St Forest	Ssx	66	C4
Target Rock Natl Wildlife Ref	Sfk	76	A1
Taylor Pond Forest Preserve	Cln	12	B1
Tenafly Nature Ctr	Brg	75	A1
Three Mile Bay St WMA	Osw	27	E3
Three Mile Bay St WMA	Osw	27	F3
Three Rivers St WMA	Ono	27	C4
Tillman Ravine St Nat Area	Ssx	66	B5
Tillman Road St WMA	Ere	35	E1
Tinmouth Channel St WMA	Rut	33	F1
Tioga Point Forest Preserve	Hml	17	E2
Tioughnioga St WMA	Mds	41	C2
Tivoli Bay St Unique Area	Dut	59	B6
Tolland St Forest	Hmp	60	F5
Tonawanda St WMA	Gns	23	A5
Tonawanda St WMA	Nia	23	A5
Trustom Pond Natl Wildlife Ref	Wgn	72	F2
Tug Hill St WMA	Lew	15	D4
Tunxis St Forest	Htf	65	F1
Tunxis St Forest	Lch	60	F6
Upper And Lower Lakes St Wildlife Area	SL	2	C5
Utica Marsh St WMA	Ond	29	C5
Vinegar Hill St WMA	Grn	58	A4
Wallkill River Natl Wildlife Ref	Ssx	66	F4
Walpack St WMA	Ssx	66	B5
Wanaque St WMA	Pas	67	C5
Ward Marsh WMA	Rut	20	B6
Ward Pound Ridge Resv	Wch	68	E3
Watts Flats WMA	Chu	48	A6
Wertheim Natl Wildlife Ref	Sfk	77	B3
West Cameron St WMA	Stu	52	A4
West Rutland St Forest	Rut	20	E5
Weybridge Cave St Nat Area	Add	13	D6
Whipple Hollow WMA	Rut	20	F5
Whittingham WMA	Ssx	66	C6
Whittingham WMA	Ssx	73	C1
Wickham Marsh St WMA	Ese	6	A6
Wilmington Notch Forest Preserve	Ese	12	B2
Wilson Hill St Fish & Game Mgmt Area	SL	2	F1
Wolf Hollow St WMA	Dlw	57	B5
Woodland Valley Forest Preserve	Uls	58	B6
Woody Hill Mgmt Area	Wgn	72	C2
Wyantenock St Forest	Lch	65	A3
Wyantenock St Forest	Lch	65	C4

Golf Courses

NAME	TERR	MAP	GRID
Adirondack G & CC	Cln	5	D5
Afton GC	Cng	55	F4
Alban Hills CC	Flt	31	C6
Alder Cr GC	Ond	29	D2
Allegheny Hills GC	Agy	50	C2
Alling Mem GC	NHv	70	B3
Amsterdam Mun GC	Mgy	44	D1
Apalachin GC	Tio	54	D6
Apple Greens GC	Uls	63	F4
Arrowhead GC	Mro	24	B4
Arrowhead GC	Ono	27	F5
Ashbrook GC	Uni	74	B5
Auburn CC	Cyg	39	F2
Barberlea GC	Lvg	37	A5
Barker Brook GC	Ond	42	A1
Basin Hbr Club	Add	13	C4
Batavia CC	Gns	36	E1
Bath CC	Stu	52	B3
Battenkill CC	Whg	33	A5
Battle Is St Pk GC	Osw	27	A2
Bay Meadows GC	Wrr	32	E2
Bay Pk GC	Nsu	75	E5
Beaver Brook GC	Hnt	73	B5
Beaver Is St Pk GC	Ere	35	A1
Bedford Cr GC	Jfs	14	E2
Beekman CC	Dut	64	C5
Beldon Hill GC	Brm	55	D4
Bellport CC	Sfk	77	A3
Bemus Pt GC	Chu	48	B5
Bend of The River GC	Srg	32	C3
Bergen Pt GC	Sfk	76	B4
Bethpage St Pk GC	Nsu	76	A3
Big Oak GC	Otr	39	A2
Birch Run CC	Cat	49	F6
Blackhead Mtn Lodge & CC	Grn	58	F2
Blair Acad GC	War	73	A1
Blue Stone GC	Cng	55	E1
Bluff Pt G & CC	Cln	6	A4
Bob O Link GC	Ere	35	D3
Bomoseen GC	Rut	20	D5
Bonavista GC	Sen	39	C4
Bowling Green GC	Mrr	66	F6
Brae Burn Rec GC	Lvg	37	D6
Braemar CC	Mro	24	C4
Brandy Brook GC	Ond	28	E5
Brentwood CC	Sfk	76	D3
Brighton Pk	Ere	22	B6
Bristol Harbour GC	Otr	38	C3
Brockport CC	Mro	24	A4
Brookhaven GC	Srg	32	B5
Brooklawn GC	Ono	27	E5
Brunswick Greens	Rns	45	E4
Burden Lake CC	Rns	45	F5
Burnet Pk GC	Ono	27	D6
Byrncliff Resort & Conference Ctr	Wyo	36	C4
Calverton Links	Sfk	77	D2
Camillus CC	Ono	27	B6
Camroden GC	Ond	29	B3
Canajoharie GC	Mgy	43	E2
Canasawacta CC	Cng	41	F6
Cantiague Pk GC	Nsu	75	F3
Cardinal Hills CC	Cat	49	A4
Casolwood GC	Mds	28	C5
Cassadaga CC	Chu	48	B2
Catatonk GC	Tio	54	C4
Cato GC	Cyg	26	F5
Catskill GC	Grn	59	B4
Cazenovia Pk GC	Ere	35	C2
Cedar River GC	Hml	18	C3
Cedar View GC	SL	3	B1
Cedars GC	Lew	15	F3
Cedars GC	Sfk	71	A6
Cee Jay CC	Ots	42	E6
Centerpointe CC	Otr	38	C2
Central Valley GC	Orn	67	E2
Champlain CC	Fkl	6	E2
Chautauqua GC	Chu	48	A4
Chautauqua Pt GC	Chu	48	A4
Chemung GC	Chm	53	E6
Chenango Valley St Pk GC	Brm	55	C4
Chili CC	Mro	24	C6
Christopher Morley Pk GC	Nsu	75	D3
Churchville GC	Mro	24	B5
Clayton CC	Jfs	7	F3
Clearview Pk GC	Que	75	C3
Cliff Pk GC	Pke	66	B3
Cobble Hill GC	Ese	12	E4
Cobleskill GC	Shh	44	A4
Colgate Univ Seven Oaks GC	Mds	41	F3
College GC	Dlw	57	A4
College Hill (Caven) GC	Dut	64	B4
Colonial CC	Grn	58	E4
Colonie Town GC	Alb	45	B3
Concord Hotel GC	Slv	62	E4
Conewango Forks GC	Cat	49	A5
Conklin Players GC	Brm	55	B6
Copake CC	Clm	59	E4
Crab Meadow GC	Sfk	76	C1
Craggie Brae GC	Mro	24	C6
Craig Wood GC	Ese	12	A4
Cranebrook GC	Cyg	39	E1
Crestbrook Pk GC	Lch	65	E5
Crestwood CC	Ond	29	C4
Cronins Golf Resort	Wrr	19	B5
Culver Lake GC	Ssx	66	D4
Dande Farms GC	Ere	23	A6
Darlington Co Pk GC	Brg	67	D6
Deerfield CC	Mro	24	B4
Deerwood GC	Ere	22	B6
Delaware Pk GC	Ere	35	B1
Delphi Falls GC	Ono	41	A2
Delta Knolls GC	Ond	29	A3
Dinsmore GC	Dut	64	A2
Dix Hills GC	Sfk	76	B3
DJs GC	Chm	53	F6
Dogwood Knolls GC	Dut	64	B5
Domenicos GC	Ond	29	B5
Dotys GC	Hrk	29	F6
Douglaston GC	Que	75	D4
Downing GC	Eri	47	A4
Drumlins GC	Ono	27	E6
Dryden Lake GC	Tmk	54	C1
Dunwoodie GC	Wch	75	B1
Durand-Eastman GC	Mro	24	E4
Dutchers GC	Dut	64	E6
Dyker Beach GC	Kng	74	F5
Eagle Crest GC	Srg	45	B2
Eagle Vale GC	Mro	25	A5
East Orange GC	Esx	74	B3
Eddy Farm Resort Hotel GC	Orn	66	D1
Eden Valley GC	Ere	35	C6
Edgewood GC	Ots	42	E6
Eisenhower Pk CC	Nsu	75	F4
Elkdale CC	Cat	49	C4
Elm Tree GC	Crt	40	D5
Elma Meadows GC	Ere	35	E2
Elms GC	Osw	14	D4
Ely Pk GC	Brm	55	B5
Emerald Crest GC	Osw	27	C2
Emerson GC	Brg	74	F1
En-Joie GC	Brm	54	E5
Endwell Greens GC	Brm	54	F5
Evergreen CC	Rns	45	D6
Evergreen GC	Agy	50	E6
Evergreen GC	Ere	22	C6
Fairchild Wheeler GC	Ffd	69	D4
Fairview Golf & Country Inn	Lvg	37	C2
Fairway Valley GC	War	73	A3
Fallsview GC	Uls	63	B4
Farmstead GC & CC	Ssx	66	E5
Fernwood GC	Esx	74	C3
Fillmore GC	Cyg	40	A4
Fishkill GC	Dut	64	B6
Flanders Valley GC	Mrr	73	D3
Ford Hill GC	Brm	55	A3
Forest Heights GC	Chu	48	C5
Forest Pk GC	Que	75	B4
Four X Four GC	SL	9	A3
Fox Fire GC	Ono	27	C5
Fox Hollow GC	Hnt	73	D5
Fox Run GC	Yts	53	A1
Francis Byrne GC	Esx	74	C3
Frear Pk & GC	Rns	45	E3
Frenchs Hollow Fairways	Alb	45	A4
Galloping Hill GC	Uni	74	C4
Galway GC	Srg	32	A6
Garrison GC & CC	Put	68	B2
Genegantslet GC	Cng	55	C3
Genesee Valley Co Pk GC	Mro	24	E5
Glen Cove GC	Nsu	75	F3
Glen Oak GC	Ere	22	D6
Golden Oak GC	Brm	55	E6
Golf Club at Wind Watch	Sfk	76	D3
Golf Club of Newport	Hrk	29	F4
Golf Knolls GC	Ond	28	F3
Gospel Hill GC	Eri	47	A5
Gouverneur GC	SL	9	A3
Governor Alfred E Smith/Sunken Meadow St Pk GC	Sfk	76	C2
Grandview Farms Bed GC	Tio	54	D3
Grandview GC	Ere	34	E5
Great Gorge GC	Ssx	66	F4
Great Gorge Golf Resort	Ssx	66	E5
Green Acres GC	Uls	63	F1
Green Knoll GC	Sms	73	E5
Green Lakes St Pk GC	Ono	28	A6
Green Mansions GC	Wrr	19	B6
Green Meadows GC	Eri	47	B4
Green Pond GC	Mrr	74	A1
Green Ridge GC	Orn	66	F2
Greenview GC	Osw	27	F3
Greenwood GC	Ere	22	E6
Griffins Greens GC	Ono	27	A5
Grossinger Golf Resort	Slv	62	D3
Grygiels Pine Hills GC	Hrk	29	E6
H Smith Richardson GC	Ffd	69	C4
Hanah CC	Dlw	57	E4
Harbour Pointe CC	Orl	23	D3
Hauppauge CC	Sfk	76	D2
Heartland Golf Pk	Sfk	76	C3
Heatherwood GC	Sfk	76	F2
Hendricks Field GC	Esx	74	E3
Hiawatha Trails GC	Alb	45	B4
Hickory Hill GC	Orn	67	C3
Hickory Ridge G & CC	Orl	23	E4
Hidden Acres GC	Ssx	66	C3
Hidden Valley GC	Cat	49	D3
Hidden Valley GC	Ond	29	C5
High Mtn GC	Brg	74	D1
High Pt CC	Ssx	66	C3
Highland Pk GC	Cyg	39	F1
Highlands CC	Put	68	A2
Hiland GC	Wrr	32	E2
Hillcrest GC	Sch	44	F3
Hillendale GC	Tmk	53	E1
Hillview GC	Chu	48	B1
Holbrook CC	Sfk	76	F3
Holland Hills GC	Ere	35	F5
Holland Meadows GC	Flt	31	C6
Hollow Hills GC	Sfk	76	B3
Homowack Hotel GC	Uls	63	A4
Hoosick Falls CC	Rns	46	B2
Hornell CC	Stu	51	E2
Hyde Pk GC	Nia	21	F5
Indian Head GC	Cyg	39	D1
Indian Hills GC	Stu	52	E5
Indian Is GC	Sfk	77	E1
Ironwood GC	Ono	27	B5
Ischua Valley CC	Cat	50	A2
Island Glenn CC	Slv	62	B3
Island Valley GC	Mro	25	A5
Islands End GC	Sfk	71	B5
James Baird St Pk GC	Dut	64	C4
Jones Beach St Pk GC	Nsu	75	F5
Katsbaan GC	Uls	59	A5
Keshequa GC	Lvg	37	C4
Kingsboro GC	Flt	31	B5
Kiss n Greens GC	Gns	36	A1
Kissena Pk GC	Que	75	C4
Knickerbocker GC	Crt	41	A6
Knoll East GC	Mrr	74	B2
Knoll West GC	Mrr	74	B2
Kutshers CC	Slv	62	D4
Kwiniaska GC	Chi	13	D2
La Tourette GC	Rmd	74	E5
Lake Isle CC	Wch	75	C1
Lake Lackawanna GC	Ssx	73	D1
Lake Lorain GC	Wyn	61	A3
Lake Pleasant GC	Hml	31	A1
Lake Saint Catherine GC	Rut	33	D1
Lake Shore CC	Mro	24	E3
Lakeside CC	Yts	38	F5
Lakeside GC	Chu	47	D4
Lakeview GC	Jfs	14	E4
LaTourette Pk GC	Rmd	74	E6
Laurel View GC	NHv	70	A2
Leatherstocking GC	Ots	43	B4
LeRoy CC	Gns	37	A1
Lido GC	Nsu	75	E5
Lima GC	Lvg	37	E2
Links at Erie Village	Ono	27	F6
Links at Hiawatha Ldg	Tio	54	E5
Liverpool GC	Ono	27	D5
Livingston CC	Lvg	37	C3
Lochmor GC	Slv	62	E3
Loon Lake GC	Frl	4	F6
Lyndon GC	Ono	27	F6
Malone GC	Frl	4	C3
Maple Crest GC	Hrk	29	E6
Maple Hill GC	Crt	54	F1
Maple Moor GC	Wch	68	D6

NAME	TERR	MAP	GRID
Maplehurst CC	Chu	48	C6
Marble Is GC	Chi	6	C6
Marine Pk GC	Kng	75	A5
Mark Twain GC	Chm	53	B5
Massena CC	SL	3	A1
McCann Mem GC	Dut	64	B4
McConnellsville GC	Ond	28	A5
Meadowbrook GC	Cyg	26	F6
Meadowbrook GC	SL	3	C4
Meadows GC	Mrr	74	C2
Mechanicville GC	Rns	45	E2
Merrick Road GC	Nsu	75	F5
Middle Is CC	Sfk	77	A2
Mill Road Acres GC	Alb	45	C3
Mine Brook GC	Mrr	73	C2
Mohawk Valley CC	Hrk	30	B6
Mohonk Mtn House GC	Uls	63	E3
Monroe CC	Orn	67	D3
Montauk Downs St Pk	Sfk	72	A6
Mosholu GC	Brx	75	B2
Mountain Top GC	Cng	42	B4
Neshobe GC	Rut	20	F3
Nevele GC	Uls	63	B4
New Course at Albany	Alb	45	B5
New Paltz GC	Uls	63	F3
Newark Valley GC	Tio	54	D3
Newman GC	Tmk	53	F1
Niagara Co GC	Nia	22	E4
Niagara Orleans CC	Nia	23	A4
Nick Stoner GC	Flt	31	A5
Nine Hole Executive Course	Srg	32	C6
North Country GC	Cln	6	B1
North Shore GC	Ond	28	B3
North Woodmere GC	Nsu	75	D5
Northern Pines GC	Ono	27	F4
Oak Hill Pk GC	Ffd	69	A5
Oak Ridge GC	Jfs	8	A2
Oak Ridge GC	Uni	74	B6
Oak Run GC	Nia	22	E4
Oakwood GC	Ere	22	D6
Old Hickory GC	Lvg	37	E3
Oneida CC	Mds	28	E6
Orange Hill CC	Ffd	69	F3
Orchard Hills GC	Brg	74	F1
Orchard Valley GC	Ono	40	D2
Oriskany Hills GC	Ond	29	B4
Otsego GC	Ots	43	B3
Otterkill CC	Orn	67	D1
Ouleout Cr GC	Dlw	56	E3
Overpeck GC	Brg	74	F2
Oyster Bay GC	Sfk	76	A3
Paramus GC	Brg	74	E1
Parkview Fairways	Otr	38	B1
Pascack Brook GC	Brg	74	F1
Passaic Co GC	Pas	74	C2
Peek n Peak GC	Chu	47	D6
Pelham/Split Rock GC	Brx	75	C2
Peninsula GC	Nsu	76	A4
Perinton G & CC	Wan	25	B5
Phillip J Rotella CC	Rck	67	F4
Pinch Brook GC	Mrr	74	B3
Pine Grove G & CC	Ono	27	C6
Pine Hills CC	Sfk	77	C2
Pine Hills GC	Hrk	29	E6
Pine Meadows G & CC	Ere	35	E1
Pinehurst GC	Chu	47	E3
Pinewood CC	Mro	24	B4
Pinnacle St Pk GC	Stu	52	D5
Plainfield West GC	Mid	74	B5
Pleasant Knolls GC	Ond	28	E5
Pleasantview GC	Grn	58	F2
Point East GC	Ono	27	E6
Popes Grove GC	Ono	27	C5
Port Bay GC	Wan	26	C3
Potsdam Town & CC	SL	3	A5
Pound Ridge GC	Wch	68	F4
Poxabogue GC	Sfk	78	C1
Proctor-Pittsford CC	Rut	20	F4
Putnam GC	Wch	68	D4
Quail Brook GC	Sms	73	F6
Queensbury GC	Wrr	32	E2
Radisson Greens GC	Ono	27	B5
Rainbow CC	Grn	58	F1
Ralph Myhre GC	Add	13	E6
Raymondville G & CC	SL	3	B2
Ricci Meadows GC	Orl	23	E2
Rip Van Winkle GC	Grn	58	F4
River Oaks GC	Ere	22	A6
River View CC	Sch	45	B2
Riverbend GC	Cng	42	C5
Riverside CC	Osw	27	D3
Riverton GC	Mro	24	D6
Rivervale CC	Brg	67	F6
Robert Moses GC	Sfk	76	C5
Robert T Jones GC at Cornell Univ	Tmk	54	A2
Robert Van Patten GC	Srg	45	C2
Rock Hill CC	Sfk	77	C2
Rockland Lake North GC	Rck	68	B5
Rockland Lake South GC	Rck	68	B5
Rockleigh GC	Brg	75	A1
Rockview GC	Ssx	66	D2
Rogues Roost GC	Mds	28	A5
Rolling Acres GC	Wyo	36	D6
Rolling Greens GC	Ssx	66	D6
Rome CC	Ond	28	F3
Rondout GC	Uls	63	D3
Rosebrook GC	Chu	34	E6
Rothland GC	Ere	22	F6
Roxbury GC	Dlw	57	F3
Rustic GC & CC	Jfs	14	E1
Rutgers GC	Mid	74	A6
Sacandaga GC	Flt	31	D4
Sag Harbor GC	Sfk	78	D1
Sagamore Resort & GC	Wrr	19	E5
Saint Bonaventure GC	Cat	50	A5
Saint Lawrence St Pk GC	SL	1	F5
Saint Lawrence Univ GC	SL	2	E5
Salmon Cr CC	Mro	24	B4
Sanctuary GC	Wch	68	C3
Sandy Pond GC	Sfk	77	D1
Saranac Inn G & CC	Frl	11	B2
Saranac Lake GC	Ese	11	F3
Saratoga Spa St Pk GC	Srg	32	C6
Sauquoit Knolls GC	Ond	42	D1
Saxon Woods GC	Wch	75	C1
Scenic Farms GC	Orn	67	C2
Schenectady Mun GC	Sch	45	A3
Scotch Hills GC	Uni	74	B5
Scotts Corner GC	Orn	63	C6
Scotts Oquaga GC	Brm	56	A6
Segalla CC	Dut	64	F2
Seneca GC	Ono	27	C5
Seneca Lake CC	Otr	39	A3
Shadow Lake GC	Mro	25	A5
Shadow Pines GC	Mro	25	A5
Shamrock GC	Ond	29	B5
Shawangunk CC	Uls	63	A4
Shawnee CC	Nia	22	C5
Shelter Is CC	Sfk	71	B6
Sheridan Pk GC	Ere	35	B1
Shore Acres GC	Mro	24	E3
Silver Cr GC	Sen	39	B2
Silver Lake Pk GC	Rmd	74	E5
Six-S CC	Agy	50	F3
Skene Valley CC	Whg	20	B6
Skyline G & CC	Ono	27	E4
Skyridge Chalet & GC	Mds	28	B6
Sleepy Hollow GC	Ond	29	A3
Smithtown Ldg CC	Sfk	76	D2
Soaring Eagles GC	Chm	53	B4
Sodus Bay Heights GC	Wan	25	F4
South Hills CC	Chu	48	C6
South Pk GC	Ere	35	B2
South Shore GC	Ere	35	B3
South Shore GC	Rmd	74	D6
Spook Rock GC	Rck	67	E5
Spooky Brook GC	Sms	73	F6
Sprain Lake GC	Wch	75	B1
Spring Lake GC	Sfk	77	A2
Springbrook Greens GC	Cyg	26	D3
Stadium GC	Sch	45	A3
Stamford GC	Dlw	57	E1
Sterling Farms GC	Ffd	68	F5
Stone Dock GC	Uls	63	E3
Stonebridge G & CC	Ond	29	C6
Stonehedges GC	Tmk	40	C6
Stony Ford GC	Orn	67	C1
Suffolk Co GC	Sfk	76	E4
Sugar Hill GC	Chu	47	F2
Sullivan Co GC	Slv	62	C3
Summit Mun GC	Uni	74	B4
Sundown GC & CC	Cng	56	A1
Sunnyhill Resort GC	Grn	58	F1
Sunset Valley GC	Chu	48	C5
Sunset Valley GC	Mrr	74	C1
Swan Lake GC	Sfk	77	C2
Swann Lake GC & CC	Slv	62	C4
Sycamore Greens GC	Sch	44	E3
Tall Tree GC	Sfk	77	A1
Tamarack GC	Mid	78	A6
Tanner Valley GC	Ono	40	C1
Taranwould GC	Wan	25	E5
Tashua Knolls CC	Ffd	69	D3
Tee-Bird GC	Srg	32	E3
Tennanah Lake GC	Slv	62	A2
Tera Greens GC	Mid	78	A6
Terry Brae GC	Slv	62	E4
Terry Hills GC	Gns	23	E6
The Heritage CC	Brm	55	B5
The Pines GC	Osw	14	D6
The Pines Resort GC	Slv	62	E4
The Ponds at Lake Grove GC	Sfk	76	E2
Thendara GC	Hrk	17	A4
Thomas Carvel CC	Dut	64	E1
Thousand Acres GC	Wrr	32	B1
Thousand Is GC	Jfs	8	A3
Ticonderoga CC	Ese	20	A2
Timber Pt CC	Sfk	76	E4
Tioga CC	Tio	54	B6
Tomacys GC	Jfs	14	F3
Tomassos GC	Tio	53	F6
Top O the World GC	Wrr	32	E1
Town Isle CC	Ono	28	A6
Town of Hamburg GC	Ere	35	C4
Town of Schroon GC	Ese	19	D3
Town of Wallkill GC	Orn	63	B6
Tri Co CC	Chu	48	E1
Triple Cr GC	Lvg	37	D5
Trumansburg GC	Tmk	39	E6
Tupper Lake GC	Frl	11	A4
Turin Highlands GC	Lew	16	B5
Twin Brooks GC	SL	2	E2
Twin Hickory CC	Stu	51	E3
Twin Hills GC	Mro	24	B4
Twin Ponds GC & CC	Ond	29	C5
Twin Willows GC	Mrr	74	C1
Two Bridges GC	Mrr	74	C2
Vails Grove GC	Wch	68	E2
Valley View GC	Ond	29	D6
Van Cortlandt Pk GC	Brx	75	A2
Vassar GC	Dut	64	B4
Vesper Hills GC	Ono	40	E3
Victor Hills CC	Otr	38	B1
Villa Roma GC	Slv	62	A3
Wa-noa GC	Ono	27	F6
Wakely Lodge & GC	Hml	17	D3
Walden Oaks GC	Crt	40	D6
Warrenbrook GC	Sms	74	A5
Watertown GC	Jfs	15	B1
Watkins Glen GC	Scy	53	A2
Wayne Hills CC	Wan	26	A6
Webster GC	Mro	25	B4
Weequahic Pk GC	Uni	74	D4
Wellesley Is St Pk GC	Jfs	7	F2
Wells Coll GC	Cyg	39	E4
Wellsville CC	Agy	51	B4
West Hill G & CC	Ono	27	B6
West Sayville GC	Sfk	76	F4
Western Hills GC	NHv	65	F6
Western Turnpike GC	Alb	45	A4
Westmoreland GC	Ond	29	A5
Westport CC	Ese	13	A4
Westvale GC	Ono	27	C6
Whispering Hills GC	Lvg	37	D4
Whiteface Inn GC	Ese	12	A3
Wildwood CC	Mro	37	E1
Wildwood GC	Ono	27	E5
Williston CC	Chi	13	F1
Willow Brook G & CC	Nia	22	E4
Willow Creek GC	Chm	53	A5
Willow Run GC	Chu	48	A4
Willowbrook GC	Crt	40	D6
Willowbrook GC	Jfs	8	B6
Willowbrook GC	Nia	22	D4
Willsboro GC	Ese	13	A2
Windham CC	Grn	58	D3
Winding Brook CC	Clm	59	D2
Winged Pheasant GC	Otr	38	C1
Woodcliff GC	Mro	25	A6
Woodcrest GC	Chu	48	A4
Woodgate Pines GC	Ond	29	B1
Woodhaven GC	Ots	56	E1

Indian Reservations

NAME	TERR	MAP	GRID
Allegany	Cat	49	B5
Allegany	Cat	49	E5
Cattaraugus	Cat	34	F6
Cattaraugus	Cat	49	A1
Cattaraugus	Chu	34	F6
Cattaraugus	Chu	35	A6
Cattaraugus	Ere	34	F6
Cattaraugus	Ere	35	A6
Oil Spring	Agy	50	C4
Onondaga	Ono	40	E1
Pequot	NLn	72	A1
Saint Regis	Frl	3	E1
Saint Regis Akwesasne	Ont	2	A3
Schaghticoke	Lch	64	F4
Shinnecock	Sfk	78	A2
Tonawanda	Ere	23	A6
Tonawanda	Gns	23	A6
Tonawanda	Nia	23	A6
Tuscarora	Nia	22	A4

Information Centers

NAME	TERR	MAP	GRID
Adirondack Pk Visitors Interpretive Ctr	Ese	18	D1
Adirondack Pk Visitors Interpretive Ctr	Frl	11	C1
Connecticut	Ffd	68	F2
Connecticut	NHv	70	C1
Dutchess Co Tourist	Dut	64	A3
Massachusetts	Brk	46	D5
Massachusetts	Brk	60	C6
New York	Brm	55	C6
New York	Cln	6	A3
New York	Ere	22	A6
New York	Ere	35	A5
New York	Ese	12	B3
New York	Gns	23	C6
New York	Grn	59	C1
New York	Hrk	30	C6
New York	Jfs	8	A3
New York	Mgy	44	E2
New York	Mro	24	D6
New York	Nsu	75	D4
New York	SL	2	A4
New York	Srg	45	C2
New York	Tio	54	A6
New York	Uls	59	A5
New York	Wrr	32	D3
Pennsylvania	Eri	47	C3
Pennsylvania	Pke	66	D2
Vermont	Add	13	A6
Vermont	Add	13	C5
Vermont	Add	13	D6
Vermont	Add	13	F5
Vermont	Add	20	C2
Vermont	Add	20	E1
Vermont	Add	20	F1
Vermont	Ben	33	E6
Vermont	Ben	33	F4
Vermont	Ben	46	C2
Vermont	Ben	46	D1
Vermont	Ben	46	D3
Vermont	Ben	46	F2
Vermont	Chi	13	D2
Vermont	Chi	13	D3
Vermont	Chi	13	E1
Vermont	Fkl	6	E1
Vermont	Fkl	6	E4
Vermont	Fkl	6	F3
Vermont	GIC	6	C1
Vermont	GIC	6	C5
Vermont	Rut	20	C6
Vermont	Rut	20	D4
Vermont	Rut	20	E3
Vermont	Rut	20	F5

Islands & Points

NAME	TERR	MAP	GRID
Alburg Tongue	GIC	6	C1
Allen Pt	GIC	6	C5
Ash Is	Ont	7	F1
Ash Is	Qub	7	B6
Association Is	Jfs	14	D2
Ault Is	Ont	2	F1
Ausable Pt	Cln	6	A6
Barcelona Pt	Sfk	71	C6
Barney Pt	Chi	6	C6
Barnhart Is	SL	3	B1
Bay Pt	NLn	71	E3
Bayfield Is	Ont	7	C3
Beadle Pt	Jfs	7	D3
Beans Pt	Chi	6	D4
Bear Is	NHv	70	D4
Bear Pt	Ont	7	A4
Bergan Pt	Sfk	76	C4
Big Bluff Is	Ont	1	A6
Big Is	Ont	8	E1
Black Rock Pt	Wgn	72	E5
Block Is	Wgn	72	F4
Blue Pt	Sfk	76	F4
Bluff Is	Jfs	7	F2
Boller Pt	Wan	25	F3
Bootleggers Pt	Wan	25	E3
Bostwick Is	Ont	7	D2
Bostwick Pt	Sfk	71	E5
Bradford Is	SL	2	E1
Bradley Pt	NHv	70	A4
Broder Is	Ont	2	E2
Brooks Pt	Sfk	72	A3
Brown Pt	Ese	13	B1
Brown Pt	Sfk	76	F4
Bull Rock Pt	Jfs	14	D1
Burt Pt	Osw	26	F1
Burtis Pt	Cyg	39	F2
Butler Is	GIC	6	D2
Calf Is	Jfs	14	B2
Campbell Pt	Jfs	14	E2
Cannon Pt	Ese	13	B3
Carleton Is	Jfs	7	C3
Carpenter Pt	Ont	7	B3
Catfish Pt	Cln	6	B1
Cayuga Is	Nia	22	A6
Cedar Beach Pt	Sfk	71	B6
Cedar Is	Sfk	76	B5
Cedar Pt	Ffd	69	B5
Cedar Pt	Sfk	71	C6
Charles Pt	Wan	26	A3
Cheney Pt	Chu	48	B5
Cheney Pt	Fkl	6	D2
Cherry Hill Pt	Sfk	71	E5
Cherry Is	Jfs	7	D5
Chimon Is	Ffd	69	B6
City Is	Brx	75	C2
Clark Pt	Jfs	14	C3
Clarke Pt	Ots	43	B3
Clay Pt	Sfk	72	A3
Clines Pt	Jfs	7	D5
Club Is	Ont	8	C3
Coates Is	Chi	6	D6
Colchester Pt	Chi	6	B6
Colligan Pt	Cln	6	B4
Coney Is	Kng	74	F5
Coney Is	Kng	75	A6
Cormorant Pt	Sfk	78	A2
Cornfield Pt	Mdx	71	B3
Cow Neck Pt	Sfk	78	A1
Crab Is	Cln	6	B5
Crane Neck Pt	Sfk	76	D1
Croil Islands	SL	3	A1
Culloden Pt	Sfk	72	A6
Cummings Pt	Jfs	7	E3
Dablon Pt	Jfs	7	B5
Davids Is	Wch	75	C2
Day Pt	Cln	6	A5
Donaldson Pt	Fkl	6	D1
Duck Pond Pt	Sfk	70	F6
Eagle Is	Wan	26	A3
East Pt	Sfk	71	E4
East Pt	Sfk	72	A3
Eastern Plain Pt	Sfk	71	F5
Eastern Pt	NLn	71	F3
Eatons Neck Pt	Sfk	76	D2
Elder Is	Sfk	76	B5
Ellis Is	Hud	74	F4
Farleys Pt	Cyg	39	D3
Farnham Pt	Ere	34	E5
Farran Pt	Ont	3	A1
Fayerweather Is	Ffd	69	D5
Fire Is	Sfk	76	F5
Fire Is	Sfk	77	A4
Fire Islands	Sfk	76	D4
Fishers Is	Sfk	71	F3
Fishers Is	Sfk	72	A3
Fisk Pt	GIC	6	B2
Fletcher Pt	Chu	34	D6
Fox Is	Jfs	7	C5
Furnace Pt	Ese	13	A4
Galloo Is	Jfs	14	B2
Galop Is	SL	2	B3
Garden Is	Ont	7	A3
Gardiners Is	Sfk	71	E5
Gilgo Is	Sfk	76	B5
Goff Pt	Sfk	71	F6
Goshen Pt	NLn	71	E3
Governor Is	NHv	70	C3
Grabell Pt	Ont	34	B2
Grand Is	Ere	22	A6
Grand Is	Ere	35	A1
Grass Is	Sfk	76	D5
Great Gull Is	Sfk	71	E4
Great Is	Sfk	76	B5
Great Is	Wch	68	D5
Great Pt	Wgn	72	F5
Grenadier Is	Jfs	7	B5
Grenadier Is	Ont	8	B2
Grindstone Is	Jfs	7	E2
Haiti Is	Cyg	26	E6
Hall Is	Osw	15	B6
Hammonasset Pt	NHv	70	E3
Harkness Is	Ont	2	C3
Hart Is	Brx	75	C2
Hatch Pt	Ese	13	B1
Hatchett Pt	NLn	71	C3
Hay Is	Ont	7	E1
Heart Is	Jfs	8	A2
Hewlett Pt	Nsu	75	C2
Hickory Is	Sfk	71	F2
High Is	NHv	70	C4
Hill Is	Ont	8	A2
Hill Pt	Chi	13	C2
Hog Cr Pt	Sfk	71	E6
Hog Is	Fkl	6	D1
Hog Isl Pt	Fkl	6	D1
Hogshead Pt	NHv	70	E3
Holcomb Pt	GIC	6	C2
Holiday Pt	GIC	6	D2
Holiday Pt	Ont	7	C3
Horse Is	Jfs	14	E1
Horse Is	NHv	70	C4
Hoveys Is	Jfs	14	D2
Howe Is	Ont	7	C2
Howland Pt	Cyg	39	D2
Hoyt Pt	GIC	6	C4
Independence Pt	Jfs	7	D5
Iroquois Is	Ont	2	B3
Isle La Motte	GIC	6	B2
Jackson Pt	GIC	6	B5
Jeffrey Pt	NHv	70	C4
Joe Indian Is	SL	10	C4
Johnson Pt	NHv	70	B4
Jones Pt	Ese	13	B2
Joshua Pt	NHv	70	D4
Kelsey Is	NHv	70	B4
Kenyon Islands	Flt	31	E5
Keshong Pt	Yts	39	A3
Kibbie Pt	GIC	6	C4
Knight Is	GIC	6	C3
Ladd Pt	GIC	6	C3
Le Roy Is	Wan	26	A3
Leek Is	Ont	7	D2
Liberty Is	Hud	74	F4
Lighthouse Pt	NHv	70	A4
Ligonier Pt	Ese	13	B2
Little Galloo Is	Jfs	14	B2
Lloyd Pt	Nsu	76	A1
Lodi Pt	Sen	39	B5
Long Beach Pt	Sfk	71	C5
Long Is	Sfk	71	A6
Long Is	Sfk	72	A6
Long Is	Sfk	76	B3
Long Is	Sfk	77	B2
Long Is	Sfk	78	C2
Long Is	Wrr	32	E1
Long Neck Pt	Ffd	69	A6
Long Pt	Cln	6	B2
Long Pt	Cyg	39	D4
Long Pt	Jfs	7	D5
Long Pt	Ont	7	A4
Long Pt	Yts	39	B5
Long Sault Islands	SL	3	A1
Lynde Pt	Mdx	71	B3
Macdonald Is	Ont	2	E1
Malletts Head	Chi	6	C6
Manursing Is	Wch	75	E1
Martin Pt	Cln	6	B4
Mashomack Pt	Sfk	71	C6
Mason Is	NLn	72	A3
Matinecock Pt	Nsu	75	E2
Mead Is	Flt	31	E4
Merwin Pt	NHv	70	A4
Mile Pt	Ono	40	A1
Mills Pt	Chi	6	C6
Mohawk Pt	Ont	34	A2
Montauk Pt	Sfk	72	B6
Morgan Pt	NHv	70	B4
Morgan Pt	NLn	72	A3
Morgans Pt	Ont	34	B2
Morrison Is	Ont	2	F1
Mud Pt	GIC	6	C1
Mulberry Pt	NHv	70	D3
Mulford Pt	Sfk	71	C5
Mumford Pt	NLn	71	F3
Napatree Pt	Wgn	72	B3
Nassau Pt	Sfk	78	A1
Navy Is	Ont	21	F6
Newark Is	Wan	26	A3
Nicholas Pt	Wan	26	A4
Nichols Pt	GIC	6	C4
Nicoll Pt	Sfk	71	C6
Nicoll Pt	Sfk	76	E4
Nine Mile Pt	Osw	14	B6
Ninemile Pt	Mro	25	A3
North Hero Is	GIC	6	C2
North Line Is	Nsu	76	A5
Oak Is	SL	8	C1
Old Field Pt	Sfk	76	E1
Old Hbr Pt	Wgn	72	F5
Orient Pt	Sfk	71	D5
Outer Is	NHv	70	C4
Paradise Pt	Flt	31	D5
Paradise Pt	Sfk	71	B6
Parsonage Pt	Wch	75	D1
Perry Pt	Yts	39	A4
Pillar Pt	Jfs	14	D1
Pine Cr Pt	Ffd	69	C5
Pine Pt	Sfk	71	D5
Plum Is	Sfk	71	D4
Point Albino	Ont	34	E2
Point Au Fer	Cln	6	B1
Point Au Roche	Cln	6	B3
Point Breeze	Ere	34	E5
Point No Pt	Ffd	69	E5
Point Peninsula	Jfs	14	C1

NAME	TERR	MAP	GRID
Centre Lake	Ont	1	B5
Chadakoin River	Chu	48	D5
Chadwick Lake	Orn	63	F6
Chain Lake	Frl	11	C1
Chair Rock Flow	SL	10	C5
Champlain Canal	Rns	45	E3
Champlain Canal	Whg	20	B6
Champlain Canal	Whg	32	F3
Champlain Canal	Whg	33	A1
Chapman Pond	Wgn	72	C2
Charleston Lake	Ont	1	A6
Charley Pond	Hml	10	D6
Charlotte Cr	Dlw	57	A1
Charlotte Cr	Shh	43	D6
Chase Lake	Flt	31	B4
Chase Lake	Lew	16	C3
Chateaugay River	Frl	4	E1
Chaumont Bay	Jfs	7	D5
Chaumont Pond	SL	10	A4
Chaumont River	Jfs	7	E4
Chaumont River	Jfs	8	A4
Chautauqua Cr	Chu	47	E4
Chazy Lake	Cln	5	C3
Chazy River	Cln	6	A1
Chemung River	Chm	53	B6
Chenango Lake	Cng	42	A6
Chenango River	Brm	55	B4
Chenango River	Cng	55	E2
Chenango River	Mds	41	F3
Cheningo Cr	Crt	41	A5
Chenunda Cr	Agy	51	B6
Cherry Cr	Chu	48	E3
Cherry Hbr	Sfk	71	E6
Cherry Valley Cr	Ots	43	B5
Cheshire Res	Brk	46	D6
Cheshire River	Brk	46	E6
Chilson Brook	Ese	20	A2
Chipman Lake	Rut	33	F2
Chipmunk Cr	Cat	49	E6
Chippawa Channel	Ere	21	F6
Chippawa Channel	Ere	35	A1
Chippawa Channel	Ont	21	F6
Chippawa Channel	Ont	35	A1
Chippewa Bay	SL	8	C1
Chippewa Cr	SL	1	E6
Chippewa Cr	SL	8	D1
Chittenango Cr	Mds	28	B5
Chittenango Cr	Mds	41	B2
Chittenango Cr	Ono	28	A5
Chittenango Falls	Mds	41	B1
Choconut Cr	Brm	54	F6
Chodikee Lake	Uls	64	B3
Chrysler Pond	Clm	59	E5
Chub Pond	Hrk	16	F6
Chuctanunda Cr North	Mgy	44	E1
Church Pond	SL	10	B6
Cincinnati Cr	Ond	29	D2
Clam River	Brk	60	E5
Clarendon River	Rut	20	F6
Claverack Cr	Clm	59	D4
Clear Cr	Chu	48	D3
Clear Cr	Ere	35	A6
Clear Cr	Wyo	36	B6
Clear Cr North Br	Ere	35	B6
Clear Lake	Ere	35	B6
Clear Lake	Hml	10	C6
Clear Lake	Hrk	17	B1
Clear Lake	Jfs	8	B3
Clear Pond	Ese	12	C6
Clear Pond	Ese	19	C1
Clear Pond	SL	10	C2
Cleveland Brook Res	Brk	60	E1
Clinton Hbr	Mdx	70	F3
Clinton Res	Pas	67	A5
Clove Brook	Ssx	66	E3
Clyde River	Wan	26	A6
Clyde River	Wan	26	C6
Cob Cr	Grn	59	A2
Cobleskill Cr	Shh	44	A4
Coggman Cr	Rut	20	B5
Coginchaug River	Mdx	70	D1
Cohocton River	Lvg	37	F5
Cohocton River	Stu	52	A1
Cohocton River	Stu	52	C3
Colchester Pond	Chi	6	E6
Cold Brook	Cln	5	B5
Cold Brook	Cln	5	E2
Cold Brook	Frl	11	E3
Cold Brook	Frl	11	F1
Cold Brook	Hml	31	A2
Cold Brook	Hrk	29	F4
Cold Brook	Ono	40	D3
Cold Brook	SL	10	D2
Cold Brook	Stu	52	C2
Cold Cr	Agy	50	E1
Cold Cr	Wyo	36	D6
Cold River	Brk	46	F4
Cold River	Ese	11	D5
Cold Spring Brook	Cng	41	F4
Cold Spring Cr East Br	Dlw	56	B5
Cold Spring Hbr	Nsu	76	A1
Cold Springs Cr	Cat	49	B4
Cold Stream	Hml	30	F1
Colebrook Brook	Lch	65	E1
Colebrook River Res	Lch	60	F6
Coles Cr	SL	2	E2
Collins Lake	Ont	7	A1
Colonel Bills Cr	Stu	51	F4
Colonie Res	Srg	45	C3
Columbia Lake	Dlw	56	B6
Community Lake	NHv	70	C1
Comstock Br	Ffd	69	A4
Cone Br	Brk	60	B2
Conesus Cr	Lvg	37	C2
Conesus Inlet	Lvg	37	D4
Conesus Lake	Lvg	37	D3
Conewango Cr	Cat	49	A2
Conewango Cr	Cat	49	A5
Conewango Cr	Chu	48	D6
Conewango Cr	Chu	48	F3
Conewango Cr North Br	Chu	48	E2
Conewango Cr West Br	Chu	48	E2
Connecticut River	Mdx	70	F1
Connecticut River	Mdx	71	A1
Connery Pond	Ese	12	A3
Converse Bay	Chi	13	C3
Converse Lake	Ffd	68	E5
Cook Cr	SL	2	C6
Cooks Res	Srg	31	F5
Cooper Lake	Uls	58	D6
Copake Lake	Clm	59	E5
Copeland Pond	Whg	32	F1
Copper Cr	Lew	16	D5
Copper Lake	Lew	16	E5
Corbeau Cr	Cln	5	F2
Corlear Bay	Ese	13	B1
Cossayuna Lake	Whg	33	A4
Cottrell Cr	Osw	15	B4
Coulombe Cr	Hml	31	C2
County Line Brook	Hml	18	D6
Cowaselon Cr	Mds	28	B5
Coxing Kill	Uls	63	D3
Coxsackie Res	Grn	59	B2
Coxton Lake	Wyn	61	A2
Crabb Kill	Sch	44	F1
Cranberry Lake	Hrk	30	C3
Cranberry Lake	Ont	1	C3
Cranberry Lake	SL	10	C4
Crane Br	Cyg	26	D6
Crane Brook	Cyg	39	E1
Crane Pond	Ese	19	E2
Crassy Brook	Ont	21	D6
Cream Hill Lake	Lch	65	C2
Cricker Br	Ffd	69	C4
Cripple Cr	Hrk	43	A2
Crooked Cr	Gns	36	A1
Crooked Cr	Jfs	8	C2
Crooked Cr	Wyn	61	C3
Crooked Lake	Hrk	17	A1
Crooked Lake	Ono	40	D3
Crooked Lake	Rns	45	F5
Crooked Lake	SL	10	C2
Cross Lake	Ono	27	A5
Cross River Res	Wch	68	E3
Crotched Pond	Hml	18	C4
Croton Falls Res	Put	68	D2
Croton River	Put	68	E1
Croton River	Wch	68	D3
Crow Cr	Wyo	36	C2
Crowfoot Brook	Ese	12	D4
Crum Cr	Flt	30	D6
Crum Cr	Hrk	30	B5
Crum Elbow Cr	Dut	64	B3
Crumhorn Lake	Ots	43	A6
Crusoe Cr	Wan	26	C5
Crusoe Lake	Wan	26	C5
Cryder Cr	Agy	51	C6
Crystal Cr	Cln	5	B1
Crystal Cr	Lew	16	B2
Crystal Lake	Alb	44	D6
Crystal Lake	Cat	50	B1
Crystal Lake	Dlw	56	B6
Crystal Lake	Jfs	8	C3
Crystal Lake	Lch	65	E1
Crystal Lake	Lew	16	C2
Crystal Lake	Slv	62	B5
Cuba Lake	Agy	50	C3
Culver Cr	Brm	54	E2
Culvers Lake	Ssx	66	C4
Cumberland Bay	Cln	6	A4
Cuthrie Run	Chm	53	A4
Dan Wright Brook	SL	3	C4
Danbury Bay	Ffd	69	A1
Danby Cr	Tmk	54	A2
Danby Pond	Rut	33	F2
Dart Lake	Hrk	17	B3
Davis Pond	Slv	62	A6
Dead Cr	Add	13	B5
Dead Cr	Cln	6	A4
Dead Cr	Ono	27	B5
Dead Cr	SL	10	C3
Dead Cr	SL	10	E4
Dead Cr East Br	Add	13	C6
Dead Cr East Br	Add	20	C1
Dead Cr Flow	SL	10	B5
Dead Cr West Br	Add	13	B6
Dead Cr West Br	Add	20	B1
Deans Cr	Ond	29	A6
Debar Pond	Frl	4	D5
Decatur Cr	Ots	43	D5
Decker Cr	Cyg	40	B4
Deer Cr	Ese	18	F3
Deer Cr	Osw	14	E5
Deer Cr East Br	Frl	4	B2
Deer Cr West Br	Frl	4	A2
Deer Kill	Rns	45	E2
Deer Lake	Brm	55	F6
Deer Lake	Mdx	70	E2
Deer Pond	Ese	18	C2
Deer Pond	Frl	11	A3
Deer Pond	Frl	11	B3
Deer River	Frl	4	A4
Deer River	Lew	15	D3
Deer River	SL	3	D2
Deer River	SL	3	E4
Deer River Flow	Frl	4	C5
Deerfield River West Br	Whg	46	F2
Deforest Lake	Rck	68	A5
Delaware Aqueduct East	Slv	62	D1
Delaware Aqueduct West	Slv	62	D1
Delaware Cr	Ere	34	F5
Delaware River	Dlw	61	C1
Delaware River	Orn	66	B1
Delaware River	Pke	66	A5
Delaware River	Pke	66	B1
Delaware River	Slv	61	F4
Delaware River	Slv	66	B1
Delaware River	Ssx	66	A5
Delaware River	War	66	A5
Delaware River	Wyn	61	C1
Delaware River	Wyn	61	F4
Delaware River East Br	Dlw	56	F6
Delaware River East Br	Dlw	57	E4
Delaware River East Br	Dlw	61	D1
Delaware River West Br	Brm	56	B6
Delaware River West Br	Dlw	56	F5
Delaware River West Br	Dlw	57	D2
Delta Res	Ond	29	A3
Derby Brook	Ese	12	E3
Deruyter Res	Mds	41	B3
Devlin Drain	Ont	2	B1
Devorse Cr	Hml	31	B3
Dexter Lake	Frl	3	F5
Dexter Lake Outlet	Frl	3	E5
Diamond Brook	Wrr	18	E5
Diamond Lake	Hml	30	D3
Dillenbeck Bay	GIC	6	C1
Dodge Cr	Agy	50	C5
Dog Pond	Lch	65	D3
Dog Pond	SL	10	D5
Doles Cr	Ont	1	C1
Donald Hanes Drain	Ont	2	C1
Doolittle Cr	Tio	54	C3
Doolittle Lake	Lch	60	E6
Doolittle Lake Brook	Lch	60	E6
Doran Cr	Ont	2	B2
Dove Kill	Clm	59	C5
Dry Brook	Ben	33	D6
Dry Brook	Chu	48	E4
Dry Brook	Dlw	57	F5
Dry Channel Pond	Frl	11	A2
Dry Mill Brook	Cln	6	A6
Dry Run	Stu	52	E4
Dryden Lake	Tmk	54	C1
Duane Lake	Sch	44	E4
Duane Stream	Frl	4	D4
Duck Hbr Pond	Wyn	61	C6
Duck Hole	Frl	11	E5
Duck Lake	Cyg	26	D5
Duck Lake	Frl	11	A5
Dudley Cr	Tio	54	E2
Dun Brook	Hml	18	B2
Dunham Res	Rns	46	A3
Dunn Bay	Cln	6	B2
Dunning Cr	Hml	31	C1
Dutch Hollow Brook	Cyg	40	A2
Dutton Brook	Add	20	F2
Dwaar Kill	Orn	63	C5
Dyberry Cr	Wyn	61	C5
Dyberry Cr East Br	Wyn	61	C4
Dyberry Cr West Br	Wyn	61	C4
Dyke Cr	Agy	51	B5
Dyken Pond	Rns	46	A4
Eagle Bay	Chu	34	D6
Eagle Crag Lake	SL	10	E4
Eagle Lake	Ese	19	E2
Eagle Lake	Hml	18	A2
Earls Cr	SL	3	B2
East Bay	Nsu	75	F5
East Bay	Rut	20	B5
East Bay	Wan	26	B3
East Br	Put	68	E1
East Br	Sqh	61	A3
East Br Ausable River	Ese	12	C5
East Br Ausable River	Ese	12	D2
East Br Basket Cr	Slv	61	F2
East Br Callicoon Cr	Slv	62	A4
East Br Canasawacta Cr	Cng	41	E5
East Br Cazenovia Cr	Ere	35	F5
East Br Cold Spring Cr	Dlw	56	B5
East Br Croton River	Put	68	E2
East Br Dead Cr	Add	13	C6
East Br Dead Cr	Add	20	C1
East Br Deer Cr	Frl	4	A2
East Br Delaware River	Dlw	56	E6
East Br Delaware River	Dlw	57	E5
East Br Delaware River	Dlw	61	C1
East Br Dyberry Cr	Wyn	61	C4
East Br Eighteenmile Cr	Nia	22	E4
East Br Fish Cr	Lew	15	E5
East Br Fish Cr	Ond	28	F2
East Br Handsome Brook	Dlw	56	E2
East Br Leadmine Brook	Lch	65	F3
East Br Leboeuf Cr	Eri	47	A6
East Br Limekiln Brook	Frl	4	B3
East Br Limestone Cr	Ono	41	B2
East Br Mohawk River	Ond	29	A1
East Br Nanticoke Cr	Brm	54	F3
East Br Otsdawa Cr	Ots	56	D1
East Br Owego Cr	Tio	54	D2
East Br Res	Put	68	F2
East Br Sacandaga River	Hml	31	D1
East Br Sacandaga River	Wrr	18	E6
East Br Saint Regis River	Frl	4	B5
East Br Shepaug River	Lch	65	C3
East Br Tioghnioga River	Crt	40	E5
East Br Tonawanda Cr	Wyo	36	C5
East Br Twelvemile Cr	Nia	22	C3
East Brook Kerrs Cr	Dlw	56	E4
East Canada Cr	Flt	30	C5
East Canada Cr	Flt	30	D4
East Canada Cr	Hrk	30	C5
East Canada Lake	Hrk	30	C6
East Cr	Add	20	B3
East Delaware Aqueduct	Dlw	56	D6
East Delaware Aqueduct	Dlw	57	B6
East Delaware Aqueduct	Dlw	61	F1
East Delaware Aqueduct	Slv	62	D1
East Fork Salmon River	Lew	15	E6
East Indies Pond	Brk	60	D6
East Kill	Grn	58	D4
East Koy Cr	Wyo	36	D4
East Koy Cr	Wyo	36	E5
East Mill Brook	Ese	12	E6
East Mongaup River	Slv	62	D3
East Pond	Frl	11	A2
East River	Brx	75	B3
East River	NHv	70	E3
East Sidney Lake	Dlw	56	D3
East Spring Br	Lch	65	D5
East Valley Cr	Agy	51	C4
East Wilcox Outlet	Hml	31	D2
East Wolf Pit Brook	Ffd	69	B2
Easton Res	Ffd	69	C3
Eaton Res	Mds	41	D2
Echo Lake	Cng	55	B2
Echo Lake	Ond	29	C1
Echo Lake	Pas	67	B6
Echo Lake	Rut	20	D4
Effley Falls Pond	Lew	16	C1
Efner Lake	Srg	32	A3
Eight Mile Cr	Ont	21	D4
Eighteen Mile Cr	Ont	21	B5
Eighteenmile Cr	Ere	35	A4
Eighteenmile Cr	Ere	35	D5
Eighteenmile Cr	Nia	22	D4
Eighteenmile Cr East Br	Nia	22	E4
Eighteenmile Cr South Br	Ere	35	C5
Eightmile Brook	NHv	69	E2
Eightmile Cr	Alb	58	E1
Eightmile Cr	Osw	26	E2
Eightmile River	NLn	71	B2
Elbow Cr	Hml	31	B1
Elevenmile Cr	Gns	36	B2
Elk Cr	Ots	43	C6
Elk Lake	Ese	12	B6
Elk Lake	Wyn	61	B5
Ellicott Cr	Ere	35	E1
Ellis Cr	Tio	54	A6
Elm Cr	Cat	49	A4
Elm Cr	SL	9	D1
Elton Cr	Cat	50	B1
Enfield Cr	Tmk	53	E2
Engleville Pond	Shh	43	E3
English Cr	Cat	49	C6
English River	Cln	5	D1
Equinunk Cr	Wyn	61	C3
Erie Canal	Hrk	29	E5
Erie Canal	Hrk	30	A6
Erie Canal	Mgy	43	D1
Erie Canal	Mgy	44	C1
Erie Canal	Mro	24	B4
Erie Canal	Mro	24	E5
Erie Canal	Nia	22	D5
Erie Canal	Ond	28	E4
Erie Canal	Ond	29	A4
Erie Canal	Ono	27	A5
Erie Canal	Ono	27	C5
Erie Canal	Ono	27	D5
Erie Canal	Orl	23	B4
Erie Canal	Orl	23	E4
Erie Canal	Sen	26	D6
Erie Canal	Srg	45	B3
Erie Canal	Srg	45	D3
Erie Canal	Wan	25	D6
Erie Canal	Wan	26	A6
Esopus Cr	Uls	58	A5
Esopus Cr	Uls	59	A6
Esopus Cr	Uls	63	E2
Essex Chain Lakes	Ese	18	D2
Evas Kill	Mgy	44	E1
Factory Brook	Crt	40	C4
Factory Brook	Hmp	60	F2
Fairview Lake	Ssx	66	B6
Fairy Lake	NLn	71	D1
Fall Brook	Lew	16	C6
Fall Brook	Uls	62	F1
Fall Cr	Cyg	40	C4
Fall Cr	Tmk	40	C6
Fall Cr	Tmk	54	A1
Fall Kill	Dut	64	B4
Fall Stream	Hml	30	F1
Falls Lake	Hrk	17	B1
Falls River	Mdx	71	A2
Farm River	NHv	70	C2
Farmingdon River	Lch	65	F1
Farmington River West Br	Brk	60	F4
Farrington Lake	Mid	78	A6
Faun Lake	Wyo	36	C5
Fawn Lake	Hml	31	A1
Fay Brook	Frl	11	D2
Fayville Br	Ben	33	E6
Fayville Br	Ben	46	E1
Featherstonhaugh Lake	Sch	44	E3
Fern Lake	Cln	12	D1
Ferris Lake	Hml	30	E3
Fifteen Mile Cr	Ont	21	B6
Fifth Lake	Ese	18	D2
Findley Lake	Chu	47	D5
Fire Is Inlet	Sfk	76	C5
First Lake	Hrk	17	A4
First Lake	Hrk	17	A5
Fish Cr	Frl	11	D2
Fish Cr	Lew	16	B4
Fish Cr	Ond	28	D4
Fish Cr	Orl	23	B3
Fish Cr	Osw	27	C3
Fish Cr	Otr	38	B1
Fish Cr	SL	1	F6
Fish Cr	SL	2	A6
Fish Cr	Srg	32	D6
Fish Cr East Br	Lew	15	E6
Fish Cr East Br	Lew	28	E1
Fish Cr West Br	Ond	28	D3
Fish Pond	Frl	11	B2
Fisher Bay	Osw	28	A4
Fishers Is Sound	NLn	72	A3
Fishing Brook	Hml	18	C1
Fishkill Cr	Dut	64	C6
Five Falls Res	SL	3	C6
Fivemile Cr	Cat	49	F5
Fivemile Cr	Ese	20	A2
Fivemile Cr	Stu	38	C6
Fivemile Cr	Stu	52	B2
Fivemile River	Ffd	69	A5
Flag Cr	Ont	2	C2
Flanders Bay	Sfk	77	E1
Flat Brook	Ssx	66	A5
Flat Cr	Mgy	43	F2
Flat Cr	Mgy	44	A3
Flatfish Pond	Hml	17	F1
Flint Cr	Otr	38	E2
Flint Cr	Yts	38	C5
Florence Cr	Ond	28	E2
Flowed Land	Ese	12	A5
Flower Brook	Rut	33	E2
Fly Cr	Brm	55	F6
Fly Cr	Mgy	44	B3
Fly Cr	Ots	43	A4
Fly Meadow Cr	Cng	41	E6
Fly Meadow Cr	Cng	55	E1
Fly Pond	Shh	43	E5
Follensby Junior Pond	Frl	11	B1
Follensby Pond	Frl	11	B4
Forest Lake	Orn	67	E3
Forest Lake	Pke	61	F6
Forest Lake	Rns	46	A4
Forked Lake	Hml	17	E2
Forks Cr	Cat	49	E4
Fort Pond Bay	Sfk	72	A6
Four Mile Cr	Ont	21	E4
Fourmile Brook	Hrk	30	B2
Fourmile Cr	Cat	50	A6
Fourmile Cr	Mro	25	A4
Fourth Lake	Flt	30	F4
Fourth Lake	Hrk	17	A6
Fourth Lake	Hrk	17	B3
Fourth Lake	Wrr	32	C2
Fox Cr	Alb	44	E5
Fox Cr	Jfs	14	F3
Fox Cr	Jfs	15	A3
Fox Hollow Lake	Ssx	66	D6
Fox Lake	Slv	62	A5
France Brook	Cat	49	C6
Francis Lake	Lew	16	E2
Franklin Falls Pond	Ese	11	F2
Franklin Falls Pond	Ese	12	A2
Franklin Lake	Brg	74	D1
Fredonia Res	Chu	48	B2
French Cr	Chu	47	D6
French Cr	Jfs	7	E3
French Cr West Br	Eri	47	C5
Frenchs Brook	Frl	12	A1
Freys Pond	Slv	62	A6
Frie Flow	Flt	31	A4
Friends Lake	Wrr	19	B5
Frisbee Cr	Clm	59	F2
Frisbee Cr	Clm	60	A2
Fry Cr	Agy	51	A1
Fulmer Cr	Hrk	43	A1
Fulton Chain Lakes	Hml	17	C3
Fulton Chain Lakes	Hrk	17	B4
Furnace Br	Rut	20	F4
Furnace Brook	Ben	46	D2
Furnace Cr	Ond	28	E2
G Lake	Hml	30	E1
Gallop Cr	Hml	31	A2
Galway Lake	Srg	31	F6
Gananoque River	Ont	7	D1
Ganargua Cr	Otr	25	B6
Gardiners Bay	Sfk	71	D5
Gardon Brook	Agy	50	F4
Garnet Lake	Wrr	18	F6
Gates Cr	Cat	50	A3
Gavord Ditch	Ont	21	A5
Gee Brook	Crt	41	A6
Genegantslet Cr	Cng	41	C6
Genegantslet Cr	Cng	55	C2
Genesee River	Agy	36	F6
Genesee River	Agy	50	E1
Genesee River	Agy	50	E2
Genesee River	Agy	51	A5
Genesee River	Lvg	37	A4
Genesee River	Lvg	37	C2
Genesee River	Mro	24	D6
Genesee River	Mro	37	C2
Georgia Cr	Hml	31	E1
Georgia Cr	Wrr	31	E1
Georgiea Pond	Sfk	78	D1
Gillette Cr	Jfs	8	B5
Glass Lake	Rns	45	F5
Glastenbury River	Ben	33	F6
Glasterbury River	Ben	46	F1
Glen Cr	Scy	53	A2
Glen Cr	Wrr	19	A6
Glen Lake	Rut	20	C5

NAME	TERR	MAP	GRID
Glen Lake	Wrr	32	D2
Glenmere Lake	Orn	67	B3
Glowegee Cr	Srg	31	F6
Golden Cr	Ont	1	C5
Golden Hill Cr	Nia	22	E3
Goldmine Stream	Hml	30	D2
Goldsmith Cr	Chm	53	C5
Golf Cr	Stu	52	A2
Good Luck Lake	Hml	30	F3
Goodnow Flowage	Ese	18	D2
Goodnow Pond	Ese	18	D1
Goodnow River	Ese	18	D1
Goodwin Res	Lch	60	F6
Goodyear Lake	Ots	43	A6
Goose Bay	Fkl	6	E1
Goose Pond	Brk	60	D3
Gooseneck Pond	Ese	19	E2
Gordon Cr	Srg	32	A6
Got Cr	Ere	22	D6
Grace Cove	Wgn	72	E4
Graham Lake	Ont	1	B6
Grampus Lake	Hml	11	A6
Grannis Brook	SL	2	E5
Grapeville Cr	Grn	59	A2
Grass Cr	Ont	7	C1
Grass Lake	SL	8	D2
Grass Pond	SL	10	C5
Grasse River	SL	2	D6
Grasse River	SL	2	E3
Grasse River	SL	3	A2
Grasse River	SL	9	D1
Grasse River Middle Br	SL	9	F2
Grasse River Middle Br	SL	10	A2
Grasse River North Br	SL	9	F1
Grasse River North Br	SL	10	B1
Grasse River South Br	SL	9	F3
Grasse River South Br	SL	10	B3
Gravely Bay	Jfs	14	C2
Graves Brook	Cln	5	C2
Great Brook	Cng	42	B6
Great Chazy River	Cln	5	C3
Great Chazy River	Cln	5	E1
Great Chazy River North Br	Cln	5	C2
Great Cove	Sfk	76	D4
Great Peconic Bay	Sfk	77	F1
Great Pond	Sfk	71	E6
Great Sacandaga Lake	Flt	31	D5
Great Sacandaga Lake	Srg	31	D5
Great Sacandaga Lake	Srg	32	A3
Great Salt Pond	Wgn	72	E4
Great South Bay	Sfk	76	C5
Great South Bay	Sfk	77	A4
Green Fall	NLn	72	C1
Green Hill Pond	Wgn	72	E2
Green Lake	Ono	40	E3
Green Pond	Mrr	73	F1
Green River	Ben	33	D5
Green River	Brk	46	D4
Green River	Clm	60	A3
Green River West Br	Brk	46	C5
Greenwood Cr	SL	9	D4
Greenwood Lake	Orn	67	C4
Gridley Cr	Crt	40	E6
Grimes Cr	Lvg	38	A4
Grindstone Cr	Osw	14	D6
Grout Brook	Crt	40	C4
Guffin Bay	Jfs	7	E5
Guffin Cr	Jfs	7	F5
Guilford Cr	Cng	56	A2
Guilford Hbr	NHv	70	D3
Gulf Brook	SL	10	A1
Gulf Pond	NHv	69	F4
Gulf Stream	Jfs	15	B2
Gulf Stream	SL	9	D5
Gull Lake	Hrk	16	F6
Gull Lake Outlet	Hrk	16	E6
Gull Pond	Frl	10	F4
Gustle Cr	Stu	52	A2
Hachery Brook	Hml	18	B6
Hackensack River	Brg	74	F3
Hackensack River	Hud	74	F3
Hadlock Pond	Whg	32	F2
Haights Cr	Crt	40	F4
Hale Brook	Ese	12	E3
Hale Cr	Flt	31	C6
Halfway Brook	Brm	55	B3
Halfway Brook	Slv	62	B6
Halfway Cr	Wrr	32	D3
Hall Cr	Flt	31	B6
Hall Meadow Brook Res	Lch	65	E2
Hamilton Brook	SL	3	D5
Hamilton Lake	Hml	31	B1
Hamilton Lake Stream	Hml	31	A2
Hammonasset River	Mdx	70	E2
Handsome Brook	Cng	42	A4
Handsome Brook East Br	Dlw	56	E3
Handsome Brook West Br	Dlw	56	E3
Handsome Pond	Hml	11	A6
Hanford Bay	Chu	34	E6
Hankins Cr	Slv	61	F3
Hannacrois Cr	Alb	59	B1
Hans Cr	Srg	31	E5
Hans Cr	Srg	32	A5
Hans Vessen Kill	Grn	59	B3
Hard Is Cr	Ont	1	A5
Harris Bay	Wrr	32	E1
Harris Lake	Ese	18	E1
Harrisburg Lake	Wrr	31	E2
Harrison Cr	Ots	42	D6
Harrison Cr	SL	2	D6
Hart Brook	Lch	65	D2
Hartshorn Brook	Whg	33	A5
Haskell Cr	Cat	50	B5
Hatch Brook	Frl	4	D4
Hatch Brook	Hml	31	C3
Hatch Lake	Mds	41	D3
Hatch Pond	Lch	65	A4
Hawkins Bay	Add	13	C4
Hawkins Cr	Jfs	8	E4
Hawkins Pond	Brm	55	E6
Hay Brook	Frl	4	C6
Hayden Cr	Ots	43	B3
Hayes Cr	Hml	18	C6
Hector Fallls Cr	Scy	53	C1
Hedges Lake	Whg	33	B5
Hemlock Cr	Tmk	40	A5
Hemlock Lake	Lvg	37	E4
Hemlock Res	Ffd	69	C4
Hempstead Hbr	Nsu	75	D2
Henderson Bay	Jfs	14	D2
Henderson Hbr	Jfs	14	D2
Henderson Lake	Ese	11	F5
Herkimer Cr	Ots	42	E3
Hesseky Brook	Lch	65	D6
Hewitt Pond	Ese	19	E4
Hickory Lake	SL	8	F1
Hidden Lake	Mdx	70	F1
Higgins Bay	Hml	30	F1
High Falls Pond	Lew	16	B1
Highland Lake	Lch	65	E2
Highland Lake	Slv	62	B6
Highlands Forge Lake	Ese	13	A2
Hill Cr	Ots	56	C1
Hill Cr	Wrr	31	E1
Hillabrandt Valley	Flt	30	F5
Hinchinbrook Brook	Frl	4	F1
Hinckley Res	Hrk	29	F2
Hinkum Pond	Rut	20	E6
Hitchins Pond	SL	10	D5
Hoasic Cr	Ont	2	D1
Hockanum Brook	NHv	69	F1
Hoel Pond	Frl	11	B2
Hogs Back Cr	Hrk	9	E6
Hogs Back Cr	Lew	15	D1
Hogs Back Cr	Lew	16	D1
Hoisington Brook	Ese	13	A4
Holbert Cr	Wyn	61	D6
Holiday Bay	Ont	7	C3
Holland Cove	Wan	25	E3
Hollister Lake	Grn	59	B3
Hollow Brook	Chi	13	D3
Hollow Cr	Put	68	B2
Home Pond	Sfk	71	E5
Honeoye Cr	Agy	50	F6
Honeoye Cr	Mro	37	D1
Honeoye Cr	Otr	37	F2
Honeoye Cr	Otr	37	F4
Honeoye Lake	Otr	37	F3
Honnedaga Br	Hrk	30	C1
Honnedaga Lake	Hrk	17	C6
Hoosic River	Rns	45	E2
Hoosic River	Rns	46	A1
Hoosic River	Whg	46	A1
Hoosic River	Whg	46	C3
Hoosic River North Br	Brk	46	F3
Hop Brook	Brk	60	D3
Hop River	Lch	65	E6
Horse Cr	Jfs	7	E5
Horseshoe Lake	SL	10	E5
Horseshoe Pond	SL	10	E4
Hospital Cr	Add	13	B6
Hothchkiss Run	Cat	49	A6
Housato River	Brk	60	E1
Housatonic River	Brk	60	B4
Housatonic River	Lch	60	B6
Housatonic River	Lch	65	E3
Housatonic River	NHv	69	D1
Housatonic River	NHv	69	E4
House Cr	Lew	16	A4
House Cr	Shh	44	A6
Howard Eaton Res	Eri	47	C5
Howells Pond	Ssx	66	D6
Hubbard Br	Brk	60	B5
Hubbardton River	Rut	20	B5
Hudson River	Alb	45	C6
Hudson River	Brg	75	A2
Hudson River	Brx	75	A2
Hudson River	Dut	68	A1
Hudson River	Ese	11	F6
Hudson River	Ese	18	D2
Hudson River	Ese	18	E1
Hudson River	Ese	18	F3
Hudson River	Grn	59	C2
Hudson River	Hml	18	F3
Hudson River	Hud	74	F4
Hudson River	NY	74	F4
Hudson River	NYC	74	F4
Hudson River	NYC	75	A2
Hudson River	Orn	64	A6
Hudson River	Orn	67	F1
Hudson River	Put	68	A1
Hudson River	Rns	45	E3
Hudson River	Srg	32	D3
Hudson River	Uls	59	A6
Hudson River	Uls	64	A3
Hudson River	Wch	68	A4
Hudson River	Wch	75	A2
Hudson River	Whg	32	E6
Hudson River	Wrr	19	B5
Hudson River	Wrr	32	B2
Hundred Acre Pond	Mro	24	E6
Hundred Acre Pond	Wgn	72	F1
Hungerford Brook	Fkl	6	F2
Hunt Lake	Srg	32	B3
Hunter Cr	Ere	35	F4
Huntington Bay	Sfk	76	A1
Hurrell Brook	Hml	30	C2
Hurricane Brook	Hrk	30	A4
Hussey Gulf	Ere	35	A5
Hutchins Cr	SL	3	A2
Hyde Bay	Ots	43	B3
Hyde Cr	Jfs	8	B4
Hyde Lake	Jfs	8	B4
Ideuma Brook	Ots	56	B2
Inddian Lake Cr	Lch	65	A2
Independence Lake	Hrk	17	A3
Independence River	Lew	16	D3
Indian Bay	Ese	13	B1
Indian Cr	Clm	59	F2
Indian Cr	Ont	1	D4
Indian Cr	SL	9	B1
Indian Cr	Sen	39	B4
Indian Lake	Frl	4	E4
Indian Lake	Hml	17	C5
Indian Lake	Hml	18	C4
Indian Lake	Lew	9	A5
Indian Pass Brook	Ese	11	F5
Indian Pass Brook	Ese	12	A4
Indian River	Ese	18	D3
Indian River	Hml	17	C5
Indian River	Hml	17	D6
Indian River	Hml	18	D3
Indian River	Jfs	8	C4
Indian River	Jfs	8	D5
Indian River	Jfs	8	F5
Indian River	Lew	9	A6
Indian River	Lew	16	B1
Indian River	Mdx	70	F2
Indian River	NHv	69	F3
Indian River	Whg	33	C2
Ingraham Lake	Frl	4	E3
Ingraham Stream	Frl	4	E4
Inman Pond	Rut	20	C5
Invary Lake	Ont	7	A1
Ira Brook	Rut	20	F6
Ireland Valley	Srg	31	F5
Irish Cr	Ont	1	A3
Irish Lake	Ont	1	A3
Iron Stream	NHv	70	D2
Irondequoit Bay	Mro	24	F4
Irondequoit Cr	Mro	25	A6
Ironwork Brook	Brk	60	C5
Irvine Bay	Ont	7	C3
Irving Pond	Flt	31	A4
Island Pond	Orn	67	E3
Ivy Mtn Brook	Lch	65	D2
Jabe Pond	Wrr	19	F4
Jabe Pond Brook	Wrr	19	F4
Jacks Pond	SL	10	E3
Jacks Pond Outlet	SL	10	D3
Jackson Summit Res	Flt	31	C5
Jamaica Bay	Kng	75	B5
Jamaica Bay	Qns	75	B5
Jamesville Res	Ono	40	E1
Java Lake	Wyo	36	B5
Jeddo Cr	Orl	23	A3
Jenkins Brook	Frl	10	F5
Jennings Cr	Crt	54	E1
Jenny Cr	SL	9	C4
Jenny Lake	Srg	32	B3
Jerseyfield Lake	Hml	30	C3
Jessup River	Hml	17	F6
Jessup River	Hml	18	A6
Jewett Brook	Whg	46	D3
Jewett Brook South Stream	Whg	46	D2
Jewett Cr	Jfs	8	C3
Jimmy Cr	Hml	31	B2
Jimmy Cr	Hml	31	D1
Jockeybush Lake	Hml	30	E3
Joe Indian Brook	SL	10	D1
Joe Indian Pond	SL	10	D1
John D Milne Lake	Wsc	69	A4
John Mack Pond	Hml	18	C5
Johns Brook	Ese	12	B5
Johnson Bay	Ont	7	C2
Johnson Cr	Cng	42	A6
Johnson Cr	Nia	22	F3
Johnson Cr	Orl	23	B3
Jones Br	Add	20	C2
Jones Cr	Ont	1	A6
Jones Cr	Ont	1	B6
Jones Cr	Ont	8	A1
Jones Cr	Ont	8	B1
Jones Inlet	Nsu	75	E6
Jordan Hbr	Ont	21	B4
Jordan Lake	SL	10	E2
Jordan River	SL	10	E2
Judson Brook	Slv	62	C4
Kaaterskill Cr	Grn	59	A4
Karner Brook	Brk	60	A5
Karr Valley Cr	Agy	51	B3
Kartright Cr	Dlw	57	B1
Kashon Cr	Otr	38	F3
Kasoag Lake	Osw	28	A1
Kayaderosseras Cr	Flt	44	C1
Kayaderosseras Cr	Srg	32	B5
Kayaderosseras Cr	Srg	32	C6
Kayuta Lake	Ond	29	D2
Kecks Ctr Cr	Flt	31	A6
Keeler Bay	GIC	6	C5
Kellum Pond	Wrr	19	C6
Kelsey Brook	Cng	55	F3
Kelsey Cr	Jfs	8	B6
Kemptville Cr	Ont	1	D1
Kemptville Cr	Ont	1	D3
Kendig Cr	Sen	39	B2
Kenisco Res	Wch	68	C6
Kennedy Cr	Ono	40	E1
Kennels Pond	Hml	30	F3
Kenney Brook	Crt	40	F3
Kennyetto Cr	Flt	31	E6
Kents Cr	Jfs	7	C4
Kerrs Cr	Dlw	56	D4
Kerrs Cr East Brook	Dlw	56	F4
Kerrs Cr West Brook	Dlw	56	E4
Keshequa Cr	Agy	51	A1
Keshequa Cr	Lvg	37	A6
Keshequa Cr	Lvg	37	B5
Keuchumville Br	Tio	54	E3
Keuka Lake	Stu	52	D1
Keuka Lake	Yts	38	E6
Key Cr East	Wyo	36	E5
Key Cr West	Wyo	36	D6
Keyport Hbr	Mom	78	D6
Kiamesha Lake	Slv	62	D4
Kill Van Kull	Hud	74	E5
Kill Van Kull	Rmd	74	E5
Killingworth Res	Mdx	70	F2
Kinderhook Cr	Clm	59	D2
Kinderhook Cr	Clm	59	E1
Kinderhook Cr	Rns	46	A6
Kinderhook Cr West Brook	Rns	46	B5
Kinderhook Lake	Clm	59	D1
King Cr	Shh	44	D4
Kings Bay	Cln	6	B1
Kinney Cr	Lvg	37	E3
Kirby Cr	Wrr	18	F5
Kirk Lake	Put	68	C2
Kiskatan Brook	Grn	59	A4
Kiwassa Lake	Frl	11	E3
Klein Kill	Clm	59	B5
Kline Kill	Clm	59	E2
Klock Cr	Flt	30	E6
Klondike Res	Hrk	30	C4
Konkapot Br	Brk	60	C3
Konkapot River	Brk	60	C5
Kunjamuk River	Hml	18	C6
Kyser Lake	Hrk	30	C6
La Motte Passage	GIC	6	C2
La Platte River	Chi	13	D2
La Rue Cr	Ont	8	A1
Labrador Cr	Crt	40	F3
Lacolle River	Qub	7	A6
Lake Abanakee	Hml	18	D3
Lake Adirondack	Hml	18	C3
Lake Aeroflex	Ssx	66	D6
Lake Algonquin	Hml	31	C2
Lake Bethany	NHv	70	A1
Lake Bomoseen	Rut	20	D5
Lake Bonaparte	Lew	9	B5
Lake Brook	Dlw	57	D2
Lake Brook	Ots	42	E6
Lake Buel	Brk	60	C5
Lake Candlewood	Ffd	65	A6
Lake Candlewood	Ffd	69	A1
Lake Chamberlain	NHv	70	A2
Lake Champlain	Add	13	B5
Lake Champlain	Add	20	B2
Lake Champlain	Chi	6	C6
Lake Champlain	Chi	13	B5
Lake Champlain	Ese	13	B5
Lake Champlain	Ese	20	B2
Lake Champlain	GIC	6	C6
Lake Champlain	Qub	7	E6
Lake Chautauqua	Chu	48	B5
Lake Clear	Frl	11	C2
Lake Clear Outlet	Frl	11	C2
Lake Colby	Frl	11	D2
Lake Colden	Ese	12	A5
Lake Cr	Shh	44	D6
Lake Delaware	Dlw	57	C4
Lake Desolation	Srg	32	A5
Lake Dunmore	Add	20	F1
Lake Durant	Hml	18	A2
Lake Eaton	Hml	18	A1
Lake Elizabeth	Rns	46	A3
Lake Eloida	Ont	1	A4
Lake Erie	Chu	34	B5
Lake Erie	Chu	48	A1
Lake Erie	Eri	47	B3
Lake Erie	Ont	34	B5
Lake Forest	Ffd	69	D4
Lake Forest	Wrr	32	C2
Lake Francis	Hml	18	D3
Lake Gaillard	NHv	70	C2
Lake Garfield	Brk	60	D4
Lake George	Wrr	19	E6
Lake George	Wrr	20	A4
Lake George	Wrr	32	D1
Lake Gibson	Ont	21	C5
Lake Girad	Ssx	66	F5
Lake Hammonasset	NHv	70	E2
Lake Hopatcong	Ssx	73	D1
Lake Hortonia	Rut	20	D4
Lake Huntington	Slv	62	A4
Lake Illif	Ssx	66	D6
Lake Iroquois	Chi	13	F2
Lake Kanawauke	Orn	67	E4
Lake Kemah	Ssx	66	C5
Lake Konomoc	NLn	71	D1
Lake Kora	Hml	17	E4
Lake Kushaqua	Frl	4	E6
Lake Lackawanna	Ssx	73	D1
Lake Lauderdale	Whg	33	B6
Lake Lila	Hml	10	C6
Lake Lila	Hml	17	C1
Lake Lillinonah	Lch	69	B1
Lake Lodore	Wyn	61	B6
Lake Lonely	Srg	32	C6
Lake Louise Marie	Slv	62	E5
Lake Ludlow	Cng	55	D1
Lake Luzerne	Wrr	32	C3
Lake Madeleine	Frl	11	A5
Lake Mahkeenac	Brk	60	B2
Lake Mahopac	Put	68	C2
Lake Marion	SL	10	D5
Lake Mohawk	Ssx	66	D6
Lake Montauk	Sfk	72	A6
Lake Moodie	Ont	21	C5
Lake Muskoday	Slv	62	A2
Lake Neatahwanta	Osw	27	A3
Lake Nebo	Whg	32	F1
Lake Ontario	Cyg	26	B2
Lake Ontario	Jfs	7	A5
Lake Ontario	Jfs	7	D5
Lake Ontario	Jfs	14	B3
Lake Ontario	Mro	24	C1
Lake Ontario	Nia	21	B3
Lake Ontario	Nia	22	B2
Lake Ontario	Ont	21	B3
Lake Ontario	Orl	23	C1
Lake Ontario	Osw	26	B2
Lake Ontario	Wan	25	B2
Lake Ontario	Wan	26	B2
Lake Owassa	Ssx	66	C5
Lake Ozonia	SL	3	E5
Lake Ozonia Outlet	SL	3	E5
Lake Paran	Ben	46	D1
Lake Parsippany	Mrr	74	A2
Lake Placid	Ese	12	A3
Lake Placid East Lake	Ese	12	A3
Lake Placid West Lake	Ese	12	A3
Lake Pleasant	Hml	31	B1
Lake Quassapaug	NHv	65	D6
Lake Ronkonkoma	Sfk	76	E2
Lake Saint Catherine	Rut	33	D1
Lake Saint Lawrence	SL	3	A1
Lake Saltonstall	NHv	70	B3
Lake Sebago	Rck	67	E4
Lake Shaftsbury	Ben	33	D6
Lake Silver Mine	Orn	67	F3
Lake Skannatat	Orn	67	E4
Lake Stahahe	Orn	67	E4
Lake Superior	Slv	62	B5
Lake Taghkanic	Clm	59	D5
Lake Tiorati	Orn	67	F3
Lake Titus	Frl	4	C4
Lake Triangle	Lch	60	E6
Lake Valhalla	Mrr	74	B1
Lake Vanare	Wrr	32	C2
Lake Waccabuc	Wch	68	E3
Lake Waramaug	Lch	65	B4
Lake Winchester	Lch	65	E1
Lake Winnemaug	Lch	65	E5
Lakeport Bay	Ond	28	B5
Lakes Kill	Dut	59	C6
Lakes Pond	Whg	32	F1
Lambs Pond	Ont	1	C5
Lamington River	Hnt	73	D5
Lamington River	Sms	73	D5
Lamoille River	Chi	6	E5
Lamoka Lake	Scy	52	F2
Landsman Kill	Dut	64	B1
Langworthy Cr	Wrr	31	F1
Lansing Kill	Ond	29	B2
Lapans Bay	Fkl	6	D3
Larkin Cr	Mro	24	C4
Laurel Cr	Dlw	56	B6
Laurel Lake	Brk	60	C3
Laurel Lake	Sfk	77	F1
Laurel Res	Ffd	68	F4
Lawrence Brook	Mid	78	B6
Lawrence Brook	SL	3	E2
Lead Pond	Frl	11	A3
Leadmine Brook East Br	Lch	65	F3
Lebanon Lake	Slv	62	C6
Leboeuf Cr East Br	Eri	47	A6
Ledge Cr	Ere	23	A6
Ledge Pond	Frl	11	A2
Ledyard Res	NLn	71	F2
Leeders Cr	Ont	1	A6
Lees Pond	Ont	1	B5
Leicester River	Add	20	E2
Lemon Fair River	Add	13	C6
Lemon Fair River	Add	20	C1
Lens Lake	Wrr	31	F2
Leonard Brook	SL	2	A6
Leonard Brook	SL	3	A6
Leonard Pond	SL	10	C3
Leroy Res	Gns	37	A2
Lester Flow	Ese	19	A2
Lewey Lake	Hml	18	A5
Lewis Cr	Add	13	F3
Lewis Cr	Chi	13	D3
Ley Cr	Ono	27	F5
Lillinonah Lake	Lch	65	B6
Lily Lake	Flt	30	F5
Lily Pond	Wrr	19	D4
Lime Lake	Cat	50	A1
Limekiln Brook East Br	Frl	4	B3
Limekiln Cr	Hrk	17	B4
Limekiln Lake	Hrk	17	C4
Limestone Cr East Br	Ono	41	A1
Limestone Cr West Br	Ono	41	A1
Lincoln Brook	Ese	12	A2
Lincoln Pond	Ese	12	F5
Lindsey Cr	Jfs	14	E4
Line Cr	Shh	44	B5
Lisbon Cr	SL	2	B5
Lissons Lake	Ont	1	C2
Little Ausable River	Cln	5	E6
Little Ausable River	Cln	12	E1
Little Beards Cr	Wyo	37	A3
Little Black Brook	Cln	12	C1
Little Black Cr	Hrk	30	A2
Little Black Cr	Mro	24	C5
Little Black Cr	Ond	29	E2
Little Br	Qub	7	C6
Little Brokenstraw Cr	Chu	48	A6
Little Buffalo Cr	Ere	35	E2
Little Chautauqua Cr	Chu	47	F3
Little Chazy River	Cln	6	A3
Little Choconut Cr	Brm	55	A4
Little Clear Pond	Frl	11	C2
Little Conesus Cr	Lvg	37	D2
Little Cr	Cyg	39	E4
Little Delaware River	Dlw	57	B3
Little Farrington Brook	Frl	3	F2
Little Forks Cr	Ont	34	A1
Little Genesee Cr	Agy	50	D6
Little Grindstone Cr	Osw	14	E6
Little Hoosic River	Rns	46	B4
Little Indian Cr	Cat	48	F1
Little Indian Cr	Chu	34	F6
Little Lake	Rut	33	D1
Little Lemon Fair River	Add	20	C3
Little Mill Cr	Stu	37	E6

NAME	TERR	MAP	GRID
Owego Cr East Br	Tio	54	D3
Owego Cr West Br	Tio	54	D3
Owl Kill	Whg	33	B6
Owl Kill	Whg	46	B1
Owl Pond	Hml	18	C5
Oxbow Lake	Hml	31	A1
Oxoboxo Lake	NLn	71	D1
Pack Forest Lake	Wrr	19	B6
Page Brook	Brm	55	C4
Paines Cr	Cyg	39	D4
Palmer Brook	Cln	12	D1
Palmer Cr	Lew	9	D6
Panther Cr	Shh	44	A6
Panther Rock Brook	Slv	62	B3
Papakating Cr	Ssx	66	D5
Paradox Cr	Ese	19	E1
Paradox Lake	Ese	19	D2
Paran Cr	Ben	46	D1
Parker Pond	Cyg	26	F5
Parkhurst Brook	SL	3	B5
Pascack Brook	Brg	67	F6
Pascack Brook	Rck	67	F6
Pasquist Pond	Wgn	72	E2
Passaic River	Brg	74	E3
Passaic River	Esx	74	C2
Passaic River	Mrr	73	F4
Passaic River	Mrr	74	C2
Passaic River	Pas	74	E3
Passaic River	Sms	73	F4
Passaic River	Uni	74	B4
Passaic River	Uni	74	C2
Patchogue Bay	Sfk	76	F4
Patenaude Br	Qub	7	B6
Pattagansett Lake	NLn	71	C2
Patterson Cr	Brm	54	F5
Patton Drain	Ont	1	D1
Paul Cr	Srg	31	F3
Paulins Kill	Ssx	66	C5
Paulins Kill	Ssx	66	D6
Paulins Kill	War	66	B6
Paultney River	Rut	33	E1
Pawcatuck River	NLn	72	B2
Payne Lake	Jfs	8	D3
Peach Lake	Put	68	E2
Peat Swamp Res	NHv	69	F2
Peck Cr	Flt	31	A6
Peck Lake	Flt	31	B5
Peconic River	Sfk	77	B2
Peeks Mill Pond	Ffd	69	E4
Peekskill Hollow Cr	Wch	68	B3
Pelots Bay	GIC	6	C3
Pepacton Res	Dlw	57	A6
Pequonnock River	Ffd	69	C3
Perch Lake	Jfs	8	A5
Perch Pond	Ese	18	F1
Perch River	Jfs	7	F5
Perch River	Jfs	8	A5
Peru River	Cln	6	A5
Peters Kill	Uls	63	C4
Pharaoh Lake	Ese	19	E3
Philips Cr North Br	Agy	51	A3
Philipse Br	Put	68	A2
Phillips Brook	Cat	49	A6
Phillips Cr	Agy	51	A4
Pickett Brook	Chu	48	C3
Pickwacket Pond	Hml	11	C6
Piercefield Flow	SL	10	F4
Pike Brook	Whg	20	A5
Pike Cr	Ere	34	F4
Pike Cr	Frl	3	E1
Pillsbury Lake	Hml	17	F5
Pine Brook	Hml	11	C6
Pine Cr	Cyg	40	A4
Pine Cr	Lew	16	D5
Pine Cr	Ond	29	E1
Pine Kill	Slv	62	F6
Pine Lake	Flt	30	F4
Pine Lake	Hml	30	E2
Pine Lake	Lew	16	E4
Pine Lake	Whg	20	A5
Pine Meadow Lake	Rck	67	E4
Pinecliff Lake	Pas	67	B5
Pinewood Lake	Ffd	69	D3
Pinnacle Cr	Flt	31	B4
Pipe Cr	Tio	54	B4
Piseco Lake	Hml	30	F2
Piseco Outlet	Hml	30	F2
Pitch Brook	Lch	65	E4
Pitch Res	Lch	65	E4
Platte Kill	Dlw	57	D4
Plattekill Cr	Uls	58	F5
Platter Kill	Shh	58	B2
Pleasant Brook	Cng	41	E4
Pleasant Brook	Mds	42	A3
Pleasant Lake	Flt	30	E4
Pleasant Lake	Jfs	15	D1
Pleasant Lake	Osw	27	D4
Pleasant Lake	SL	8	E2
Pleasant Lake	SL	10	B2
Pleasant Lake Stream	SL	10	B2
Pleasure Lake	Slv	62	E4
Plum Brook	SL	3	A4
Plum Hollow Cr	Ont	1	A5
Plumadore Pond	Frl	4	E5
Plumb Brook	SL	9	E2
Plymouth Res	Cng	41	E5
Pochuck Cr	Orn	67	A3
Poesten Kill	Rns	45	E4
Point Judith Pond	Wgn	72	F2
Point Rock Cr	Lew	28	F1
Pomperaug River	NHv	65	D6
Pomperaug River	NHv	69	C1
Pompton River	Mrr	74	C1
Pompton River	Pas	74	C1
Pond Brook	Add	13	E3
Pond Brook	Ffd	69	B1
Pontoosuc Lake	Brk	60	C1
Pool Brook	Ots	42	E5
Pootatuck River	Ffd	69	C2
Port Bay	Wan	26	B3
Port Jefferson Hbr	Sfk	76	E1
Port Weller Hbr	Ont	21	D4
Post Cr	Stu	52	F4
Potash Bay	Add	13	B5
Potic Cr	Grn	59	A3
Potter Bay	Osw	28	B4
Potter Pond	Frl	10	F2
Potter Pond	Wgn	72	F2
Poultney River	Rut	20	C6
Power Res	Nia	21	F5
Power Res	Nia	22	A5
Power Res	Ont	21	F5
Powers Lake	NLn	71	D2
Preston Ponds	Ese	11	E5
Prince Brook	Lew	15	D6
Prompton Lake	Wyn	61	B5
Pumpelly Cr	Tio	54	C6
Pumpkin Hook Cr	Whg	33	C6
Punch Brook	Clm	59	E6
Punsit Cr	Clm	59	F3
Putnam Br	Cyg	26	F6
Putnam Cr	Ese	19	F2
Putnam Cr	Ese	20	A1
Putnam Lake	Ffd	68	E5
Putnam Pond	Ese	19	E2
Pyramid Lake	Ese	19	E2
Quacken Kill	Rns	45	F4
Quaker Cr	Orn	67	B3
Quaker Lake	Cat	49	B6
Quaker Pond	Mro	24	F6
Quaker Run	Cat	49	B6
Quebec Brook	Frl	4	A6
Quebec Pond	Frl	11	B1
Queechy Lake	Clm	60	A2
Queer Lake	Hml	17	C3
Quinnipiac River	NHv	70	B2
Quonnipaug Lake	NHv	70	D2
Ragged Lake	Frl	4	F4
Ragged Lake Outlet	Frl	4	E4
Rahway River	Mid	74	C5
Rahway River	Uni	74	C5
Rainbow Falls Res	SL	3	C6
Rainbow Falls Res	SL	10	C1
Rainbow Lake	Frl	11	D1
Ramapo River	Brg	67	D6
Ramapo River	Orn	67	D4
Ransom Cr	Ere	22	D6
Ransom Cr	Hrk	30	B5
Raquette Brook	Hml	18	E3
Raquette Lake	Hml	17	E2
Raquette Pond	Frl	11	A4
Raquette River	Frl	11	B4
Raquette River	Hml	18	A2
Raquette River	SL	2	F4
Raquette River	SL	3	A2
Raquette River	SL	3	A6
Raquette River	SL	10	F4
Raritan Bay	Mom	78	D6
Raritan Bay	Rmd	74	D6
Raritan River	Mid	78	B6
Raritan River	Mrr	73	D3
Raritan River	Sms	73	F6
Rattlesnake Cr	Wyn	61	E6
Raven Lake	Hrk	16	F1
Ray Bay	Jfs	14	C2
Ray Brook	Ese	11	F3
Raystone Cr	Jfs	14	F3
Raystone Cr	Jfs	15	A4
Read Cr	Dlw	56	D6
Reall Cr	Ond	29	D5
Red Cr	Ots	43	B4
Red Cr	Wan	25	C5
Red Cr	Wan	25	D4
Red Cr	Wan	26	D3
Red House Brook	Cat	49	D6
Red House Lake	Cat	49	D5
Red Kill	Dlw	57	F4
Red Lake	Jfs	8	D3
Red River	Hml	17	C4
Reeder Cr	Sen	39	A3
Reeds Bay	Ont	7	A4
Reeds Cr	Ont	7	A4
Reservoir No 3	Orn	66	D2
Reuben Har Res	Lch	65	D2
Rhinebeck Kill	Dut	64	A1
Rice Brook	Cat	49	D6
Rice Cr	Osw	26	F1
Rice Lake	Frl	4	C6
Rich Lake	Ese	18	D1
Richelieu River	Cln	6	B1
Richelieu River	GIC	6	B1
Richelieu River	Qub	7	B6
Richmond Pond	Brk	60	C2
Rickerson Brook	Frl	11	D1
Rideau Cr	Ont	1	B1
Rideau River And Canal	Ont	1	A2
Riga Lake	Lch	60	A6
Riley Brook	Cln	5	F4
Rio Res	Slv	62	C6
Roaring Br	Ben	33	E6
Roaring Br	Brk	60	D2
Roaring Br	Wrr	32	A2
Roaring Br South Fork	Ben	33	F6
Roaring Brook	Ese	11	F5
Roaring Brook	Hml	18	B1
Roaring Brook	Lew	15	E4
Roaring Brook	Lew	16	A4
Robbs Cr	Hml	18	C6
Robinson Pond	Clm	59	F5
Robinson River	Hrk	10	A6
Rochester Cr	Uls	63	C3
Rock Br	Lch	65	F4
Rock Lake	Hml	18	C3
Rock Lake	Hrk	17	B1
Rock Lake	Wyn	61	C3
Rock Pond	Hml	17	E1
Rock River	Fkl	6	F1
Rock River	Hml	18	B2
Rock River	Qub	7	D6
Rock Stream	Scy	53	A1
Rockaway Inlet	Que	75	A6
Rockwell Cr	Jfs	8	F4
Rockwell Cr	Lew	9	A4
Rockwood Lake	Ffd	68	E5
Rockwood Lake	Flt	30	F6
Rocky Run	Otr	38	D2
Roeliff Jansen Cr	Clm	59	C6
Roeliff Jansen Kill	Clm	59	F5
Rogers Lake	NLn	71	C2
Rollins Pond	Frl	11	A3
Rondout Cr	Uls	63	A2
Rondout Cr	Uls	63	B4
Rondout Cr	Uls	63	D3
Rondout Res	Uls	63	A3
Roods Cr	Dlw	56	B6
Rooster River	Ffd	69	D4
Rosedale Cr	Ont	1	A1
Rosemond Lake	NLn	71	F1
Round Lake	Ese	12	B4
Round Lake	Hml	10	F6
Round Lake	Srg	45	C1
Round Pond	Hml	11	C6
Round Pond	Hml	18	C4
Round Pond	Lew	16	D1
Round Pond	Mro	24	E3
Round Pond	Wrr	18	F6
Round Pond Brook	Hml	18	C4
Round Pond Cr	Mro	24	D4
Round Valley Res	Hnt	73	B5
Rudd Pond	Brk	60	E3
Rush Cr	Agy	50	F1
Rush Cr	Agy	51	A1
Rushford Lake	Agy	50	D2
Russ Pond	Osw	27	D2
Russell Brook	Dlw	57	A6
Russell Brook	Dlw	62	A1
Rutgers Cr	Orn	66	F3
Rye Lake	Wch	68	D6
Sacandaga Lake	Hml	31	A1
Sacandaga River	Hml	18	B6
Sacandaga River	Hml	31	C1
Sacandaga River	Hml	31	C3
Sacandaga River	Srg	31	F3
Sacandaga River	Srg	32	B3
Sacandaga River East Br	Hml	31	D1
Sacandaga River East Br	Wrr	18	E5
Sacandaga River West Br	Hml	30	F3
Sacandaga River West Br	Hml	31	B2
Sackett Brook	Brk	60	D1
Saddle River	Brg	67	E6
Saddlemire Drain	Ont	2	D2
Sag Hbr Bay	Sfk	71	C6
Sagaponack Pond	Sfk	78	C2
Sage Cr	Osw	27	D1
Saint Albans Bay	Fkl	6	E3
Saint Johnsville Res	Flt	30	F6
Saint Josephs Lake	Slv	62	D5
Saint Lawrence River	Jfs	7	C4
Saint Lawrence River	Jfs	8	B2
Saint Lawrence River	Ont	1	D6
Saint Lawrence River	Ont	2	B3
Saint Lawrence River	Ont	7	B3
Saint Lawrence River	SL	1	D6
Saint Lawrence River	SL	2	B3
Saint Lawrence Seaway	Frl	3	D1
Saint Lawrence Seaway	SL	3	A1
Saint Regis Pond	Frl	11	B1
Saint Regis River	Frl	4	A5
Saint Regis River	Frl	11	A1
Saint Regis River	Frl	11	A2
Saint Regis River	SL	3	C3
Saint Regis River	SL	3	D4
Saint Regis River East Br	Frl	4	B5
Saint Regis River West Br	SL	3	B3
Saint Regis River West Br	SL	3	C5
Saint Regis River West Br	SL	10	F1
Salisbury Swamp	Add	20	E2
Salmon Cr	Lch	65	B1
Salmon Cr	Mro	24	C3
Salmon Cr	Tmk	39	F5
Salmon Cr	Wan	25	D4
Salmon Cr	Wan	25	E4
Salmon Lake	Hml	17	D1
Salmon Lake	Hrk	17	A1
Salmon Pond	Hml	18	B2
Salmon River	Cln	5	D5
Salmon River	Frl	4	B1
Salmon River	Frl	4	D4
Salmon River	Hml	18	A2
Salmon River	Lew	28	D1
Salmon River	Mdx	71	A1
Salmon River	Osw	14	E6
Salmon River	Osw	15	A6
Salmon River	Osw	15	C6
Salmon River East Fork	Lew	15	E6
Salmon River North Br	Osw	27	F2
Salmon River Res	Osw	15	B6
Salmon River South Br	Osw	27	E2
Sampson Lake	Hml	17	F6
Sampson Pond	SL	10	C3
Sand Cr	Srg	31	E3
Sand Lake	Hml	30	F2
Sand Lake	Hrk	9	F6
Sand Lake	Hrk	17	A6
Sand Lake Outlet	Hml	30	F2
Sand Pond	Dlw	61	D1
Sand Pond	Slv	62	B6
Sand Pond Brook	Ese	19	B1
Sands Cr	Dlw	56	C6
Sands Cr	Dlw	61	C1
Sandwich Res	Brk	60	E6
Sandy Br	Brk	60	E6
Sandy Cr	Jfs	14	E3
Sandy Cr	Jfs	15	C2
Sandy Cr	Mro	24	A3
Sandy Cr	Ont	2	A1
Sandy Cr	Orl	23	F3
Sandy Cr North Br	Jfs	15	B2
Sandy Cr South	Jfs	14	F3
Sandy Cr South	Jfs	15	A3
Sandy Hook Bay	Mom	78	E6
Sanford Brook	Add	20	C3
Sangerfield River	Mds	42	A3
Santanoni Brook	Ese	11	E5
Saranac River	Cln	5	B6
Saranac River	Cln	5	E4
Saranac River	Ese	11	E2
Saranac River North Br	Frl	4	D6
Saranac River North Br	Frl	5	A6
Saratoga Lake	Srg	32	D6
Saratoga Lake	Srg	45	C1
Saugatuck Res	Ffd	69	B3
Saugatuck River	Ffd	69	A2
Saugatuck River	Ffd	69	B4
Saugatuck River West Br	Ffd	69	B4
Sauquoit Cr	Ond	29	C6
Saw Kill	Dut	59	B6
Saw Kill	Uls	58	E6
Saw Kill	Uls	58	F6
Saw Mill River	Wch	68	D6
Sawyer Bay	Jfs	14	C3
Sawyer Cr	SL	9	A4
Sawyer Kill	Uls	59	A5
Schenevus Cr	Ots	43	B6
Schenob Brook	Brk	60	B6
Schoharie Cr	Grn	58	C4
Schoharie Cr	Mgy	44	C1
Schoharie Cr	Shh	44	B5
Schoharie Res	Shh	58	A2
School House Pond	Wgn	72	E2
Schroon Lake	Ese	19	C3
Schroon River	Ese	12	D6
Schroon River	Ese	19	D1
Schroon River	Wrr	19	C4
Schroon River	Wrr	32	C1
Sconondoa Cr	Ond	28	F6
Scott Cr	Chu	48	C1
Scriba Cr	Osw	27	F3
Sears Pond	Lew	15	D4
Second Cr	Wan	26	A5
Second Lake	Hrk	17	A5
Second Lake	Wrr	32	C2
Second Pond	Rns	46	A3
Second Pond Brook	Wrr	18	E5
Seeley Cr	Chm	53	B6
Seeley Cr	Stu	51	E2
Seely Brook	Orn	67	D2
Seneca Lake	Scy	53	B1
Seneca Lake	Sen	39	A4
Seneca Lake	Yts	39	A4
Seneca River	Cyg	26	E5
Seneca River	Ono	27	A5
Seneca River	Ono	27	C4
Separator Brook	Cln	5	A4
Seventh Lake	Hml	17	D4
Shadigee Cr	Wyn	61	A2
Shallow Lake	Hml	17	D3
Shandelee Lake	Slv	62	B2
Shanty Brook	Hml	17	C1
Shanty Brook	Wrr	18	E6
Shanty Cr	Ont	7	B4
Shawangunk Kill	Orn	63	B5
Shawler Brook	Cng	42	B4
Shehawken Cr	Wyn	61	C2
Shekomeko Cr	Clm	59	D6
Shekomeko Cr	Dut	64	E1
Shelburne Bay	Chi	13	C1
Shelburne Pond	Chi	13	E2
Sheldon Cr	Wyo	36	A4
Sheldrake Cr	Sen	39	C5
Shelter Is Sound	Sfk	71	B6
Shepaug Res	Lch	65	C4
Shepaug River	Lch	65	B5
Shepaug River	Lch	65	C5
Shepaug River	NHv	69	C1
Shepaug River East Br	Lch	65	C2
Shequaga Cr	Scy	53	A3
Sheriff Lake	Hml	30	E2
Sherman Lake	Ese	19	F1
Sherman Lake	Wrr	19	D5
Shingle Kill	Orn	66	D1
Shinnecock Bay	Sfk	77	F3
Shinnecock Bay	Sfk	78	A2
Shinnecock Inlet	Sfk	78	A2
Shohola Cr	Pke	66	A1
Short Pt Bay	Osw	27	F4
Shunock River	NLn	72	B1
Siamese Ponds	Wrr	18	D5
Silver Cr	Chu	34	E6
Silver Cr	Chu	48	E1
Silver Cr	Sen	39	B3
Silver Cr Res	Chu	48	E1
Silver Lake	Add	20	F2
Silver Lake	Cln	5	B6
Silver Lake	Cln	12	B1
Silver Lake	Dlw	56	B6
Silver Lake	Dut	64	C2
Silver Lake	Hml	31	A3
Silver Lake	SL	10	C4
Silver Lake	Wyo	36	F4
Silver Lake Outlet	Hml	31	A3
Silver Lake Outlet	Wyo	37	A4
Silver Run	Hml	17	E4
Silver Stream Res	Orn	67	E1
Silvermine River	Ffd	69	A4
Simon Pond	Frl	11	A4
Sing Sing Cr	Chm	53	B4
Sister Cr	Ere	34	F4
Six Mile Cr	Ont	21	E4
Sixmile Brook	Hml	18	B1
Sixmile Cr	Eri	47	A5
Sixmile Cr	Ond	29	B3
Sixmile Cr	SL	10	B5
Sixmile Cr	Tmk	54	B2
Sixteen Falls Cr	Sen	39	B5
Sixteen Mile Cr	Ont	21	A6
Sixteen Mile Pond	Ont	21	C4
Sixth Lake	Hml	17	C4
Sixtown Cr	Agy	50	C1
Skaneateles Cr	Ono	40	A1
Skaneateles Lake	Ono	40	B2
Sky Lake	Brm	55	F5
Skylight Brook	Ese	12	A6
Slab City Cr	Cat	48	F2
Sleepy Hollow Lake	Grn	59	C3
Slim Pond	Hml	10	F6
Slocum Brook	Lch	60	F6
Slocum Cr	Whg	32	F5
Smith Brook	Crt	40	F6
Smith Cove	Sfk	71	C6
Smith Mill Brook	Slv	62	A5
Smithtown Bay	Sfk	76	D1
Smoke Cr	Ere	35	C3
Snake Cr	Osw	14	D6
Snake Cr	Osw	27	E1
Snake Cr North Br	Osw	27	F1
Snake Cr South Br	Osw	27	F1
Snook Kill	Srg	32	C5
Snook Kill	Srg	32	E4
Sodus Bay	Wan	26	A3
Sodus Cr	Wan	26	B4
Sodus Ditch	Wan	26	B5
Soft Maple Res	Lew	16	D1
Somerset Lake	Dlw	61	D2
Song Lake	Crt	40	E3
South Bay	Ond	28	C4
South Bay	Whg	20	A6
South Br Calkins Cr	Wyn	61	E5
South Br Catatonk Cr	Tio	54	A4
South Br Cattaraugus Cr	Cat	49	B2
South Br Eighteenmile Cr	Ere	35	B4
South Br Grasse River	SL	9	F2
South Br Grasse River	SL	10	A3
South Br Moose River	Hrk	16	F5
South Br Moose River	Hrk	17	B5
South Br Raritan River	Hnt	73	B4
South Br Raritan River	Hnt	73	B5
South Br Raritan River	Sms	73	D6
South Br Salmon River	Osw	27	E2
South Br Snake Cr	Osw	27	E1
South Br South Nation River	Ont	1	F3
South Br South Nation River	Ont	2	A2
South Br Tuscarora Cr	Stu	52	A6
South Br Van Campen Cr	Agy	50	E4
South Br West Canada Cr	Hml	30	C2
South Brook	Wrr	31	F2
South Colton Res	SL	3	B6
South Cr	Chm	53	C6
South Cr	Lew	9	C5
South Fork Roaring Br	Ben	33	F6
South Lake	Hml	17	E6
South Lake	Hrk	17	B6
South Lebanon Brook	Mds	41	D3
South Meadow Brook	Ese	12	A4
South Nation River	Ont	1	E4
South Nation River	Ont	2	A1
South Nation River North Br	Ont	1	F1
South Nation River South Br	Ont	1	F3
South Nation River South Br	Ont	2	A2
South Norwalk Res	Ffd	69	A4
South Oyster Bay	Nsu	76	A5
South Pond	Hml	18	A1
South Pond	Lch	60	A6
South Pond	Osw	14	D5
South Ponds	Hrk	16	F1
South Res	Ond	29	D6
South River	Mid	78	B6
South Sandy Cr	Jfs	14	E3
South Sandy Cr	Jfs	15	A3
South Spectacle Pond	Lch	65	A4
South Stream Jewett Brook	Whg	46	D3
Spafford Cr	Ono	40	D3
Spaulding Brook	Cln	5	E6
Spectacle Cr	Ffd	69	A4
Spectacle Lake	Hml	30	F4
Sperry Pond	Hml	10	F5
Split Rock Pond	Ese	18	E2
Splitrock Res	Mrr	74	A1
Spooner Cr	Ere	35	D6
Sprague Brook	Hml	18	B3

NAME	TERR	MAP	GRID
Sprague Pond	Hml	18	B3
Spring Brook	Ere	35	E6
Spring Brook	Lvg	37	E1
Spring Cr	Ere	36	A2
Spring Cr	Gns	23	E6
Spring Lakes	Dut	59	C6
Spring Mile Cr	Ont	21	A5
Springwater Cr	Lvg	37	E5
Sprite Cr	Flt	30	E5
Sprite Cr	Flt	30	F6
Sprout Cr	Dut	64	B5
Spruce Cr	Hrk	30	B4
Spruce Hill Brook	Ese	12	C4
Spruce Lake	Hml	17	E6
Spruce Lake	Hrk	30	B4
Spruce Mill Brook	Ese	12	E3
Spruce Mill Brook	Ese	12	F3
Spruce Run	Hnt	73	A4
Spruce Run Res	Hnt	73	B5
Spuytenduivel Brook	Wrr	19	E3
Spy Lake	Hml	30	F2
Squaw Brook	Hml	18	B4
Squaw Lake	Hml	17	D5
Squeak Brook	SL	3	C2
Stacy Brook	Ese	13	A5
Stamford Hbr	Ffd	68	F6
Stammer Cr	SL	9	D3
Staplin Cr	Jfs	15	C1
Star Br	Srg	32	B6
Star Lake	SL	9	F5
Stark Falls Res	SL	10	D1
State Drainage Ditch	Cat	48	F4
Steele Br	Lch	65	E5
Steele Cr	Hrk	42	E1
Steele Res	Srg	31	F5
Stephens Pond	Hml	18	A3
Sterling Cr	Cyg	26	E3
Sterling Cr	Hrk	29	E5
Sterling Lake	Orn	67	C4
Sterling Valley Cr	Osw	26	E3
Steuben Cr	Ond	29	C3
Stewart Br	Wrr	32	C2
Stewarts Bridge Res	Srg	32	B3
Stickle Pond	Mrr	74	B1
Still River	Lch	65	B6
Stillwater Cr	Chu	48	C6
Stillwater Pond	Lch	65	E2
Stillwater Res	Hrk	16	F2
Stillwater Res	Hrk	17	A2
Stillwell Lake	Orn	67	F2
Stockbridge Bowl	Brk	60	B2
Stocking Cr	Stu	52	C3
Stoddard Cr	Cat	49	C6
Stoner Lakes	Flt	30	F4
Stoney Brook Res	NLn	71	E1
Stony Br	Brk	60	C4
Stony Br	Stu	51	D1
Stony Brook	SL	3	E6
Stony Brook	SL	10	B3
Stony Brook	Shh	44	C5
Stony Brook	Stu	37	D6
Stony Brook	Wyo	36	C3
Stony Brook Hbr	Sfk	76	D2
Stony Clove Cr	Grn	58	C5
Stony Cr	Cat	49	C6
Stony Cr	Cat	49	F1
Stony Cr	Clm	59	B6
Stony Cr	Jfs	14	E2
Stony Cr	Jfs	15	A2
Stony Cr	Ond	28	E5
Stony Cr	Shh	44	A5
Stony Cr	Shh	44	C5
Stony Cr	Wrr	31	E2
Stony Cr	Wrr	32	A1
Stony Cr	Wyo	36	D3
Stony Cr Ponds	Frl	11	C4
Stony Cr West	Flt	31	C4
Stony Cr West	Hml	31	C4
Stony Kill	Clm	59	F2
Stony Lake	Lew	16	D3
Stony Pond	Hml	10	E6
Streeter Lake	SL	9	F5
Streets Pond	Ffd	69	A4
Stringer Brook	Ond	29	B2
Stump Pond	Crt	55	B1
Stuyvesant Brook	Clm	59	D2
Sucker Brook	Add	20	F2
Sucker Brook	Hml	17	C3
Sucker Brook	Lew	15	F6
Sucker Brook	SL	2	B4
Sucker Brook	SL	10	C5
Sucker Brook	Sen	39	C2
Sugar Cr	Lvg	37	B6
Sugar Cr	Yts	38	E5
Sugar Hollow Brook	Rut	20	F3
Sugar River	Lew	16	B6
Sulphur Springs Cr	Tio	54	A4
Summit Lake	Ots	43	B2
Summit Lake	Shh	43	F5
Sumner Stream	Hml	17	E4
Sunset Bay	Osw	14	B6
Susquehanna River	Brm	55	A5
Susquehanna River	Brm	55	E5
Susquehanna River	Cng	56	A3
Susquehanna River	Ots	43	A5
Susquehanna River	Tio	54	B6
Sutherland Pond	Clm	59	E2
Swamp River	Dut	64	E5
Swarte Kill	Uls	63	F3
Swartswood Lake	Ssx	66	B6
Swede Pond	Wrr	19	F4
Swennen Br	Qub	7	F6
Swinging Bridge Res	Slv	62	C5
Swiss Cr	Lew	15	F1
Swiss Cr	Lew	16	A1
Switz Kill	Alb	44	E5
Sylvia Lake	SL	9	A3
Sympaug Br	Ffd	69	A2
Taft Bay	Osw	28	A4
Taghkanic Cr	Clm	59	D5
Taghkanic Cr	Clm	59	E5
Talbot Cr North Br	Stu	52	A4
Tallette Cr	Mds	42	B3
Tanner Brook	Ben	33	E5
Tanner Cr	SL	9	C2
Taughannock Cr	Scy	53	D1
Taunton Pond	Ffd	69	B2
Taylor Pond	Cln	12	B1
Taylorville Pond	Lew	16	C1
Tea Cr	Ont	21	E6
Temperance Lake	Ont	1	A5
Tenant Cr	Srg	31	E2
Tenmile Cr	Alb	58	E1
Tenmile Cr	Stu	52	B1
Tennanah Lake	Slv	62	A2
Terry Brook	Ben	33	D4
Thames River	NLn	71	E2
Thatcher Brook	Cat	49	A1
Thayer Lake	Hml	17	C1
The Bove	Qub	7	D6
The Br	Ese	12	B6
The Br	Ese	12	D4
The Br	Ese	19	B1
The Brochets River	Qub	7	E6
The Cove	Srg	32	E6
The Great Bay	Qub	7	E6
The Gulf	NHv	69	F4
The Gut	GIC	6	C3
The Narrows	Add	13	B4
The Whirlpool	Ont	21	F5
The Wide Waters	Wan	25	E6
Third Lake	Ese	18	C2
Third Lake	Flt	30	F4
Third Lake	Hrk	17	A5
Third Lake	Wrr	32	B2
Thirteenth Lake	Wrr	18	E4
Thompsons Pond	Whg	46	D3
Thousand Acre Swamp	Brk	60	D5
Three Mile Bay	Jfs	7	D4
Three Mile Cr	Jfs	7	E4
Three Mile Hbr	Sfk	71	D6
Threemile Bay	Osw	27	F4
Threemile Pond	Brk	60	C5
Thumb Pond	Ese	18	E2
Thunder Bay	Ont	34	F2
Thurman Pond	Ese	19	C3
Timmerman Cr	Mgy	30	D6
Tinmouth Channel	Rut	33	F1
Tioga River	Stu	52	E5
Tioghnioga Cr	Crt	41	A4
Tioughnioga River	Brm	55	B3
Tioughnioga River	Crt	40	E5
Tioughnioga River	Crt	54	F1
Tioughnioga River East Br	Crt	40	E5
Tioughnioga River West Br	Crt	40	D5
Tirrell Pond	Hml	18	B2
Titicus Res	Wch	68	E3
Tobaccolot Bay	Sfk	71	F5
Tobechanna Cr	Scy	52	F1
Tobsey Pond	Lch	65	D1
Tomahawk Lake	Orn	67	D2
Tomhannock Res	Rns	45	F2
Tonawanda Cr	Ere	22	C6
Tonawanda Cr	Ere	23	A6
Tonawanda Cr	Gns	23	C6
Tonawanda Cr	Gns	36	D2
Tonawanda Cr	Nia	22	C6
Tonawanda Cr	Wyo	36	C3
Tonawanda Cr East Br	Wyo	36	C4
Tooley Pond	SL	10	A3
Toronto Res	Slv	62	C5
Towbridge Brook	Frl	11	E2
Town Brook	Brk	46	C6
Town Brook	Dlw	57	E2
Town Farm Bay	Chi	13	C3
Tracy Brook	SL	2	F5
Tracy Brook	SL	3	A5
Tracy Cr	Brm	54	E6
Train Pond	Frl	3	F6
Trammel Cr	Hrk	30	C4
Transylvania Brook	Lch	65	C6
Trap Falls Res	Ffd	69	E3
Treadwell Cr	Dlw	56	E2
Tremper Kill	Dlw	57	C5
Trendwell Bay	Cln	6	B3
Trombley Bay	Cln	6	B2
Troups Cr	Stu	51	F6
Trout Brook	Brk	60	F1
Trout Brook	Crt	40	F4
Trout Brook	Crt	40	F5
Trout Brook	Dlw	56	F6
Trout Brook	Dlw	61	F1
Trout Brook	Ese	19	B3
Trout Brook	Ese	19	F3
Trout Brook	Ese	20	A3
Trout Brook	Frl	4	A5
Trout Brook	Osw	14	F6
Trout Brook	Osw	15	A5
Trout Brook	Otr	38	A1
Trout Brook	SL	2	E5
Trout Brook	SL	3	B4
Trout Brook	SL	3	C3
Trout Cr	Dlw	56	C4
Trout Lake	Hml	30	D2
Trout Lake	SL	9	C2
Trout Lake	Wrr	19	D6
Trout Pond	Ese	18	F1
Trout Pond	Hmp	60	F5
Trout River	Frl	4	C2
Trowbridge Cr	Brm	55	D6
True Brook	Cln	5	B5
Tub Mill Pond	Ese	12	F6
Tully Lake	Ono	40	E3
Tupper Lake	SL	10	F4
Turkey Hill Res	Mdx	70	F1
Turner Cr	Cng	55	F1
Tuscarora Cr	Stu	52	A5
Tuscarora Cr South Br	Stu	52	A6
Tuscarora Lake	Mds	41	C2
Tuxedo Lake	Orn	67	D4
Twelvemile Cr	Nia	22	A3
Twelvemile Cr	Stu	38	B6
Twelvemile Cr	Stu	52	A1
Twelvemile Cr East Br	Nia	22	B3
Twentyeighth Cr	Chu	48	E4
Twentymile Cr	Chu	47	D4
Twin Lakes	Hrk	30	A1
Twin Lakes	Pke	66	B2
Twin Lakes Stream	Hrk	29	F1
Twin Lakes Stream	Hrk	30	A1
Twin Ponds	Frl	4	B4
Twitchell Cr	Hrk	17	A3
Twitchell Lake	Hrk	17	B2
Two Mile Cr	Ont	21	E3
Twomile Cr	Lvg	37	C5
Tyler Lake	Lch	65	D2
Unadilla River	Cng	42	B6
Unadilla River	Mds	42	D2
Unadilla River	Ots	42	B6
Unadilla River	Ots	56	B2
Unadilla River West Br	Ond	42	D2
Uncas Pond	NLn	71	C2
Union Falls Pond	Frl	5	A6
Union Falls Pond	Frl	12	A1
Upper Ausable Lake	Ese	12	B6
Upper Bay	Hud	74	F5
Upper Bay	Kng	74	F5
Upper Blenheim Gilboa Res	Shh	58	A1
Upper Chateaugay Lake	Cln	5	A4
Upper Duck Hole	Ese	11	E6
Upper Goose Pond	Brk	60	D3
Upper Greenwood Lake	Pas	67	B4
Upper Pond	Hml	17	F2
Upper Rhoda Pond	Clm	59	E5
Upper Saint Regis Lake	Frl	11	C1
Upper Saranac Lake	Frl	11	C3
Upper Shepaug Res	Lch	65	C3
Upper Sister Lake	Hml	17	C2
Upper Spectacle Pond	Brk	60	E4
Usshers Cr	Ont	21	F6
Utowana Lake	Hml	17	F2
Valatie Kill	Clm	59	D1
Valatie Kill	Rns	45	E6
Valentine Pond	Wrr	19	C4
Valley Brook	Lch	65	B3
Valley Cr	Cat	49	C4
Valley Cr	Cat	49	E3
Valley Cr	Dlw	57	F4
Valley Cr	Dlw	58	A4
Valley Cr	Rns	46	A5
Van Campen Cr	Agy	50	E4
Van Der Linden Pond	Agy	50	C3
Vandenburgh Pond	Flt	31	B5
Vandermark Cr	Agy	51	B4
Vanderwhacker Brook	Ese	18	F2
Vav Wie Cr	Mgy	44	B1
Venise Bay	Qub	7	E6
Vernooy Kill	Uls	63	B2
Viele Pond	Wrr	32	C1
Virgil Cr	Crt	40	D6
Virgil Cr	Tmk	40	B6
Virgil Cr	Tmk	54	C1
Vlockie Kill	Rns	45	D6
Vloman Kill	Alb	45	D1
Vrooman Cr	Jfs	8	D3
Wager Pond	Rns	46	A4
Wahconah Brook	Brk	60	D1
Wainfleet Marsh	Ont	34	C1
Walker Lake	Pke	66	B1
Wallkill River	Orn	63	D6
Wallkill River	Orn	66	F3
Wallkill River	Orn	67	A3
Wallkill River	Orn	67	B1
Wallkill River	Ssx	66	E6
Wallkill River	Ssx	66	F3
Wallkill River	Uls	63	F3
Walloomsac River	Whg	46	C1
Walnut Cr	Chu	34	D6
Walnut Cr	Chu	48	D2
Wampecack Cr	Whg	46	A1
Wampus River	Wch	68	D5
Wanaksink Lake	Slv	62	F5
Wanaque Res	Pas	67	C5
Wanaque River	Pas	67	C5
Waneta Lake	Scy	52	E1
Wangum Lake	Lch	65	C1
Wappinger Cr	Dut	64	B5
Wappinger Cr	Dut	64	D2
Ward Brook	Frl	11	D4
Wards Cr	Add	13	B6
Warm Brook	Ben	33	D6
Warner Cr	Uls	58	C5
Warner Lake	Alb	44	E5
Washinee Lake	Lch	60	A6
Washington Canal	Mid	78	B6
Washington Lake	Slv	62	B6
Washington Mtn Lake	Brk	60	D2
Washining Lake	Lch	60	B6
Wassaic Cr	Dut	64	E2
Watchaug Pond	Wgn	72	D2
Watson Pond	Brk	60	F4
Wawayanda Cr	Orn	67	B4
Weaver Lake	Hrk	43	A1
Webster Brook	Cyg	40	C5
Weekeepeeme River	Lch	65	D5
Welch Lake	Rck	67	F4
Welland Canal	Ont	21	D4
Welland Canal	Ont	21	D6
Welland Canal	Ont	34	C2
Welland River	Ont	21	D6
Welland River	Ont	34	B1
Weller Pond	SL	3	E6
Wells Brook	Rut	33	D2
Welmet Lake	Slv	62	B5
West Beaver Brook	Whg	33	B4
West Br	Htf	65	F1
West Br Ausable River	Ese	12	A4
West Br Ausable River	Ese	12	C2
West Br Batten Kill	Ben	33	F4
West Br Beaver River	Hrk	17	A2
West Br Black Cr	Jfs	8	E6
West Br Black Cr	Whg	33	B3
West Br Cazenovia Cr	Ere	35	D5
West Br Conewango Cr	Chu	48	D2
West Br Dead Cr	Add	13	B6
West Br Dead Cr	Add	20	B1
West Br Deer Cr	Frl	4	A2
West Br Deerfield River	Whg	46	F2
West Br Delaware River	Brm	56	A6
West Br Delaware River	Dlw	56	D5
West Br Delaware River	Dlw	57	C3
West Br Dyberry Cr	Wyn	61	B4
West Br Farmington River	Brk	60	E4
West Br Fish Cr	Ond	28	C2
West Br French Cr	Eri	47	B6
West Br Green River	Brk	46	C5
West Br Handsome Brook	Dlw	56	E3
West Br Keuka Lake	Yts	38	E6
West Br Lackawaxen River	Wyn	61	B4
West Br Limestone Cr	Ono	41	A1
West Br Mongaup River	Slv	62	C4
West Br Onondaga Cr	Ono	40	D1
West Br Oswegatchie River	Lew	9	B5
West Br Oswegatchie River	Lew	16	C1
West Br Otsdawa Cr	Ots	56	D1
West Br Owego Cr	Tio	54	C3
West Br Res	Lch	65	F1
West Br Res	Put	68	D1
West Br Sacandaga River	Hml	30	F3
West Br Sacandaga River	Hml	31	A2
West Br Saint Regis River	SL	3	B4
West Br Saint Regis River	SL	10	E1
West Br Saugatuck River	Ffd	69	B4
West Br Tioughnioga River	Crt	40	E4
West Br Unadilla River	Ond	42	D2
West Br Westfield River	Brk	60	F3
West Brook	Uls	62	F1
West Brook Kerrs Cr	Dlw	56	E4
West Brook Kinderhook Cr	Rns	46	B5
West Canada Cr	Hml	17	C6
West Canada Cr	Hrk	30	A2
West Canada Cr	Hrk	30	A5
West Canada Cr	Ond	29	E4
West Canada Cr South Br	Hml	30	E1
West Caroga Lake	Flt	30	F5
West Cr	Jfs	8	C5
West Cr	Mro	24	A3
West Cr	Mro	24	C3
West Cr	Shh	43	E3
West Delaware Aqueduct	Slv	62	C1
West Ditch	Lvg	37	C5
West Fork Little Snake Cr	Brm	55	A6
West Fork Moorman Cr	Mro	24	A4
West Hill Pond	Lch	65	F2
West Kill	Grn	58	B4
West Kill Cr	Shh	57	F1
West Kill Cr	Shh	58	A1
West Lake	Flt	30	F4
West Lake	Hml	17	E5
West Lake Res	Ffd	68	F2
West River	NHv	70	A2
West River	NHv	70	A3
West River	NHv	70	D2
West River	Otr	38	D3
West Stony Cr	Flt	31	B5
West Stony Cr	Hml	31	B4
Westcolang Lake	Pke	61	F6
Westcott Cove	Ffd	68	F6
Westfield River	Brk	46	F5
Westfield River West Br	Brk	60	F3
Wet Brook	Brk	60	F3
Wetland River	Ont	21	A6
Wewaka Brook	Lch	65	B6
Whaley Lake	Dut	64	E6
Whallon Bay	Ese	13	B3
Wharton Cr	Ots	42	C5
Wharton Cr	Ots	42	E6
Wheeler Pond	NLn	71	E1
Wheelers Cr	Ond	29	A4
Whetstone Cr	Lew	15	F4
Whetstone Cr	Lew	16	A4
Whitaker Lake	Hml	18	B6
White Bay	Add	13	B5
White Br	Stu	51	D6
White Cr	Gns	36	F1
White Cr	Hrk	30	A4
White Cr	Ond	29	B6
White Cr	SL	9	A2
White Cr	Whg	33	B6
White Lake	Ond	16	E6
White Lake	Slv	62	B4
White Oak Pond	Wyn	61	B5
Whiteside Cr	Whg	45	F1
Whitford Brook	NLn	72	A2
Whiting River	Lch	60	C6
Whiting Swamp	Add	20	D2
Whitney Cr	Gns	23	A5
Whitney Lake	Hml	17	F5
Whitney Pt Lake	Brm	55	A2
Whortekill Cr	Dut	64	C5
Whortleberry Pond	Ese	19	D3
Wickham Lake	Orn	67	C3
Wigwam Res	Lch	65	E4
Wilber Lake	Ots	42	F6
Wilcox Lake	Wrr	31	E2
Wilcox Outlet East	Hml	31	D2
Willeysville Cr	Tio	54	B3
Williams Pond	Wyn	61	E6
Williams River	Brk	60	B3
Willis Brook	Frl	10	F2
Willis Pond	Frl	11	A2
Willow Br	NHv	70	B1
Willsboro Bay	Ese	13	B2
Wilmurt Lake	Hml	30	D1
Wilson Cr	Otr	38	F3
Wilson Cr	Tio	54	E3
Wilson Hollow Brook	Dlw	56	F5
Wiltse Lake	Ont	1	A5
Windfall Brook	SL	10	C3
Windfall Pond	Frl	11	A2
Windover Lake	Wrr	18	F5
Windsor Res	Brk	60	E1
Winfield Cr North	Hrk	42	D1
Winona Pond	Add	13	E4
Winooski River	Chi	6	C6
Winooski River	Chi	13	F1
Wiscoy Cr	Agy	36	E6
Wiscoy Cr	Wyo	36	C6
Wolcott Cr	Wan	26	C4
Wolf Cr	Ese	18	E2
Wolf Cr	Wyo	36	F5
Wolf Hollow Cr	Hrk	30	A4
Wolf Is Cut	Ont	7	D2
Wolf Lake	Slv	62	E5
Wolf Pond	Ese	11	D6
Wolf Pond	Frl	4	F5
Wolf Pond	Frl	10	F1
Wolf Pond	Frl	11	A3
Wolf Pond	Hrk	10	A6
Wolf Pond Outlet	Hrk	10	A6
Wononpakook Lake	Lch	65	A1
Wononskopomuc Lake	Lch	65	A1
Wood Cr	Ond	28	E4
Wood Cr	Whg	32	F3
Wood Cr Pond	Lch	60	D6
Wood River	Wgn	72	D1
Woodbridge Lake	Lch	65	D3
Woodcliff Lake	Brg	67	F6
Woodhull Cr	Hrk	16	E6
Woodhull Cr	Ond	29	D1
Woodhull Lake	Hrk	17	A5
Woodland Cr	Uls	58	B6
Woodland Lake	Srg	32	B4
Woods Lake	Flt	31	C3
Woods Pond	Brk	60	C2
Woodward Lake	Flt	31	D4
Worden Pond	Wgn	72	E1
Wrights Cr	Cat	49	F4
Wylie Brook	Cng	55	E3
Wyneoop Cr	Chm	53	E6
Wyomanock Cr	Clm	60	A1
Yankee Lake	Slv	62	F5
Yankeetown Pond	Uls	58	E6
Yanty Cr	Mro	24	A3
Yanty Cr	Orl	23	F3
Yatesville Cr	Mgy	44	A2
Yellow Lake	SL	8	E3
Yokum Brook	Brk	60	E3
Yokum Pond	Brk	60	E3
York Lake	Brk	60	D5
Young Lake	Hrk	43	B2
Zimmerman Cr	Flt	30	E6

Military & Federal Features

NAME	TERR	MAP	GRID
Ava Test Annex	Ond	29	B2
Belle Mead General Depot	Sms	73	D6
Bullville Army Reserve Ctr	Orn	63	B6
Camp Johnson	Chi	6	E6
Canadian Forces Base Kingston	Ont	7	A2
Coast Guard Acad	NLn	71	E2
Connecticut St Mil Camp	NLn	71	D3
Fort Drum Mil Resv	Jfs	8	E5
Fort Hamilton	Kng	74	F5
Fort Wadsworth	Rmd	74	F5
Galeville Army Airport	Uls	63	D5
Griffiss AFB	Ond	29	B4
Hancock Field USAF Base	Ono	27	E5

NAME	TERR	MAP	GRID
Knolls Atomic Power Lab	Sch	45	B3
Mattituck Airbase	Sfk	77	F1
Mid-Orange Correctional Facility	Orn	67	C3
Moriches Coast Guard Station	Sfk	77	C3
New York St Atomic & Space Development Authority	Srg	45	C1
New York St Mil Resv Camp Smith	Wch	68	A3
Picatinny Arsenal (US Mil Resv)	Mrr	73	F1
Plattsburgh AFB	Cln	6	A5
Port of Entry	Cln	5	A1
Port of Entry	Cln	5	C1
Port of Entry	Cln	5	E1
Port of Entry	Cln	7	A6
Port of Entry	Cln	7	B6
Port of Entry	Fkl	7	E6
Port of Entry	Frl	3	F1
Port of Entry	Frl	4	C1
Port of Entry	Frl	4	D1
Port of Entry	Frl	4	E1
Port of Entry	GlC	7	C6
Port of Entry	GlC	7	D6
Port of Entry	Nia	21	F5
Port of Entry	Ont	2	A4
Port of Entry	Ont	8	A2
Port of Entry	Ont	21	F5
Port of Entry	SL	2	A4
Port of Entry	SL	3	C1
Raritan Prison	Mid	74	C5
Royal Mil Coll	Ont	7	A3
Seneca Army Depot	Sen	39	B3
Sing Sing St Corr Facility	Wch	68	B5
Stockbridge Test Site (USAF)	Mds	28	E6
Stone Ranch Mil Resv Connecticut Natl Guard	NLn	71	C2
US Dept of Agriculture	Sfk	71	D4
US Mil Acad at West Pt	Orn	67	F2
US Mil Acad at West Pt	Orn	68	A2
US Mil Resv	Fkl	6	F3
US Mil Resv	Mrr	67	A6
US Mil Resv	Mrr	74	A1
US Mil Resv	Nia	22	B5
US Mil Resv (Camden Test Annex)	Ond	28	B3
US Mil Resv (Verona Test Site)	Ond	28	E5
US Mil Resv (Youngstown Test Site)	Nia	22	A4
US Naval Resv	Hud	74	E4
US Naval Resv Earle Ammunition Depot	Mom	78	F6
US Naval Resv Supply Depot	Sch	45	A2
US Naval Resv Supply Depot	Sch	45	A3
US Navy Submarine Base & Library	NLn	71	F2
US Resv (Kenneth A Kesselring Site)	Srg	32	A6
US Resv Brookhaven Natl Laboratory	Sfk	77	B1
US Resv Brookhaven Natl Laboratory	Sfk	77	B2
Veterans Admin Ctr	Stu	52	B2
Watervliet Arsenal	Alb	45	D4
Western New York Nuclear Service Ctr	Cat	49	E1
Wheeler Sack Field	Jfs	8	D6

Mountain Peaks

NAME	TERR	MAP	GRID
Adler Bed Mtn	Hrk	9	F6
Alder Brook Mtn	Cln	5	B6
Algonquin Peak	Ese	12	A5
Alma Hill	Agy	50	F6
Ampersand Mtn	Frl	11	D4
Arab Mtn	SL	10	E4
Azure Mtn	Frl	3	F6
Bald Mtn	Brg	67	D5
Bald Mtn	Hrk	17	A4
Bald Peak	Ese	13	A5
Baldhead Mtn	Wrr	32	A1
Balsom Lake Mtn	Uls	57	E6
Baxter Mtn	Dlw	56	F6
Bear Mtn	Ben	33	E4
Belleayre Mtn	Uls	57	F5
Bennett Hill	Alb	45	A6
Berlin Mtn	Brk	46	C4
Berlin Mtn	Rns	46	C4
Berry Hill	Cng	41	D6
Black Dome	Grn	58	E3
Black Spruce Mtn	Wrr	32	C1
Blue Mtn	Hml	18	B2
Borden Mtn	Brk	46	F5
Brewster Mtn	Ese	11	E2
Bullhead Mtn	Wrr	18	D4
Call Hill	Stu	51	D4
Catamount	Cln	12	B1
Cathead Mtn	Hml	31	C3
Chapel Hill	Cat	49	F4
Clove Mtn	Dut	64	D4
Crane Mtn	Wrr	19	A6
Cushetunk Mtn	Hnt	73	C5
Debar Mtn	Frl	4	D5
Denman Mtn	Slv	62	F2
Diamond Mtn	Rck	67	E4
Dix Mtn	Ese	12	C5
Dorset Peak	Rut	33	F3
Eleventh Mtn	Wrr	18	F5
Ellenburg Mtn	Cln	5	B3
Equinox Mtn	Ben	33	E4
Fivemile Mtn	Wrr	19	F5
Fort Noble Mtn	Hml	30	C2
Fort Noble Mtn	Hrk	30	C2
Garner Hill	Brk	60	F2
Giant Mtn	Ese	12	D5
Glastenbury Mtn	Ben	46	F1
Gomer Hill	Lew	16	A5
Gore Mtn	Wrr	18	F4
Graham Mtn	Orn	66	F1
Green Mtn	Ben	33	F6
Hall Mtn	Hnt	73	C4
Hamilton Mtn	Hml	31	B2
Herrick Mtn	Rut	20	E6
Hickory Mtn	Pas	67	C5
High Mtn	Brg	67	D5
High Mtn	Pas	74	D1
High Peak	Grn	58	F5
High Point	Ssx	66	D3
High Point	Uls	63	B4
High Point	Uls	63	C1
Hoffman Mtn	Ese	19	C2
Hooker Mtn	Ots	43	B5
Hunter Mtn	Grn	58	D4
Irish Hill	Stu	52	D3
Jay Mtn	Ese	12	D3
Kinners Knob	Stu	52	A4
Kittatinny Mtn	Ssx	66	B5
Lead Mine Mtn	Rut	20	F3
Loon Lake Mtn	Frl	4	E6
Lyon Mtn	Cln	5	B4
McCarthy Hill	Cat	49	C6
Middle Mtn	Dlw	57	C6
Mongaup Mtn	Uls	62	D1
Mother Myrick Mtn	Ben	33	E4
Mount Ararat	Wyn	61	A3
Mount Donaldson	Frl	11	D5
Mount Everett	Brk	60	A5
Mount Frissell	Lch	60	A6
Mount Greylock	Brk	46	D5
Mount Haystack	Ese	12	B5
Mount Irvine	Cat	49	E6
Mount Marcy	Ese	12	A5
Mount Matumbla	SL	10	F3
Mount Morris	Frl	11	A5
Mount Nimham	Put	68	D1
Mount Philo	Chi	13	D3
Mount Pisgah	Dlw	57	C4
Mount Skylight	Ese	12	A5
Mount Tobias	Uls	58	D6
Mount Tuscarora	Cat	49	B6
Mount Van Hoevenberg	Ese	12	A4
Netop Mtn	Ben	33	F3
North Dome	Grn	58	B4
October Mtn	Brk	60	D2
Panther Mtn	SL	9	E1
Pharaoh Mtn	Ese	19	E3
Pillsbury Mtn	Hml	17	F5
Pilot Knob	Whg	32	E1
Pine Hill	Ese	19	B3
Pinnacle Point	Clm	60	A3
Pokamoonshine Mtn	Ese	12	F2
Prospect Mtn	Ben	46	F2
Prospect Mtn	Wrr	32	C1
Puffer Mtn	Wrr	18	D4
Robert Frost Mtn	Add	13	F6
Rock Rift Mtn	Dlw	56	D5
Saint Regis Mtn	Frl	11	B2
Samson Mtn	Uls	63	B2
Santanoni Peak	Ese	11	E5
Schunnemunk Mtn	Orn	67	E2
Seward Mtn	Frl	11	D5
Seymour Mtn	Frl	11	E5
Slide Mtn	Uls	63	B1
Smith Mtn	Brk	60	B1
Snake Mtn	Add	13	C6
Snowy Mtn	Hml	18	B4
South Beacon Mtn	Dut	68	A1
South Mtn	Add	13	F5
Split Rock Mtn	Ese	13	B4
Spruce Mtn	Srg	31	E2
Spruce Mtn	Srg	32	B4
Spruce Mtn	Whg	20	A5
Spruce Peak	Ben	33	D6
Sterling Mtn	Orn	67	C4
Stillwater Mtn	Hrk	16	F2
Stissing Mtn	Dut	64	D1
Stony Cr Mtn	Frl	11	C4
Street Mtn	Ese	11	F4
Taylor Mtn	Orn	67	B4
Terry Mtn	Cln	5	D6
The Dome Mtn	Ben	46	D3
Tolman Mtn	Cln	5	C6
Tomany Mtn	Hml	30	F3
Twin Lakes Mtn	Hml	30	E1
Upper Pohatcong Mtn	War	73	A3
Valley Mtn	Grn	58	A4
Vanderwhacker Mtn	Ese	18	E2
Wakley Mtn	Hml	17	F4
Washburn Mtn	Clm	59	F5
Whiteface Mtn	Ese	12	A2
Woodhull Mtn	Hrk	17	A5
Woodlawn Mtn	Rut	33	E2

Parks & Recreation

NAME	TERR	MAP	GRID
Above All St Pk	Lch	65	B4
Adirondack Pk	Ese	6	A6
Adirondack Pk	Ese	12	D3
Adirondack Pk	Ese	19	C3
Adirondack Pk	Frl	4	D4
Adirondack Pk	Frl	11	B4
Adirondack Pk	Hml	18	A3
Adirondack Pk	Hml	30	C2
Adirondack Pk	Hml	31	B3
Adirondack Pk	Hrk	17	B4
Adirondack Pk	Hrk	29	F1
Adirondack Pk	Lew	16	D3
Adirondack Pk	SL	3	D6
Adirondack Pk	SL	9	E3
Adirondack Pk	SL	10	B3
Adirondack Pk	Whg	20	A4
Adirondack Pk	Whg	32	A1
Adirondack Pk	Wrr	19	C3
Adirondack Pk	Wrr	32	A1
Akron Falls Pk	Ere	23	A6
Allamuchy Mtn St Pk	Ssx	73	C1
Allamuchy Mtn St Pk	War	73	C2
Allegany St Pk	Cat	49	B6
Allegany St Pk Admin Bldg	Cat	49	C5
Artpark	Nia	21	E5
Ashbrook Resv	Uni	74	B5
Ausable Pt Forest Preserve	Cln	6	A6
Battle Is St Pk	Osw	27	A2
Bayard Cutting Arboretum St Pk	Sfk	76	D3
Bear Mtn St Pk	Rck	67	F3
Bear Mtn St Pk	Rck	68	A3
Beaver Is St Pk	Ere	35	A1
Beaver Lake Co Pk	Ono	27	B4
Becket Hill St Pk	NLn	71	C2
Beeman Cr Pk	Ere	22	E6
Belmont Lake St Pk	Sfk	76	B4
Belmont Pk	Nsu	75	D4
Bennington Batl St Hist Site	Whg	46	C1
Bethpage St Pk	Nsu	76	A3
Black Cr Pk	Mro	24	C6
Black Rock St Pk	Lch	65	E5
Blauvelt St Pk	Rck	68	A6
Bluff Pt St Pk	NLn	71	F3
Bomoseen St Pk	Rut	20	C4
Bonds Lake Co Pk	Nia	22	B4
Boston Forest Co Pk	Ere	35	C5
Bowman Lake St Pk	Cng	41	E6
Bradbury St Pk	Add	20	F2
Bradbury St Pk	Rut	20	F2
Branch Brook Pk	Esx	74	D3
Brighton Pk	Ere	22	B6
Bristol Beach St Pk	Uls	59	A5
Bronx Pk	Brx	75	B2
Brookdale Pk	Esx	74	D2
Browns Bay Pk	Ont	8	C1
Buckhorn Is St Pk	Ere	22	A6
Burlingame St Pk	Wgn	72	D2
Burnet Pk	Ono	27	D6
Burnham Pt St Pk	Jfs	7	C3
Burton Is St Pk	Fkl	6	D3
Buttermilk Falls St Pk	Tmk	53	F2
Buttermilk Falls St Pk	Tmk	54	A2
Button Bay St Pk	Add	13	B4
Caleb Smith Preserve St Pk	Sfk	76	C2
Campbell Falls St Pk	Lch	60	D6
Campgaw Mtn Co Resv	Brg	67	D6
Canandaigua Lake St Marine Pk	Otr	38	C2
Canoe-Picnic Pt St Pk	Jfs	7	F2
Captree St Pk	Sfk	76	C5
Captree St Pk	Sfk	76	D5
Castleton Is St Pk	Rns	45	C6
Catskill Pk	Dlw	57	C6
Catskill Pk	Dlw	61	F1
Catskill Pk	Grn	58	C4
Catskill Pk	Slv	62	D1
Caumsett St Pk	Sfk	76	A1
Cayuga Lake St Pk	Sen	39	C2
Cedar Beach Pk	Sfk	76	B5
Cedar Is St Pk	SL	8	C1
Cedar Pt St Pk	Jfs	7	D3
Central Pk	NYC	75	A3
Charleston Lake Provincial Pk	Ont	1	A6
Charleston Lake Provincial Pk	Ont	8	A1
Chatfield Hollow St Pk	Mdx	70	E2
Cheesequake St Pk	Mid	78	C6
Chenango Valley St Pk	Brm	55	C4
Cherry Plain St Pk	Rns	46	B5
Chestnut Ridge Co Pk	Ere	35	D4
Chimney Bluffs St Pk	Wan	26	A3
Chittenango Falls St Pk	Mds	41	B1
Clarence Fahnestock Mem St Pk	Put	68	B1
Clark Resv St Pk	Ono	27	F6
Clark Resv St Pk	Ono	40	F1
Clarksburg St Pk	Brk	46	E4
Clausland Mtn Co Pk	Rck	68	A6
Clay Pit Ponds Preserve	Rmd	74	D6
Clermont St Pk	Clm	59	B6
Cockaponset St Pk	Mdx	70	E1
Coles Cr St Pk	SL	2	E2
Collins Pk	Sch	45	A3
Colonial Pk	Sms	73	F6
Como Lake Co Pk	Ere	35	E2
Conesus Lake St Pk	Lvg	37	D3
Connetquot River Preserve St Pk	Sfk	76	E3
Croton Pt Pk	Wch	68	B4
Crown Pt Resv	Ese	13	A6
Crysler Farm Batl Pk	Ont	2	E1
Cumberland Bay St Pk	Cln	6	B4
Cunningham Pk	Que	75	C4
DAR St Pk	Add	13	B6
Darien Lake St Pk	Gns	36	A2
Darlington Co Pk	Brg	67	D6
Davella Mills Co Pk	Esx	74	D2
Delaware Water Gap Natl Rec Area	Pke	66	A4
Delaware Water Gap Natl Rec Area	Pke	66	B3
Delaware Water Gap Natl Rec Area	War	66	A4
Delta Lake St Pk	Ond	29	B3
Dennis Hill St Pk	Lch	65	D1
Devils Hopyard St Pk	Mdx	71	B1
DeWolf Pt St Pk	Jfs	8	A3
Duke Is Pk	Sms	73	D6
Durand-Eastman Pk	Mro	24	E4
Eagle Rock Resv	Esx	74	C3
East Sidney Lake Rec Area	Dlw	56	D2
Edgelake Pk	Uni	74	B5
Eel Weir St Pk	SL	2	A5
Eighteen Mile Cr Pk	Ere	35	B4
Eisenhower Pk	Nsu	75	F4
Ellison Co Pk	Mro	24	F5
Elma Meadow Co Pk	Ere	35	E2
Emerald Lake St Pk	Ben	33	F3
Emery Pk	Ere	35	E4
Evangola St Pk	Ere	34	E5
Fair Haven Beach St Pk	Cyg	26	D2
Farny St Pk	Mrr	67	A6
Farny St Pk	Mrr	74	A1
Fillmore Glen St Pk	Cyg	40	B4
Flushing Meadows Corona Pk	Que	75	B3
Forest Pk	Que	75	B4
Fort George Natl Hist Pk	Ont	21	E4
Fort Niagara St Pk	Nia	21	F3
Fort Shantok St Pk	NLn	71	E1
Fosters Pond St Pk	Mdx	70	F2
Four Mile St Campsite	Nia	21	F3
Four Mile St Campsite	Nia	22	A3
Franklin D Roosevelt St Pk	Wch	68	B3
Frear Pk	Rns	45	E3
Galloping Hill Pk	Uni	74	C4
Ganondagan St Hist Site	Otr	38	A1
Garret Mtn Resv	Pas	74	D2
Gateway Natl Rec Area	Kng	75	B5
Gateway Natl Rec Area	Mom	78	F6
Gateway Natl Rec Area	Que	75	B5
Gateway Natl Rec Area	Rmd	74	E6
Genesee Co Pk and Forest	Gns	36	E2
Genesee Valley Co Pk	Mro	24	E5
George Waldo St Pk	NHv	69	C1
Georges Is Pk	Wch	68	A4
Gilbert Lake St Pk	Ots	42	E5
Gilgo St Pk	Sfk	76	C5
Glimmerglass St Pk	Ots	43	B3
Golden Hill St Pk	Nia	23	A2
Goosepond Mtn St Pk	Orn	67	D3
Governor Alfred E Smith/Sunken Meadow St Pk	Sfk	76	C1
Grafton Lakes St Pk	Rns	46	A3
Graham Hill Co Pk	Wch	68	C5
Grand Isle St Pk	GlC	6	C4
Grass Cr Pk	Ont	7	C2
Grass Pt St Pk	Jfs	7	F2
Grass Pt St Pk	Jfs	8	A3
Greece Pk	Mro	24	D4
Green Lakes St Pk	Ono	28	A6
Green Mtn Pk	Ben	46	D3
Greenwich Pt Pk	Ffd	68	F6
Grenville Pk	Ont	2	A3
Hacklebarney St Pk	Mrr	73	C4
Haddam Is St Pk	Mdx	70	F1
Haley Farm St Pk	NLn	71	F2
Hamlin Beach St Pk	Mro	24	A2
Hammonasset Beach St Pk	NHv	70	E3
Harkness Mem St Pk	NLn	71	E3
Harriet Hollister Spencer Rec Area	Otr	37	F4
Harriman St Pk	Orn	67	F3
Harriman St Pk	Orn	68	A2
Harriman St Pk	Rck	67	F3
Haystack Mn St Pk	Lch	65	D1
Haystack Mtn St Pk	Lch	60	D6
Heckscher St Pk	Sfk	76	E4
Hempstead Lake St Pk	Nsu	75	D4
Herkimer Home St Hist Site	Hrk	30	B6
High Pt St Pk	Ssx	66	D3
High Tor St Pk	Rck	67	F4
High Tor St Pk	Rck	68	A4
Highland Lakes St Pk	Orn	67	B1
Highland Lakes St Pk	Uls	63	B6
Higley Flow St Pk	SL	3	A6
Higley Flow St Pk	SL	10	B1
Hinckley Res Picnic Area	Hrk	29	F3
Historic New Bridge Ldg Pk	Brg	74	F1
Hither Hills St Pk	Sfk	71	F6
Hook Mtn St Pk	Rck	68	B5
Hopatcong St Pk	Ssx	73	D1
Housatonic Meadows St Pk	Lch	65	B3
Housatonic St Pk	Lch	65	B2
Hudson Highlands St Pk	Put	68	A1
Hudson Highlands St Pk	Put	68	A2
Hudson River Islands St Pk	Clm	59	C2
Hunter Cr Pk	Ere	35	F3
Huntington St Pk	Ffd	69	B2
Hunts Pond St Pk	Cng	42	B5
Hyde Pk	Nia	21	F5
Indian Well St Pk	Ffd	69	E2
Irondequoit Bay St Marine Pk	Mro	24	F4
Ivy Mtn St Pk	Lch	65	D2
Jacques Cartier St Pk	SL	1	D6
James Baird St Pk	Dut	64	C4
Jamesville Beach Co Pk	Ono	40	F1
John Boyd Thacher St Pk	Alb	44	F4
Johnson Co Pk	Mid	74	A6
Jones Beach St Pk	Nsu	75	F5
Joseph Davis St Pk	Nia	21	F4
Keewaydin Pt St Pk	Jfs	8	A3
Kent Falls St Pk	Lch	65	A3
Kettletown St Pk	NHv	69	D1
Keuka Lake St Pk	Yts	38	E6
Kingsland Bay St Pk	Add	13	C4
Kissena Pk	Que	75	C4
Kittatinny Valley St Pk	Ssx	66	D6
Knight Pt St Pk	GlC	6	C3
Kring Pt St Pk	Jfs	8	B2
La Tourette Pk	Rmd	74	E6
Lake Erie St Pk	Chu	48	A1
Lake George St Pk	Wrr	32	D2
Lake Saint Catherine St Pk	Rut	33	D1
Lake Superior St Pk	Slv	62	A5
Lake Taghkanic St Pk	Clm	59	D5
Lake Waramaug St Pk	Lch	65	B4
Lakeside Beach St Pk	Orl	23	C2
Lenape Pk	Uni	74	C4
Letchworth St Pk	Lvg	37	A4
Letchworth St Pk	Wyo	36	F5
Letchworth St Pk	Wyo	37	A4
Liberty St Pk	Hud	74	F4
Lincoln Pk	Hud	74	E4
Lodi Pt St Pk	Sen	39	B5
Long Pond Ironworks St Pk	Pas	67	C5
Long Pt on Lake Chautauqua St Pk	Chu	48	B4
Long Pt St Pk	Cyg	39	D4
Long Pt St Pk	Jfs	7	D5
Louis Morris Pk	Mrr	73	F3
Macedonia Brook St Pk	Lch	64	F3
Macedonia Brook St Pk	Lch	65	A3
Macomb Resv St Pk	Cln	5	E5
Malletts Bay St Pk	Chi	6	D5
Margaret Lewis Norrie St Pk	Dut	64	A3
Marine Pk	Kng	75	A5
Mary Is St Pk	Jfs	8	A2
Max V Shaul St Pk	Shh	44	A6
Mendon Ponds Co Pk	Mro	37	E1
Mendon Ponds Pk	Mro	24	F6
Millers Pond St Pk	Mdx	70	E1
Mine Kill St Pk	Shh	58	A1
Minisink Battleground Natl Hist Site	Slv	66	A1
Minnewaska St Pk	Uls	63	C4
Mohansic Co Pk	Wch	68	B3
Montauk Downs St Pk	Sfk	72	A6
Montauk Pt St Pk	Sfk	72	B6
Moreau Lake St Pk	Srg	32	D4
Morningside Pk	Slv	62	D4
Morristown Natl Hist Pk	Mrr	73	F3
Mount Bushnell St Pk	Lch	65	B4
Mount Philo St Pk	Chi	13	D3
Mount Riga St Pk	Lch	60	A6
Mount Tom St Pk	Lch	65	C4
Mount Van Hoevenberg Rec Area	Ese	12	B4
Mountain Reserve Pk	Pas	74	D1
Mountainside Pk	Slv	62	F4
Napeague St Pk	Sfk	71	E6
Napeague St Pk	Sfk	78	F1
Naugatuck St Pk	NHv	70	A1
Newtown Batl St Pk	Chm	53	D6
Nomahegan Pk	Uni	74	C4
North Br Pk	Sms	73	D6
North Hero St Pk	GlC	6	D2
North Hudson Pk	Hud	74	F3
North Hudson Pk	Hud	75	A3
Nyack Beach St Pk	Rck	68	B5
Oak Orchard Marine Pk	Orl	23	D2
Oatka Cr Pk	Mro	24	C6
Oatka Cr Pk	Mro	37	C1
Ogden & Ruth Mills St Pk	Dut	64	B2
Old Croton Trailway St Pk	Wch	68	B6
Old Erie Canal St Pk	Ono	27	F6
Old Erie Canal St Pk	Ono	28	E5
Old Troy Pk	Mrr	74	B3
Oneida Shores Co Pk	Ono	27	E4
Onondaga Lake Co Pk	Ono	27	D5
Onondaga Pk	Ono	27	D6

NAME	TERR	MAP	GRID
Oquaga Cr St Pk	Dlw	56	B4
Orient Beach St Pk	Sfk	71	D5
Osborndale St Pk	NHv	69	E2
Overpeck Co Pk	Brg	74	F2
P & C Stadium	Ono	27	D6
Palisades Interstate Pk	Brg	75	B1
Passaic River Pk Area	Sms	73	F4
Peebles Is St Pk	Alb	45	D3
Peebles Is St Pk	Srg	45	D3
Pelham Bay Pk	Brx	75	C2
Pinnacle St Pk	Stu	52	D5
Pixley Falls St Pk	Ond	29	C2
Planting Fields Arboretum St Hist Pk	Nsu	75	F2
Point Au Roche St Pk	Cln	6	B3
Powder Mill Pk	Mro	25	A6
Pratts Falls Co Pk	Ono	41	A1
Preakness Valley Pk	Pas	74	D1
Prompton Lake Pk	Wyn	61	C5
Prospect Pk	Kng	75	A5
Putnam Mem St Pk	Ffd	69	B2
Quinnipiac River St Pk	NHv	70	B1
Rahway River Pkwy	Uni	74	B4
Rahway River Pkwy	Uni	74	C5
Ringwood St Pk	Pas	67	D5
Riverbank St Pk	NYC	75	A3
Robert H Treman St Pk	Tmk	53	E2
Robert Moses St Pk	SL	3	B1
Robert Moses St Pk	Sfk	76	C5
Roberto Clemente St Pk	Brx	75	A2
Rockefeller St Pk	Wch	68	C5
Rockland Lake St Pk	Rck	68	A5
Rocky Glenn St Pk	Ffd	69	C1
Rocky Neck St Pk	NLn	71	D3
Roosevelt Co Pk	Mid	74	B6
Roscoe Conkling Pk	Ond	29	C6
Round Valley Rec Area	Hnt	73	B5
Royalton Ravine Co Pk	Nia	22	E4
Sackets Hbr Batl	Jfs	14	D1
Saddle River Pk	Brg	74	E1
Sagamore Hill Natl Hist Site	Nsu	75	F2
Saint Albans Bay St Pk	Fkl	6	D3
Saint Lawrence Islands Natl Pk	Jfs	8	A2
Saint Lawrence Islands Natl Pk	Ont	7	B3
Saint Lawrence Islands Natl Pk	Ont	7	E2
Saint Lawrence Islands Natl Pk	Ont	8	B1
Saint Lawrence Seaway	SL	3	C1
Saint Lawrence St Pk	SL	1	F5
Sampson St Pk	Sen	39	B4
Sand Bar St Pk	Chi	6	D5
Saratoga Natl Hist Pk	Srg	32	E6
Saratoga Natl Hist Pk	Srg	45	E1
Saratoga Spa St Pk	Srg	32	C6
Schenectady Central Pk	Sch	45	B3
Selden Neck St Pk	NLn	71	B2
Selkirk Shores St Pk	Osw	14	D6
Seneca Lake St Pk	Sen	39	A2
Seneca Pk	Mro	24	E4
Seth Pierrepont St Pk	Ffd	68	F2
Seth Pierrepont St Pk	Ffd	69	A3
Shaftsbury St Pk	Ben	33	D6
Sherwood Is St Pk	Ffd	69	C5
Silver Lake St Pk	Wyo	36	F4
Skylands Pk	Ssx	66	D5
Sleeping Giant St Pk	NHv	70	B1
South Mtn Resv	Esx	74	C4
Southwick Beach St Pk	Jfs	14	D3
Spring Lake Co Pk	Uni	74	B5
Spruce Run Rec Area	Hnt	73	A5
Squantz Pond St Pk	Ffd	64	F6
Squantz Pond St Pk	Ffd	65	A6
Stephens St Pk	Mrr	73	C2
Stoddard Hill St Pk	NLn	71	F1
Stony Brook St Pk	Stu	37	D6
Stony Pt St Pk	Rck	68	A4
Storm King St Pk	Orn	67	F1
Storm King St Pk	Orn	68	A1
Swartswood St Pk	Ssx	66	C6
Taconic Trail St Pk	Brk	46	C4
Taconic/Copake Falls St Pk	Brk	60	A5
Taconic/Copake Falls St Pk	Clm	59	F5
Taconic/Copake Falls St Pk	Clm	59	F6
Taconic/Copake Falls St Pk	Dut	59	F6
Taconic/Rudd Pond St Pk	Dut	64	F1
Taconic/Rudd Pond St Pk	Dut	65	A1
Tallman Mtn St Pk	Rck	68	B6
Tamaques Resv	Uni	74	B5
Taughannock Falls St Pk	Tmk	39	E6
Tenafly Nature Ctr	Brg	75	A1
Thomas Bull Mem Co Pk	Orn	67	C1
Thompson Pk	Jfs	15	B1
Thompsons Lake St Pk	Alb	44	F5
Thrall Dam Pk	Ese	12	F3
Trimountain St Pk	NHv	70	D1
Upper Delaware Natl Scenic Rec River	Pke	61	F5
US Mil Acad at West Pt Michie Stadium	Orn	68	A2
Valley Stream St Pk	Nsu	75	D4
Van Cortlandt Pk	Brx	75	A2
Vernon Valley Great Gorge Action Pk	Ssx	67	A4
Verona Beach St Pk	Ond	28	D4
Voorhees St Pk	Hnt	73	A4
Ward Pound Ridge Resv	Wch	68	E3
Warinaco Pk	Uni	74	C5
Washington Rock St Pk	Sms	74	A5
Watchung Mtn Pk	Sms	73	E5
Watchung Resv	Uni	74	B4
Waterson Pt St Pk	Jfs	7	F1
Watkins Glen St Pk	Scy	53	A2
Wawayanda St Pk	Pas	67	A5
Wawayanda St Pk	Ssx	67	A4
Webster Pk	Mro	25	A4
Weequahic Pk	Esx	74	D4
Wellesley Is St Pk	Jfs	7	F2
West Essex Pk	Esx	74	B3
West Essex Pk	Esx	74	C2
West Hills Co Pk	Sfk	76	A3
West Rock Ridge St Pk	NHv	70	A2
Westcott Beach St Pk	Jfs	14	E2
Wharton Brook St Pk	NHv	70	C2
Whetstone Gulf St Pk	Lew	15	F4
Whetstone Gulf St Pk	Lew	16	A4
Wildwood St Pk	Sfk	77	C1
Wilson-Tuscarora St Pk	Nia	22	B3
Wilson-Tuscarora St Pk	Nia	22	D2
Winding Hills Pk	Orn	63	C6
Windsor James St Pk	Brk	46	F6
Windsor St Pk	Brk	46	E6
Woodford St Pk	Ben	46	F2
Woods Is St Pk	Fkl	6	D3
Wooster Mtn St Pk	Ffd	69	A2
Wyantenock St Pk	Lch	65	B3

Points of Interest

NAME	TERR	MAP	GRID
Adirondack Ctr Mus	Ese	12	F4
Adirondack Mus	Hml	18	A2
Adventureland Amusement Pk	Sfk	76	A3
African American Mus	Nsu	75	E4
Agricultural Mus	Jfs	8	A5
Akwesasne Mus	Frl	3	D1
American Labor Mus	Pas	74	D1
American Merchant Marine Mus	Nsu	75	C3
American Mus of Firefighting	Clm	59	C3
Amherst Mus Colony Pk	Ere	22	D6
Antique Boat Mus & Uncle Sam Boat	Jfs	7	E3
Arcade & Attica RR Mus	Wyo	36	A6
Arnot Art Mus	Chm	53	B5
Artpark	Nia	21	E4
Ausable Chasm	Cln	6	A6
Bakers Falls	Srg	32	E3
Bartlett Arboretum	Ffd	68	F5
Bayonne Bridge	Rmd	74	E5
Beaver Lake Nature Ctr	Ono	27	A4
Beekman Arms	Dut	64	B1
Bellport-Brookhaven Hist Mus	Sfk	77	A4
Bennington Batl St Hist Site	Whg	46	C1
Berkshire Bird Paradise	Rns	46	B3
Biathlon Area	Ese	12	A4
Blue Trail Range	NHv	70	C1
Boldt Castle	Jfs	8	A2
Boscobel Mansion Restoration	Put	68	A1
Bridgehampton Hist Mus	Sfk	78	B1
Bronx Zoo	Brx	75	B2
Bronx-Whitestone Bridge	Que	75	C3
Brooklyn Battery Tunnel	NYC	74	F4
Brooklyn Bridge	NYC	75	A4
Brooklyn Mus	Kng	75	A4
Buffalo & Erie Co Botanical Gardens	Ere	35	C3
Buttermilk Falls	Tmk	53	F1
Caleb Smith House	Sfk	76	E2
Canajoharie Falls	Mgy	43	F2
Canajoharie Gorge	Mgy	43	E2
Caramoor Ctr For Music & The Arts	Wch	68	E4
Carousel Ctr	Ono	27	D6
Carrier Dome	Ono	27	E6
Catskill Game Farm	Grn	59	A3
Catskill Mtn Railroad	Uls	58	C6
Cattaraugus Co Mem & Mus	Cat	49	C3
Champlain Canal Lock 4	Rns	45	E1
Chateaugay High Falls Pk	Frl	4	E2
Chautauqua Inst	Chu	48	A4
Chemung Co Hist Soc	Chm	53	C5
Cherry Grove Ferry	Sfk	76	F4
Chittenango Falls	Mds	41	B1
Clermont St Hist Site	Clm	59	B5
Conklin House Mus & Huntington Hist Soc	Sfk	76	A2
Connecticut Marine Research Lab	NLn	72	A3
Cornell Plantations	Tmk	54	A1
Corning Glass Ctr	Stu	52	F5
Cradle of Aviation Mus	Nsu	75	E4
Cross Bay Bridge	Que	75	C5
Crown Pt St Hist Site	Ese	13	A6
Culinary Institute of America	Dut	64	A4
Delaware & Hudson Canal Mus	Uls	63	E3
Delaware and Ulster Rail Ride	Dlw	57	E5
Delaware Co Hist Association Mus	Dlw	57	B3
Denison Homestead	NLn	72	A2
Dunkirk Hist Lighthouse & Veterans Mus	Chu	48	B1
Durham Ctr Mus	Grn	58	E2
Dwight D Eisenhower Lock	SL	3	B1
Earlville Opera House	Cng	41	F4
East Hampton Marine Mus	Sfk	78	E1
East Jersey Olde Towne	Mid	74	A6
Eatons Neck Lighthouse	Sfk	76	A1
Edison Natl Hist Site	Esx	74	D3
Eells-Stow House	NHv	69	F4
Eisenhower Mem Pk Mus	Nsu	75	F4
Eleanor Roosevelt Natl Hist Site-Val-Kill	Dut	64	B3
Electronics Communication Mus	Otr	38	A2
Ellis Is Ferry	NYC	74	F4
Empire Expo Ctr	Ono	27	C6
Empire St Plaza	Alb	45	C5
Erie Canal Lock 6	Srg	45	D3
Erie Canal Village	Ond	28	F4
Erie Co Fairground	Ere	35	C4
Erpf Catskill Cultural Ctr	Dlw	57	E5
Erwin Indian Heritage Mus	Stu	52	E5
Ethan Allen Homestead	Chi	6	D6
Falaise-Guggenheim Estate	Nsu	75	D2
Fenimore House	Ots	43	A4
Fenton Hist Ctr	Chu	48	C5
Fire Is Pines Ferry	Sfk	76	F4
Fly Cr Cider Mill	Ots	43	A4
Fort Crailo	Rns	45	C5
Fort George Natl Hist Pk	Ont	21	E4
Fort Hancock	Mom	78	F6
Fort Henry	Ont	7	A3
Fort Ontario St Hist Site	Osw	26	F1
Fort Stanwix Natl Monument	Ond	29	A4
Fort Ticonderoga	Ese	20	B2
Fort Wellington	Ont	1	F4
Fort William Henry	Wrr	32	D2
Frederic Remington Art Mus	SL	2	A4
Frelinghuysen Arboretum	Mrr	74	A3
Frontier Town	Ese	19	D1
Fulton Co Mus	Flt	31	C6
Ganondagan St Hist Site	Otr	38	A1
General Grant Natl Mem	NYC	75	A3
General McCullough Mansion	Ben	46	C1
Genesee Country Village & Mus	Mro	37	A1
Geographic Ctr of New York St	Mds	41	E1
George Washington Bridge	NYC	75	A2
Giffard Cider Mill	Slv	62	A3
Gingerbread House	Ssx	66	E5
Glenn H Curtis Mus	Stu	52	C2
Glimmerglass Opera	Ots	43	A3
Goethals Bridge	Rmd	74	D5
Goshen Hist Track & Harness Racing Hall of Fame	Orn	67	C2
Grandma Moses Grave	Rns	46	B2
Graves Pt Mus & Preserve	Nsu	75	E2
Great Falls & Natl Landmark District	Pas	74	D2
Gregory Mus	Nsu	75	F3
Greig Farm	Dut	59	B6
Greyton H Taylor Wine Mus	Stu	52	D1
Grover Cleveland Birthplace	Esx	74	C2
Guil Hall	Sfk	78	D1
Guilderland St Training Station	Alb	45	A4
Guy Pk	Mgy	44	D1
H Lee White Marine Mus	Osw	26	F1
Hamilton Fish Jr Mem Bridge	Dut	64	A6
Hamilton Fish Jr Mem Bridge	Orn	64	A6
Hamilton Grange Natl Mem	NYC	75	A3
Hammond Mus & Oriental Stroll Gardens	Wch	68	F3
Hanford Mills Mus	Dlw	57	B1
Harriet Tubman Home	Cyg	39	E2
Herkimer Diamond Mines	Hrk	30	A5
Herschell Carrousel Factory Mus	Nia	22	B6
High Falls	Ese	12	B2
Holland Tunnel	NYC	74	F4
Home of F D Roosevelt-Natl Hist Site Mus & Library	Dut	64	A3
Home Sweet Home Mus	Sfk	78	D1
House of History	Clm	59	D2
Howe Caverns	Shh	44	A4
Hubbardton Battle Monument & Mus	Rut	20	E4
Hudson River Maritime Mus	Uls	64	A1
Hudson River Mus	Wch	75	B1
Huguenot Mus House	Uls	63	E4
Hunterdon Co Arboretum	Hnt	73	B5
Hyde Collection	Wrr	32	E3
Hyde Hall	Ots	43	B3
Hyde Log Cabin	GIC	6	C4
Ice Caves Mtn	Uls	63	B4
Industrial Monument	Lch	60	C6
Iroquois Indian Mus	Shh	44	B4
Jamestown Audubon Nature Ctr	Chu	48	D6
John Brown Farm	Ese	12	A4
John Burroughs Mem Hist Site	Dlw	57	E3
John Jay Homestead	Wch	68	E3
John Mason Monument	NLn	72	A2
Johnson Mus of Art	Tmk	54	A1
Joseph Smith Home	Wan	25	D6
Kaatskill Kaleidoscope	Uls	58	C6
Keansburg Amusement Pk	Mom	78	E6
Kingston Rhinecliff Bridge	Dut	64	A1
Knox Hdq	Orn	67	F1
Lake Champlain Maritime Mus	Add	13	B4
Lake George Steamboat Company	Wrr	32	D1
Lake Placid Ctr for the Arts	Frl	11	F3
Land of Make Believe	War	73	A2
LeRoy House	Gns	37	A1
Liberty Is	Hud	74	F4
Lincoln Tunnel	NYC	74	F3
Long Is Game Farm	Sfk	77	C2
Long Is Marine Mus	Sfk	76	E4
Lorenzo St Hist Site	Mds	41	B1
Luge Run	Ese	12	A4
Lyndhurst	Wch	68	B6
Madison Barracks	Jfs	14	E1
Manhattan Bridge	NYC	75	A4
Manitoga Nature Ctr	Put	68	A2
Marine Pkwy Bridge	Kng	75	B6
Maritime Aquarium at Norwalk	Ffd	69	B5
Martin Van Buren Natl Hist Site	Clm	59	D2
Massena Hist Ctr & Mus	SL	3	B1
Mather Homestead	Agy	51	A5
Michael Rockefeller Arts Ctr	Chu	48	B1
Mid-Hudson Bridge	Dut	64	A4
Millard Fillmore Log Cabin	Cyg	40	B4
Millard Fillmore Mus	Ere	35	E3
Mills Mem St Pk	Dut	64	B2
Miniature Kingdom	War	73	A3
Minisink Battleground Natl Hist Site	Slv	66	A1
Montauk Pt Lighthouse	Sfk	72	B6
Morgan Horse Farm	Add	13	D6
Museum Village	Orn	67	D2
Museums at Stony Brook	Sfk	76	E2
Mystic Aquarium	NLn	72	A2
Mystic Sea Port	NLn	72	A2
Nannen Arboretum	Cat	49	D3
Nassau Co Mus of Art	Nsu	75	E3
Nassau Vets Mem Coliseum	Nsu	75	E4
National Baseball Hall of Fame & Mus	Ots	43	A4
National Bottle Mus	Srg	45	B1
National Mus of Racing and Hall of Fame	Srg	32	D5
National Soaring Mus	Chm	53	A5
National Soccer Hall of Fame	Ots	56	F1
Natural Bridge Caverns	Jfs	9	A6
Natural Stone Bridge & Caves	Wrr	19	B3
New England Maple Mus	Rut	20	F4
New Jersey Ctr for the Visual Arts	Uni	74	B4
New Jersey Meadowlands Sports Complex	Brg	74	E3
New Paltz Planetarium	Uls	63	F4
New Windsor Cantonment St Hist Site	Orn	67	F1
New York & Lake Erie RR Depot	Cat	49	A1
New York Botanical Garden	Brx	75	B2
New York Mus of Transportation	Mro	24	D6
New York St Capitol	Alb	45	C5
New York St Fairgrounds	Ono	27	C6
Newark St School	Otr	25	F6
Newark St School	Wan	25	F6
Newburgh Beacon Bridge	Dut	64	A6
Newburgh Beacon Bridge	Orn	64	A6
Niagara Falls Convention Ctr	Nia	21	F5
Northport Hist Mus	Sfk	76	B2
Obadiah Smith House	Sfk	76	D2
Olana St Hist Site	Clm	59	C4
Old Bethpage Village Restoration	Nsu	76	A3
Old Fort Erie	Ont	35	A2
Old Fort Niagara	Nia	21	F3
Old Rhinebeck Aerodrome	Dut	64	B1
Old Stone Fort Mus	Shh	44	B4
Old Westbury Gardens	Nsu	75	E3
Olympic Bobsled Run	Ese	12	A4
Olympic Ctr Ice Arenas	Ese	12	A3
Olympic Ski Jump	Ese	12	E3
Olympic Village	Ese	11	E3
Oppenheim Pk & Zoo	Nia	22	A5
Original Woodstock Festival Site	Slv	62	B4
Oriskany Batl	Ond	29	B4
Outerbridge Crossing	Rmd	74	D6
Oysterpond Hist District & Mus	Sfk	71	C5
P & C Stadium	Ono	27	D6
Pakatakan Farmers Market	Dlw	57	D5
Paper Mill Playhouse	Esx	74	B4
Parrish Art Mus	Sfk	78	B2
Peace Bridge	Ere	35	B2
Peace Bridge	Ont	35	B2
Peters Valley Craft Ctr	Ssx	66	B4
Petrified Creatures Mus	Hrk	43	A2
Petrified Sea Gardens	Srg	32	B5
Philipsburg Manor	Wch	68	B5
Point Lookout	Grn	58	E2
Port Alexandria	Ont	7	B4
Port Kent Burlington Ferry	Chi	13	C1
Port Metcalf	Ont	7	D3
Prospect Mtn Scenic Overlook	Wrr	32	C2
Queens-Midtown Tunnel	NYC	75	A3
Queensboro Bridge	NYC	75	A3
Remington Firearms Mus	Hrk	29	F6
Rich Stadium	Ere	35	C3
Richardson Bates House Mus	Osw	26	F1
Rip Van Winkle Bridge	Clm	59	B4
Rip Van Winkle Bridge	Grn	59	B4
Roberson Mus & Science Ctr	Brm	55	A5
Robertson-Kopernik Observatory	Brm	54	E6
Rochester Mus & Science Ctr	Mro	24	F5
Rockefeller Ctr	NYC	75	A3
Rockwell Mus	Stu	52	F5
Ross Pk Zoological Gardens	Brm	55	B6
Royal Lipizzan Stallions of Austria	GIC	6	C3
Royal Mil Coll	Ont	7	A3
Sackets Hbr Batl	Jfs	14	D1
Saddle Rock Grist Mill	Nsu	75	D3
Sag Hbr Whaling Mus	Sfk	71	C6
Sagamore Hill Natl Hist Site	Nsu	75	F2
Sagamore Lodge Natl Hist Site	Hml	17	E3
Saint Annes Shrine	GIC	6	B2
Saint Lawrence-FDR Power Project Visitors Ctr	SL	3	C1
Saint Paul Natl Hist Site	Wch	75	B2
Salamanca Rail Mus	Cat	49	D5
Sandy Hook Lighthouse	Mom	78	F6
Santas Workshop	Ese	12	B2
Saratoga Co Mus	Srg	45	B1
Saratoga Performing Arts Ctr	Srg	32	C6
Schenectady Mus & Planetarium	Sch	45	A3
Schoharie Crossing	Mgy	44	C1
Seabreeze Amusement Pk	Mro	24	F4

NAME	TERR	MAP	GRID
Secret Caverns	Shh	44	B4
Senate House St Hist Site	Uls	63	F1
Seneca Pk Zoo	Mro	24	E4
Seneca-Iroquois Natl Mus	Cat	49	C5
Seven Falls Of Wiscoy	Agy	36	E6
Seward House	Cyg	39	E1
Shaker Mus	Clm	59	F1
Shea Stadium	Que	75	C3
Shelburne Mus	Chi	13	C2
Sheldon Mus	Add	13	D6
Shushan Covered Bridge Mus	Whg	33	B5
Silver Stadium	Mro	24	E4
Six Nations Indian Mus	Frl	11	E1
Skenesborough Mus	Whg	20	B6
Sleepy Hollow Cem & Old Dutch Church	Wch	68	B5
Snell Lock	SL	3	C1
Sonnenberg Gardens	Otr	38	C2
Southampton Hist Mus	Sfk	78	B2
Southeast Mus	Put	68	E2
Southern Vermont Art Ctr	Ben	33	E4
Space Farms Zoo & Mus	Ssx	66	D4
State Agricultural Experiment Station	Otr	38	F2
State Ofc Campus	Alb	45	B4
Staten Is Ferry	NYC	74	F5
Statue Of Liberty Natl Monument	Hud	74	F4
Sterling Hill Mine & Mus	Ssx	66	E6
Sterling Hist Soc	Sfk	71	B5
Steuben Mem	Ond	29	D2
Stonington Lighthouse	NLn	72	B3
Stony Pt Batl	Rck	68	A4
Storm King Art Ctr	Orn	67	E1
Stratford Festival Theater	Ffd	69	E4
Suffolk Co Hist Mus	Sfk	77	D1
Sugar Loaf Village	Orn	67	C3
Sunnyside	Wch	68	B6
Swamp Fight Monument	Ffd	69	C5
Syracuse Burnet Pk Zoo	Ono	27	D6
Tappan Zee Bridge	Wch	68	B6
The Farmers Mus	Ots	43	A4
The Original American Kazoo Co Mus & Factory	Ere	35	B5
Thomas A Edison Mem Tower And Mus	Mid	74	B6
Thomas Lee House	Sfk	71	D3
Thousand Islands Intl Bridge	Jfs	8	A2
Throgs Neck Bridge	Que	75	C3
Timespell	Scy	53	B2
Tioga Gardens	Tio	54	D5
Tioga Transportation Mus	Tio	54	D5
Tomsco Falls Colony	Slv	62	F4
Topping Tavern Mus	Ben	33	D6
Triborough Bridge	NYC	75	A3
Troy Savings Bank Music Hall	Rns	45	D4
Troy-US Lock	Alb	45	D3
Troy-US Lock	Rns	45	D3
Tuthilltown Grist Mill	Uls	63	D4
Ulster Co Court House	Uls	63	F1
UN Hdq	NYC	75	A3
Uncle Sams Grave	Rns	45	E3
Upper Canada Village	Ont	2	F1
US Mil Acad at West Pt Michie Stadium	Orn	68	A2
USGA Natl Hdq Golf House & Mus	Sms	73	E5
Valentown Mus	Otr	25	A6
Van Cortlandt Manor	Wch	68	B4
Vanderbilt Mansion Natl Hist Site	Dut	64	A3
Vanderbilt Planetarium & Mus	Sfk	76	A2
Verkeerder Kill Falls	Uls	63	C4
Vermont St Craft Ctr	Add	13	E6
Vernon Valley Great Gorge Action Pk	Ssx	67	A4
Verrazano Bridge	Kng	74	F5
Victorian Doll Mus	Mro	24	B5
Village Green	Sfk	71	A6
Walt Whitman House	Sfk	76	B3
Walter Elwood Mus	Mgy	44	D1
Walworth Mus/ Casino/Hist Soc	Srg	32	C6
Washburn Mtn Lookout	Clm	59	F5
Washington Hdq Hist Site	Orn	67	F1
Washingtons Hdq-Hasbrouck House	Wch	68	C6
Waterloo Village	Ssx	73	C1
Webbs Candy Factory	Chu	48	A4
Whaling Mus	Sfk	76	A2
Wick House	Mrr	73	F3
Widmark Honey Farms	Uls	63	D4
Wild West City	Ssx	73	D1
William Floyd Estate	Sfk	77	C3
Williamsburg Bridge	NYC	75	A4
Willowwood Arboretum	Mrr	73	D3
Womens Hall of Fame	Sen	39	C1
Womens Rights Natl Hist Pk/Stanton House	Sen	39	C1
World Trade Ctr	NYC	74	F4
Wurtsboro Soaring Planes	Slv	63	A5
Yankee Stadium	Brx	75	B3
Young-Morse Hist Site	Dut	64	A4

Racing Tracks

NAME	TERR	MAP	GRID
Accord Speedway	Uls	63	D3
Airborne Intl Raceway	Cln	5	F5
Apple Valley Speedway	Wan	25	D4
Aqueduct Race Track	Que	75	B4
Batavia Downs	Gns	23	D6
Belmont Pk Race Track	Nsu	75	D4
Bridgehampton Race Circuit	Sfk	78	B1
Buffalo Raceway	Ere	35	C4
Canandaigua Speedway	Otr	38	D2
Cayuga Co Fair Speedway	Cyg	26	F6
Dundee Raceway Pk	Yts	39	A6
Finger Lakes Race Track	Otr	38	B1
Flemington Speedway	Hnt	73	B6
Fonda Speedway	Mgy	44	B1
Goshen Hist Track & Harness Racing Hall of Fame	Orn	67	C2
Island Dragway	War	73	A2
Lancaster Natl Speedway	Ere	35	E1
Lebanon Valley Speedway	Clm	60	A1
Monticello Raceway	Slv	62	D5
Orange Co Fair Speedway	Orn	67	B1
Oswego Speedway	Osw	27	A1
Ransomville Speedway	Nia	22	B3
Riverhead Raceway	Sfk	77	D1
Rolling Wheels Raceway Pk	Cyg	26	F6
Saratoga Harness Raceway	Srg	32	C6
Saratoga Race Course	Srg	32	C6
Vernon Downs	Ond	28	F6
Watkins Glen Intl Race Track	Scy	53	A2
Yonkers Raceway	Wch	75	B2

Scenic Highways & Trails

NAME	TERR	MAP	GRID
Adirondack Northway	Ese	12	E5
Adirondack Northway	Ese	19	C3
Adirondack Tr	Frl	4	C4
Adirondack Tr	Frl	4	C6
Adirondack Tr	Frl	11	A4
Adirondack Tr	Frl	11	B3
Adirondack Tr	Frl	11	C1
Adirondack Tr	Hml	10	F5
Adirondack Tr	Hml	18	A1
Adirondack Tr	Hml	18	B5
Appalachian Tr	Ben	33	F5
Appalachian Tr	Ben	33	F6
Appalachian Tr	Ben	46	E2
Appalachian Tr	Ben	46	E4
Appalachian Tr	Brk	46	E6
Appalachian Tr	Brk	60	A6
Appalachian Tr	Brk	60	D3
Appalachian Tr	Brk	60	E1
Appalachian Tr	Dut	64	D6
Appalachian Tr	Lch	65	A3
Appalachian Tr	Lch	65	B1
Appalachian Tr	Orn	67	B4
Appalachian Tr	Orn	67	E3
Appalachian Tr	Put	68	B2
Appalachian Tr	Ssx	66	D4
Appalachian Tr	Ssx	66	F3
Appalachian Tr	War	66	A6
Barge Canal Rec Way	Mro	24	A4
Barge Canal Rec Way	Nia	22	E4
Barge Canal Rec Way	Orl	23	C4
Barge Canal Recreationway	Alb	45	C3
Bear Mtn Beacon Hwy	Put	68	A1
Black River Tr	Lew	9	B6
Black River Tr	Lew	16	B2
Black River Tr	Lew	16	B4
Black River Tr	Ond	29	A3
Black River Tr	Ond	29	B2
Black River Tr	SL	2	A5
Black River Tr	SL	9	A2
Black River Tr	SL	9	B4
Central Adirondack Tr	Hml	17	C4
Central Adirondack Tr	Hml	18	A2
Central Adirondack Tr	Hml	18	D3
Central Adirondack Tr	Ond	16	E6
Central Adirondack Tr	Ond	29	B4
Central Adirondack Tr	Ond	29	D1
Central Adirondack Tr	Wrr	19	A5
Central Adirondack Tr	Wrr	32	D1
Champlain Tr	Cln	6	A2
Champlain Tr	Cln	6	A5
Champlain Tr	Ese	13	A2
Champlain Tr	Ese	13	A4
Champlain Tr	Whg	20	A5
Champlain Tr	Whg	32	F3
Champlain Tr	Whg	33	A2
Dude Ranch Tr	Wrr	32	B1
Dude Ranch Tr	Wrr	32	B3
Erie Canal Tr	Mds	28	B6
Erie Canal Tr	Ond	28	E4
Finger Lakes Tr	Agy	37	A6
Finger Lakes Tr	Agy	51	C1
Finger Lakes Tr	Cat	49	C6
Finger Lakes Tr	Cat	49	D4
Finger Lakes Tr	Cat	50	B2
Finger Lakes Tr	Lvg	37	A6
Finger Lakes Tr	Stu	51	E2
Finger Lakes Tr	Stu	52	A3
Finger Lakes Tr	Wyo	36	F6
Garden St Pkwy	Brg	67	F6
Garden St Pkwy	Esx	74	D3
Garden St Pkwy	Mid	74	C5
Garden St Pkwy	Mid	78	C6
Garden St Pkwy	Mom	78	C6
Garden St Pkwy	Rck	67	F6
Greenville Tour	Grn	59	A2
I 87	Wrr	19	D6
I 88	Ots	43	B6
I 88	Sch	44	D4
I 88	Shh	43	F5
Jewett Tour	Grn	58	C3
Lake George-Lake Placid Tr	Ese	12	C4
Lake George-Lake Placid Tr	Ese	12	F5
Lake George-Lake Placid Tr	Ese	20	A1
Lake George-Lake Placid Tr	Whg	32	F4
Lake George-Lake Placid Tr	Wrr	19	E5
Lake George-Lake Placid Tr	Wrr	32	D1
Lake Ontario St Pkwy	Mro	24	A2
Lake Rd	Mro	25	A4
Lake Rd	Nia	22	D2
Lake Shore Rd	Ere	34	F4
Lake Shore Rd	Ere	35	A4
LaSalle Arterial	Nia	22	A6
Lincoln Pond Rd	Ese	12	F4
Long Path	Grn	58	F3
Long Path	Orn	67	D1
Long Path	Uls	58	C6
Long Path	Uls	63	B1
Long Path	Uls	63	B5
Military Tr	Cln	5	A1
Military Tr	Cln	5	D1
Military Tr	Cln	6	A1
Military Tr	Frl	3	D1
Military Tr	Frl	4	A1
Military Tr	Frl	4	D2
Military Tr	SL	3	B2
New York St Thruway	Chu	47	D3
New York St Thruway	Chu	48	B1
North Country Natl Finger Lakes Tr	Cng	55	D1
North Country Natl Finger Lakes Tr	Cng	56	A3
North Country Natl Finger Lakes Tr	Crt	41	A5
North Country Natl Finger Lakes Tr	Scy	53	C2
North Country Natl Finger Lakes Tr	Stu	52	E3
North Country Natl Finger Lakes Tr	Tmk	54	A3
Northern Foothills Tour	Grn	58	D2
Northern Mtn Tour	Grn	58	B3
Northville Lake Placid Tr	Hml	11	B6
Northville Lake Placid Tr	Hml	17	E6
Northville Lake Placid Tr	Hml	18	A4
Northville Lake Placid Tr	Hml	30	F1
Notch Tour	Grn	58	B5
NY 5	Chu	34	C6
NY 5	Ere	35	B2
NY 5	Hrk	29	F6
NY 5	Ond	29	D5
NY 9N	Cln	12	F1
NY 9N	Ese	12	D2
NY 12	Cng	41	F5
NY 12	Cng	42	A5
NY 12	Mds	42	A3
NY 12	Ond	29	C6
NY 12	Ond	42	C1
NY 28	Ond	29	D3
NY 28	Ots	43	A5
NY 49	Ond	29	D5
NY 73	Ese	12	C4
NY 80	Ots	43	B3
NY 97	Slv	66	A1
NY 266	Ere	35	A1
NY 418	Wrr	32	C1
Olympic Tr	Ese	12	B2
Olympic Tr	Frl	11	B4
Olympic Tr	Jfs	8	E6
Olympic Tr	Jfs	14	F1
Olympic Tr	Jfs	15	B1
Olympic Tr	Lew	9	A6
Olympic Tr	SL	9	E4
Olympic Tr	SL	10	B4
Olympic Tr	SL	10	D3
Prospect Mountain St Hwy	Wrr	32	C1
Revolutionary Tr	Alb	45	B3
Revolutionary Tr	Hrk	30	A6
Revolutionary Tr	Mgy	43	E1
Revolutionary Tr	Mgy	44	A1
Revolutionary Tr	Ond	28	E3
Revolutionary Tr	Ond	29	A4
Revolutionary Tr	Osw	14	E6
Revolutionary Tr	Osw	28	B1
Revolutionary Tr	Sch	44	F2
River Tour	Grn	59	B1
River Tour	Grn	59	B4
Robert Moses Pkwy	Nia	21	F4
Robert Moses Pkwy	Nia	21	F6
Roosevelt-Marcy Mem Hwy Tr	Hml	18	C1
Roosevelt-Marcy Mem Hwy Tr	Wrr	19	A4
Seaway Tr	Chu	34	C6
Seaway Tr	Chu	34	F5
Seaway Tr	Chu	47	E3
Seaway Tr	Chu	48	A2
Seaway Tr	Cyg	26	D4
Seaway Tr	Ere	35	A5
Seaway Tr	Ere	35	B4
Seaway Tr	Jfs	7	D3
Seaway Tr	Jfs	7	E5
Seaway Tr	Jfs	8	B2
Seaway Tr	Jfs	14	D2
Seaway Tr	Mro	24	A3
Seaway Tr	Nia	21	F4
Seaway Tr	Nia	22	B3
Seaway Tr	Nia	22	D2
Seaway Tr	Nia	23	A2
Seaway Tr	Orl	23	B2
Seaway Tr	Orl	23	E3
Seaway Tr	Osw	14	C6
Seaway Tr	Osw	14	D6
Seaway Tr	Osw	14	E5
Seaway Tr	Osw	26	E2
Seaway Tr	Osw	27	B1
Seaway Tr	SL	1	D6
Seaway Tr	SL	1	E5
Seaway Tr	SL	2	B4
Seaway Tr	SL	2	E2
Seaway Tr	SL	3	A1
Seaway Tr	SL	3	B1
Seaway Tr	Wan	25	E3
Seaway Tr	Wan	26	B4
Southern Foothills Tour	Grn	58	F3
Southern Tier Expwy	Cat	49	A5
Southern Tier Expwy	Chu	48	D5
State Hwy Tour	Grn	58	B3
State Hwy Tour	Grn	58	C4
State Hwy Tour	Grn	58	D3
Stony Clove Tour	Grn	58	C5
Taconic St Pkwy	Put	68	C2
US 9	Ese	12	D5
US 9	Put	68	B1
US 9W	Brg	75	A1
US 9W	Orn	67	F1
US 9W	Orn	68	A2

Ski Areas

NAME	TERR	MAP	GRID
Belleayre Mtn	Uls	57	F5
Big Tupper	Frl	11	A4
Bobcat	Dlw	57	D4
Bousquet	Brk	60	C2
Brantling Ski Slopes	Wan	25	F4
Bristol Mtn	Otr	38	A4
Brodie	Brk	46	C5
Butternut Basin	Brk	60	B4
Campgaw Mtn Co Resv	Brg	67	D6
Catamount	Brk	60	A5
Catamount	Clm	60	A5
Cochran	Chi	13	F2
Cockaigne	Chu	48	D3
Concord Resort	Slv	62	E5
Cortina Valley	Grn	58	E4
Craigmeur	Mrr	67	A6
Dry Hill	Jfs	15	B1
East Mtn St Forest	Brk	60	C4
Four Seasons	Ono	28	A6
Frost Ridge	Gns	24	A6
Gore Mtn	Wrr	18	F4
Greek Peak Ski Resort	Crt	40	E6
Hickory	Wrr	32	C1
Hidden Valley	Ssx	67	A4
Holiday Mtn	Slv	62	E5
Holiday Valley	Cat	49	D3
Hunter Mtn	Grn	58	D4
Jiminy Peak	Brk	46	C6
Kissing Bridge	Ere	35	E6
Kutshers CC	Slv	62	D5
Labrador Mtn	Crt	40	F4
Maple Ski Ridge	Alb	44	E5
McCauley Mtn	Hrk	17	A4
Mount Peter	Orn	67	C4
Mount Pisgah	Ese	11	E2
Mount Tone Ski Resort	Wyn	61	C2
Northampton Pk	Mro	24	B4
Oak Mtn	Hml	18	B6
Orange Co	Orn	67	C1
Otis Ridge	Brk	60	E4
Peek n Peak	Chu	47	D6
Pines Ski Area	Slv	62	E4
Plattekill Mtn Ski	Dlw	57	E3
Powder Mill Ski Slopes	Mro	25	A6
Prospect Mtn	Ben	46	F2
Ridin-Hy	Wrr	19	D5
Rocking Horse	Uls	64	A4
Royal Mtn	Flt	30	F5
Sawkill Family Ski Ctr	Uls	63	E2
Scotch Valley	Shh	57	E1
Shu-Maker Mtn	Hrk	43	B1
Ski Tamarack	Ere	35	D4
Ski Windham	Grn	58	C3
Snow Ridge	Lew	16	A5
Song Mtn	Crt	40	D3
Sterling Forest	Orn	67	D4
Swain	Agy	51	B1
Thunder Ridge	Put	64	F6
Titus Mtn	Frl	4	D3
Toggenburg	Ono	41	A3
Val Bialas	Ond	29	D5
Vernon Valley/Great Gorge	Ssx	66	F4
Villa Roma	Slv	62	A3
West Mtn	Wrr	32	D3
Whiteface Mtn	Ese	12	B2
Willard Mtn	Whg	32	F6
Woods Valley	Ond	29	B3

Towns & Townships

NAME	TERR	MAP	GRID
Adams	Jfs	14	F2
Adams	Jfs	15	A2
Addison	Add	13	B6
Addison	Stu	52	C5
Afton	Cng	55	F4
Afton	Cng	56	A4
Alabama	Gns	23	B6
Albion	Orl	23	D4
Albion	Osw	14	F6
Albion	Osw	15	A6
Albion	Osw	27	F1
Albion	Osw	28	A1
Alburg	GIC	6	C1
Alburg	GIC	7	D6
Alden	Ere	35	F1
Alden	Ere	36	A2
Alexander	Gns	36	D2
Alexandria	Hnt	73	A5
Alexandria	Jfs	8	B3
Alford	Brk	60	A3
Alfred	Agy	51	C4
Allamuchy	War	73	B1
Allegany	Cat	49	F6
Allegany	Cat	50	A5
Allen	Agy	50	F2
Alma	Agy	50	F6
Almond	Agy	51	C2
Altamont	Frl	10	F3
Altamont	Frl	11	A3
Altona	Cln	5	E2
Amboy	Osw	28	A2
Amenia	Dut	64	F2
Amherst	Ere	22	D6
Amherst	Ere	35	D1
Amity	Agy	50	F4
Amsterdam	Mgy	44	D1
Ancram	Clm	59	E6
Ancram	Clm	64	E1
Andes	Dlw	57	C5
Andover	Agy	51	C5
Andover	Ssx	66	D6
Angelica	Agy	50	F3
Annsville	Ond	28	E2
Ansonia	NHv	69	F1
Antwerp	Jfs	8	E4
Antwerp	Jfs	9	A4
Ararat	Sqh	61	A3
Arcade	Wyo	36	B6
Arcadia	Wan	25	E5
Argyle	Whg	33	A4
Arietta	Hml	17	F5
Arietta	Hml	18	A2
Arietta	Hml	30	E3
Arietta	Hml	31	A3
Arkwright	Chu	48	C1
Arlington	Ben	33	D6
Ashford	Cat	35	E6
Ashford	Cat	49	E1
Ashland	Chm	53	C6
Ashland	Grn	58	B3
Athens	Grn	59	A3
Attica	Wyo	36	D2
Augusta	Ond	29	A6
Augusta	Ond	41	F1
Augusta	Ond	42	A1
Aurelius	Cyg	39	D1
Aurora	Ere	35	E4
Ausable	Cln	5	F6
Ausable	Cln	6	B6
Ausable	Cln	12	E1
Austerlitz	Clm	60	A2
Austerlitz	Grn	59	F3
Ava	Ond	29	A1
Avoca	Stu	51	F2
Avoca	Stu	52	A2
Avon	Lvg	37	C2
Babylon	Sfk	76	B4
Bainbridge	Cng	55	F3
Bainbridge	Cng	56	A3
Baldwin	Chm	53	D6
Ballston	Srg	45	B1
Bangor	Frl	4	A3
Barker	Brm	55	B3

NAME	TERR	MAP	GRID
Barkhamsted	Lch	65	F2
Barre	Orl	23	D4
Barrington	Yts	38	F6
Barrington	Yts	52	F1
Barton	Tio	53	F5
Barton	Tio	54	A6
Batavia	Gns	23	D6
Batavia	Gns	36	D1
Bath	Stu	52	B3
Beacon Falls	NHv	69	F1
Becket	Brk	60	E3
Bedford	Wch	68	D4
Bedminster	Sms	73	D4
Beekman	Dut	64	D5
Beekmantown	Cln	5	E3
Beekmantown	Cln	6	A3
Belfast	Agy	50	E3
Bellmont	Frl	4	E3
Bellmont	Frl	5	A5
Bennington	Ben	46	C2
Bennington	Wyo	36	A2
Benson	Hml	31	B3
Benson	Rut	20	C4
Benton	Yts	38	F4
Benton	Yts	39	A4
Bergen	Gns	23	F5
Bergen	Gns	24	A5
Berkeley Heights	Uni	74	A4
Berkshire	Tio	54	C4
Berlin	Rns	46	B4
Berlin	Wyn	61	D6
Bernards	Sms	73	F5
Berne	Alb	44	E5
Bethany	Gns	36	E2
Bethany	NHv	69	F1
Bethany	NHv	70	A2
Bethel	Ffd	69	B2
Bethel	Slv	62	B4
Bethlehem	Alb	45	B6
Bethlehem	Hnt	73	A4
Bethlehem	Lch	65	D5
Big Flats	Chm	53	A4
Binghampton	Brm	55	A6
Birdsall	Agy	51	B2
Black Brook	Cln	5	C6
Black Brook	Cln	12	D1
Blairstown	War	66	A6
Blairstown	War	73	A1
Blandford	Hmp	60	F4
Bleecker	Flt	31	B4
Blenheim	Shh	43	F6
Blenheim	Shh	44	A6
Blenheim	Shh	57	F1
Blenheim	Shh	58	A1
Block Island	Wgn	72	E4
Blooming Grove	Orn	67	D2
Bolivar	Agy	50	E6
Bolton	Wrr	19	D6
Bolton	Wrr	32	D1
Bombay	Frl	3	E2
Boonton	Mrr	74	A1
Boonville	Ond	16	C6
Boonville	Ond	29	C1
Boston	Ere	35	C5
Bovina	Dlw	57	D3
Boylston	Osw	15	A5
Bradford	Stu	52	E3
Branchburg	Sms	73	D6
Brandon	Frl	4	B4
Brandon	Rut	20	E3
Branford	NHv	70	C3
Brant	Ere	34	F6
Brant	Ere	35	A6
Brasher	SL	3	D2
Bridgewater	Lch	65	B6
Bridgewater	Lch	69	B1
Bridgewater	Ond	42	C2
Bridgewater	Sms	73	E5
Bridport	Add	13	C6
Bridport	Add	20	C1
Brighton	Frl	4	C6
Brighton	Frl	11	D1
Brighton	Mro	24	E5
Bristol	Add	13	F5
Bristol	Otr	38	A3
Broadalbin	Flt	31	D6
Brookfield	Ffd	65	B6
Brookfield	Ffd	69	B1
Brookfield	Mds	42	B3
Brookhaven	Sfk	76	E2
Brookhaven	Sfk	77	B2
Broome	Shh	44	C6
Broome	Shh	58	C1
Brownville	Jfs	7	E5
Brownville	Jfs	8	A6
Brownville	Jfs	14	D1
Brunswick	Rns	45	E3
Brutus	Cyg	26	F6
Buckingham	Wyn	61	C2
Burke	Frl	4	D1
Burlington	Htf	65	F4
Burlington	Ots	42	E4
Burns	Agy	51	C1
Busti	Chu	48	C6
Butler	Wan	26	C4
Butternuts	Ots	42	B6
Butternuts	Ots	56	B1
Byram	Ssx	73	D1
Byron	Gns	23	E5
Cairo	Grn	58	F3
Caledonia	Lvg	37	C1
Callicoon	Slv	61	F3
Callicoon	Slv	62	A2
Cambria	Nia	22	B4
Cambridge	Whg	33	A6
Cambridge	Whg	45	F1
Cambridge	Whg	46	A1
Camden	Ond	28	C2
Cameron	Stu	52	B4
Camillus	Ono	27	C6
Campbell	Stu	52	D4
Canaan	Clm	59	F2
Canaan	Clm	60	A2
Canaan	Lch	65	B1
Canaan	Wyn	61	B6
Canadice	Otr	37	F4
Canajoharie	Mgy	43	E2
Canandaigua	Otr	38	B2
Candor	Tio	54	C4
Caneadea	Agy	50	E2
Canisteo	Stu	51	F4
Canisteo	Stu	52	A3
Canton	SL	2	D6
Canton	SL	9	D1
Cape Vincent	Jfs	7	C4
Carbondale	Lak	61	A6
Carlisle	Shh	43	F3
Carlisle	Shh	44	A4
Carlton	Orl	23	D3
Carmel	Put	68	D2
Caroga	Flt	30	F5
Caroga	Flt	31	A4
Caroline	Tmk	54	B2
Carroll	Chu	48	E6
Carrollton	Cat	49	E6
Castile	Wyo	36	F5
Castile	Wyo	37	A4
Castleton	Rut	20	E5
Catherine	Scy	53	C2
Catlin	Chm	53	A3
Cato	Cyg	26	F5
Cato	Cyg	27	A5
Caton	Stu	52	F6
Catskill	Grn	59	A4
Cayuta	Scy	53	D3
Cazenovia	Mds	28	B6
Cazenovia	Mds	41	B2
Cedar Grove	Esx	74	D2
Centerville	Agy	36	C6
Centerville	Agy	50	D1
Champion	Jfs	8	D6
Champion	Jfs	15	D1
Champlain	Cln	5	F1
Champlain	Cln	6	A1
Champlain	Cln	7	A6
Charleston	Mgy	44	C2
Charlestown	Wgn	72	D2
Charlotte	Add	13	D3
Charlotte	Chu	48	C3
Charlton	Srg	45	A1
Chateaugay	Frl	4	F2
Chatham	Clm	59	E1
Chatham	Mrr	74	A4
Chautauqua	Chu	47	F4
Chautauqua	Chu	48	A3
Chazy	Cln	5	F2
Chazy	Cln	6	B2
Cheektowaga	Ere	35	C2
Chemung	Chm	53	E6
Chenango	Brm	55	B4
Cherry Creek	Chu	48	E3
Cherry Ridge	Wyn	61	C6
Cherry Valley	Ots	43	D3
Cheshire	Brk	46	E6
Cheshire	NHv	70	A1
Chester	Mdx	70	F1
Chester	Mdx	71	A2
Chester	Mrr	73	D3
Chester	Orn	67	C3
Chester	Wrr	18	F4
Chester	Wrr	19	B4
Chesterfield	Ese	6	B6
Chesterfield	Ese	12	F1
Chesterfield	Ese	13	A1
Chili	Mro	24	C6
Chittenden	Rut	20	F3
Cicero	Ono	27	F5
Cicero	Ono	28	A5
Cincinnatus	Crt	41	A6
Cincinnatus	Crt	55	A1
Clare	SL	9	F2
Clare	SL	10	A2
Clarence	Ere	22	E6
Clarence	Ere	35	D1
Clarendon	Orl	23	F6
Clarendon	Rut	20	F6
Clarendon	Rut	33	F1
Clark	Uni	74	B5
Clarksburg	Brk	46	E4
Clarkson	Mro	24	A3
Clarkstown	Rck	67	F5
Clarkstown	Rck	68	A5
Clarksville	Agy	50	C5
Claverack	Clm	59	D4
Clay	Ono	27	D6
Clayton	Jfs	7	F3
Clayton	Jfs	8	A5
Clermont	Clm	59	B6
Clifford	Sqh	61	A4
Clifton	SL	9	F4
Clifton	SL	10	A4
Clifton Park	Srg	45	B2
Clinton	Cln	5	B1
Clinton	Dut	64	B2
Clinton	Frl	4	F1
Clinton	Hnt	73	B5
Clinton	Mdx	70	F3
Clinton	Wyn	61	A5
Clymer	Chu	47	F6
Cobleskill	Shh	43	F6
Cobleskill	Shh	44	A4
Cochecton	Slv	61	F4
Cochecton	Slv	62	A4
Coeymans	Alb	45	B6
Coeymans	Alb	59	B1
Cohocton	Stu	37	F6
Cohocton	Stu	38	A6
Cohocton	Stu	51	F1
Cohocton	Stu	52	A1
Colchester	Chi	6	D6
Colchester	Chi	13	D1
Colchester	Dlw	57	A5
Colchester	Dlw	61	F1
Colchester	Dlw	62	A1
Cold Spring	Cat	49	B5
Colden	Ere	35	E5
Colebrook	Lch	60	E6
Colebrook	Lch	65	E1
Colesville	Brm	55	D4
Collins	Ere	35	B6
Collins	Ere	49	B1
Colonie	Alb	45	B3
Colton	SL	3	B6
Colton	SL	10	C2
Columbia	Hrk	42	F1
Columbus	Cng	42	B4
Concord	Ere	35	D6
Concord	Ere	49	C1
Conesus	Lvg	37	E4
Conesville	Shh	58	C2
Conewango	Cat	49	DA4
Conklin	Brm	55	B6
Conquest	Cyg	26	E5
Constable	Frl	4	C1
Constantia	Osw	27	F3
Constantia	Osw	28	A3
Copake	Clm	59	F5
Copake	Clm	60	A5
Corinth	Srg	32	B4
Corning	Stu	52	F5
Cornwall	Add	13	C6
Cornwall	Add	20	D1
Cornwall	Lch	65	B3
Cornwall	Orn	67	E2
Cornwall	Orn	68	A1
Cortlandt	Wch	68	B3
Cortlandville	Crt	40	B6
Coventry	Cng	55	E3
Covert	Sen	39	D6
Covington	Wyo	36	F3
Covington	Wyo	37	A3
Coxsackie	Grn	59	B2
Cranford	Uni	74	C5
Crawford	Orn	63	B6
Croghan	Lew	9	B6
Croghan	Lew	15	F1
Croghan	Lew	16	A1
Crown Point	Ese	13	A5
Crown Point	Ese	19	F1
Crown Point	Ese	20	A1
Cuba	Agy	50	B6
Cuyler	Crt	41	A4
Dalton	Brk	46	E6
Dalton	Brk	60	D1
Damascus	Wyn	61	E4
Danby	Rut	33	F2
Danby	Tmk	53	F3
Danby	Tmk	54	A2
Dannemora	Cln	5	B4
Dansville	Stu	37	E6
Dansville	Stu	51	E1
Danube	Hrk	30	B6
Danube	Hrk	43	C1
Darien	Ffd	68	F6
Darien	Ffd	69	A5
Darien	Gns	36	B1
Davenport	Dlw	43	B6
Davenport	Dlw	57	A1
Day	Srg	31	F3
Day	Srg	32	A3
Dayton	Cat	49	A2
Decatur	Ots	43	D5
Deep River	Mdx	71	A2
Deerfield	Ond	29	D5
Deerpark	Orn	66	D1
DeKalb	SL	9	A1
Delaware	Hnt	73	A6
Delaware	Pke	66	A4
Delaware	Slv	61	F3
Delaware	Slv	62	A3
Delaware Kalb	SL	2	B6
Delaware Peyster	SL	1	F6
Delaware Peyster	SL	2	A6
Delaware Ruyter	Mds	41	B3
Delhi	Dlw	57	B3
Denmark	Lew	15	E2
Denning	Uls	57	F6
Denning	Uls	58	A6
Denning	Uls	62	E1
Denning	Uls	63	A1
Denville	Mrr	73	F2
Denville	Mrr	74	A2
DePeyster	SL	9	A1
Deposit	Dlw	56	B5
Deposit	Dlw	61	C1
Derby	NHv	69	F3
Dewitt	Ono	27	F6
Dewitt	Ono	40	E1
Diana	Lew	8	F5
Diana	Lew	9	B5
Dickinson	Brm	55	A5
Dickinson	Frl	3	F4
Dickinson	Frl	4	A4
Dingman	Pke	66	A3
Dix	Scy	53	B3
Dorset	Ben	33	E3
Dover	Dut	64	F4
Dresden	Whg	19	F5
Dresden	Whg	20	A5
Dryden	Tmk	40	B6
Dryden	Tmk	54	B1
Duane	Frl	4	D5
Duanesburg	Sch	44	D3
Dunkirk	Chu	34	C6
Dunkirk	Chu	48	B1
Dunkirk	Chu	48	C1
Durham	Grn	58	D2
Durham	Mdx	70	D1
Dyberry	Wyn	61	C5
Eagle	Wyo	36	C6
East Bloomfield	Otr	38	A1
East Brunswick	Mid	78	B6
East Fishkill	Dut	64	C6
East Fishkill	Put	68	B1
East Greenbush	Rns	45	E5
East Haddam	Mdx	71	B1
East Hampton	Sfk	71	D6
East Hampton	Sfk	72	A6
East Hampton	Sfk	78	D1
East Hanover	Mrr	74	B2
East Haven	NHv	70	B2
East Lyme	NLn	71	C2
East Otto	Cat	49	C2
East Rochester	Mro	25	A5
Eastchester	Wch	75	C1
Easton	Ffd	69	C4
Easton	Whg	32	F6
Easton	Whg	45	F1
Easton	Whg	46	A1
Eaton	Mds	41	E2
Eden	Ere	35	B5
Edinburg	Srg	31	F4
Edinburg	Srg	32	A4
Edison	Mid	74	B6
Edison	Mid	78	B6
Edmeston	Ots	42	C4
Edwards	SL	9	C3
Egremont	Brk	60	A4
Elba	Gns	23	E5
Elbridge	Ono	27	A6
Elizabethtown	Ese	12	D4
Ellenburg	Cln	5	B3
Ellery	Chu	48	B4
Ellicott	Chu	48	D5
Ellicottville	Cat	49	E3
Ellington	Chu	48	E4
Ellisburg	Jfs	14	E4
Elma	Ere	35	E3
Elmira	Chm	53	C5
Enfield	Tmk	53	E1
Ephratah	Flt	30	F6
Ephratah	Flt	43	F1
Erin	Chm	53	D4
Erwin	Stu	52	E5
Esopus	Uls	63	F3
Esopus	Uls	64	A3
Esperance	Shh	44	B4
Essex	Chi	6	F6
Essex	Chi	13	F1
Essex	Ese	13	A3
Essex	Mdx	71	A2
Evans	Ere	34	E5
Evans	Ere	35	A4
Exeter	Ots	42	E3
Fabius	Ono	40	F3
Fair Haven	Rut	20	C5
Fairfax	Fkl	6	F4
Fairfield	Ffd	69	C4
Fairfield	Fkl	6	F2
Fairfield	Fkl	6	F3
Fairfield	Hrk	30	A5
Fallsburg	Slv	62	E3
Farmersville	Cat	50	A2
Farmington	Otr	25	C6
Farmington	Otr	38	C1
Fayette	Sen	39	B2
Fell	Lak	61	A5
Fenner	Mds	28	C6
Fenner	Mds	41	C1
Fenton	Brm	55	C4
Ferrisburg	Add	13	C4
Fine	SL	9	E5
Fine	SL	10	A5
Fishkill	Dut	64	A6
Fishkill	Put	68	A1
Fleming	Cyg	39	E2
Florence	Ond	28	D1
Florida	Brk	46	F4
Florida	Mgy	44	D2
Floyd	Ond	29	C3
Forestburgh	Orn	66	D1
Forestburgh	Slv	62	D6
Forestport	Ond	16	D6
Forestport	Ond	29	E1
Fort Ann	Whg	19	E6
Fort Ann	Whg	20	A6
Fort Ann	Whg	32	F1
Fort Covington	Frl	3	F1
Fort Covington	Frl	4	A1
Fort Edward	Whg	32	F4
Fowler	SL	9	A3
Frankford	Ssx	66	C5
Frankfort	Hrk	29	D6
Frankfort	Hrk	42	E1
Franklin	Dlw	56	E3
Franklin	Frl	4	F5
Franklin	Frl	5	A5
Franklin	Frl	11	E1
Franklin	Frl	12	A1
Franklin	Hnt	73	A6
Franklin	Sms	73	F6
Franklin	Sos	78	A6
Franklinville	Cat	49	F3
Franklinville	Cat	50	A3
Fredon	Ssx	66	C6
Freedom	Cat	36	B6
Freedom	Cat	50	B1
Freetown	Crt	40	F6
Freetown	Crt	54	F1
Frelinghuysen	War	73	A1
Fremont	Slv	61	E2
Fremont	Slv	62	A2
Fremont	Stu	51	E2
French Creek	Chu	47	D6
Friendship	Agy	50	E4
Fulton	Shh	43	F6
Fulton	Shh	44	A6
Gaines	Orl	23	D3
Gainesville	Wyo	36	D4
Galen	Wan	26	B5
Gallatin	Clm	59	D6
Galway	Srg	31	E6
Galway	Srg	32	A6
Galway	Srg	44	F1
Gardiner	Uls	63	E4
Garwood	Uni	74	C5
Gates	Mro	24	D4
Geddes	Ono	27	D6
Genesee	Agy	50	C6
Genesee Falls	Wyo	36	F6
Geneseo	Lvg	37	C3
Geneva	Otr	39	A3
Genoa	Cyg	39	E5
Genoa	Cyg	40	A5
Georgetown	Mds	41	C3
Georgia	Fkl	6	E4
German	Cng	41	B6
German	Cng	55	B1
German Flatts	Hrk	29	E6
German Flatts	Hrk	30	A6
German Flatts	Hrk	43	A1
Germantown	Clm	59	B5
Gerry	Chu	48	D4
Ghent	Clm	59	E3
Gilboa	Shh	57	F1
Gilboa	Shh	58	B1
Glastenbury	Ben	33	E6
Glastenbury	Ben	46	F1
Glen	Mgy	44	B2
Glenville	Sch	44	F2
Gorham	Otr	38	D3
Goshen	Add	20	F2
Goshen	Lch	65	D2
Goshen	Orn	67	B2
Gouverneur	SL	8	F2
Gouverneur	SL	9	A2
Grafton	Rns	45	F4
Grafton	Rns	46	A3
Granby	Osw	27	A3
Grand Island	Ere	21	F6
Grand Island	Ere	22	A6
Grand Island	Ere	35	A1
Grand Isle	GIC	6	C4
Granger	Agy	36	F6
Granger	Agy	37	A6
Granger	Agy	50	F1
Granville	Whg	33	B2
Great Barrington	Brk	60	B4
Great Valley	Cat	49	E4
Greece	Mro	24	D4
Green	Ssx	73	C1
Green Island	Alb	45	D3
Greenbrook	Sms	74	A5
Greenburgh	Wch	68	B6
Greene	Cng	55	D3
Greene	Eri	47	A6
Greenfield	Eri	47	C5
Greenfield	Srg	32	A5
Greenport	Clm	59	C4
Greensburgh	Wch	75	B1
Greenville	Grn	58	F2
Greenville	Orn	66	E2
Greenwich	Ffd	68	E6
Greenwich	Ffd	75	E1
Greenwich	Whg	33	A5
Greenwood	Stu	51	D4
Greig	Lew	16	C4
Groton	NLn	71	F2
Groton	NLn	72	A2
Groton	Tmk	40	B5
Grove	Agy	37	A6
Grove	Agy	51	B1
Groveland	Lvg	37	C4
Guilderland	Alb	45	A4
Guilford	Cng	55	F2
Guilford	Cng	56	A1
Guilford	NHv	70	D2
Haddam	Mdx	70	E1
Haddam	Mdx	71	A1
Hadley	Srg	32	B2
Hague	Wrr	19	F4
Hague	Wrr	20	A3
Halcott	Grn	57	F4
Halcott	Grn	58	A4
Halfmoon	Srg	45	D2
Hamburg	Ere	35	B4
Hamden	Dlw	56	F4
Hamden	Dlw	57	A4
Hamden	NHv	70	A1
Hamilton	Mds	41	F3
Hamilton	Mds	42	A3
Hamlin	Mro	24	B3
Hammond	SL	1	D6
Hammond	SL	8	D1
Hampton	Ssx	66	C5
Hampton	Whg	20	C6
Hampton	Whg	33	C1
Hamptonburgh	Orn	67	C1
Hancock	Brk	46	C5
Hancock	Brk	60	B1
Hancock	Dlw	56	D6
Hancock	Dlw	61	E1
Hannibal	Ssw	26	F3
Hanover	Chu	34	E6
Hanover	Chu	48	E1
Hanover	Ere	35	A6
Hanover	Mrr	74	A3
Harbor Creek	Eri	47	A5
Hardenburg	Uls	62	E1
Hardenburgh	Uls	57	E6
Hardenburgh	Uls	58	A5
Harding	Mrr	73	F4
Harding	Mrr	74	A3
Hardwick	War	66	A6
Hardwick	War	73	A1
Hardystown	Ssx	66	F6
Harmony	Chu	47	F6
Harmony	Chu	48	A6
Harmony	Sqh	61	A1
Harpersfield	Dlw	57	D1

NAME	TERR	MAP	GRID
Harpersvield	Dlw	43	D6
Harrietstown	Frl	11	D4
Harrisburg	Lew	15	E3
Harrison	Wch	68	D6
Harrison	Wch	75	D1
Hartford	Crt	54	D1
Hartford	Whg	33	A2
Hartland	Htf	65	F1
Hartland	Nia	22	F3
Hartland	Nia	23	A3
Hartsville	Stu	51	D4
Hartwick	Ots	42	F5
Harwinton	Lch	65	E3
Hastings	Osw	27	D3
Haverstraw	Rck	67	E4
Haverstraw	Rck	68	A4
Hazlet	Mom	78	D6
Hebron	Whg	33	C3
Hector	Scy	39	C6
Hector	Scy	53	C1
Hempstead	Nsu	75	E4
Hempstead	Sfk	76	A5
Henderson	Jfs	14	E2
Henrietta	Mro	24	E6
Herkimer	Hrk	29	F5
Herkimer	Hrk	30	A6
Hermon	SL	9	C2
Herrick	Sqh	61	A3
Highgate	Fkl	6	F1
Highgate	Fkl	7	F6
Highland	Slv	62	B6
Highland	Slv	66	A1
Highlands	Orn	67	F2
Highlands	Orn	68	A2
Hillsborough	Sms	73	D6
Hillsdale	Clm	59	F4
Hillsdale	Clm	60	A4
Hillside	Uni	74	D4
Hinesburg	Add	13	E3
Hinsdale	Brk	60	E1
Hinsdale	Cat	50	B5
Holland	Ere	35	F5
Holland	Ere	36	A5
Homer	Crt	40	E5
Hoosick	Rns	46	B2
Hope	Hml	31	D3
Hope	War	73	A2
Hopewell	Otr	38	D1
Hopkinton	SL	3	D5
Hopkinton	SL	10	E1
Hopkinton	Wgn	72	C1
Horicon	Wrr	19	D4
Hornby	Stu	52	F3
Hornellsville	Stu	51	D3
Horseheads	Chm	53	C5
Hounsfield	Jfs	7	E5
Hounsfield	Jfs	14	F1
Howard	Stu	51	F3
Howard	Stu	52	A3
Hubbardton	Rut	20	D4
Hume	Agy	36	F6
Hume	Agy	50	E1
Humphrey	Cat	49	F4
Humphrey	Cat	50	A4
Hunter	Grn	58	E4
Huntington	Chi	13	F2
Huntington	Sfk	76	B2
Hurley	Uls	58	D6
Hurley	Uls	63	E1
Huron	Wan	26	B4
Hyde Park	Dut	64	B3
Independence	Agy	51	C6
Independence	War	73	B2
Indian Lake	Hml	17	F3
Indian Lake	Hml	18	B4
Inlet	Hml	17	D4
Ira	Cyg	26	F4
Ira	Cyg	27	A4
Ira	Rut	20	E6
Ira	Rut	33	F1
Irondequoit	Mro	24	E4
Ischua	Cat	50	B4
Isle La Motte	GIC	6	B2
Islip	Sfk	76	D3
Italy	Yts	38	C5
Ithaca	Tmk	53	F1
Ithaca	Tmk	54	A1
Jackson	Whg	33	A5
Jasper	Stu	51	F5
Jasper	Stu	52	A5
Java	Wyo	36	B5
Jay	Ese	12	D2
Jefferson	Lak	61	A6
Jefferson	Mrr	66	F6
Jefferson	Mrr	67	A6
Jefferson	Mrr	73	F1
Jefferson	Shh	43	E6
Jefferson	Shh	57	E1
Jericho	Chi	6	F6
Jericho	Chi	13	F1
Jerusalem	Yts	38	D5
Jerusalem	Yts	52	E1
Jewett	Grn	58	E3
Johnsburg	Wrr	18	F5
Johnsburg	Wrr	19	A5
Johnstown	Flt	31	A6
Johnstown	Flt	44	A1
Junius	Sen	26	B6
Junius	Sen	39	B1
Keene	Ese	12	C4
Kendall	Orl	23	F2
Kent	Lch	65	A4
Kent	Put	64	D6
Kent	Put	68	D1
Kiantone	Chu	48	D6
Killingworth	Mdx	70	E2
Kinderhook	Clm	59	D1
Kingsbury	Whg	32	F6
Kingston	Uls	58	F6
Kingston	Uls	63	F1
Kingwood	Hnt	73	A6
Kirkland	Ond	29	A6
Kirkland	Ond	42	A1
Kirkwood	Brm	55	C5
Knox	Alb	44	E4
Kortright	Dlw	57	C2
La Grange	Dut	64	B4
Lackawaxen	Pke	61	E6
Lackawaxen	Pke	62	A6
Lafayette	Ono	40	E2
Lafayette	Ssx	66	D5
Lake George	Wrr	32	D2
Lake Luzerne	Wrr	32	C3
Lake Pleasant	Hml	17	F4
Lake Pleasant	Hml	18	A5
Lake Pleasant	Hml	31	B1
Lancaster	Ere	35	E1
Lanesborough	Brk	46	C6
Lanesborough	Brk	60	D1
Lansing	Tmk	39	F5
Lansing	Tmk	40	A6
Lansing	Tmk	53	F1
Lansing	Tmk	54	A1
Lapeer	Crt	54	E1
Laurens	Ots	42	E6
Laurens	Ots	56	F1
Lawrence	SL	3	D4
Le Ray	Jfs	8	C6
Le Ray	Jfs	15	B1
Le Roy	Gns	23	F6
Le Roy	Gns	24	A6
Le Roy	Gns	36	F1
Le Roy	Gns	37	A1
Lebanon	Hnt	73	B4
Lebanon	Mds	41	E3
Lebanon	Wyn	61	D4
Ledyard	Cyg	39	E4
Ledyard	NLn	71	F1
Ledyard	NLn	72	A1
Lee	Brk	60	D3
Lee	Ond	28	F3
Lee	Ond	29	A2
Lehman	Pke	66	A4
Leicester	Add	20	E2
Leicester	Lvg	37	A3
Lenox	Brk	60	C2
Lenox	Mds	28	C5
Leon	Cat	48	F3
Lewis	Ese	12	E3
Lewis	Ese	13	A3
Lewis	Lew	15	F6
Lewis	Lew	28	F1
Lewis	Lew	29	A1
Lewisboro	Wch	68	E3
Lewiston	Nia	21	F4
Lewiston	Nia	22	A4
Lexington	Grn	58	C4
Leyden	Lew	16	B6
Leyden	Lew	29	A1
Liberty	Slv	62	C2
Liberty	War	73	A2
Lima	Lvg	37	E2
Lincklaen	Cng	41	B4
Lincoln	Add	13	F5
Lincoln	Mds	28	D6
Lindley	Stu	52	E6
Lisbon	SL	2	C4
Lisle	Brm	54	F2
Litchfield	Hrk	29	D6
Litchfield	Hrk	42	D1
Litchfield	Lch	65	D3
Little Falls	Hrk	30	B6
Little Falls	Hrk	43	B1
Little Falls	Pas	74	D2
Little Valley	Cat	49	C4
Livingston	Clm	59	C5
Livingston	Esx	74	B3
Livonia	Lvg	37	E3
Lloyd	Uls	63	F4
Lloyd	Uls	64	A3
Locke	Cyg	40	B5
Lockport	Nia	22	D5
Lodi	Sen	39	C5
Long Hill	Mrr	73	F4
Long Hill	Mrr	74	A4
Long Lake	Hml	10	D6
Long Lake	Hml	11	B5
Long Lake	Hml	17	D2
Long Lake	Hml	18	B1
Lorraine	Jfs	15	A4
Louisville	SL	2	F2
Louisville	SL	3	A2
Lowville	Lew	15	F3
Lowville	Lew	16	A3
Lumberland	Slv	62	B6
Lumberland	Slv	66	B1
Lyme	Jfs	7	E4
Lyme	Jfs	14	C1
Lyme	NLn	71	C1
Lyndon	Cat	50	B3
Lyons	Wan	25	F5
Lyons	Wan	26	A5
Lyonsdale	Lew	16	D5
Lysander	Ono	27	A4
Macedon	Wan	25	C5
Machias	Cat	49	F2
Machias	Cat	50	A2
Macomb	SL	1	F6
Macomb	SL	8	F1
Madison	Mds	41	F2
Madison	Mds	42	A2
Madison	NHv	70	E2
Madrid	SL	2	E3
Maine	Brm	54	F4
Malone	Frl	4	C3
Malta	Srg	32	C6
Malta	Srg	45	C1
Mamakating	Slv	63	A5
Mamaroneck	Wch	75	D1
Manchester	Ben	33	E4
Manchester	Otr	25	D6
Manchester	Otr	38	D1
Manchester	Wyn	61	D2
Manheim	Hrk	30	B5
Manlius	Ono	27	F5
Manlius	Ono	28	A6
Manlius	Ono	41	A1
Mansfield	Cat	49	B3
Mansfield	War	73	A3
Maplewood	Esx	74	C4
Marathon	Crt	54	F1
Marbletown	Uls	63	D2
Marcellus	Ono	27	C6
Marcellus	Ono	40	B1
Marcy	Ond	29	C4
Marilla	Ere	35	F2
Marilla	Ere	36	A3
Marion	Wan	25	D4
Marlborough	Uls	63	F5
Marlborough	Uls	64	A5
Marshall	Ond	29	B6
Marshall	Ond	42	B1
Martinsburg	Lew	15	E4
Martinsburg	Lew	16	A4
Maryland	Ots	43	B6
Maryland	Ots	57	B1
Masonville	Dlw	56	B4
Massena	SL	3	B1
Mayfield	Flt	31	C4
McDonough	Cng	41	C6
McDonough	Cng	55	C1
Mendham	Mrr	73	F3
Mendon	Mnr	38	A1
Mendon	Mro	24	F6
Mendon	Mro	37	F1
Mentz	Cyg	26	E6
Meredith	Dlw	57	A2
Mexico	Osw	14	C6
Mexico	Osw	27	D1
Middleburgh	Shh	44	C5
Middlebury	Add	13	E6
Middlebury	Add	20	D1
Middlebury	NHv	65	E6
Middlebury	NHv	69	E1
Middlebury	Wyo	36	E2
Middlefield	Hms	60	F2
Middlefield	Mdx	70	D1
Middlefield	Ots	43	B4
Middlesex	Yts	38	C4
Middletown	Dlw	57	D4
Middletown	Grn	58	A4
Middletown	Mom	78	E6
Middletown Springs	Rut	20	E6
Middletown Springs	Rut	33	D1
Mihwah	Brg	67	D5
Milan	Dut	59	C6
Milan	Dut	64	C1
Milford	Ots	43	A6
Milford	Ots	57	A1
Milford	Pke	66	B2
Mill Creek	Eri	47	A5
Millburn	Esx	74	C4
Milo	Yts	39	A5
Milton	Chi	6	D5
Milton	Srg	32	A6
Milton	Srg	45	A1
Mina	Chu	47	D5
Minden	Mgy	43	D2
Mine Hill	Mrr	73	E2
Minerva	Ese	18	D2
Minerva	Ese	19	A2
Minisink	Orn	66	F3
Mohawk	Mgy	44	B1
Moira	Frl	3	E2
Moira	Frl	4	A3
Monkton	Add	13	E4
Monroe	Ffd	69	C2
Monroe	Fkl	46	F4
Monroe	Orn	67	D3
Montague	Lew	15	D4
Montague	Ssx	66	D3
Monterey	Brk	60	C4
Montezuma	Cyg	26	D6
Montezuma	Cyg	39	D1
Montgomery	Orn	63	C6
Montgomery	Orn	67	D1
Montour	Scy	53	B3
Montville	Mrr	74	B2
Montville	NLn	71	D1
Mooers	Cln	5	E1
Moravia	Cyg	40	A4
Moreau	Srg	32	E4
Morehouse	Hml	17	D6
Morehouse	Hml	30	D1
Moriah	Ese	12	F6
Moriah	Ese	13	A6
Morris	Lch	65	D4
Morris	Mrr	73	F3
Morris	Mrr	74	A3
Morris	Ots	42	C6
Morris	Ots	56	C1
Morristown	SL	1	D6
Morristown	SL	8	E1
Mount Hope	Orn	63	A6
Mount Hope	Orn	66	F1
Mount Kisco	Wch	68	D4
Mount Morris	Lvg	37	B5
Mount Olive	Mrr	73	D2
Mount Pleasant	Wch	68	C5
Mount Pleasant	Wyn	61	B3
Mount Washington	Brk	60	A5
Murray	Orl	23	F3
Nanticoke	Brm	54	F3
Naples	Otr	38	A5
Napoli	Cat	49	B4
Nassau	Rns	45	F6
Nassau	Rns	46	A5
Nassau	Rns	59	E1
Naugatuck	NHv	65	E6
Naugatuck	NHv	69	F1
Nelson	Mds	41	D2
Neversink	Slv	62	E2
New Albion	Cat	49	B3
New Ashford	Brk	46	D5
New Baltimore	Grn	59	B1
New Berlin	Cng	42	A6
New Bremen	Lew	16	B2
New Canaan	Ffd	68	F5
New Canaan	Ffd	69	A5
New Castle	Wch	68	C4
New Fairfield	Ffd	65	A6
New Fairfield	Ffd	68	F1
New Fairfield	Ffd	69	A1
New Hartford	Lch	65	F2
New Hartland	Ond	29	C6
New Haven	Add	13	E5
New Haven	Osw	14	B6
New Haven	Osw	27	C1
New Hudson	Agy	50	D3
New Lebanon	Clm	46	B6
New Lebanon	Clm	59	F1
New Lebanon	Clm	60	A1
New Lisbon	Ots	42	E5
New Marlborough	Brk	60	C5
New Milford	Lch	65	B5
New Paltz	Uls	63	E3
New Scotland	Alb	45	A5
New Windsor	Orn	63	D6
New Windsor	Orn	67	D1
Newark Valley	Tio	54	E4
Newburgh	Orn	63	F6
Newburgh	Orn	64	A6
Newburgh	Orn	67	E1
Newcomb	Ese	11	E6
Newcomb	Ese	12	A6
Newcomb	Ese	18	E1
Newcomb	Ese	19	A1
Newfane	Nia	22	D3
Newfield	Tmk	53	E3
Newport	Hrk	29	F4
Newport	Hrk	30	A4
Newstead	Ere	22	F6
Newstead	Ere	23	A6
Newstead	Ere	35	F1
Newstead	Ere	36	A1
Newtown	Ffd	69	C2
Niagara	Nia	21	F5
Niagara	Nia	22	A5
Nichols	Tio	54	C6
Niles	Cyg	40	A3
Niskayuna	Sch	45	B3
Norfolk	Lch	60	D6
Norfolk	Lch	65	D1
Norfolk	SL	2	F3
Norfolk	SL	3	A3
North Bergen	Brg	74	F3
North Branford	NHv	70	C2
North Brunswick	Mid	78	A6
North Canaan	Lch	60	C6
North Canaan	Lch	65	C1
North Castle	Wch	68	D5
North Collins	Ere	35	B6
North Dansville	Lvg	37	D6
North East	Dut	59	F6
North East	Dut	60	A6
North East	Dut	64	E1
North East	Eri	47	C4
North Elba	Ese	11	E3
North Elba	Ese	12	A3
North Greenbush	Rns	45	E5
North Harmony	Chu	47	F5
North Harmony	Chu	48	A5
North Haven	NHv	70	B2
North Hempstead	Nsu	75	D2
North Hero	GIC	6	C2
North Hudson	Ese	12	C6
North Hudson	Ese	19	C1
North Norwich	Cng	41	F5
North Norwich	Cng	42	A5
North Salem	Wch	68	E3
North Stonington	NLn	72	B1
Northampton	Flt	31	D4
Northumberland	Srg	32	E5
Norway	Hrk	30	A4
Norwich	Cng	41	F6
Norwich	Cng	42	A6
Norwich	Cng	55	F1
Norwich	Cng	56	A1
Nunda	Lvg	37	B6
Oakfield	Gns	23	C5
Ogden	Mro	24	C5
Ohio	Hrk	16	F6
Ohio	Hrk	17	B5
Ohio	Hrk	29	F1
Ohio	Hrk	30	A2
Old Bridge	Mid	78	C6
Old Lyme	NLn	71	C3
Old Saybrook	Mdx	71	B3
Olean	Cat	50	A6
Olive	Uls	58	D6
Olive	Uls	63	C1
Oneonta	Ots	42	F6
Oneonta	Ots	56	F1
Onondaga	Ono	27	C6
Onondaga	Ono	40	D1
Ontario	Wan	25	C4
Oppenheim	Flt	30	D6
Orange	NHv	69	F3
Orange	NHv	70	A3
Orange	Scy	52	F3
Orangetown	Rck	67	F6
Orangetown	Rck	68	A6
Orangeville	Wyo	36	C4
Orchard Park	Ere	35	D3
Oregon	Wyn	61	D5
Orleans	Jfs	7	F2
Orleans	Jfs	8	A4
Orwell	Add	20	C3
Orwell	Osw	14	F5
Orwell	Osw	15	A6
Osceola	Lew	15	D6
Osceola	Lew	28	D1
Ossian	Lvg	37	C6
Ossian	Lvg	51	C1
Ossining	Wch	68	B5
Oswegatchie	SL	1	F5
Oswegatchie	SL	2	A5
Oswego	Osw	26	F2
Otego	Ots	56	D1
Otis	Brk	60	E4
Otisco	Ono	40	D2
Otsego	Ots	43	A4
Otselic	Cng	41	D4
Otto	Cat	49	B2
Ovid	Sen	39	C5
Owasco	Cyg	39	F1
Owasco	Cyg	40	A2
Owego	Tio	54	D6
Oxford	Cng	55	E2
Oxford	NHv	69	E1
Oxford	War	73	A3
Oyster Bay	Nsu	75	E2
Oyster Bay	Sfk	76	A3
Pahaquarry	War	66	A6
Palatine	Mgy	43	E1
Palatine	Mgy	44	A1
Palermo	Osw	27	C2
Palmyra	Wan	25	D5
Palmyra	Wyn	61	D6
Pamela	Jfs	15	B1
Pamelia	Jfs	8	B6
Panton	Add	13	C5
Paris	Ond	29	C6
Paris	Ond	42	C1
Parish	Osw	27	E1
Parish	Osw	28	A1
Parishville	SL	3	B6
Parishville	SL	10	C1
Parma	Mro	24	C3
Parsippany	Mrr	74	A2
Patterson	Put	64	E6
Patterson	Put	68	E1
Pavilion	Gns	36	F1
Pavilion	Gns	37	A1
Pawlet	Rut	33	D2
Pawling	Dut	64	E6
Pelham	Wch	75	C2
Pembroke	Gns	23	A6
Pembroke	Gns	36	B1
Pendleton	Nia	22	D5
Penfield	Mro	25	A4
Pequannock	Mrr	74	C1
Perinton	Mro	25	B5
Perry	Wyo	36	F3
Perry	Wyo	37	A3
Perrysburg	Cat	34	F6
Perrysburg	Cat	48	F1
Persia	Cat	49	A2
Perth	Flt	31	D6
Perth	Flt	44	D1
Peru	Brk	60	F1
Peru	Cln	5	F6
Peru	Cln	6	A5
Petersburg	Rns	46	C3
Pharsalia	Cng	41	D5
Phelps	Otr	25	E6
Phelps	Otr	26	A6
Phelps	Otr	38	F1
Philadelphia	Jfs	8	D5
Philipstown	Put	68	A1
Pickney	Lew	15	C2
Piercefield	SL	10	E3
Pierrepont	SL	2	F6
Pierrepont	SL	3	A6
Pierrepont	SL	9	F1
Pierrepont	SL	10	A1
Pike	Wyo	36	E6
Pine Plains	Dut	59	D6
Pine Plains	Dut	64	D1
Piscataway	Mid	74	A6
Pitcairn	SL	9	C4
Pitcher	Cng	41	B6
Pittsfield	Ots	42	C5
Pittsford	Mro	24	F6
Pittsford	Rut	20	E4
Pittstown	Rns	45	F2
Pittstown	Rns	46	A2
Plainfield	Ots	42	D3
Plattekill	Uls	63	F5
Plattsburgh	Cln	5	E4
Plattsburgh	Cln	6	A5
Pleasant Valley	Dut	64	C3
Plymouth	Cng	41	E5
Plymouth	Lch	65	F5
Poestenkill	Rns	45	F4
Poestenkill	Rns	46	A4
Poland	Chu	48	E5
Pomfret	Chu	48	B2
Pompey	Ono	41	A2
Portage	Lvg	36	F6
Portage	Lvg	37	A6
Porter	Nia	21	F3
Porter	Nia	22	A3
Porter	Pke	66	A3
Portland	Chu	47	F3
Portland	Chu	48	A2
Portville	Cat	50	B6
Potsdam	SL	2	F4
Potsdam	SL	3	A5
Potter	Yts	38	D4
Poughkeepsie	Dut	64	A5
Poultney	Rut	20	D6
Poultney	Rut	33	D1
Pound Ridge	Wch	68	E4
Pownal	Ben	46	D3
Prattsburg	Stu	38	C6
Prattsburg	Stu	52	B1
Prattsville	Grn	58	A2
Preble	Crt	40	E3
Preston	Cng	41	E6

NAME	TERR	MAP	GRID
Preston	Cng	55	E1
Preston	NLn	71	F1
Preston	NLn	72	A1
Preston	Wyn	61	B2
Princetown	Sch	44	E3
Proctor	Rut	20	F5
Prospect	NHv	65	F6
Prospect	NHv	69	F1
Prospect	NHv	70	A1
Providence	Srg	31	F5
Providence	Srg	32	A5
Pulteney	Stu	38	D6
Pulteney	Stu	52	D1
Putnam	Whg	20	A3
Putnam Valley	Put	68	B2
Queensbury	Wrr	32	D3
Ramapo	Rck	67	E5
Randolph	Cat	49	A5
Randolph	Mrr	73	E2
Raritan	Hnt	73	B6
Rathbone	Stu	52	B5
Reading	Scy	53	A2
Readington	Hnt	73	C6
Readsboro	Ben	46	F4
Red Hook	Dut	59	B6
Red Hook	Dut	64	B1
Red House	Cat	49	C5
Redding	Ffd	69	B3
Redfield	Osw	15	B5
Redfield	Osw	28	C1
Remsen	Ond	28	E2
Rensselaerville	Alb	44	D6
Rensselaerville	Alb	58	D1
Rhinebeck	Dut	64	A2
Richfield	Ots	42	F2
Richford	Tio	54	D2
Richland	Osw	14	E6
Richland	Osw	27	D1
Richmond	Brk	60	B2
Richmond	Chi	13	F2
Richmond	Otr	37	F3
Richmond	Wgn	72	D1
Richmondville	Shh	43	E5
Richmondville	Shh	44	A5
Ridgefield	Ffd	68	F3
Ridgefield	Ffd	69	A3
Ridgeway	Orl	23	B3
Riga	Mro	24	B6
Ripley	Chu	47	D4
Ripton	Add	13	F6
Ripton	Add	20	F1
River Vale	Brg	67	F6
River Vale	Brg	74	F1
River Vale	Brg	75	A1
Riverhead	Sfk	77	C1
Rochelle Park	Brg	74	E2
Rochester	Uls	63	B2
Rockaway	Mrr	67	A6
Rockaway	Mrr	73	F1
Rockaway	Mrr	74	A1
Rockland	Slv	62	C1
Rodman	Jfs	15	B2
Romulus	Sen	39	C4
Root	Mgy	43	F3
Root	Mgy	44	A2
Rose	Wan	26	B5
Roseboom	Ots	43	D4
Rosendale	Uls	63	E2
Rossie	SL	8	E2
Rotterdam	Sch	44	F2
Roxbury	Dlw	57	E3
Roxbury	Dlw	58	A3
Roxbury	Lch	65	C6
Roxbury	Mrr	73	D2
Royalton	Nia	22	F5
Royalton	Nia	23	A4
Rupert	Ben	33	D3
Rush	Mro	24	E6
Rush	Mro	37	E1
Rushford	Agy	50	C1
Russell	SL	2	E6
Russell	SL	9	E2
Russia	Hrk	29	E3
Rutland	Jfs	8	C6
Rutland	Jfs	15	C1
Rutland	Rut	20	F5
Rye	Wch	68	D6
Rye	Wch	75	D1
Saddle Brook	Brg	74	E2
Saint Albans	Fkl	6	E3
Saint Armand	Ese	11	F2
Saint Armand	Ese	12	A2
Saint George	Chi	13	E2
Saint Johnsville	Mgy	30	D6
Saint Johnsville	Mgy	43	E1
Salamanca	Cat	49	C4
Salem	NLn	71	C1
Salem	Whg	33	C5
Salina	Ono	27	D5
Salisbury	Add	20	E1
Salisbury	Hrk	30	C4
Salisbury	Lch	60	A6
Salisbury	Lch	65	A1
Sand Lake	Rns	45	E5
Sand Lake	Rns	46	A5
Sandgate	Ben	33	D4
Sandisfield	Brk	60	E5
Sandy Creek	Osw	14	F5
Sandyston	Ssx	66	C4
Sanford	Brm	55	F6
Sanford	Brm	56	A5
Sangerfield	Ond	42	A2
Santa Clara	Frl	4	B5
Santa Clara	Frl	11	B2
Saranac	Cln	5	C5
Saratoga	Srg	32	D6
Sardinia	Ere	35	E5
Sardinia	Ere	36	A6
Saugerties	Uls	58	F6
Savannah	Wan	26	C5
Savoy	Brk	46	F5
Scarsdale	Wch	68	C6
Scarsdale	Wch	75	C1
Schaghticoke	Rns	45	E2
Schodack	Rns	45	D6
Schodack	Rns	59	C1
Schoharie	Shh	44	B4
Schroeppel	Osw	27	C3
Schroon	Ese	19	C2
Schuyler	Hrk	29	C5
Schuyler Falls	Cln	5	E4
Scio	Agy	50	F5
Scipio	Cyg	39	F3
Scipio	Cyg	40	A3
Scotch Plains	Uni	74	B5
Scott	Crt	40	D4
Scott	Wyn	61	B1
Scriba	Osw	14	B6
Scriba	Osw	27	B1
Searsburg	Ben	46	F3
Sempronius	Cyg	39	B4
Sempronius	Cyg	40	B4
Seneca	Otr	38	F2
Seneca Falls	Sen	39	B1
Sennett	Cyg	26	F6
Sennett	Cyg	39	F1
Sennett	Cyg	40	A1
Seward	Shh	43	E4
Seymour	NHv	69	E2
Shaftsbury	Ben	33	D6
Shaftsbury	Ben	46	D1
Shaghticoke	Rns	46	A1
Shandaken	Uls	57	F5
Shandaken	Uls	58	B6
Shandaken	Uls	63	B1
Sharon	Lch	65	A2
Sharon	Shh	43	E3
Shawangunk	Uls	63	C5
Sheffield	Brk	60	B5
Shelburne	Chi	13	D2
Shelby	Orl	23	B4
Sheldon	Fkl	6	F2
Sheldon	Wyo	36	B4
Shelter Island	Sfk	71	C6
Shelton	Ffd	69	E3
Sherburne	Cng	41	F4
Sherburne	Cng	42	A4
Sheridan	Chu	34	C6
Sheridan	Chu	48	D1
Sherman	Chu	47	F2
Sherman	Ffd	65	A6
Shohola	Pke	66	B2
Shoreham	Add	20	C2
Sidney	Dlw	56	C3
Skaneateles	Ono	27	B6
Skaneateles	Ono	40	A1
Smithfield	Mds	28	D6
Smithfield	Mds	41	D1
Smithtown	Sfk	76	C2
Smithville	Cng	55	C1
Smyrna	Cng	41	E4
Sodus	Wan	25	E4
Sodus	Wan	26	A4
Solon	Crt	40	E6
Somers	Wch	68	D3
Somerset	Nia	22	F2
Somerset	Nia	23	A2
South Bristol	Otr	38	E4
South Canaan	Wyn	61	B6
South Hackensack	Brg	74	F2
South Hero	GIC	6	E5
South Kingstown	Wgn	72	F1
South Orange	Esx	74	C3
South Valley	Cat	48	F6
Southampton	Sfk	71	B6
Southampton	Sfk	78	B1
Southbury	NHv	65	D6
Southbury	NHv	69	F1
Southeast	Put	68	E2
Southold	Sfk	70	F6
Southold	Sfk	71	A6
Southold	Sfk	77	F1
Southold	Sfk	78	A1
Southport	Chm	53	B6
Spafford	Ono	40	C3
Sparta	Lvg	37	D5
Sparta	Ssx	66	E6
Spencer	Tio	53	F4
Spencer	Tio	54	A4
Springfield	Ots	43	B3
Springfield	Uni	74	B4
Springport	Cyg	39	D3
Springwater	Lvg	37	F5
Springwater	Lvg	38	A5
Stafford	Gns	23	E6
Stafford	Gns	36	F1
Stamford	Ben	46	E3
Stamford	Dlw	57	E2
Stanford	Dut	64	D2
Stark	Hrk	43	C1
Starkey	Yts	39	A6
Starkey	Yts	53	A1
Starksboro	Add	13	F4
Stephentown	Rns	46	A6
Stephentown	Rns	60	A1
Sterling	Cyg	26	D3
Steuben	Ond	29	C2
Stillwater	Srg	32	E6
Stillwater	Srg	45	E1
Stillwater	Ssx	66	B5
Stockbridge	Brk	60	B3
Stockbridge	Mds	28	E6
Stockbridge	Mds	41	E1
Stockholm	SL	3	B3
Stockport	Clm	59	C3
Stockton	Chu	48	B3
Stonington	NLn	72	A2
Stony Creek	Wrr	31	E1
Stony Creek	Wrr	32	A1
Stony Point	Rck	67	F3
Stony Point	Rck	68	A3
Stratford	Ffd	69	E4
Stratford	Flt	30	E4
Stuyvesant	Clm	59	C2
Sudbury	Rut	20	D3
Sullivan	Mds	28	B5
Summerhill	Cyg	40	B5
Summit	Eri	47	A6
Summit	Shh	43	E6
Sunderland	Ben	33	D6
Swanton	Fkl	6	E2
Swanton	Fkl	7	D6
Sweden	Mro	24	A5
Taghkanic	Clm	59	E5
Taylor	Crt	41	A5
Teaneck	Brg	74	F2
Teaneck	Brg	75	A2
Tewksbury	Hnt	73	C4
Texas	Wyn	61	C6
Theresa	Jfs	8	C3
Thomaston	Lch	65	E4
Thompson	Slv	62	D5
Thompson	Sqh	61	A2
Throop	Cyg	26	E6
Throop	Cyg	39	E1
Thurman	Wrr	18	E6
Thurman	Wrr	19	B6
Thurman	Wrr	31	E1
Thurman	Wrr	32	A1
Thurston	Stu	52	C4
Ticonderoga	Ese	19	F2
Ticonderoga	Ese	20	A2
Tinmouth	Rut	33	F1
Tioga	Tio	54	B5
Tolland	Hmp	60	F5
Tompkins	Dlw	56	D5
Tonawanda	Ere	22	A6
Tonawanda	Ere	35	B1
Torrey	Yts	39	A4
Trenton	Ond	29	D4
Triangle	Brm	55	A2
Troupsburg	Stu	51	E6
Troupsburg	Stu	52	A6
Troy Hills	Mrr	74	B2
Trumbull	Ffd	69	D3
Truxton	Crt	40	F4
Tryingham	Brk	60	D4
Tully	Ono	40	E3
Turin	Lew	16	A4
Tuscarora	Stu	52	D6
Tusten	Slv	61	F5
Tusten	Slv	62	A6
Tuxedo	Orn	67	D3
Tyre	Sen	26	C6
Tyre	Sen	39	C1
Tyrone	Scy	52	F1
Ulster	Uls	58	F6
Ulster	Uls	63	F1
Ulster	Uls	64	A1
Ulysses	Tmk	39	D6
Ulysses	Tmk	53	D1
Unadilla	Ots	56	B2
Union	Brm	54	F5
Union	Hnt	73	A5
Union	Uni	74	C4
Union Vale	Dut	64	D4
Urbana	Stu	52	C1
Van Buren	Ono	27	B5
Van Etten	Chm	53	F4
Varick	Sen	39	B3
Venango	Eri	47	C6
Venice	Cyg	39	F4
Venice	Cyg	40	A4
Vernon	Ond	28	F6
Vernon	Ond	29	A6
Vernon	Ssx	66	F4
Vernon	Ssx	67	A4
Verona	Ond	28	E4
Vestal	Brm	54	F6
Vetran	Chm	53	C3
Victor	Otr	25	A6
Victor	Otr	38	A1
Victory	Cyg	26	D4
Vienna	Ond	28	D3
Villenova	Chu	48	E2
Virgil	Crt	40	E6
Virgil	Crt	54	E1
Volney	Osw	27	B2
Waddington	SL	2	D3
Wales	Ere	35	F4
Wales	Ere	36	A4
Wallingford	NHv	70	C1
Wallingford	Rut	33	F1
Wallkill	Orn	63	A6
Wallkill	Orn	67	A1
Walpack	Ssx	66	A5
Waltham	Add	13	C5
Walton	Dlw	56	E5
Walworth	Wan	25	C4
Wantage	Ssx	66	E3
Wappinger	Dut	64	B5
Ward	Agy	51	A4
Warren	Hrk	43	A2
Warren	Lch	65	B3
Warren	Sms	73	F5
Warren	Sms	74	A5
Warrensburg	Wrr	19	C6
Warrensburg	Wrr	32	B1
Warsaw	Wyo	36	E3
Warwick	Orn	67	B3
Washington	Brg	74	F1
Washington	Brk	60	D2
Washington	Dut	64	D3
Washington	Lch	65	B5
Washington	Mrr	73	C3
Washington	War	73	A4
Waterford	NLn	71	E2
Waterford	Srg	45	D3
Waterloo	Sen	39	A1
Watertown	Jfs	15	A2
Watertown	Lch	65	E5
Watson	Lew	16	C3
Waverly	Frl	3	F5
Waverly	Frl	4	A5
Waverly	Frl	10	F1
Waverly	Frl	11	A1
Wawarsing	Uls	63	A3
Wawayanda	Orn	67	A2
Wayland	Stu	37	E6
Wayland	Stu	51	E1
Wayne	Pas	74	D1
Wayne	Stu	52	E1
Webb	Hrk	9	E6
Webb	Hrk	10	A6
Webb	Hrk	16	F3
Webb	Hrk	17	B2
Webster	Mro	25	A4
Weehawken	Brg	74	F3
Wells	Hml	18	C6
Wells	Hml	31	D2
Wells	Rut	33	D1
Wellsville	Agy	51	B5
West Abington	Lak	61	C6
West Almond	Agy	51	B3
West Bloomfield	Otr	37	F2
West Bloomfield	Otr	38	A2
West Haven	Rut	20	B5
West Milford	Pas	67	B5
West Monroe	Osw	27	F2
West Rutland	Rut	20	F5
West Seneca	Ere	35	D3
West Sparta	Lvg	37	C5
West Stockbridge	Brk	60	B3
West Turin	Lew	15	F5
West Turin	Lew	16	A6
West Union	Stu	51	D6
Westbrook	Mdx	71	A3
Westerlo	Alb	44	F6
Westerlo	Alb	58	F1
Westerly	Wgn	72	C2
Western	Ond	29	B3
Westfall	Pke	66	C2
Westfield	Chu	47	E3
Westford	Chi	6	F5
Westford	Ots	43	B5
Westmoreland	Ond	29	A5
Weston	Ffd	69	B4
Westport	Ese	13	A5
Westport	Ffd	69	B5
Westville	Frl	4	B1
Wethersfield	Wyo	36	C5
Weybridge	Add	13	C6
Wheatfield	Nia	22	A5
Wheatland	Mro	24	B6
Wheatland	Mro	37	C1
Wheeler	Stu	52	B1
White	War	73	A2
White Creek	Whg	33	B6
White Creek	Whg	46	B1
Whitehall	Whg	20	B5
Whitehall	Whg	33	B1
Whitestow	Ond	29	B5
Whiting	Add	20	D2
Willet	Crt	55	A1
Williamson	Wan	25	D4
Williamstown	Brk	46	D5
Williamstown	Osw	15	A6
Williamstown	Osw	28	B1
Willing	Agy	51	B6
Williston	Chi	13	E1
Willsboro	Ese	13	A2
Wilmington	Ese	12	B3
Wilna	Jfs	8	E6
Wilna	Jfs	15	F1
Wilson	Nia	22	C3
Wilton	Ffd	69	A4
Wilton	Srg	32	D5
Winchester	Lch	65	E1
Windham	Grn	58	D3
Windsor	Brk	46	E6
Windsor	Brk	60	F1
Windsor	Brm	55	D6
Winfield	Hrk	42	D1
Winfield	Uni	74	C5
Wirt	Agy	50	E5
Wolcott	NHv	65	F5
Wolcott	Wan	26	C4
Woodbridge	Mid	74	C6
Woodbridge	NHv	69	F1
Woodbridge	NHv	70	A2
Woodbury	Lch	65	D5
Woodbury	Orn	67	E3
Woodford	Ben	46	E2
Woodhull	Stu	52	B6
Woodstock	Uls	58	D6
Worcester	Ots	43	D6
Worth	Jfs	15	C4
Worthington	Hms	60	F2
Wright	Shh	44	D4
Wyckoff	Brg	67	D6
Wyckoff	Pas	74	D1
Yates	Orl	23	A2
York	Lvg	37	B2
Yorkshire	Cat	35	F6
Yorkshire	Cat	36	A6
Yorkshire	Cat	49	F1
Yorkshire	Cat	50	A1
Yorktown	Wch	68	C3

Wineries

NAME	TERR	MAP	GRID
Adair Vineyards	Uls	63	E4
Amberg Wine Cellars	Otr	38	E2
Americana Vineyards Winery	Sen	39	D6
Anthony Road Wine Co	Yts	39	A4
Applewood Winery	Orn	67	B3
Arbor Hill Grapery	Otr	38	B4
Arcadian Estate Vineyards	Scy	53	B1
Baldwin Vineyards	Orn	63	C5
Banfi Vintners-Old Brookville Vineyards	Nsu	75	E2
Barrington Cellars-Buzzard Crest Vineyards	Yts	38	E5
Batavia Wine Cellars	Gns	36	E1
Bedell Cellars	Sfk	71	A6
Benmarl Winery & Vineyards	Uls	64	A5
Bidwell Vineyards	Sfk	70	F6
Brimstone Hill Vineyard	Uls	63	B5
Brotherhood Americas Oldest Winery Ltd	Orn	67	E1
Bully Hill Vineyards	Stu	52	D1
Canandaigua Wine Co	Otr	38	B2
Casa Larga Vineyards	Mro	25	A6
Cascade Mtn Winery & Restaurant	Dut	64	F2
Cascata Winery at the Professors Place	Scy	53	B2
Castel Grisch Estate Winery	Scy	53	A2
Cayuga Ridge Estate Winery	Sen	39	D4
Chateau LaFayette Reneau	Scy	53	B1
Clinton Vineyards	Dut	64	C2
Cory Cr Vineyards	Sfk	71	C5
Delmonicos Winery	Kng	75	A4
Doctor Konstantin Franks Vinifera Wine Cellars	Stu	52	D1
Duck Walk Vineyards	Sfk	78	B2
Eagle Crest Vineyards Inc	Lvg	37	E4
Earle Estates Meadery	Cyg	40	A5
El Paso Winery	Uls	64	A2
Four Chimneys Farm Winery	Sen	39	A5
Fox Run Vineyards	Yts	39	A4
Frederick S Johnson Vineyards	Chu	47	E3
Frontenac Pt Vineyard	Tmk	39	D6
Fulkersons Winery & Juice Plan	Yts	53	B1
Glenora Wine Cellars	Yts	53	A1
Goose Watch Winery	Sen	39	C3
Great Western Winery Vis Ctr & Pleasant Vly Wine	Stu	52	D2
Gristina Vineyards	Sfk	77	F1
Hargrave Vineyard	Sfk	70	F6
Hazlitt 1852 Vineyards	Scy	39	B6
Heritage Wine Cellars	Eri	47	C4
Herman J Wiemer Vineyard Inc	Yts	39	A5
Heron Hill Vineyards	Stu	52	D1
Hosmer Wine Cellar	Sen	39	C4
Hudson Valley Draft Cider	Dut	64	B2
Hunt Country Vineyard	Yts	38	E5
Jamesport Vineyards	Sfk	77	E1
Johnstons Winery	Srg	32	A6
Joseph Zakon Winery	Kng	75	A4
Keuka Overlook Wine Cellars	Yts	38	E6
King Ferry Winery	Cyg	39	E5
Knapp Vineyards Winery & Restaurant	Sen	39	C3
Lakeshore Winery	Sen	39	C3
Lakewood Vineyards	Scy	53	B1
Lamoreaux Ldg Wine Cellars	Sen	39	B5
Larrys Vineyard & Farm Winery	Alb	44	F4
Leidenfrost Vineyards	Scy	39	B6
Lenz Winery	Sfk	71	A6
Loughlin Vineyards Inc	Sfk	76	F4
Loukas Wines	Brx	75	B2
Lucas Vineyards	Sen	39	D5
Macari Vineyards & Winery	Sfk	77	E1
Magnanini Winery	Uls	63	E5
Mazza Vineyards	Eri	47	C4
McGregor Vineyard & Winery	Yts	52	F1
Merritt Estate Winery	Chu	48	D1
Millbrook Vineyards & Winery	Dut	64	D2
Mogen David Wine Corporation	Chu	47	F2
New Land Vineyard	Sen	39	A2
North Salem Vineyard	Wch	68	E2
Olde Germania Wine Cellars	Stu	52	D1
Onondaga Winery Inc	Ono	27	E4
Ospreys Dominion Vineyards	Sfk	71	A6
Palmer Vineyards	Sfk	77	E1
Paumanok Vineyards Ltd	Sfk	77	E1
Peconic Bay Vineyards	Sfk	71	A6
Pellegrini Vineyards	Sfk	71	A6
Penn Shore Vineyards	Eri	47	B4
Pindar Vineyards	Sfk	71	A6
Pleasant Valley Winery	SL	2	F6

Key to Abbreviations

Acad .... Academy	Dr .... Drive	Mem .... Memorial	Resv .... Reservation
Admin .... Administration	E .... East	Mgmt .... Management	RI .... Rhode Island
Al .... Alley	Envir .... Environment	Mil .... Military	RR .... Railroad
Alt .... Alternate	Est/Ests .... Estates	Mt .... Mount	S .... South
Ave .... Avenue	Expwy .... Expressway	Mtn .... Mountain	SC .... South Carolina
Batl .... Battlefield	Ext .... Extension	Mun .... Municipal	Sch .... School
Bldg .... Building	Frwy .... Freeway	Mus .... Museum	SHA .... State Highway Administration
Bltwy .... Beltway	GA .... Georgia	N .... North	Soc .... Society
Blvd .... Boulevard	GC .... Golf Club/Golf Course	Nat .... Natural	Sq .... Square
Boro .... Borough	Govt .... Government	Nat Res .... Natural Resource	St .... State/Street
Br .... Branch/Bridge	Hbr .... Harbor	Natl .... National	Sta .... Station
Bus .... Business	Hdq .... Headquarters	Natl Balt Pk .... National Battlefield Park	Tech .... Technical
By-P .... By-Pass	Hgts .... Heights	NC .... North Carolina	Terr .... Terrace
CC .... Country Club	Hist .... Historic/Historical	NH .... New Hampshire	Theol .... Theological
Cem .... Cemetery	Hlth Ctr .... Health Center	NJ .... New Jersey	TN/Tenn .... Tennessee
Cir .... Circle	Hwy .... Highway	No .... Number	Tpk .... Turnpike
Co .... Company/County	I .... Interstate	NY .... New York	Tr .... Trail
Coll .... College	Ind .... Industrial	Ofc .... Office	Trk .... Truck
Comm .... Community	Inst .... Institution	OH .... Ohio	Twp .... Township
Conn .... Connector	Intl .... International	PA/Penn .... Pennsylvania	Univ .... University
Cr .... Creek	Is .... Island	Pk .... Park	US .... Federal Route
Cres .... Crescent	Jct .... Junction	Pkwy .... Parkway	Utd .... United
CT/Conn .... Connecticut	Jr Coll .... Junior College	Pl .... Place	VA .... Virginia
Ct .... Court	KY .... Kentucky	Pt .... Point	Vil .... Village
Ctr .... Center	La .... Lane	Rt .... Road	Voc .... Vocational
DE/Del .... Delaware	Ldg .... Landing	Rec .... Recreation	VT .... Vermont
Dept .... Department	Lp .... Loop	Rec Ctr .... Recreation Center	W .... West
Dev .... Development	MA/Mass .... Massachusetts	Ref .... Refuge	WMA .... Wildlife Management Area
DMV .... Department of Motor Vehicles	MD .... Maryland	Reg .... Regional	WV .... West Virginia
DOT .... Department of Transportation	ME .... Maine	Res .... Reservoir	

Notes